HISTORY OF THE CHURCH

IX

HISTORY OF THE CHURCH

Edited by
HUBERT JEDIN
and
JOHN DOLAN

Volume IX

THE CHURCH
IN THE
INDUSTRIAL AGE

by
Roger Aubert
Günter Bandmann
Jakob Baumgartner
Mario Bendiscioli
Jacques Gadille
Oskar Köhler
Rudolf Lill
Bernhard Stasiewski
Erika Weinzierl

Translated by
Margit Resch

CROSSROAD • NEW YORK

1981

The Crossroad Publishing Company

18 East 41st Street, New York, NY 10017

Translated from the *Handbuch der Kirchengeschichte*

Vol. VI/2: *Die Kirche in der Gegenwart: Die Kirche zwischen*

Anpassung und Widerstand (1878 bis 1914)

© Verlag Herder KG Freiburg im Breisgau 1973

English translation © 1981 by The Crossroad Publishing Company

Printed in the United States of America

Library of Congress Cataloging in Publication Data

Main entry under title:

The Church in the industrial age.

(History of the church; v. 9)

Translation of Die Kirche in der Gegenwart, part 2:

Die Kirche zwischen Anpassung und Widerstand (1878 bis

1914)

Bibliography: p.

Includes index.

1. Catholic Church—History—19th century.

2. Catholic Church—History—20th century. 3. Church

history—19th century. 4. Church history—20th

century. I. Aubert, Roger. II. Series: Jedin,

Hubert, 1900– ed. Handbuch der Kirchengeschichte.

English; v. 9.

BR145.2.J413 1980 vol. 9 [BX 1386] 270s [282'.09'034] 80-27313

ISBN 0-8245-0012-1 Previously: 0-8164-0448-8

CONTENTS

CONTENTS

CONTENTS

CONTENTS

PART THREE: THE EXPANSION OF CATHOLIC MISSIONS FROM THE TIME OF LEO XIII UNTIL WORLD WAR II
(Jakob Baumgartner)

PREFACE

This preface must begin with an apology or rather a justification. The pontificates of Leo XIII and Pius X, treated in this volume, were given much more attention than had originally been intended because they lead directly to the problems with which the Church of the twentieth century has had to struggle. The authors have attempted to trace the roots of today's problems to events and developments in the first half of the century. Unlike previous volumes, the following chapters include investigations of political parties, parliamentary governments, social trends, ecclesiastical alliances, and theological problems. Europe still exercises its spiritual leadership. Yet other continents are beginning to pose their problems. Although the secret archives of the Vatican generally do not allow access to the holdings pertaining to this era, documents are more abundant now than they used to be. Therefore a more thorough treatment is possible. Those readers who consider the studies of Leo XIII's encyclicals and the description of the dispute over modernism to be too extensive should bear in mind that these chapters deal with problems that are still keeping us in suspense today.

This work is not a history of Popes but of the Church. Even though the two pontificates are often said to be antitheses, their simultaneous investigation seemed to be appropriate. Likewise, it seemed appropriate to go beyond the period of the two pontificates in regard to topics such as the Roman question (chap. 34), the development of the Eastern Churches (chap. 25), and the missions (chaps. 38 and 39). Is the allegation of some critics true that there was a lack of necessary planning?

Between 1956 and 1959, we designed the master plan for the series. During several meetings arranged by the publishing house of Herder, the staff developed the basic guidelines, subject matter, and technical aspects of the work. At that time, the Second Vatican Council had not yet set in motion the tidal wave that was to seize, shake, and transform the Church. We planned to treat the history of the Church between the two World Wars as if it were a contemporary phenomenon in ecclesiastical terms: with the conciseness demanded by the lack of historical distance, with expedient constraint in judgment, and with confinement to the most important and urgent facts. Such an approach would have permitted us to master the subject matter within a relatively small space, i.e., within the framework of this volume. This is no longer possible. The events that took place between World War I and the death of Pope Pius XII have turned into history. The Church has left the calm waters in which it navigated for centuries, probably since the Council of Trent. It is heading toward the open sea and we do not know where it will land. Church history takes its course in longer intervals than political history. For the latter, the two World Wars, even the Third Reich, constitute events which are historically accessible. Information about them is available in open archives; they can, indeed, they must be assessed historically. Church history faces more difficulties. It does not gain historical perspective as quickly as political historiography and, unable to forego judgement entirely, has to practice restraint in regard to its evaluations. Therefore, it seemed prudent to dedicate a complete volume to the history of the Church from World War I to the Second Vatican Council.

Hubert Jedin

PREFACE TO THE ENGLISH EDITION

Insofar as the time period covered in this volume overlaps with the era known as the Victorian Age, there is a temptation to draw a comparison. For many even to this day it was the Golden Age of European Civilization. The Enlightenment of the seventeenth and eighteenth centuries had then reached high noon. Science had triumphed for the benefit of humankind. Wealth and universal education were guaranteed for all. The age witnessed what is often called the last outbreak of imperialism as well as a phase of the industrial revolution that was scientific rather than technical. There were no major wars. From it all the Church drew consolation and confidence. The press and the tremendous strides in transportation by way of pilgrimages strengthened the image of a highly centralized Church. The Europeanization of the world through the cooperation between the industrial revolution and the Christian missionary enterprises had become a common goal.

While economic problems no longer solvable by traditional means appeared world wide, efforts to control them still centered on political institutions based on a system of independent states.

Yet Leo XIII's envisioned *res publica Christiana* was not the answer. His role as *arbiter mundi* and his efforts to revive medieval social and economic theories and the theology of Thomas Aquinas now appear unrealistic. To proclaim Joseph the Carpenter the model of the worker when the effort of the laboring masses to gain full membership in the community was the major political event of the generation reflects this lack of historical sense. Yet to their credit neither Leo nor Pius exercised their recently proclaimed infallibility. Their missionary efforts, laudable as they were, too often fall under Kipling's couplet: "By all you leave or do, the silent sullen peoples shall weigh your Gods and you."

While this volume presents a more objective view of the pontificates of Leo and Pius, it also sheds light on the problem of modernism and the decree *Lamentabili* and the encyclical *Pascendi*. Finally its account of Rome's effort toward reunion with the Eastern Churches and its diplomatic dealings with the three archaic empires are a valuable addition to European history on the eve of the First World War.

John P. Dolan

LIST OF ABBREVIATIONS

Acta Leonis *Acta Leonis XIII. Allocutiones, epistolae, constitutiones, aliaque acta praecipua,* 8 vols., Bruges 1887–1911.

Acta Pii *Acta Pii X Pontificis Maximi,* Vol. V, Graz 1971.

AFrH *Archivum Franciscanum Historicum,* Florence–Quaracchi 1908ff.

AHC *Annuarium Historiae Conciliorum,* Paderborn 1969ff.

AHPont *Archivum historiae pontificiae,* Rome 1963ff.

AHR *The American Historical Review,* New York 1895ff.

AHVNrh *Annalen des Historischen Vereins für den Niederrhein, insbesondere das alte Erzbistum Köln,* Cologne 1855ff.

AkathKR *Archiv für Katholisches Kirchenrecht,* (Innsbruck) Mainz 1857ff.

AKG *Archiv für Kulturgeschichte,* (Leipzig) Münster and Cologne 1903ff.

ALW *Archiv für Liturgiewissenschaft* (formerly: *JLW*), Regensburg 1950ff.

AMrhKG *Archiv für mittelrheinische Kirchengeschichte,* Speyer 1949ff.

AnGr *Analecta Gregoriana cura Pontificiae Universitatis Gregorianae edita,* Rome 1930ff.

Anthropos *Anthropos. Internationale Zeitschrift für Völker- und Sprachenkunde.* Mödling 1906ff.

ArchSR *Archives de Sociologie des religions,* Paris 1956ff.

ArSKG *Archiv für schlesische Kirchengeschichte,* ed. K. Engelbert, I–VI Breslau 1936–41, VIIff. Hildesheim 1949ff.

ASS *Acta Sanctae Sedis,* Rome 1865–1908.

Aubert, Pie IX R. Aubert, *Le pontificat de Pie IX* (ed. A. Fliche and V. Martin, *Histoire de l'Église depuis des origines jusqu'à nos jours,* 21), Paris 1962.

BGPhMA *Beiträge zur Geschichte der Philosophie* (as of no. 27, 1928–30: *und Theologie*) *des Mittelalters,* ed. M. Grabmann, Münster 1891ff.

Bihlmeyer-Tüchle K. Bihlmeyer and H. Tüchle, *Kirchengeschichte* I: *Das christliche Altertum,* Paderborn 1955, II: *Das Mittelalter,* Paderborn 1955, III: *Die Neuzeit und die neueste Zeit,* Paderborn 1956

BLE *Bulletin de littérature ecclésiastique,* Toulouse 1899ff.

BZThS *Bonner Zeitschrift für Theologie und Seelsorge,* Düsseldorf 1924–31.

Catholicisme *Catholicisme. Hier–Aujourd'hui–Demain,* ed. G. Jacquemet, Paris 1948ff.

CH *Church History,* New York–Chicago 1932ff.

CHR *The Catholic Historical Review,* Washington 1915ff.

CICfontes P. Gasparri–I. Serédi, *Codicis Iuris Canonici Fontes,* 9 vols., Rome 1923–39.

CivCatt *La Civiltà Cattolica,* Rome 1850ff. (1871–87 Florence).

D   H. Denzinger, *Enchiridion Symbolorum, Definitionum et Declarationum de rebus fidei et morum*, Freiburg i. Br. 1955.

DDC   *Dictionnaire de droit canonique*, ed. R. Naz, Paris 1935ff.

Delacroix *Histoire universelle des missions catholiques*, ed. S. Delacroix, 4 vols., Paris–Monaco 1957–59.

DHGE   *Dictionnaire d'histoire et de géographie ecclésiastiques*, ed. A. Baudrillart et. al., Paris 1912ff.

DLZ   *Deutsche Literaturzeitung*, Berlin 1880ff.

DR   *Downside Review*, Stratton on the Fosse n. Bath 1880ff.

DSAM   *Dictionnaire de Spiritualité ascétique et mystique. Doctrine et Histoire*, ed. M. Viller, Paris 1932ff.

DSP   *DSAM*

DThC   *Dictionnaire de théologie catholique*, ed. A. Vacant and E. Mangenot, continued by É. Amann, Paris 1930ff.

DZKR   *Deutsche Zeitschrift für Kirchenrecht*, Tübingen 1861–1917.

ECatt   *Enciclopedia Cattolica*, Rome 1949ff.

ED   *Euntes docete (Commentaria urbana)*, Rome 1948ff.

EE   *Estudios eclesiásticos*, Madrid 1922–36, 1942ff.

EHR   *English Historical Review*, London 1886ff.

ELit   *Ephemerides Liturgicae*, Rome 1887ff.

Engel-Janosi F. Engel-Janosi, *Österreich und der Vatikan*, 2 vols., Graz 1958–60.

ÉO   *Échos d'Orient*, Paris 1897ff.

EThL   *Ephemerides Theologicae Lovanienses*, Bruges 1924ff.

Études   *Études*, Paris 1856ff. (until 1896: *Études religieuses*).

FreibThSt *Freiburger Theologische Studien*, Freiburg i. Br. 1910ff.

Gebhardt-Grundmann B. Gebhardt, *Handbuch der deutschen Geschichte*, 8th ed. by H. Grundmann, Stuttgart, I: 1954, II: 1955

GrabmannG M. Grabmann, *Die Geschichte der katholischen Theologie seit dem Ausgang der Väterzeit*, Freiburg i. Br. 1933.

Heimbucher M. Heimbucher, *Die Orden und Kongregationen der katholischen Kirche*, 3 vols., Paderborn 1907–8; in 2 vols., Paderborn 1932–34.

HistCathFr A. Latreille, J. R. Palanque, É. Delaruelle and R. Rémond, *Histoire du catholicisme en France* III: *La période contemporaine*, Paris 1962.

HJ   *Historisches Jahrbuch der Görres-Gesellschaft*, (Cologne 1880ff.) Munich 1950ff.

HM   *Historia Mundi*, founded by F. Kern, 10 vols., Bern–Munich 1952ff.

Hocedez E. Hocedez, *Histoire de la Théologie au XIXᵉ siècle*, Brussels–Paris, I: 1948, II: 1952, III: 1947.

Hochland *Hochland*, Munich 1903ff.

HZ   *Historische Zeitschrift*, Munich 1859ff.

IKZ   *Internationale Kirchliche Zeitschrift*, Bern 1911ff.

Irénikon *Irénikon*, Amay–Chevetogne 1926ff.

Jungmann MS J. A. Jungmann, *Missarum sollemnia. Eine genetische Erklärung der römischen Messe* I–II, Vienna ⁵1962.

Kißling   J. B. Kißling, *Geschichte des Kulturkampfes,* 3 vols., Freiburg i. Br. 1911–16.

KmJb   *Kirchenmusikalisches Jahrbuch* (formerly: *Cäcilienkalender*), Cologne 1886ff.

KuD   *Kerygma und Dogma,* Göttingen 1955ff.

Kyrios   *Kyrios. Vierteljahresschrift für Kirchen- und Geistesgeschichte Osteuropas,* Königsberg–Berlin 1936–43: n.s. Berlin 1960ff.

LJ   *Liturgisches Jahrbuch,* Münster 1951ff.

LThK   *Lexikon für Theologie und Kirche,* Freiburg 1957–68.

Mansi   J. D. Mansi, *Sacrorum conciliorum nova et amplissima collectio,* 31 vols., Florence–Venice 1757–98; reprinted and continued by L. Petit and J. B. Martin in 60 vols., Paris 1899–1927.

Mercati   A. Mercati, *Raccolta di Concordati su materie ecclesiastiche tra la Santa Sede e le autorità civili,* 2 vols., Rome 1919–54.

MGG   *Die Musik in Geschichte und Gegenwart,* ed. F. Blume, 10 vols., Basel–Kassel 1949ff.

MOP   *Monumenta ordinis Fratrum Praedicatorum historica,* ed. B. M. Reichert, 14 vols., Rome 1896–1904; Paris 1931ff.

MSR   *Mélanges de science religieuse,* Lille 1944ff.

MthSt(H)   *Münchner theologische Studien,* ed. F. X. Seppelt, J. Pascher, and K. Mörsdorf, *Historische Abteilung,* Munich 1950ff.

MThZ   *Münchner Theologische Zeitschrift,* Munich 1950ff.

NDB   *Neue Deutsche Biographie,* Berlin 1953ff.

NRTh   *Nouvelle Revue Théologique,* Tournai–Louvain–Paris 1879ff.

NZM   *Neue Zeitschrift für Missionswissenschaft,* Beckenried 1945ff.

ÖAKR   *Österreichisches Archiv für Kirchenrecht,* Vienna 1950ff.

OstkSt   *Ostkirchliche Studien,* Würzburg 1951ff.

PhJ   *Philosophisches Jahrbuch der Görres-Gesellschaft,* Fulda 1888ff.

QFIAB   *Quellen und Forschungen aus italienischen Archiven und Bibliotheken,* Rome 1897ff.

QLP   *Questions liturgiques et paroissiales,* Louvain 1921ff.

RACHS   *Records of the American Catholic Society,* Philadelphia 1884ff.

RB   *Revue biblique,* Paris 1892ff. n.s. since 1904.

RevSR   *Revue des Sciences Religieuses,* Strasbourg 1921ff.

RGG   *Die Religion in Geschichte und Gegenwart,* Tübingen 1909–13; 1927–32; 1956ff.

RH   *Revue historique,* Paris 1876ff.

RHE   *Revue d'histoire ecclésiastique,* Louvain 1900ff.

RHÉF   *Revue d'histoire de l'Église de France,* Paris 1910ff.

RHM   *Revue d'histoire des missions,* Paris 1924ff.

RHMC   *Revue d'histoire moderne et contemporaine.*

RicRel   *Ricerche Religiose,* Rome 1925ff.

RNPh   *Revue néoscolastique de philosophie,* Louvain 1894ff.

Rohrbasser   *Heilslehre der Kirche. Dokumente von Pius IX bis Pius XII,* ed. P. Cattin and H. T. Conus, trans. A. Rohrbasser, Fribourg 1953.

RPhL	*Revue philosophique de Louvain*, Louvain 1945ff.
RPol	*Review of Politics*, Notre Dame (Indiana) 1939ff.
RSPhTh	*Revue des sciences philosophiques et théologiques*, Paris 1907ff.
RSR	*Recherches de science religieuse*, Paris 1910ff.
RSTI	*Rivista di storia della chiesa in Italia*, Rome 1947ff.
RStRis	*Rassegna storica del Risorgimento*, Rome 1913ff.

Saeculum	*Saeculum. Jahrbuch für Universalgeschichte*, Freiburg i. Br. 1950ff.
SC	*Scuola Cattolica*, Milan 1873ff.
Schmidlin M	J. Schmidlin, *Katholische Missionsgeschichte im Grundriß*, Steyl 1925.
Schmidlin PG	J. Schmidlin, *Papstgeschichte der neuesten Zeit* I–IV, Munich 1933–39.
Schmitz	Ph. Schmitz, *Histoire de l'ordre de saint Benoît* I–VII, Maredsous 1948–56.
SM	*Studien und Mitteilungen aus dem Benediktiner- und Zisterzienserorden bzw. zur Geschichte des Benediktinerordens und seiner Zweige*, Munich 1880ff. (n.s. since 1911).
SMB	*Societas Missionum Exterarum de Bethlehem in Helvetia* (Schweizer Missionsseminar Immensee).
SPM	*Sacrum Poloniae Millennium*, Rome 1954ff.
StdZ	*Stimmen der Zeit* (before 1914: *Stimmen aus Maria-Laach*), Freiburg i. Br. 1871ff.
StL	*Staatslexikon*, ed. H. Sacher, Freiburg i. Br. 1926–32; 1957ff.
Streit	*Bibliotheca Missionum*, started by R. Streit, continued by J. Dindinger (Münster, Aachen) Freiburg i. Br. 1916ff. (up to 1971: 28 vols.).

ThGl	*Theologie und Glaube*, Paderborn 1909ff.
ThPQ	*Theologisch-praktische Quartalschrift*, Linz a.d.D. 1848ff.
ThQ	*Theologische Quartalschrift*, Tübingen 1819ff.; Stuttgart 1946ff.
ThRv	*Theologische Revue*, Münster 1902ff.
ThSt	*Theological Studies*, Baltimore 1940ff.
TThZ	*Trierer Theologische Zeitschrift* (until 1944: *Pastor Bonus*), Trier 1888ff.

Wetzer-Welte	*Wetzer und Welte's Kirchenlexikon*, 12 vols. and 1 index vol., Freiburg i. Br. 1882.
WZ	*Westfälische Zeitschrift. Zeitschrift für vaterländische Geschichte*, Münster 1838ff.

ZAGV	*Zeitschrift des Aachener Geschichtsvereins*, Aachen 1879ff.
ZAM	*Zeitschrift für Aszese und Mystik* (since 1947: *Geist und Leben*) (Innsbruck, Munich) Würzburg 1926ff.
ZChK	*Zeitschrift für christliche Kunst*, founded and ed. by A. Schnütgen, continued by F. Witte, 34 vols., Düsseldorf 1888–1921.
ZGAE	*Zeitschrift für Geschichte und Altertumskunde Ermlands*, (Mainz, Leipzig, Braunsberg) Osnabrück 1858ff.
ZKG	*Zeitschrift für Kirchengeschichte*, (Gotha) Stuttgart 1876ff.
ZKTh	*Zeitschrift für katholische Theologie*, (Innsbruck) Vienna 1877ff.
ZM	*Zeitschrift für Missionswissenschaft* 1–17, Münster 1911–27.

ZMR   *Zeitschrift für Missionswissenschaft und Religionswissenschaft,* vols. 34ff., Münster 1950ff.; *Zeitschrift für Missionswissenschaft und Religionswissenschaft* 18–25, Münster 1928–35; *Zeitschrift für Missionswissenschaft* 26–27, Münster 1935–37; *Missionswissenschaft und Religionswissenschaft* 28–33, Münster 1938–41, 1947–49.

ZSavRGkan *Zeitschrift der Savigny-Stiftung für Rechtsgeschichte, Kanonistische Abteilung,* Weimar 1911ff.

PART ONE

The Problem of Adapting to the Modern World

The World Plan of Leo XIII: Goals and Methods

The Conclave

The conclave after the death of Pius IX[1] meant a turning point in the history of papal elections because, for the first time, the head of the Catholic Church was to be elected after the factual loss of the *Patrimonium Petri*. The late Pope had explicitly indicated his choice as to the election site. A strong group of cardinals, especially Ledóchowski, Franzelin, and Manning, had spoken against the elections in Rome. Pius VII had been elected in Venice because in February 1798 French troops under General Berthier occupied Rome. But in the following eighty years the Christian world had changed dramatically and there was not a single place in Italy for refuge during the interim. The alternative was to meet in Rome or in a foreign country. During the first congregation (8 February 1878), a minority of only eight cardinals voted for Rome as the election site. The following day, Cardinal di Pietro indicated in a speech that, even though no foreign power had issued an invitation, Italy had been given a guarantee of nonintervention. The cardinal had been nuncio in Lisbon and belonged to the politically "liberal" group of the College of Cardinals. When the matter was put to the vote, five cardinals voted for Spain and thirty-two for Rome. Camerlengo (since 1877) Gioacchino Vincenzo Pecci, an experienced organizer, who prepared the election and shielded it diplomatically against Italy, had to undertake considerable renovations in the Vatican for the conclave.

Although Cardinal Pecci, who was well informed, had voted for an election outside of Italy on 8 February, it appears questionable at first glance whether such a far-reaching step, though discussed at length, was in fact pursued after the foreign powers had refused. Italy was not interested in it, despite radical efforts to expel the Pope from Rome. The guarantee was, therefore, trustworthy. The foreign powers had, for different reasons, an interest in a smooth transition and a politically obliging successor to the Holy See. Vienna seems to have agreed with Berlin that "a fanatical Jesuit pope" was not wanted. Despite the decrease of Republican representatives from 363 to 323, French President MacMahon had experienced the political defeat of the "conservative republic" after the Chamber was dissolved in 1877. And he had witnessed the effect of the slogan *le cléricalisme, voilà l'ennemi*. In Spain,

---

[1] Engel-Janosi, *Österreich und der Vatikan* I, 200–14, including the preceding history since 1872.

the liberal-conservative politician Antonio Cánovas, who had revived the constitutional monarchy in 1876, was intent on good relations with the *Moderados*. Great Britain was occupied with the problems of Catholic Ireland, even though in 1874 the imperialist Disraeli succeeded Gladstone (until 1880), who was friendly toward Ireland. For Bismarck, the *Kulturkampf* had become burdensome for several reasons. Even Russia, in the middle of a successful war against Turkey, was interested in easing tensions, though it had brutally deprived Poland of all autonomy since the uprising of 1863 and employed the harshest measures against the Catholic Church (rupture of diplomatic relations between the Pope and Saint Petersburg in 1877). Imminent peace and the impending international conference in Berlin had priority in international politics. Therefore, the new situation of the Catholic Church was distinctive in world history because the conclave played a minor role this time in diplomatic correspondence.[2] A conciliatory Pope was wanted. Even the "Catholic powers," who stood in the background, would consider the idea of exercizing the right of exclusion only if a disciple of Pius IX's politics were to be elected.

Did the Curia assess the situation correctly when discussing whether the election should take place outside of Italy? Four years after his election and after the riots which occurred one night in 1881 during the transferal of Pius IX's body from Saint Peter's to S. Lorenzo fuori le Mura, the new Pope would discuss with a delegate from the court in Vienna whether Trent or Salzburg could offer him asylum. He received an invitation which implied, however, that he should not accept it (1882).[3] The alternative of having the papal elections in Rome or in a foreign country, which was apparently deemed serious on 8 February 1878, turned out to be no alternative. One could continue to reject the Italian guarantee law of 13 May 1871, but one had to live with it and worry that it was here to stay.

On 18 February sixty of the sixty-four cardinals moved into the Vatican for the conclave. Twenty-five of them were non-Italians, in accord with the ecclesiastical world plan of Pius IX. The preparatory congregation had decided on 10 February to elect an Italian; probably the only possible solution in this situation. The insinuation in Paris that a non-Italian, but certainly not a German, could be elected met with no support in Vienna. Pius IX had chosen the cardinals for the thirty-five positions created since 1868 mainly from the zealots. But even they tended to lean toward a man who would be capable of easing the

---

[2] Schmidlin, *PG* II, 341; in reference to Schmidlin, see Engel-Janosi I, 212.

[3] Schmidlin, *PG* II, 414f., with documents against E. Soderini's presentation; Engel-Janosi I, 226–31; see also, ". . . how much the situation had changed [since 1870]" (Engel-Janosi I, 230).

political and theological tensions which had increased during the previous pontificate. Due to the efforts of Cardinal Bartolini, the conclave's leading member (since 1875 secretary for the Congregation of Rites), the conclave was able to focus quickly on one candidate. Gioacchino Vincenzo Pecci had been bishop in Perugia since 1846 (cardinal since 1853). During the lifetime of Pius IX, Pecci had moved up to a promising position within the papacy because he was regarded as the representative of the moderate line. However, he was not allowed to enter Rome until Antonelli died. Pecci's competitor, Cardinal Bilio, had been close to Pius IX and had participated in drafting the *Syllabus*. He had, apparently, been chosen by Pius to be his successor. But because of Bartolini's attitude, the intransigents were unable to agree upon a candidate from their midst, and Bilio was threatened with a French and Spanish veto. The candidate of the "liberal faction" was Cardinal Franchi. He had become a legate to Spain in 1850, nuncio in 1871, and was respected in matters related to Church policies. His side was taken by the Spanish cardinals, in accordance with their government. Bartolini was able to win their votes for Pecci (Franchi was appointed secretary of state on 5 March 1878, but he died that August).

At the first ballotting (the morning of 19 February 1878), which was declared invalid for technical reasons, Pecci received 19 votes, Bilio 6, and Franchi 4. But neither Bilio nor Franchi could claim the majority of the remaining fragmented votes. In the afternoon, Pecci's share increased to 26 votes, Bilio's to 7, while Franchi only received 2. On the morning of 20 February, Pecci was elected Pope with 44 votes, a two-thirds majority. So far, this was the shortest papal election, a few hours shorter than that of Pius IX. Among the cardinals who remained Pecci's rivals to the end were Flavio Chigi, the offspring of the old Sienese landed gentry (1850–61 nuncio in Munich, then in Paris until 1873), L. Oreglia, and the Tyrolese Jesuit Johann Baptist Franzelin (1850–76 professor at the Gregoriana). To the latter (since 1876 cardinal of the Curia) is attributed a considerable share in framing the constitution *De fide catholica* of Vatican I.

The new Pope chose his name after Leo XII (1823–29), to whom he was grateful for furthering his studies at the Roman seminary. Observers felt he indicated his program in the fact that he did not call himself Gregory or Pius.[4]

Leo XIII did not deliver the benediction *urbi et orbi* from the outer loggia toward the Saint Peter's Square but toward the Basilica. There

---

[4] Schmidlin, *PG* II, 346; Schmidlin calls Leo XII especially "peaceful and moderate," while Tüchle-Bihlmeyer and other authors emphasize the reactionary policies of the Papal State.

were indications that the problem of relations between the Church and the postrevolutionary world articulated itself most strongly in the Holy City: festive illuminations stood in contrast to protest demonstrations. This was true also during the coronation (3 March), held in the Sistine Chapel and not in St. Peter's because the Italian authorities could not or would not guarantee security. The Pope's choice of a name inspired the mockery, "Non è Pio, non è Clemente, Leone senza dente." Leo sent individual inaugural letters to Catholic as well as non-Catholic heads of state in which he indicated his desire to settle disputes. The Italian government was ignored and in turn did not recognize the new Pope officially.

Despite the strong positive response of the world to Leo XIII's election, it is questionable whether the Catholic Church really began "to develop into a great world power which politics had to take into account." Above all, Catholicism certainly had to incorporate domestic politics, especially as long as it was capable of establishing itself as a social group. But it was the goal of the Pope, sixty-eight years old at his coronation, to present the Catholic Church and the papacy to all of mankind as *the* "great world power" with an intellectual and spiritual mission.

The Career of Gioacchino Pecci

In March 1814 the four-year-old Gioacchino Pecci was able to witness the triumphal inauguration of Pius VII after the end of the Napoleonic era. His aristocratic family temporarily had to leave their residence in Carpineto, a small town in the rocky mountains south of Rome, because of insurgent activities. Gioacchino was born on 2 March 1810, the son of Colonel Lodovico Pecci. The bishop of Anagni was his godfather. Together with his older brother Giuseppe, he attended the Jesuit school in Viterbo from 1818 on. After his graduation with honors in 1824, he studied rhetoric, philosophy, and theology at the Roman seminary which Leo XII had just returned to the Jesuits (among his teachers were Perrone and Patrizi). His brother entered the *Society of Jesus* the same year.[5] It was in accord with his talents that Gioacchino Pecci, during the jubilee in 1825, was allowed to head a delegation to the protector Leo

---

[5] G. Pecci, professor of philosophy, came to blows with the order which opposed the Thomistic revival for some time to come, and consequently resigned in 1848. He collaborated with his papal brother, who appointed him cardinal in 1879, in the development of a program to renew the "Christian philosophy" which had been ushered in by the encyclical *Aeternis Patris* (see chap. 20). Two years before his death (1890), he was reinstated by the Society of Jesus.

XII and deliver a Latin address of gratitude.[6] As was in keeping with someone who had a church career in mind, Gioacchino Pecci studied law at the *Accademia dei nobili.* He concluded his doctoral studies in 1837 with the remarkable topic of appeals to the Pope. The same year, Cardinal Odescalchi ordained the promising young man to the priesthood. Pecci had found influential patrons in Cardinal J. A. Sala, who had distinguished himself as prelate in the politics of restoration under Pius VII, in Cardinal Bartolomeo Pacca, leader of the zealots, and in Secretary of State Lambruschini.

The year of his ordination, the twenty-seven-year-old Pecci was appointed domestic prelate by Gregory XVI and given three offices, one of which was consultant at the Congregation of the Council. In 1838, the very next year, Pecci was sent as a delegate to Benevento, an enclave of the Papal State in the Kingdom of Naples. The situation there, dominated by gangs of bandits and smugglers in the service of the landed gentry, was anarchistic. But Pecci ruled with an iron fist and organized the tariff system in such a way that the enclave lost its reputation as a smuggler's paradise. In June 1841 he was transferred to Spoleto as a delegate and in July to Perugia where he also busily reformed the administration. The visit of Pope Gregory XVI to the Umbrian city was a great opportunity, of which the delegate Pecci took advantage. The Via Gregoriana was finished on time, and the reception proceeded so splendidly that the Pope promised to think of his delegate in Rome.[7] In January 1843 Pecci was appointed nuncio to Belgium. In later years, his career was attributed to the character of Leo XII, though Pecci himself certainly knew how skillfully to further it. Even though the tempo of his rise was above average, one has to bear in mind that the will to excel was a frequent phenomenon in young Roman prelates, which is only particularly striking when one becomes historically significant.

The nunciature in Belgium was Gioacchino Pecci's first failure

---

[6] Gioacchino Pecci began his *Carmina* in Viterbo. A humanistic eduation had determined his way of thinking (Dante, Cicero, Virgil, Horace, Tacitus, and Sallust were considered proper reading). In his letter to Cardinal Parocchi (20 May 1885) concerning the education of the clergy in Rome, he urged them to study Thomas Aquinas and to develop a good style, ". . . nihil est fere ad iuvandam intelligentiam maius, quam scribendi virtus et urbanitas. Nativo quippe et eleganti genere dicendi mire invitantur homines ad audiendum, ad legendum" (*Acta Leonis* V, 62). In his encyclicals, Leo XIII had enjoyed eloquent rhetoric, since he had so ardently participated in writing them. The Romans, who valued a humanistic education, talked about the *pontificato dei dotti* (L. Teste, *Léon XIII et le Vatican* [Paris 1880], 103).

[7] See Schmidlin, *PG* II, 334, with quotations from other biographers.

(1843–46).[8] The task demanded too much from the scarcely thirty-three-year-old man, despite his efforts to adjust to the situation he faced. After all, he had acquired his experience under totally different circumstances. In Belgium, the understanding, developed since the nation's founding between so-called Liberals, the liberal Catholics, and the moderate ultramontanes, began to crumble. Pecci's predecessor, who had been transferred to Paris, knew very well how to maneuver in this terrain and had been on good terms with Prime Minister Nothomb. When Nothomb was overthrown by the Conservatives in 1845, he blamed the new nuncio. Pecci's generally fine relationship with Leopold I and the royal family had its drawbacks because the conservative attitude of the monarch was not the only one in the web of political forces. This prompted the ultramontane clergy to accuse the nuncio of opportunism. The fact that Pecci did not avoid Vincenzo Gioberti, who was living in Brussels at the time, pleased neither the liberals nor the clergy. It was even more difficult for the nuncio to get along with the University of Louvain, which was Catholic but not papal. During this time, the confrontation of the ontologists and the representatives of philosophical traditionalism with the Scholastic renaissance began to develop at the university, and its leading publication was opposed by the Jesuits. By demand of the royal court, Archbishop Pecci was recalled in 1846 because he had supported the episcopate against the King in the question of the university's examination commission.

One had to have a great deal of imagination to predict the tiara for the failing nuncio.[9] In January 1846 he was given the bishopric of Perugia, located "in remote tranquility" (Schmidlin). He was honored with the cardinalate *in petto* in 1853. It is not without reason that we call Gioacchino Pecci an outstanding bishop who was especially concerned with the education of his clergy (which includes the founding of the Academy of Saint Thomas). He intensified pastoral work through the establishment of missions and he furthered charitable institutions through his strong administrative talents. As a result of such activities, he would hardly have received emphasis in Italian Church history. His decisive

---

[8] In addition to the general literature, see *Lettres de Pecci 1843–46* (Brussels 1959); in reference to V. Gioberti: Schmidlin, *PG* II, 334f.

[9] According to Narfon, cited in Schmidlin, *PG* II, 335, n. 10.—It is a difficult question to answer whether Pecci's future concepts were "decisively influenced by the entirely new and unfamiliar environment" into which the Italian was placed after "having lived in the traditional atmosphere of the Papal State" (Schmidlin, *PG* II, 334). This break in his career may have possibly been a shock for G. Pecci. R. Aubert (*LThK* VI/2, 953) points out that Pecci's visit of Belgian industrial works, a journey to the Rhineland, and sojourns in London and Paris while returning to Rome "were the future Pope's only contacts ever with industrial and parliamentary Europe".

opposition to the revolutionary movement (1848, destruction of the papal castle) and to the Piedmontese regime (established 1860 in Perugia) shows a dedicated bishop, who had the same experiences as his fellow bishops. Pecci simply expressed the general ecclesiastical conviction in his pastoral letter of 12 February 1860, when he wrote that the time before Constantine the Great was a legitimate epoch, "because the highest spiritual power of the papacy carried the seed of secular power from its inception."[10] Though he did not even enjoy the favor of Pius IX, Bishop Pecci was also instrumental in the efforts which brought about the *Syllabus.* A characteristic new tone, however, was sounded in the pastoral letters of 1874–77, which maintain that a reconciliation between the Church and modern culture, provided modern culture is understood correctly, is possible and desirable. The letters spoke of human progress, e.g., relaxation of the penal code, and they praised technological accomplishments in a very poetic language,[11] which the Pope did not employ once he had become familiar with the reality of industrialism through the social sciences. He also omitted poetic prose from his new and not at all reactionary cultural critique.

Long before such demonstration of insight, however, Cardinal Giacomo Antonelli, secretary of state since 1850, had put the bishop of Perugia on the list of men within the hierarchy who seemed suspect to him. Antonelli did not even allow Pecci to venture to suburbanized Albano. His attempt to do so indicated that he did not possess the kind of nature which would be satisfied with the ecclesiastical duties facing him in Perugia. On the other hand, one can conclude from Antonelli's opposition that he sensed in Pecci an important personality and opponent of his politics. After Antonelli's death, Pius IX, who had to reckon with his own death, appointed Cardinal Pecci camerlengo on 21 September 1877. Through this gesture, the Pope documented his evaluation of the man from Perugia and his confidence that Pecci possessed the skills necessary to meet the danger of the interregnum. The appointment somewhat diminished the feasibility of Pecci becoming Pope be-

[10] Cited from Tischleder, *Staatslehre,* 346f. Leo XIII expressed his convictions somewhat differently in a letter to Rampolla of 15 June 1887 (after the persecutions, "a particular situation arose from the convergence of circumstances, shepherded by destiny itself, which resulted in the establishment of temporal authority"); but it is hardly justified to see here, as Tischleder does (p. 349), a corrected image of the seed of the Pope's temporal power.

[11] Schmidlin, *PG* II, 337, n. 16: the inventor of the lightning rod "seems majestic"; the telephone is the "messenger of man's desire" across oceans and mountains; man harnessed steam so it "may carry him across land and sea with the speed of the wind." Technology is seen as liberation from the hardest of labor; creativity of man as "a spark from the Creator himself."

cause, traditionally, the camerlengo has virtually no chance in the conclave. Gioacchino Pecci lived in Umbria more than thirty-one years.

The Pontificate

Pope Leo XIII led the Catholic Church into a world which had risen from revolution. With an attitude which can only adequately be termed "optimistic," he attempted to reconcile an uncompromised tradition with the modern spirit. One may say that he opened up a new epoch in the history of the Catholic Church and set a precedent with courage deeply rooted in faith, without which his successors to the see of Saint Peter would not have been conceivable. An interpretation today faces the understandable danger of misjudging the greatness of this Pope after almost a century, of even blaming him for the failure of the courageous plan for reconciliation which was to embrace the whole world, of overlooking the fact that it had to fail because each period in history makes its own imprint. We might add that even the achievements of this pontificate (i.e., the formation of Catholicism into autonomous groups within a society which was growing increasingly secular) have been discredited for a long time by the term "ghetto Catholicism." But such a sweeping judgment does not grasp the historical accomplishments relative to the pontificate itself and to society as a whole.

On the other hand, it should be noted that the image of Leo XIII in Catholicism, as it was passed on in popular and in scholarly history, was instilled with success by some sort of pressure, which may be informative about the situation and historical self-awareness of Catholics after this pontificate. "Peace Pope" and "Pope of the Workers" are the two most significant appositions crystallizing the tradition of his image. The twenty-fifth anniversary of German Emperor Wilhelm II in 1913 compelled Sebastian Merkle, understandably, to impose a certain style on his essay about the Catholic Church which was proper for the event. It was, however, more than style when he called the Emperor's visit to the Vatican in the fall of 1888 "a dialogue between the representatives of the *sacerdotium* and the *imperium*," or when he labeled as a "thoughtful present" the glass painting which Wilhelm II donated to the Cathedral of Münster (it shows Charlemagne and Leo IX meeting in Paderborn in 799).[12] Placed between Pius IX, Pope of the *Syllabus,* and Pius X, Pope of the Borromeo encyclical, Leo XIII is historically illuminated in a fashion which does not correspond to the reality of the concluding *Kulturkampf.* Josef Schmidlin characterized this pontificate more com-

---

[12] In *Deutschland unter Kaiser Wilhelm II* II, 61, 64 (biblio., chap. 12).

prehensively in 1934. After "the harmony between the two spheres [Church and culture] dissipated, and after both were alienated from each other because of the polemical attitude toward modern philosophical accomplishments under the papacy of Pius and Gregory, the progressive peace Pope considered it his foremost task to restore a close union and understanding to the realm of ideas" and to re-build a "Christian *Weltanschauung*" based on speculative reason and positive history. In his scholarly writings, he was supposed to have developed in a unique way "the governmental program of gain and conciliation, which means Christianization of modern life and modernization of Christian life," a program which he outlined in his inaugural encyclical. "With inner ties he chained the modern world again to the tiara" and strengthened the moral greatness and authority of the papacy even more "than the medieval *dominium temporale* had been able to do" and more than the "anti-revolutionary reactive faction" was intending to do. J. Schmidlin speaks about the "indestructible accomplishment of Leo's pontificate," which "was to imprint upon the twentieth century his domination of modern man and mankind's reconciliation with the Church."[13] Fernand Hayward, in 1937, considered the reconciliation of Catholicism with the age, without the abandonment of Catholic teachings, to be the hallmark of this pontificate. According to Hayward, even in France, the echo of Leo's teachings finally effected an inner balance and some sort of neutralization within the secular state, despite the failure of *ralliement* and the continuation of Catholicism's inner conflicts.[14] Such evaluations, like most others from the first half of the twentieth century, have their roots in the obvious need of a group to escape isolation while remaining true to itself and while having to live within the confines of a society to which it belongs but to which, in the final analysis, it cannot belong. Leo XIII appeared to be the Pope who had created this possibility which seemed so vital that, to a large extent, its realization had to be historically verified. There are also considerations, however, usually presented as qualifications, which delve deeply into the problems of this pontificate. Wilhelm Schwer, who dealt with the social teachings of Leo XIII, noted that the Pope, for quite some time, tended "to attribute all material progress to Christian and ecclesiastical influences, more than a precise analysis of the participating forces will permit."[15] This insinuates more than an incidental error in historical interpretation.

Leo XIII was a political Pope and it is, therefore, correct to say that he enjoys a position among the "masters of politics." To be sure, he was

---

[13] Schmidlin, *PG* II, 393, 352, 589.—"The peace Pope" is the repeated synonym for Leo XIII. In reference to Schmidlin's criticism of this pontificate, see the following.
[14] F. Hayward, op. cit., 322f.
[15] W. Schwer (biblio., chap. 12), 16.

fortunate that Bismarck himself had an interest in terminating the *Kulturkampf* in Germany. The political chance had to be taken advantage of and had to be pursued to its very end with determination and skill. In so doing, papal politics could not deal exclusively with Bismarck but also had to take into account the ideas of the German episcopate and those of the Center Party, the latter not seeing itself as an extension of the Curia. There is no question about the personal credit due to Leo XIII for the termination of the *Kulturkampf*. In Switzerland, the relatively limited *Kulturkampf* was essentially ended at the onset of the pontificate, thanks to the election victories of the Conservatives and the cooperation of moderate Liberals. After 1883, only the Geneva question and the nomination to the bishopric of Basel-Solothurn had to be settled; but even that was not possible without compromise. In Belgium, however, at the beginning of his administration, Leo XIII had to face the severe school conflict, and as a result of his intention to avoid intensification, differences with the Belgian episcopate emerged. In this case, success was due, first of all, to the Belgian Catholics, who, strengthened by their devotion to the Pope, brought about a devastating defeat for the Liberals in the elections of 1884. But the style in which diplomatic relations were resumed in 1885, after they had been discontinued in 1880, was typical for the polite ways of Leo XIII. Much more difficult was the task facing the Pope in Spain. The problem was not so much the various governments during the era of the Spanish "restoration," which vacillated between liberal-conservative and moderate left; nor the tensions which resulted from the censorship of text books, and the admission of religious who had been expelled from France. The problem was rather a group who believed themselves to be more papal than the Pope and who fought their political enemies as if they were traitors. With political perspicacity, the Pope recognized that the constitution of 1876 provided the Church with relatively optimal operating possibilities. Papal politics also avoided unnecessary aggravation in Portugal, the land of Pombal, while negotiating the new circumscription of the dioceses (1881) and the rights of patronage in the Indian mission (1886). From the central-European perspective, Leo XIII's success with his stance toward the changing conditions in the Latin American republics was generally underestimated. It was the prerequisite for the possible success of the pastoral plans of the plenary council of 1899.

It was in keeping with the confessional, ethnic, and political situation in the Slavic world that the politics of Leo XIII could only obtain slight relief for the Catholic population there. But it is probable that the arrangement with Russia, which the Austro-Hungarian ambassador to the Vatican, Revertera, called a "Midsummer Night's Dream," was all that could be achieved. In this matter Leo XIII also had to deal with the concerns in Vienna, where the strengthening of Pan-Slavism and additional tensions were feared. The situation was most delicate in areas where the Pope collided with the union of national and Catholic consciousness, especially in the Russian and Prussian parts of Poland. The clergy and the population believed themselves betrayed by the Pope to Russification, particularly because Leo XIII encountered very little understanding for his cooperation in Petersburg. The case is similar for the Prussian area: The German archbishop of Gnesen-Posen, Julius Dinder, who had been appointed in 1886 by Leo XIII after the resignation of Lédochowski, wanted a settlement between Berlin's ruthless policy of Germanization and the historical identification of Polish culture and Catholic faith; but he was unsuccessful. In view of the serious differences between Czechs and Germans in Bohemia and Moravia, the Pope had hardly a choice but to admonish the episcopate, in 1901, to keep the Catholic faith out of those differences. Like the Poles, the Slovenes and the Croatians had found their historical identity within the Slavic world in a union of confessionality and nationality. The idea of a Catholic Greater Croatia was completely contradictory to the Pope's intentions. He wanted the Croatian College in Rome, which was just being changed and renamed, to be a center for the movement to unify the Church. Aside from the confessional questions in Hungary, which had been increasing since 1886, the policy of Magyarization was a difficult component of Leo XIII's religious policy in Eastern Europe.

One can compare the attitude of Leo XIII toward Polish Catholicism under Russian influence with his attitude toward the Irish, who were suppressed by Great Britain. In both instances, there was a revolutionary situation. The difference was that Britain had Gladstone, which gave the Pope a chance to pursue an effective pro-Irish policy. Thus the question should be asked as to which the Pope better understood: the principles according to which every revolution needs to be rejected or the terribly violent resistance of the Irish toward the injustices inflicted upon them. In view of the French Revolution, Leo himself later said that it is difficult from the beginning for such changes to occur within the framework of justice. The relations of Leo XIII with Great Britain were even better when the liberal de-anglicanization of public life provided greater freedom for Catholics. The reputation of the papacy in the Anglo-Saxon world grew remarkably during this pontificate; and it was more than just an act of courtesy when Cleveland, then president of the United States of America, sent a copy of the Constitution to Leo XIII for the anniversary of his ordination in 1887. The Know-Nothing Party and the Ku Klux Klan were to fight Catholicism publicly and secretly for a long time to come, but their influence on public opinion was counterbalanced by the prestige of Leo XIII.

At the jubilees in 1883, 1887, 1893, and 1903, the Pope could enjoy the Catholics' demonstrations of loyalty and the good wishes of almost all other nations. However, it characterizes the historical situation that the original countries of the Christian West, France and Italy, could not be listed in the index of success, even though Leo XIII considered these countries especially important in the perspective of his world design.

Perhaps the central question in the historical evaluation of this pontificate deals with the opportunism which even benevolent historians denote as a characteristic of Leo XIII. Léon Gambetta was filled with hatred for the clergy. But although hate can sharpen the eye, this alone is not sufficient for the appropriate assessment of his charge that Leo was an "opportuniste sacré." Walter Goetz also supported this judgment in his sympathetic analysis. However, he distinguished such opportunism from "ordinary" opportunism, which marks the commonplace politician, noting Leo XIII's magnificent political personality, "political instinct and true leadership," especially in regard to social questions, and, last but not least, to the limits the Pope placed on his activities where demanded by his position. This question can only be answered in the context of Leo XIII's total concept. Is it correct to say that his policies and his ecclesiastical leadership were solely determined by the desire to restore the Papal State? No doubt this was a legitimate goal, and even those who considered it anachronistic had no right to call Leo XIII a "Tantalus who yearned after a small Italian principality which was to be cut from the body of the dynasty of Savoy."[16] But if this had been the ultimate goal of Leo XIII, according to which his devotion to modern society is to be judged, then he would have been neither a "master of politics" nor an important Pope.

It is obvious that the Italian question is a primary motif which, with extreme fluctuations from cautious hope to inscrutable resignation, ran through the life of Gioacchino Pecci after he was enthroned on the chair of Saint Peter. It would be misleading to see his advances toward Bismarck from this perspective only. From an agreement with the "great conservative statesman," this "ingenious, courageous, strong-willed man, who knows how to procure obedience,"[17] Leo XIII expected the establishment of a bastion against the revolutionary tendencies in Europe. But the papal words *finis impositus,* from his address on the

---

[16] H. Hermelink, *Das Christentum in der Menschheitsgeschichte* III (1955), 92. This remark is not only "too harsh" (G. Maron, op. cit., 205), but also evidence of surprising historical ignorance.

[17] Engel-Janosi I, 215–323; here: 220f. According to the topic of this book, Austrian affairs are given preference. Nevertheless, based on unpublished documents, this book is fundamental for the assessment of this pontificate's policies. For Leo XIII's appraisal of Bismarck, see chap. 3.

termination of the German question (23 May 1887), were spoken in the fatal year when, after many disappointments for the Pope, the end of a greater alliance had come. After the shameful events of 13 July 1881 (see p. 0), Austria as well as other powers refused the expected help against Italy; and in October King Umberto was a celebrated guest in Vienna. What other hope had he placed on Bismarck, a Protestant, yet an admired politician? At first, the Pope was not alone in his opinion of the weakness of the House of Savoy. But just when the Pope spoke of an asylum in the Habsburg Monarchy with the Austrian special emissary (1882), the Triple Alliance between Germany, Austria, and Italy was about to be ratified. The support of the House of Savoy—a child of the revolution to Leo XIII—was presented to the Pope as an act of conservative politics,[18] and Austria pressured the Vatican to settle the German question. The Pope's reliance on Bismarck grew considerably when the latter asked him to mediate the negotiations with Spain concerning the Caroline Islands, one of Leo XIII's most important functions in the last phase of the *Kulturkampf.* Its conclusion was announced in a papal address of 23 May 1887, ending with the expression of hope that "harmony" could now also be restored to Italy stressing the condition that the Pope's authority should be subject to no one else's.[19] Obviously, the Pope felt, at that moment, that the time for such a solution to the "Roman question" had come: crowning the peace with Germany. However, Crispi refused immediately. In October the Italian prime minister was Bismarck's welcome guest, and the Triple Alliance was renewed. The Pope, though "abandoned by the powers,"[20] returned to his old demands. But with what political power could they be realized? On 2 June 1887 Mariano Rampolla[21] was appointed secretary of state. On 4 October 1887 the French ambassador reported to the Vatican that the Cardinal had spoken with France *d'une entente cordiale.* At the end of the year Pope Leo XIII himself called France *sa fille privilegiée* in the presence of the ambassador. As early as 1884, the letter *Nobilissima Gallorum gens* had intonated such language. In the year 1888, when Wilhelm II visited the Pope, the Pope called Bismarck a great revolutionary during an audience with the French ambassador. After the report of the Austrian special emissary (6 August 1888), Leo XIII told him, "If the government cannot dispatch any troops for my protection,

---

[18] At the Catholic Convention in Freiburg, 1888, Windthorst interpreted the Triple Alliance, renewed in 1887, as a situation favorable to the Pope; as a result, the German and Austrian Catholics could exert more influence on Italy (Kißling II, 234f.).

[19] *Acta Leonis* VII, 112–16; here: 115.

[20] Engel-Janosi I, 251: Leo XIII's words to the Austrian ambassador to the Vatican.

[21] On Rampolla, see bibliography and the appraisals of diplomats in Engel-Janosi I, 245, 257ff.

they should at least hoist their flags on the walls of the Vatican when danger is imminent." In connection with a war feared at that time, the Pope advised Vienna and Paris that an alliance with the Vatican would be to their advantage.[22] In 1890 the policy of *ralliement* began: reconciliation with the French Republic. Rampolla explained to the French delegate that the establishment of an Italian republic might clear the situation for the Vatican because the Pope would not have to reckon with a monarch next to him in Rome.[23] The second political alliance failed with the *ralliement*.[24] That it had little to do with a trend toward democracy as such can be deduced from the report by Revertera, the Austrian ambassador to the Vatican, according to which the Pope, two weeks after the encyclical *Au milieu des sollicitudes* (1892), declared his principal support for a "monarchical restoration in France," were it at all possible.[25]

During the New Year's reception in 1897 at Count Revertera's, Leo XIII expressed two hopes: before the end of his days, he wanted to see the dawn, at least, of a unification with the Christian peoples outside of the Church and the beginning of a solution to the Roman question. So as not to diminish the political problems of the Papal State or to cloud one's view of the greatness of the Pope by isolating the problem from his total portfolio,[26] it is necessary to see both hopes as one. Naturally, one must understand the Pope's hope for unification from the perspec-

---

[22] Engel-Janosi I, 256, 266.

[23] Ibid., 256.

[24] Toward the end of the year 1895, when the law against congregations became an issue, Nuncio Ferrata tried to combine the two alliances by reminding the French president of the cooperation with the monarchies (*Mémoires* III, 306f.).

[25] Leo XIII to Count Revertera, "I would like to tell you confidentially what I can, naturally, only confide to few people: I regret that a monarchal restoration in France is impossible under present circumstances. . . . The future of the monarchy there depends on the predominance due to the Catholics within the state" (Engel-Janosi I, 272f.). For a description of Revertera ("honest nobleman"), see ibid., 257.—Cf. chap. 2.—On the change of course: Ward, 60.

[26] Walter Goetz (op. cit., 397f.) also considers this aspect most problematic in view of the question of opportunism. He emphasizes how seriously the Pope took the restoration of the Papal State, unbelievable as this may seem. He wanted to hold Rampolla responsible for the " scrupulous attempts to restore Europe" after 1887. "One cannot simultaneously assent to democracy in France and forbid participation in elections in Italy" (von Aretin, op. cit., 166), since this is based on a relationship to democracy which did not exist; similarly, Fülöp-Miller, op. cit., 130—The papal relations to the American episcopate of Cardinal Gibbons and its development must be seen in this context. From the beginning, there were basic differences, since this episcopate consisted of confirmed democrats.—Whatever could be reconciled by most of the didactic letters which Leo XIII was undoubtedly responsible for, did not preclude conflicts in a certain historical situation (cf. chaps. 10 and 24). The personal sacrifices which the Pope demanded in his policies, during the *Kulturkampf* as well as the *Ralliement,* are aspects of the general problem of political power. Cardinal of the Curia (since 1875) Ledóchowski

tive of what was then historically feasible. The Pope did not expect mutual sympathy from the separated Christians, but rather a mass movement toward conversion. The movement was the horizon on which the validity of the Anglican ordinations was discussed. After he received reports from the Balkans in 1887, Leo XIII believed he could count on the movement. He had oriented his policies toward Russia according to his expectations.[27] Even without calling Leo XIII a "mortal enemy of Protestants,"[28] one could reject such a perception of Christian ecumenism. But given the Catholic self-concept, the city of Saint Peter was the essential component of a Christian unification. However Leo XIII may have envisioned the solution to the Roman question at different times, in detailed or in general terms, it was not only a matter of a "small principality," but of the Holy City as the center of the world Church and the episcopal see of its sovereign, subject to no other power. Rome of Saint Peter's successor and Christ's deputy—or Rome of the Freemason "plague"; that was the question. "La Roma nostra," Leo XIII used to say. And when the Pope spoke about finding asylum in Austria or Spain, he repeatedly used Ambrose's words "Ubi Papa, ibi ecclesia"; however, he thought primarily of a future triumphant return to Rome.[29]

---

had to renounce the archbishopric of Gnesen in 1886. Archbishop Melchers of Cologne, imprisoned during the *Kulturkampf,* had to resign in 1885 when promoted to cardinal of the Curia. Bishop Lachat of Basel-Solothurn was demoted when transferred to Ticino as apostolic administrator. The often bitter reactions in the French episcopate are rather understandable.—Bismarck was satisfied with Leo XIII's mediation in the question of the Caroline Islands and he thanked him by addressing him with "sire" in the letter of 31 January 1886 (which the Pope considered significant in reference to the Roman question). Pragmatism and his high opinion of Bismarck, in spite of disillusionments, compelled Leo XIII to award this statesman, whom he later called a revolutionary, the Medal of Christ.

[27] Cf. chaps. 9, 11, and 25. For his expectations as to conversions in the East, see Engel-Janosi I, 222f., 248f., 268ff., 321f.

[28] R. Seeberg, *Aus Religion und Geschichte* I (1906), 332–51.—In several encyclicals, Leo XIII declared the Enlightenment and the Revolution a result of the Reformation. On 1 August 1897, the three hundredth anniversary of Peter Canisius's death, Leo XIII sent the encyclical *Militantis Ecclesiae* to the Austrian, German, and Swiss episcopates. He compared the situation of Canisius, when the corruption of morals was followed by the "craze for innovations," with the present and spoke of the *rebellio lutherana* (*Acta Leonis* XVII, 248–59; here: 248f.).

[29] The idea of finding asylum for the papacy outside of Italy came up four times: 1881–82 when Austrian Trent was considered; 1888 (again looking toward Austria), when the Crispi government played its intrigues and the Pope found his hopes for a conclusion of the *Kulturkampf* disappointed because the visit of Emperor Wilhelm II had gone badly, primarily because of Prince Henry; 1889, after the demonstrations at the unveiling ceremonies of the Giordano Bruno memorial, this time with Spain in mind; in the summer of 1891, when Emperor Franz Joseph discouraged the Pope (Schmidlin, *PG,* 414f., 417, 421; Engel-Janosi I, 226–31, 255, 266f.).

If one wants to understand all aspects of this pontificate, it seems necessary to start with Leo XIII's very pronounced awareness of the history of the papacy. This awareness did not have a trace of historicism. He repeated, again and again, in his encyclicals that the papacy formed the Christian West, and what the nations, especially Italy, owed to the papacy.[30] It is self-evident that the Popes Leo the Great and Gregory the Great were especially mentioned, and, likewise, that Leo's predecessors since the French Revolution occupy the most space in the list. Upon examination of the actual content of the frequent traditional mentioning of predecessors,[31] one might find it worthy of note that quotes by Innocent III abound, almost all of which show the personal handwriting of Leo XIII. In the encyclical *Inscrutabili Dei* (28 May 1878), Innocent III appears together with Leo the Great, Alexander III, and Pius V as models for the new pontificate. Leo XIII, referring to Innocent III and other popes in connection with his unification plans for Eastern Churches, provokes historical comparisons which were, of course, not intended. *Nobilissima Gallorum gens* (1884), written after the conclusion of the Triple Alliance, anticipates subsequent French policy (in the introduction, the *Gesta Dei per Francos* is mentioned). Interestingly, Innocent (together with Gregory IX) is cited in a quotation from the letter to the archbishop of Rheims. In it he speaks of the preferential love of France and her obedience to the Apostolic See, which outdoes all other empires.[32] In 1892 Leo XIII had the remains of Innocent III transferred from Perugia to the oldest and most sacred church in Rome, the Lateran Basilica, which he had been restoring and expanding in grand style since 1881. In the same year, the *ralliement,* the second big attempt to solve the Roman question, was in progress, as well as the creation of a papacy which would, in this revolution-ridden world, resume the universal historic task from which it had profited during the Middle Ages. With the appropriate adjustments, the papacy could win back "moral-religious hegemony in a new Christian world empire."[33] In 1892, on the anniversary of his coronation (3 March 1878), Leo XIII justified the transfer of the remains of his great predecessor, Innocent III, in a speech to the cardinals.[34] During his episcopate in Perugia, his favorite idea had been to honor the memory of this man, and he realized the idea that year, so that his voice might be heard from the Lateran Basilica, the "symbol of Christian unity." Immediately afterwards, he

---

[30] Cf. chap. 22.
[31] Gregory XIII is mentioned often, which is only important because of the calendar reform in connection with outfitting the observatory (*Acta Leonis* XI, 62).
[32] *Acta Leonis* IV, 11.
[33] Schmidlin, *PG* II, 353.
[34] *Acta Leonis* XII, 383–85.

mentioned the great goals of Innocent's pontificate: the "conquest of the Holy Land and the independence of the Church." Under the "freedom of the papacy," he said, the Christian faith, "like our blood, revitalized the social and political organism" and tied the "peoples" to the authority of the Church, the "moral center of the world." Is not "a strong faith, verified in the conscience of the peoples, rather than the restoration of medieval institutions," the way to achieve final victory? The differentiation of medieval and contemporary conditions reflects the discussions about the guilds which were conducted in socialist circles and paid attention to in *Rerum novarum* (1891). It seems especially important that, in these instances, peoples rather than nation states were referred to. This was in line with hopes placed on the "Catholic masses" since 1887 and with a remark by Rampolla on the "clearly democratic trend of an era, which the Church should not face with animosity.[35] Rampolla's opinion was supported by the worker pilgrimages. We do not know, specifically, what Leo XIII knew about the pontificate of Innocent III, whose great universal goal it had been to lift the papacy "in the realm of *christianitas* to a sacerdotal-royal position," with himself "as head of the super-national *populus christianus,* which would be his direct responsibility."[36] It would be misleading to single out Innocent III merely on the basis of the quotations from Leo's predecessors. But Innocent III's memory accompanied Leo XIII from his birth (Anagni was the native bishopric of Gioacchino Pecci) to Perugia, to a dramatic turning point, the transfer of Innocent III's body to the Lateran Basilica (1892), to Leo's own burial (on the right side of the Basilica opposite the tomb of Innocent III).[37] Thus, Innocent III offers access to the universal conception of Leo XIII, who felt that another personality from the Middle Ages, Thomas Aquinas, had completed "Christian philosophy," a return to which would be the way to cure modern society. Perhaps this explains Leo XIII's "temptation to theocracy."

From this background it is understandable that, in an age of imperialism, against all political reality, Leo XIII highly valued the prospects of an international office for arbitration. Such an office he claimed

[35] Engel-Janosi I, 259f.—Rampolla's remark was directed to Count Revertera, the Austrian ambassador.

[36] F. Kempf, *LThK* V, 688.

[37] Two other Popes were buried in the Cathedral of Perugia (Urban IV [1261–64] and Martin IV [1281–85]). To Friedrich Kempf I owe the information that "at some time, the remains of all three Popes were buried together"; thus, it was a remarkable act to transfer the remains of the most important Pope (after all, the Romans forced Martin IV to be crowned in Orvieto). On the transfer (the remains are supposed to have been taken to Rome by a prelate; he carried them in a box and traveled by railway), see Schmidlin, *PG* II, 405.—Leo XIII pointed to Anagni, in 1897, as the birthplace of Innocent III and Gregory IX.

principally for the papacy. Already, in *Diuturnum illud* (1881), one is reminded that, at the time of the Holy Roman Empire, the Church as *conciliatrix* had tamed the political passions of peoples partly through clemency, partly by exerting authority.[38] Bismarck's offer of papal mediation (1885) in the dispute between Germany and Spain over the Caroline Islands was, naturally, significant for Leo XIII, mostly because he interpreted the gesture of the Chancellor as recognition of his temporal sovereignty. The Pope, who tended to attach high hopes to the offer, underwent the experience of Spain's refusing his arbitration under international law and conceding merely to mediation.[39] In his letter of 29 May 1899, Leo XIII referred specifically to this diplomatic action. He was answering a letter from the Dutch Queen Wilhelmina, who, at the initiative of the Tsar, had wanted to include the Pope in the peace negotiations in the Hague, and had asked him for "moral support."[40] Leo XIII explained in his letter that it was the duty of the papal office not only to provide the conference with moral support, but also to "play an effective and active part in it." This, he wrote, was in keeping with the tradition of the papacy, whose authority transcended all national borders. Despite opposition, he was going to pursue this duty and not seek any fame other than "de servir la cause sacrée de la civilisation chrétienne." The invitation failed because of Italy. Other countries were also perplexed over this view of papal duties. They believed it to be limited to arbitration. Confirmation of the papal mission had been drawn into demonstrations of loyalty by Catholic congregations, yet it would lead to complications if it was to be applied to a concrete situation.[41] It was a delusion to project this political world onto a "Christian

---

[38] *Acta Leonis* II, 282.

[39] Leo XIII appointed a commission of cardinals. Their proposal of 22 October 1885 to acknowledge Spain's sovereignty over the islands, but to grant Germany free trade, was accepted by the political powers (1899, after the Spanish-American War, Germany bought the islands from Spain as a protectorate). U. Stutz (op. cit., 60) speaks of a "diplomatic masterpiece" by Bismarck; E. Born (Gebhardt-Grundmann III, 236), emphasizes that this step signifies "the recognition of the Pope's worldly sovereignty, which has not happened since the occupation of the Papal State in 1870"; on the critical assessment of the papal expectations by the Austrian embassy to the Vatican, see Engel-Janosi I, 240; on Spain, R. Konetzke (biblio., chap. 8), 521. On a malicious German caricature, showing the Pope holding a sword and trying to destroy the inscription "Honor-Profit—he is scornfully looking at a Spanish woman to his left; on the right, massively, the triumphant Bismarck—see von Aretin, op. cit., 127.

[40] *Acta Leonis* XIX, 83–85.

[41] In 1890, at the Catholic Convention in Coblenz, Windthorst pleaded for recognition (Kißling II, 246). At the Catholic Convention in Munich in 1895, another motion by Prince Löwenstein was defeated (Siebertz, op. cit., 203–9).

civilization" and to want to redesign it as a union of nations unified in the Christian faith.[42]

The significance of the encyclical *Rerum novarum* (1891)[43] is correctly evaluated and not in the least diminished if placed in the context of Leo XIII's great world design. Certainly the experiences the Pope had with the conservative monarchies, specifically in the years 1887/88, play a role. The monarchies did not want to assist him against the Italian upstart. And Leo XIII, despite his general utterances in reference to political philosophy, was adverse to democracy. Likewise, the change in tone after 1901 toward *Graves de communi* is evident. The negative turn of events exposes the overall goal: a cure for the social and political disruptions in the modern world, which was plunging into a state of deep resignation around the end of the nineteenth century. The cure was hoped to be the recognition of the moral authority of the *vicarius Christi*. It involved the inevitable liberation of the *proletarii* from oppression by *classes dirigeantes* as well as their right to unionize. The "question of the workers" is only one part of the general renovation of society based on Neo-Scholastic social philosophy. For Leo, renovation was feasible only if the authority of the Church would be respected again by everyone. As much as the workers' pilgrimages to Rome[44] meant to the Pope in view of the Piedmontese sovereignty, it is absurd to interpret the patriarchal papal involvement in the workers' question as a mere means of pragmatic politics in the "Roman question."[45]

Leo XIII was not only a political but also a seigneurial Pope.[46] His

---

[42] Tischleder, *Staatslehre*, 404ff.—H. Hermelink (op. cit., 107) remarked that it was too late "to subjugate liberated peoples to the centralistic leadership of a celibate international priesthood"; this remark, made in 1955, shows a curious Protestant feeling of resentment.

[43] Rightfully, K. O. von Aretin (op. cit., 158) calls this encyclical "a great deed" which is directed against the paternalistic slander of the Christian social movement.

[44] French pilgrimages 1887, 1888, 1889, 1891 (the words "vive le Pape!" resulted in disturbances during which a picture of the Pope was burned). In 1892, a medallion was issued displaying a picture of the Pope and a figure, symbolic of religion, carrying the encyclical of 1891 in the right hand and the cross in the left, while smashing the head of the hydra (greed). A poor woman and her child are sitting at the feet of this female figure. A strong workman with his tools is looking up to her, while wealthy gentlemen approaching from the other side bring presents (Schmidlin, *PG* II, 378). One has to consider here the popular taste of the time.

[45] Cf. chaps. 12 and 13.

[46] It would be presumptuous to undertake even a sketch of Gioacchino Pecci's portrait. The reports of people who met him are contradictory (cf. Engel-Janosi I, 217, 231, 263). Optimism, naturally greater at the beginning of his office than at the end, seems to have been intertwined with scepticism, something rather unexpected in view of Leo XIII's expansive concepts. Emotional features were, probably, not foreign to this strong,

first secretary of state, Alexander Franchi,[47] whose appointment may have had something to do with the papal elections, was the most distinguished secretary of state before Rampolla. In 1880, two years after Franchi's death, Lorenzo Nina, who also belonged to the intransigents, incurred displeasure and was in office only a short time.[48] Secretary of State Ludovico Jacobini (1880–87), formerly nuncio to Vienna, had a cautious nature and "his personality could neither succeed in the Vatican nor with the Pope himself" (Engel-Janosi). He had to follow the changing initiatives of the Pope in his policy toward Bismarck. Leo XIII also expected that his nuncios would be recognized as executive representatives of his authority, through which he ruled the world Church in a centralized manner.[49] To strengthen his position toward the ecclesiastical opponents of the Spanish constitution, the Pope stated the point clearly in a letter on 15 April 1885, delivered by Secretary of State Jacobini to Rampolla, nuncio to Madrid since 1882.[50] "In respect to the faithful in the country and their ecclesiastical affairs," the nuncios have an "authoritative mission," whose extent is determined by the Pope—the constitution *Pastor aeternus* is referred to. Domenico Ferrata, one of Leo XIII's outstanding diplomats, became nuncio to Paris after his duties in Switzerland and Belgium (1891–96). In 1894 he declared to French President Périer that the nuncio represents the Pope as the "true spiritual sovereign of the Catholics in the respective country," and that he, the nuncio, differed fundamentally from other ambassadors.[51] Another man especially favored by the Pope was the diplomat Luigi Galimberti. As special emissary of the Pope, he played a major role in the conclusion of the *Kulturkampf,* and his behavior toward Windthorst, which he could not have afforded at his own expense, documented the individual style of government of this pontificate.[52] That his rival Rampolla became secretary of state in 1887 and that he himself had to go to

---

humanistic rationalist ("cool and sober": Schmidlin, *PG* II, 587). According to a report by the Austrian delegate, Leo XIII interrupted Secretary of State Jacobini while the latter was voicing objections concerning an administrative question, saying, "Ego sum Petrus!" Leo XIII's mood, prompted by Emperor Franz Joseph's evasive reply (1881), was characterized by Jacobini as follows, "J'en ai été navré." Naturally, the physical strength of the Pope, born in 1810, had diminished. But caution should be exercised over talk about his "senility." In 1901 the Austrian ambassador found the Pope to be more energetic and fresher than twelve years earlier.

[47] Cf. chap. 3, n. 3.
[48] Cf. chap. 3, n. 12.
[49] Leo XIII asserted "the weight of his authority even in nonecclesiastical matters" and thus practiced the *potestas directa* indirectly (Schmidlin, *PG* , 583).
[50] *ASS,* 17, 561ff.; cf. cit., chap. 8, n. 5.
[51] *Mémoires* II, 455.
[52] Cf. chap. 3, n. 43.

Vienna as nuncio (until 1893) were the result of the major policy changes in papal politics.[53] As long as the Vatican archives until 1903 are not generally accessible, it cannot be determined accurately, among other matters, which position Secretary of State Rampolla took toward Leo XIII.[54] It is possible that he had great influence on Leo XIII's activities during the final years.

With this diplomatic apparatus, Leo XIII sought to assert the power of his moral authority. In the beginning of the 1880s, he had to realize that the conditions for such assertion were not present because the conservative forces did not consider this authority indispensable to their survival in the face of revolutionary tendencies. Not even the Habsburg Monarchy wanted to or could face the consequences in reality. After the nineties Leo XIII noticed that turning directly to the people could strengthen his authority over Catholicism. But his hopes for the expansion to turn into conversion movements were not fulfilled, much less his expectation that he would be respected as the moral authority by all men. It was one of his favorite plans to establish diplomatic relations with China. He had already designated Antonio Agliardi, later nuncio to Vienna, as the apostolic delegate when his letter to the Emperor of China (1 February 1885) received a positive response. His immediate motive had been the protection of the Catholic missionaries. But the ultimate goal was the inclusion of this world culture into his universal concept.[55] The plan failed because France, the only power generally recognized to protect the Christians in the Orient, saw her interests endangered and threatened the Vatican with a break in diplomatic relations.

One must see the consecration of the entire human race to the Sacred Heart, on the occasion of the jubilee in 1900, in the perspective of Leo's world plan. Even though Leo XIII was a "political Pope" and as such subjugated to the conditions of politics, this pontiff cannot be understood if his goal is defined as "the domination of all of mankind by the Catholic Church,"[56] unless one understands "domination" as the kind of mutual permeation of religious and political concepts which charac-

---

[53] On Galimberti, see Engel-Janosi I, 261f. The "mysterious" diplomat was considered a supporter of a rapprochement with Italy. This is contradicted by a report of the French ambassador in Vienna. It says that Galimberti supported an aggressive liquidation of the *Non Expedit* and would have liked to see the Pope leave the Vatican together with his cardinals in order to prove the alleged fallacy of the freedom of the Pope.

[54] On Rampolla, see this chap., n. 21.

[55] *Acta Leonis* V, 10–12. On Leo XIII's relations to the missions, ibid., III.

[56] W. Goetz, op. cit., 403. Engel-Janosi I, 264, maintains that "Leo XIII wanted to be and was more than the 'Pope of diplomacy.' " Ward, 61: great as a Pope, not as a politician.

terized the political theory of the West before it dissolved in the later medieval period. One cannot say that his pontificate distinguished itself through the creative forces of spirituality,[57] even though Leo XIII's deep religious piety is proven beyond doubt. Traditional forms, which Marie-Thérèse of Lisieux picked up and internalized during her life of suffering, were developed further and incorporated in the service of public worship. But the character of this pontificate is distorted if one misunderstands the "politicization" as an ideological manipulation of religiosity. This is contradicted by the astonishing attraction which most religious orders and congregations exerted, so that they were able to keep winning many young people for extensive social work with religious motivation.

The world design of Leo XIII found its most magnificent expression, revealing its innermost moments, in the apostolic letter *Praeclara gratulationis* of June 1894.[58] It is one of those utopias without which historical greatness is not possible. The end is marked by the bitter letter *Annum ingressi sumus* of 19 March 1902,[59] in which Leo XIII bemoans the insults inflicted upon the Church. But it was not just the fanatic hatred of individual Freemasons and the animosity of the whole organization toward the Catholic Church. Reconciliation of the modern world with tradition was no longer in anyone's power. The so-called "tragic failure"[60] of Leo stood under a world signature. His successes were fewer than he had hoped. But that he had hoped for much was the basis for his achievements. To the faithful "he gave a new feeling of inner security toward the world."[61] This constitutes his historical significance. "Though his reign, in retrospect, may not appear to be as unique as it was presented elsewhere, Leo XIII is unquestionably the most important Pope of his century and the most important Pope between Benedict XIV and Pius XI" (G. Schwaiger).[62] His policies and the changes in his policies, his political and social encyclicals, his reclaiming the great philosophy of Thomas Aquinas, his centralized orientation of Catholicism and the Church toward Rome, his involvement in the world mis-

---

[57] Cf. chap. 16.
[58] *Acta Leonis* XIV, 195–214; A. Harnack calls this letter "the testimonial of Leo XIII": *Reden und Aufsätze* II (2nd ed., 1906), 267–93; one cannot expect "any concessions (toward the non-Catholics), other than a friendly tone."
[59] *Acta Leonis* XXII, 52–80.
[60] Fülöp-Miller, op. cit., 152.
[61] W. Goetz, op. cit., 402—W. von Loewenich, (*Moderner Katholizismus* [Witten a.d. Ruhr 1955], 69f.) speaks of the "disunity of modern Catholicism" becoming evident in Leo XIII, whom he portrays very objectively. On this "disunity," see chaps. 12–14. The real problem is not "abundant authoritative preliminary decisions." The problem is much more complex and not confined to Catholicism.
[62] G. Schwaiger, op. cit., 49.

sion, his hopes for a great conversion movement: all these were testimony to his grandiose desire for *restauratio;* no longer by way of political restoration as at the beginning of the century, but by turning to the modern world because of his basic concern for the salvation of mankind. The fact that the election of the new Pope after Leo's death on 20 July 1903 stirred the political powers much more than those in the year 1878 was a result of the respect which Leo XIII had gained in the world for the papacy.

The Situation in the Various Countries until 1914

CHAPTER 1

The Kulturkampf *in Prussia and in the German Empire until 1878*

Nowhere in Europe was the struggle between Church and state fought as vigorously as in the German Empire of 1871. This battle considerably impeded inner consolidation for the next two decades. Since most of the controversial issues continued to be subject to the legislation of the individual states, the struggle took place on their terrain, and most vigorously in Prussia, the dominating power in the new Empire. There were two momentous determining factors: ideological contrast between the ultramontane Catholic Church and liberalism, which was controlling spiritual and political life, peaking in the years of the *Syllabus;* and the continued disparity within the Prussian state. The confessional disputes had further increased; the Prussian bureaucracy, partly Protestant, partly liberal, had only reluctantly executed an ecclesiastical policy of parity, as defined by the constitutions of 1848 and 1850.[1] The strengthening of Catholicism as a social force awakened old and new adversaries. In the late sixties, attacks against confessional schools, cloisters, and other Church institutions occurred more and more often. Mutual misunderstandings due to insufficient knowledge of the opponent and the German lack of flexibility and moderation were contributing factors.

One direct cause of the conflict was the creation of the Center Party, which Bismarck falsely regarded as a conglomerate of the Empire's adversaries. Other causes were the dispute over the dogma of infallibility, the alliance with the National Liberals, designed by the chancellor to

---

[1] V. Conzemius, *Die Briefe Aulikes an Döllinger. Ein Beitrag zur Geschichte der "Katholischen Abteilung" im preußischen Kultusministerium* (Rome, Freiburg, Vienna 1968), passim.—On occasion, Bismarck himself had reprimanded high Prussian civil servants for their animosity towards Catholics. Cf. his direct report of 30 September 1865: O. v. Bismarck, *Die gesammelten Werke* V (Berlin 1928), no. 185. In regard to tensions in Prussia after 1866, see K. Bachem, *Zentrumspartei* III, 26–47; R. Morsey, *Probleme der Kulturkampfforschung,* 221–24.

consolidate the Empire, and his fear of an anti-German coalition of Catholic states.

The political tensions within the Church increased and were nurtured continuously since the end of 1869 by news from the Council in Rome.[2] These tensions and the fear of more severe anti-Catholic measures, as demanded by the Liberals, seemed to necessitate the political consolidation of Catholics in Prussia as well. The movement seeking to found a party since the summer of 1870 was headed by Hermann von Mallinckrodt and Peter Reichensperger. Against the opposition of integralistic circles, they insisted on a political, not primarily a Catholic, party: a principle they had already defended in the fifties.[3] Nevertheless, in response to the particular initial situation, Church affairs took precedence in the first program of the Center Party: the immunity of the Church as defined in the Prussian constitution, the guarantee of confessional schools and freedom of instruction. Other, more important resolutions demanded the preservation of the federal constitution of the German Empire, governmental decentralization, protection of workers, and social welfare. On the basis of this program, fifty-eight deputies were elected to the Prussian Diet in November 1870.

The founding of the Center Party coincided with the Franco-Prussian War. Even the majority of the German Catholics and their leaders regarded this war as a legitimate opportunity to ward off ever increasing threatening pressures. In a similar vein was the pastoral letter of the episcopal conference in Fulda in the summer of 1870, which was addressed particularly to the opponents of the dogma of infallibility. In contrast to the fraternal strife of 1866, the war against the "arch-enemy" was quite popular, especially in the Catholic west and southwest of Germany.

Those who had approved the war could not reject its predictable consequence, the founding of the Empire. Indeed, in 1871 the sentiments of most Catholics differed from those of most other Germans only by reason of an increasing fear of Church conflicts. They also wanted close contact between the Empire and Austria. At the Catholic Convention in Mainz (September 1871) its President Friedrich Baudri and Bishop Ketteler gave recognition to the Emperor and the Empire.[4] Urgently responding to the actual increase of controversies caused by

[2] V. Conzemius, "Preußen und das 1. Vatikanische Konzil," *AHC* 2 (1970), 353–419.
[3] Concerning the founding of the Center Party, see K. Bachem, *Zentrumspartei* III, 99–151; L. Bergsträsser, *Geschichte der politischen Parteien in Deutschland* (Munich, 10th ed., 1960), 133–37; T. Nipperdey, *Die Organisation der deutschen Parteien vor 1918* (Düsseldorf 1961), 265ff.; E. R. Huber, *Verfassungsgeschichte* IV, 50ff.; R. Morsey, *StL* VIII, 966f.
[4] F. Vigener, *Ketteler,* 653–58.

the dogma of infallibility, which had already invaded imperial legal territory, they demanded from the state justice for the Church and protection from assaults by the Liberals. Similarly, Ketteler expressed himself in a political program written in 1871, but not published until 1873.[5] He welcomed the "partial unity of the German people," created by the founding of the Empire, "because it satisfied, partially, a right of the German people and it made amends for the injustice inflicted upon them."

At the first session of the *Reichstag* (March 1871), the Center Party already represented the second strongest faction (with fifty-eight deputies). The program, which had not been substantially modified since the previous year,[6] and Ketteler's words mentioned above (in 1871/72 he was a member of the *Reichstag*) showed the reservations of the Center Party as it proceeded with its work. They were sufficient to create an almost irreconcilable opposition to the dominant National Liberals. This was clearly proven by the exclusion of the Center Party from the Presidium. The situation was intensified when the Center immediately accepted some Guelph guest listeners and, soon afterwards, supported other minorities as well (Poles, Alsatians). Continual controversies about the new dogma, about the ecclesiastical censure of orthodox adversaries, and about the growing Old Catholic Church were part of the efforts of the new Empire to gain a historical self-understanding. After 1866 National-Liberal, National-Protestant, and also Protestant-Conservative writers presented the results of 1870/71 as a victory for the social principles essential to Protestantism and a consequence of Protestant Prussian history.[7] The Habsburg dynasty, the papacy, the Jesuits, and the Counter Reformation were held responsible for actually or allegedly leading German history astray. Now and then, Catholics were advised to establish a National Church.

The Center Party itself had introduced these disputes over principles into the first session of the *Reichstag*. This was instigated by the problems of the Papal State, which stirred everyone's emotions, especially after the annexation of Rome (September 1870). The numerous demonstrations and pilgrimages of the Catholics were meant to assure the Pope of their solidarity and to ask their governments for support. The

[5] "Die Katholiken im neuen Reich. Entwurf zu einem politischen Programm" (Mainz 1873).
[6] Text: K. Bachem, *Zentrumspartei* III, 137f.
[7] T. Schieder, *Das deutsche Kaiserreich von 1871 als Nationalstaat* (Cologne, Opladen 1961), 22–26, 58f., 76–82, 125–30; K. G. Faber, *Die nationalpolitische Publizistik Deutschlands von 1866 bis 1871* II (Düsseldorf 1963) nos. 883, 885, 890, 907–10, 913f., 921f., 930; E. Fehrenbach, *Wandlungen des deutschen Kaisergedankens 1871–1918* (Munich, Vienna 1969), 23–40, 52–56, 60–65, 223–27, etc.

Liberals took this as a challenge, since they considered the completion of unity in Germany and Italy as a victory of the modern concept of the state.[8]

Since help could neither be expected from Austria, which tried to come to terms with Italy, nor from now Republican France, Pius IX had asked the King of Prussia for assistance in the fall of 1870. Archbishops Melchers and Ledóchowski had turned to Wilhelm I and Bismarck with the same request. In Berlin Queen Augusta (Empress since 1871) expressly supported the papal desires. She was guided by a conservative awareness of the law as well as the wish to integrate Catholics into the Prussian-German state. The conservative Minister of Religious Affairs Heinrich Mühler (1813–74) agreed with her, but intended to intervene only together with other political powers.[9] King Wilhelm I (Emperor since January 1871) was not disinclined toward the considerations of his spouse, but had to agree with Bismarck's arguments, who, during the persisting war with France, strictly refused any anti-Italian intervention. However, he was willing, if necessary, to grant asylum to the Pope.

In the Emperor's speech before the first *Reichstag,* Wilhelm disavowed any kind of intervention into the domestic affairs of other peoples. In the draft of a reply addressed to the Monarch, the National-Liberal majority formulated the principle of non-intervention, which was in accord with the national self-understanding and the needs of the Empire in regard to her foreign policies, but clearly oriented against the Pope and the Papal State.[10] The Center Party attempted a modification which would not fundamentally exclude intervention in favor of the Pope. Constitution-minded Ludwig Windthorst (1812–91), former cabinet minister of Hannover, stood out in this debate. In the following years, especially after Mallinckrodt's death in 1874, Windthorst became the great leader of the Center Party and Bismarck's most important parliamentary adversary in the *Kulturkampf.* Windthorst declared papal independence, as guaranteed by the Papal State which was created under Charlemagne, founder of the First German Empire, to be of vital interest to German Catholics. In the debate, arguments by politicians

---

[8] Concerning the controversies of 1870/71, see E. Portner, *Die Einigung Italiens im Urteil liberaler deutscher Zeitgenossen* (Bonn 1959), 66ff., 111ff., 148ff.; K. Buchheim, *Ultramontanismus und Demokratie,* 213f., 237, 243f., 248ff., etc.; K.-G. Faber, op. cit.; K. O. von Aretin and R. Lill, *La fine del potere temporale . . . Atti del XLV congresso di storia del risorgimento italiano* (Rome 1972), 79–87, 291–301.

[9] The point of view of Augusta, Wilhelm I, and Mühler, see A. Constabel, *Vorgeschichte,* nos. 14, 16, 19, 21, 25, 32, 35, 43, 53, 68, 80, 84, 87, 91.

[10] Concerning the address debate, see T. Schieder, *Kaiserreich,* 80f. Cf. also K. Bachem, *Zentrumspartei* III, 193–98; G. Stoltenberg, *Der deutsche Reichstag 1871 bis 1873* (Düsseldorf 1955), 39–43.

wishing for a united Germany excluding Austria were brought forth, sympathy for liberal Italy was declared, and impetuous invectives against the Catholic Church and its latest developments were voiced. The majority's address to the Monarch was approved with 243 to 63 votes. Although the failure of the Center Party's motion was predictable, the fact that it was pursued anyway was not only due to the anti-papal tone of the majority draft. The deputies of the then strongest Catholic party seemed to believe that they could draw inopportune conclusions from the commitment of solidarity with the Pope, which had always been part of an ultramontane Church concept. Once again, more trenchantly than in 1866, did the Roman-Italian aspect of the decision of 1870 affect and burden German Catholics and their relations to the nation-state.

The debate on the address resulted in the isolation of the Center Party, which was immediately intensified during the deliberation about the constitution.[11] The faction reiterated demands for the inclusion of certain fundamental rights in the federal constitution, among them articles 15 and 18 of the Prussian constitution, guaranteeing immunity for the Church. As early as 1867, after the creation of the North German Confederation, several Catholic deputies had voiced these demands. The main supporters of the hopeless initiative were Ketteler and Peter Reichensperger. Mallinckrodt and Windthorst had dissuaded them in vain. They felt that it would be more profitable for the Church to assign responsibilities for religious policies to the individual states than to the liberally governed Empire.

The debates on the address and the constitution anticipated the parliamentary fronts of the *Kulturkampf*. Bismarck found his suspicions concerning the Catholic party verified. It seemed to him that the party's alleged "international" character and its first initiatives endangered the consolidation of national unity. He hated the "Guelph" Windthorst. He was particularly suspicious of the protection which the party provided the Poles who had been forced into total opposition since the founding of the Empire. Attempts to denounce the Center Party in Rome as conspirators of revolution and compel the Pope to chastise the party were only partially successful. After some ambiguous remarks, Cardinal Antonelli expressed his appreciation for the party in a letter which Ketteler had effected.[12] Bismarck thereupon fought an open battle,

---

[11] K. Bachem, *Zentrumspartei* III, 198–201; G. Stoltenberg, *Reichstag,* 43–46.

[12] F. Vigener, *Ketteler,* 650f. The demarches in the Vatican were carried out by the Bavarian delegate Count Tauffkirchen, who was also representing the Empire there for a while. G. Franz-Willing, *Die bayrische Vatikangesandtschaft 1803–1934* (Munich 1965), 63ff.; O. von Bismarck, *Gesammelte Werke,* VIc, no. 9, cf. also ibid., no. 3.

which was primarily motivated by political, not by religious reasons.[13] The Center Party did not suit Bismarck's plans; confessionally based on the masses, it was socially heterogeneous. It had also legitimized itself as a democratic body and was therefore intent on parliamentary rule, which Bismarck despised. The "ultramontane" party was the first which the Chancellor embellished with the term "foes of the Empire," fighting them with unreasonable vehemence. Bismarck's opposition to these groups was responsible for the integration of the other parties in accordance with his governmental policies.

The Prussian government, especially Bismarck and the conservative Minister of Religious Affairs Heinrich Mühler, regarded the Vatican Council and its resolutions as domestic affairs of the Catholic Church. A position was not taken until the bishops began inflicting penalties upon opponents to the impairment of their civil or social status. Mühler completely avoided conflict, regretted the recent internal developments within Catholicism and sided with the reprimanded professors in Bonn and Breslau and the other clerical teachers.[14] Prince-Bishop Förster of Breslau[15] had acted especially harshly, though he had been a vehement opponent of the dogma of infallibility himself. He had submitted, finally, and expected the same from his clergy.

Bishop Krementz of Ermland[16] took steps not only against Professor

---

[13] "Declarations of war" by the Chancellor were his letter to Count Frankenberg (19 June 1871), published a few days later in the *Nationalzeitung,* and an article against the "clerical faction" inspired by Bismarck, published in the *Kreuzzeitung* (also 19 June 1871). Frankenberg belonged to a minority of the Catholic nobility, predominantly represented in Silesia, which was very close to the Prussian state.

[14] Concerning the controversies about the professors, see A. Constable, *Vorgeschichte,* nos. 2f., 7f., 10–13, 15ff., 22f., 26, 28–31, 33f., 36–42, 45, 47, 51, 54–57, 63f., 77, 81, 83.

[15] Heinrich Förster, cathedral vicar and chaplain since 1837, a leading figure in the ecclesiastical liberation movement, continued as bishop (since 1853) the restoration efforts of his predecessor Diepenbrock. Because of his resistance to the May laws, Förster was dismissed in October 1875. In order to avoid arrest, he moved to the Austrian part of his bishopric, where he was able to perform the duties of his office. (A. Nowack, *ArSKG* 2 [1937], 207–18; K. Engelbert, ibid. 7 [1949], 147–88; H. Hoffmann, ibid. 12 [1954], 257–62; V. Schurr, *LThK²* IV, 218f; a study by T. Lissek soon to be published.

[16] Philippus Krementz (1819–99), 1848: priest in Koblenz, 1867: bishop in Ermland. His conflict with the government intensified in 1872 until his income was withheld (suspension of temporalities). In the subsequent struggle, Krementz stayed in the background. Therefore, and because of protection by Empress Augusta, he was able to remain in office and to succeed Melchers as archbishop of Cologne in 1885, and as cardinal in 1893. "Philippus Krementz. Ein Lebensbild," *Festschrift zur Kardinalserhebung* (Cologne 1893); *Atlpreußische Biographie,* ed. by C. Krollmann (Königsberg 1941–44), 364; B. M. Rosenberg, *ZGAE,* 30 (1960), 191–97; F. Lauchert, *LThK¹* VI, 237.

Michelis of Braunsberg, but also against all the teachers of the local Catholic high school. The principal and Wollmann, the religion teacher, were excommunicated. Students subsequently boycotted religious instruction and were forced by the government to leave the school.[17]

The government used the controversy for its first administrative maneuver of far-reaching consequences. On 8 July 1871 the Catholic department of the Ministry of Religious Affairs was dissolved and combined with the Protestant department to form a department for ecclesiastical affairs.[18] Bismarck and the liberal press accused the functionaries of the Catholic department, vainly defended by Mühler, of two offenses: in the latest controversy they did not adequately represent the position of the state and they did not energetically combat the expansion of the Polish clerical influence in the schools of the eastern provinces.

In the meantime, Bismarck's alliance with the National Liberals had solidified because the Conservatives had taken a reserved stand toward his domestic policies, fearing a diminution of Prussian autonomy. The radical political program directed against the Church, which the Chancellor explained to Mühler in August 1871, a few weeks after his official "declaration of war,"[19] was completely in accord with the new constellations. The program combined Bismarck's typical desire to restore the old Prussian sovereignty over the Church with the extensive adoption of the ecclesiastical maxims of liberalism. Bismarck wanted to combat the ultramontane party, especially in the eastern provinces. He was aiming at separation of church and state and of church and school. He wanted to transfer school inspections to nonclerical supervisors and abolish religious instruction in the schools. Henceforth, ecclesiastical affairs were to be administered by the Ministry of Justice.[20]

The Prussian bishops under the chairmanship of Paulus Melchers met again in September 1871 in Fulda. In a direct petition they tried to prove the legitimacy of their measures against the Old Catholics and to clarify the misunderstandings caused by dogma. But they were unable to accomplish anything against Bismarck's intentions.[21] His fight was

---

[17] Concerning the Braunsberger controversy and the subsequent conflict with Krementz, see. A. Constabel, *Vorgeschichte,* no. 46ff., especially nos. 52, 62, 65–76, 78f., 90, 107, 117, 141f., 158ff., 166–71, 205f., 208ff., 213ff., 224ff., 240–58.
[18] Concerning the abolishment of the Catholic department, see A. Constabel, *Vorgeschichte,* nos. 85f., 89, 92ff., Cf. O. von Bismarck, *Gesammelte Werke,* VIc, no. 10.
[19] See n. 13.
[20] W. Reichle, *Mühler,* 333.
[21] A. Constabel, *Vorgeschichte,* nos. 106, 109, 112f., 115; R. Lill, *Die ersten deutschen Bischofskonferenzen* (Freiburg, Basel, Vienna 1964), 112–18.

not directed against the infallability of the Pope as much as against the Center Party and the ultramontane "conspiracy." To the Liberals, the dogma meant simply the ultimate confirmation of their ecclesiastical policies. Ketteler, after a conversation with Bismarck in November 1871, had to recognize that the conflict had become irreconcilable. The Chancellor seemed to be convinced that the Curia and the Center Party were conspiring against the Empire.[22]

A legal strategical initiative had meanwhile emanated from Bavaria. In October 1871 the *Reichstag* opened its second session. Minister Johann Lutz presented a bill introducing a pulpit paragraph which was ratified 10 December 1871 (ARTICLE 130a of the penal code). The clergy was forbidden, when in office, to deal with public affairs "in a way which would endanger the peace of public life."[23] In previous passionate debates, Windthorst, Peter Reichensperger, and Ketteler had justified the opposition of the Center Party. Lutz had explained that it was a question of who was in command: the state or the Roman Church. Almost all National Liberals agreed. Their chairman, Rudolf von Bennigsen, admitted in confidential consultation that he wanted to provoke the clerical faction to act with more rigor.

Meanwhile, Bismarck and his colleagues had proceeded to realize their program in Prussia. Only with reservations did the Emperor join in. But Bismarck was able to convince him that the interests of the state left no choice. Augusta's numerous and well-founded warnings of the conflict accomplished nothing.[24] Mühler resisted Bismarck consistently. He wanted to introduce the law on school supervision by the state, which Bismarck desired so urgently, only under the provision that a general school law be passed which would preserve the Christian character of the school system. Mühler had to resign in January 1872. He was succeeded by Adalbert Falk (1827–1900), a disciple of the liberal political concept. He had strong support from the National Liberal Party and was the driving force next to Bismarck in the *Kulturkampf.* On 11 March 1872, the school supervision law was passed. Now, the state had the right to supervise all public and private schools and to appoint school inspectors (ART. 2), who had previously been employed by the Church.[25] This law, like the Baden school law of 1868, was not so much a result of the *Kulturkampf* as of the liberal desire to remove all ecclesiastical influence from public affairs. It was discriminatory because

[22] F. Vigener, *Ketteler,* 662ff.

[23] Text: J. B. Kißling, *Kulturkampf,* II, 460.—Concerning the previous debate, see G. Stoltenberg, *Reichstag,* 101–14.

[24] Concerning Augusta's warnings, see. A. Constabel, *Vorgeschichte,* nos. 68, 80, 91, 108, 156, 172, 177, 183, 188, 202, 220, 252, 258.

[25] Text: J. B. Kißling, *Kulturkampf* II, 460f.

of the circumstances under which it was passed. Bismarck, Falk, and the liberal press left no doubt that they wanted to strike out against the Catholic Church and the Polish population of Prussia. Nevertheless, this law caused the break with the Conservatives which embittered the Chancellor. The Conservative majority rejected the new dogmatic developments within Catholicism. But they also rejected a conflict knowing that it would turn against the Protestant Church and, generally, against the alliance of throne and altar.

In the following months, the government increased antiecclesiastical administrative measures introduced under Mühler. Prominent victims were Bishop Krementz, whose salary was withheld in spite of the Emperor's reluctance, and Bishop Namszanowski, military ordinary to the armed forces.[26] Namszanowski had discontinued services in the garrison's church, St. Pantaleon in Cologne, which the state had allowed to the Old Catholics. He had also forbidden a curate, who opposed the dogma, to perform the duties of his office. The Defense Department did not understand the clerical responsibilities of the military ordinary and considered his actions illegal transgressions from his area of competence. When Namszanowski participated in the episcopal conference in Fulda (April 1872), the Department charged him with leaving Berlin without permission "on unofficial business."[27] The government suspended the bishop, but the disciplinary court did not confirm it. The appeal was decided by the Ministry of State itself. On 26 June 1873, the Bishop was placed under suspension, after the cabinet decree of 15 March 1873 had already dissolved the military ordinariate. A diplomatic protest by the Vatican (Antonelli's letter of 28 August 1872), with whom the establishment of the ordinariate to the armed forces had been arranged, received no answer. This diplomatic insult of the Vatican had been preceded by a worse one in the spring of 1872. Bismarck had tried to force Cardinal Hohenlohe as ambassador upon the Pope, though in 1870 he had fallen out of favor with Rome.[28] After papal rejection of

---

[26] Franz Adolf Namszanowski (1820–1900), provost in Königsberg, in 1868 titular bishop and military ordinary to the Prussian armed forces, after his provisional retirement he resided in Frauenburg (Ermland), where he became cathedral vicar. H. Pohl, *Die katholische Militärfürsorge Preußens 1797–1888* (Stuttgart 1926, reprint Amsterdam 1962), 209ff., 229, 236–39, 250–344, 363, 369–72, 387; *Altpreußische Biographie* (see n. 16), 455; B. M. Rosenberg, ibid., 197f.

[27] Concerning the controversy over Namszanowski and the military ordinariate, see H. Pohl, op. cit., 250–344; A. Constabel, *Vorgeschichte,* no. 105, 148, 152, 161f., 165, 168, 173f., 179–82, 184f., 187f., 191ff., 196ff., 201, 207, 236, 261.

[28] E. Deuerlein, "Bismarck und die Reichsvertretung beim Heiligen Stuhl," *StdZ* 164 (1959), 203–19, 256–66; H. Philippi, "Beiträge zur Geschichte der diplomatischen Beziehungen zwischen dem Deutschen Reich und dem Heiligen Stuhl," *HJ* 82 (1963), 219–62, see esp. 219–39.

the cardinal, only a chargé d'affaires remained in the Vatican. By the end of 1872, he was also recalled because of Pius IX's vehement protests against the unrelenting execution of the Jesuit laws. In 1875, at the peak of the *Kulturkampf,* funds for the embassy to the Vatican were stricken from the state budget.

Intensification of the already tense situation in 1872, painfully felt by the Vatican and the majority of the German Catholics, brought about the Jesuit law, the second federal law of the *Kulturkampf* (4 July 1872).[29] The Society of Jesus and related orders (Redemptorists, Lazarists) were forbidden in the Empire and existing foundations were dissolved (ART. 1). The members were subjected to residence restrictions, and the foreigners among them faced expulsion from the country. This was precipitated by a storm of petitions by Old Catholics, the Association of Protestants, and many National Liberal groups. The Jesuits were charged with responsibility for the *Syllabus* and for the dogma of infallibility, and they were exposed as opponents of the modern state and civil liberties. The leaders of south German liberalism, Lutz and his predecessor Hohenlohe, launched concrete initiatives in opposition to the law, but confined them to residence restrictions for the Jesuits. In spite of the strong resistance by the Center and some Conservatives, the National Liberal majority of the *Reichstag* pushed through a law of prohibition without any time limitations. Like the Socialist law, passed in 1878, the Jesuit law was an exceptive law which violated the constitutional principles of liberalism. Nevertheless, only a few National Liberals advised against it, e.g., Ludwig Bamberger, Eduard Lasker,[30] Johannes von Miquel, and the majority of the leftist-liberal Progressive Party. The fact that the majority of the National Liberals voted for the exceptive laws damaged their credibility and prepared the party's crisis, facilitating the conclusion of the *Kulturkampf.*

The Catholic reactions to the Jesuit law were sharp. Shortly before its passage, Pius IX, in an address to the German Catholics, urged resistance to the "persecution of the Church."[31] In June 1872 Felix von Loë (1825–96) founded the "Society of German Catholics" in Mainz. He declared as his primary task the defense against a liberal state-church policy.[32] The most important protest was contained in a memorandum

---

[29] Text: J. B. Kißling, *Kulturkampf* II, 461; E. R. Huber, *Dokumente zur deutschen Verfassungsgeschichte* II, 363.—Concerning the previous debate, see K. Bachem, *Zentrumspartei* III, 252–57; G. Stoltenberg, *Reichstag,* 144–52.—B. Duhr, *Das Jesuitengesetz* (Freiburg 1919).

[30] The reference to Bamberger and Lasker contradicts the generalization by many Catholics that "the Jews" were responsible for the *Kulturkampf.* About the participation of many Jews, see K. Bachem, *Zentrumspartei* III, 417f.

[31] Text: N. Siegfried, *Aktenstücke,* 132f.

[32] K. Buchheim, *Ultramontanismus und Demokratie,* 255–70.

drafted by Ketteler and accepted by the entire German episcopate in Fulda in September.[33] The memorandum called the recent measures of Prussia and the Empire violations of Church immunity, as defined by the constitution and international law, and highly detrimental to the current judicial system. In no uncertain terms the bishops brought to mind ARTS. 15–18 of the Prussian constitution, which guaranteed ecclesiastical autonomy. From the divine endowment of the Church the bishops derived the claim that the Church "existed within the integrity of its constitution and its very essence." The charge that the Church, Jesuits, and Center Party were enemies of the Empire, and therefore dangerous to the state, was rejected once and for all.

The Prussian government had to concede that its religious policies, practised since 1871, were in violation of the constitution. But since the government intended to adhere to its program, it answered the Fulda memorandum with the law which limited the guarantees of ARTS. 15–18 (5 April 1873).[34] ARTICLE 15 was amended to the effect that the autonomy of the churches recognized therein would remain "subject to the laws of the state and to its jurisdiction." The state's prerogative to regulate by law the rights of the Church regarding the training and employment of the clergy and its disciplinary authority restricted the Church's freedom to staff ecclesiastical offices (ART. 18).

Thereby the conditions for the actual laws of the struggle were set. They were passed in May 1873 after stormy debates in the Prussian Provincial Diet and in the House of Lords, imposing upon the Church a closed system of governmental supervision.[35] Since taking office, Falk had prepared these laws, diligently aided by Emil Friedberg, professor of civil and canon law, by Rudolf Gneist, Paul Hinschius, and Otto Mejer.

The law regarding training and appointment of the clergy (11 May 1873)[36] made the appointment to a clerical office dependent on German citizenship, on education at a German university, and on approval by the state (ARTS. 1–3). All clerical educational institutions were placed under the control of the state (ARTS. 6,7,9–14). Theology students had to pass an additional state examination in philosophy, history, and Ger-

---

[33] Text: N. Siegfried, *Aktenstücke*, 133ff. Cf. F. Vigener, *Ketteler*, 665ff.; R. Lill, *Bischofskonferenzen*, 119ff.

[34] Text: J. B. Kißling, *Kulturkampf* II, 461f.

[35] For the most thorough description of the Church laws enacted in 1873–75, see E. R. Huber, *Verfassungsgeschichte* IV, 709–20, 723–31, 733–42. Concerning liberal justification of the May laws, see P. Hinschius, *Die preußischen Kirchengesetze des Jahres 1873* (Berlin 1873).

[36] Text: J. B. Kißling, *Kulturkampf* II, 462–67.

man literature (culture examination ART. 8). The bishops had to report each candidate for clerical office to the appropriate functionary (Notification Law). In case of objections, the appointment could not take place. Objections could be made on the basis of facts justifying the assumption that the candidate might violate the law or disturb the peace (ART. 15–17). Each vacant incumbency was to be filled within a year (ART. 18). Violations were punished with stiff fines (ARTS. 22–24).

The law regarding both ecclesiastical disciplinary power and the establishment of a Royal Tribunal of Ecclesiastical Affairs[37] (12 May 1873) excluded all non-German Church institutions, primarily the Pope and the Curia, from disciplinary power over the German clergy (ART. 1). Consequently, all ecclesiastical disciplinary measures could be made subject to the control of the state (ARTS. 5–9). Those affected by such measures had the right to appeal to the newly created Tribunal of Ecclesiastical Affairs, which could declare the appealed decisions void (ART. 10–23). The Tribunal could also dismiss clergymen who had violated the law or a civil regulation to such a degree that their activity appeared incompatible with law and order (ARTS. 24–31).

Above all, the state veto of clerical appointments and the right to remove clergy from office were severe attacks on the constitution of the Church as well as freedom of belief and conscience. Both the National Liberals, whose animosity toward the Church had been strengthened by the dogma of infallibility, and the bureaucracy, which was still adhering to the common provincial law, cooperated in reimposing a historically obsolete state church in an expanded fashion, enabled to do so by the political power of the modern state. The Church was of course compelled to oppose these measures, and thus these first two May laws kindled a long and passionate fight. Less trenchant was the law limiting the right to use ecclesiastical disciplinary and penal means (13 May 1873).[38] It prohibited punishing violations of the civil honor code, which, after 1870, included the extensive excommunication of the opponents of the new dogma. Also less incisive was the law regarding secession from the Church (14 May 1873),[39] which became valid by simply declaring secession to a civil judge.

The Prussian bishops decided quickly, justified by the memorandum of Fulda in 1872, to practice passive resistance to the May laws. They rejected and forbade any kind of cooperation in their enforcement.[40] With the exception of a small minority (so-called state priests, state

[37] Text: ibid., 467–73.
[38] Text: ibid., 473f.
[39] Text: ibid., 474f.
[40] Collective petition by the Prussian bishops, 26 May 1873. Text: N. Siegfried, *Aktenstücke*, 188f.

Catholics), the clergy and the laity followed these directives. Directors of seminaries refused state supervision, theology students rejected the culture examination. The bishops themselves appointed priests, ignoring the provisions of the May laws. The state reacted by closing most clerical seminaries. In December 1873 a new oath was ordered for bishops and episcopal functionaries, which required absolute submission to all laws.[41] Soon indictments began against bishops and clergymen who had been appointed illegally. According to the May laws, they were liable to punishment for just saying Mass or administering sacraments. Prohibition of appointments turned into termination of office.[42] Falk, the liberal lawyers supporting him, and the Prussian bureaucracy enforced these laws relentlessly and without constraint. As they wanted to gain the Church's submission to the supremacy of the state, they agreed completely with Bismarck's intentions, despite some of his statements. The Chancellor also appreciated the useful aid of many journalists who, contrary to Bismarck's political goals, brought the ideological struggle into the limelight, and who advocated the supremacy of the national state and the superiority of the "German mentality" against the "Rome-serving" Catholics.[43] Many aberrations in recent German history partially stem from this period.

Bismarck, Falk, and their aides completely misjudged the Church's will and strength to resist. Under the concentric pressure by the state, Catholics from all walks of life flocked around their bishops and the Center Party, which was able to increase its mandate considerably (*Reichstag* 1871: 58; 1874: 91 deputies; Prussian Diet 1870: 58; 1873: 90 deputies). Under Windthorst's leadership, the Center became the primary opponent to the Chancellor, fighting him uncompromisingly on constitutional grounds. The Vatican persistently supported the Prussian Catholics. Pius IX and Antonelli, finally forced into the defensive by 1870, confined themselves to fruitless protests, hardly adequate in view of their opponents' arguments. They refused to recognize that their intransigence had contributed to the intensification of the differences. The Pope acted very unwisely, when, in a letter to Wilhelm I, he jus-

---

[41] Text of the new and the old oath: *AkathKR,* 31 (1874), 345ff.

[42] Falk's decree of 24 October 1873, addressed to the presiding judges, demanded criminal procedures be taken against active clergymen who had been illegally employed and therefore prosecuted previously. Text: J. B. Kißling, *Kulturkampf* II, 241f.

[43] One among many typical documents: In the *Preußische Jahrbücher* (II [1873], 596), the *Kulturkampf* was praised as a "double battle . . . the fight of modern freedom of thought against the last spiritual heritage of the Middle Ages, the papal subjugation of faith; and the fight of the modern state against the last judicial vestige of the Middle Ages, the immunity of the Roman Church."

tified his right to criticize the May laws with the questionable identification of Papal Church and Christianity: "Everyone who has been baptized belongs in some way to the Pope."[44] This hurt the Emperor, who personally did not exactly favor the *Kulturkampf,* and the conservative Protestants, who felt likewise but remained silent because of their deeply rooted loyalty to the Prussian state. They were forced into the camp that was fighting the *Kulturkampf* and trying everything to exploit the confessional differences.

In order to break the Catholic resistance, the May laws were intensified in 1874. However, this step was unsuccessful. Since the penal sanctions of the law of 11 May 1873 had proven insufficient, the Prussian government passed an expatriation law for the whole Empire (4 May 1874),[45] which violated the bill of rights severely. Clergymen who continued practicing in office after their dismissal by the state were threatened with expulsion from certain places or areas. In case of extreme insolence or contravention, they would be threatened with exile or loss of citizenship. On 20 May 1874, the Prussian Diet passed a law concerning the administration of suspended bishoprics.[46] According to this law, an episcopal administrator (capitulary vicar) could only operate until the state-approved appointment of a bishop, provided he could document his qualifications according to the law of 11 May 1873, and provided he swore an oath of obedience to all laws. If no capitulary vicar was elected by the chapter, a state commissioner had to administer the bishopric. Since no chapter was willing to execute the law, such commissioners had to be appointed for all vacant dioceses. Immediately, the law concerning the declaration of the law of 11 May 1873 (21 May 1874)[47] followed. It placed the burden of proof on the clergymen who had been charged with illegally taking office, and threatened to confiscate all property if an office was filled against the provisions of the May laws. The judicial and administrative struggle against the Church seemed complete.

The National Liberals used the intensification of the conflict to realize an old postulate of their social doctrine. By law (9 March 1874), civil marriage became obligatory in Prussia. Wilhelm I approved, with seri-

---

[44] Pius IX to Wilhelm I, 7 August 1873. Text: N. Siegfried, *Aktenstücke,* 197f. Ibid., 198f., the Emperor's response (3 September 1873), in which the May laws are attributed to the "intrigues against the state" by a political party supported by the clergy, and in which the papal claims towards the non-Catholics are rejected with reference to the Evangelical faith.

[45] Text: J. B. Kißling, *Kulturkampf* II, 475ff.

[46] Text: ibid., 477–81.

[47] Text: ibid., 481ff.

ous reservations.[48] A year later, civil marriage became an imperial law—the culmination of the *Kulturkampf* (6 February 1875).

In the meantime, prosecution of the bishops and priests in violation of the laws was continued. Since bishops were fined whether they did or did not fill an office illegally, the sum of fines reached proportions which could neither be paid through compulsory auctions nor with voluntary contributions from the faithful. In this situation, the Prussian bureaucracy did not refrain from employing imprisonment. In 1874/75, five out of eleven Prussian bishops[49] spent several months in prison: Archbishops Ledóchowski and Melchers, Bishops Eberhard (Trier), Martin (Paderborn), and Brinkmann (Münster).[50] Förster avoided imprisonment by moving to the Austrian part of his bishopric. The imprisoned bishops were worshipped as martyrs. However, since the summer of 1874, Catholic demonstrations, societies, and newspapers were subject to strict police control.[51]

The Catholics' political convictions suffered disillusionment, and they grew increasingly bitter when the government decided to apply even the most extreme May laws, forcing the royal tribunal, created in 1873, to dismiss the bishops who were still practising resistance. Dismissals began with Ledóchowski in 1874. In the next three years, Melchers, Martin, Förster, Brinkmann, and Blum (Limburg) were dismissed. Eberhard died during the trial. In 1878, only Bishops Krementz (Ermland), von der Marwitz (Kulm), and Sommerwerck (Hildesheim) were still in office. The episcopates of Fulda, Osnabrück, and Trier had been vacant since the death of their incumbents. According to Church law, the six dismissed bishops remained in office, but they could not administer officially and, thus, went into exile,[52] where they tried to rule over their dioceses with the help of secret delegates.[53]

---

[48] H. Conrad, "Zur Einführung der Zwangszivilehe in Preußen und im Reich 1874/75," *Das deutsche Privatrecht . . . Festschrift für H. Lehmann* (Berlin 1956).

[49] The bishopric of Fulda was vacant since the death of Bishop Kött (1873).

[50] Ledóchowski was imprisoned for two years, which was by far the longest time. During his imprisonment he was appointed cardinal. It was characteristic of the particular severity of the *Kulturkampf* in the provinces of Poland that Ledóchowski's suffragans Janiszewski (Posen) and Cybichowski (Gnesen) were sentenced to prison in 1875 and later expelled from their dioceses. Janiszewski was also officially dismissed in 1877.

[51] The Catholic Society in Mainz was forbidden (see above, p. 39). An assassination attempt on Bismarck in July 1874 served as a pretext to intensify the control of the press and societies. The assassin acted on his own, because, contrary to premature statements by the Chancellor, collaboration with backers could not be verified.

[52] Aside from Förster, Blum had also gone to Austria. Ledóchowski found asylum in the Vatican. Melchers, Brinkmann, and Martin lived in Holland and Belgium, close to their dioceses.

[53] In three canonically vacant dioceses, such delegates were active by papal decree. The police searched for them in vain.

The final phase of the *Kulturkampf* was ushered in, at the end of 1874, during the trial of former ambassador and Bismarck opponent Count Arnim,[54] when the text of a "papal election telegram" became known. It was sent by the Chancellor in May 1872. Bismarck therein suggested to the European governments an agreement regarding conditions for the recognition of a new Pope. He justified his initiative by stating that, since the Vatican Council, the bishops of all countries were merely functionaries of the Pope. In February 1875, the German episcopate responded with a declaration based on a thorough analysis of the Vatican decrees. It stressed the direct authority of each bishop within his diocese, justified by apostolic succession, and was, soon thereafter, approved by Pius IX.[55] Shortly before, the Pope had used the sharpest means at his disposal against the Prussian religious policies. The encyclical *Quod numquam* (5 February 1875)[56] declared the May laws invalid, insofar as they contradicted the divine constitution of the Church, and decreed excommunication of everyone who participated in their creation and execution. At the same time, Pius rejected any kind of dissent against the authorities in secular matters.

Prussia answered with a new series of penal laws. The so-called breadbasket law (22 April 1875)[57] decreed discontinuation of all state funds to the Catholic Church (ART. 1). It provided the possibility of resumption in individual dioceses only in the case of a written assurance by the responsible bishop or episcopal administrator that the laws would be obeyed (ART. 2). Individual clergymen also could only receive the state funds due to them if they provided such declarations (ART. 6). Few state priests were willing to make such promises, and, therefore, an almost total cessation in state payments occurred, welcomed by the Liberals as an important step in the separation of church and state.

The law concerning religious orders of 31 May 1875[58] hurt the

---

[54] F. Hartung, "Bismarck und Graf Harry Arnim," *HZ* 171 (1951), 47–77.

[55] Text of the collective declaration: N. Siegfried, *Aktenstücke,* 264–67; D 3112–16. Cf. R. Lill, *Bischofskonferenzen,* 121f. The papal approval (12 March 1875): N. Siegfried, *Aktenstücke,* 270f.; D 3117. In the discussions concerning the primate and the episcopate (begun by the Second Vatican Council), the declaration of the German bishops approved by Pius IX was rightfully used as an important document of the ecclesiastical self-understanding of 1870. However, it must be added that Pius IX himself did not attempt to interpret the dogma of infallibility in such a moderate and clarifying manner. Had he done so, he might have avoided or alleviated many a controversy after 1870. (cf. *Constitutio dogmatica de Ecclesia* [21 November 1964], chap. III, ART. 27, no. 95: *LThK*². "The Second Vatican Council," I, 246f.—J. Ratzinger, *K. Rahner–J. Ratzinger, Episkopat und Primat* [Freiburg 1961], 29f.; W. Kasper, "Primat und Episkopat nach dem Vatikanum I," *ThQ* 142 [1962], 48f.).

[56] Text: N. Siegfried, *Aktenstücke,* 267ff.

[57] Text: J. B. Kißling, *Kulturkampf* III, 438ff.

[58] Text: ibid., 440f.

Catholics most. It excluded orders and congregations from Prussian state territory. Existing settlements were not allowed to accept new members and were to be dissolved within six months. In case of orders whose members were teaching, the deadline could be extended up to four years (ART. 1). Exempted from the decree were hospital orders, whose place of residence, however, could be seized at any time and placed under state control (ART. 3). This brought restoration, proceeding rapidly since the 1850s, to a standstill. The members of male orders with pastoral duties, who had survived the Jesuit laws, went either to the United States or to Belgium and Holland,[59] where they could, at least, maintain contact with their home country. For many of the female orders remaining in Prussia, Empress Augusta effected some relief.

On 18 June 1875, ARTS. 15 and 18 of the Prussian constitution were abolished. On 20 June, a comprehensive law regarding the administration of the estate of Catholic parishes was passed.[60] Its aim was to debilitate the hierarchic system of the Church and extensively adopt evangelical parish principles. The administration of Church estates was democratized (ART. 1) and turned over to a vestry board consisting of the pastor and elected members (ARTS. 5–8). Important decisions were dependent on the approval of a board of local representatives (ART. 21). The Church could tolerate this law, since most elected mayors tried to cooperate with the ecclesiastical authorities.

The final law dealt with the ecclesiastical property of the Old Catholic parishes (4 July 1875). It assured the Old Catholics the use of property and churches belonging to the Catholic parishes wherever they had gained a "considerable number" of new members (ARTS. 1,2). Priests who had become Old Catholic could keep their benefices (ART. 3).[61] Since the Catholics continued to reject the use of their churches by the seceded minority, and since the bureaucracy usually interpreted the law in favor of the Old Catholics, serious controversies occurred. Catholic services were discontinued in churches given to the Old Catholics.

The year 1876 brought only amendments to the pulpit paragraph and to the law regarding the administration of diocesan property.[62] Also, a

---

[59] Arnold Janssen also founded and developed the first German mission in Holland (Steyl, S. V. D., 1875). F. Bornemann, *Arnold Janssen, der Gründer des Steyler Missionswerkes 1837–1909* (Steyl 1969).—Since the Jesuit laws survived the *Kulturkampf*, the German Jesuits moved their study center, after their escape to Ditton Hall, England (in 1872), to Valkenburg, Holland, in 1894.

[60] Text: J. B. Kißling, *Kulturkampf* III, 441–52.

[61] Text: ibid., 452f.

[62] Federal law of 26 February 1876, Prussian law of 7 June 1876. Texts: J. B. Kißling, *Kulturkampf* III, 454–57.

ministerial order was issued by Falk, subjecting religious instruction in elementary schools to state supervision (18 February 1876).[63]

Otherwise, the struggle began to stagnate. The Catholic Church organization in Prussia was demolished, more than one thousand parishes were without pastors. But the passive resistance of the Catholic population, their cooperation with the clergy and the hierarchy, and the active resistance of the Center Party remained unbroken. These were not the only reasons why, in the middle of the 1870s, the *Kulturkampf* turned out to be a failure. Liberal ideology and bureaucratic perfection had given the *Kulturkampf* an edge, originally not intended by Bismarck, which deeply affected internal peace and forced Catholics and other minorities into a ghetto, to the disadvantage of the Empire. The struggle against the Catholic Church furthered de-Christianization of society, which did not suit Bismarck's authoritarian concept. Favored by the *Kulturkampf*, a new and dangerous adversary appeared—social democracy.[64] The warnings of the Empress, the doubts of the Emperor and many Conservatives had been fully confirmed. In addition, Prussia had lost its reputation as a tolerant state, a reputation twice as valuable in the impending age of public opinion. The arrests and expulsions of bishops, clergymen, and members of orders deepened the mistrust toward Bismarck outside of Germany, even in anticlerical circles. The Napoleonic methods of his "founding the Empire from above" had had the same effect.

Slowly and strategically motivated, the Chancellor, therefore, turned away from the *Kulturkampf*. It is yet to be proven that he intended to keep the more important positions obtained during the *Kulturkampf*, and that he merely changed his methods, especially in dealing with the Center Party. If the Party could not be conquered in open battle, then he had to try to integrate it into government politics or separate it from its roots among the masses either via political concessions or agreements with the Vatican.[65]

Bismarck's experiences, resulting from the *Kulturkampf*, contributed greatly to his estrangement from the National Liberals, which was further determined by the renewed disagreements over parliament, constitutionalism, and economic policies. Another contributing factor was

---

[63] Text: N. Siegfried, *Aktenstücke,* 315ff., excerpt: J. B. Kißling, *Kulturkampf* III, 138ff.

[64] When he fought this second mass movement of the opposition, starting in 1878, with means similar to but more ruthless than those employed by the Catholics, he proved his inability to draw the correct conclusions from the failure of the *Kulturkampf*. Combatting "the foes of the Empire" was part of his domestic policies because he hoped it would result in a greater cohesiveness within the other groups and a further consensus regarding his politics.

[65] Cf. chap. 3, pp. 57, 62, 71, 74.

the crisis of the liberal system, beginning in the middle of the seventies, the cause of which cannot be discussed here. At any rate, the Chancellor was preparing a conservative turn of events which would determine his domestic policies from 1878/79 on. He did not take an initiative for a compromise in religious policies because he wanted to avoid, at any cost, the impression of a pilgrimage to Canossa, and because a settlement under Pius IX seemed impossible to him (and to other politicians). Both sides strengthened their positions.

The political failure was completed by the fact that Bismarck had not succeeded in involving foreign countries in the *Kulturkampf.* Bismarck had placed high hopes on the leading statesmen of Austria and Italy because of local disputes involving religious policies.[66] But they were too realistic and too familiar with the nature and the strength of the Catholic Church to agree to a bureaucratic persecution in the Prussian fashion.

During the liberal five years after the founding of the Empire, the *Kulturkampf* was able to spread to other federal states, however with characteristic differences. Most similar to the Prussian development, though less consequential, was the one in Baden. Its school, marriage, and Church laws of 1868–74[67] were fashioned after the Prussian laws or followed them verbatim.—In Bavaria, "a covert *Kulturkampf*" had begun already before 1870, rooted in the tradition of a liberal-Catholic regalism. It was led by Lutz's ministry (1870–90) with consistency and the intent to avoid open conflict.[68] He did not go beyond restoration of previous state supervision (1873). Bavarian parishes and seminaries accepted clergymen and theology students who had to leave Prussia. Only because they were vacant for several years did the bishoprics of Speyer and Würzburg attract some attention. Pius IX had rejected the appointment of candidates for these sees who were nominated by the King and leaned toward the state-church concept.—Following Prussia's example, Hesse-Darmstadt and Saxony passed liberal religious laws in the years 1874–76.[69]

The two other German states with a large Catholic population, Württemberg and Oldenburg, refused to become involved in the *Kulturkampf.* In Württemberg, within the boundaries set by the Church law of 1862, there existed an exceedingly good relationship between Church and state, cultivated carefully by King Karl I (1864–91) and

[66] Austria: see below, chap. 2.
[67] Cf. Bachem, *Zentrumspartei* IV, 357–418.
[68] Cf. Bachem, op. cit., 316–46.
[69] Hessen-Darmstadt: Kißling, III, 406–15; Vigener, *Ketteler,* 612–722; Bachem, op. cit., 419–37. Saxony: Kißling, III, 418–22; W. Rittenbach, *LThK*² IX, 201f.

Bishop Hefele. In Alsace-Lorraine, whose very difficult integration into the Empire would have been complicated even more by the *Kulturkampf,* the administration, dependent on Berlin, backed away from sharp measures.

CHAPTER 2

Tensions in the Austro-Hungarian Monarchy (1878–1914)

After the denominational laws of May 1874 came into force, all further attempts by the Liberals to design the Cisleithan legislation concerning religious policies according to their concepts failed. The bill to regulate the exterior judicial system of the monastic societies miscarried. It had been passed by both the House of Representatives and the House of Lords but was not sanctioned by Emperor Franz Joseph. The marriage clause, passed by the House of Representatives in 1876, also miscarried. It failed because it was vetoed by the House of Lords. The Confessional Committee of the House of Representatives began once again, in February 1877, to draft a marriage law. This led to a debate, early in 1878, about the draft of a bill introducing obligatory civil marriage.[1] But such projects were tabled in favor of other legislative tasks and the occupation of Bosnia and Herzegovina. All other attempts by the Liberals to achieve a change in legislation regarding religious policy came to nothing.

The Catholics, on the contrary, had considerable success concerning the school question. On 5 February 1880, Prince Aloys Liechtenstein, deputy of the Conservatives (but a decade later a member of the Christian Socialists), introduced a school resolution in the House of Representatives requesting the government to revise the elementary school law. The goals of Liechtenstein's reform plan were: decrease of expenditures, increase of the individual states' influence on the school system, and consideration of the population's religious, moral, and national needs. These goals were further specified by a motion proposed the same day by the Catholic deputy Georg Lienbacher. Both motions urged the government's draft of a school law. Participating in the draft was the original designer of the elementary school law of 1869, Section Chairman Alois Hermann. A friend of Adalbert Stifter, he was a disci-

---

[1] G. Kolmer, *Parlament und Verfassung in Österreich von 1848–1904* II (Vienna, Leipzig 1903), 339.

ple of the parochial school.[2] The government bill was finally passed by Parliament in April 1883 and ratified by the Emperor in the following month.[3] The amendment was significant for the organization of the school system and gave particular consideration to the religious denomination of the students. However, Prince Liechtenstein's second school bill of 28 January 1888, which was supported by a memorandum from the Austrian episcopate and which demanded that the schools be placed under the supervision of the Church, was unsuccessful.[4] The government's attitude of rejection was emphatically reinforced by the Austrian Social Democrats, who were then on their way to unification.[5] Until the decline of the Monarchy under the presidency of Count Kasimir Badeni (1895–97), the demand for denominational schools had only one chance to be at least partially realized. However, the Christian Socialists, heeding their voters from the German-speaking parts of Czechoslovakia, denied Badeni their support for his attempt to oblige the Czechs with his language ordinances. Thus, the Christian Socialists contributed to Badeni's overthrow.[6] Their leader, Dr. Karl Lueger (1844–1910), had meanwhile become mayor of Vienna despite the resistance of the upper clergy and the royal court. This did not prevent the radical German Nationalists under the leadership of Georg Ritter von Schönerer from exploiting the sympathies of the Alpine Catholic People's Party for the Slavs' desire to propagate the Away-from-Rome movement.[7] Thus, for the Liberals, the desired elaboration of the denominational legislation became unattainable. According to the judgement of a liberal historian, they remained "unrealized and were, in reality, hardly worth the paper on which they were written."[8] Even if this assessment is not entirely correct, there is no doubt that the Emperor and, finally, both the government and the bureaucracy respected the feelings of the enraged Catholics who had decided seriously to resist the state. The denominational appeasement is partially due to the understanding which Cardinal Rauscher and his successors, the Viennese Archbishops Kutschker, Ganglbauer, and Gruscha, had offered to the state even after the repeal of the concordat of 1870. In addition, the Liberals suffered an almost total loss of their nearly omnipotent position after Auersperg's ministry was overthrown in 1879.

---

[2] W. Goldinger, "Das Verhältnis von Staat und Kirche in Österreich nach Aufhebung des Konkordates von 1855," *Religion, Wissenschaft, Kultur* 9 (1957/III), 144.
[3] *Reichsgesetzblatt 1883*, no. 53.
[4] *Beilagen zu den Stenographischen Protokollen des Abgeordnetenhauses 1883*, no. 490.
[5] P. M. Zulehner, *Kirche und Automarxismus* (Vienna, Freiburg, Basel 1967), 38f.
[6] B. Sutter, *Die Badenischen Sprachverordnungen von 1897* I (Vienna 1960), 247.
[7] J. Wodka, *Kirche in Österreich* (Vienna 1959), 350.
[8] G. Kolmer, op cit. II, 343.

The neutral conservative cabinet of Eduard Taaffe maintained good relations with the conservative Right in the Parliament and had mostly Christian social reformers such as Count Egbert Belcredi and Aloys Liechtenstein work out the social legislation set in motion by Taaffe. This legislation was compatible both with the previously mentioned clause regarding the elementary school law of 1883 and the Catholics' school demands. In July 1883, the endowments of Gleink and Garsten, which had been taken away from Bishop Rudigier of Linz by the liberal government during the *Kulturkampf,* were reinstated. During Taaffe's era (1885) there followed provisionary legislation by the Congruists to improve the poor material condition of the clergy.[9]

This spirit of conciliation marks the ecclesiastical legislation of all Cisleithan governments after Taaffe. In this area, laws were only enacted when it was absolutely necessary for practical reasons or to avoid hardships,[10] and as such included the amendment to the law regarding religion teachers (1888),[11] the so-called Forensen law (1894),[12] and the Congruist law (1898),[13] which still did not quite fulfill the wishes of the lower clergy and was therefore improved in 1902 and 1907 through amendments.[14] Both amendments were the work of Max Hussarek, a specialist in canon law, later a historian dealing specifically with the concordat of 1855. Beginning in 1897, he was head of the Department for Affairs of Catholic Worship.[15] Until the collapse of the Monarchy, the Austrian religious legislation was essentially based on the denominational laws of 1868 and 1874, whose moderation and generally benevolent execution by the government finally compelled the Catholics to be more or less content with them. The episcopate of the German-speaking states, coming, with few exceptions, from the bourgeoisie,[16] distinguished itself by its loyalty to the Emperor. In 1891, on the occasion of the elections, the bishops issued a pastoral letter to the faithful

[9] *Reichsgesetzblatt 1885,* no. 47.
[10] R. Höslinger, "Das Kultuswesen in der Zeit von 1867–1948," *100 Jahre Unterrichtsministerium 1848–1948* (Vienna n.d.), 429.
[11] *Reichsgesetzblatt 1888,* no. 99.
[12] Landed proprietors who are not members of the parish, but whose property is completely or partially located in this parish, are, according to canon law, obligated to contribute toward the church building fund. This obligation was not recognized until the enactment of the law of 31 December 1894. *Reichsgesetzblatt 1895,* no. 7.
[13] *Reichsgesetzblatt 1896,* no. 176.
[14] *Reichsgesetzblatt 1902,* no. 48.
[15] W. Plöchl, "Max von Hussarek als akademischer Lehrer," *ÖAKR* 5 (1954), 82f.
[16] E. Saurer, *Die politischen Aspekte der österreichischen Bischofsernennungen 1867–1903* (Vienna, Munich 1968), 230.

advising them "to vote for an electorate which would be loyal to the Emperor."[17]

In the ensuing open controversy between the Conservatives and the Christian Socialist Party, as it was called since 1889, almost all of the bishops—as well as the Emperor—faced the new Catholic party with utter mistrust, if not animosity. Since the beginning of the 1890s, the upper clergy, represented by Cardinal Schönborn of Prague, together with the Emperor's diplomats, continually brought charges against the Christian Socialists in Rome. However, thanks to the mediation of the Viennese Nuncio Agliardi and the good will of Secretary of State Cardinal Rampolla, these accusations had no disadvantageous consequences, but resulted in Rampolla's explicit approval of the Christian Socialist program, provided, to be sure, that the radical anti-Semitism propagated by the party during its rise and endorsed by many priests[18] be alleviated.[19] Nevertheless, Cardinal Gruscha probably gave moral support to Franz Joseph, with whom he got along splendidly, when the Emperor tenaciously refused to confirm Lueger's election as mayor of Vienna. Gruscha bitterly opposed the Christian Socialists, because to him "democracy for the price of Christianity appeared to be the great ensuing danger."[20] Lueger, in turn, at a campaign meeting in 1901, did not refrain from severely criticizing the "obedient" attitude of the Austrian episcopate regarding religious policies.[21] Only under Archbishops Nagl and, above all, Piffl, did the relations of the episcopate to the party substantially improve. After all, the party had started out representing the middle classes; then it won over the farmers, united with the Conservatives in 1907 and was finally the only representative of Church interests in the Republic. Of course, these were also advocated by the Catholic organizations springing up in the last two decades of the nineteenth century (Catholic University Society 1884, Catholic School Society 1886, Christian Workers Movement 1892). In 1905, through the initiative of Viktor Kolb, S. J., the Pius Society was founded to protect the Catholic press, which, after the First World War, joined the Catholic People's Union (founded in 1909).[22] Around the turn of the

[17] W. Goldinger, op. cit., 145.

[18] *Kirche und Synagoge, Handbuch zur Geschichte von Christen und Juden,* ed. by K. H. Rengstorf and S. von Kortzfleisch, II (Stuttgart 1970), 499ff.; also: I. A. Hellwing, *Der konfessionelle Antisemitismus im 19. Jahrhundert in Österreich* (Vienna, Freiburg, Basel 1972).

[19] F. Funder, *Vom Gestern ins Heute* (Vienna 1952), 138ff.

[20] O. Posch, "Anton Josef Gruscha und der österreichische Katholizismus 1820–1911" (unpub. diss., Vienna 1947), 185, 208.

[21] R. Sieghart, *Die letzten Jahrzehnte einer Großmacht* (Berlin 1932), 318.

[22] J. Wodka, op. cit., 345f.

century, Catholic farmers' unions were organized. In 1917, several Catholic youth groups from the prewar years were combined in the Imperial Union of Catholic German Youth of Austria.[23] Also the Austrian Catholic conventions, taking place at irregular intervals after 1877, served from the beginning as a platform to declare ecclesiastical (specifically Catholic) demands, even though they might not coincide with the government's policy, for reasons relating to foreign politics. This was the case in 1889, when the second Catholic convention made the need of freedom for the Holy See the subject of a memorandum directed against Italy, a member of the Triple Alliance. The convention even incited President Taaffe to declare in the House of Representatives that the foreign policies of the Monarchy were determined by the close friendly relations with the Kingdom of Italy and its vital interests.[24]

The Habsburg Monarchy's position regarding Italy and its problem of nationalities was the dominant question arising in the discussions between Austria-Hungary and the Vatican during the pontificate of Leo XIII. According to information from the Austrian Legate Johannes von Montel (1831–1910),[25] Cardinal Manning and Cardinal Simor, primate of Hungary, were instrumental in the election of Leo XIII.[26] The newly elected Pope soon complained in his first political letter to Franz Joseph about "the constantly increasing hostility" of Italy against the Holy See; he asked the Emperor to intervene on behalf of the threatened papacy.[27] The Emperor responded favorably but without committing himself. Since it was decided in Vienna to include Italy—arisen from revolution—in the circle of conservative powers, Austria, among others, refrained from condemning the scandal occasioned by the transport of Pius IX's body in July 1882. In the spring of 1882, through his special legate, Baron Hübner, the Emperor offered the deeply disappointed Pope the Monarchy's hospitality in case of need. However, Hübner was also to prevent the Pope from making use of the offer for asylum.[28] This difficult assignment was successful enough for Leo XIII

---

[23] G. Schultes, *Der Reichsbund der katholischen deutschen Jugend Österreichs* (Vienna 1967) 132ff.

[24] A. Hudal, *Die österreichische Vatikanbotschaft 1806–1918* (Munich 1952), 234.

[25] Concerning Montel, see primarily A. Hudal, op. cit., 250ff.

[26] L. Freiherr von Pastor, *Tagebücher, Briefe, Erinnerungen* (Heidelberg 1950), 374.

[27] *Die politische Korrespondenz der Päpste mit den österreichischen Kaisern 1804–1918,* ed. by F. Engel-Janosi in cooperation with R. Blaas and E. Weinzier! (Vienna, Munich 1964), no. 145.

[28] F. Engel-Janosi, *Österreich und der Vatikan 1846–1918* I (Vienna, Graz, Cologne 1958), 230.

to say to Hübner: "My hopes, my love, and my trust I place, next to God, in his Majesty, the Emperor of Austria."[29]

As a matter of fact, within the Triple Alliance Austria refused to guarantee Italy the possession of Rome.[30] In 1888, the Emperor, through Hübner, again offered the Pope, who was being pressured by the Crispi government, asylum in Austria. Once again, quite in line with Austria's expectations, Leo XIII did not accept, but he gave serious thought to Salzburg in 1882 while still considering Trent as his place of asylum.[31]

Under Secretary of State Rampolla, however, relations between the Monarchy and the Vatican cooled down considerably. The Vatican's pro-French and pro-Slavic politics had been noted with dismay in Vienna.[32] Aside from that, there were continuous frictions with the Curia over a series of questions regarding the Monarchy's ecclesiastical policies, as, for instance, in the case of appointments of bishops. The Emperor's right to nominate was largely claimed by the royal and imperial bureaucracy. The Emperor nearly always agreed with its political leanings and, after 1880, was more and more oriented toward the problem of nationalities. Therefore, Italians and Slavs from the coastal areas and Dalmatia, unpopular Ruthenians in Galicia, but mainly men whose loyalty to the government was believed to be absolute were nominated bishops.[33] Above all, the Curia created difficulties when bishoprics in Hungary and in the coastal areas were to be filled. Compromises were often reached only after exhaustive negotiations and mutual rejection of the candidates, as in the case of Hungarian Primate Simor's succession in 1891 and the occupation of Zagreb (1894)[34] or Zadar (1902).[35] In Zadar, there was a question of the imperial right of transfer of bishops, a matter which was energetically defended by Catholics as ardent as Max von Hussarek, who functioned as adviser to the Division of Religious Affairs in the Department of Education.[36] Occasionally, there were also tough battles about the appointment of cardinals, as in the case of Archbishop Dr. Josef Samassa of Erlau, who had been nominated by the government. Samassa, in the opinion of the Vatican, had not appropri-

---

[29] *Die politische Korrespondenz,* op. cit., 48f.

[30] F. Engel-Janosi, op. cit. I, 232.

[31] Ibid., 255f.

[32] Ibid., 268ff.

[33] E. Saurer, op. cit., 235ff.

[34] F. Engel-Janosi, op. cit. I, 278ff.

[35] G. Adriányi, "Friedrich Graf Revertera, Erinnerungen (1888–1901)," *AHPont* 10 (1972), 326f.

[36] W. Goldinger, "Eine Auseinandersetzung Österreich-Ungarns mit der Kurie über das kaiserliche Nominationsrecht für Bischofsstühle," *ÖAKR* 6 (1955), 213.

ately opposed the Hungarian bill about civil marriage. He had also come out in favor of the imperial veto regarding the papal election to the Hungarian delegation in 1894. Therefore, Samassa was not granted the honor of cardinal until Pius X's pontificate.[37] The efforts of Foreign Secretaries Aehrenthal and Berchtold to raise the number of cardinals in the Monarchy from six (four in the Austrian and two in the Hungarian part of the Empire) to seven were not successful.[38]

On the other hand, those bishops of the Monarchy, "whose voices were gladly heard in the Vatican,"[39] did not enjoy the sympathies of the Austrian government. Among them were Bishop Stadler of Sarajevo and Bishop Stroßmayer of Djakovo, both spokesmen and protectors of the Croatians. Important was the question of the national liturgical languages, especially of the Slavic language in the Croatian-Dalmatian dioceses with Latin rites. The government considered it a means, intentionally employed by many bishops (e.g., Stroßmayer), to unite the Slavs or at least the southern Slavs on a national level "through the bond of the Catholic Church."[40]

Another source of political and scholarly controversies between the Vatican and Vienna was the use of Hungarian as the liturgical language in the Greek dioceses of Munkács and Epirus by Magyarized Ruthenians. The Vatican finally forbade the use of the Hungarian liturgy.[41] This did not prevent Rome from quietly tolerating its usage in the bishopric which was established in 1912 for the Greek-Catholic Hungarians in Hajdudorog, although the successor to the throne, Franz Ferdinand,[42] had explicitly disapproved of it.[43]

The Austrians also reacted sensitively to the Monarchy's right to protect the Christians of the Balkans and the Middle East. The Vatican's negotiations with Turkey about the conclusion of a concordat for Albania failed because of Austro-Hungarian opposition. Austria-Hungary saw a violation of its protectoral rights in such an agreement.[44]

All these differences lose their importance when compared with the most consequential controversy the Monarchy had with the Holy See

[37] F. Engel-Janosi, op. cit. II (Graz, Vienna, Cologne 1960), 79ff.
[38] E. Weinzierl-Fischer, *"Die letzten Ernennungen österreichisch-ungarischer Kardinäle"*, *Östterreich und Europa (Festgabe für Hugo Hantsch)* (Graz, Vienna, Cologne 1965), 411ff.
[39] F. Engel-Janosi, op. cit. I, 296.
[40] Kálnoky to Revertera in 1881, VII, 23; F. Revertera, *Erinnerungen*, op cit., 260, n. 17.
[41] Ibid., 264.
[42] F. Engel-Janosi II, 122, 156f.
[43] F. Revertera, *Erinnerungen,* op. cit., 266.
[44] A. H. Benna, "Studien zum Kultusprotektorat Österreich-Ungarns in Albanien im Zeitalter des Imperialismus (1888–1918)," *Mitteilungen des österreichischen Staatsarchivs* 7 (1954), 28f.

during the pontificates of Leo XIII and Pius X: the fight over Hungary's legislation regarding religious policy. It goes back to 1890, to the so-called decree of abatement of former religion through baptism.[45] Its goal was to obtain obedience to the law of 1868 pertaining to the religious denomination of children from denominationally mixed marriages. According to this law, children were to follow by sex their father's or mother's denomination; but it became common practice for the Catholic priest to "abate" the denomination through baptism. Already at that time, Rome had refused the transfer of baptismal records to the appropriate clergymen as was required by the state. This stand was evident in 1891, when the demands for civil marriage, civil matriculation, and general religious freedom were recapitulated in the Hungarian Parliament. Secretary of Religious Affairs in the Wekerle cabinet, Albin Count Csáky, also adopted this program. Following its first resignation and subsequent reinstatement without Csáky, the government succeeded at the end of 1894 in pushing through both houses of Parliament civil marriage, civil matriculation, and an amendment to the law of 1868. The Emperor ratified the new laws. Subsequently, Wekerle resigned for good, having lost the Emperor's confidence in the success of another anticipated judicial reform. In contrast to the radical-conservative Hungarian People's Party (founded in November 1894) and to many tendencies of the liberal Bánffy government, both Secretary of Foreign Affairs Count Kálnoky and the Austrian Ambassador to Rome Count Revertera tried to prevent an open quarrel with the Holy See.[46] When Nuncio Agliardi of Vienna came to Hungary in April 1895 for an official visit, he pleaded with the Catholic leaders of Hungary in several speeches to side with the clergy in the ensuing fight with the government. This was followed by an interpellation in the Hungarian House of Representatives. In his answer, President Bánffy declared that the nuncio had overstepped his authority and that Kálnoky was of the same opinion and had already protested to the Curia. Since this was not the case, Kálnoky hotly denied Bánffy's statements in a telegram and resigned. Still, in a letter to Bánffy, he termed the nuncio's behavior "tactless." Rome, on the other hand, refused to recall Agliardi, "provided that the insult inflicted upon the Holy Father in the person of His deputy be compensated," as Secretary of State Cardinal Rampolla explained to Revertera.[47] Even though Rome disregarded an expressed apology by Vienna, it was not until 1896 that Agliardi was appointed cardinal and thus recalled from Vienna. Meanwhile in Hungary, the

---

[45] M. Csáky, *Der Kulturkampf in Ungarn* (Graz, Vienna, Cologne 1967), 41ff.
[46] F. Engel-Janosi, op. cit. I, 287.
[47] Ibid., 292.

laws concerning the acceptance of Judaism and general freedom of religion had been enacted and, at the end of 1896, ratified by the Emperor. One could argue whether the changes in the Hungarian legislation regarding religious policy from 1894 to 1895 should be assessed as a *Kulturkampf* or a reform.[48] Without a doubt, however, the long and at times dramatic controversy between Church and state could have been at least alleviated. Its acuteness was probably rooted in the fact that the Church was not only interested in defending the sacrament of matrimony and Catholic education, but also its dominant position in the Empire of Saint Stephen, which, according to Rampolla, "was never to be relinquished to the Calvinists and Jews."[49]

The longer Leo XIII's pontificate lasted, the more powerful the secretary of state became. In Vienna, he grew more and more unpopular, not to say hated. Even the Imperial Ambassador Revertera, extremely loyal to church and Vatican, differed with him again and again.[50] It was certainly not easy to get along with the proud and sensitive Sicilian. The animosities of the Austrian diplomatic corps seem to have originated in the burden imposed upon the Monarchy's domestic policy by the problem of nationalities, which was constantly increasing, especially during Leo XIII's pontificate, and reached a climax during the Badeni crisis of 1897. Rampolla sympathized with the Slavs, the Italians, the Christian-Socialists, and the respective Catholic democratic parties within Austria and Hungary. He granted France and Russia an important role in the foreign policies of the Vatican. Therefore, he had to be *persona ingrata* not only with the conservative and liberal politicians and with several Austrian bishops, but also with the Emperor himself. It remains to be decided whether, through the years, the Emperor remembered the cardinal's initial refusal to give his son Rudolf a church funeral.[51] One thing is certain: never before had there been such accord on the use of the imperial veto as during the papal elections of 1903. As of the evening of 1 August, Rampolla was ahead with twenty-nine out of sixty-two votes,[52] and was already greeted as the new Pope. One has to assume, then, that the Austrian veto announced by Cardinal Puzyna of Cracow on 2 August[53] deprived him of the tiara. Giuseppe Sarto, patriarch of Venice, was finally elected Pope on 4 August 1903. He quickly fulfilled several of Austria's long-standing wishes; for instance, the promotion of Archbishop Samassa to cardinal. Yet more quickly (in January 1904,

---

[48] M. Csáky, op. cit., 103ff.
[49] Ibid., 110.
[50] For example, F. Revertera, *Erinnerungen,* op. cit., 309.
[51] A. Hudal, op. cit., 250, and F. Engel-Janosi II, 2.
[52] Ibid. II, 37.
[53] Ibid. II, 38.

through the constitution *Commissum Nobis*), Pius X declared invalid the right of veto which France, Spain, and Austria had traditionally claimed, and imposed extremely harsh penalties upon participation in such an act.[54]

The battle against "modernism," which Pius X fought so passionately within the Church, "was of no great consequence for the relations of this pontificate to the Habsburg Monarchy."[55] Indeed, there was a "literary battle" in Austria; there were people who were accused of "modernism" and suffered harm because of it, e.g., writers like Enrica von Handel-Mazzetti, scientists like Albert Ehrhard, priests like Josef Scheicher, who was a representative of Lower Austria, and Franz Martin Schindler, the theoretician of the Christian Social Party. Ehrhard[56] had to leave the University of Vienna; Schindler was not promoted to bishop because of his friendship with Ehrhard.[57] Even the Viennese Archbishop Gustav Piffl was denounced in Rome as a modernist by integralists from the Viennese Commer-Kralik group. He had opposed the establishment of a Viennese subsidiary of Benigni's infamous organization *Correspondance de Rome,* whose purpose was denunciation.[58] The tempest over modernism which, in regard to Austria, is just now being researched,[59] never reached the dimensions it did in France, Germany, or Italy. However, the Austrian public took an enormous interest in a case which was supposedly dramatized by the unauthorized and certainly undiplomatic action of Granito Pignatelli di Belmonte, nuncio to Vienna. Professor Ludwig Wahrmund, specialist in canon law from Innsbruck,[60] who had published a study about the veto right of the Catholic powers in 1888, interceded in favor of reform Catholics Ehrhard and Schell in his lectures of 1902. On 18 January 1908, he gave a "scientific" speech for the general public in Innsbruck about the "Catholic world view and free scholarship," which was directed against the *Syllabus* and Pius X's encyclical *Pascendi* and was a masterpiece of massive anticlericalism. Moreover, Wahrmund published this speech in Munich after it was confiscated in Austria. Consequently, Nuncio Belmonte did not just call on Foreign Secretary Aehrenthal, but also announced to several newspapers that he

[54] Ibid. II, 52.
[55] Ibid. II, 142.
[56] A. Dempf, *Albert Ehrhard. Der Mann und sein Werk* (Colmar 1944).
[57] F. Funder, *Aufbruch zur christlichen Sozialreform* (Vienna, Munich 1953), 126ff.
[58] A. Hudal, op. cit., 289.
[59] O. Schroeder, *Aufbruch und Mißverständnis. Zur Geschichte der reformkatholischen Bewegung* (Graz, Vienna, Cologne 1969), 392–411ff., and *Der Modernismus. Beiträge zu seiner Erforschung,* ed. by E. Weinzierl (Thomas-Michels commemorative ed.) (Graz, Vienna, Cologne 1973).
[60] M. Höttinger, "Der Fall Wahrmund" (unpub. diss., Vienna 1950), and F. Engel-Janosi II, 86ff.

had asked Aehrenthal to remove Wahrmund from his teaching position. He insisted on the truth of this statement even after Aehrenthal's official denial. As a result, Wahrmund became the hero of an enraged liberal public, and the Department of Education could not afford to dismiss Wahrmund had it wished to do so.[61] Aehrenthal, in turn, demanded that Belmonte be recalled. Even Legate Montel, always attempting to mediate, asked the Pope "imploringly" to recall Belmonte. Pius X, apparently feeling offended himself, pounded the table and declared: "I am not a diplomat, but I am immovable. I cannot allow Monsignor Belmonte to leave Vienna now. If his mother were on her deathbed, I would not give him leave at this time." Then he deplored the Josephinism which continued to exist in the Habsburg Monarchy.[62] In 1911, when it was his turn, Belmonte became cardinal and was thus officially recalled from Vienna, though he was not received any longer by the Austrian foreign secretary. Nevertheless, Pius X generally expressed himself with benevolence towards the Monarchy, giving it his unequivocal sympathy at the outbreak of the world war he had feared for many years.[63]

On the Austrian side, in those "last years of a great power," when the bishops of the Monarchy paid homage to Franz Joseph on the occasion of his sixtieth anniversary of government in 1908, the Emperor once more emphatically acknowledged the alliance of throne and altar which he had strived for since the beginning of his reign. The aging Emperor concluded his avowal with the words: "You can be assured of the protection of the state while teaching your faith and administering your duties. I myself am a loyal son of the Church which taught me humility in difficult hours, offered me consolation in bad times, and guided me and my House loyally through all paths of life."[64]

[61] In tedious negotiations, Wahrmund was therefore forced to take leave for several semesters. He was finally transferred to Prague.
[62] F. Engel-Janosi II, 96.
[63] Ibid. II, 151.
[64] O. Posch, op. cit., 208f.

CHAPTER 3

The Conclusion of the Kulturkampf
in Prussia and in the German Empire

Leo XIII[1] considered himself to be a political Pope and wanted to break the isolation of his predecessor as quickly as possible. Considering his foremost task to be the conclusion of the German *Kulturkampf,* then the

[1] Concerning the personality and the program of Leo XIII, see pp. 6–25 above.

most pressing political burden of the Church, he initiated immediate action. On the day of his election (20 February 1878), he wrote a letter to Emperor Wilhelm I and other princes of states struggling with tensions concerning religious policy in which he suggested mutual attempts to restore the previously good relations.[2] Berlin's unwillingness to compromise did not deter him. Supported by a few trusted men, such as Secretary of State Cardinal Franchi[3] and Monsignor Czacki,[4] he hurriedly drafted his program. The Pope and his advisers appreciated Bismarck's anti-revolutionary policies and were convinced that only a statesman of his caliber was capable of ending the *Kulturkampf*, which he himself had started.

The Pope's immediate and constant goal was to restore his freedom of movement, which the Church needed for its spiritual mission. If necessary, he was willing to grant the state concessions consistent with the Church constitution. An equally legitimate task, in his opinion, was the preservation and strengthening of the conservative social order. In an alliance between the papacy and a monarchal power such as Prussia and the Empire, Leo saw the most effective defense against socialism and revolution. He hoped for a comprehensive contractual agreement. Convinced of the state's need for peace, he prematurely expected that Bismarck would more or less share his views and meet a conciliatory Pope halfway in these urgent controversies.[5] The self-conception of the modern state, the complex political structure of Prussia and Germany, and the numerous psychological obstacles in the way of appeasement found little consideration in the Vatican. Neither the nuncios in Vienna and Munich who were fairly informed about the situation in Germany, nor the Prussian bishops were consulted. The politicians of the Center Party who were carrying the main burden of the struggle were not

---

[2] Concerning the first exchange of letters between Leo XIII and Wilhelm, see Siegfried, *Aktenstücke,* no. 183f.

[3] Alessandro Franchi (1819–78), 1856: nuncio to Florence, 1860: secretary of the Congregation for Special Ecclesiastical Affairs (AES), 1868: nuncio to Madrid, 1873: cardinal, 1874: prefect for propaganda; in 1877, Franchi had already participated in attempts to initiate talks with Germany. *ECatt* V, 1622 (biblio.); R. Lill, *Vatikanische Akten* (henceforth: *V.A.*) 3, n. 1.

[4] Wladimir Czacki (1834–88), 1877: secretary of the Congregation of the AES, 1879: nuncio in Paris, 1882: cardinal. Czacki, a Pole, was often suspected by the German *Kulturkampf* fighters of being an "enemy of the Empire". He was of firm convictions and he collaborated in the peace politics of the new Pope. He was particularly interested in France; aside from the Pope, he was the true initiator of the policy of understanding toward the Republic (U. Stutz, *Die päpstliche Diplomatie unter Leo XIII . . . .* [AAB (1925), nos. 3–4], 7ff., 62–67, etc.; *V.A.*, 116, n. 1).

[5] Concerning programmatic statements by Leo XIII and his close advisers, see *V.A.*, nos. 12, 33, 58, 61, 75, 85, 90, 94, 103, 127, 130, 142a, 144, 147, 152, 180, 187, 207, 215, 225.

consulted either. The Pope considered himself, and only himself, the appointed guardian of ecclesiastical rights, believing that he alone was competent to conduct negotiations and make decisions in a struggle of such fundamental significance as the *Kulturkampf*. This proves the centralistic-autocratic tendency of Leo's pontificate, which is a direct continuation of the Curia's development in the nineteenth century. This tendency is often overlooked in view of Leo's relative intellectual openness and his ability to adjust. From a treaty between papacy and Empire, Leo also expected a strengthening of his claim to sovereignty, which he decided to cultivate more rigorously than his predecessor, who tended to give way to resignation. In addition, an agreement with the strongest European powers could facilitate the conclusion of the conflicts with other states.

The strength of Leo XIII's program lay in his insight that the Church should not be permitted to be content with the belligerent situation which it had inherited from Pius IX. Its weaknesses were the exaggerated assessment of his own possibilities and his insufficient knowledge of the situation in the various states, such as Germany. Only after setbacks which could have been avoided had the situation been analyzed in time and with realism did the Vatican come to the understanding that political reverses had to be accepted. The Pope, attributing greatest significance to appeasement, was more willing in a tight situation to compromise than his collaborators. Only in the last phase of the development described in this chapter did the Pope find a close coworker in Monsignor Luigi Galimberti, who was far more compliant than the Pope himself.

Of the reasons which compelled Bismarck not to reject Rome's peace attempts, only one partially agreed with the Pope's motives: the weakening of the monarchal state system through the *Kulturkampf* was increasing and filled the imperial court and many conservative circles with concern. More important for the Chancellor were the failure of the *Kulturkampf*, the changed situation as a whole, and his new domestic plans.[6] The change of course from free trade to protective tariffs, which he initially thought necessary, could only be enforced against the will of the liberal allies in the *Kulturkampf* and required new alliances. Bismarck was used to discarding partners who had done their duties. He was already reapproaching the Conservatives. Now he planned to either attract the Center Party or to pass them over through negotia-

[6] Concerning programmatic statements by the Chancellor, see Bismarck, *GW* VIc, nos. 120, 143, 174, 178, 183f, 217, 220, 222ff., 229, 231, 241, 243f., 259, 261ff., 267, 279, 290f., 301, 306, 306, 322, 324f., 328ff., 332–35, 338, 347–53, 355, 357, 360, 367; XII, 11f., 299–305; XIII, 181–92, 194–202, 282–315. *V.A.* nos. 6a, 13, 19, 24, 49–52, 62, 70, 99, 112, 152f., 155, 198, 218, 222, 229, 233, 237, 244, 255.

tions with the Pope and to separate them from their ecclesiastically motivated mass base. Since the change of pontificate, the conditions for this move seemed more favorable than previously. His speculations on the Center Party and his consideration of the Conservatives indicate the larger framework of domestic politics primarily determined by the growth of social democracy. The change of economic policy was only part of the conservative turn and consolidation of the Empire's structures which were introduced by the Chancellor in the spring of 1878. Included are the socialist law and the repression of all efforts to parliamentarize the Empire.[7] A modus vivendi with the papacy and the Catholic Church suited this new domestic turn, as did the simultaneous new direction in foreign policy taken through the Dual Alliance with Austria-Hungary. However, Bismarck and the Prussian bureaucracy did not intend to yield in regard to ecclesiastical matters as much as Leo XIII had hoped. The open struggle was to be ended, but the state's supervision over the Church was to remain. The harshest features of the May laws were to be eliminated; this was to be done, however, through unilateral laws. Bismarck never contemplated the treaty which the Pope envisioned.

The problem-ridden conclusion of the *Kulturkampf* took place in three stages: in the first, through negotiations between the Holy See and Prussia (1878–80); in the second, through discretionary mitigation laws (1881, 1882, 1883); in the third through the two Peace Laws (1886, 1887).

1. Bismarck reacted to the signals from the Vatican with utmost dispatch as he did not have to fear giving the impression of a pilgrimage to Canossa. He knew how to keep the Pope in the dark about his true intentions for a long time and entice him down the path of concessions through harmless advances, as for example the Roman question. Leo's obvious desire for peace put the trumps in the hands of the adversary.

Nuncio Aloisi Masella of Munich,[8] the Prussian delegate Count Werthern, and Bismarck's Bavarian adviser Count Holnstein established the first contacts, expressing the Chancellor's wish for an honorable peace. Crown Prince Friedrich Wilhelm, representing his father,

---

[7] Concerning the conservative turn of German domestic politics 1878–80, see especially N. Böhme, *Deutschlands Weg zur Großmacht . . . 1848–1881* (Cologne 1966), 446–579; H.-U. Wehler, *Bismarck und der Imperialismus* (Cologne, 1969), 101–11, 127–35, 139–51, 168–93; E. R. Huber, *Verfassungsgeschichte* IV, 67f., 104, 146f., 152–57, 772f., 882f., 1044–49, 1063ff., 1068, 1153–64; R. Lill, *Wende im Kulturkampf,* 232ff., 245f., etc.

[8] Gaetano Aloisi Masella (1826–1902), 1877: nuncio in Munich, 1879: in Lisbon, 1883: cardinal of the Curia. *ECatt* I, 916 (biblio.).

who had been hurt in an assassination attempt, wrote a letter which led to the main negotiations. It also contained Bismarck's program in its entirety, the implications of which were at first not understood in the Vatican. The Crown Prince explained that the laws of the state could not be adjusted to the Catholic dogmas and that a fight over principles was out of the question. He suggested, however, solving practical controversies together.[9] In the summer of 1878, a meeting between Bismarck and Aloisi Masella was arranged in Kissingen, where the incompatibility of the two viewpoints became clear for the first time.[10] The nuncio asked for the return to the status quo of 1871, which was characterized by the legal rule of the state Church. The Chancellor demanded papal recognition of the May laws regarding the duty to announce to the state candidates for clerical office and, in turn, offered restoration of diplomatic representation to the Holy See in order to conduct further negotiations about practical solutions. The prospect of a nunciature in Berlin was also held out. Though Leo XIII was very interested in diplomatic relations with Berlin,[11] he could not agree to this offer because it preserved the entire legislation of the *Kulturkampf*. In addition, his peace policy had at that moment, in the days of the meeting in Kissingen, lost its strongest supporter when Franchi suddenly died. Therefore, Aloisi's talks led to an atmospheric improvement. In place of negotiations, intentionally dilatory letters by Bismarck were exchanged between the new Secretary of State Cardinal Nina[12] and the Chancellor until the summer of 1879. By order of the Pope, Nina demanded contractual guarantees for the autonomy of the Church, especially a free exercise of their ministry for bishops and clergy and the return of those who were expelled including religious as well as clergy. He also asked the state to waive its claim to interfere in the education of the clergy and religious instruction in schools.

While Bismarck's anti-Polish attacks were skillfully handled by the Vatican,[13] the Chancellor's hopes for papal influence on the Center Party seemed to have a chance of being fulfilled.[14] Leo XIII's program left no room for independent action by the party. It was to perform secondary services. Above all, so the Vatican soon indicated, the party

[9] Crown Prince Friedrich Wilhelm to Leo XIII, 10 June 1878, text: Siegfried, *Aktenstücke*, no. 185.

[10] The meeting in Kissingen: Bismarck, *GW*, VIc, no. 124; *V.A.*, nos. 47–58.

[11] Under Pius IX, the Holy See had just been increasingly isolated diplomatically. In 1878, only four embassies and nine legations were accredited there; he entertained six nunciatures, two internunciatures, and four delegatures.

[12] Lorenzo Nina (1812–85), associate of the Holy Office, 1877: cardinal, 1878: secretary of state, 1880: prefect of propaganda. *V.A.*, 115, n. 4.

[13] *V.A.* nos. 19, 24, 26, 32, 37, 44, 47, 52.

[14] *V.A.* nos. 18, 13f., 17, 19f., 22, 25, 27, 34, 40, 45, 49, 52, 55ff., 62ff., 72.

was to oblige Bismarck politically in order to facilitate the negotiations between Rome and Berlin. Only if these negotiations should stagnate was the party to exert pressure on the Chancellor. The first differences between the Curia and the Center Party occurred in the summer of 1878, when the party, against Rome's wish, refused to approve the socialist law and was derided as a conspirator of the revolution by the government press. Matters did not improve when the Cathedral Canon Moufang of Mainz,[15] a respected man in Rome, explained the motives of the Center to the Curia. He said that the party wanted to keep political and ecclesiastical questions separate, that it was willing to appropriately fend off the socialistic danger, but that it did not want to approve Bismarck's exception laws because of its constitutional principles. At the end of 1878, Windthorst himself approached the Curia several times through the Viennese Nuncio Jacobini,[16] who was rather open-minded toward the party, and suggested parliamentary procedures to revise the May laws. He believed that the cooperation between Center Party and the Conservatives favoring Bismarck's new economic policies had created propitious conditions. He concluded that, in a constitutional state, a party, with its influence on the parliament and the public, was able to offer better guarantees for the Catholic minority than treaties between the Vatican and the government could. To Windthorst, the time for a separation of Church and state seemed to be right.[17] He and his friends did not expect much from Bismarck. Such proposals were not in keeping with Leo's wish to come to terms about the question of sovereignty. From the improved parliamentary constellations, the Vatican drew the opposite conclusion. The Center was urged to form a close coalition with the Chancellor. This was the first climax in the attempts to influence the party, but they were as unsuccessful as the fight over the septennate eight years later. The leadership of the party, supported by the episcopate,[18] insisted on its political independence.[19]

---

[15] Moufang was deputy for the Center Party in the *Reichstag* during 1871–77 and 1878–90. For his letters for the Curia from 1878–79, see *V.A.* nos. 54, 73, 78, 88, 110f., 122, 129, 145, 160a, and appendix no. 1.

[16] Lodovico Jacobini (1832–87), undersecretary of state of the First Vatican Council, 1874: nuncio to Vienna, 1879: cardinal and pronuncio, 1880: secretary of state; due to illness, his influence decreased in the last two years of his life. *V.A.* 9, n. 1; Weber, *Kirchliche Politik,* 29ff., 39–45, 48–51, 115–18, 128–31, 135–38, 149–58.

[17] *V.A.* nos. 83, 86, 100 (n. 3), 106–09, 116, 123, 143, 162, 164f., 167, 169f., 177, 185, 259, 261f.

[18] The Prussian bishops, lead by Archbishop Melchers of Cologne, repeatedly warned of concessions to Bismarck, see *V.A.* nos. 63, 77–81, 97f., 117–21, 156, 181, 184a, 212, 249.

[19] *V.A.* nos. 111, 116, 122 (incl. n. 4), 129, 143.

As a result, Leo XIII agreed to negotiate details as Bismarck had demanded since Kissingen. New hopes were raised when Falk, Minister of Religious Affairs and the embodiment of the *Kulturkampf,* resigned and was replaced by highly conservative Robert von Puttkamer (1828–1900),[20] who disliked the *Kulturkampf.* Falk's resignation was primarily caused by his differences with the orthodox faction of the Protestant Church, which was influential at the imperial court.[21] In the negotiations conducted since the summer of 1879 in Vienna by Jacobini, the German Ambassador Prince Reuß, and canonical experts, both positions regarding the resolutions of the May laws were formulated. Both standpoints continued to be essentially irreconcilable, Jacobini maintained in a meeting with Bismarck (Gastein, September 1879). The Chancellor, however, did openly declare his sympathy for the papal claim of sovereignty.[22] Henceforth, several concessions were announced during the talks in the following months. The ecclesiastical tribunal was to be abolished, the state was to resume payments, the extradition law was not to be enforced any longer, the oath for administrators of bishoprics was to be eliminated. Under state supervision, convents and seminaries were to be reopened. Denominational organization of elementary schools and teacher training were allowed, the prospect of assigning local school inspection to the pastors was held out.[23]

Before the Pope was able to make his objections, Bismarck broke off negotiations. Apparently, he had just wanted to ascertain the positions of his opponent. His pretext was the opposition of the Center to several bills proposed by the government. Bismarck and his aides, among them Secretary of State Hohenlohe, exaggerated this resistance by claiming it to be a fundamental opposition to state and Empire. In order to save some portions of his concept, Leo XIII went so far as to concede his duty to announce clerical appointments in advance and thus to make the very concession which both the Prussian bishops and the Center feared would result in the subjugation of the entire ecclesiastical life to the state bureaucracy.[24]

---

[20] Puttkamer, as minister of the interior (1881–88), supported the consolidation of the conservative system of government with all the means at his disposal; E. Kehr, *Das soziale System der Reaktion in Preußen unter dem Ministerium Puttkamer,* now in: E. Kehr, *Der Primat der Innenpolitik, Ges. Aufsätze . . . ,* ed. by H.-U. Wehler (2nd ed., Cologne 1970), 64–86; Weber, *Kirchl. Politik,* 67f.

[21] Bismarck, *GW* VIc, nos. 137, 139, 161f.; Förster, *Falk,* 553–652.

[22] Concerning the meeting in Gastein, see Bismarck, *GW* VIc, no. 167; *V.A.* nos. 152f.

[23] Concerning the negotiations in Vienna, see *V.A* nos. 136, 141f., 155–90; Heckel, *Beilegung,* 243–63.

[24] Concerning the papal announcement of this concession and the reaction of government, episcopate and Center, see *V.A.* nos. 201f., 207, 212ff., 218–26, 229, 231. When Bismarck did not concede, Leo retracted his announcement: *V.A.* nos. 245, 254.

2. Meanwhile, the Chancellor decided to move ahead unilaterally. Even his close advisers were surprised about his about-face. In March 1880, discretionary legislation was announced, which was to empower the government to apply several resolutions of the May laws with moderation. It determined the development of the next five years. Placing the enforcement of the existing laws within the discretion of the Ministry violated fundamental legal principles and was as injurious to the constitutional awareness in Germany as were the exceptive laws of the *Kulturkampf* themselves. But this was not atypical for Bismarck's style of government. To the Curia and the Center, the discretionary powers of authority seemed unacceptable because they aimed at regulating pending controversies without cooperation from the Church and substituted the arbitrary decisions of the bureaucracy for the severity of the current laws.[25] Over the joint reactions to Bismarck's new plan there arose a relatively good collaboration between the Vatican and the party. Now the party could begin to struggle for ecclesiastical interests in the Provincial Diet, which was once again responsible for the *Kulturkampf*.

The bill, introduced in May 1880, was to make possible the state-controlled organizational reconstruction of the Catholic Church. The most important enabling acts proposed by Bismarck and Puttkamer pertaining to new regulations of the culture examinations and the readmission of dismissed bishops had to be stricken because the National Liberals believed that they went too far, and the Center, upon instructions from Rome, continued to reject them. The first moderation law, passed on 19 June 1880 by a four-vote majority,[26] authorized the government (until the end of 1881) to employ episcopal administrators and bishops without an oath of obedience, to terminate the state's administration of the property belonging to newly filled dioceses, and to resume financial support by the state. The time limitation was proposed by the Conservatives, who wanted to characterize the discretionary legislation as a temporary arrangement. The law enabled state-approved clergymen to perform office as substitutes in vacant parishes and reinstated nursing orders without a time limit.

Concessions in social politics, announced during talks in Vienna, had meanwhile been decreed by Puttkamer. After his transfer to the Department of the Interior (1881), the new Minister of Religious Affairs, conservative Gustav Goßler (1838–1902), continued the strategy of gradual concessions. However, against the Center's wishes, he insisted on the state's authority in all matters concerning schools. In 1891, Goß-

---

[25] Concerning Bismarck's move toward discretionary legislation and his renewed polemics against the Center, see *V.A.* nos. 196, 198, 206, 222, 233ff., 237–44, 246–70.
[26] Text: Kißling III, 457f.

ler became the highest civil official of West Prussia. But only in the eastern provinces did Goßler proceed with his usual harshness. The second moderation law (31 May 1882)[27] was prepared by Goßler and through agreements between the Center and the Conservatives. It was also approved by the Catholic deputies. This law extended the enabling acts of the summer of 1880 to 1 April 1884 and contained the concessions which had earlier failed because of Liberal opposition.

The definite revision of the *Kulturkampf* laws demanded by Rome and the Prussian Catholics was postponed again. The government required complete realization of the May laws appertaining to the announcement of clerical candidates before it would consider revisions. Several initiatives by the Center were unsuccessful. In April 1883 Winthorst received the majority in the Provincial Diet for a resolution which demanded the "organic revision of the May laws." It was more than a moral victory because it proved that the majority in Parliament had grown tired of Bismarck's policy of obstruction. Bismarck and Goßler, however, succeeded in parrying the effects of the resolution by quickly enacting the third moderation law (11 July 1883).[28] According to this law, conferring of clerical offices whose incumbents could be recalled and the arrangements for a substitution were no longer subject to report to the bureaucracy, and the state's right to veto the nomination was abolished. This was a rather remarkable accomplishment toward progress. The temporary filling of vacant parishes was now possible without time limitations. The Church had to be content with having to apply for the candidate's dispensation from the culture examination demanded by the May laws. The law was passed by an overwhelming majority, opposed only by part of the Liberal Conservatives and the National Liberals, who were weakened by the turn of domestic politics. The Progressive Party continued to be viewed with suspicion in Church-related circles. Nonetheless, the party voted for this as well as other moderation laws, delineating once again the principles it had adhered to since the seventies: it welcomed the *Kulturkampf* laws insofar as they had a liberal motive; but the Progressives rejected repressive measures.

The first moderation law rendered possible the filling of the bishoprics of Fulda, Osnabrück, Paderborn, Trier, and Breslau,[29] which, through the death of their incumbents, were canonically vacant. This required new negotiations between Berlin and the Vatican. Leo XIII was still disappointed about Bismarck's change of course. He agreed to

---

[27] Text: Kißling III, 458f.
[28] Text: Kißling III, 459f.
[29] Breslau only became vacant after Förster's death on 20 October 1881.

negotiate only after some hesitation and upon the advice of the Center's leadership. The party pleaded for constructive use of the present accomplishments while reiterating further demands from the state. In the summer of 1881, Kurd von Schlözer (1822–94), then the Empire's envoy in Washington, negotiated with Cardinal Jacobini, who had meanwhile become Leo XIII's secretary of state. In December of the same year, Clemens August Busch (1834–95),[30] under secretary of state in the Foreign Office, conducted the negotiations. Schlözer, liberal and well versed in history, had been legation secretary in Rome (1864–69), where he acquired a thorough knowledge of the Church's situation in Rome and Italy[31] and of Catholicism, which he basically despised. This was exceptional for a Protestant from Northern Germany. Schlözer knew how to deal with the prelates, and therefore Bismarck wanted him in Rome at all times. As the first head of the Prussian Legation to the Holy See, reopened in February 1882, he energetically participated in negotiations for the following five years. The restoration of diplomatic relations was a clear step toward normalization, though Leo XIII had hoped for more in this important area: he had hoped that the Empire would establish an embassy.[32] The Chancellor tried to appease the Liberal opposition in the Provincial Diet by stressing that the function of the legation to the Vatican was simply one of concern with Church matters and, thus, with domestic affairs. At the same time, he had to convince the Vatican that the legation did indeed mean recogni-

[30] Aside from Hohenlohe, Busch was one of the very few Catholics among the leading civil servants of the Foreign Office. Here, as in other high administrative offices of the Empire, the Catholics, in the Bismarck period and later (cf. chap. 35), only had a chance for promotion if they belonged to the governmental minority generally tending toward the Free Conservative Party, and if they kept a distance from "ultramontanism" and the Center (R. Morsey, *Die oberste Reichsverwaltung unter Bismarck 1867–1890* [Münster 1957], 116–22, 248f., 268f).

[31] This was documented by his "Roman letters" with the impressive description of papal Rome and its leading personalities in the last years of the Papal State (ed. by K. v. Schlözer [Suttgart, Berlin 1913]). In German-speaking countries, these letters can only be compared to the historical passages in *The Years of Travel in Italy* by F. Gregorovius (last ed. by H.-W. Kruft [Munich 1967]).

[32] This accreditation was in keeping with the competence, pertaining to Church politics, of the German federal states. Of these states, Bavaria maintained a legation to the Holy See because she was interested in continuous relations with the Vatican. The creation of a nunciature in Berlin, discussed several times during the negotiations of 1878–79, failed because of the opposition of the Emperor and influential Evangelical circles. However, the Center politicians and the Prussian bishops were clearly against this project. They feared that a nunciature would become a tool for Berlin's Church politics and that it would hinder the independent actions of the episcopate and the Center (*V.A.* nos. 19, 47, 49ff., 57, 62, 114 [incl. n. 2], 116 [n. 4], 152, 168, 183, 233, 237, 239 [n. 4], 240 [n. 1], 262 [n. 11]; cf. also Bismarck, *GW* VIc, nos. 176, 223).

tion of papal sovereignty. To stress this point, Bismarck avoided, as did his Austrian colleague Kálnoky, giving Italy a formal guarantee of her territorial claims, which had been requested during the negotiations for the Triple Alliance in the spring of 1882. This would have meant a direct recognition of the annexation of the Papal State.[33] Nevertheless, the treaty of the two imperial powers with Italy deeply disappointed the Pope, because it consolidated Italy and raised her political value. Now the Pope could not expect from Bismarck effective help on the question of the Papal State.

The concrete goal of Schlözer's and Busch's mission was only reached gradually and with new difficulties. At first, the Holy See enabled only the cathedral chapters in Osnabrück and Paderborn to elect capitular vicars, who were able to assume office in February 1881 without state interference.[34] In Trier, where an election was subsequently ordered, Philipp de Lorenzi, who had been chosen by that chapter, was rejected by the government. The negotiations were difficult and complicated by the differences between the liberal, progovernment minority[35] and the ultramontane-intransigent majority.[36] But the government and the Curia agreed to appoint bishops in Trier and Fulda who were nominated by the Pope directly, circumventing the chapter's right of elections. In choosing the candidate, a momentous compromise was arrived at: in Trier the Curia insisted on the staunchly ultramontane Alsatian Michael

---

[33] Factually, the Italian wishes were fulfilled. In the first treaty of the Triple Alliance (20 May 1882, ART. 2), Germany and Austria promised Italy their full military support in case of an unprovoked attack by France, probably the only power still interested in the restoration of the Papal State. Now, the Roman question was an affair exclusively between Italy and the Vatican (Italicus, *Italiens Dreibundpolitik 1870–1896* [Munich 1928], 52–61; L. Salvatorelli, *La Triplice Alleanza* [Milan 1939], 62–72).

[34] In Osnabrück Bernhard Höting, in Paderborn Kaspar Drobe. In the fall of 1882, both took full responsibility of their dioceses as bishops. In Breslau, after Förster's death, Suffragan Bishop Hermann Gleich was elected capitulary vicar. Since the election of bishops did not take place because the government withdrew several candidates, the Pope, after negotiations with the government, appointed Prior Robert Herzog of Saint Hedwig in Berlin as prince bishop (March 1882).

[35] Their leaders were Cathedral Prior Karl Josef Holzer and his close friend Church historian Franz Xaver Kraus, professor in Freiburg. Kraus especially fought ultramontanism and the "political Catholicism" of the Center, accusing them of secularizing religious interests (cf. chap. 29; F. X. Kraus, *Tagebücher,* ed. by H. Schiel [Cologne 1957]; H. Schiel, *Im Spannungsfeld von Kirche und Politik, Franz Xaver Kraus* [Trier 1951]; H. Schiel, *Trierer Bischofskandidatur von Korum und Kraus* [Trier 1955]; on the same subject: Weber, *Kirchl. Politik,* 33–58; on Holzer: E. Hegel, *Festschrift für Alois Thomas* [Trier 1967], 151–62).

[36] It was endorsed by Windthorst; more importantly, it had direct contacts to Secretary of State Cardinal Jacobini through one of its members, Seminary Professor Peter Alexander Reuß.

Felix Korum;[37] in Fulda, the government insisted on compliant Georg Kopp.[38] Korum established close contacts with exiled Archbishop Melchers, with Bishop Krementz from Ermland, and with the Center Party. He also led the opposition of the episcopate's majority to Berlin's religious policy. Kopp, ready to make concessions, represented the other side of papal policy. He felt just as responsible to the state as he did to the Church. Reconciliation of state and Church was of great concern to him. But since he felt that considerable concessions were necessary to realize this goal, he soon found himself in opposition to his colleagues and to the Center, which he accused of sterile opposition.[39]

When these bishops were appointed, when Bishops Blum (Limburg) and Brinkmann (Münster) were pardoned and returned (in 1883–84), when government payments to the dioceses with state-approved bishops[40] were resumed, and when vacant parishes were filled temporarily, the restoration of the Catholic Church organization as desired by the government had indeed begun. After 1883 the shortage of priests was rapidly relieved. However, many important questions were still unresolved. The *Kulturkampf* continued to smolder, while the involvement of the faithful due to granted relief threatened to decrease in time. The gravest difficulties were caused by the state's continuous claim to the right of veto regarding the filling of offices, the training of the clergy, the question of religious orders, and the new appointments for the bishoprics of Cologne and Gnesen-Posen. According to the government, seminarians were to study only in the theology faculties of the state universities, a choice also preferred by liberal Catholics,[41] while the Curia and the majority of the bishops insisted on seminaries controlled by them. The state bureaucracy and the National Liberals resisted the

[37] Michael Felix Korum (1840–1921), 1865: seminary professor, 1872: cathedral preacher, 1880: cathedral vicar in Strasbourg, 1881: bishop in Trier; biography by J. Treitz (Munich 1925); Weber, *Kirchl. Politik,* passim.

[38] Georg Kopp (1837–1914), vicar general in Hildesheim, made efforts to achieve détente regarding the *Kulturkampf;* 1881: bishop of Fulda, 1884: member of the Prussian State Council, 1887: member of the House of Lords (for life), also prince bishop of Breslau, 1893: cardinal (Morsey, *Probleme;* Morsey, "Georg Kard. Kopp. Fürstbischof von Breslau, Kirchenfürst oder 'Staatsbischof'?," *Wichmann-Jahrbuch für Kirchengeschichte im Bistum Berlin,* XXI–XXIII (1967–69), 42–65; Weber, *Kirchl. Politik,* chap. IVff.; E. Gatz, *Bischöfliche Einheitsfront . . . .* [cf. chap. 1]).

[39] Cf. chap. 35.

[40] Only the archbishoprics of Cologne and Gnesen-Posen remained without state-approved bishops until 1885 and 1886, respectively, and therefore they had no official diocesan administration and no state funds.

[41] The example of the university and seminary education shows that liberal Catholics were dependent on the alliance with the state in order to assert at least some parts of their concept against ultramontanism (*V.A.* nos. 193[including n. 16], 231 [including n. 4], appendix no. 3 [including n. 8]).

return of the religious orders with a vehemence that had nothing in common with liberal principles. In Berlin reinstatement of Archbishops Melchers and Ledóchowski was felt to be a question of the state's prestige and was categorically refused, even though neither archbishop reacted any differently to the *Kulturkampf* laws and Leo XIII's concessions from the majority of his colleagues. In Gnesen the government wanted to name a German archbishop.

For the time being, neither side was willing to give in. In 1883 and 1884, the Pope and Secretary of State Jacobini declared several times that freedom in the matter of ecclesiastical jurisdiction and the training of priests was essential. According to the old curial maxim that you should adhere to your principles and rather sacrifice the person, if necessary, the Pope and his advisers wanted to consent to the resignation of the archbishops only if the state would concede in those central questions. Essentially, Leo XIII took the same position in this matter that the majority of the episcopate, led by Melchers and Korum, and the Center faction under Windthorst maintained. In the summer of 1885, Rome still repudiated the fact that Bishop Drobe of Paderborn had given in to the state's regulations regarding the training and assignment of the clergy. But that was the last substantial victory the Prussian Catholic leaders who were averse to Bismarck could report to the Vatican.

3. In 1885 Leo XIII changed his mind, which led to the last phase of the conclusion of the *Kulturkampf.* Bishop Kopp had prepared the Pope diplomatically, corroborating his old notion that the *Kulturkampf* should be terminated as soon as possible in cooperation with rather than in opposition to Bismarck. He also declared the resignation of the archbishops a prerequisite for salvaging a situation that had run aground. He regarded preliminary concessions as inevitable, even as justifiable, since he trusted Bismarck. Just as important were the power shifts within the Vatican. As a result of his illness, Secretary of State Cardinal Jacobini, who tended toward the Center, had lost some of his influence. In 1885 the Pope was busy defending himself against severe criticism from intransigent Catholics,[42] and therefore decided to continue his strategy of negotiations with even more persistence. Last but not least, because of the intensification of Italy's anticlerical politics, the Pope desired more and more urgently immediate and evident successes.

---

[42] A great sensation was caused by the attacks of the French scholar, Cardinal of the Curia Jean-Baptiste Pitra, O.S.B. He charged Leo with having deviated from the tested path of his predecessors and with having furthered the liberal deterioration (C. Crispolti, G. Aurelia, *La politica di Leone XIII,* 87–90; Weber, *Kirchl. Politik,* 113–17; U. Engelmann, *LThK²* VIII, 527).

Monsignor Galimberti,[43] of Cardinal Franchi's school, had taken over the factual direction of the Congregation for Extraordinary Affairs in the summer of 1885. The Pope found in Galimberti an adviser who was as devoted as he was able, though it was difficult to see through his motives.[44] Monsignor Boccali, head of the papal secret cabinet, eagerly supported him. Both monsignors entertained close relations with the Prussian delegate, with Montel, Austrian Auditor of the Rota, who was also a friend of Schlözer's, frequently mediating.[45]

Strengthened by his advisers, the Pope made his old program more concrete. Like the leaders of the Center and the majority of the Prussian bishops, he feared only the continuation of the *Kulturkampf*. While the former deduced from this that one should continue to demand the *status quo ante* and that compromises would eventually end in the Church's submission to the state, the Pope drew the opposite conclusion. He did not believe, as Windthorst did, that time would work in favor of the Church. In order to prevent the incalculable "bogginess" of the conflict, he decided to make concessions in several areas. As soon as possible, he wanted to achieve a solution which would guarantee at least the more important ecclesiastical demands. On this level he met Bismarck, who was also interested in a speedy appeasement, considering the consolidated alliance with Austria and the impending international crisis in 1885.[46] Research today has confirmed that the policy of ap-

---

[43] Luigi Galimberti (1836–96), professor at the College of Propaganda since 1860. As an enemy of the intransigents and the disciples of the Italian nation state, he was without influence for a long time. With the election of Leo XIII he became his political writer, in 1882 editor of the *Moniteur de Rome,* in 1885 pro-secretary, in 1886 secretary of the congregation of the AES, in 1887 nuncio in Vienna, and in 1893 cardinal and prefect of the Vatican archives (G. Grabinski, "Il Cardinale Galimberti," *Rassegna Nazionale* 89 (1896), 376–416; C. Crispolti and G. Aurelia, *La politica di Leone XIII,* passim; Weber, *Kirchl. Politik,* chap. VIff.; *ECatt* V, 1881).

[44] In the period of time between October 1886 and May 1887, which was decisive for the conclusion of the *Kulturkampf* and during which Galimberti was primarily responsible for papal politics, due to Jacobini's progressing illness and subsequent death (28 February 1887), Galimberti accepted payments from Bismarck's "reptile funds" (cf. above p. 22; R. Lucius von Ballhausen, *Bismarckerinnerungen* [4th and 6th eds., Suttgart 1921] 364; *Staatssekretär Graf Herbert von Bismarck. Aus seiner politischen Privatkorrespondenz,* ed by W. Bußmann [Göttingen 1964], 401f.).

[45] Johannes von Montel-Treuenfest (1831–1910), 1877: auditor, 1889: dean of the Rota, consultant to the Holy Office and other congregations, clerical adviser to the ambassador of the Austro-Hungarian Vatican Embassy, representative of various Austrian and German affairs in the Vatican, whose influence decreased when Rampolla was appointed secretary of state (*V.A.* no. 66, n. 2; biblio.); Weber, *Kirchl. Politik,* passim).

[46] The Bulgarian crisis of 1885 led to a catastrophic deterioration of Austro-Russian relations. At the same time, new German-French tensions occurred and a French-Russian alliance was under way. The crisis, to which Bismarck devoted most of his

peasement in the years 1885–87 was a personal achievement of the Pope and Bismarck.[47] Both had to overcome the resistance of the intransigents within their respective camps[48] and, therefore, used only the reliable aides mentioned above. Kopp especially, who was trusted by both sides and who in 1887 had been appointed to the Prussian House of Lords with the Pope's approval, henceforth mediated between Rome and Berlin, bypassing his colleagues and the Center.

The deadlock was overcome in the summer of 1885, when Leo called Melchers to Rome as a cardinal of the Curia and appointed Bishop Krementz his successor in Cologne, even though no satisfactory solution was in sight for Gnesen.[49] Krementz followed the principles of his predecessor, but that was not as relevant as the prestige the government had gained by removing the speaker of the episcopate in the years of struggle. Krementz was also weaker than Melchers. Nevertheless, the decisive impetus came from Bismarck a few months later, when he offered the Pope to mediate between Germany and Spain in the controversy over the Caroline Islands, an offer he accepted with alacrity. The "prisoner of the Vatican" was officially recognized thereby as sovereign, and, for the first time, Leo could perform the international office of arbitration in the service of peace, a function which he hoped to secure for the papacy for good by way of returning to politics.[50] The Pope thanked Bismarck for his help by awarding him the Order of

---

energies in the following two years, could only be settled through a Mediterranean *entente* and a German-Russian guarantee-treaty (both 1887) (A. Hillgruber, *Bismarcks Außenpolitik* [Freiburg 1972], 175–93).

[47] Morsey, *Probleme*, 225–45; Weber, *Kirchl. Politik*, 107ff., 120–25, 138ff., 188ff., etc.; Morsey, *Kopp*, 46f.

[48] On the side of the state: the National Liberal Party, the sympathetic news media, and strong powers in the Prussian bureaucracy; on the Roman side: most cardinals of the Curia, among them Ledóchowski and Johann Bapt. Franzelin,S. J. (1816–86), who were especially familiar with Germany and endorsed the policies of the Center. Both belonged to the commission for Germany, established by Leo XII, which was, however, practically without any influence since Galimberti's rise. Nevertheless, the Pope appreciated the advice of the educated and sharp Franzelin, whose death, therefore, gave the pro-Prussian groups a lift. Melchers, called to Rome in 1885, was not able to replace him, in spite of identical views. He could not influence the Vatican's politics, which were meanwhile conducted by Galimberti (on Franzelin: *V.A.* no. 69, n. 1; M.-G. von Twickel, *LThK²* IV, 272f.).

[49] Concerning the circumvention of the cathedral chapter, the appointment of Krementz and his cooperation with Korum (which the government did not want), see N. Trippen, *Das Domkapitel und die Erzbischofswahlen in Köln 1821–1929* (Cologne, Vienna 1972), 257–66.

[50] This seems to have been the major interest of Leo XIII. He used it to begin a line of papal policies which goes back to Benedict XV and Pius XII (cf. p. 22f.).

Christ, an act that was interpreted, not only in governmental publications, as a demonstration of reconciliation.

During the following months, the foundations for the two decisive peace laws were laid in secret meetings, from which were excluded the Center Party, the majority of the Prussian bishops, Cardinal Jacobini, and the members of most of the duly qualified authorities of the Vatican. The original alternative of appeasement by treaty or law was replaced by a combination of both, as Bismarck had wanted. After consultation with the Vatican about what could be demanded from either side, the state enacted laws which legally validated the content of those consultations.

The draft of the first of these two laws[51] was debated from February until March 1886 and encountered reservations similar to the first moderation law six years earlier. For the National Liberals the concessions in this draft went too far; for the Center and the bishops (with the exception of Kopp) they did not go far enough. But now the changed constellation had its effect in the localities where the decisions had to be made. Contrary to parliamentary procedure the draft was initially not debated in the Provincial Diet, but in the House of Lords, where Kopp and some aristocratic "state Catholics" could appear and conservative governmental forces were in charge. Windthorst, Korum, and Krementz were ignored, even though they continued to be backed by the great majority of the Prussian Catholics. In previous years, visits and letters from Trier to the Curia had been welcomed, but now the attempt to send one of the bishops to the Vatican and convince the Pope to take a stricter stance failed. Bismarck and Leo XIII, Galimberti and Kopp succeeded and achieved a great deal: the law (21 May 1886)[52] disposed of the ecclesiastical tribunal and the culture examination for theology students. In most dioceses, seminaries and convents were allowed to reopen without the state supervision required by May law, thus widening the restricted work of the religious orders. Even before the law was published, Leo XIII assented to Bismarck's renewed request appertaining to the duty to report candidates for permanent positions in pastorates. In vain, Windthorst again warned against accepting this important requirement by the state.

---

[51] Concerning the first peace law, see Bachem, *Zentrumspartei* IV, 132–47; Heckel, *Beilegung,* 317–33; Schmidt-Volkmar, 300–16; Weber, *Kirchl. Politik,* 122–47. During the debate of the law, new intense controversies about the Polish question came up because the Center opposed the settlement law which furthered the Germanization of the Polish-speaking provinces (Bismarck, *GW* VIc, nos. 323, 325; XII, 166–78; J. Mai, *Die preußisch-deutsche Polenpolitik 1885–1887* [Berlin 1962], 75–82, 115–32; H. Neubach, *Die Ausweisungen von Polen und Juden aus Preußen 1885/1886* [Wiesbaden 1967], 92–112).

[52] Text: Kißling III, 460ff.

The fierce discussion over the second law was also encumbered by the septennate controversy.[53] Bismarck maneuvered the Center Party into this struggle, assisted by Leo XIII and his advisers, who critically transgressed the limits of their clerical competence. The Chancellor used the crisis in foreign policy to further enlarge the armed forces and, above all, to effect another septennate, i.e., the commitment of the military budget for seven years. As on similar former occasions, Bismarck wanted to limit the *Reichstag's* right to appropriate funds. The antiparliamentary course of 1878 was consistently pursued. Under the pretext that a Franco-German war was on the way, Bismarck persuaded the Pope to exert massive influence on the Center in favor of the septennate.[54] In this matter, as in the question of the Caroline Islands, Leo was guided by his exaggerated concept of the papal mission of order and peace. The Center, however, insisted upon its political independence. According to its constitutional fundamental concept, the party, along with the Freethinkers,[55] did not want to sanction more than a three-year military budget. Such a compromise did not satisfy Bismarck. The *Reichstag* was dissolved; the government presented the new elections (21 February 1887) as being a decision for or against Germany's defense preparedness. Through this demagogical tactic, the Chancellor accomplished the alliance of the National Liberals and the Conservatives, the so-called cartel. It was not difficult to accuse the two opposing parties of animosity toward the Empire. At the height of the election campaign, Bismarck published the Vatican's comments on the septennate, which Galimberti and Schlözer had delivered into his hands. The Center appeared to have been compromised by the Pope. Windthorst's superior tactics,[56] the determination of its active members, and the support by

[53] The septennate controversy, forming fronts which affected more than the *Kulturkampf*, and the subsequent negotiations about the second peace law have been researched more thoroughly than most phases of the *Kulturkampf* and its conclusion (see mainly Bachem, *Zentrumspartei* IV, 148–326; Heckel, *Beilegung*, 333–49; Morsey, *Probleme*, 225–35; Schmidt-Volkmar, 324–41; Weber, *Kirchl. Politik*, 148–71).

[54] The Pope and Galimberti conceived two decrees for Nuncio Di Pietro of Munich (3, 21 January 1887), which were signed by Jacobini, but which were supposed to have been sent to Baron Georg Arbogast von Franckenstein (MdR), who worked closely with Windthorst and had good contacts to the nunciature in Munich. The second decree had been initiated by a letter from Franckenstein in which he had extensively explained and justified the politics of the Center.

[55] The Progressive Party and other left Liberals. Groups which had defected from the National Liberals had joined the Freethinkers in 1884.

[56] He proved his tactic in his famous election speech in Cologne's Gürzenich (6 February 1887) two days after the unexpected announcement of the second Vatican decree, which was immediately exploited by the government press. He interpreted it completely in accord with Leo XIII's wish, expressed therein, for a strong continuation of the Center and his recognition of what the party had accomplished in the interest of the

the Rhenish-Westphalian bishops helped the party to survive the crisis. It was in its favor that Nuncio Di Pietro[57] of Munich did not belong to Galimberti's but to Jacobini's group and that the Pope himself modified his earlier statements. The Pope did not wish a catastrophe for the party and was alarmed by the startling criticism on the part of Korum and Bishop Senestréy of Regensburg.[58] Therefore the Center endured but an insignificant defection, mostly noble Catholics from the right, who sympathized with Kopp's course in any case. Thanks to his solid voting block, he could return to the *Reichstag* with ninety-eight deputies (previously ninety-nine), while the Freethinkers, under pressure by governmental propaganda, lost half their mandate. In March 1887, the cartel parties, who had emerged from the election campaign with new strength, helped the septennate to victory.

The Pope directly intervened in the final preparations for the second law by sending Galimberti to Berlin,[59] where he also expressed the Pope's wider political desires. They ranged from the restoration of the Papal State to papal arbitration for the purpose of avoiding war. As had happened on former occasions, Bismarck's simple and polite approval awakened exaggerated hopes and further willingness to compromise in as yet unresolved controversies. The Pope did not realize that he was just playing the role which the Chancellor had designed for him in his political concept. Again, there were serious disputes over the next moves between Galimberti and Kopp, who were essentially satisfied with Bismarck's offers, and Windthorst and his faction, who wanted to continue fighting in order to gain more. By order of the Pope, whose competence to decide ecclesiastical matters was not questioned by the Catholic deputies, the Center finally supported the bill of the Chancellor, who took great efforts to overcome the resistance of the liberal advocates of the *Kulturkampf.* Minister of the Interior Puttkamer energetically supported this bill, but even Minister of Religious Affairs Goßler feared the sacrifice of too many state prerogatives. The law, enacted on 29 April 1887,[60] limited, as far as the state was concerned, the duty to report candidates and the government's right to veto the

---

Church (Hüsgen, *Windthorst,* 288–301 [with the text of the speech]; Bachem, *Zentrumspartei* IV, 189–97 [with excerpts]).

[57] Angelo Di Pietro (1828–1914), 1877: delegate in Buenos Aires, 1879: internuncio in Rio de Janeiro, 1882: nuncio in Munich, 1887: in Madrid, 1893: cardinal of the Curia (De Marchi, *Le Nunziature Apostoliche,* 278 [index]).

[58] Senestréy (bishop of Regensburg since 1858) was very respected in Rome for his long-lasting efforts on behalf of the ultramontane principles.

[59] A welcome occasion was the festivities for Emperor Wilhelm I's ninetieth birthday (22 March 1887).

[60] Text: Kißling III, 462f.

permanent filling of pastorates. At the same time, it waived the obligation to fill them permanently. Seminaries and convents were allowed again in all German-speaking dioceses; most religious orders could return and were given back their property, which had been taken into custody by the state.

The state had thus abandoned most of the discriminatory measures of the *Kulturkampf*. Remaining from the Kulturkampf legislation, but in moderated form, were the state supervision of schools,[61] civil marriage, the pulpit paragraph, the Jesuit law (until 1917), and the duty to announce candidates, but in moderated form; the Church paragraphs of the constitution were not reinstated. The state's control over the Church was consequently preserved to a degree which went far beyond the situation of 1871, but Bismarck was not able to reinforce this control. His attempt proves that he still did not completely understand the vitality which the Church had been able to maintain. In similar fashion, he often failed to realize the importance of a historical evolution in terms of domestic politics, especially when dealing with opponents. One century of Church emancipation had passed over the Prussian claim for control over the Church. At the most, control could be enforced for a short period in an anachronistic struggle of attrition if all of the powers of the state were employed. The Church, relieved of the shackles of the *Kulturkampf,* could no longer be kept dependent through the remaining restrictions. In the following years, a status quo of balance between Church and state, acceptable to both sides, was reached. In that respect, Windthorst, Korum, and their disciples had been too pessimistic. Leo XIII handled the concrete controversies quite realistically. The relatively favorable conclusion of the *Kulturkampf* did indeed increase the Vatican's diplomatic prestige, which Leo was particularly interested in, since, in 1887, Francesco Crispi became the head of the Italian government. He was strongly anticlerical and desirous of further isolating the Vatican. The Pope rightfully called the second peace law an *aditus ad pacem,* expressing in this manner his hopes for further moves by the state. His hopes for such moves were fueled by the enforcement of his pro-Prussian politics of 1886–87 through important decisions pertaining to personnel. Circumventing the suffrage of the cathedral chapters, which primarily tended toward the Center's course, he appointed progovernment bishops in Limburg and Kulm.[62] In Gnesen-Posen, for the first time, he appointed a German archbishop

---

[61] Henceforth, the local state inspection of schools was usually assigned to the priests.
[62] In Limburg Karl Klein, who, in 1887, was the only Prussian bishop (aside from Kopp) to support the septennate; in Kulm Leo Redner.

in the person of Julius Dinder from Königsberg. Kopp, so bitterly opposed by the Center, was promoted to Prince-Bishop of Breslau a few months after the achievement of the compromised peace which he had supported so diligently. Following Cologne, Breslau was Prussia's most prestigious episcopal see. But Leo XIII's other wishes and far-reaching political expectations remained unfulfilled. The Chancellor had reached his goal and, therefore, did not think of further concessions. Thus, Leo's wishful thinking took its toll. So did the hastiness, entirely unnecessary after the relief in 1880–83, with which, at the end, Leo fulfilled the opponents' wishes, thus burdening German Catholicism with needless inner tensions which continued to have an effect for some time to come. The Pope made it easy for the Chancellor to deceive him. Nevertheless, Bismarck, in complete command of the current situation, did not sufficiently contemplate the long term effects of his actions. The Pope's final disappointment in Bismarck and German politics form the background for the pro-French reorientation, which Leo XIII and Jacobini's successor Rampolla launched soon after.

Bismarck also did not succeed when he attempted for the last time, on the occasion of the septennate, to force the Center Party into submission and thus force a strong opponent out of the front which was pressing for parliamentarism. The party of the Catholics had supported the Chancellor on many issues, such as his fledgling policies of worker protection. In the eighties the party had already become an important and stable factor in German politics, which could only be hampered for a few years by the cartel of 1887.

Therefore, the *Kulturkampf* was one of Bismarck's worst mistakes in regard to domestic politics, aside from the persecutions of the Socialists. However, he was able partially to compensate for it through a skillful termination of the conflict. The *Kulturkampf* laws and the exceptive laws diminished the trustworthiness of the state and the ideas concerning law of the Germans. The timely evolution of state structures as well as the integration of the Catholics into the nation-state was delayed unnecessarily. The relations between the denominations as well as between the Germans and Poles were lastingly affected, especially as the fight in the eastern provinces was continued as a struggle between nationalities. Thanks to the mobilization of new political forces and Leo XIII's diplomacy, which was dependent on these forces, German Catholicism survived this test of strength. Nevertheless, militant liberalism reached a goal which it had pursued since the sixties: the Catholics had been completely isolated spiritually and socially in those years of struggle.[63]

[63] Cf. K. Erlinghagen, *Katholisches Bildungsdefizit* (Freiburg 1965), 17 etc.

As groups tend to do when pushed into a ghetto, they reacted by relying on their own strength and by refusing to recognize that some of the liberal initiatives merely corresponded to increasing secularization, which negation could not forestall in the long run. Henceforth, the Catholics tried harder than ever to expand the legal foundation, again assured since 1886–87, relative to various organizations. The most important new creations of the *Kulturkampf* period were the *Görres-Gesellschaft* and the *Volksverein*. That the defensive attitude of most Catholics was not unjustified was proven, last but not least, by the founding (1886) and activities of the *Evangelischer Bund*. It embraced those Protestants who felt the termination of the *Kulturkampf* to be a capitulation to the Catholic Church, and initially enkindled extreme denominational polemics.

The beginning of Baden's renunciation of the *Kulturkampf* and its motives have already been mentioned. In 1878 under the ministry of Turban-Stößer, appointed in 1876, the tedious reduction of *Kulturkampf* laws began. It was not concluded until 1918. The archbishopric of Freiburg, which, since 1868, had been administered by a capitulary vicar, was filled again in 1882 by Johann Baptist Orbin (1806–86)[64] from the irenic circle of J. B. Hirscher. Hessen-Darmstadt followed the Prussian example in the decade of the struggle as well as in its conclusion. Between 1880 and 1887, the *Kulturkampf* laws were largely revised. The conciliatory Paul Leopold Haffner (1829–99)[65] became bishop of Mainz in 1886. Moufang, who had been too exposed during the struggle and temporarily administered the bishopric after Ketteler's death (1877), had to withdraw. In Saxony, tensions also relaxed gradually, even though the law of 1876 pertaining to state supervision of churches remained in force. In Alsace-Lorraine, the conservative Governor Edwin Manteuffel after 1879 practiced a consistent policy of reconciliation.[66]

---

[64] *Badische Biographien* IV, 289–310; W. Müller, *LThK*² VII, 1196.
[65] L. Lenhart, *Paul Leopold Haffner (1829–99). Der schwäbische Philosoph auf dem Mainzer Bischofsstuhl (1886–99). Sonderdruck aus dem Jahrbuch für das Bistum Mainz* VIII (Mainz 1960); L. Lenhart, *LThK*² IV, 1312.
[66] In 1881 Manteuffel recommended Prebendary Korum of Strasbourg as candidate for bishop in Berlin.

CHAPTER 4

The Development of Catholicism in Switzerland

The defeat of the Catholic cantons in the War of 1847 significantly determined for generations to come not only the external but also the internal situation of Swiss Catholicism. The federal constitution of 1848 assigned the regulation of Church relations to the cantons on a federalistic basis, in spite of increased centralism. But in the elections, majority suffrage (election by proportional representation first in 1918), deliberate division of constituencies, and, last but not least, domestic differences among Catholics rather favored the Liberal candidates.[1] The occurrences after 1848 were especially radical in the canton of Fribourg. But the reaction of Catholics was just as resolute: in the parliamentary elections of 1856, the Conservatives were overwhelmingly victorious (sixty-four versus three radical representatives). Bishop Marilley of Lausanne-Geneva, expelled in 1848, was able to return. The development in the canton of Lucerne was similar. There, the teaching sisters of Baldegg had to be readmitted, and the Conservatives were successful in May 1871 despite the First Vatican Council. Special problems existed in Ticino because it belonged to the dioceses of Como and Milan. In the canton of Saint Gall, the future Bishop Karl Johann Greith[2] was the political leader in the school controversy (next to some prominent representatives of the laity). In 1861 a law regarding schools could be enacted which was favorable to the Catholics. In the 1859 elections in Unterwallis, the Conservatives were successful. It should be noted, however, that liberal cantons with Catholic minorities (e.g., Basel, Zurich, Winterthur, Berne, Lausanne, Geneva) practiced toleration (moderated, to be sure, by the ecclesiastical law of the state) even though the denominations were frequently financed through secularizations. These were the external conditions for intensive pastoral work in respect to the diaspora.

To find the pragmatic middle of the road between centralism and political federalism, essential to the Catholic cantons, was a difficult task for Swiss Catholicism in view of this cantonal situation. The Catholic

---

[1] Cf. K. Müller, op. cit., 169–99; T. Schwegler, op. cit., 213–27.

[2] K. J. Greith from Rapperswil (1807–88) had proved his worth in the battles of the thirties; but at the First Vatican Council (1834–36, he was in exile in Rome) he belonged to the group which opposed the dogmatization of the infallibility. He wrote (studied theology at the Sorbonne) a handbook of philosophy, was interested in Dominican mysticism and the Old Irish Church, and was bishop of the diocese of Saint Gall (1862–82) in existence since 1823 (Cf. K. Müller, op. cit. 194f).

Schweizerischer Studentenverein (Swiss Student Association), founded in 1841 in Schwyz, was the first organization to expand throughout all the cantons. Patrician Theodor Scherer-Boccard (1816–85) of Solothurn directed the editor's office of the *Schweizerische Kirchenzeitung* and became chairman of the *Schweizerischer Pius-Verein* (Swiss Pius Society),[3] founded in 1857 in Beckenried. The Benedictine monks transformed the cantonal school in Sarnen (Obwalden) into a reputable secondary school, and the monasteries at Einsiedeln and Engelberg enlarged their curriculums. In 1856 one of the leading personalities in this period of Swiss Catholicism, the enterprising friar of the Capuchin order, A. K. (Theodosius) Florentini,[4] restored the college of Maria-Hilf in Schwyz, which had been under the supervision of the bishops of Chur, Basel, and Saint Gall since 1884. Similar progress was made with Saint Michael in Fribourg. Florentini earned everlasting fame even outside of Switzerland when he founded the house of the Sisters of Mercy of the Holy Cross in Ingenbohl (Mother Superior Theresa Scherer, 1825–88). The house had separated from the Menzingen educational institute after one of the frequent controversies over congregations and had devoted itself (following Florentini's example) to caring for the sick.

The *Kulturkampf*,[5] occurring at the same time as the First Vatican Council, is closely related to the occurrences in Germany. Before it ended, *Die katholische Stimme aus den Waldstätten* (The Catholic Voice of Waldstätten) appeared in Lucerne, following Döllinger's argumentation. After 1873, professor J. H. Reinkens of Breslau, since 1873 bishop of the Old Catholics in Germany, founded in many cities in Switzerland "societies of free-thinking Catholics," from which sprung the Christian Catholic Church of Switzerland, founded in 1875–76 in Olten.[6] But one should consider the specific social differences within Swiss Catholicism, the resistance of Catholic patrician families to the constitution of 1848, and the differences between agrarian Catholic

---

[3] T. Schwegler, op. cit., 223; a survey of the history of Catholic societies in K. Müller, op. cit., 299–312, and G. Beuret, op. cit., 13–59.

[4] Anton Krispin Florentini (1808–65), born in Müstair (Graubünden), in the monastery of Solothurn since 1830, was one of the heroes in the battle with the Liberals and vicar general in Chur (1859). Concerning his utopian industrial enterprises, cf. chap. 13; M. Künzle, *Die schweizerische Kapuzinerprovinz* (Einsiedeln 1928); T. Schwegler, op. cit., 221.

[5] K. Müller, op. cit., 231–94; T. Schwegler, op. cit., 227–37. The *Kulturkampf* in Switzerland renewed the animosity, "in which Catholicism and anti-Church radicalism—both, at that time, pressured into extreme positions—confronted each other for decades to come," even though *Kulturkampf* was forestalled in many parts of the country thanks to the restraint of the local episcopate (Hanno Helbling, *Schweizer Geschichte* (Zurich 1963), 141. This ecclesiastical restraint was in accord with the cantons' governments.

[6] Müller, op. cit., 286–94; O. Gilg, *Christkatholizismus* (Lucerne 1945).

cantons and the predominently liberal urban bourgeoisie, whose Catholics, to a large extent, had rejected Pius IX's *Syllabus*. Eduard Herzog, professor of theology in Lucerne, born in Schongau, was a very devout representative of the Christian Catholics, but had hesitated to accept his election as bishop in Olten.[7] Local conflicts usually broke out because the Christian Catholics demanded the right to use the Catholic churches.

While the cantonal governments in Zurich, Lucerne, and Saint Gall exercised restraint, severe conflicts flared up in Berne and in cantons belonging to the diocese of Basel-Solothurn, especially at the bishop's see of Solothurn, where, in 1870, Eugen Lachat was forced to accept the closing of the seminary (which had just been opened in 1858) by the "Diocesan Body" (representatives of the canton governments). On 29 January 1873 the "Body" dismissed Lachat because he refused to keep in office the clergy who opposed the dogma of infallibility. The cantons of Lucerne and Zug did not support his dismissal. In Aargau and Solothurn convents and monasteries were closed and the many developing Christian Catholic congregations were favored (especially in the canton of Aargau, where whole congregations often followed their priests on the path away from the Roman Catholic Church). The Benedictine monks from Maria-Stein who emigrated across the French border were able to continue to administer their parishes in the canton of Solothurn. The canton of Berne proceeded with severity against the priests in the Jura who were loyal to deposed Bishop Lachat (living in Lucerne). Eighty-four priests were expelled from Switzerland; others had to conduct services in secret hiding places.

Aside from Bishop Lachat of Basel-Solothurn, Gaspard Mermillod (1842–92) was also the object of harsh struggles regarding ecclesiastical policies. In Geneva, the overthrow of the patrician government by the Liberals turned out to be advantageous for the Catholics. Subsequently, the congregations, strengthened by immigrants, expanded quickly in the fifties. In Notre Dame, a church dedicated in 1859, Mermillod delivered moving sermons, and in 1864 Pius IX appointed him titular bishop of Hebron, suffragan bishop of the diocese of Lausanne, and vicar general of Geneva, replacing Bishop Marilley of Lucerne, who resigned in 1879. The cantonal government regarded this as a circumvention of the constitutional decree forbidding the establishment of new bishoprics. Oriented toward the leftist Liberals since 1870, the government dismissed Mermillod in September of 1872 as priest of Geneva's Notre

---

[7] T. Schwegler, op. cit., 232; insight into Swiss Old Catholicism, though prejudiced against the papacy in the biography by R. Dederen, *Un réformateur catholique au 19ᵉ siècle - Eugène Michaud, 1839–1917* (Geneva 1963), also: Küppers, *ZKG* 75 (1964), 418f; and V. Conzemius, *ZSKG* 58 (1964), 177–204.

Dame. In January 1873 the Pope responded to this move by appointing Mermillod apostolic vicar in Geneva. In February 1873, the government, having already enacted a radical state-church law in 1872, expelled Mermillod from the country. He continued his activities, however, from Ferney, on the other side of the French border. The Federal Council immediately answered a papal letter to the Swiss Catholics of 21 November 1873 by severing diplomatic relations. A centralistic revision of the constitution in 1874 intensified the state's Church law.

The *Kulturkampf* in Switzerland did not last as long as in Germany. At the end of 1875, the Federal Council gave permission to the clergymen who had been expelled from the Berne Jura to return, and after 1878 they were allowed to perform their office without disturbance. The leftist liberal canton government in Geneva suffered several defeats in 1878. In Bellinzona (Ticino) a conservative government was formed in 1875. Thus Leo XIII's diplomat Domenico Ferrata[8] found a favorable situation when he came to Switzerland as a result of the Federal Council's appeal to the Vatican. The Geneva question had already been solved in 1883: when the successor of Bishop Mermillod (who had resigned) passed away, Leo XIII was able to appoint Mermillod bishop of Lausanne-Geneva, gaining approval of the Federal Council, but sacrificing Pius IX's Geneva plans (the apostolic vicariate was abolished). That Ferrata had difficulties later on adjusting to the local situation was due to internal affairs within the Catholic Church. The Basel and Ticino questions were resolved through pragmatic unification. At first, the person of Bishop Eugen Lachat presented a problem: the non-Catholic cantons of the diocese of Basel-Solothurn wanted peace, but rejected Lachat's return from exile in Lucerne. Gioacchino Pecci, as bishop of Perugia, had demonstrated his sympathy for papally loyal Lachat, and now, as Pope, he had to sacrifice Lachat for the sake of a political arrangement. Informally, Lachat showed willingness to submit, even though his position in Ticino was rather undefined; officially he declined. This produced a great deal of embarrassment for the Curia, which Ferrata was to alleviate. His investigative mission resulted in Lachat's being persuaded to resign. Ferrata's visit permitted the bishop to save face before the outraged members of the diocese. In Ticino, separated by the Provincial Diet from the dioceses of Como and Milan (in 1859, Austria had lost Ticino to Piedmont), the problem was that the Catholic conservatives of Bellinzona wanted their own bishopric, while the Federal Council insisted on annexation to the German-Swiss diocese of Basel-Solothurn. Ferrata and Swiss politicians, led by the Protestant Conservative deputy Emil Welti (of Aargau), agreed at a

[8] *Mémoires* I U. Stutz, op. cit., 29–46.

conference (12 August to 1 September 1884) that the Pope should appoint a persona grata (F. Fiala) to the bishopric of Basel-Solothurn, at least for the time being (the constitution of 1874 was ignored), and that Lachat should become apostolic administrator in Ticino with a temporary office in Balerna. The Ambrosian liturgy was to be preserved together with the Roman liturgy. After Bishop Lachat's death (1886) the Ticino question had to be renegotiated. In 1887 Ferrata (meanwhile named nuncio to Belgium) had to deal with two Freethinkers in Berne, discretely indicating to them that the administrator from Ticino could be expelled and possibly govern from Italy. It was agreed that the parish church of Saint Laurenz in Lugano be elevated to the Cathedral of Ticino, and that an apostolic administrator be appointed who had to be from Ticino (triple nomination) and required the approval of the bishop of Basel.

In the eighties, a new generation of Swiss Catholics came to the forefront. They distinguished themselves politically from those men for whom Senator Philipp Anton Segesser (1817–88) from Lucerne was representative. He came from an old patrician family, was decidedly conservative and federalistic and, like Bishop Greith from Saint Gall, he had reservations about the definition of infallibility.[9] In 1888 three fellow students, Kaspar Decurtins from the Grisons (1855–1916), twenty-six years old and the youngest senator,[10] Ernst Feigenwinter, a lawyer from Basel (1853–1919),[11] and theologian Josef Beck (after 1891 professor in Fribourg) founded the *Verband katholischer Männer-und Arbeitervereine der Schweiz.* This group intentionally addressed itself to Swiss Catholicism as a whole, turning away from the Pius societies of the Catholic cantons with their traditional leadership. The first plenary meeting in 1889—held in Zurich—behaved as if it were a Catholic convention with an address by the Pope, so that the president of the Pius societies, A. Wirz, had occasion to complain. In the course of the growing conflict, Wirz pleaded for "the kind of prudent policy following conservative Catholic principles we inherited from our forefathers."[12]

---

[9] T. Schwegler, op. cit., 214; G. Beuret, op. cit., 61.

[10] The Decurtins family is an interesting example of the political differences among the Swiss Catholics. The mother of Kaspar, daughter of the papal General K. A. T. de Latour, was a highly political lady. In Truns, she was the focal point of a liberal club. She was filled with resentment toward her father's former commander-in-chief, Pius IX, and toward the Jesuits. In the canton of Chur, she was the candidate opposing her own son Kaspar, who had been expelled from his liberal student fraternity because of obstinacy and had joined the radical clerical faction, probably out of opposition to his mother (K. Fry I, 17, 41) (G. Beuret, 62–64, an objective, positive assessment of this man who "was looking for allies wherever he could find them" in order to save Catholicism from isolation).

[11] Feigenwinter founded the *Basler Volksblatt* in 1874; T. Schwegler, 229.

[12] K. Fry, op. cit. II, 220.

This was an allusion to the fact that Decurtins and his friends had been founding members of the *Schweizerischer Arbeiterbund*[13] in Aarau, which had a large membership of Social Democrats. For Decurtins, Catholicism was a house with many mansions, and he lived in the "left" wing. Thus he said during the founding ceremonies: "I am ultramontane through and through, but in social questions . . . I am on your side; hunger is neither Catholic nor Protestant."[14] This was certainly intended as a polemic against the Conservatives, who, in social questions, usually joined the moderate liberal Center. (In 1891, the Catholic-Conservative faction was able to bring a Catholic member into the Federal Council, Dr. Joseph Zemp, born in 1834. He was a member until his death in 1908).

In the nineties, the competition between the Pius society, now calling itself *Schweizerischer Katholikenverein,* and *Männer- und Arbeiterverband* increased rapidly. A union of both organizations was rejected. The idea to direct the rural and the conservative urban population toward the *Katholikenverein* and the industrial areas toward the *Männer- und Arbeiterverband*[15] was utopian as well as characteristic. During the meeting of the *Arbeiterverband* in Schaffhausen in 1898, Decurtins presented the plan to transform the Catholic People's Party, established in 1894 in Lucerne, into a socially oriented Catholic Center Party patterned after the German Center Party. His attempt did not succeed. A new initiative emanated from Saint Gall, where, in 1899, Prebendary Johann B. Jung (1861–1922) founded the first *Christlich-soziale Arbeiterverein* and where the first *Christliche Gewerkschaft* was formed. Both organizations were combined in 1903 in the *Zentralverband christlich-sozialer Organisationen,* whose president was Dr. Alois Scheiwiler (1930 bishop of Saint Gall). The *Christliche Gewerkschaften* were interdenominational, though the Protestants were rather in low profile. Starting in 1903, the Christian-social *Zentralverband* spread from east Switzerland throughout the entire Swiss confederation. In 1904, upon Feigenwinter's proposal, the *Katholikenverein* and the *Männer- und Arbeiterverband* were combined. This move was introduced in September 1903 at the first "general" Catholic Convention in Lucerne. In 1905, the *Katholikenverein* counted 40,983 members. Kaspar Decurtins remained stubborn.[16] In a

---

[13] H. Farner, *Die Geschichte des schweizerischen Arbeiterbundes* (diss., Zurich 1923).

[14] K. Fry, op. cit. II, 96ff.; Beuret classifies the Catholic movement in Switzerland within the total movement of social Catholicism (70–127).

[15] K. Fry, op. cit. II, 223; G. Beuret, op. cit., 128–4.

[16] The conflict within Catholicism was involved with the Swiss Workers' Union, whose existence Decurtins considered very important because he deeply mistrusted the ecclesiastical modus vivendi with the Liberals and expected coverage by the Social Democrats. He furiously defended himself against a vitriolic anticlerical article in the *Arbeiterbund* (K. Fry, op. cit. II, 231ff.). In 1899, in Lucerne, the political and religious

letter from the period of his audience with Pius X (1904)—Decurtins had gained a reputation in Rome for his involvement in the social-political Catholic *Union de Fribourg*—he said: "Reactionaries (by that I mean feudal lords of the large countries, great capitalists, the delegates of the Catholic political powers to the Vatican)" want the Pope "to disavow Christian democracy."[17] After 1906, the Christian social groups in various cantons began to form a political party which cooperated, in spite of differences, with the Conservative People's Party established throughout the cantons in 1912. The separation of church and state proceeded essentially without problems. In the city of Basel the Catholics were compensated with 200,000 francs. They received the status of an association under civil law; the Protestants and Old Catholics fell under the law applying to public bodies—a distinction that was generally made according to the individual cantonal situation. Bishops' conferences took place annually.

Even though the *Katholische Volksverein* in Switzerland was a relatively weak imitation of the German model, the Swiss Catholics accomplished a goal to which the Germans had aspired in vain: they created a Catholic university. It was established in spite of the misgivings of Bishop Mermillod of Lausanne-Geneva, who desired an independent institution designed after the French *Institutes catholiques.* It was also opposed by the Catholic federalists, except Augustin Egger (bishop of Saint Gall 1882–1906) who finally supported it. Even Leo XIII hesitated, as can be seen by his "cold and short" treatment of the intermediary on 6 June 1889.[18] His behavior was not based upon monetary demands. On 4 November 1889 statesman Georges Python succeeded in prevailing upon the cantonal government in Fribourg to found and finance a department of law and philosophy. Mermillod was absent during its creation. Behind his back, Decurtins traveled to Rome in December 1889 to solve the delicate matter of the theological faculty which Mermillod wanted to have established by the bishops. Python and Decurtins miraculously persuaded President Ruchonnet to have the Pope appoint

---

neutrality of the union was once again affirmed, though it was constantly threatened by the Social Democrats' trade union, which had existed since 1888. On the other hand, the founding of the union in Saint Gall was now called a violation of neutrality. In vain, Decurtins declared at the convention of the union in 1903: "Capitalism does not rest on denominational grounds, it is the same everywhere." The Social Democrats grew more radical under the sign of the class struggle. Isolated from his own friends, Decurtins left the executive committee of the Workers' Union in 1910 (after the general strike of 1918, the Christian-social and Catholic groups separated from the Workers' Union and formed their own organization) (cf. G. Beuret, op. cit., 166–202).

[17] K. Fry, op. cit. II, 249.
[18] K. Fry, op. cit. II, 23.

the professors of the theological faculty from members of the Dominican Order (he was interested in preventing students from studying theology in foreign countries). On 21 January 1890 the Pope gave his approval and donated 100,000 francs and a golden chain for the president. Bishop Mermillod, though still resisting, was appointed cardinal to the Curia. It had not been easy to recruit professors for this university. After a fruitless attempt in Louvain, Decurtins concentrated his efforts especially in Germany, where Gustav Schnürer (a student of Grauert) accepted a position in history. This resulted in 1898 in the "German crisis" at the university: eight professors submitted a collective resignation because they felt encroached upon by Dominican censorship. Decurtins acted rather pompously in this matter and spoke about the German "royal gibberish."[19] The Dominicans' lust for power was proven by the fact that they demanded from the Swiss theology professor J. Beck that he propagate the order's mission. It was necessary to find a replacement in Austria. In 1906 Pius X had occasion to praise the university and the Dominican order for their theological position.

In the battle over reform Catholicism, one should not regard a man like Decurtins as representative of Switzerland, even though Merry del Val supported him and Umberto Benigni spent several weeks in the summer of 1910 in Truns.[20] However, it was no accident that *Hochland* failed to find a favorable climate within Swiss Catholicism. The publications *Vaterland* and *Ostschweiz* rejected Decurtins's efforts, partly because they had grown weary of this man. However, in the *Neue Züricher Nachrichten,* the talented writer Heinrich Federer, under the pseudonym "Senex," sharply condemned the extremely conservative contemporary Catholic literature. He made common cause with Bishop Schmid von Grüneck of Chur, who called Carl Muth a "modernist" when he visited the bishop on the advice of the prior of Einsiedeln.[21]

---

[19] K. Fry, op. cit. II, 68, 74.

[20] K. Fry, op. cit. II, 348. Decurtins, since 1905 professor of cultural history in Fribourg, wrote (during 1907–10) three "letters" against Fogazzaro, Handel-Mazzetti, and the *Hochland,* for which Pius X praised him on 15 September 1910 (K. Fry, op. cit. II, 331). He denounced (theology) Professor Zapletal in vain, because the general of the order intervened (Zapletal was elected president in Fribourg in 1910). When A. Gisler, dogmatics professor in Chur, whose book on Modernism was not acrimonious enough for the "lion from Truns," was publicly exposed in the *Correspondance de Rome,* even the arch-conservative Bishop Georgius Schmid of Grüneck was indignant.

[21] K. Fry, op. cit. II, 235ff. It is a surprising anachronism that Karl Fry in his otherwise deserving book places Albert Ehrhard in the "fifth column" emerging in the Catholic countries.

CHAPTER 5

Italian Catholics between the Vatican and the Quirinal

The *Non expedit* at the Time of Leo XIII

The political and sociological situation in unified Italy did not show any fundamental changes. Attempts were made to adjust to the new institutions, which were very liberal and lay oriented. Suffrage was rather limited: in 1871, of a total population of 25 million, only 600,000 were listed on the register of voters. The parliamentary deputies came from well-to-do social classes, where the different interests of the industrialized North and the rural South clashed. They also did not stand up, to the same extent, for the lay orientation as represented by the state. The Catholics, obedient to the hierarchy, maintained a critical distance from the unified state because it had annexed the Papal State and enacted anti-clerical laws (church marriage was not recognized by civil law; the orders were supressed and their properties confiscated; ecclesiastical welfare organizations were secularized; religious instruction in schools eliminated). In this manner, Catholics declared their solidarity with the protests of the Holy Father and the excommunications imposed by him on the "usurpers". These intransigent Catholics developed their ecclesiastical societies according to the uniform directives formulated by the *Opera dei Congressi e dei Comitati Cattolici;* but, obeying the *Non expedit* of the Vatican, they refrained from political life and election campaigns. With their newspapers, they wanted to be the spokesmen of the "real country," demanding, above all, freedom from want. This was quite in contrast to the "legal country" of the parliament, the government, and government-dependent authorities, which represented only 2 percent of the population due to the electoral system and which were under the influence of Masonic anti-clericalism. Therefore, the "obedient" Catholics were happy with the symptoms of weakness which the new state demonstrated, because they felt it was indicative of its decline. The political development of Italian society and the state, proceeding hand in hand with the economic development, brought about changes precipitated in the Catholic movement through new directives and several new structures.[1]

---

[1] The customary division into periods according to the pontificates of Leo XIII and Pius X is determined externally in respect to the Roman question and the *Non expedit.* The papal directives should be seen via the forces which were pushing up from below (from the movement) and which gained independence and self-awareness, first on the social level and then in the political field until, in 1919, the nondenominational Italian People's Party ("Partito popolare italiano") was founded.

But there were also the "liberal," "disobedient" Catholics, who disapproved of the lay principles of the state derived from the *Risorgimento*. However, they were of the opinion that this state represented the historical reality to which one needed to adjust. They therefore founded a conservative party in order to support the principles and institutions of the national Catholic traditions in the spirit of loyal cooperation with the official authorities.[2]

Some of the ways in which the open attitude of Pius IX's successor expressed itself were: the fact that he resumed and strengthened diplomatic relations with the states, that he approved and furthered Catholic initiatives in social and political areas, and that he used gestures and words to address the Italian people and their statesmen which were conciliatory or, at least, efforts toward easing the tensions. The *Non expedit,* strongly adhered to in 1886 (participation in political elections was not allowed), was gradually regarded as a tactic in the relations between conscientious Catholics and the national unified state. In 1880 the official *Osservatore Romano* (11 June) was already interpreting the *Non expedit* as an active element, as "preparazione nell'astensione" ("preparation with temperance"). Expanding voting rights to new segments of the population (1882) worried several bishops, such as Bonomelli of Cremona, who feared that the leftists, under the influence of the Freemasons, could be strengthened and that anticlerical politics could be radicalized, unless the voices of the Catholics, excluded through the *Non expedit,* were able to create a countermeasure for the purpose of defending the religious and social order. The Holy See used this as a means to force a solution to the Roman question according to its liking.

On 23 May 1887, Leo XIII chose conciliatory words when he expressed the wish: "May Heaven grant that the desire for peace among all nations which We hold dear to Our hearts will be of value . . . to Italy . . . . For a long time, We have desired security and peace for all Italians and We wished that the disastrous battle with the Roman papacy would finally be terminated without detriment to the legal claims and the dignity of the Apostolic See . . . . We mean to say that the path to harmony is subject to the condition that the Pope not be subjugated to any authority and enjoy absolute and true freedom, as is his right."[3] This declaration received enthusiastic praise and was followed by concrete proposals in the writings of the Benedictine Prior Tosti and ex-Jesuit C.

---

[2] Cf. C. M. Curci, *Il moderno dissidio tra Chiesa e l'Italia considerato in occasione di un fatto recente* (Florence 1878), and A. Stoppani, *Gli intransigenti alla stregua dei fatti vecchi, nuovi e nuovissimi* (Milan 1886).

[3] *Acta Leonis XIII* VII (Rome 1888), 115, quoted from H. Bastgen, *Die Römische Frage. Dokumente and Stimmen* III (Freiburg i. Br. 1919), 43f.

M. Curci. But Minister President Crispi rejected the offer to negotiate and claimed once again that, according to the guarantee law of 1871, a Roman question no longer existed. He was apparently under the influence of the anticlerical political forces, which held a majority in Parliament. Subsequently, Pope Leo returned to his rigid position and demanded the restoration of the temporal power of the Pope and, especially, the return of Rome (15 June 1887).[4] He also disapproved of mediating publications, particularly the "Pensieri d'un prelato italiano" by Bonomelli (1891), which, in March 1889, had appeared anonymously in the "Catholic-national" paper *La rassegna italiana* under the title "Roma, l'Italia e la realtà delle cose."[5]

The directive "preparation with temperance," which exceeded the rather passive and polemical motto "nè eletti nè elettori" ("neither the elected nor the voters"), expressed by the *Osservatore cattolico* of Milan, entertained the idea of prospects for political activities, however remote they might be, and created the division of militant Catholics into three groups: some concentrated on purely religious activities; others waited for an occasion to expand these activities to the political sector; while others turned to social areas. But the Holy See immediately expressed its preference, requesting action in the service of the defense and preservation of the faith, love for one's fellow man, and traditional Christian morality. The Pope adhered to the same opinion Pius IX had expressed in 1877: "The desire for political renovations is a bait cast out by the enemy to divide the Catholic front, because he is afraid of the unity in its intentions and the sanctity of its goals."[6] The arbitration proposals, intended at least partially to restore the Papal State and grant to the Kingdom of Italy the remaining territory, were rejected, even by less sectarian politicians, for instance R. Bonghi, who affirmed Italy's claim to all of Rome. The antiecclesiastical lay legislation also hurt the works of charity, emanating from faith and animated by it. It forced them to be absorbed in congregations of charity, which excluded the pastor and were administered by the community (1890). This happened at a time when Catholics increasingly concentrated their efforts on the administration of congregations for which the *Non expedit* was invalid.

Thus the Italian Catholics were called upon to apply their strength and abilities to religious social activities. For this purpose, the existing organizations were further developed, especially the Catholic youth society, certified in 1886, the *Società della Gioventù cattolica italiana*, which

[4] *Acta Leonis XIII* op. cit., 134–53.
[5] Cf. C. Bellò, *Geremia Bonomelli* (Brescia 1961), 101–17, and *Dokumente,* 288.
[6] In the letter *Non sine moerore* of 29 January 1877, addressed to the president and the council of the Catholic youth in Italy (*Insegnamenti pontifici.* 4. *Il laicato,* 78–81).

had been joined by the more polemically oriented *Associazione Cattolica per la libertà della Chiesa* of 1866. According to its motto "prayer, action, sacrifice," the association was especially active in the area of piety and edification, following a line which was soon considered "old-fashioned," meaning narrow-minded. Aside from this, Catholic parish committees *(Comitati cattolici parrocchiali)* sprang up (in the northern and central regions of Italy more than in the south), which were religiously active and often joined the traditional confraternities which were not affected by the suspension laws. They referred their members to new areas of activity and bound them more strictly to obedience toward the Pope and the bishops and to solidarity with the protests of the "prisoner of the Vatican." Soon, in Rome, Pavia, Genoa, Milan, and Pisa, Catholic university groups were formed *(Circoli universitari cattolici),* organizations which were to constitute the fertile soil for those whose enthusiasm put them in the forefront. In all these associations, a stronger social sensitivity—the new sign of loyalty to the Catholic faith—was combined with religious activities and strict adherence to ecclesiastical regulations regarding the observance of holidays and fast days. This expressed itself primarily in new institutions, like the "Vincent Conferences" which Ozanam also organized in Italy. A certain militant spirit was included; respect for religious practices and institutions was demanded and their reputation and traditional sphere of activity were defended.

For the purpose of coordinating these parish and diocesan committees, the *Opera dei Congressi e dei comitati cattolici* was added in 1874. Soon this league became the driving and constructive force of the Catholic movement in Italy. In 1884 Leo XIII gave this organization, established under the pontificate of Pius IX, a new structure, which reflected its progress. It was divided into five sections: Organization and Catholic Action, Christian Social Economy, Instruction and Education, Press, Christian Art. Because of the industrial development, which caused the workers to demand social legislation, the second section *(Dell'economia sociale cristiana)* was of special importance. At first it was headed by the Bergamo nobleman Medolago Albani, who did research in social problems. Later on it was led by Giuseppe Toniolo from Veneto, professor at the University of Pisa. Both were active in overcoming the paternalistic orientation of love for one's fellow man and charity. In dealing with liberal and socialist economic theories, Toniolo designed a Christian social program in which he presented the medieval guilds of the Christian past as models of socioeconomic institutions. A *Unione cattolica per gli studi sociale* was responsible for developing and applying this theory according to the examples in France, Belgium, Germany, and Switzerland.

The *Opera dei congressi*—the name implied the annual meetings of the diocesan and regional committees—was supported by the more active parish clergy of northern and central Italy, which was receptive to the call for an organization to defend the faith. It was further aided by the "notables" who followed, according to family traditions and by conviction, the directives of the hierarchy and did not relate to the new political leadership class (landed proprietors, noblemen, independent professionals). The *Opera dei congressi* was also endorsed by the people, especially the rural population, who identified with the Church institutions which were affected by the suspension laws, because they did not see their standard of living improved by the new laws, particularly by the tax laws and the military draft. Therefore, they were willing to lend an open ear to the Pope's protests against the secular state and to agree with them. Thus the *Opera dei congressi* was able to pursue detailed action for the purpose of deepening the consciousness of faith and to inspire the activities of Catholic societies by enforcing and coordinating local diocesan and regional initiatives.

The Catholic movement, stimulated in this fashion, not only made use of the hostile press in the large metropolitan centers of Turin, Milan, Florence, Naples, and Venice, but also in provincial cities like Brescia and Bergamo. The polemics and ridicule of scandals, which resulted in confiscations and law suits, were followed by discussions of the actual problems and the possible solutions according to the principles of the Christian conscience and the institutions inspired by it. The *Osservatore cattolico* of Milan excelled in the critical examination of methods and goals. Its young editor, Filippo Meda, gained more and more influence over the boisterous editor Davide Albertario, who was bold enough to subject even bishops to public criticism.

Aside from Medolago Albani and Toniolo, the following leaders are worthy of mention: G. B. Paganuzzi, born in Veneto, G. Acquaderni of Bologna, G. Radini Tedeschi of Emilia (later bishop of Bergamo), L. Bottini of Lucca, N. Rezzara of Bergamo, G. B. Casoni of Bologna, G. Tovini of Brescia, Giovanni Grosoli of Emilia, and the Jesuit Gaetano Zocchi. They were all strong personalities, firmly rooted in their convictions. Therefore they often had differences of opinion regarding organizational questions, the interpretations of papal decrees, or the selection of the cadre. Most of all, they fought over merging the Catholic movement into the sociopolitical reality of the Italian state under the regime of the *Non expedit*. The new orientation took the sociopolitical efforts of the Catholics north of the Alps as a model and tried resolutely to promote Catholic action in the social and economic area (banks, companies, publishing houses, trade schools, etc.). The encyclical *Rerum novarum* of Leo XIII was cited. This group, however, encountered the opposition of the intransigent wing, which feared infection by the liberal spirit and compromises with the institutions of the secular state.[7] The area most likely to cause controversies between the two positions was the administration of communities and provinces which were open to Catholics. But, as was frequently the case, second ballots were necessary; their elections had to be assured by consultations with other parties. It was the task of the Catholics, voted into these administrations, to protect the primary schools, which were subject to the community, from sectarian and laic influences, to appoint as administrators of charitable institutions men who would respect their religious goals and arrangements regarding church services, and to make sure that the hospitals, especially psychiatric clinics (which were subordinate to the provinces), were staffed with members of religious orders. The need of gaining control in the communities and provinces by appropriate election preparations played an increasingly important role for the Catholic movement in Italy and created emotional tensions.[8]

Along with the intransigents, who strictly adhered to the papal decree forbidding cooperation with the secular state, there were the transigents, who, like the intransigents, relied upon their own religious conscience. They were, however, of the opinion that the interest and the duty of the Church demanded that they not seek refuge in the ghetto, so to speak, and flee the world and its progress in the socioeconomic and political institutions. Instead, they were to delve into the new realities and work from the inside out, in order to bring to bear the motives and forces of the Christian tradition and thus to shape these realities in the Christian spirit. These transigents were partly spiritual heirs of the "New Guelphs," of the first Gioberti, like Cantù and Tosti, and partly confirmed supporters of the liberal Catholicism in accord with the ideas of Montalembert, Lacordaire, Görres, Newman, and Lord Acton. Many of them had shared the patriotic enthusiasm of 1848. They had held political offices in the decade of 1848–59 and in the first years of the Italian kingdom and had thus participated in the *Risorgimento* movement. Some of them, e.g., Lambruschini and Capponi, identified spiritually with Jansenist circles of the early nineteenth century or they advocated the reform programs of A. Rosmini[9] (which were both religious and sociopolitical). They were members of the educated clergy, as for example the natural scientist A. Stoppani; personalities who had a

[7] Significant for this is the publication by the bishop of Fossano, E. Manacorda, *Movimento cattolico, errori democratici e relativi doveri dei sacerdoti* (Fossano 1897).

[8] Cf. M. Belardinelli, "Motivi religiosi nell' attività amministrativa dei cattolici organizzati," *Spirito ed azione del laicato cattolico italiano* I (Padua 1969), 177–214.

[9] Cf. E. Passerin d' Entrèves, "L'eredità della tradizione cattolica risorgimentale," *Aspetti della cultura cattolica dell'età di Leone XIII* (Rome 1961), 235–87.

reputation because of their education, their profession, or their wealth, like Alessandro Manzoni, Niccolò Tommaseo, Cesare Cantù; reputable members of one of the two chambers, like Senators Canonica, Lampertico, and Stefano Jacini, mostly Liberal Conservatives who had many supporters, particularly among the middle class. There were also personalities of the hierarchy among the transigents, such as Cardinal Capecelatro of Naples, Cardinal Svampa of Bologna, Bishop Bonomelli of Cremona, and the founder of the institution for the spiritual emigrants, Bishop Scalabrini of Piacenza.[10] The transigents had certain elements of the press at their disposal, among them respected daily papers, such as the Milanese *La lega Lombarda.* They were also heard by papers of the conservative right, like the *Perseveranza,* appearing also in Milan, where they could present the intentions and motives of their "moderate" position compared to the anticlerical radicalism of many proposed laws and several divisions of the state bureaucracy. The numerous faithful Catholics who held offices in the administration, in the military, and in the different branches of government were able to effect a moderate interpretation of the anticlerical laws and apply them appropriately. Moreover, these transigents were in the position of offering their services as arbitrators to the state authorities, to the politicians, and to the public administration. They were also able to negotiate formulas and procedures which made it possible for Vatican-appointed bishops, for instance, to maintain their sees and to receive the appropriate revenue without having to expressly submit to the statute of the guarantee law requiring the *Exequatur* by the government.

There were also issues on which the transigents (liberal, middle-of-the-road Catholics) and the intransigents agreed: they both pointed to the necessity of public order; both fought socialism as a sociopolitical doctrine and as an organization devoted to class struggle. The majority of their "notables" came from the same circles, primarily in Piedmont and in certain areas in southern Italy. Both sides respected the monarchy and relations with the personalities of the House of Savoy. Beyond the polemics of the Roman question and the legal regulations, which were to be valid for the ecclesiastical institutions, these common features found expression in the election alliances between clerical and moderate groups. In the administrative elections, they seriously defeated the coalitions of radicals and Socialists and their lay program, for example in Venice, during Cardinal Sarto's patriarchate, and later on even in Rome itself.

During the last two decades of the nineteenth century, in a unified Italy, further crass economic and sociopolitical disparities appeared, not

[10] Cf. chap. 10, n. 4.

only between the north and the south, but also between the different social classes. The transition from an artisan to an industrial economy, which had to compete with the more productive branches of industry north of the Alps and was largely dependent on their finances, their machines, and their technicians, occasioned constant disquiet and anxiety. The organization of the working class under both the flag of Marxist socialism and the banner of the most radical revolutionary syndicalism, as represented by the anarchist Bakunin, took place even in the rural areas. Strikes, civil unrest, and suppressive measures followed one after another in all parts of the country and found a strong echo in the press. The expansion of suffrage, which in 1882 increased the number of eligible voters from 2 to 10 percent of the population, provided the Socialists, in coalition with the Radicals, representation in parliament. In 1891, the official founding of the Italian Socialist Party took place. Its program represented the demands of the workers, but also contained a lay anticlerical policy. All this favored the draft of a social legislation which was in line with the encyclical *Rerum novarum* and was therefore energetically promoted by the Catholic movement, especially by the Christian Social Economy section of the *Opera dei congressi* and by the *Unione cattolica di Studi sociali,* founded by Tonioli. With this kind of sponsorship, the Catholic societies, in accordance with the demands of the social-political situation, produced new institutions: workers' cafeterias, parish houses, employment agencies, trade schools, societies for mutual assistance, production, credit, and consumer agencies, banks for the support of various professions and institutions, and workers' associations with a union character, which competed with their efforts toward socialistic associations. On the theoretical level, the *Unione cattolica di Studi sociali* formulated in 1894 a "program of Catholics in regard to Socialism" which mirrored the demands and the experiences of the agricultural and industrial world of Lombardy, Emilia, and Tuscany.[11]

All this had an effect on the *Opera dei congressi,* whose organization and program was severely criticized by the young. They insisted that the defensive attitude, the predominantly religious and devotional orientation, the nagging paternalism, and the gap between the secular state and the democratic organizational forms should be abandoned in favor of greater latitude regarding decisions and freedom of movement. Even the *Non expedit* was now open to various interpretations: distance from the secular state meant obligation to an autonomous social and political organization, which obviously had to agree completely with the principles of Christian morality. On the basis of the formula "preparation with

[11] D. Secco Suardo, *Da Leone XIII a Pio X* (Rome 1967), 20; cf. L. Gerevini, *Democrazia socialista e democrazia cristiana* (Treviso 1899).

temperance," this line was already being presented by the three most active centers of the Catholic movement: in Bergamo with Medolago Albani and the newspaper *L'Eco di Bergamo,* in Milan with Filippo Meda and the *Osservatore cattolico,* in Brescia with G. Tovini, G. Montini and the *Cittadino di Brescia.* This increased the demand for more extensive efforts in the political field. The motives were provided, on the one hand, by the need to insure the socioeconomic principles of the movement in legislation and to enforce social laws which would agree with the Christian maxims of cooperation between the various social classes. The other motive was the need to fight socialism and its associations on their own ground. The contentions between the young and the old (of which the one between the priest Romolo Murri from the Marches and the layman Filippo Meda from Milan stood out in particular) increasingly vitalized the Catholic congresses, with the result that the Vatican more and more emphatically demanded harmony and unity.

In 1898 (the year of war between Spain and the United States) disturbances flared up here and there in Italy because of an increase in bread prices. In Milan, they were violently suppressed with the help of military forces dispatched solely for that purpose. Among other measures, the radical Socialist and Catholic opposition newspapers were suppressed and their editors imprisoned (e.g., Don Albertario, editor of the *Osservatore cattolico,* who was subsequently sentenced by a court in Milan). Thus the year 1898 put the Catholic movement to the test: personalities of the intransigent wing tried to keep their distance from the mass disturbances and their spokesmen and made efforts to restore the Church and Catholicism as guarantors of the existing social order. Therefore, the government in Rome took measures only against some Catholic organizations in the north, not, however, against the presidency of the *Opera dei congressi,* which was still dominated by such socially backward intransigents as Count Paganuzzi. This resulted in rapprochement between the conservative intransigents and the conservative governmental authorities. The young, however, saw in the need of the people an opportunity to attack the "secular hunger state" even more vehemently and were preoccupied with the idea that social action could serve as a springboard for seizing power for the benefit of the masses.

The Holy See took careful note of everything that was going on in the Catholic movement. It was obvious that the Curia harbored differing opinions. Some supported a trend which tolerated or even favored the expansion of Catholic action in the social field and, though with more constraint, even in the political arena. Among them were Cardinals Rampolla and Agliardi and the less eminent Monsignors Gasparri and della Chiesa, who pointed to the model and the accomplishments of the

Catholic movement in Belgium, Germany, Austria, and the United States, and to whom Leo XIII gave ear. But there was also an opposition group (consisting of Cardinals Respighi, Vicar of Rome, and Vives of the Holy Office) which still regarded every political and social action employed to overcome the tensions present in Italy, every instance of cooperation with the existing authorities, and every exploitation of state laws as support of the "Italian revolution," a minimization of the problem of the Roman question, and an undermining of the *Non expedit.* According to their opinion, the *Non expedit* was to be strictly adhered to, so that the Vatican could exert pressure on the Quirinal. Particularly in view of the energetic demands from outside their ranks (meaning the laity), these opponents of the movement liked to point to the fact that quite a few bishops rejected it also. The Holy See and Pope Leo XIII himself were frequently asked by the activists of both persuasions, the conservatives and the progressives, to intervene. They were supposed to approve the program of one of the parties and to condemn the principles and proponents of the opposing party. This often caused embarrassment for the men in the Vatican. They preferred to confine themselves to the confirmation of general directives and to the admonishment to activity in the spirit of harmony.[12]

That very year, 1898, a new leader of the Catholic movement appeared with the publication *Cultura sociale,* which was intended to be for the Italian Catholics what the *Neue Zeit* represented for the German Socialists. This leader was Don Romolo Murri. Born in August 1870, he received his doctorate in theology from the Università Gregoriana in Rome and founded the Catholic university circle there in 1894. But soon he extended his activities to the social field. He remained intransigent in regard to the Roman question, considering it a symptom of the deep schism between the Christian and the modern "heathen and materialistic" concept of life and culture. The contrast between the dome of Saint Peter's Basilica and the tricolors upon the Quirinal were for him the "sign of conflict between two different and mutually antagonistic cultures," "the secret of the inner history and the future of the Church."[13] With this statement, he removed himself from Filippo Meda as well and he recommended fighting the liberal, secular state to the bitter end. The boycott of the ballot boxes was, therefore, not just an act of obedience toward the Pope, but also the conscious rejection of the freedom-persecuting state.

[12] D. Secco Suardo, op. cit., 72ff.
[13] "Cultura sociale," 16 September 1898. On the circumstances, cf. F. Fonzi, "Dall'intransigentismo alla democrazia cristiana," *Aspetti della cultura . . .,* op. cit., 323–88.

Murri's general promotion of social action was close to Toniolo's heart. Yet Murri's call for autonomy was more urgent and he demanded the expansion of social programs in the area of politics, suffrage, and legislation. Thus, the demands for autonomous action in the spirit of a "Christian democracy" were voiced more and more at the congresses of the *Opera dei congressi* in Milan (1897), Ferrara (1899), and Taranto (1901). It encountered vehement reactions by the individuals and currents which, in this ferment, were forced to reformulate their motives and forge new alliances, not only in the central, but also in the regional diocesan and local committees and related organizations. There were passionate controversies concerning the expansion of the Christian democratic action programs, the priority of political-religious questions versus the social question, the opportunism of preparing for a political life, the right of the Holy See to intervene in political and social matters, the question of whether it is prudent to separate the Catholic action, dependent on the hierarchy, from the political action of a Catholic party, and the autonomy of the democratic movement."[14]

At stake was the traditional domination of Paganuzzi, Medolago Albani, and both Scottons from Venetia, who were all in contact with militant groups in Venetia, Lombardy, Piedmont, Tuscany, and Rome. In 1899, a Christian democratic union *(Fascio democratico cristiano)* was formed in Milan, and in Turin an "action program" containing twelve points was formulated outside of the *Opera dei congressi.* They all referred to the papal decrees, the *Rerum novarum* and the subsequent "instructions." They interpreted them as they saw fit and mobilized their friends in high Vatican circles to have their program confirmed.

From within the Congregation for Special Church Affairs, Leo XIII appointed a "permanent commission to regulate the Catholic movement in Italy" and entrusted it with the task of examining the many documents pertaining to the presidency of the *Opera dei congressi,* to its various sections, the subgroups, and the numerous bishops who had expressed their need for help and had asked for directives. The main point of controversy was "Christian democracy" as a name and a program. It was typical for the methods of Leo XIII that he was able to assert his already clearly defined decision. Basically, he was siding with the young, in whom he saw vital energies of the Church. But even though he approved and recommended the social action arising from below, "he was intent on having the inspiration and coordination filter down from above, from his will."[15] With a view toward the German

[14] A. Gambasin, *Il movimento sociale nell'Opera dei Congressi (1874–1904)* (Rome 1958), 467.
[15] D. Secco Suardo, op. cit., 126.

model of the *Volksverein* and the Catholic Center in the German *Reichstag,* Agliardi and Gasparri intervened with the Pope on behalf of Murri.

In this manner, Leo XIII prepared his intervention, followed by the encyclical *Graves de communi* (18 January 1901).[16] With reference to *Rerum novarum,* his circular letter insisted that the action of the Catholics proceed in unity, to the exclusion of all politics, in conjunction with a central organization, and in submission to the Pope and the bishops, who had the right to take practical measures "according to the local and personal situations." In the "fundamental theoretical and practical points", which were to be publicized among the people, the following was declared: "Christian democracy shall not have any political significance; it advocates the welfare of the lower classes, but also pays attention to the upper classes; it does not support plans for insubordination and opposition to public authority; rather, it proposes to put all its energies into easing the hard lot of the manual laborers, gradually enabling them to provide their own livelihood."[17]

One of the directives, which was enacted by the Congress of Taranto (1901), demanded the granting of greater latitude to the young and their inclusion in the social initiatives of men like Medolago Albani, Toniolo, Radini Tedeschi, and Rezzara. This demand alarmed the still powerful group of the older generation who took up a position behind the customary loyalty to the Pope and were opposed to innovations. The new statutes of 1901 still required abstinence from politics. Therefore, Murri's initiatives seemed at least inopportune and were deleted by Cardinals Vives y Tutó and Respighi, who were entrusted with formulating the program of the second section on Christian charity and social economics.

The success of the movement's social and religious action, which enforced the people's loyalty to the Pope, affected the people's conscience and procured more political impact for the movement. This provided the Vatican with greater influence on the Italian government. In December 1901, as a result of its concern for public order, the government proceeded toward a policy of exceptive laws, which both the socialist radicals and the younger members of the Catholic movement rejected with determination.

Leo XIII's attempts to mediate between the various factions of the Catholic movement in order to preserve unity and identity encountered difficulties. The customary compliancy toward the Pope was not able to break the opposition of the conservatively inclined older generation,

---

[16] Italian text in *Insegnamenti pontifici.* 4. *Il laicato,* 171–94.
[17] D. Secco Suardo, op. cit., 135–136.

who tried to justify the existing economic and social order by referring to the events of 1898. They alluded essentially to paternalistic motivations, since they were only concerned with love and charity. The boisterous younger generation, on the other hand, was reluctant to adhere to the institutions organized and ruled from above. Inspired by Murri, they undermined the homogeneous structure of the *Opera dei congressi,* which was less and less representative of the Catholic movement in Italy. Pius X was to experience this and to institute a change which would seal the demise of the congressional organization.

CHAPTER 6

The Failure to Reconcile
Catholics and the Republic in France

The Ecclesiastical Policy of the Republicans

During the enthronement of Leo XIII, everything indicated that the existence of the Republic in France, formed in 1875 under such tremendous difficulties, was secure. The elections of 1876 brought a Republican majority into parliament which held 64 percent of the seats in the Chamber of Deputies. Moreover, the failure of the *coup de main* of 16 May 1877, shortly before the papal elections, was a successful prologue to the take-over of the provincial diets and the offices of the mayors. These victories of Gambetta's friends were bound to be followed by the overthrow of the senate majority in January 1879 and by the massive invasion of a group of deputies who held, after the elections in the summer of 1881, 83.6 percent of the seats. In the following years, the government successfully survived an economic crisis and an attack by the Boulangists. But now, the Church leaders had to recognize that it would be prudent to come to an understanding with a Republic on whose demise they could not count.

The Republicans, in turn, were eager to secure their election victory through a "republicanization" of the upper administration (e.g., the State Council and the large institutions, the army and the judiciary). The Catholic Church was especially affected by this policy of the "Republican defensive" in view of the farspread social influence which it had gained through preaching and charity, through its schools and, most of all, through the religious orders. This impact was feared by the leaders of the Republican majority, and therefore they placed systematic secularization of public life at the top of their ideological and political program. During the budget debate of 1877, V. Guichard presented this plan in his report, and consequently a fund was provided to finance an investigation into the significance of the orders. This investigation was carried out in 1878. It showed that the total number of order members amounted to at least 30,000, among them 3,350 Jesuits. The congregations of women included about 128,000 persons who cared for approximately 16,500 girls schools. There were three times as many religious priests as secular ones, and it was discovered that this number approximated that of 1765, when the number of religious priests had peaked in the eighteenth century. Most of the congregations were not legally authorized.[1] This explains why, on 15 May 1879, the Minister of Education Jules Ferry supplemented his bill regarding the introduction of a generally obligatory, secular primary education with ARTICLE 7, which prohibited the nonauthorized congregations from any kind of instruction. It also explains why he enforced this prohibition through appropriate decrees, at first directed against the Jesuits, who were expelled in 1880, and then, in the following November, also directed against the other nonauthorized male congregations.

The struggle between the Republic and the Church erupted most vehemently over the issues of religious orders and schools. The bishops, in turn, waged a campaign against the laicization of elementary education, which was resolved on 28 March 1882, and against the cancellation of payment in connection with the abolition of official manuals for public instruction (Louis Capéran). But in many other areas, religious demonstrations in public were forbidden or strictly regulated. Processions, preaching, lay societies, courts, hospitals, and cemeteries were supervised, and the Magnet Law regarding divorce was finally passed after intensive debates (19 July 1884). The cardinals of Rouen and Paris declared in festive *Observations* (1 June 1882) "that more than twenty bills regarding the regulation of religion had been proposed." Bishop-Deputy Freppel before the Parliament defended the rights of the Church pertaining to this legislation, concluding with the exclamation: "Separation, that is your goal. Yesterday it was the separation of Church and school, today it is the separation of parish and congregation, tomorrow or the day after tomorrow it will be the separation of Church and state (enthusiastic applause on the left). Always and everywhere separations."[2]

The aim of such a policy was, in fact, the suspension of the concordat. Separation had already been the main theme of the election campaign in the summer of 1881, and, when the two chambers were combined, Paul Bert introduced a bill, reiterating the proposals of four deputies who

---

[1] In September 1880, the Secretary of the treasury estimated the estates of the orders to be 628 million francs, which appears to be rather exaggerated.

[2] Chambre des Députés, meeting of 5 November 1883 (*Journal Officiel,* 6 November 1883).

had also demanded the dissolution of the concordat. Those responsible for Republican policies, however, hesitated to make this extreme move. Ferry especially adhered to a concordat policy which, in June 1879, he had called "a strict application of the treaty of 1801 and which was to satisfy everything and to secure a rigorous defense of the rights of the state."

This caution resulted from an analysis of the country's religious and political situation deduced from the three important series of reports[3] which were demanded by the prefects and the attorneys general in the years 1879, 1881, and 1888. They clarified the very obvious regional differences in the religious practices in urban areas, which, from the vicinity of Paris, extended toward the north up to Normandy and to the northern and northeastern region bordering the Central Mountains and which were characterized by increasing separation from the Church; as well as in the wooded and mountainous rural areas (Lyon and the eastern border of the Central Mountains, the Savoy Alps, etc.), where a general religious practice continued to dominate. In addition, the reports listed a stronger tendency for separation in the areas bordering the *departements* Yonne, Sâone-et-Loire, and, above all, in the Mediterranean region from Narbonne to Nice. This separation rarely affected the religious situation directly, and even in the most de-Christianized areas, as in Haute-Vienne, religious practices continued. Among the peasants, there was a general and widespread mistrust of the priests' meddling in the political and social arena, and of everything conventionally called the "government of priests." This mistrust existed even in the most devout areas. It increased according to the extent to which the clergy itself demonstrated through remarks and behavior that it was intransigent, generally in southern areas. In the vicinity of the bishops' sees, the reports often detected a social class with such intransigent and vehemently anti-Republican sentiments, where the lay dignitaries and society ladies were competing with each other. These groups were often under the leadership of the respective vicar general, who, simply on the basis of his age, often controlled large elements of the clergy. They were also able to make themselves heard in the *Semaines religieuses*,[4] and were intent on exerting direct influence on the leadership of the dioceses. The only authority which these circles obeyed and which was able to

[3] The reports are preserved in the *Archives Nationales* (F 19. 5610). They were analyzed by L. Capéran, *Histoire contemporaine de la laïcité française* II (Paris 1959), 157, and by J. Gadille, *La pensée and l'action politiques des évêques français* . . . I (Paris 1967), 144 (cf. especially the map in this work).

[4] Cf. H. Sempér, "Propagande et action catholiques dans le seconde moitié du XIXᵉ s. et au debut du XXᵉ s., "*La Semaine religieuse de Toulouse;* coll.: *Publications de l'Université de Toulouse-Le-Mirail* (Toulouse 1973); H. Taine, *Les Origines de la France contemporaine: Le regime moderne* II (Paris 1894), 80.

suppress the opposition of the clergy was the bishop, mainly through the full powers of authority which the concordat had bestowed upon him. This was the reason why the government had conceded special importance to the figure of the bishop and the role he could play as a mediating factor. The prefect emphatically pointed out the advantages of a direct agreement with the bishop in order to avoid unpleasant incidents. This was especially true in the southwest, Cahors, the territories with a strong Protestant minority (e.g., Nîmes), and in the mountain areas like the Hautes-Alpes, where Monsignor Guilbert had imposed on the clergy in Gap his views about the necessity of a religious activity free of any political claims (1876). For dioceses where the clerical opposition could possibly increase, the responsible agencies of the Republic systematically appointed bishops who were interested in a settlement, (e.g., Guilbert in Amiens, later in Bordeaux; Meignan in Arras, later in Tours). The reports finally showed that alongside the priests in Mayenne who were strongly influenced by the nobility, a new generation of priests was growing from among the lower clergy, mainly in the western parts of the country, who were conciliatory and Republican like Abbé Frémont, a well-known priest from Poitou, whose diary was then being published.[5] In the poorest areas, the intransigence of the clergy was moderated by the traditional high esteem for the ruling authority, which, in the eyes of the people, was the guarantor of an ordered life and of respect for the individual.

Thus the concordat treaty continued to be firmly rooted in the political reality of the country, in the almost universal loyalty of the peasantry toward their religion, and in the desire of a certain segment of the upper and the lower clergy to be cooperative. The Republicans were aware of this fact, especially the prefects, who were much closer to the daily realities of life, and who condemned the radical candidates' demands for a separation as utopian. "One of our representatives, a confirmed advocate of the separation, explained to me that he had arrived at the conviction that the majority of his voters did not agree with the separation . . .," wrote the prefect of Jura in December 1885 to the minister. In response to Ernest Renan, who in November 1881 had developed the idea of a separation of the two powers in modern society, Paul Cambon wrote that the Republic should not deprive itself of this indispensable instrument of control which the decrees of the concordat provided: "Dominating or dominated—there is no middle of the road for the Catholic Church."[6]

---

[5] A. Siegfried, *L'abbé Frémont* (1852–1912), two vol. (Paris 1932).
[6] Prefect of Jura with the powers of a secretary, 31 December 1885 (*Archives Nationales*, F 19. 2576) (Renan, *Corr.* II [Paris 1924], 215–18, and Cambon, *Corr.* I [Paris 1905], 139–40).

This attitude was clearly expressed in the arguments which the government presented in May 1882 to the Concordat Commission formed under the chairmanship of Paul Bert. This commission was entrusted with the examination of all proposals by the extreme left regarding the suspension of the concordat. Paul Bert himself asked them to consider that the clergy, due to their influence on society, would regain their estates and means of action immediately after the separation, and that it would intensify their demands for support by the people, whose discontent could easily turn against the Republic. "Consequently, one would gain all the disadvantages of the separation, but none of the advantages." Thus, various reasons existed for the objections to the separation. The government, however, announced that it would reject every new demand for a reduction of the budget for cultural affairs. It even went so far as to disapprove of Paul Bert's plan for the future. The government wanted to preserve the concordat in letter and in spirit.[7]

Thus the French found themselves in the paradoxical situation of having to deal with two powers which, in theory, had opposing political and philosophical principles, but, in practice, made efforts to bring about a reconciliation. In spite of those representatives of the Republican state and the Church who regarded the separation as inevitable, both parties had one interest in common: preventing the break as long as possible. Thus this alliance was only a temporary endeavor based upon expediency and de facto situation, a weak base, which was threatened as soon as the conflicts were stronger than the desire to agree.[8]

The Politics of Reconciliation (1878–92)

The further development in the relations between the two powers was also subject to fluctuations which were based upon both French domestic politics and the opposing influences within the Curia which affected Leo XIII. In the first period, embracing the years 1878–90, politics was marked by mutual efforts to avoid alienation. The French government and especially the Foreign Office made attempts at the Vatican to diminish the significance of anticlerical pronouncements and the majority's legislation. The kind of politics which part of the Concordat Commission expressed in their definite rejection of the desire for separation asserted itself on every occasion. In the spring and summer of 1880, attempts were made to incite the congregations' political declaration of loyalty, which would have limited the application of ARTICLE 7 and thus allowed a reduction of expatriations. After the enactment of

[7] Cf. L. Capéran, op. cit. III (Paris 1960), 135–41.
[8] Regarding Church politics between 1891 and 1902, cf. J.-M. Larkin, "The Church and the French Concordat, 1891 to 1902," EHR (Oct. 1966), 717–39.

the law of March 1882, pertaining to obligatory and laicized elementary instruction, Jules Ferry's pronouncements defined the neutrality of schools in a way which paid respect to the freedom of conscience. The government tried to negotiate the cancellations of salaries which it had ratified after the incidents regarding the manuals for state instruction. Finally, the government seized every opportunity to emphasize that it was willing to pay a certain price to prove that its foreign policy served the defense of the Catholic interests. While Archbishop Charles de Lavigerie of Algeria, appointed cardinal in 1882, was working in Tunisia, the Near East, and in Africa, his activities were determined by this perspective. This also explains his equally great influence in the Vatican and at the Quai d'Orsay.

The Holy See and the ecclesiastical hierarchy were intent on preventing the defense of the Church's rights against the anticlerical laws from developing into an open opposition to overall policies. In this respect, Leo XIII's efforts to keep the ultramontane press in check and to counterbalance it with the "liberal" press were of great importance. So was his attempt to tie the leadership of the Church once again closer to a responsible hierarchy. On every occasion, the Pope protected the Nuncios Czacki and di Rende against the attacks of the intransigent Catholics. He did the same for those bishops who championed the policy of reconciliation, for example, Monsignor Louis Édouard Pie and Henri Bellot des Minières,[9] the successor to Cardinal Pie in Poitiers. He advised the French Catholics to resist only when it was a question of conscience. In this manner, he created conditions for solving serious controversies by way of negotiations, as in the case of the conflict regarding education, which would have otherwise resulted in a break.

When the elections of October 1885 seemed to offer a favorable chance for the formation of a Catholic party, Leo XIII expressed himself negatively, because the well-known statements of its main advocate, Albert de Mun, would have, without doubt, stamped the party with an anti-Republican imprint. In 1889, the Pope, encouraged by French domestic politics and the international situation, believed that the time had come amicably to conclude his policy of reconciliation with France. To be sure, a law had been passed that same year which obligated the seminarians to serve one year of military duty. On the other hand, this was also the year of failure for Boulanger's politics and of a truce in the controversy. The philosophy of Henri Bergson, *Les données immédiates de la conscience,*" and the literary prose by E. M. de Vogüé and Paul Bourget had undergone a spiritual renaissance. Finally, the Holy See felt that the policy of coalition within the Triple Alliance made the need

[9] J. B. Woodall, "Henri Bellot des Minières . . .", *CHR* (1952).

for close cooperation even more urgent. Leo XIII requested Monsignor Domenico Ferrata, whom he appointed nuncio to Paris in June 1891, to report to him personally about the state of these efforts. Called upon for comment, the cardinals of Paris, Lyon, and Rennes declared that they were not competent. It took no less than five appeals until Cardinal Charles de Lavigerie, in October 1890, was willing to deliver a declaration, ignoring the dangers which such an involvement entailed for his missionary work. When, on 12 November 1890, he received the officers of the Mediterranean fleet in Algeria, he proposed a toast to the French navy, suggesting to the French Catholics the "unconditional acceptance of the Republic," and added that "they would surely not have to experience the disapproval of any authority as a consequence." Rome endorsed this viewpoint only semiofficially, and Leo XIII let fifteen months pass before he expressed himself similarly in his encyclical *Au milieu des sollicitudes* of 17 February 1892, following a brief to the French cardinals on 3 May 1891. This hesitation can certainly be explained by the cool reception with which the leaders of French Catholicism responded to the papal attitude.

The term *Ralliement* had a different significance in the deliberations for Leo XIII and for the French Catholics. For the Pope, in line with his "political" encyclicals of 1881, 1885, and 1888, it was not at all a question of "baptizing" the Republic, but rather of accepting this government as a tool to re-Christianize legislation and the social institutions. For him, it was also not a question of founding a Catholic party, but rather of combining the Catholics of all persuasions and the Republicans in one comprehensive conservative union. This union, with the parliamentary power it represented, was to contribute to re-Christianization within its constituency. Such a concept, however, was difficult to accept for the majority of the bishops and the leading lay representatives of the Catholic public. The tradition of the "religious defensive," which they embraced, compelled them rather to form a Catholic party. In it, all were to come together who were concerned with the defense of the Church and who would not be readily willing to abandon the anti-Republican conviction from which they drew the strength to act. From this position arose the *Union de la France chrétienne,* which was founded in April 1891 by Charles Chesnelong, Lucien Brun, and Émile Keller and which refused the succession to Charles de Lavigerie, archbishop of Algeria.

In the Catholic public, however, the pressure in favor of the policy of the "toast" became more and more noticeable. Several bishops, e.g., Cardinal Adolphe Perraud, had already taken such a position; and some newspapers and individual groups from Paris and Bordeaux were working toward a reconciliation. The appearance of *Rerum novarum,* primarily, introduced a change in the political attitude of the Catholics. The existence of groups which had formed years ago and wanted to take the same path of social action accounts for the response which this encyclical encountered. Among them was the *Association Catholique de la jeunesse française* (ACJF), which, under the leadership of Albert de Mun, was able to fill even part of the aristocracy with enthusiasm and, above all, the committees which had been established by the newspaper *La Croix* since 1887. In Paris, almost seven hundred of these committees were combined under one general office (1891). With the help of these committees, Abbé Théodore Granier awakened the interest of the Catholic public to the fate of the workers and farmers, which created the foundation for a union which was constituted in 1892 as the *Union Nationale*. At this time, Catholics like Émile Duport and Louis Durand founded cooperative societies for farmers in the area of Lyon.

The Pursuit
and the Failure of Reconciliation
(1892–99)

At the time when Leo XIII commented on the occurrences in France, the voices within the Catholic public, for the reasons already known, had become more conciliatory. The intransigent wing of the newspaper *L'Univers* defected and founded the paper *La Vérité*. On 12 May 1892 the *Assemblée des Catholiques* dissolved the *Union de la France chrétienne*. Two of their most important leaders, Albert de Mun and Armand Mackau, joined the *Ralliement,* ignoring the criticism of their friends from the monarchic right. The moderation of these men during the Panama crisis and during the anarchist crisis was received by the Republicans with satisfaction, and they gave their official approval to this policy. Everything seemed to indicate that the reconciliation would be confirmed by the people's vote at the elections in August 1893.

These elections, however, turned out to be a disappointment. Only about thirty advocates of *Ralliement* were elected, and not one of the Catholic leaders who had so courageously expressed their opinion was among them. The reason for this may lie in the fact that they had not succeeded in agreeing on a parliamentary level, which would have enabled them to form a "unified front" in the election campaign. Earlier Jacques Piou, a deputy from Anjou, had formulated the reconciliation in its most comprehensive form, terming it the "constitutional right." But Albert de Mun, leader of the *Association Catholique de la jeunesse Française* wanted primarily to stress the common denominator of Catholicism in regard to the constitutional engagement of the *Ralliement,* and he opposed the ACJF to the Catholic League. Another deputy, Étienne Lamy, supported by several liberal Catholics mainly from the southwest of the country, finally began paving the way to the moderate Republicans through the Catholic League. There was no election coalition between the two groups, and even after the election, no link could guarantee the cohesion between the various groups of the *Ralliement*. They divided and dispersed, joining the various factions of the Chamber, and (since their leader did not belong to the Chamber and they were without help) were finally absorbed by the moderate majority which, at the time of Minister Jules Meline, enjoyed relative stability. "We needed a French Windthorst," Lecanuet said.

After the failure of the attempt of 1893, there was no more hope for the success of a policy which aimed at a parliamentary coalition. Thus a second phase began, during which, in view of the impending elections of 1898, the reconciliation was to take place on the stage of public opinion. This phase was, indeed, the great time of the "second Christian democracy." Representative of this trend was a group of young clergymen who tried to create new possibilities for pastoral work (Abbé Charles Calippe; clergy congresses in Rheims in 1896 and Bourges in 1900). They recognized the political power of their apostolic involvement. Fruits of their work were the organization of congresses for the Christian Democrats, the first of which took place in May 1903 in Rheims, and the founding of newspapers like *La Justice sociale* by Abbé Paul Naudet in Bordeaux, *Le Peuple française* by Abbé Théodore Garnier, and *La Démocratie chrétienne,* which appeared until 1908 under the editorial leadership of Abbé Paul Six. In September 1893, in the northern area of Hazebrouck, one of these democratic clergymen, Jules Auguste Lemire, was elected in place of a respected Catholic. This election was an example of the awakening of the Republican consciousness of a large part of the clergy and the farmers of this area marked by Christian faith.[10] Through this mandate, Lemire became the leader of the Christian Democrats, even though this movement had emerged from a series of individual initiatives which were neither carried by a substantial desire for coordination nor by a strong support through the episcopate. Their centers were in the north, where there was a connection to the Belgian Catholic social movement, and in the area of Lyon close to the *Chronique du Sud-Est* (V. Berne, M. Gonin, L. Crétinon). The impact of this newspaper extended over the *departements* of Ain, Loire, and Ar-

---

[10] J.-M. Mayeur, *Un prêtre démocrate, l'abbé Lemire (1853–1928)* (Paris 1968), 133. This election has to be seen in connection with the election of Abbé Hippolyte Gayraud, who was elected in Brittany in 1897, another area determined by the Christian spirit. The election of Gayraud attracted even more attention because he competed with Msgr. Maurice d'Hulst, a member of the higher clergy. After being declared invalid, the election was finally confirmed.

dèche and into the Mediterranean area, where Abbé Sahut founded a paper in Montpellier with the significant title *La sociologie catholique.*[11] Another active center existed in the area around Bordeaux. From 1894 until 1898, annual congresses took place in Rheims, Paris, and Lyon, where the representatives of the young clergy and the lower middle class met. Simultaneously, and often in connection with the Christian Democrats, the local boards of the newspaper *La Croix,* whose owners were Assumptionists, reached the peak of their development in the year 1895 with 3,000 local subsidiaries. The great number of local editions of *La Croix* (approximately 100 in 1897) and its wide circulation, which secured a total of almost 700,000 issues, made this press organ an important support of these committees. *La Croix* did also reach the middle classes, but mainly the lower middle class, the workers, and the rural population. Having the same basis as the Christian Democrats and the ACJF, the members of these committees insisted on a definite political engagement. At a congress held in 1895 an election committee of *La Croix* was formed under the name *Comité Justice-Égalité.*

Now the congresses of the Christian Democrats, in turn, founded an election federation in Rheims (1896) and Lyon (1897). It was actually a question of organizing all those groups, which had grown rapidly since 1890, and of placing them under a common leadership while preserving a certain autonomy. The man who took the leadership was Étienne Lamy. Cardinal Rampolla had asked him in March 1896 to take on this task. Unfortunately, the influence of the *Comité Justice-Égalité* and the Assumptionists' authority, which was in control of the *Bonne Presse,* was much stronger, and the election federation of the Christian Democrats was unable to bring the Catholics to back their plan of endorsing a promising moderate Republican. On the contrary, the various political factions of the Catholics often fought against each other, a fact which was finally put to good use by a radical candidate. Lamy himself refused the candidacy because he would not have been able to find a constituency. The elections of May 1898 resulted in the same failure of the *Ralliement* as the elections of 1893. To be sure, the number of elected representatives of the *Ralliement* was larger now (seventy-six), but the majority of the "moderates" decreased correspondingly. This fact was confirmed on 14 June of the following year, when they succeeded, with the help of a majority, to henceforth exclude the representatives of the *Ralliement* from the governing coalition. The following months brought the end for the federation and the decline of "Christian democracy" in France.

Very much to the disadvantage of the "new spirit," there continued to

---

[11] G. Cholvy, *Géographie religieuse de l'Hérault contemporain* (Paris 1968), 386.

be considerable sources of tension between the Catholics and the Republicans. They were passionately nurtured by the readers of *La Croix.* Two points were of importance: the government of Alexandre Ribot had imposed additional taxes on the religious congregations, the so-called *Abonnement,* which had incited a wave of protest. Primarily, as Capéran demonstrated, it was anti-Semitism which provoked the Catholic masses against the Republic. Édouard Drumont charged the Republic with being in the grip of a "Jewish-Masonic" conspiracy, which was sneaking into the higher ranks of the military, thus threatening religious values and national integrity. This partly explains why the revision of the sentence for the Jewish Captain Dreyfus, attaché in the War Ministry, had drawn such attention from the public. Dreyfus had been falsely accused of delivering military secrets to Germany and, in 1894, had been sentenced to deportation for life. The episcopate did practice noteworthy constraint in this affair; but this cannot be said about the lower clergy and the masses of Catholics, among whom only a small minority courageously confessed to be *"dreyfusards."* Recent research has shown that Edouard Drumont's articles in the newspaper *Libre Parole* had found an undeniable echo in Catholic circles, and that the anti-Semitism of *La Croix* was indeed of a different nature, but nonetheless very real. The newspaper unconditionally took the side of the army when, in 1899, heated debate flared up about the trial of the Court of Justice of Rennes. Even among the Christian Democrats anti-Semitism was strongly represented. Also people like Abbé Hippolyte Gayraud confessed to it, and the agenda of the congresses carried the mark of an exaggerated assessment of the national beliefs and the condemnation of "anti-French and anti-Christian Jewish intrigues." This is proven by the fact that Cardinal Pierre Coullié, the archbishop of Lyon, on the occasion of the congresses in Lyon in 1896 and 1897, warned his clergy of such programmatic terminology, which he believed to be contradictory to the Christian spirit, and that he himself denounced any participation.

The nationalistic excesses in the spring of 1899 turned against the person of President Émile Loubet. That was not unexpected, since a coalition had been formed in Parliament whose anti-clerical program was directed against the religious congregations. It was the motto of the "Republican concentration" which achieved a majority for Pierre Waldeck-Rousseau on 26 June. Their Republican leaders did not hesitate to blame the Catholics' intrigues for the sentence which prevented Dreyfus' acquittal in August and resulted merely in a reduction of his punishment. In November, the houses of the Assumptionists in Paris and the offices of *La Croix* were subject to a police search. The suppression of the Assumptionists, following a trial in the District Court, and

Leo XIII's decision to deprive them of the direction of the *Bonne Presse* have to be seen in the context of the influence they had had in the previous ten years. The Assumptionists were the first religious congregation to be affected by the measures which finally led to the separation of Church and state.

Now the Republic returned to its policy of persecution, which, in the eyes of the general Catholic public, it had never completely given up. This poses the question of whether French Catholicism in its majority was ever really ready for reconciliation. The anti-Semitic wave and the corresponding press propaganda allow the conclusion that the Catholic population itself was, to a large extent, responsible for the failure of the reconciliatory efforts by causing an anticlerical feeling within the committees and the administration of the Republicans.

CHAPTER 7

On the Road to Conservatism:
Belgium, the Netherlands, and Luxemburg

Belgium

Around the turn of the century, thanks to the constitution of 1831, Belgian Catholicism had been able to flourish so intensely that Belgium was practically a Catholic country, at least in regard to the classical arena of struggle against liberalism: the school system. This constitutional reality, however, deviating from the liberal statutes, was endangered. The ecclesiastical circles, on the one hand, regarded the political status quo merely as an opportunity; and the Liberals, on the other hand, forgot the time of common resistance to the Dutch Monarchy and reacted with increasing anticlericalism. There were also indications of considerable differences between the agrarian and the early industrial areas, between the Flemish and the Walloon areas regarding religious practices. The radical-liberal government of Rogier and Frère-Orban (1857–70) was overthrown because the powerful Catholic congressional movement, organized by the laity, was also politically transformed, and the domestic differences within Catholicism pertaining to the question of the constitution could temporarily be settled.

But the conflict continued to intensify. The head of the Catholic constitutional opponents was economist Charles Périn (1815–1905) of Louvain, who, in the area of economics, represented a mixture of liberalism and moral patronage and strongly influenced the group around Bishop Freppel in Angers.[1] Van Humbeeck, who was the minister of Cultural Affairs in the radical-liberal government of Frère-Orban, which had come to power in 1878, coined the phrase: "Un cadavre est sur la terre, il barre la route au progrès . . . le cadavre du passé—c'est le catholicisme."[2] Pope Leo XIII, who was familiar with the Belgian circumstances through his nunciature (1843–46), believed, when taking office, that peace could be preserved in Belgium. After the June 1878 election victory of the Liberals, he still tried to prevent an intensification of the situation, while requesting respect for the constitution. The good wishes of Secretary of State Nina for the twenty-fifth anniversary of the newspaper *Le Bien Public* (published since 1853), which followed an intransigent ultramontane course, was played off against papal politics and had to be interpreted.[3] A pastoral letter by the Belgian episcopate in December, quite contrary to the intentions of Leo XIII, was composed in a sharp tone, which coincided with the belligerent attitude of Archbishop Victor-Auguste Dechamps of Mechelen (archbishop since 1867, cardinal since 1875), who had also intervened in the German *Kulturkampf*. On 10 July 1879 the law regarding nondenominational elementary schools was enacted, followed by a law pertaining to public secondary and high schools. The Belgian bishops excommunicated those parents who sent their children to public elementary schools and did the same to teachers who taught there. In vain the Pope attempted moderation. A papal letter to Dechamps of 2 April 1880 finally recognized the attitude of the episcopate, which Leo could not disavow. But since he had promised the Belgian ambassador to the Vatican a compromise, the government felt deceived and broke off diplomatic relations in June 1880.

The school laws were simply a failure, especially in Flanders. By the end of 1880, 580,680 children went to free Catholic schools and only 333,401 to public schools, which were being increased to no purpose. The ecclesiastical sanctions against the communal school system could usually anticipate religious obedience and willingness to make sacrifices (e.g., dismissal of civil servants). The people also complained about the financial burdens which were the consequence of the state's rather irrational school policies.[4] In the elections of 10 June 1884 the Liberals

---

[1] "The worker is a brother in Jesus Christ whom God has entrusted to the employer: C. Périn, *Die Lehren der Nationalökonomie seit einem Jahrhundert* (Freiburg 1882), 277.—M. Becqué, A. Louant, "Le dossier 'Rome et Louvain' de Charles Périn" (incl. a biographical sketch), *RHE* 50 (1955), 36–124.

[2] Quoted in F. Petri, op. cit., 476.

[3] Schmidlin, *PG* II, 437.

[4] F. Petri, op. cit., 477, incl. biblio.

suffered a devastating defeat, which was to be a determining factor for a long time to come. On 20 September 1884 the minister of Cultural Affairs, Charles Woeste, tried to thoroughly revise the school law of 1879, but President Beernaert (1884–94) solved the controversy, which had badly shaken the Belgian public, through a compromise.[5]

In February 1885 the Belgian government sent a special delegate to the Vatican, and in May, Domenico Ferrata, who had earned diplomatic credits in Switzerland, came discretely to Brussels as nuncio. On 21 June, during the Te Deum on occasion of the jubilee of the Belgian kingdom, he was already able to function as the doyen of the diplomatic corps. He preluded Lavigerie's famous toast by a toast to the royal couple during the anniversary of the railroad, receiving the applause of the Liberals who had approved the budget for the Vatican Embassy in 1886.[6] The discussion of two questions pertaining to canon law during the nunciature of Ferrata (until 1889) is indicative of the Leonic pragmatism. The liberal government of Frère-Orban had suspended denominational cemeteries in 1879. Since Beernaert hesitated to change this, the Pope recommended to his nuncio to wait and see.[7] More crucial was the fact that in 1876 the Holy Office, via the French episcopate, had prohibited the Catholic judges in France from cooperating in divorces (legalized again in 1884) even if it required their resignation. Neighboring Belgium, where divorce had been legalized in 1809, was worried about this, and therefore Ferrata informed them that the decree was only binding for the French bishops, not for Belgium.[8]

In reference to Belgium it was noted that the difference between liberal and social Catholicism was not as general as it seemed. The delay in social activity was said to have to do with the Lamennais crisis of Catholic Liberalism in Belgium.[9] As a matter of fact, it was a political anti-Liberalist, Charles Périn, who had obscured the need for a reform with his morally moderate economic liberalism, which was only later attacked by the Catholic Democrats. The Catholic bourgeoisie was energetically involved in the enormous industrial growth going on since

---

[5] The communal administrations were empowered to fully recognize the Catholic schools ("accepted schools") and to make decisions regarding religious instruction in public schools (however, the child's father was entitled to exempt his child from it). The teachers' training was no longer restricted to state seminaries.

[6] Stutz, 46–54.

[7] When Dechamps's (died 1883) successor, Archbishop Pierre-Lambert Goossens of Mechelen (cardinal since 1889) inquired in Rome about this matter, he was given a canonical answer, but was urged to practice tolerance.

[8] Ferrata, *Mémoires* I, 334ff.

[9] "Social Catholicism and liberal Catholicism are not so opposed to each other as they have often pretended to be"; Henri Haag: J. N. Moody (ed.), *Church and Society* (New York 1953), 294f.

the sixties, which after 1880 could continue only with strict economic concentration because of the European protective tariff policies. Therefore King Leopold II, who had done much for the country, encountered strong resistance when he wanted to introduce compulsory military service within the framework of his military policy, because he did not anticipate again having the good fortune which had guided him in the war of 1870. The socio-political aspect amounted to the fact that everybody could free himself from military duty by financing a substitute, which was naturally not possible for a worker or a small craftsman. Interestingly, the bill of 1887 miscarried, mainly because of the Catholic Conservatives who were backed by the episcopate because it feared the suspension of the clergy's exemption from military service. In contrast to the question of the septennate dicussed in Berlin the same year, Leo XIII was reserved toward the Belgian king's plea for intervention, even though he did not share the opinion of the episcopate.[10]

Moreover, the gradual removal of the property qualification had to be accomplished in spite of the opposition of the Catholic Conservatives and their allies, the Liberals of Frère-Orban's persuasion. The pioneers in this struggle were the younger Liberals, but it was primarily the Socialists whose demonstrations forced the government, dominated by the Catholic party, to introduce general though still limited suffrage in 1893.[11] The Conservatives did not expect that the Catholics, rather than the Socialists, would profit from this law, especially in the Flemish-speaking areas.

The signal for a social reform which could no longer be ignored (unusually low wages, long working hours) was the general strike, starting in Liège on 18 March 1886 and commemorating the Parisian uprising of the commune in 1871. There was violence, and military forces were dispatched under General van der Smissen. The Beernaert government was now forced to design reform laws against the opposition of the extreme right, led by Charles Woeste, an intransigent convert. Liège became the center of the Catholic social movement which recognized that traditional paternalism, often enough just a phrase, was no longer adequate for the growing industrial society. An early attempt was made in 1871 by the Catholic industrialist Gustave de Jaer. But he could not assert himself in the politically dominating ranks of Belgian Catholicism.[12] In East Flemish Ghent in 1875 a group of young workers came

---

[10] Ferrata, *Mémoires* I, 334ff.; Stutz, 51ff.; H. Pirenne, *Histoire de Belgique* VII (1932), 221, 309f.; F. Petri, op. cit., 471f.

[11] This caused the number of eligible voters to increase from 137,000 to 1,370,000; F. Petri, op. cit., 478.

[12] M. Vaussard, *Histoire de la Démocratie chrétienne* (Paris 1956), 143; about paternalism in Belgium, see R. Reszohazy, op. cit., 47–98; about de Jaer, ibid., 70.

together, from which the Anti-Socialist League emerged. By 1911 the organization had one hundred thirty-five staff members, its own daily paper, and productive social institutions. The Socialists felt that this organization was breaking class solidarity and consequently collisions occurred. Among the first of the Catholic labor leaders who belonged to the working classes themselves was the weaver Léon Bruggeman from Ghent, who, together with printers, founded a Christian-oriented union in 1882.[13] In 1886 and 1887, the first two socio-political congresses took place in Liège, endorsed by Bishop Doutreloux, who was a good-natured priest but not a fighter. Charles Woeste called these events "exaggerations,"[14] but he assessed them correctly as an opposition, since people were a great deal more realistic in Liège than in France. Abbé A. Pottier was the focal point there. He was a theoretician as well as a practioner, but in 1898 he turned his back on the internal conflicts and went to Rome.[15] The Liège Congress (1890) enjoyed sizable international participation and was quite lively. The discussions concentrated around the generally controversial state intervention, which Woeste exposed as *"Césarisme,"* and the equally delicate question of whether employers and employees should form joint or separate organizations. It was this question which again divided Belgium's Catholics into two vehemently opposed groups. Without meaning to establish their own party, the approximately one hundred Catholic workers' societies combined to form the *Ligue Démocratique Belge.* The initiative came from Professor G. Helleputte of Louvain (1852–1925) and the engineer A. Verhaegen (1847–1917), who had collaborated with the Vincent Conferences. Charging Woeste with being interested only in an increase of the state budget for the Church's sake and the public support of the Catholic schools is probably a polemical exaggeration.[16] But there is no doubt that the power of the *Parti Catholique* was determined until World War I by the strong interests of the middle-class Catholics, against whom the Christian social forces had difficulties bringing their interests to bear, especially since they were often enough in disagreement and looked for a coalition with either the Conservatives or the Christian social movement on the left. It was also due to the abstract style of the encyclical *Rerum novarum* (1891) that it could become the object of particularly serious controversies in respect to its interpreta-

[13] M. P. Fogarty, *Christian Democracy in Western Europe* (London 1957, Freiburg i. Br. 1959), 218ff.

[14] Vaussard, 143; with a great amount of objectivity R. Reszohazy, op. cit. 201–86, describes the political differences within Belgian Catholicism from C. Woeste at the extreme right wing to A. Daens.

[15] C. Cardolle, *Un précurseur, un docteur, un pionnier social: Msgr. Pottier* (Brussels 1951).

[16] M. P. Fogarty, op. cit., 364.

tion. Bishop Doutreloux had defined papal principles in a pastoral letter in the beginning of 1894. Leo XIII, in a letter to the Belgian episcopate of 10 July 1895 suggested a conference which took place in March 1896 in Mechelen and decided on a rather inappropriate compromise.[17] Meanwhile a group of young Catholic deputies had formed to the left of the Democratic League, indebted with respect to its definite social demands to the Dominican Rutten, one of the "social chaplains" of that era, later the first secretary general of the *Confédération des Syndicats chrétiens,* which had grown out of local groups between 1904 and 1912.[18] The small Flemish Christian People's Party faltered soon because Abbé Daens, charged with having endorsed ideas of class warfare, was suspended in 1897.[19] Significant for the existing insecurity was Cardinal (since 1889) Goossens's inquiry in Rome in connection with the Congress of Mechelen in 1896: did the employer commit a sin, and to what extent, if he preferred cheaper labor and did not pay family-adequate wages in the fight to compete on the market? It was the Belgian primate's inquiry, rather than this particular problem (widely discussed among western European Catholics), which was remarkable, as well as Cardinal Zigliara's answer that a "fair wage" was to be paid according to equity.

Leo XIII in 1895 refused to receive Abbé Daens, and in a conversation with Duc d'Ursel, the cousin of Albert de Mun,[20] he is supposed to have said: "Quant à Daens, c'est fini, et s'il recommence, je le frappe."[21] But the ultraconservative Charles Woeste also was by no means persona grata. However, the Pope's chances of alleviating the extremes within Catholicism were even more limited in France than in Belgium. The Conservatives were in power and had the financial means, which the bishops used for ecclesiastical projects and did not intend to relinquish. This situation intensified critically in 1898 when A. Verhaegen implored the Church in Rome to authorize a political oath.[22] There he encountered the opposition of Woeste, but also the benevolence of Rampolla, who mediated his audience with the Pope. Leo XIII promised to send a letter on behalf of Verhaegen to the Belgian episcopate. But while Cardinal Goossens and the bishops again assured the *Ligue Démocratique*

[17] Schmidlin, *PG* II, 439f; M. P. Fogarty, op. cit., 345f.
[18] M. P. Fogarty, op. cit., 345.
[19] H. Haag, op. cit., 297; for an objective view of the hearing by the Inquisition, see R. Reszohazy, op. cit., 223f., 231f., 239ff; 261–68, about the League's relations to the "Daensistes"; 279–85, about the decline of the movement (Abbé Daens submitted to his bishop).
[20] Cf. chap. 12, n. 45.
[21] According to C. Woeste in his memoirs, quoted in R. Reszohazy, op. cit., 240.
[22] R. Reszohazy, op. cit., 286–90.

of their friendly disposition, they did not want to risk a public congress for the purpose of unification. As in the case of Abbé Daens, the Belgian episcopate in view of these tensions was chiefly interested in preserving the unity of the *Parti Catholique* and its majority in Parliament.

The social differences within Belgian Catholicism were difficult to overcome because, in contrast to comparable parties in other countries, the Catholic party had the clear majority and external forces of integration were lacking. In 1905 a majority of Christian-Social and Socialist deputies carried through the Sunday-rest law in spite of the opposition by the Catholic chief of the cabinet, M. de Smet de Naeyer;[23] and in 1907 the government was defeated in the question of the eight-hour day for miners, which enraged the middle-class Catholic press.[24] Professor Helleputte, whose position in the *Ligue Démocratique* had been questionable, now joined the young conservative cabinet of de Trooz.[25] But Secretary of State Cardinal Merry del Val's influence provided new complications, which lasted until 1914. Verspeyen, editor of the *Bien Public,* received papal commendation in 1910. But the Conservatives were disappointed by Pius X, because the Pope had respected the independence of the league, provided, to be sure, that it would follow the directives of the bishops. While most of them remained reserved, Désiré Mercier favored the Christian Democrats, so that they were able to score a victory over Woeste at the Congress of Mechelen in 1904.

The Catholic societies developed slowly under the dominance of the *Parti Catholique,* which seemed to offer security for the Church. In 1903 the *Association de la Jeunesse belge* was founded in Louvain. At first it was a loose group, whose goals were not particularly directed toward the youth. A change was effected by young Abbé A. Brohée, a student of Cardinal Mercier. He sharply separated religious from political action, and at the congresses of 1911 and 1913 almost no one but young people gathered. The first beginnings of the *Jeunesse ouvrière chrétienne,* developed by J. Cardijn (1882–1967) in the vicinity of Brussels and itself an appeal to the youth, was interrupted by World War I.[26] In contrast to the societies, religious orders and congregations flourished, especially when the Belgian Congo offered them new tasks. In 1829, 4,791 religious were counted, as compared to 38,140 in 1910.[27] The Jesuits could do their work here undisturbed. The society of the Salvatorians, founded in 1881 by the Alemannian Johann Baptist Jordan

[23] Vaussard, 148.

[24] M. P. Fogarty, op. cit., 345.

[25] R. Reszohazy, 359ff.

[26] R. Aubert, "Organisation et Caractère des mouvements de jeunesse cath. en Belgique," *Politica e storia* 28 (Rome 1972) especially 275–79, 287f.

[27] M. Dierickx, *LThK*² II, 157.

and expanding rapidly, also took root in Belgium. A flourishing center of monastic life was the Benedictine priory in Maredsous (abbey since 1878), which Maurus Wolter had founded in 1872 with the help of the Desclée family (entrepreneurs from Tournai). The priory was closely associated with the abbey at Beuron, whose hindrance by the German *Kulturkampf* forced attention to foreign affairs. Abbot Maurus Wolter of Beuron (since 1875) appointed his brother Placidus abbot of Maredsous and became the instrument of the liturgical inspiration which he had during a sojourn in Solesmes (1862). In 1878 Gérard van Caloen published the first lay missal in Maredsous (*Missel des fidèles*).[28] At this time, Anselm Schott of Beuron resided in the Belgian abbey. In 1888 the abbey's church was consecrated by a cardinal legate in the presence of Nuncio Ferrata and the entire Belgian episcopate. When Maurus Wolter died (1890) and his brother Placidus succeeded him as archabbot of Beuron, Hildebrand de Hemptinne took over the direction of Maredsous. When he was consecrated abbot by Cardinal San Felice in Montecassino, he was also given a comprehensive papal commission.[29] In the same year, a priory was founded in Steenbrugge (1896, abbey). The priory of Mont-César in Louvain (1890) would later become, next to Maredsous, an important abbey in the Belgian congregation. From here emanated, in 1909, the liturgical movement inspired by Lambert Beauduin. The priory of Saint André in Bruges (1901) is related to the Brazilian congregation.[30]

That the first eucharistic congress did not take place in Belgium was due to reservations Cardinal Dechamps had during the Frère-Orban government. But after the third congress, which took place in Liège in 1883, where E. Marie Tamisier had a protector in Bishop Doutreloux, Belgium and France became the main areas of this movement (after Antwerp, Brussels was the city where the congress took place in 1898 under Cardinal Goossens).[31]

The Catholic University of Louvain enjoyed the special benevolence of Leo XIII[32] and had a financial patron in Cardinal Goossens. In 1882, Désiré Mercier, who had studied theology there, became the first professor to hold the chair for Thomistic philosophy which had been estab-

---

[28] W. Trapp, *Vorgeschichte und Ursprung der liturgischen Bewegung* (Regensburg 1940), 363; in 1884, van Caloen founded the periodical *Messager des fidèles,* since 1890 *Revue bénédictine;* cf. chap. 16.

[29] Cf. chap. 17.

[30] P. Weißenberger gives information about the development of the order in the form of excerpts from documents, *Das benediktinische Mönchtum im 19. und 20. Jahrhundert* (Beuron 1953).

[31] Cf. chap. 16.

[32] Schmidlin, *PG* II, 440 with documentation.

lished upon the Pope's request, and after the ontological crisis he inaugurated a new phase in the history of the institution, which, after 1899, under its president Monsignor Abbeloos, gained great significance in historical and biological studies as well. Between 1890 and 1905, the theological faculty received acclaim especially in the fields of biblical research and patristics.[33] As archbishop of Mechelen (cardinal, 1907), Mercier determined the ecclesiastical situation in Belgium on the basis of a neoscholastic interpretation of society. In 1909, Pius expressly praised the University of Louvain.

In spite of all this, an increasing de-Christianization of life in Belgium cannot be overlooked, even in rural areas, but mainly in the industrial regions, where only a few churches were built in the workers' quarters. Not only did the attendance of Sunday services decrease, but even birth, marriage, and death were often no longer included in ecclesiastical life.[34]

Amidst the mostly decadent spiritual literature of these decades, the poetry of the Flemish priest and poet Guido Gezelle (1830–90) shone like a star. Filled with the intimate experience of nature and an original religiosity, Gezelle broke with all conventions and kept aloof from all fashionable styles. It is significant that the poetic genius of Gezelle was only appreciated rather late.[35]

The Netherlands

Catholicism in the Netherlands, after the area's separation from Belgium, constituted a sizable minority of nearly 40 percent. The liberal circumstances permitted the development of religious orders and schools, and in the forties the establishment of a press. Next to these ecclesiastical issues, economic considerations were decisive for the coalition with the Liberals. The leading ranks of Dutch Catholicism were comprised of men from business and trade. Thus the Catholics had a remarkable share in the success of the Liberals under the leadership of Thorbecke and in the state's basic law of 18 September 1848, which fundamentally strengthened the power of Parliament and ended the

[33] Cf. chaps. 21 and 23.—R. Aubert, *Le grand tournant de la faculté de théologie de Louvain à la veille de 1900: Mélanges offerts à M.-D. Chenu* (Paris 1967), 73–109.—About Mercier, 324f.

[34] Around 1910, 23 percent of the children in Seraing near Liège were not baptized, 46 percent of the marriages were only performed in civil ceremonies, and 64 percent of the funerals took place without a priest—an extreme case, but it shows the trend of the workers' alienation from the Church.

[35] A. Vermeylen, *De Vlaamse letteren van Gezelle to heden* (⁴1949); Joris Taels, *Lexikon der Weltliteratur* I (Freiburg i. Br. 1960), 655.

Calvinistic character of the Netherlands. The Catholics profited from the freedom of association in all areas of life. In the Netherlands, as elsewhere, the question of schools was the key issue in the relationship of Catholics to modern society. As an alternative to the Calvinistic parochial school, a group of Catholic politicians endorsed the school law of 1857, which indicated a radical ideological neutralization. However, this resulted in the *verzuiling*,[36] which characterized Dutch society, because of a-Christian, even atheistic beliefs developing within liberalism, and because of the Calvinistic and Catholic orthodoxy's joint opposition. A letter drafted by both in 1868 requested the increase of free Catholic schools.

Shortly before the school conflict in Belgium, the left-liberal Kappeyne government enacted a law which was emphatically and successfully opposed by the Reformed clergyman Abraham Kuyper (he gathered 470,000 signatures).[37] In 1888, as leader of the Anti-Revolutionary Party, he established connections with the Catholic priest H. J. M. Schaepman (1844–1903), who had been voted into Parliament in 1880. The Kappeyne government was overthrown. This conservative coalition, rather than Leo XIII's[38] admonition directed toward the Dutch Catholics in April 1888, effected the school law of 1889, which placed the principle of free schools on a realistic foundation: free schools would receive state support and, after 1920, unconditional equality. The church-minded Protestants and Catholics, who were in agreement over the necessity of parochial schools, constituted a political cooperation which repeatedly resulted in formations of government. In 1896, Monsignor Schaepman founded the *Katholieke Staatspartij*, which developed into an exceedingly powerful factor in Dutch politics. Leo XIII made use of the now strong and pro-Rome Catholicism of the Netherlands for his fight in Italy (letter to the episcopate of 24 September 1895). His relations with the royal court were friendly, and neither the widowed Queen nor Leo are to blame for the failure to invite the Pope to the first general peace conference, which took place in The Hague in 1899 and was opposed by Italy.

Since industrialization, at that time, was much slower than in Belgium and socialism did not play as important a role there, social Catholicism lagged behind for a long time. This was not Monsignor Schaepman's fault, who had indeed recognized this growing problem, but the fault of the lobby within his party.[39] The occasion which led to the founding of

---

[36] F. Petri, op. cit., 482–86.
[37] F. Petri, op. cit., 482f.; J. T. de Visser, *Kerk en Staat* III (1927), 387–479.
[38] Schmidlin, *PG* II, 486.
[39] M. P. Fogarty, op. cit., 348f.; Verluis, *Beknopte Geschiedenis van de Katholieke Arbeidersbeweging* (1949).

the Catholic People's Union by W. J. Pastoors, later deputy to the Parliament, was trivial: the Catholic workers and the lower middle class were angered by the high price of tickets which the wealthy prominent Catholics had charged in 1888 for the celebrations in Amsterdam of the tenth anniversary of Leo's pontificate.[40] That same year the Catholic social priest A. Ariens organized a workers' league in the textile city of Enschede, whose goals were religious education, social gatherings, and financial assistance through a relief fund. The Socialist propaganda prompted him by means of a strike (1890) to transform the league into a denominational union. His alliance with the Protestant group of 1895 seemed to be the beginning of an interdenominational Christian union in the Netherlands, and for several years the union, with its joint executive board and treasury, had considerable success. But the denominational party structure as well as the ecclesiastical opposition, especially of the Catholic episcopate,[41] gave this attempt no chance. In 1895, a congress of the Catholic workers' movement combined forty-nine Catholic unions which had emerged locally since 1891. In 1910 Monsignor H. Poels, an exegete who had just returned from Washington, founded a Catholic workers' union in Limburg, a city which had recently been discovered by industry. Thanks to Poels, de-Christianization of the workers did not proceed as quickly in the Netherlands as in other countries.

Compulsory elementary education was not enacted until 1900, which was partly due to the opposition of the conservative parties and their press, from which Monsignor Schaepman was completely isolated. In 1905, parochial high schools also received state subsidies.

Dutch Catholicism retained its conservative hallmark (developed since the middle of the nineteenth century) far beyond World War I. The Catholic Convention in Utrecht in 1889, where H. van de Wetering was archbishop from 1882 until 1928, strengthened the religious self-identity in connection with the political victory, which was little touched by the problems of the era. The awareness of unconditional dependence on the papacy increased during the pontificate of Pius X, who established a regular hierarchy in the Netherlands in 1908. The *Maasbode* represented an extreme integralism, and Pius X found himself able to

---

[40] M. P. Fogarty, op. cit., 218f.

[41] The "union struggle" in Germany was also carried across the border. In view of the directive of the Dutch episcopate which stated that it was only permissible to join Catholic unions, a Catholic union leader from Germany said at a conference in the Netherlands in 1908: "With all due respect for our spiritual fathers, the bishops, we must say: this far, but no farther" (quoted in M. P. Fogarty, 225; cf. P. H. Winkelmann in S. H. School [ed.], *150 ans de mouvement ouvrier chrétien en Europe de l'Ouest* [Paris, Bonn 1966]).

praise the Dutch episcopate when, thanks to its alertness, the "modern-istic plague" did not find a stronghold there. The Catholic University of Nijmegen, founded in 1923, is historically rooted in the educational system which was created by H. Moller at the beginning of the century. Its spiritual open-mindedness was along the lines of the publication *Van onzen tijd,* which had been founded by laymen, especially by the Klarenbeekse Club.

In the history of the Catholic Church, the Netherlands enjoyed the reputation of being, at that time, a haven for the persecuted, who were of a different persuasion than those during the time of the Enlighten-ment. Arnold Janssen, born in the Lower Rhine area, founded the *Societas Verbi Divini* (Society of the Divine Word), which was to grow into the most important missionary institute. With the approval of Bishop J. A. Paredis of Roermond and Archbishop A. J. Schaepman of Utrecht, he transferred the institute across the Dutch-German border to Steijl (1874).[42] The Jesuits, who were absolutely forbidden in Ger-many from the conclusion of the *Kulturkampf* until 1904 and officially forbidden in Switzerland until just recently, could work in the Nether-lands and Belgium without interference, and therefore they transferred their exile college in Ditton Hall, England, to Valkenswaard in 1894. The same year, during the Catholic Convention in Cologne, Schaepman praised Dutch liberty.[43]

Luxemburg

The Concordat of 1801 made Luxemburg part of the bishopric of Metz; but after its promotion to grand-duchy in union with the Netherlands in 1815, it was assigned to the bishopric of Namur (1823). Following the Belgian revolution, it lost its position as a diocese because King Willem I of the Netherlands did not want to divide Namur. Following a provi-sionary arrangement for the city of Luxemburg and after the surrender of the Walloon area to Belgium (1839), the rest of the country became an independent apostolic vicariate (1840). The appropriate desire to promote Luxemburg to a bishopric, which Willem II favored on account of the concession for free papal appointments, failed because the pro-posals of the concordat were not sanctioned by Rome.[44] Pius IX's un-ilateral move of 27 September 1870 encountered the opposition of the Luxemburg State Council. Not until 23 June 1873 was the establish-ment of a bishopric ratified through a royal grand-ducal resolution by Willem III. Vicar Apostolic N. Adames was the first bishop of Luxem-

[42] Chap. 17; see also J. M. Gijsen, *Joh. Aug. Paredis 1795–1886* (Assen 1968).
[43] Kißling, *Katholikentage* II, 267.
[44] E. Donckel, op. cit., 132–34, 136f., 161f.

burg (1870–83).[45] The school law of 1881 suspended the inspection in which the clergy participated, as well as the right of the local priest to supervise the teacher, and it authorized community commissions, including a priest, to supervise the schools. This law, which was revised in 1898 in favor of the Church, demonstrated the delayed development in Luxemburg. But the law of 1912, which Bishop J. J. Koppes (1883–1918) opposed, though it did respect the Christian faith, caused the separation of school and Church. Consequently, religious instruction was administered outside of the school.[46] According to the example of the neighboring countries, the Catholic organizations now developed.

The desired course of the interdenominational Christian union in Luxemburg did not succeed. During World War I, however, the workers left the weak specialized sections of the workers' societies and joined neutral associations, which is why in 1920 independent but denominational Christian unions were founded.[47] The development of the iron industry in the region of Esch caused an increase in the membership of the Social Democratic Party, founded in 1900. The ecclesiastical alienation of large segments of the population was due less to the relatively moderate Luxemburg Liberals of the eighties than to the Socialists. But Luxemburg did not lose its Catholic character.

ARTICLE 26 of the Constitution of 1848 resolved that the religious societies needed a legal license. But the regulation was usually interpreted amicably, so that, during the *Kulturkampf* in Germany and in the wake of the laws of 1901 and 1904 in France, the faithful could find refuge in Luxemburg.

[45] E. Donckel, op. cit., 157–60, 165f.
[46] E. Donckel, 149, 170f., 194. The amendment of the law of 1921 caused the reintroduction of religious instruction in the schools (ibid., 173). About the law of 1912, see Schmidlin, *PG* III, 85.
[47] E. Donckel, 185f.

CHAPTER 8

*The Church of the Iberian World
between Revolution and Reaction*

Spain

The leading ranks of Catholicism in Spain were preoccupied with waging war against each other, in spite of Leo XIII's constant admonitions. The descendents of the "Apostolic Party" and the Carlists, such as the journalist Nocedal in his *Siglo futuro* or the publication *Ciencia Cris-*

tiana, charged the liberal conservative Catholics with betrayal of the faith. In 1881, under the aegis of Cardinal Moreno of Toledo, a national pilgrimage to Rome with many committees was organized. It was to serve as a demonstration of their own power rather than of their loyalty to the successor of Saint Peter. This caused Secretary of State Jacobini, on 13 February 1878, to request purely diocesan groups of pilgrims.[1] The rather reform-oriented *Partido Socialista Obrero Español,* founded in 1878 under the leadership of Pablo Iglesias, was not adequately assessed by the belligerents, at least not at first; but it flourished. So did the violent anarchism which had sympathizers and disciples especially among the totally impoverished farm hands on the large latifundia in Andalusia and in Catalonia. There were numerous assassinations and terrorism. The activities reached a climax on 7 June 1896 in Barcelona when, during a Corpus Christi procession, a bomb killed six people and seriously wounded forty-two.[2]

An indirect victim of this incident was a politician who, after the brief First Republic in Spain (1873–74), had restored the Bourbon Monarchy under Alphonso XII and given the period of restoration (1875–1902) its political and spiritual character: Antonio Cánovas del Castillo. He was murdered in 1897 for the tough trial regarding the assassination in Barcelona. Cánovas[3] was the representative of the liberal-conservative line, which was so passionately combatted by the intransigents. This was in agreement with the constitution of 1876, which recognized the basic laws and consequently endeavored to include the Liberals. In reference to religion, the constitution contained a compromise between the Catholic state religion and the freedom of religion, but in spite of this and despite the significant ecclesiastical rights regarding education, Pius IX and the Spanish clergy rejected it.[4] The governments between 1875

[1] Schmidlin, *PG* II, 442; only the pilgrimages from Toledo and Saragossa took place.
[2] R. Konezke, *Europäische Geschichte,* 512. Concerning the failure of the Spanish hierarchy and the greater part of the clergy in the social question, see J. N. Moody, *Church and Society* (New York 1953), 721–807. The words of a Catalan poet are characteristic for the attitude of sympathetic intellectuals: "The bomb and blasphemy are the same thing, a destructive expression of rage in the face of the inability to be creative. The angel who wanted to be like God but could not slandered God; whoever hates society and doesn't feel strong enough to change it throws a bomb in the middle of the market place" (J. Vicens Vives, *Cataluña en el Siglo XIX* [1961], 436; F. Soldevila, *Historia de España* VIII [1959], 349, quoted according to R. Konetzke, op. cit., 512).
[3] R. Konetzke gives an impressive portrait, op. cit., 505. Cánovas intended a creative restoration which was to lead Spain out of this *circulus vitiosus* of anticlerical liberalism and reaction to it. He wanted to continue the development of the nation, which he considered the work of divine providence.
[4] ARTICLE 11 of the constitution says: "The Roman Catholic religion is a state religion. The nation is obligated to support the worship and its servants. Nobody on Spanish soil

and 1902 were alternately formed by Cánovas's party and by the monarchal Liberals under the leadership of Sagasta. The censorship of books was either introduced or abolished, depending on the government. But both parties had their political base in the Bourbon monarchy and in the representative constitution.

A serious conflict between Church and state arose in 1899 when, in violation of the law of 1880, numerous members of the orders and congregations from France had immigrated to Spain because of persecution. The question of civil inscription of orders, which were not licensed as was required by the laws of 1867, was solved in 1901 through the conciliatory stance of Secretary of State Rampolla and the Spanish nuncio. The vitality of the Church in Spain during Leo XIII's pontificate was demonstrated by the exceedingly strong development of the female congregations.

The chief theme of Church history during this period in Spain involved the political differences within Catholicism itself. In January 1882, Rampolla occupied the nunciature in Spain, and on 8 December, Leo XIII, in an encyclical, implored the politically divided Spanish Catholics to make religious peace, and requested that they develop Catholic organizations under the direction of the bishops, as was done in other countries. But in 1884 and 1885, Rampolla was exposed to vicious attacks in the press by Nocedal, who could be called a Spanish Veuillot. A minister of the Cánovas government had given a speech in Parliament about the temporal sovereignty of the Pope, which complicated relations with the Italian government and upset the Vatican. In this context Nocedal wrote that the nuncio evaluated the circumstances in Spain regarding ecclesiastical conditions much too optimistically instead of fighting the entire system of Cánovas, including the constitution of 1876. The controversy became a matter of principle when Nocedal characterized the function of the nuncio as a purely diplomatic one, which required his subordination to the episcopate in questions pertaining to the domestic affairs of the Spanish Church. Bishop Casas of Plasencia had written a strongly worded pastoral letter. In a note of April 1885 to Nuncio Rampolla, Secretary of State Jacobini termed Nocedal's ideas Febronianism and declared, in reference to the constitution *Pastor aeternus,* that the Pope had the right to interfere at any time in the affairs of the bishoprics, even through the nuncios whose competence he alone determined.[5] In the case of Bishop Casas, Ram-

---

will be molested because of his religious belief or his corresponding form of worship, provided the Christian morals are being respected. However, no other public ceremonies nor demonstrations other than those of the state religion are allowed."

[5] *ASS* XVII, 561ff. "Is it true that the Pope delegates to his legate only purely diplomatic missions without any authority over the shepherds and faithful of those states to

polla also received the desired letter from Jacobini, in which the bishop was reprimanded for disturbing the internal peace of the Church.

Around this time, it was Leo XIII's general intent to prevent the formation of exclusively Catholic parties. He became increasingly reserved toward the *Unión Católica,* led by Alejandro Pidal, which he had still recommended in 1881, because he wanted to be considerate of the Carlists whom Pidal had failed to win for his union. In their press, the Carlists waged a venomous war against the *Unión Católica* because they did not regard it as sufficiently Catholic, since it recognized the Bourbon Kingdom.[6] The Pope's support of the *Unión Católica* could have only increased the tensions in Spanish Catholicism. Leo XIII brought his authority with the Spanish episcopate to bear in order to prevent the Carlists from acting up after the death of Alphonso XII (26 November 1885) and to assure the reign of the widowed Queen María Cristina.[7] In March 1887, a minister spoke in Parliament about the great respect of the Spanish people for Leo XIII, who had secured the peace between Church and state.

The Pope concentrated his special attention on the internal renovation of the Church, especially on the improvement of clerical education, which was to be handled by the following metropolitan seminaries: Toledo, Tarragona, Seville, Valencia, Granada, Burgos, Valladolid, Santiago de Compostela, Saragossa. The Jesuit seminary in Salamanca was authorized to award doctorates. The University of Comillas (near Santander) was established in 1890 as a papal institute and gained influence in Latin America.[8] In 1892, the "Spanish College" was opened in Rome.

After Rampolla's appointment as secretary of state (1887), the conflicts within Spanish Catholicism increased considerably. In 1889, the Pope had reason to write to the bishop of Madrid, the cardinal of Saragossa, and the bishop of Urgel; and he urged the *Revista popular* to end its polemics. The great pilgrimage to Rome in 1894 was tarnished by the previous Carlist disturbances in Seville, which caused vehement

---

which they are assigned? Should we admit that the Holy Father delegates his nuncios in the same manner ministers and representatives of the state are delegated by their government? Rather, the appropriate directives and official orders show that the apostolic nuncios have not only a diplomatic mission, but also an authoritative mission regarding the faithful and ecclesiastical affairs" (U. Stutz, op. cit., 56; Schmidlin, *PG* II, 443).

[6] R. Konetzke, op. cit., 506; cf. Schmidlin, *PG* II, 442, n. 6.

[7] The Pope sent her the "Golden Rose" and became the godfather of Alphonso, born 10 May 1886 (later Alphonso XIII). Rampolla performed the baptism (Schmidlin, *PG* II, 443f.).

[8] The theological revival becomes apparent around the turn of the century in the establishment of publications: 1899: *Ciudad de Dios,* 1901: *Razón y Fé,* 1907: *Estudios franciscanos,* 1910: *Ciencia tomista.*

discussions in the press and in Parliament. In spite of the intransigent ecclesiastical attitude of the Carlists, the Pope refrained from taking sides and asked the Spanish pilgrims to accept the constitution of 1876 and to devote themselves to religious and cultural tasks.[9]

There was no lack of the kind of tasks the Pope had spoken of. In 1887, 81.16 percent of the Spanish population was illiterate. (1900: 71.43 percent). The negligence of the state and the communities was not compensated for by the efforts of the Church. The initiative emanated from the liberal philosopher of law Francisco Giner de los Ríos of Madrid (1839–1915), who rejected any kind of political agitation. But his *Institución Libre de Enseñanza* (since 1876) had developed a small but tremendously effective school complex, in which the liberal intelligentsia was nurtured.[10] The outstanding representative of ecclesiastical Catholicism at that time was a professor of literary history in Madrid, Marcelino Menéndez y Pelayo (1856–1912). In rediscovering the *Siglo de Oro,* he wanted to overcome the contemporary controversies within Catholicism, which were paralyzed with clichés, and he intended to resurrect the great traditions of Spain. In his speech commemorating Calderon, he recalled the great ideals of Spanish history: the Catholic faith, the Spanish monarchy, the Latin race, and Iberian liberty.[11] In his *Historia de los heterodoxos españoles* (1881), he wanted to present a sharp critique of all the spiritual phenomena which endangered Spain's tradition. He refrained from actual disputations because he relied on a creative restoration which would speak for itself. In his later work, *Historia de las ideas estéticas,* he attempted a Christian interpretation of Hegel.

The defeat of Spain in the war with the United States in 1898[12] meant the political and intellectual end of the restoration period which was passionately criticized by the "generation of 98." But a figure like

---

[9] Schmidlin, *PG* II, 444f.

[10] R. Konetzke, op. cit., 514, with biblio. (p. 526). Combining a high school with an elementary preparatory school, vocational training (towards a vocational school), and excursions shows the influence of Friedrich Fröbel's pedagogy. Such schools were also founded in other Spanish cities.

[11] *La conciencia española* (Madrid 1948), 9f.; *Obras completas,* 65 vols. (Madrid 1941–62); J. F. Pastór, op. cit., 41–45.

[12] Cuba's War of Independence had already begun in 1868 and was interrupted in 1878 by concessions to the Liberals. The conflicts increased because the conservative landed proprietors hesitated to realize the concessions and the Liberals began demanding absolute autonomy. The rebels operated from the United States, which intervened on 24 January 1898 (claiming an obligation to protect its citizens in Cuba). President McKinley wanted to avoid war, but the Congress insisted. After war had broken out, Archbishop Ireland established contact with the president by order of the Pope, but his attempts were in vain (Schmidlin, *PG* II, 445). The destruction of the Spanish fleet occurred in July.

Miguel de Unamuno (1864–1936) makes clear the complexity of the new spiritual development then breaking through which cannot be imagined without Spanish Catholicism.[13] However, the fanatical integralism of the *Siglo futuro* continued to live, and Cardinal Sancha y Hervas of Toledo was accused of liberalism because of his counsel urging internal peace. Consequently, he had to ask for the Pope's protection, who, on 22 August, clearly reprimanded those people who wanted to determine autocratically who was Catholic and who was not. Leo XIII witnessed the enthronement of sixteen-year-old King Alphonso XIII on 17 May 1902 and he had reasons to worry about Spain's future. During Pius X's pontificate, the internal controversies within Catholicism continued. The Jesuits had supported the integralistic line of Nocedal until Leo XIII intervened through the general of the order. But when the Jesuits, in their publication *Razón y Fé* (since 1901), endorsed some sort of probabilism in the election of the deputies, they were defended by the Pope against the intransigent Conservatives.

It was not surprising that the encyclical *Rerum novarum* (1891) encountered little interest in Spain. The *Círculos Católicos Obreros,* which copied the institutions founded by Albert de Mun in France and were promoted after 1876 by Bishop Ceferino Gonzáles of Córdoba, developed very slowly. Another single-handed effort was made by Antonio Vicent, S.J. At the Church Congress of Tarragona in 1894, the encyclical was on the agenda, among other things; and in 1895, the *Consejo Nacional de las Corporaciones Obrero-Católicas,* the central organization of the worker societies was formed. Its lack of efficiency has to be judged in view of the fact that the interest for social problems was rather slim in all parties down to the leftist Liberals; the strongest interest existed in Cánovas's party. Around 1900, only about 30 percent of the population belonged to the industrial complex of the Spanish economy.[14] But it was especially devastating that the agrarian production did not correspond to the increase of the population, which was negligible compared to other countries. The ruling class knew, without admitting it, that the anarchistic assassinations were by no means singular incidents. This is proven by the fact that there was hesitation in publishing the result of an investigation by the workers in 1884.[15] This made it even more neces-

---

[13] F. Niedermayer, "Two Spains?", *Saeculum* 3 (1952), 444–76; also: H. Jeschke, see bibliography.

[14] In the Basque provinces, iron ore was mined and mostly exported, but it was also smelted, using coal from England and later from Asturias, and it became the basis for a shipbuilding industry. A strong textile industry developed in Catalonia (R. Konetzke, op. cit., 508).

[15] J. M. Jóvez, *Conciencia obrera y conciencia burguesa en la España contemporánea* (Madrid 1952).

sary for the Church to get involved. But, to Leo XIII's sorrow the interests of the Church were almost completely absorbed by the differences within the ruling ranks. The de-Christianization in the middle class, increasing since the sixties, began to extend into the industrial world. The bombing attack during the Corpus Christi procession in Barcelona in 1896 had only been a prologue. The great crises of the twentieth century drew closer.[16] In the left wing of the dividing parties appeared the group of Alejandro Levroux, who, in the name of the Republic, proclaimed the now fashionable version of *"Écrasez l'infâme!"* and incited his *jóvenes bárbaros* to act.[17] Thirteen years after the strike against the Corpus Christi procession, the masses of workers of Barcelona burnt seventeen churches, twenty-three monasteries, sixteen parochial schools, and four asylums. They brutally shot monks and nuns who tried to flee through a city blocked with street barricades and desecrated their bodies.[18] The uprising of July 1909, following a general strike, was suppressed by the military forces dispatched from Valencia and Madrid. The repeated call for a dictatorship became louder and louder.

In the years following 1902, ecclesiastical policies of the alternately conservative or left-liberal governments were concerned with the question of admitting or limiting the religious communities, a question which was intensified by the return of Spanish missionaries from Cuba and the Philippines. The overthrow of the liberal government made possible the Convention of 1908, which was followed by the creation of a Vatican-Spanish commission, under the chairmanship of the archbishop of Toledo, empowered to investigate the monastery and school question. The conflict came to a head again when J. Canalejas (murdered in 1912) prohibited the founding of religious orders for the next two years, abolished the religious vow in December 1910, limited religious instruction in public schools, and recalled the ambassador to the Vatican. During the Eucharistic Congress in Madrid in 1911, King Alphonso XIII consecrated the Spanish people to the Sacred Heart. By this act and by its festive repetition in 1919, he won the Carlists for the Bourbon monarchy. The *Asociación Católica de propagandistas,* founded in 1909 by the young Jesuit Ángel Ayala, gained great significance during the time between the two world wars.

---

[16] E. Comín Colomer, *Historia del anarquismo español,* 2 vols. (Madrid 1956).
[17] "The barbaric youth of today plunder and murder the decadent and miserable civilization of this country, they destroy its temples, they put an end to its gods . . . . There is nothing sacred on this earth. The people are slaves of the Church. The Church should be destroyed." (R. Konetzke, op. cit., 528)
[18] R. Konetzke, op. cit., 529.

Portugal

The often noted parallel between Spain's and Portugal's development continued into the last third of the nineteenth century, but in the beginning of the twentieth century remarkable differences developed. The agreement of 1848 between state and Church could essentially be preserved and was hardly impaired by the alternation of the two monarchal parties heading the government of the apolitical King Luis I (1861–89); the conservative *Regeneradores* and the *Progresistas*. The economic difficulties of the sixties under the conservative ministry of Antonio María de Fontes (1871–77) were turned into a brilliant recovery. The exhaustive negotiations between the Vatican and Lisbon under the liberal government of Braacamp (1879–81) resulted in a new circumscription of the dioceses through the papal constitution of 30 September 1881: the seventeen dioceses were reduced to three archbishoprics (Lisbon, Evora, and Braga) with nine suffragans. At the end of another conservative government came the new convention of 7 August 1886 regarding the rights of royal patronage in the Indian missions.[19] At the University of Coimbra, having been anticlerical since Pombal, the theology faculty renounced Church supervision in 1885, solidly supported by the other faculties.

In the last decade of the century, Portugal's crisis began in spite of the political wisdom of King Carlos I, who refrained from visiting King Umberto I in 1895 because, as Rampolla had indicated, it would be against the Pope's wishes.[20] The crisis was partly due to public debts (bank crisis) and partly to the erosion of the two-party system and the resulting power of the radical forces. The liberal-conservative ministry of Hintze Ribeiro decreed in 1901 that the clerical societies be limited to those which were devoted to teaching, charity, and mission in the colonies. Leo XIII had opened a Portuguese College in Rome in 1900. In a brief of Easter 1902 addressed to Cardinal Neto of Lisbon, he praised the episcopate for having sent an address to the King concerning the religious orders' legislation. Carlos I and the Crown Prince fell victim to an assassination on 1 February 1908. This was the actual end of the Portuguese representative system. In the land of Marquis de Pombal, all radical forces had gathered around the Republican party, founded in 1876. Its partners were the Freemason lodge *Gran Oriente Lusitano Unido* (formed from scattered groups in 1869) and the violent *Carboneria*. While revolutionary groups were organizing in the underground, willing to lay their lives on the line, Portuguese Catholicism had spiritually collapsed despite its membership in the rural areas. Shortly

[19] Schmidlin, *PG* II, 447; cf. part III.
[20] Schmidlin, *PG* II, 448.

before the revolution, one deputy in the House of Representatives declared: "On the one hand, we have the Jesuits, the clergy and even the Parliament. On the other hand, we have the liberal people, and they have to employ all means available."[21]

The Republic, proclaimed on 5 October 1910, experienced terrorist acts against the churches and monasteries, robberies, arson, and murder (as it had during the Spanish uprising in 1909).

The minister of justice declared: "Within two generations, Portugal will have eliminated Catholicism totally."[22] The law of 20 April 1911, following the French model, carried out the separation of Church and state. The bishop of Oporto, Antonio Barroso, was arrested because of a pastoral letter; the archbishops of Lisbon and Braga, the bishops of Portalegre and Lamego were expelled. The constitution of 21 August 1911 limited the freedom of religion and suspended religious instruction.[23] On 24 May 1911 Pius X sharply condemned the separation law in an encyclical to the Portuguese episcopate. The regime favored compliant clergymen and excluded the young priests who had been educated in the Portuguese College in Rome. After the tensions in the Sidonio Paes government had eased somewhat, Pius X recommended to the Catholics the recognition of the Republic. In 1913, the papal nuncio was expelled. Portugal's long internal turbulence ended with the Conservatives' coup d'état in 1918, resulting in the dictatorship of General Carmona (resumption of diplomatic relations to the Vatican).

Latin America

The *Collegio Pio latino-americano,* founded in 1858 in Rome, was not very successful in changing the religious situation in Latin America. To be sure, the orders and congregations tried to strengthen their establishments with immigrants from Europe or with new foundations.[24] They wanted to ease the chronic and extreme lack of priests, which was a result of earlier negligence in training the native clergy and had been intensified drastically by the expulsion of the Jesuits and subsequent revolutionary occurrences, especially since the clergy was concentrated in the cities. The population of the South American continent increased

---

[21] J. Pabón, *La Revolución Portuguesa,* 2 vols. (Lisbon 1941, 1945), I, 82, quoted from R. Konetzke, op. cit., 356.

[22] J. Pabón, op. cit., 131; R. Konetzke, op. cit., 538.

[23] ARTICLE 4 decrees freedom of religion, but it places worship in general "under a special law" in the interest of public order, freedom, and security of the citizens." ARTICLE 10: "Education offered in public and private institutions under state supervision is to be neutral in regard to religion."

[24] Cf. biblio., chap. 17.

from 20 million in 1825 to 65.7 million in 1900. But a religious revitalization could only be expected if the ecclesiastical forces within the Latin American countries themselves were activated. With this insight and after amazingly thorough preparations, Leo XIII convened the Latin American Plenary Council, which met from 28 May until 9 July 1899 in Rome and organized twenty-nine general congregations and nine solemn sessions.[25] Within several years, a comprehensive report of more than one thousand articles had been worked out. It was sent to the Latin American episcopate for comments, which, in turn, were examined by the consultants in Rome. The strongest influence came from the Catalan Capuchin Vives y Tutó (1854–1913), who had endorsed a staunch antiliberalist line in the Curia (since 1884) and was promoted cardinal in 1899.[26] Twelve archbishops and forty-one bishops of the one hundred four Latin American hierarchies came to Rome, which seemed to be the only feasible place for a meeting in view of the political situation (the majority of the prelates had voted for Rome). The welcoming address was given by Cardinal di Pietro. Mariano Soler,[27] since 1897 the first archbishop of Montevideo (the capital of Uruguay), paid tribute to the Holy Father. The chairmanship of the concluding session was given to Archbishop Tovar of Lima (the capital of Peru). The primate of Brazil gave the address in the audience with the Pope on 10 July after the conclusion of the Council. The constitutions of the Council, which included sixteen titles with 998 decrees, were sanctioned by Leo XIII on 1 January 1900. The Council's resolutions dealt with: bishops' conferences and provincial as well as diocesan synods, the canonical conduct of the often undisciplined clergy, the regionally varied pastoral work (especially in reference to the young), the charitable institutions, the dangers to the faith which secular books and newspapers, neutral schools, and the Freemasons represented, and with positivism (which had gained significance in Latin America). The Council also ruled on the principles of relations between Church and state, whereby the full authority of the nuncios in reference to the country's episcopate was emphasized, on the temporal rights of the Church regarding property, and on the claim for ecclesiastical jurisdiction. All these issues had long been the object of public debate in the Latin American states. The decrees were preceded by the consecration to the Sacred Heart and to the Immaculate Conception.

Toward the end of Leo XIII's pontificate, the Plenary Council had without doubt touched upon the main ecclesiastical problems in the

---

[25] Schmidlin, *PG* II, 449f.; see the Council's files above.
[26] His immense knowledge was book knowledge. Concerning his role under Pius X, see p. 390; concerning his contribution to the encyclical *Pascendi,* see chap. 33, n. 15.
[27] J. M. Vidal, *El primer arzobispo de Montevideo,* 2 vols. (Montevideo 1935).

Latin American countries. But the structures of society were and continued to be so rigid that the social prerequisites for a fundamental religious renovation were absent, especially since the Christianization of the people had stagnated and the European enlightenment had seduced the intelligentsia. As history proves, it was only natural in such a situation that as a rule the Church had its alliance with the great landholders in the provinces representing the Federalists in contrast to the liberal Centralists in the urban centers. The masses, even the poor white population, remained passive until the end of the nineteenth century, and the Church was unable to activate them because they were either not willing or too weak. For a long time, there was no middle class. Until World War I, there was little social welfare.[28] Even if the Church had acted with less conformism after the secularizations, it would hardly have been in the position to effect a change of circumstances beyond its conventional Christian work of charity.[29] It made no difference in those times whether a regime which favored the Church was in power or not. Nor were the Liberals interested in social questions.

By 1880, Argentina, Chile, and Brazil were the leading Latin American countries, chiefly because of their economic growth,[30] but also thanks to a relationship between Church and state which was essentially peaceful, in spite of repeated tensions. The Argentinian constitution of 1853 remained in force until 1920. It declared the Catholic Church to be the state religion and provided financial compensations for secularizations. It did, however, tolerate other denominations. President Domingo Sarmiento (1868–74), who was greatly interested in improving the backward educational system,[31] opened the country to European influences. After his overthrow and emigration to Chile, the political anticlericalism of the Liberals was strengthened by a minor, but intellectual group.[32] Nevertheless, Leo XIII was able to establish, with the approval of the government, the bishoprics in La Plata, Santa Fé, and Tucumán. Argentina's situation was strongly determined by immigrants: in 1869, 1.8 million inhabitants were counted; from 1874 to 1880, approximately 45,000 people, from 1880 to 1886 approximately

---

[28] E. Samhabera, op. cit. (1949), 93: "There existed a state, but it was a feudal state, ruled by an aristocratic society which had to fulfill certain tasks, but which strictly maintained its position."

[29] Cf. J. N. Moody, *Church and Society* (New York 1953), 750–807.

[30] Argentina was able to increase its cattle and wheat export in the last third of the century; Chile secured for itself through belligerent means the world monopoly for saltpeter. Brazil, whose population had grown more than the average, was expanding its coffee production continuously.

[31] For a long time, the University of Buenos Aires, founded in 1821, suffered from a lack of students.

[32] C. Bruno, *El derecho público de la iglesia en la Argentina,* 2 vols. (Buenos Aires 1956).

70,000 people came into the country annually, mostly Italians and Spaniards. At times, in the following period of speculation, 300,000 people immigrated per year. It was difficult to organize proper pastoral work, and the increase of bishoprics (under Pius X three additional ones) was actually a facade. In 1910, a Catholic University was established in Buenos Aires. In the same year, the liberal lawyer and politician Joaquín V. González, founder of the University of La Plata, wrote his book *El Juicio del Siglo,* in which he analyzed the path the country took from the culture of the Spanish aristocracy via barbarism down to the "return": it emphasized the continuity of *hispanidad,* transcending anticlericalism.[33]

The ecclesiastical situation in Chile resembled the one in Argentina because it had a similar constitution (1865). Basically tolerant of other religions, Catholicism was still the official religion, even for the regalists, whose belief in regard to the state church law was rooted in the tradition of the patronate's law. During the pontificates of Leo XIII and Pius X, the Chilean ecclesiastical situation was characterized by the fact that the masonic anticlericalism of the Radical-Liberals eased up considerably. An example of such curious alliances is the purely political one of 1890 between the strictly Church-oriented Conservatives and the Radicals. It was aimed at the Liberal José Balmaceda, who was rather authoritarian as president and lost the belligerent conflict in Parliament.

The establishment of the Republic in Brazil by the Radical-Liberals came about peacefully. This can be partly credited to the Pope's diplomacy; he was, however, totally ill-disposed toward Emperor Pedro II (1831–88) and his tolerance of non-Catholic sects.[34] The Pope recognized the Republic and diplomatic relations were resumed. The constitution of 1891 guaranteed the Church freedom and property, but, following the separation law, all financial aid was disallowed. The Brazilian Church now had to rely on its own resources (like the Church in the United States), and it had to centralize the revenues and donations of its diocesan treasuries. Of greatest concern, however, was the augmentation of the clergy, whose number (in 1872 not quite one thousand priests) was especially depressing compared to the rapid growth of the population under Pedro II because of heavy immigration (from approx-

---

[33] Cf. quotation in W. v. Schoen, op. cit., 570.

[34] Catholic Church historiography considered Pedro II an "enemy of the Church" (Schmidlin, *PG* II, 453). The main reason is his action against the two bishops whose attitude toward the directives of Pius IX regarding the question of the Freemasons was just as correct as that of the King toward the constitution. Pedro II, who granted amnesty to the two bishops in the following year, was not a politician, but an important person, and his relation to the Church is hardly any different from that of Joseph II (cf. W. v. Schoen, op. cit., 359f.).

imately 6 to 14 million). The Church was also interested in raising the standards of religious education, which had suffered greatly in the era of rationalism. The Pope favored the settlements of European orders in Brazil, such as those of the Premonstratensians of Averbode in São Paulo and the Benedictines of Maredsous, who strove to renovate the Brazilian congregation of Olinda. In 1894 and 1895, G. van Caloen made visitations, the results of which were discussed in Beuron's mother house in Maredsous. Leo XIII employed his authority to this end *(est mea voluntas)*.[35] In 1899, the Pope appointed van Caloen vicar general to the Brazilian Archabbot Machado[36] with the right of succession for life. From 1892 until 1902, Leo XIII established eight new bishoprics in Brazil. In 1905, Pius X appointed the archbishop of Rio de Janeiro, Arcoverda Cavalcanti, cardinal, the first one in Latin America. The successful foreign minister, Baron Rio Branco, made sure that this honor was recompensed properly. The Republic, again and again shaken by disturbances, sent the Pope a de luxe edition bound in pure gold, with the Pope's signature laid out in precious stones and his portrait framed by ninety diamonds.[37]

Bolivia was weakened by frequent military revolts and the loss of its coastal province of Atacama to Chile. Only after World War I did it recoup on account of its tin production. Even in the last third of the nineteenth century, the ecclesiastical situation remained unchanged and the Franciscans continued their missionary work among a population which consisted mainly of Indians and half-castes.[38] Though freedom of religion existed in principle, the Catholic Church was the only one supported by the state. Coupled with this support, however, was a large amount of interference, against which the Pope protested in 1906. In Peru, where a papal delegate was allowed to reside in Lima (also responsible for Bolivia and Ecuador), conditions similar to Bolivia prevailed until the turn of the century, when the situation was clouded by the introduction of civil marriage (1898). But in 1899, an agreement with the government concerning three apostolic prefectures was signed. Serious domestic controversies ended under the dictatorship of A. Leguía (1908–12; 1919–30). In 1913, a provincial council met in Lima in order to deal with the devastating shortage of priests.

It is interesting to compare ecclesiastical development in Colombia and Venezuela with that in Ecuador and Guatemala. Colombia was the first Latin American country which instituted a radical separation of Church

---

[35] P. Weißenberger, *Das benediktinische Mönchtum im 19. u. 20. Jahrhundert* (Beuron 1959), 59; cf. chap. 17.

[36] M. E. Scherer, "Domingos Machado—der Restaurator," *SM* 74 (1964), 7–162.

[37] Described extensively in Schmidlin. *PG* III, 92.

[38] L. Lemmens, *Geschichte der Franziskanermissionen* (Munich 1929), 316ff.

and state (1853). Since the presidency of R. Núñez (1880), relations with the Church were exceedingly friendly, and, in 1885, diplomatic relations with the Vatican were resumed (General Vélez as ambassador). After the constitution of 1887/88, amended in 1892, the Catholic Church became the official religion and enjoyed independence. Compromises were agreed upon in controversial questions, such as the clergy's civil jurisdiction and the Church's competence in regard to cemeteries. The separation law of 1853, however, was not suspended. In the years from 1880 until 1900, Leo XIII established six new dioceses. Between 1899 and 1902, the country was once again shaken by a violent civil war, resulting in the secession of Panama, supported by the United States, from Colombia. E. Moreno y Díaz played a mediating role between the state and the Church. In 1888 he had come to Colombia from the Philippines as provincial of the Augustinian hermits. From 1895 until 1906, he was bishop of Pasto.[39] After 1904, General Rafael Reyes ruled rather dictatorially. But he is fondly remembered because he removed the consequences of civil war. He demonstrated his good relations to the Catholic Church by constructing a building for the nunciature in Bogotá (1908), where a Eucharistic Congress took place in 1913 under Archbishop Herrera Restrepo.

Venezuela also experienced the evolution of religious toleration after the regime of Guzmán, who was hostile toward the Church and had expelled Archbishop Guevara from the country in 1870. The activities of the religious orders flourished under his reign; not, however, under the dictatorship of Cipriano (1899–1908), at least not in respect to foreign relations. The seminary which was planned at a bishops' conference in Caracas (1904), was opened in 1913.

The relationship between Church and state fluctuated in Ecuador[40] and Guatemala. Even after the murder of Ecuador's President García Moreno (1875), whose work created what was called a "model Christian state,"[41] the Church continued to be favored under the more or less conservative governments. In 1881, the Concordat of 1862 was revised and Roman Catholicism in its capacity as the state religion was given extraordinary rights, as in regard to the supervision of schools. An additional agreement in 1890 alotted 3 percent of the state's property to the episcopate. In return, Leo XIII promised to use his influence on the bishops during the elections; this was generally the quid pro quo in Latin America, and it was particularly difficult because the appointment

---

[39] T. Minguella y Arnedo, *Biographie* (Barcelona 1909).

[40] J. I. Larrea, *La Iglesia y el Estado en el Ecuador* (Seville 1954).

[41] Schmidlin, *PG* II, 451; the effects of the Church situation at that time on the relations between Ecuador and the then anticlerical Colombia are remarkable (W. v. Schoen, op. cit., 456).

of priests was often under the direction of the ruling classes. However, the radical-liberal revolution of 1895, under the government of the otherwise moderate General Eloy Alfaro, produced severe measures against the previously favored Church, confiscating properties and expelling religious orders. After the enactment of civil marriage in 1902, the separation of Church and state was declared official (1904).

The development in the Central American republic of Guatemala proceeded more quickly. Following the presidency of Carrera and Cerna, who were amicable toward the Church and dominated by the Conservatives of the white minority, the Liberals introduced a lay regime with the new constitution of 1879. With prophetic pathos, Archbishop Casanova y Estrada excommunicated President Justo Rufino Barrios, who had confiscated ecclesiastical estates, expelled the Jesuits, forbidden clerical dress in public, and mobilized the Indians and half-castes constituting the great majority of the population.[42] He was exiled in 1887. The subsequent presidents essentially followed the same line. Dictator Estrada Cabrera (1899–1919) built a "Minerva Temple" for state celebrations.

Probably the most extreme changes in the relations between Church and state took place in Mexico. After the failure of the politically respectable program of pure-blooded Indian Benito Juárez[43] the lay laws regarding the separation of Church and state, constitutionally validated by his successor, remained in force. But this separation had rather advantageous effects during the economically successful dictatorship of Porfirio Díaz (1877–81, 1884–1911). The wife of Díaz, Carmelita, who was friendly toward the Church, played an important role. The members of the orders and congregations were allowed to return more or less legally, and in the period between 1880 and 1902 Leo XIII established the bishoprics of Oaxaca, Monterrey, and Durango, as well as eleven bishoprics. It was in accord with the Indian tradition that Leo XIII decreed the consecration of the shrine of Nuestra Señora de Guadalupe in 1886, whose veneration (the name was taken after a Spanish shrine) was never disturbed by political disorders after 1531.[44] In 1896, a provincial council took place. According to the European model, Catholic Congresses were organized in Puebla (1903), Mérida

---

[42] "The so-called Justo Rufino Barrios was expelled from our blessed community. I forbid him from henceforth bearing the name of one of our Roman martyrs. We warn the faithful of any communication with the so-called Justo Rufino Barrios, who was deprived of God's mercy" (W. v. Schoen, op. cit., 419)

[43] R. Roeder, *Juárez and His Mexico*, 2 vols (New York 1947).

[44] In 1894, the office was expanded; in 1910, she became the patroness of all Latin America; R. V. Ugarte, *Historia del Culto de María en Ibero-América* I (Madrid ³1956), 190–207.

(1904), Guadalajara (1906), and Oaxaca (1909). Especially remarkable is the Catholic Congress of Tulancingo (1904), during which the social problems of Mexican agriculture were discussed for the first time from a religious perspective. At the Congress of Zamora (Mexico) of 1913, the program of the *Confederación Nacional de los Círculos Católicos Obreros* was developed, to which Father Alfredo Méndez Medina contributed a great deal. Some of the social principles may have had an influence on the constitution of 1917 which arose from revolutionary chaos. However, ARTICLE 3 contained resolutions regarding the radical laicization of education and ART. 27 the nationalization of Church property.

There are many reasons for the failure of the religious regeneration of Latin America during this period. Without a doubt, the ecclesiastical forces concentrated too much on the relations between Church and state and on the hope of finding protection from the conservative governments, which, when given, was often rather questionable. Unfortunately, it is just as certain that the native clergy was qualitatively and quantitatively too weak, and that help from Europe not only came too late but brought ideas which did not match the Latin American circumstances. It was said that the wives of the politicians of all colors did go to church and that an open belligerence toward religion did not exist until the twentieth century.[45] One may add that Latin American Catholicism is so basic a phenomenon that it is evident even in the non-Christian literature, not to mention the Chilean poet Gabriele Mistral (Lucila Godoy Alcayaga). But this traditional Catholicism was exposed to consistent erosion after the middle of the nineteenth century due to the philosophy of Auguste Comte. Around 1880, positivism was the acknowledged faith of nearly the entire intellectual elite and of a large part of the liberal politicians (though with a different interpretation); it prevailed far beyond the turn of the century. Whoever lifted himself into the educated classes, which expanded considerably in the decades after 1880, would generally go the same route. The revolutions at the beginning of the nineteenth century had been a great disappointment, especially to Simón Bolívar. Now, it was hoped, the breakthrough would proceed past traditional Catholicism and succeed with the help of education.

[45] E. Samhaber, op. cit. (1949), 92; similarly in A. Bellesheim, *AkathKR* 81 (1901), 38: "The unifying factor in this multitude of peoples and states is the higher interests of the Catholic religion, which has remained the faith of the overwhelming majority of the South American states to this day in spite of the destructive efforts of the Freemasons and Liberalism."

CHAPTER 9

Catholic Self-Awareness in the British Empire

England and Scotland

In 1912 England had 1.79 million Catholics and Scotland .54 million, totalling 2.33 million within a population of 40.8 million (not counting Ireland). Around 1878, approximately .35 million Catholics lived in Scotland. Ireland aside (80 percent Catholic including Ulster), the Catholics were a small minority, which was concentrated for a long time in certain areas: in England, in Lancashire, London, and the Midlands; in Scotland, mainly in the vicinity of Glasgow and Edinburgh. After England had been granted an official hierarchy in 1850, Leo XIII, as one of the first acts of his pontificate (4 March 1878), established in Saint Andrews-Edinburgh the Scottish metropolitan see with four suffragans and in Glasgow an archbishopric which was directly responsible to Rome. This division was implemented with consideration for the significance of Irish immigration relative to the English Catholics, who were frequently of Irish descent. This explains why most Catholics were poor. To be sure, there were a large number of wealthy Catholics in England, which increased as a result of the conversion movement, but there was only a small representation in the middle class.

It is due in part to these sociological conditions that growing Catholicism was imprinted with the political genius of Henry Edward Manning rather than with the spirit of John Henry Newman. Manning (born in 1808), was the son of an entrepreneur, an English patriot who was shocked by Newman's conversion in 1845, and a friend of Gladstone, who also could not understand Manning's conversion in 1875.[1] The archbishop of Westminster (1865) was elevated to cardinal in 1875. That Manning was able to smoothly combine his English patriotism with his activism on behalf of Pius IX is, on the one hand, based on the religious tolerance of the Victorian period; on the other hand, it rested on Manning's social involvement which he considered a Christian as well as a national matter. This was facilitated by the fact that in Great Britain only a fool could have conceived of the idea of instituting a Catholic social movement. It was quite natural that Manning appeared as the speaker at the anniversary celebration of the British and Foreign Anti-Slavery Association in 1884 and that he was a member of the "royal commission for securing better housing for the poor." His main concern was not Catholicism as such, but social problems which were

---

[1] Gladstone to Wilberforce on 11 April 1851.

becoming increasingly urgent and had major political relevance in view of the election reforms. Manning, not withstanding his religious motivation, was interested in the matter itself, which can be said of only relatively few Catholics. By no means did he prefer political action to social action;[2] in fact, he refused to combine secular politics with ecclesiastical politics. For Manning, as for his friend William E. Gladstone (1809–98), the great leader of the Liberals, Irish home rule was a matter of both fairness and political prudence. To sacrifice it for the sake of the papal diplomacy of the eighties[3] was just as unthinkable to Manning as the idea of developing the overtures, exchanged during the fiftieth jubilee of Queen Victoria (1887), into diplomatic relations as envisioned by the conservative English Catholics. He had no confidence in missionary work conducted from above. "So far, the world has been ruled by the dynasties. Now it is time for the Holy See to negotiate with the peoples."[4]

In close cooperation with Leo XIII, Cardinal Manning resolved the difficulties which regularly occurred in the process of transition from the ecclesiastical structure under the Propaganda Fide to that of an official hierarchy. There were especially tensions between the episcopate and the Benedictine monks as well as the Jesuits, whom Manning disliked. In the constitution of 8 May 1881, pastoral work and the administration of Church property were reserved exclusively to the episcopate. The new Scottish hierarchy organized a plenary council in August 1886. Manning's concept of the spirituality of the secular priesthood,[5] whose activities he protected against the criticism of the religious orders, must be seen in this. Neither theological speculation, one of the elements of tension between him and Newman, nor the isolated priesthood was of interest to Manning. "The clergy are in danger of becoming mere Mass priests and hucksters of sacraments."[6] What he wanted was a simple profile of Catholic basic principles, which were not to be concealed by secondary issues; no useless disputations, but expansive directives for action.

As everywhere else, the educational system was an important issue.

---

[2] Schmidlin, *PG* II, 488.

[3] Leo XIII's letters to the archbishop of Dublin, Eduard McCabe, of 3 January 1881 (*Acta Leonis* II, 187–90), to the Irish episcopate of 1 August 1882 (*Acta Leonis* II, 129–33), to Cardinal McCabe of 1 January 1883 (*Acta Leonis* III, 187–91), to the Irish episcopate of 24 June 1888 (*Acta Leonis* VIII, 249–53).

[4] Quoted from K. Buchheim (biblio., chap. 12), 332.

[5] Manning, *The Eternal Priesthood* (London 1884); also P. Pourrat, *La spiritualité chrétienne* IV (Paris ⁶1951), 579ff.

[6] Trapp (*Vorgeschichte und Ursprung der liturgischen Bewegung* [Regensburg 1940]) quotes from the biography of Purcell, p. 360.

The liberal religious policies of Gladstone, who even in his later years adhered to his Christian persuasion,[7] contained an ambivalent aspect for Catholicism in Great Britain. On the one hand, it was to its advantage that the Anglican Church, which dominated the school system and received public funds for it, began to lose its preeminence. On the other hand, the education law of 1870, which required that public non-denominational schools were to be financed by the state, resulted in the "provided schools" of the state dominating the field (general compulsory education was not introduced until 1880). The parochial private schools decreased, except for the Catholic ones, which dominated in Saint Leonard's on the Sea (Sussex), among other places. There, they were cared for by the Sisters of the Child Jesus, whose society had been organized by Cornelia Connelly[8] upon Nicholas Wiseman's suggestion. But it was not until 1902 that the Catholic schools received state funds (if they followed the general school curriculum).

In Great Britain, there were at least two different ways of dealing with the status of a minority; in fact, there were two sociologically different philosophies of Catholicism facing each other in the ecclesiastical world as it developed in the eighties and in the mentality of those who favored the attempts of an alliance with the Anglican Church (1895).

Wilfrid Ward wrote in his biography of Wiseman that the Catholics and Protestants had become "seemingly different races" in the period before 1829.[9] This is still true, when one considers the annual processions which loudly recited the Rosary as they proceeded from Newgate (East London) to Tyburn (West London), retracing the path which the English martyrs of the time of the Reformation (beatified by Leo XIII in 1886) were forced to march from prison to the place of their execution. Parliament permitted these processions, but for the people of London they were a version of the otherwise familiar nonconformism which belonged to a "different race." In 1887, clergyman Philip Fletcher and lawyer Lister Drummond,[10] two converts, founded The Guild of our Lady of Ransom and gave the society the prayer "Jesus, convert England!" At the procession's destination, the convent of the Sisters of Perpetual Adoration, Cardinal Vaughan founded an educational center for converts (1903). The Society Our Lady of Salvation declined around the turn of the century and was taken over by the Catholic Evidence Guild. The Catholic Truth Society, founded in 1884 by a

---

[7] P. Kluke, op. cit., 276.

[8] J. Bolten, *C. Connelly* (Munich 1928).

[9] W. Ward, *Life and Times of Cardinal Wiseman* I (London 1897), 438.

[10] With permission of Cardinal Vaughan he preached in Hyde Park and set an example.

converted layman, James Britten, was devoted to literary apologetics and, after 1887, set up stands in churches for pamphlets dealing with controversial religious questions, with English Church history, and also with the social question.

That was the kind of Catholicism in Great Britain which, with great sacrifice, supported the clergy[11] and its schools. It was the Catholicism of the lower classes, much more so than in the United States. This social climate was a determining factor in Cardinal Manning's activities. "The coming age will belong neither to the capitalists nor to the commercial classes, but to the people. The people are yielding to the guidance of reason, even to the guidance of religion. If we can gain their confidence, we can counsel them, if we show them a blind opposition, they will have power to destroy all that is good."[12] What is characteristic in this statement is that Manning was able to see the social problems of the industrial revolution as a universal problem. In 1880 he had already formed a theoretical foundation in *The Catholic Church and Modern Society.*[13] In this sober analysis, the son of an entrepreneur identified himself with the cause of the industrial worker. This, not esteem for the high priest of the papal Church, is the background for the popular story dealing with the arbitration of the dockworkers' strike which broke out in London on 13 August 1889.[14] In this instance, Manning fulfilled the "duties of citizens and patriots," whose rejection by the Catholics even after 1828 he called "a dereliction of duties in and of itself illegal."[15] The question of denominational or Christian unions was of little importance in Britain, since the trade unions were not oriented toward Marxism.[16]

[11] "To contribute to the support of our pastors" is one of the commandments of the English catechism.

[12] Letter to A. de Mun of 25 January 1891, in the new edition of *The Dignity and Rights of Labour and other Writings on the Social Questions* (London 1934), 68.

[13] His important contribution regarding the position of the industrial worker appeared in London in 1891; in the same year his comment on *Rerum novarum:* "Leo XIII on the condition of Labour." About Manning's contribution regarding the social theory of Catholicism see chap. 12, n. 58.

[14] Two hundred thousand dock workers were on strike because of their low wages after their moderate demands had been denied by the dock directors. Along with the lord mayor of London and the Anglican bishop, Manning was also a member of the arbitration commission, especially since there were numerous Catholics among the strikers. The compromise which had been negotiated one weekend did not materialize because of deadline difficulties regarding the obtainment of signatures. Consequently, the workers went on strike on Monday. Manning negotiated single-handedly with the strikers and was chosen as their arbitration representative. The strike was of importance because of the masses of unskilled laborers aroused there. John Burns, one of the leaders in the union of highly qualified workers (P. Kluke, op. cit., 287), cooperated well with Cardinal Manning during the arbitration procedures of the strike.

[15] According to E. Taylor, op. cit., 49.

[16] H. A. Clegg and others, *History of the British Trade Unions since 1889* I (London 1964).

The membership of Catholic workers was taken for granted. The Catholic Social Guild, founded in 1909 by H. Parkinson,[17] president of Oskott College, and by the Jesuit C. Plater, was devoted to the religious training of workers for the purpose of halting the spreading de-Christianization. Following the model of the *Katholischer Volksverein* in Germany, "penny-pamphlets" were to be distributed. The beginnings of the Catholic Social Guild were difficult. Five thousand members had been expected, but by 1912 there were only a thousand, though some were group memberships. After 1900 the National Conference of Catholic Trade-Unionists pursued similar goals.

The rest of organizational activity in Great Britain was rather limited, even though it extended over a multiplicity of social groups: 1910, The Catholic Medical Guild, with 200 members; 1911, The Catholic Stage Guild. The Catholic Young Men's Society of Great Britain had 22,000 members in 1912, including the Catholic Boy Scouts. The Catholic Women's League reached a membership of 8,000 in 1912.[18] A very bourgeois-conservative affair was The Catholic Association, founded in 1891 under the presidency of the Earl of Denbigh. It was related to the Catholic Confederation, which appeared in 1910 and was socially more embracing and above partisanship.

It was said that Manning's social activity stands isolated,[19] and that is true to a certain extent, because Catholicism's scholarly exchanges in the social question in Britain were not intensified until after 1900, in conjunction with the political growth of the Socialists.[20] But this has to be placed in the context of general history. Gladstone, who was consumed by the Irish question and in a legal sense favored the development of the trade unions, "was not a social reformer in the strict sense of the word, and the needs of the working class hardly concerned him."[21] Benjamin Disraeli, who is said to have had sympathies for Manning,[22] was a rather unique figure among the Tories for his social sensibilities (the Labour Party was founded in 1900). There was only a small number of Catholics to be found in the upper reaches of society. During the

---

[17] H. Parkinson, *A Primer of Social Science* (London 1913).

[18] K. Wanninger, op. cit., 110–30.

[19] "Manning's contribution was unique, for the majority of the older English Catholics were remote from the social struggle and unsympathetic towards the Irish laborers in factory and mine": C. Hollis: J. N. Moody, *Church and Society* (New York 1953), 822.

[20] Following the outsider E. G. Bagshawe (bishop of Nottingham) with his book *Mercy and Justice to the Poor* (London 1885); J. Mooney, *Catholic Principle of Social Reform* (London 1912); H. Parkinson, op. cit.; G. S. Devas, *Social Question and the Duty of Catholics* (London 1907); id., *Political Economy* (London 1911); the *Catholic Social Yearbook* appeared since 1912.

[21] P. Kluke, op. cit., 276.

[22] Cardinal Grandison in his *Lothair* is supposed to have certain features of Manning. K. Waninger, op. cit., 56.

nineteenth century, the following had a seat in the government: Lord Ripon (1870, converted Freemason), in several liberal cabinets until 1909; Lord Llandaff, in the conservative cabinet of Lord Salisbury from 1886 until 1909; and the Duke of Norfolk, mediator of the papal response to the Queen during the jubilee of 1887, in the conservative cabinet of 1894.

The Catholicism of the upper classes was somewhat sympathetic toward the English Church Union, an organization founded in 1844 by the Anglo-Catholics within the Anglican Church. Its president (after 1868), Lord Halifax, personally inclined toward the Roman Catholic Church, had met the French Lazarist Fernand Portal, a student of Dupanloup, in 1890 on Madeira. In their correspondence during 1892, they searched for a way to unify the Roman Catholic and the Anglican Church in the near future. A discussion about the validity of Anglican orders was to serve as "a means toward that goal."[23] In July 1892, Halifax paid the archbishop of Westminster a visit in order to present his plan. Herbert Alfred Vaughan (in 1872 bishop of Salford, after March 1892 archbishop of Westminster, after 1893 cardinal) came from an old Catholic aristocratic family. In 1857 he had joined the Ambrosians, a society of the secular clergy, founded under Charles Borromeo, which Manning had introduced in Bayswater the same year. Vaughan differed from Manning and had lifted the prohibition for Catholic students to study in Cambridge and Oxford, which Manning had effected in Rome in 1895.[24] Nevertheless, he was in agreement with his predecessor in terms of ecclesiastical policy and definitely endorsed the doctrine of infallibility in the *Tablet,* which he purchased in 1866. Compared to Manning, he was less interested in social questions.[25] From the beginning Vaughan made it clear that, in contrast to the Anglicans, the recognition of papal primacy was the decisive element. Portal published *Les ordinations anglicanes* under a pseudonym in 1893 in Paris, in which he termed the consecration of Matthew Parker (appointed archbishop of Canterbury in 1559 by Elizabeth I) valid in terms of the "historical facts," but expressed doubt concerning the "intentions" of the consecrator. Church historian L. Duchesne used Catholic teaching on the sacraments to argue against this treatment of the question of intention and declared that one could consider the ordination as valid. Since Portal

---

[23] J. J. Hughes, *Absolutely Null and Utterly Void* (London 1968); German: "Absolut Null und Nichtig. Zur Ablehnung der anglikanischen Weihen . . .," *Studia Anglicana* 2 (Trier 1970), 39.

[24] Not until 1872 did Gladstone abolish the law which made being a member of the Anglican Church a prerequisite for the obtainment of an academic degree. P. Kluke, op. cit., 278.

[25] C. Hollis, op. cit., 823.

was able to anticipate the Catholics' objections to his arguments concerning the intention, as one would expect from an educated theologian, his essay was termed "a tactical move"[26] to get the discussion going. In 1894, Portal visited Halifax, who introduced him to the Anglican bishops. The archbishop of Canterbury, E. W. Benson, was very cool and just as aware of his convictions as Cardinal Vaughan, who was also annoyed because Portal did not follow up his invitation to visit him.[27] In September 1894, Portal was asked by Cardinal Secretary of State Rampolla to come to Rome and be introduced to the Pope. Portal's suggestion that Leo XIII should propose a conference to the Anglican episcopate was discarded. Instead, Rampolla wrote a letter to Portal, praising his desire for ecclesiastical unity and expressing hopes for "England's return to the only center cf unity." Portal's second visit with the archbishop of Canterbury was even cooler than the first one. On 21 March 1895, Lord Halifax had an audience with the Pope, in which he proposed a direct offer (not through Cardinal Vaughan) to the Anglican episcopate, which was graciously noted. But in February, F. A. Gasquet, O.S.B., a Vaughan aide, was given the task of composing a papal letter[28] which was not to be addressed to the Anglican episcopate. Vaughan, who had arrived in Rome in 1895, used all means at his disposal to exert pressure against Portal's intentions. Basically his and Lord Halifax's plan had already failed in view of the apostolic letter *Amantissimae voluntatis* of 14 April 1895,[29] which was addressed *Ad Anglos* and urged using the "means" of discussing the ordinations in order to achieve a conference which could initiate the reunification. The letter, recalling Pope Gregory the Great, spoke with restraint about the Reformation ("Anglia . . . gravissimum vulnus accepit . . ., divulsa a communione Apostolicae Sedis, dein ab ea fide sanctissima abducta est"), praised the efforts toward unity of all Christians, and finally granted indulgence in a prayer to the Virgin Mary which was intended for the *Fratres dissidentes* and asked that they unite *summo Pastori, Vicario in Terris Filii tui*. The

---

[26] J. J. Hughes, op. cit., 56.

[27] J. J. Hughes, op. cit., 59f.—One should probably ask why Portal did not request an audience after his invitation by Vaughan was lost.

[28] According to the literary remains of Gasquet. Aso: K. Connelly, "An Unheard-of Thing: An Historical Study of the Apostolical Letter . . ." (unpubl. diss., Louvain 1967); J. J. Hughes, op. cit., 97.—Critical analysis of the historian Gasquet (1900: abbot of Downside, 1907: chairman of the commission to revise the Vulgate, 1914: cardinal): D. Knowles, *Cardinal Gasquet as an Historian* (London 1957); id., *The Historian and Character . . .* (Cambridge 1963), 240–63.—Concerning Leo XIII's perspective in this matter, see "The Union's favorite dream of the universal empire with Rome," Schmidlin, *PG* II, 489.

[29] *Acta Leonis* XV, 138–55; concerning its development, see J. J. Hughes, op. cit., 97f.

conclusion of the letter was composed by Merry del Val, who, as a young man, had been much favored by Leo XIII.[30] In spite of this conclusion, the letter was generally well received in England; even Benson spoke of an "honest appeal," but noted the important fact that it did not mention the Anglican Church. In the papal commission, appointed in 1896 for the purpose of investigating the question of Anglican orders, Merry del Val played a significant role as secretary to the president, Cardinal Mazzella, and as middleman to Vaughan. The six (later eight) members were selected equally from both parties; the one side was led by Gasquet, the other by Duchesne. However, Cardinal Mazzella, who rejected an application for admission of the Anglicans then present in Rome, and his secretary were definite opponents of the recognition of Anglican orders. The vote took place on 7 May. Voting for recognition were Duchesne and the Jesuit A. M. de Augustinis (professor of dogmatics at the Roman College); Pietro Gasparri (in 1880 professor of canon law at the *Institut Catholique* in Paris, later cardinal secretary of state) and another member expressed through their vote that the validity of the ordinations was "doubtful". The Vaughan group voted against it. The validity of Anglican orders was rejected in the papal bull *Apostolicae curae* of 13 September 1896, which was composed by Merry del Val.[31] The expectations of some that the conversions would increase if submission to the authority of the Pope was clearly demanded were not fulfilled. The hopes of others for an impending reunification of the Churches as such was an illusion in view of the contemporary historic situation. Except for the situation of the Anglican Church, oscillating between conservative and liberal tendencies, Wilfrid Ward, a moderate disciple of Vaughan and mediator to Halifax, analyzed the situation in England and Ireland clearly: "Should we be surprised that the descendants of those whose lives were ruined . . . or who died the death of a martyr . . . could muster only little understanding for the argument that their persecutors and judges belonged to a Church which, all in all, was possibly in agreement with them?"[32]

Leo XIII's conciliatory pragmatism was also responsible for the existing illusions, which include the Pope's own on unification. It is interest-

---

[30] J. J. Hughes, op. cit., 32; also below, Introduction to Pt. II, n. 19.

[31] *Acta Leonis* XVI, 258–75.—Concerning the theological controversy, see F. Clark: *LThK*² I, 554f, incl. biblio.; also: J. de Bivort de la Saudée, *Anglicans et catholiques* (Paris 1949). In opposition to Clark, see J. J. Hughes, *Stewards of the Lord. A Reappraisal of Anglican Orders* (London 1970); id., "Zur Frage der anglikanischen Weihen. Ein Modellfall festgefahrener Kontroverstheologie," *Quaestiones disputatae* 59 (Freiburg i. Br. 1973; the original in German).

[32] J. J. Hughes, *Absolut und Nichtig*, 49. Concerning W. Ward and the Synthetic Society, see chap. 31.

ing that nearly one month before the papal bull, on 23 August 1896, Leo XIII sent a letter to Cardinal Vaughan dealing with the problem of the economic situation of converted Anglican clergymen. Here, his intentions were clearly expressed. He speaks about the "heroism" of those clergymen who converted without any consideration of the economic consequences. But there were also others who did "not possess as much courage," but yet were close to taking this step. Therefore he suggested establishing a relief fund.[33] The Converts Aid Society, however, was not very successful because of the extraordinary financial burden placed upon the Catholics and because its purpose was misunderstood. Cardinal Francis Bourne (1903–35) organized this action after World War I with great interest. In 1898, analogous to other national institutions, Leo XIII founded the Beda College in Rome, and on 13 November he elevated the Venerable Bede to the rank of Father of the Church.

In 1905, following the victory of the Liberal Party, which had been rejuvenated by youthful forces, the question of schools came up again. The objective of the education law of 1870 was reiterated insofar as the Rosebery cabinet wanted to further repress the traditional Anglican predominance in education.[34] But now Cardinal Bourne aligned with the Anglicans and the conservative opposition in the fight against the deconfessionalization of schools (religious instruction was to be given in the classroom, but not to belong to the general curriculum)[35] and, consequently, the bill miscarried in the House of Lords. But these were tactical alliances. The Eucharistic World Congress of 1908 in London, which was attended by Cardinal Legate Vannutelli, was correctly analyzed as a "brilliant expression of the unified power" of the island's Catholics.[36] But this was also the way a large part of the London public understood it, and thus protests occurred, and Lord Herbert Asquith, promoted from chancellor of the treasury to prime minister (1908), warned against carrying the monstrance in the procession.[37] It was clear to the seasoned episcopate in Great Britain, which also held back in the dispute over modernism,[38] that the founding of a Catholic party, as Leo XIII desired, would only harm ecclesiastical life. On 28 October 1911 the Pope reorganized the hierarchy. Henceforth, the Church province of Westminster was to incorporate the dioceses of Northhampton, Nottingham, Portsmouth, and Southwark; the new province of Liverpool

---

[33] *Acta Leonis* XVI, 246ff.; cf. I. Bolten, op. cit., 80f.
[34] P. Kluke, op. cit., 291.
[35] Schmidlin, *PG* III, 112.
[36] K. Waninger, op. cit., 99.
[37] He referred to several existing prohibitions; but there were numerous ones, and ignoring them had not resulted in any complications (cf. Schmidlin, *PG* III, 113, n. 13).
[38] Cardinal Bourne expressed himself to that effect to von Hügel; see chap. 31.

was to add the dioceses of Newcastle, Leeds, Middlesbrough, and Salford; and the province of Birmingham included the dioceses of Clifton, Menevia, Newport, Plymouth, and Salisbury.

Ireland

During the first year of Leo XIII's pontificate, Cardinal Paul Cullen, the head of the episcopate in Ireland, died. In 1880 Gladstone took over the government after the victory of the Liberals in the elections, in which the Irish National Party was able to increase its seats from fifty-nine to sixty-five. In spite of Gladstone's conflicts with the Irish episcopate over the question of the universities in 1873 and his reaction to it (published in a flyer which became known all over Europe),[39] his personal involvement and current events entangled him once again in the Irish question. Bad harvests and the intensification of the political battle resulted in 1882 in nearly one hundred attempted assassinations and twenty-six murders. The terrorism in the battle for justice was also directed against those Irish who did not obey the directives of the organization.[40] This has to be taken into consideration as well as the impoverishment of the Irish tenant farmers, whose lot could only gradually be improved by a land act which Gladstone enacted in spite of the terrorism.[41] Otherwise, the solidarity of a large part of the episcopate[42] and Leo XIII's interventions cannot be adequately assessed.

On 3 January 1881 the Pope sent a letter to Archbishop MacCabe of Dublin, no doubt repeating, in reference to Gregory XVI, more of the *debita obedientia* and the *Cupiditates in seditiones flammam,*[43] than was prudent in view of the situation created by the recently enacted land act. The letter of 1 August 1882, addressed to the entire Irish episcopate, endorsed the condemnation of the terrorist acts; however, in blaming them on the "secret societies,"[44] he showed little understanding of the necessity for organized resistance in such a situation, even though the Pope generally approved of the desire for justice. Incidentally, the Irish episcopate had good reason to suggest that Rome should not altogether trust the information from London. After MacCabe had been elevated to cardinal on 27 March 1882, the Pope, in a

[39] The Vatican decrees in their bearing on civil allegiance (1874).
[40] C. C. O'Brien, *Parnell and his Party* (London 1957).
[41] The only way out was emigration, so that the 8 million inhabitants had decreased to about 4 million from the beginning of the century until the end.
[42] Even in 1890, Manning's attitude is expressed in his words: "If the government treats its people the way lords and country squires treat their herdsmen and workers, then the free Englishmen will rebel against it;" quoted by E. Taylor, op. cit., 161.
[43] *Acta Leonis* II, 188.
[44] *Acta Leonis* III, 130.

letter of 1 January 1883, admonished the episcopate to act in concord and the clergy to obey the bishops.[45] The intrigues of the conservative Catholic deputy from Ireland, Errington, at the Vatican showed what kind of impact the massive interests of the landlords had, even on the Church's treatment of the Irish question.[46] How venomous the atmosphere was in the Church itself is documented by the case of Archbishop Walsh of Dublin, who had to undergo an interrogation in 1885 in Rome before he was confirmed.[47] The Vatican critic Gladstone was able to foresee for the next decades that the Irish question could not be solved merely by improved reform laws, but that the request for home rule had to be granted. In the beginning of 1886, he failed to win support for his bill providing for the suspension of the union of 1801 and for Ireland's own Parliament (with the exclusion of trade, foreign affairs, and the military). The bill miscarried because of imperialistic resistance, even within his own ranks.[48] The Home Rule law of 1912/14 came too late because of the war. It brought revolution. Leo XIII carried part of the responsibility for this. The old grievances did not return after Gladstone's defeat, but Ireland's being chained to Great Britain and the interests of the Unionists persisted, so that the unrest was aggravated, a consequence from which the episcopate could not escape. Nevertheless, the Pope, counseled by the Prefect for Propaganda Simeoni and the Irish College, showed little understanding for Ireland's increasing national, rather than economical demands.[49] On 20 April 1888, the Congregation on the Inquisition answered negatively an inquiry about whether a boycott by the tenant farmers was permissible, and requested an attitude of charity and fairness. However, in a letter of 24 June 1888, addressed to the entire episcopate, Leo XIII emphasized that the matter was not only subject to the authority of the bishops but also to his own authority, and he resented being insufficiently informed.[50] The Irish question had critically entangled political issues, characterized by a mixture of right and wrong, with ecclesiastical aspects on all sides. At the same time, it was an example of the dilemma of Leo's direct policies, and thus it continued to smolder. Furthermore, the legation of Vannutelli in 1904[51] only intensified the ecclesiastical situation.

[45] *Acta Leonis* III, 188f.
[46] Schmidlin, *PG* II, 488.
[47] Ibid., 493.
[48] P. Kluke, op. cit., 285.
[49] Schmidlin, *PG* II, 493.—D. H. Akenson, *The Church of Ireland. Ecclesiastical Reform and Revolution, 1800–1885* (Yale 1971).
[50] *Acta Leonis* VII, 253, 251 ("Num igitur in eo temeritas inest, quod aiunt, de caussa Nos iudicavisse non satis cognita?").
[51] Schmidlin, *PG* III, 111.

The liberal Asquith was able to achieve in 1909 what the liberal Gladstone had failed to accomplish in 1873. In addition to the Queen's University of Belfast, he established the National University of Ireland, with its three colleges in Dublin, Cork and Galway, which were both fundamentally supra-denominational, but the school in Dublin was, for all practical purposes, Catholic.[52]

At that time, Catholicism in the United Kingdom of Great Britain and Ireland was sociologically hardly homogeneous. This is evidenced by the biographies of a line of significant writers who knew they belonged to Catholicism, but cannot be regarded as its exponents without serious reservations. C. K. Patmore (born in 1823 in Woodfore, died in 1896) grew up without any religious training; the poet of the "Unknown Eros" (1877) converted to Catholicism in Rome in 1864. His younger friend G. M. Hopkins (born in 1844 in Stratford, Essex, died in 1889) converted in 1866 under the influence of Newman and joined the Society of Jesus in 1868. Dedicated to the art of "inscape," he is one of the most original religious poets. A marginal figure was Francis Thompson (born in 1859 in Preston, Lancaster, died in 1907), the son of convert parents. He attended the seminary of Ushaw at a young age, but after 1885 became a homeless person in London, addicted to opium. In the nineties, he grew to feel somewhat at home in the Franciscan monastery Pantasaph in North Wales, where he became known as the poet of God's love, which one cannot escape ("The Hound of Heaven," 1890). G. K. Chesterton (born in 1874 in London, died in 1936) converted to Roman Catholicism in later years; but his socially grounded opposition to the representatives of the "heretics" (1905) is documented in a nonconformist fashion in his *Orthodoxy* (1908) and in his story about the Catholic farm boy from Scotland and the atheist who are prevented by the eternal compromisers from fighting each other (*The Ball and the Cross,* 1909). Together with his friend Hilaire Belloc (1870–1953), a student of the Oratorians in Birmingham, he wielded a sharp apologetic sword against British society. The fact that Belloc was of French-Irish descent (he was fascinated by Charles Maurras) fits into the continental orientation of the Irish "revival," whose most important members, however, were alienated from the Church (indicative of the problem of Irish Catholicism).[53]

---

[52] Cf. A Bellesheim, *AkathKR* (1910).

[53] J. C. Reid, *The Mind and the Art of C. K. Patmore* (London 1957); J. G. Ritz, *Le poete G. M. Hopkins* (Paris 1960); R. Hill, "F. Thompson," *Lexikon der Weltliteratur* II (Freiburg i. Br. 1961), 1074f.; M. Ward, *G. K. Chesterton* (London 1944); R. Hill, op. cit., 330–32; J. B. Morton, *H. Belloc* (London 1955).

Canada

In Canada, the Catholic part of the total population decreased slightly from 42.9 percent in 1871 to 39.4 percent in 1911.[54] The Franco-Canadian Catholicism in the province of Quebec, which had developed a pronounced conservative stance during Pius IX's pontificate and actually dominated public life with its strong ecclesiastical authority, was suffering from serious tensions in the last quarter of the century, which were at least partly ignited by its relations with France. The French-Canadian economic relations were increased after 1890, and at that time, Franco-Canadian society was more and more influenced by an image of France based on the Restoration rather than the Revolution. It was the spirit of Victor Hugo. As a result, the controversies within French Catholicism, the pro and con in reference to Leo XIII's *Ralliement* politics, and the ecclesiastical policy of the Third Republic were considered by the Canadian Catholics to be much their own affair. These backlashes combined with inner Canadian differences in the episcopate. E.-A. Taschereau, from 1871 until 1898 archbishop of Quebec,[55] held from the beginning of his episcopate a more differentiated opinion of the relationship between the civil society and the Church than Bishop J. Bourget of Montreal, who had died in 1876. The Conservatives, therefore, suspected him of liberalism, and he had to defend himself against immigrant extremists by demanding their return to France. The owner and editor of *La Vérité*, J.-P. Tardivel (1851–1905), had chosen Louis Veuillot as his model. After 1881 he fought, together with his friend Fr. J. Grenier, S.J., anyone who, in his opinion, was not exclusively oriented toward Rome. Both Veuillot and Tardivel inspired a comparison with Taschereau and Dupanloup.[56] In reference to the Spanish Catholics' disputations in *Siglo futuro* and the insolent behavior of Nocedal, the "Spanish Veuillot,"[57] Leo XIII wrote a letter in 1882 asking the Spanish Catholics to make peace. Archbishop Taschereau did not miss the opportunity to pass this letter on to his clergy, including a comment relative to the local situation. The writer Tardivel was too radical even for Monsignor Laflèche, Bishop of Trois Rivières and leader of the strictly conservative bishops of Canada. In his "Mandement sur

---

[54] Saint-Denis, tables V and VI. The population of Irish descent decreased during that time from 24.3 percent to 14.9 percent, while the population of French descent increased from 37.9 to 41.7 percent. Immigration played an important role for a long time: in 1914, every fourth Canadian was born outside of the dominion.
[55] P. Savard, op. cit., index.
[56] P. Savard, op. cit., 84.
[57] This vol., p. 121.

les sociétés secrètes" of 1883, he reserved for himself the right to decide which societies would be subject to the ecclesiastical prohibition. On the occasion of the publication of the encyclical *Humanum genus* of 1884, he emphasized the need for a fight against the Freemasons, conceding, however, that there were only very few of them in French Canada.[58] But the basic attitude of Archbishop Taschereau was more in line with Leo XIII's intentions than those of his opponents, and thus Leo appointed him cardinal in 1887.[59]

In the nineties French Canada also experienced a school struggle. But it differed from similar conflicts because of the conditions there: the dominant position of the Church in education. In 1886 the Sulpicians had been accused of undermining the congregations of teaching brothers by supporting a stronger participation of laymen in education.[60] In 1893 it was demanded that the clergy pass the same examination as the laymen, from which they had been exempted in 1846. Moreover, the traditional humanistic curriculum became more and more the object of controversy. The Prime Minister of the Dominion of Canada, John A. Macdonald, who had been in office since the British North America Act (1867), was replaced in 1891 by the liberal Wilfrid Laurier. When the liberal president of Quebec, F.-G. Marchand wanted to establish a department for education in 1889, a furious public reaction occurred and the project was unable to secure a majority in Parliament.[61] In 1889 Leo XIII seized the initiative and elevated the ecclesiastical University of Ottawa (founded in 1849), where Archbishop J.-T. Duhamel taught (1874–1909), to a papal institution. The University, recognized by the state in 1866, was the first in Canada to teach in English and French. An example of the increase in tensions was

---

[58] Taschereau rejected the Knights of Labor, in contrast to Archbishop J. J. Lynch of Toronto (1860–88) (1883: inquiry in Rome with negative answer, 1886: another inquiry, because the answer had only been applied to Quebec. The response this time was that the answer was a general one); P. Savard, op. cit., 212–20.—Regarding the further development, see J. Hulliger, *L'enseignement social des évêques canadiens, 1891–1950* (Paris 1958); M. Têtu, "Les premiers Syndicats cath. canadiens. 1900–1921" (diss., Laval University 1961).

[59] Tardivel tried in vain to obtain an audience with Leo XIII in 1888–89; although he was received benevolently in 1896, he does not seem to have been satisfied with the result of the audience.

[60] F. S. Louis, *Les frères des Écoles chrétiennes au Canada. 1837–1900* (Montreal 1921).— In regard to the school conflict in general, see P. Savard, op. cit., 177–86.

[61] An example of the change after an extreme conservative reign is the path which the politician J.-I. Tarte, who was once a friend of Tardivel and later his enemy took (L. Lapierre, "Relation between the French Canadian Episcopacy and a French Canadian Politician, 1874–96," *Rapport de la Société Canad. d'Histoire de l'Église Catholique* (1958), 23–39.

the unreasonable request (in 1889) that Cardinal Taschereau appeal to Queen Victoria on behalf of the Roman question and the partisan interpretation of his refusal as being a betrayal of the Pope. On the other hand, an increase in animosity toward the Church is evident, which came partly from Ontario, whence anti-Jesuitism spread to Quebec, and partly from France. The anti-Catholic Equal Rights Association founded a group in Montreal and the radical Grand Orient lodge founded a branch in French Canada. The conflicts survived the death of Cardinal Taschereau (his successor in Quebec was L.-N. Bégin, 1898–1925), corresponding to the political development in France. An example is the embarrassment of the successful French preacher J.-F.-R. Rozier in 1902 in Montreal, when he was charged (in a newspaper interview) with having failed to divorce himself sufficiently from the French government. In 1911 the first plenary synod was aimed at demonstrating the inner cohesiveness of French and English Catholicism in Canada. The opening address of the premier of Quebec, L. Gonin, at the Eucharistic Congress of 1910 showed what kind of authority the Church still possessed in spite of a certain intensification of liberalism: "The Canadian State does not consider the Church an enemy to be fought as a rival; it considers the Church an ally and its best support."[62]

Australia

Catholicism in Australia entered a new period of growth, when P. F. Moran[63] was appointed archbishop of Sydney (in 1885 he became Australia's first cardinal). In spite of a decrease in Irish immigration, the portion of the Catholics in the growing white population remained fairly constant: 1841: 40,000 out of 211,000; 1901: 850,000 out of 3.78 million.[64] It was of great significance in 1888 that Cardinal Moran could found and open Saint Patrick's Ecclesiastical College in Manly (north of Sydney), thus providing for the training of the native clergy. This contributed to easing the tensions which the religious orders and secular clergy from Europe had brought into the country. It also diminished the Australian Englishmen's fear of French settlements. But the process of deconfessionalizing education had more negative consequences for the Catholic schools in Australia than it did in Britain. The cancellation of

---

[62] A. Touchet, "Le congrès eucharistique de Montréal," *Correspondant* 141 (October 1910), 3–30.

[63] P. F. Moran, born in Ireland (1830–1911), studied at the Irish College in Rome and served after 1866 as secretary to Cardinal Cullen, his uncle. He wrote the *History of the Catholic Church in Australia*, 2 vols. (Sydney 1896).

[64] Around 1927, the proportions changed considerably: 1.1 million–6.3 million; 480,000 in the Church province of Sydney 320,000 in the province of Melbourne.

state subsidies could not easily be compensated for by individual efforts, and the Australian bishops had to solicit the assistance of European teaching orders. Until the middle of the twentieth century, the congregations were usually represented in branch foundations.

Among the original Australian foundations are the Sisters of Saint Joseph (in 1882 in Goulburn and in 1883 in Lochinvar) and Our Lady's Nurses of the Poor (1913). Cardinal Moran followed the example of Leo XIII's pontificate and organized regular plenary synods in Sydney (1885, 1895, 1905). The growing social awareness of Australian Catholicism expressed itself in the congresses taking place after 1900, having an active leader in their cardinal, who was a supporter of the constitution of the Commonwealth of Australia. It was in accord with the social status of most Catholics in Australia that Moran favored the Australian Labor Party and showed sympathy for the strikes of the nineties, even though that gained him the reputation among the Conservatives of being a socialist.[65]

Like the rest of the population, the Catholics concentrated in New South Wales and in Victoria. There were difficulties in establishing an ecclesiastical organization in West Australia, where natural conditions in the southwestern part favored a stronger density of population. There, the Irishman M. Gibney, who had been a priest in West Australia since 1863, was appointed Bishop of Perth in 1887 (a bishopric since 1845). The use of Trappists from the abbey of Sept-Fons in the Beagle Bay Mission proved to be impractical. In 1901 they were replaced by the Pallotines (under the generalate of Fr. Whitmee). Lacking crucial internal or external tensions, Catholicism was able to develop favorably, and Cardinal Cerretti, during his visits in 1915/17, found a flourishing Church.

[65] P. Ford, *Cardinal Moran and the A. L. P.—A Study in the Encounter between Moran and Socialism* (Melbourne 1966).

CHAPTER 10

The American Way

In 1820 there were one hundred ninety thousand Catholics among the total white population of 7.8 million. By 1870 the total population had risen to 33.5 million with 4.5 million Catholics. This growth rate, mainly due to Irish immigration, decreased in the seventies when 600,000 out of 2.8 million immigrants were Catholics (180,000 Irish, 175,000 German, and 82,000 Canadian). In the eighties, 1.2 million of the 5.2

million immigrants were Catholic (400,000 German, 300,000 Irish, approximately 200,000 East European, 130,000 Italian). In this time period the number of births within the Catholic population almost equalled that of the immigrants. In the following years, however, the largest portion of immigrants were Italians, who often came without their families and returned to their homeland. In 1900, there were about 12 million Catholics in the total population of 78 million; they had tripled since 1870.[1] For the year 1957, there was an estimate of 25.7 percent Catholics.[2]

In view of the growing mobility of the industrial age, pastoral work in regard to immigrants, especially in the United States, had been recognized as an important task. At the Catholic Convention in Mainz in 1871, the Saint Raphael Society for the Protection of German Emigrants was founded, mainly upon suggestion of the businessman Peter Paul Cahensly (1838–1923; 1885 deputy of the Center Party). Journeying to the United States in 1874, he occupied steerage in order to investigate the situation of the emigrants. Encouraged by Leo XIII, he repeated this trip in 1883. In Italy, which was harder hit than Germany, G. B. Scalabrini, bishop of Piacenza after 1876,[3] took the initiative and founded the *Pia Società dei Missionari di S. Carlo per gli Italiani emigranti* (1887). Cahensly, who had presented his case to the Congress of Liège in 1887, made contact with Scalabrini, who founded the *Società S. Raffaele* in 1890. It is the name of the rather active German Cahensly that comes to mind in connection with the controversy about "Cahenslyism" (which was unreasonable, but its proponents had good intentions), rather than the name of the diligent Scalabrini, in whose spirit Francesa Saveria Cabrini (1850–1917) worked.[4] During the Saint Raphael's Convention in Lucerne in 1890, the international character of which was somewhat diminished by the absence of the Americans, a

---

[1] Data according to J. T. Ellis: *New Catholic Encyclopedia* 14 (1967), 434f. All numbers are dubious because the American Constitution prohibits questions about one's faith. During the time of immigration, the denomination index of the home country was used, among other things.

[2] The statistician controversy is not finished yet. The calculations of G. Shaughnessy, *Has the Immigrant Kept Faith?* (New York 1925), are accepted by some or rejected by others (L. Hertling, op. cit., 162–66).

[3] I. Felici, *G. B. Scalabrini* (Monza 1954); M. Caliaro, M. Francesconi, *L'Apostolo degli emigranti, G. B. Scalabrini* (Milan 1968).

[4] She founded the *Missionarinnen vom Heiligsten Herzen* (confirmed in 1881) and devoted her life to the Italian emigrants, first in New York, later in several other cities (died in Chicago); canonized on 7 July 1946. The miserable conditions which she encountered and tried to alleviate by establishing schools, hospitals, and orphanages, should not be blamed on the American pastoral work (Hertling, op. cit., 171f; C. Caminada, *Una Italiana per le vie del mondo* [Turin 1946]).

memorandum was composed which stated that, as a result of the pastoral situation in the United States, 10 million Catholic immigrants had been deprived of the practice of their faith. Cahensly sent the memorandum to the Pope and increased the number of victims in a letter to Rampolla to 16 million. As a remedy he suggested placing the national parishes under the authority of a bishop of their respective countries.[5]

The reaction of the episcopate as well as the general public in the United States was vehement. In 1891, through Rampolla and Ledóchowski, the Pope rejected the idea of a nationally differentiated American episcopate[6] and limited the measures to pastoral care of the Italians by Italian priests, as he had already recommended in 1888.[7] But the incident in Lucerne could not easily be repaired, and Leo XIII's benevolence in this matter was, among other things, an indication that European ideas obscured the view of the New World. Of course, national emotions played an intensifying role. Senator Cushman C. Davis brought the matter to the attention of Congress in 1891 and spoke favorably of the Pope, Cardinal Gibbons, and Archbishop Ireland, but was critical of the Germans. In January 1892 the *Catholic World* attacked the Italians, declaring that they should relieve the Pope of his burden. Denis Joseph O'Connell, then rector of the American College in Rome,[8] wrote to his friend Gibbons in 1891: For us, it is simply a clerical matter, but for it [the Curia] it is a political matter, it is part of its policy in regard to the Central Powers."[9] It is correct, however, to say that the pastoral question was not handled as carefully as would have been proper under the given circumstances. It is also true that the political calculation of the pontificate (or what was taken as such) could play a disturbing role, as was the case in other situations.[10] As for an objective diagnosis, Archbishop Ireland, who was probably more aware because of his pride in America, came closest to the truth in his estimation that 1 to 1.5 million immigrants had lost the practice of their Catholic faith, and this figure should be considered accurate.

The controversy concerning the immigrants' pastoral care was already on the horizon of the great conflict of the nineties, and it illuminates the

[5] L. Hertling, op. cit., 162–66.
[6] *ASS* 24, 685: "Cum enim tunc temporis inanes rumores spargi in vulgus cepissent de Catholicae Hierarchiae in Statibus Foederatis ratione ita immutanda isthuc Catholicis ex variis Europae nationibus populares Episcopi praefici deberent. . . ." Schmidlin, *PG* II, 497.
[8] R. McNamara, *The American College in Rome, 1855–1955* (New York 1956).
[9] L. Hertling, op. cit., 216–21; here, 217f.
[10] With some resignation we have to acknowledge that T. Maynard, in 1941, talks about "Teutonic hubris" in this context; quoted by Hertling, op. cit.

central problem of Catholicism in the United States at that time. The difficulties of a minority in an often aggressively hostile society[11] were intensified by its national heterogeneity. On the other hand, the groups of the various immigrants found a certain security in their national parishes, so that the development of a total Catholic consciousness as well as its acculturation to American society was problematic. But these tendencies, fostered by the European mother countries, stood in contrast to existing social conditions, especially for the second generation of immigrants. The result was the emergence of problems related to parochial jurisdiction whenever there was the desire to change the parish and thus the *rector ecclesiae.* The language problem seems to have played a relatively minor role. The Irish spoke English, and the Germans, next to the Irish the most important group up to the eighties, quickly learned the language of the country, at least in the second generation.

The situation was more difficult for the Italians and the Eastern Europeans. But the command of the English language did not erase the differences which were, last but not least, a matter of clerical estate. The German Roman Catholic Central Society (founded in 1857), for a long time the only Catholic umbrella organization in the United States, played an important role in American Catholicism. This caused understandable resentment among the Catholics of Irish descent, who were highly influential in the hierarchy, constituted the great majority, and refused to tolerate special groups. The question of parish membership[13] was delayed by the Propaganda Fide in 1887 and finally resolved in 1897, with the understanding that children of non-English-speaking immigrants born in America could, upon reaching maturity, leave the parish of their parents and join an English-speaking parish; and that English-speaking immigrants could become members of an English-speaking parish and were not subject to the pastor of their national congregation.[13] The increasing social mobility gradually drew the Catholics into the American melting pot. An unreliable census in 1916 counted 5,660 Catholic national parishes. English sermons were delivered in 3,502 of them, and

[11] In regard to the agitation by the American Protective Association (APA) in the nineties, see L. Hertling, op. cit., 194.

[12] Memorandum by Ireland and Keane in 1886 regarding the "German question": "The fight for the rights of the Germans is carried on with the kind of stubborness and aggressiveness which is characteristic of Bismarck's countrymen"; regarding the language question, see L. Hertling, op. cit., 166–72. Ireland and Keane were in Rome at the same time (1886) as Pastor Peter Abbelen, who advocated the maintenance of the German parishes. He had a recommendation by Gibbons, which Hertling (188) does not seem to consider sincere.

[13] *ASS* 30, 256.

sermons in one additional language were even delivered in some.[14] The Irish episcopate aimed at the sensible goal of totally Anglicizing Catholicism in the United States, but this achievement was hampered by national emotions.[15]

The leaders of the Church in the United States during Leo XIII's pontificate were born in the thirties and were mostly of Irish descent. James Gibbons (1834–1921) was the son of an Irish immigrant in Baltimore, though he grew up in Ireland between 1837 and 1853, because his parents had returned there. A priest since 1861, he was consecrated bishop in 1868 and participated as the youngest council father in the first Vatican Council. In 1872, he was appointed bishop of Richmond.[16] His book, *The Faith of Our Fathers,* appeared in 1876 and was a great success among American Catholics, even though, theologically, it was insignificant. Gibbons was a master of well adjusted apologetics.[17] As coadjutor of J. R. Bayley, an Anglican clergyman who converted in Rome in 1842, Gibbons succeeded him in 1877 as archbishop of Baltimore. Cardinal (since 1886) Gibbons was in many respects Manning's American counterpart, and was repeatedly helped by him in his ecclesiastical endeavors. He was convinced of the papacy's mission and entertained no doubts concerning his episcopal responsibility, as he saw it, in the framework of the specific situation of Catholicism in the United States. The constitution of the United States was for him a sort of secular Bible: "I would not expunge or alter a single paragraph, a single line, or a single word" (1897).[18] His reserve toward some German-speaking Catholics was not unfounded. He contributed considerably to the development of American Catholicism and to its esteem in the total society.[19]

---

[14] Only one language was spoken in the 530 Spanish (in the Southwest), 466 Polish, 206 German, 200 French (mostly Canadians), and 149 Italian parishes (L. Hertling, op. cit.).

[15] The German clergyman Peter Rosen published an essay in 1897 (forbidden by the Church), "Archbishop Ireland, as He Really Is." In it he attacked the man who tried everything to be an American and to be accepted as such; in 1891, when Cardinal Gibbons handed the Austrian Archbishop Katzer the pallium, he had emphatically rejected a national division of the Catholic Church in the United States.

[16] In addition to the biography by J. T. Ellis, cf. the more objective character description by L. Hertling, op. cit., 190–95, 200–02; Schmidlin, *PG* II and III several times (index).

[17] This book copies a French book, including the title. It was translated into German, like the book for priests *The Ambassador of Christ* (Baltimore 1897). In 1917, Gibbons presented an autobiographical retrospect.

[18] Quoted according to J. T. Ellis: *New Catholic Encyclopedia,* 6 (1967), 468.

[19] L. Hertling, op. cit., 210. Hertling does not do Gibbons justice when he calls him "more adroit, successful, important" than M. Corrigan, while attributing more character to Corrigan. They are both two entirely different hierarchs, whom one cannot compare. The "more adroit" man has to be more adroit as a politician, that is in the nature of things.

It is much more difficult to assess John Ireland (1838–1918). Born in Ireland (Burnchurch), he came to the United States with his parents in 1848. The French bishop of St. Paul sent him to study at the preparatory seminary of Meximieux in France, which gave him an education in the spirit of Dupanloup. Upon his return to St. Paul, he was ordained a priest in 1861; in 1875 he was named auxiliary coadjutor and in 1884 bishop. In 1888 he persuaded other bishops to sign a petition to elevate St. Paul to an archbishopric. His patriotism was not as natural as that of Cardinal Gibbons and often approached exaltation.[20] In spite of their different opinions and temperaments, Gibbons and Ireland were united in their efforts toward an indigenous American Catholicism. Ireland's address to the Council of Baltimore (1884), "The Catholic Church and Civil Society," became famous. His love for writing was documented by the collection of essays *The Church and Modern Society.* Ireland's endorsement of the missionary concept of I. T. Hecker was probably less controversial in respect to the dispute over "Americanism" than was his behavior after Leo XIII's letter of condemnation to Gibbons, *Testem benevolentiae,* of 22 January 1899.[21] The Irishman John Keane (1839–1918) also belonged to this influential group of the American episcopate. It was thanks to his initiative, supported chiefly by Ireland, that the Catholic University of America was founded in Washington in 1889.[22] He was its first president, but also one of the first victims of the "Americanism" disturbances, and was relieved of office in September 1896. From 1900 to 1911 he was archbishop of Dubuque. An important role in the controversies, intensifying in the nineties, was played by the president of the American College in Rome, Denis Joseph O'Connell (1849–1927). He was born in Ireland and was a close

[20] In 1889, during the centennial in Baltimore: "The Americans do not wish a Church with a foreign flair which could not have an impact upon them . . . I would like all Catholics to be enthusiastic patriots" (quoted according to L. Hertling, 213). All his life he told of his part in the battle of Corinth as a military chaplain of the Northern states (J. P. Shannon: *New Catholic Encyclopedia* 7 [1967], 611). As a member of the Republican party he fought for President McKinley.

[21] In regard to "Americanism", cf. chap. 24. Regarding Ireland's behavior after 1899, see Moynihan (chap. biblio), L. Hertling (1954), 238, and the *Tagebuch* (publ. in 1957) by F. X. Kraus, 739f. Kraus, who was a friend of Denis Joseph O'Connell and John Keane, assesses Ireland much more critically than Hertling, who has no objections toward the attitude of the Curia in this crisis. Regarding Ireland's behavior during a reception of the cardinals, in August 1900, where the Pope chose him to report about America, Kraus says: "And all this is just a comedy. Ireland was motivated by but *one* idea: to take revenge on his enemies . . . . All his concessions only served to get him the red hat . . . ." (Kraus was informed through Denis O'Connell). Regarding criticism of Ireland after 1899, see F. X. Kraus, op. cit., 749.

[22] P. H. Ahern, *The Life of John J. Keane, Educator and Archbishop* (Milwaukee 1955).

friend of Gibbons and his liaison man at the Vatican, where he was considered a "Liberal." Gibbons had to agree to O'Connell's dismissal from the College in 1895, and he could only save his friend's and his own reputation by appointing him rector of his titular church in Trastevere. In 1903, he made him president of Catholic University and continued to maintain the friendship.[23] The limitations of the cardinal became obvious when, in 1890, he wanted to promote John Lancaster Spalding, bishop of Peoria and cofounder of Catholic University, to archbishop of Milwaukee, but failed because of the Curia's opposition.[24] The leader of the opposition in the American episcopate was Michael A. Corrigan (1839–1902), whose Irish father had immigrated in 1828. Between 1859 and 1863, he studied at the North American College in Rome (founded by Pius IX) and was ordained a priest in the Lateran by Cardinal Patrizi. Under the patronage of Vicar-General McQuaid (later the bishop of Rochester), he was consecrated bishop (at age thirty-four) in Newark, where he had taught dogmatics since 1864. He promoted the Jesuit College in New Jersey and organized the first American pilgrimage to Rome (1874). After the Council of Baltimore (1884), he published the pastoral letter on "true freedom." Coadjutor, by 1880, Corrigan was appointed archbishop of New York in 1885. In various controversial questions he held a very intransigent view.[25] While Gibbons, Ireland, and Keane were upset about the approbation of Charles Maignen's devastating book, which increased the American tensions coupled with the French ones, it was welcomed by Corrigan.

In this milieu of people and movements, Catholicism in the United States matured. The issues of the first Plenary Council of Baltimore in 1866 were, to a large extent, still discussed at the third Council in 1884.

[23] A misunderstanding during the publication of the diaries by F. X. Kraus created the ironical situation that *Denis* was mistaken for his namesake *William Henry* (p. 688), who became the new rector of the American College (1895), was a protégé of the Pope and Rampolla, and completely unsuited for closer contact with F. X. Kraus (cf. chap. 29, n. 5). *Denis* J. O'Connell became bishop of Richmond in 1912, suffragan of Gibbons, giving rise to the suspicion that he would be his successor (cf. C. J. Barry: *New Catholic Encyclopedia,* 10 [1967], 635f.). Concerning William Henry O'Connell, see the biography by D. G. Wayman (New York 1955).
[24] J. L. Spalding was a nephew of the archbishop of Baltimore, Martin John Spalding; F. X. Kraus, op. cit., 734, recorded a "very strange sermon" of Spalding in the Gesù, commenting that with him the "spectator" entered the pulpit.
[25] L. Hertling, op. cit., 208, regarding the controversy about the Protestant land reformer Henry George, whose indictment Corrigan wanted to achieve: "Here, as always, he believed adamantly in the *Roma locuta, causa finita.*"—J. J. Zwierlein, *Letters of Archbishop Corrigan to Bishop McQuaid and Allied Documents* (Rochester 1946); cf. J. T. Ellis in the Gibbons biography.—Corrigan favored the presentation of American Church history by J. G. Shea, because it was in accordance with his concept (cf. J. T. Ellis).

In the previous year, Leo XIII had invited part of the episcopate to Rome in order to give the archbishops directives through the Propaganda Fide,[26] and he planned to have the council chaired by a cardinal of the Curia. The Americans were able to realize their desire to entrust the chairmanship to James Gibbons, who occupied the see of Baltimore, the most prestigious archbishopric, but was rather indifferent toward the project (J. T. Ellis). Symptomatic of the change in the structure of American Catholicism is the portion of American-born bishops at the Council: in 1852, there were 9 out of 32; 1866, 14 out of 45; 1884, 25 out of 72, 15 of them of Irish descent. Aside from these 15 prelates, there were 20 who were born in Ireland, so that the Irish almost had the majority (8 Germans, 6 Frenchmen, 4 Belgians).

A specifically American question concerned the procedure for the appointment of bishops. While the Curia wanted to transfer the European model of the cathedral chapters to America, there were also strong efforts to introduce an election system by the clergy.[27] The council decided that the "diocesan consultors" (half appointed by the bishop and the other half elected by the clergy) together with irremovable pastors[28] were to make a list, to which, however, the bishops of the ecclesiastical province were not obligated when making a proposal to the Pope. This remarkable procedure was in effect until 1918 (new codex). In the years between 1880 and 1903, Leo XIII intensified the ecclesiastical organizations by establishing 23 dioceses and 3 prefectures. After Pius X's establishments, there were now 82 bishoprics in 14 ecclesiastical provinces.[29] While the Plenary Council of 1884 took place without a papal legate, Leo XIII used the occasion of the centennial of the American Catholics in 1889 to send Francesco Satolli (1839–1910), an adviser from Perugia and a strict neoscholastic,[30] as his representative to Baltimore. On the occasion of the World's Columbian Exposition in Chicago in 1893 (a celebration of the four-hundredth anniversary of the discovery of America), organized by the United States, Satolli, now titular archbishop, came a second time in order to deliver Vatican documents. While the episcopate appreciated this as an honorable ges-

---

[26] Schmidlin, PG II, 495f.

[27] Representative of this is the publication by P. Corrigan (not the Archbishop of New York!): *What the Catholic Church Most Needs in the U.S. or: the Voice of the Priests in the Election of the Bishops* (1884).

[28] "Tenured" were only the church rectors, because there were no canonical benefits; in Baltimore it was decided that at least one tenth of the diocesan clergy was to be elevated to this rank.

[29] Schmidlin, PG II, 495, III, 114.

[30] In 1880, Leo XIII recalled Satolli from Perugia and appointed him professor of dogmatics at the College of the Propaganda Fide and the Roman Seminary.

ture (Gibbons had transmitted the government's desire to the Pope), the archbishops, except Ireland, were embarrassed that Satolli would thenceforth be an official Apostolic Delegate. The attitude of Satolli, who returned to Rome in October 1896 and was replaced by Archbishop Sebastiano Martinelli (1889 Prior-General of the Ausgustinian Hermits, 1901 cardinal), is difficult to assess.[31]

More crucially than in Catholicism elsewhere, the school question stood in the foreground of American interests. The constitutional right to found private schools, its necessity for the Catholic minority's development of self-awareness, the financial difficulties in this extensive country form the background for the history of the school system.[32] At the Plenary Council of 1884, the responsibility of the parents was emphatically defined as an episcopal decree, and the tendency to excommunicate offenders was repressed. Episcopal dispensation had to be mentioned because there were not nearly enough Catholic schools. By 1900, the two hundred primary schools of 1840 had increased to 3812 (nine hundred thousand students out of approximately 17 million); yet, more than half the children went, more or less by necessity, to other schools. Moreover, the standards of public schools improved considerably.[33] The Jesuits were particularly concerned with higher education. Around 1880, they had four thousand students altogether, and in 1890, five thousand five hundred. The small increase was caused by the fact that the Jesuits had not adjusted their organization and curriculum to the public schools, which was partly corrected by the initiative of the second president of Catholic University, Thomas Conaty. An increase of scientific subjects failed in spite of the efforts by Notre Dame University, founded in 1842 under the direction of the Congregation of the Holy Cross. The Sisters of the Sacred Heart, who from the middle of

---

[31] Schmidlin, *PG* II, 498, says simply that Satolli was received "triumphantly." In accord with his attitude toward the Pope's wishes as of 1885, Gibbons did indeed ask the Pope on 4 January 1893, in the name of all archbishops (with the exception of Ireland), to disregard the establishment of a permanent apostolic delegation. On 14 January, Leo XIII wired his orders (cf. J. T. Ellis in the Gibbons biography; also *New Catholic Encyclopedia* 14 [1967], 441, where he speaks about a *fait accompli*). Incidentally, since Satolli appeared in November 1892 at the conference of the archbishops in New York as a de facto delegate, the question arises of what the meaning is of "proposing" (Ellis) such a delegation. It is remarkable that Satolli arrived in the company of Denis O'Connell, kept close contact with Gibbons and Ireland, and lived at Keane's, whose dismissal as rector of the university (1896) he had initiated before he himself was recalled. F. X. Kraus (*Tagebücher,* 714) notes that Satolli, who had become cardinal in 1895, had irritated Keane in Rome. There were also "American news stories" about his conduct. L. Hertling (op. cit., 225f. and 232f.) speaks about a "change in Satolli" around 1894.
[32] More information in L. Hertling, op. cit., 245–62; ibid. 221–24.
[33] Cf. E. Angermann: *HM* 10 (Berne 1961), 305f.

the century until 1890 had founded ten girls' high schools, tried to adjust within limits. It is natural that education became one of the areas of conflict in American Catholicism's attempt to gain identity. During the congress of the National Education Association in 1890, John Ireland surprised the public and his friends-in-faith with the suggestion to integrate the Catholic parochial schools with the system of the public schools, whereby religious instruction was to be given outside of the general lessons. To some, this seemed like a betrayal, to others a malicious Roman attack on the free republic. Patriotism and the worry of increasing the Catholic schools' incompatibility had joined hands in Ireland. The idea was realized in the parochial schools of Faribault and Stillwater in the Archdiocese of St. Paul, which were leased on notice to the local school board for one dollar a year as part of the public school system. The school board was also responsible for the salary of the Catholic teaching sisters (except for the religious instruction to be given in the schools). The professor of ethics at the Catholic University of America, Thomas Bouquillon, and the group of the episcopate around Gibbons supported the "Faribault plan," but Bouquillon's colleague, the German professor of dogmatics J. Schroeder, and the Jesuits opposed it vehemently. The majority of the German Catholics' resentment was based upon the *Kulturkampf*, rather than concern about the preservation of the German language. Rome, to which the controversy had been transferred, decided (in April 1892) in favor of a *tolerari posse*, referring at the same time to the resolution of the Council of Baltimore. But Ireland's idea had failed.

In Baltimore, in 1884, the founding of a Catholic national university was planned, an idea which Gibbons viewed with reservations (J. T. Ellis). At first Bishop John Lancaster Spalding and Bishop John Keane supported the idea. Opposed to the plan were Archbishop Corrigan and the bishop of Rochester, Bernard J. McQuaid, as well as a good part of the Jesuits, because they feared a liberal spirit. The donation of a young female convert amounting to three hundred thousand dollars facilitated the efforts to gain the Vatican's approval. On 13 November 1889, the Catholic University of America in Washington (the founders had wanted this location, while Gibbons had favored Philadelphia—outside of his dioceses) was inaugurated in the presence of President Harrison.[34] Keane relinquished his bishopric in favor of the presidency. But internal

---

[34] J. T. Ellis, *The Formative Years of the Catholic University of America* (Washington 1946); id., *The Catholic University of America. The Rectorship of John J. Keane. 1887–96* (Washington 1949). Keane tried in 1887–88 to have Ludwig Pastor appointed (*Tagebücher*, 203, 210), who declined because the place was not suited for his papal history. This was probably no great misfortune for Keane, who was a man of feeling, according to F. X. Kraus (*Tagebücher*, 683) (cf. P. E. Hogan [chap. biblio.]).

Catholic animosities within the institute continued. Within the faculty, the German Joseph Schroeder, who taught dogmatics, was the head of the opposition against Keane and his friends in the episcopate. He had emphatically supported Cahensly's criticism of America and created the teaching chair for German literary studies, which was to be filled in accord with his ideas defined in the essay "Liberalism in Theology and History" (1881).[35] Ireland succeeded through the Apostolic Delegate S. Martinelli[36] in having Schroeder, who was supported by Corrigan, recalled. The German dogmatist Josef Pohle had already returned to Europe in 1894. Leo XIII's recall of Keane from the presidency on 15 September 1896 is part of the crisis of American Catholicism.[37] In 1904, after the presidency of T. Conaty, the university, in spite of the efforts by Denis O'Connell, was driven into a catastrophic situation due to the mismanagement of its treasurer, a situation which it could not overcome until ten years later. The comparatively older universities in Georgetown (since 1805) and St. Louis had trouble adjusting to the general development. Most successful was the University of Notre Dame.

Another complex problem discussed at the Plenary Council of 1884 was the question of which societies with Freemason-like rituals Catholics would be allowed to join. This was an old problem, with which the Provincial Council of 1875 in San Francisco had dealt. They suggested that the father confessors permit membership in a society in doubtful cases, but demand withdrawal as soon as the respective "secret" society was forbidden by the Church. The discussion was bound to get more serious after the encyclical *Humanum genus* (1884), which contained an especially sharp condemnation of the Freemasons. But since their rituals were customary in many American societies, there was only the alternative of leaving the decision to the conscience of the faithful or to proclaim a list of forbidden societies, which was exceed-

---

[35] Schroeder's character is hard to define in view of the distorted sources. Hertling: his opponents described him as a heavy drinker. F. X. Kraus *(Tagebücher,* 697), records with satisfaction (Schroeder had instigated his censure) a piece of information from Denis O'Connell, according to which the German professor "disappeared for months from his apartment at the university in order to spend the night in wretched bars, drinking and frequenting the company of questionable ladies . . . ." From Washington, Schroeder went to the theological academy in Münster (died 1903) (cf. chap. 29).

[36] F. X. Kraus, *Tagebücher,* 697 (February 1898).

[37] The Pope appointed Keane adviser to the Propaganda Fide in Rome. But the fight against this man, who was later called "a rationalist, throwing all dogma over to modern ideas" (quoted according to P. H. Ahern, op. cit.), continued, and he returned to the United States. His friends convinced the Pope to elevate him in 1900 to archbishop of Dubuque.

ingly difficult. An archiepiscopal conference in 1886 approved the Grand Army of the Republic (a society of Civil War veterans whose president was a Catholic and the brother of a bishop) and the Ancient Order of Hibernia. The explicit prohibition of other societies was debated at the conferences, but no agreement was reached. In Boston, in 1890, the majority around Gibbons decided to forbid only Freemasons, a rule that was protested by other episcopal parties (Corrigan, McQuaid, and others). Archbishop Katzer of Milwaukee complained in Rome. After the Church provinces of New York and Philadelphia had autocratically forbidden, respectively, three and four societies, the question was turned over to the Curia in November 1892 (meanwhile Satolli had arrived as papal delegate), since no agreement had been reached. After some time, on 20 August 1894, the Holy Office proscribed three societies. Rampolla's simultaneous letter to Satolli, stating that the execution of this decree was left to the judgment of the metropolitans, only caused confusion. In December 1894, Leo XIII, through Satolli, ordered the promulgation of the decree.[38] Gibbons traveled to Rome in vain (1895)—the crisis was on the way. Now, societies like The Knights of Saint John or the more important Knights of Columbus were promoted—a separation which was against the principle of accomodation.[39] The fact that individual bishops were suspicious of such organizations, and that the entire episcopate did not support a federation of the individual Catholic societies until 1905, is indicative of the social attitude of American Catholicism before World War I. On the parochial and diocesan levels, the Catholics, in spite of their economic weakness, were considerably active in the educational and social spheres.

The struggle over a closer definition of the "secret societies" was also one of the elements in the controversy about the association of the Noble and Most Holy Order of the Knights of Labor, which was founded in Philadelphia in 1869 and spread quickly under the leadership of the Catholic Irishman Terence Powderly (since 1879). Two thirds of its members were Catholics. When Gibbons was able to prevent Rome's condemnation of this society in February 1887, it was already (for several reasons) on the decline. Therefore, the historical significance of these events was not embedded in the history of this association as much as in the relation of American Catholicism to the

---

[38] L. Hertling, op. cit., 202–06.
[39] L. Hertling, op. cit., 206: ". . . here the Catholics were among themselves and there was no danger that they would be pulled unnoticed into the wake of the lodges." (Cf. F. McDonald [chap. biblio.].)

socio-political question of which association was representative.[40] It was said that the "ever-present and recurring earning potential" of the United States had prevented the social embitterment that had occurred in Europe.[41] Although the question of salaries and working conditions was pertinent, the main long-term problem was the accumulation of capital in the hands of the lower classes and the way in which this wealth was accumulated.[42] Concentration in the agrarian sector produced a growing rural proletariat, which was welcomed by industry. There, however, the workers were victims of a ruthless labor market and had to pay the price in times of crisis as a result of legislation, jurisdiction, and an administration which exclusively served the interests of the entrepreneurs. Cheap labor was plentiful among immigrants, "freed" black slaves, and children.[43] The formation of unions was hampered by legislation and the lack of solidarity among the heterogeneous labor force. The Knights of Labor was the first significant worker movement, though vehemently attacked by American society as a whole, in spite of its sensible demands (equal wages for women and blacks, an eight-hour day, a labor arbitration court) and its reserved attitude in regard to strikes. The same sentiments were shown by the conservative segment of the clergy,[44] who, moreover, associated the Knights of Labor with the "secret societies" which were forbidden by the Church because they copied the secular "mores" of the Freemasons. Because the Catholic workers were urged, on the occasion of parish missions, to leave the associations, T. Powderly (son of an Irish worker with twelve children) changed the title of his association. In 1884, upon his inquiry in Rome, Taschereau (archbishop of Quebec, after 1887 cardinal) received the reply that membership in the Knights of Labor was forbidden by the

---

[40] Henry Brown, *The Catholic Church and the Knights of Labor* (Washington 1949); Sister Joan Leonard, *Catholic Attitude forward American Labor. 1884–1919* (Columbia Univ. 1946); F. Downing: J. N. Moody (ed.), *Church and Society* (New York 1953), 843–904; L. Hertling, op. cit., 196–202; A. M. Knoll (biblio., chap. 12), n. 236; P. Mourret (biblio., chap. 12), 292.

[41] L. Hertling (op. cit., 196), who, nevertheless, immediately discusses the economic crisis of 1885 and its consequences.

[42] E. Angermann, op. cit. (op. cit., n. 33), 295–302. During the "Erie War" (speculations with the Erie railroad), Jay Gould obtained huge amounts of money from the railroad king C. Vanderbilt, and when he died in 1892, he left his heirs 92 million dollars (both parties bribed the politicians). The famous pioneers of capitalism, A. Carnegie and J. D. Rockefeller, collected their wealth not just by way of diligence, but also because they fought a brutal competition, to which the small businessmen fell victim. In 1895, the banker J. P. Morgan gave the government a 60 million dollar loan, which brought his syndicate earnings of 72 million dollars.

[43] In 1870, 750,000 ten- to fifteen-year-old children were employed; in 1910, almost 2 million; in 1910, a sixty-hour-week was the rule for adults; E. Angermann, op. cit., 302.

[44] J. Leonard, op. cit., 56.

Church. The American episcopate discussed whether this prohibition applied to Canada only and decided to present the question again to the prefect of the Propaganda Fide, Cardinal Giovanni Simeoni. In Canada, where Archbishop Lynch of Toronto favored the organization, it was discussed whether the reply referred to Quebec only. The answer from Rome in 1886 was "general prohibition."[45] Gibbons's letter of 20 February 1887, which he signed himself, but had composed in collaboration with Ireland, Keane, and Denis O'Connell, effected in Rome a toleration of the Knights of Labor.[46] Gibbons' recollections thirty years later showed which internal and public problems in regard to Church affairs he had had to face. But soon more radical organizations successfully competed with the Knights of Labor.[47] The radicalization of the social differences was one of the causes for increasing de-Christianization slightly veiled with Christian slogans.[48] The encyclical *Rerum novarum* (1891) found little attention among the American Catholics.[49] But there were a few clergymen who called the social problems by their names, in the first place John Ryan (1869–1945), son of an Irish immigrant, who had already attracted attention at the Catholic University of America in 1906 with his dissertation "A Living Wage: Its Ethical and Economic Aspects." In 1916, his main work, *Distributive Justice,* was published. During the twenties he reached the peak of his public career.[50] One of

[45] Cf. chap. 9, n. 58.

[46] In "My Memories," *Dublin Review* 160 (April 1917), 171, quoted according to J. T. Ellis: "If the Knights of Labour were not condemned by the Church, then the Church ran the risk of combining against herself every element of wealth and power . . . . But if the Church did not protect the working man she would have been false to her whole history; and this the Church can never be."—In the *Catholic Quarterly Review,* G. D. Wolff said openly in April 1886 what forces Gibbons had to fear: "It is futile for the public press to be constantly preaching platitudes concerning patience and respect for the law, whilst evasions and defiant violations, constantly practiced by mammoth capitalists and corporations, are ignored, condoned and approved de facto."

[47] See E. Angermann, op. cit., 309, who quotes the motto of the organization: "Everyone be his own master—everyone be his own employer," which suggests a certain parallel to the Vogelsang school (chap. 12); F. Downing (op. cit., 852) does not exclude the possibility that the expressed ecclesiastical toleration was one of the factors for the decline.

[48] T. Powderly, in 1893 dismissed by his organization as first master workman, joined the Freemasons in 1901 and died in 1924, excommunicated. L. Hertling (op. cit., 202) assesses him basically negatively, while F. Downing (op. cit., 852) shows some psychological understanding of this personal development.

[49] F. Downing, op. cit., 856.

[50] F. L. Broderick, *Right Reverend New Dealer: John A. Ryan* (New York 1963); Ryan was very critical about the social interest of the major part of the clergy. In regard to Ireland he said: "The archbishop's associations were with the pillars of the contemporary economic order"; the big businessmen, with whom he was friends, he considered "good men" (*Social Doctrine in Action* [New York 1941], 21–27).

his allies was Peter E. Dietz (1878–1947), son of a German immigrant, who cooperated successfully with some of the union leaders and founded a social section in the *Deutscher Katholischer Centralverein*. The fact that he founded a Catholic union (Militia of Christ for Social Service), in accord with the encyclical *Singulari quadam* of 1912, should be viewed in this context. In 1923, the Catholic members of the Chamber of Commerce persuaded Archbishop J. T. McNicholas of Cincinnati to force Dietz to close his Social Academy.[51]

The case of the New York priest Edward McGlynn (1839–1900)[52] turned into a theoretical social conflict with strong ecclesiastical and political overtones. McGlynn had lobbied for the land reform theory of Henry George and for his candidacy (1886) as mayor of New York.[53] The fact that Archbishop Corrigan had forbidden it only promoted fanaticism. After two citations ordering him to come to Rome, which he did not obey, McGlynn was suspended (1887). But in 1892, as a result of Gibbons's approval (mediated by Delegate Satolli), he was reinstated. Since Corrigan had failed to secure approval for his proposal to place the writings of Henry George on the Index because Gibbons's group opposed it,[54] this act was a serious disavowal of the archbishop.

The concept which Gibbons and his friends held of the relationship between the Church and society as a whole finds its most definite expression in their active participation in the Religion Congress of 1893 in Chicago, which was organized in the context of the World's Columbian Exposition. Jews, Moslems, Hindus, and followers of other religions had been invited.[55] Its president was the Presbyterian J. H. Barrows, who declared that no one was expected to sacrifice even the most insignificant part of his faith. Gibbons's position in the public of the United States of America is illuminated by the fact that he recited the Lord's Prayer after his welcoming speech. John Keane, one of the twenty speakers (among them Ireland and Hecker's biographer, Elliot), gave the concluding speech, which he repeated in 1894 at the Catholic Congress of Scholars in Brussels. None of the participating Catholics was

---

[51] M. H. Fox, *Peter E. Dietz, Labor Priest* (Notre Dame 1953).

[52] S. Bell, *Rebel, Priest and Prophet. A Biography of E. McGlynn* (New York 1937).

[53] The Single Tax Theory of Henry George provides that real estate tax be paid to the government as the only tax. In this respect, he criticizes the papal social doctrine in his essay "The Condition of Labour" (1894), which was published as an "open letter to his Holiness Pope Leo XIII" (H. Pesch, "Henry George und die Enzyklika 'Rerum novarum,'" *StdZ* 74 [1894], 365–82, 523–44; L. Hertling, op. cit., 206–08, 226).

[54] In April 1889, only a few sentences in an unpublished letter to the American episcopate by George were censored.

[55] L. Hertling, op. cit., 226ff.

religiously indifferent,[56] but they were all of the conviction that the Roman Catholic faith could not be absent from the register of world religions in the United States of America. Writing to Satolli in September 1895, Leo XIII stated that so far he had tolerated interdenominational conventions quietly; he preferred, however, Catholic events to which non-Catholics were invited.[57]

It was the first year of the crisis. The long brief *Longinqua Oceani* of 6 January 1895 was full of praise for the United States and the religious zeal of the Catholics. However, it contained a paragraph which was understandable in view of the Pope's opinion of the relation between Church and state in "Catholic" countries and especially in view of his expectations in regard to France. At the same time, it questioned the sociological foundations of American Catholicism.[58] It may be acceptable to say that the separation of Church and state as practiced in America was not the best of all possibilities under any circumstances. But the Pope's remark that the fruits of the development of ecclesiastical life would be a lot more plentiful if the Church would enjoy, aside from freedom, the favor of the law and the patronage of the public authorities,[59] offended the secular creed of every citizen in the United States. Even Corrigan wrote to Gibbons that it was fortunate that the non-Catholics had not taken offense.[60] But this was not only a matter of concern for the non-Catholics. One cannot assume that the paragraph in the Pope's letter was incidental. That same year, Denis O'Connell was recalled from Rome; in November the same happened to Satolli, and in September 1896, Keane was dismissed as president of the university. In connection with the conditions in France and the situation in general, the "American way" turned into the ecclesiastical problem of "Americanism".

Gibbons's concept had failed. On 6 June 1911, the fiftieth anniversary of his ordination, thousands of visitors assembled, among them President W. H. Taft and former president T. Roosevelt, whose visit in Rome the previous year had resulted in complications with the Vati-

---

[56] L. Hertling, op. cit., 228: "The dominant theme [of the congress] stated that all religions are equally good, this being the kind of religious indifferentism which Gibbons in his opening address had wanted to exclude"; one should hardly assume that any religion would be termed inferior at this congress. That Gibbons participated in the opening was an expression of his concept; that he stayed away from the other meetings was in consideration of his office.

[57] Quoted according to L. Hertling, op. cit., 233.

[58] *ASS* 27, 387–99, here 390.

[59] "Longe tamen uberiores [Ecclesia] editura fructus, si, praeter libertatem, gratia legum fruatur patrocinioque publicae potestatis." (cf. chap. 14.)

[60] Quoted according to L. Hertling, op. cit., 233.

can.[61] But Gibbons no longer held center stage. In 1911, William H. O'Connell (1859–1944), whom Gibbons had made the successor of Denis J. O'Connell at the American College (1895),[62] was elevated to cardinal of Boston, after an official hierarchy had been established in the United States in 1908 through the apostolic constitution *Sapienti consilio*. In 1905, following the Russo-Japanese War, William H. O'Connell visited the Emperor of Japan on a special mission for Pope Pius X. He diligently supported the organization and funding of missions at the congress of 1908 in Chicago and of 1913 in Boston. He was a man of the new era.[63] The construction of Saint Patrick's Cathedral in New York, begun in 1858 in a neo-Gothic style (like most Catholic churches), was completed in 1906.

[61] Schmidlin, *PG* III, 66, 116; cf. below, Introduction to Pt. II, n. 6.
[62] Cf. n. 24.
[63] "I have never hesitated to speak as plainly as possible . . . whenever direction was needed"; quoted according to D. G. Wayman: *Catholic Encyclopedia* 10 (1967), 637.

CHAPTER 11

Catholicism in the Slavic World until 1914

Russia, as one of the great powers, lost its supremacy in Europe after its defeat in the Crimean War, but it preserved its leadership over all Slavs and propagandized for the liberation of all Slavic peoples in the Austro-Hungarian Empire and Turkey by employing, aside from foreign politics, pan-slavic idealism. The Orthodox Russian State Church, with its representation at the Holy Synod, left little chance for development to the Catholics within the Russian area of influence; the Poles especially were oppressed. Because of the impact of liberalism and nationalistic tensions, Catholic Slavs found themselves in a difficult position in the Austro-Hungarian Dual Monarchy, in the small countries in southern Europe, and in the areas of Turkey remaining after the Balkan Wars. Their efforts to preserve the mother tongue in education and preaching, which they had a right to according to Church laws and decrees,[1] created widespread conflicts, which had been caused by state orders and which could only partially be resolved.

The Russian Empire

Following the Polish uprising in 1863/64, the introduction of the Russian language into schools and church services in 1869–77, and the

[1] T. Grentrup, op. cit., 121–381.

close collaboration of some Polish prelates and the Russian government, a break between the Holy See and Russia occurred. When the Russian diplomatic agent Prince Leon Urosov refused to accept the memorandum of 11 July 1877 which had been drafted and delivered by Cardinal Secretary of State Giovanni Simeoni and contained fifteen complaints concerning the persecution of Catholics in Russia and Poland, he was pronounced persona non grata by the Vatican.

By announcing to the "Highest Emperor and King" Alexander II (1855–81) his coronation on 20 December 1878, Pope Leo XIII tried to loosen the rigid political fronts and establish diplomatic relations with Russia. He gave his Nuncio Ludovico Jacobini full authority to conduct preliminary talks in Vienna. These resulted in a provisional agreement on 31 October 1880[2] and, after exhaustive negotiations between Jacobini (meanwhile elevated to secretary of state) and the Russian negotiators, a settlement was reached on 24 December 1882.[3] The partners agreed on the administration of the bishoprics of Minsk, Podlachia, and Kamieniec under the jurisdiction of the archbishop of Mogilev and bishop of Luck-Zytomierz, on the subordination of seminaries and the Clerical Academy of Saint Petersburg to ecclesiastical direction and state supervision, and on lifting the government strictures against the clergy decreed in 1865–66. The regulation requiring that studies in Russian language, history, and literature should be increased in ecclesiastical academic institutions and indifference to the controversial problems of the oppressed Uniates foreshadowed future conflicts in spite of the agreements achieved. Moreover, the Chief Procurator, Constantin Petrovich Pobedonostsev, made no secret of his dislike of the agreement and deplored the concession to the Catholic Church, which he presented as a danger to the existence of the Russian state. As the tutor of Alexander III (1881–94), who came to power after the assassination of Alexander II, he exerted great influence on the young Tsar. He was filled with the ideals of the "Holy Russia" of the old Moscow, and wanted to overcome the internal strife within Russia by reenforcing the Orthodox State Church and by fighting against the liberal reforms and revolutionary elements. Since he rejected Catholicism, which had, traditionally, deep roots in many areas in the country, he regarded the agreement with the Vatican as pandering to revolutionary elements. He considered disastrous an alliance between the Pope and the Orthodox State Church, which, in his opinion, offered the only defense against the autocracy of the Tsar, even though Foreign Minister Prince Alexander Gortšakov and others recog-

---

[2] A. Boudou, op. cit., 553–55.
[3] Ibid., 556–58; Mercati I, 1016–18.

nized the restoration forces of the papacy. Anxious to offer moral support against revolutionary currents and to conlcude the *Kulturkampf* in Germany and Russia, Leo XIII endeavored to come to an understanding with Alexander III. His first success was the reorganization of the Church hierarchy by preconization of twelve prelates with whom he filled the vacancies in the archbishopric of Mogilev, in the suffragan bishoprics of Kovno, Luck-Zytomierz, Tiraspol, and Vilnius, as well as in the archbishopric of Warsaw, in the suffragan bishoprics of Kalisz, Kielce, Lublin, Plock, Sandomierz, and Seyny. The new pastors, especially Kazimierz Gintovt of Mogilev (1883–89) and Vincenty Teophil Popiel of Warsaw (1883–1912), tried to eliminate the obstacles to ecclesiastical life posed by the Russian State Church.

The measures of the state against the Uniates and the pressures to employ the Russian language in preaching and instructions as well as the regulations of 16 January 1885 regarding the appointment of clergy (who could function only after the respective governors or governors-general in the Vistula regions had given their approval), effected another break in diplomatic relations between Russia and the Vatican. They were not resumed until after 1887/88.[4] In 1890, Leo XIII appointed a number of new bishops for Russia. On 18 June 1894, Alexander Izvolski, Imperial Russian diplomatic agent in the Vatican since 1888, became resident minister to the Holy See. Count Frederick Revertera, the Austro-Hungarian ambassador to the Vatican, called the papal efforts in regard to an understanding with Russia a "midsummer night's dream,"[5] but Leo XIII was able to ordain seven more bishops for Russia in 1896. The accession of Nicholas II (1894–1917) seemed to warrant new hopes. In 1899 the Tsar gave his permission for the construction of a new church in Saint Petersburg. But the erection of a nunciature, which the Pope desired, did not follow. In a letter to the Tsar of 21 September 1899, Chief Procurator Pobedonostsev appointed himself spokesman for the widespread mistrust toward the papacy. He ended the letter with the words: "May God save Russia from a papal nuncio."[6] He did not want to diminish the competency of the Holy Synod and of the dominant position of Orthodoxy in Russia.

By 1900, 70 percent of the Russian population were members of the Orthodox Church. After them, the Moslems and the Roman Catholics formed the strongest religious groups. Of the approximately 10 million Catholics, two-thirds were Poles;[7] the rest were Lithuanians, White

[4] E. Winter, *Rußland und das Papsttum* II, 381–454; Winter emphasizes the Vatican's part in the French-Russian treaty in its ecclesiastical policies toward Russia.
[5] F. Engel-Janosi, op. cit. I, 268.
[6] E. Winter, *Rußland und das Papsttum* II, 478.
[7] In 1889, there were 9,679,818 Catholics in Poland and Russia, 5,932,123 of whom lived in the Russian part of Poland; cf. W. Urban, op. cit., 255.

Russians, Ukranians, Latvians, and Germans.[8] At the beginning of the twentieth century, state funds for the Orthodox Church amounted to about 30 million rubles, while the Catholics received only about 1.5 million rubles. Payment of state salaries to the Catholic clergy through the Roman Catholic Clerical College in Saint Petersburg considerably limited their independence. The entire correspondence between the Church administration and the Curia was conducted through the Ministry of the Interior. The preconized bishops (in each case it took exhaustive negotiations in order to find a candidate who was acceptable to both the tsarist government and the Vatican) were appointed by the Tsar. He also had to confirm in office all canons and other dignitaries. An instruction from the minister of education of 1900 demanded that the topics for final examinations in seminaries be in the Russian language and include history. Since this regulation was not followed by the Polish bishops, numerous clergymen could not be employed. Archbishop Józef Elias Szembek of Mogilev (1903–05) conducted a bishops' synod in 1904, during which the Roman Catholic episcopate of Russia compiled its demands to present to the government.

A manifesto, issued on 22 February 1903 by Nicholas II, expressed religious toleration and acknowledged the freedom of the Catholic Church to act, but it did not alleviate the distress of the Catholics in any way. Only after defeat in the Russo-Japanese War of 1904/05 and the proclamation of a constitutional system of government at the end of 1904 did the Tsar decide to issue a statement in which reforms were promised (e.g., freedom of belief and conscience). On 30 April 1905, he published a belief and toleration edict, which was followed by amnesties for religious offenders; this filled the Catholics with confidence. The Orthodox Church was termed the prevailing Church; it was allowed to maintain the right of propaganda; the penalties against those who left the Church and converted to another religious congregation were abolished. The Russian Old Believers, who had been cruelly persecuted since their separation from the Orthodox Church in the second half of the seventeenth century, could relax. The situation of the Catholics seemed particularly to improve, since the Tsar, in a man-

---

[8] For the Catholic settler who had migrated to the south of Russia in the second half of the eighteenth century, the bishopric of Cherson was made a suffragan bishopric of the archbishopric of Mogilev (1848). It was transferred to Tiraspol in 1852. Saratov on the Volga River became an episcopal see. Under the leadership of Bishops Franz Xaver Zottmann (1872–89), Eduard Baron von Ropp (1902–04), and Joseph Aloysius Keßler (since 1904, resigned 1929) a favorable development commenced, despite the fact that the Catholics suffered from Russification measures. In 1914, the diocese included 350,000 faithful, 90 percent of whom were Germans (cf. B. Stasiewski, *Die kirchliche Organisation,* 279–83).—The total number of German Catholics in Russia before World War I was 500,000; 80,000 lived in Siberia.

ifesto of 30 October 1905, ordered the government "to give the population immovable foundations of civil freedom according to the principles of absolute inalienable personal rights, freedom of conscience and speech, and the right of assembly."[9] Also, the resignations of Chief Procurator Pobedonostsev and his deputy C. V. Sabler were interpreted as a weakening of the supremacy of the Russian Orthodox Church over all other Christian confessions.

The optimism of the Catholics was soon shaken. At first, some relief was given them, for instance in the controversial language question. In 1906, the Curia yielded to the pressures to use the Russian language in preaching, and on 22 July 1907 it came to an agreement with Russia[10] concerning Russian language, history, and literature in the Catholic seminaries in Poland. After 1908, the Catholic monthly publication *Truth and Faith* appeared in Russian in Saint Petersburg. From the beginning, its editorial office had to struggle with censorship and in 1912 its publication was forbidden. It was replaced by the Russian paper *Words of Truth* (1913), which lobbied for the preservation of the Uniates's rites, among other things, but which collapsed in 1915.

The regime survived the year of crisis (1905/06). But after its stabilization, it stunted the growth of parliamentary life by suspending the First and Second Duma (1906/07), and through certain regulations and administrative measures it turned the relief granted to the non-Orthodox churches into an illusion. At the fourth Missions Congress in Odessa in 1908, Orthodox bishops demanded that the bishops be reprimanded and that the toleration edict be voided. In 1907, Eduard Baron von Ropp, since 1904 bishop of Vilna and a member of the First Duma and of the Catholic Conservative party, which he had founded, was recalled by Nicholas II because he had resisted the introduction of the Russian language into Catholic church services. He was replaced by an administrator sent by the Curia. In 1909, Bishop Cyrtovt of Kovno, together with three hundred clergymen, was accused of having failed to comply with the required formalities when converting from the Orthodox to the Roman Catholic Church. In 1910 the Catholic bishops were forbidden to deal directly with the Curia and to publish papal decrees without the permission of the government. The marriage decree *Ne temere* of the Council Congregation of 2 August 1907, the encyclical *Pascendi dominici gregis* of 8 September 1907 (concerning modernism), and the motu proprio *Sacrorum antistitum* of 1 September 1910 (concerning the antimodernist oath) were not allowed to be pub-

---

[9] P. Scheibert (ed.), *Die russischen politischen Parteien von 1905 bis 1917. Ein Dokumentationsband* (Darmstadt 1972), 29.
[10] Mercati I, 1097–98.

lished. In 1911, the nearly eighty-year-old administrator of the arch-bishopric of Mogilev, Titular Archbishop Stefan Anton Denisovič, was held responsible in Saint Petersburg for having established a Marianist Congregation in Moscow. His successor as archbishop of Mogilev, Vincenty Kluczyński (1910–14), was so worn down by the government's reprisals that he resigned in 1914.

On the eve of World War I, the Catholics were being suppressed in Russia just as they had been in the nineteenth century. The Roman Catholic Clerical College in Saint Petersburg, which was responsible for the joint affairs of the dioceses, consisted of the archbishop of Mogilev and two members appointed by the Tsar from among the higher clergy and from assistants elected in the various dioceses.[11] The government maintained a controlling influence, especially the Department of Foreign Cults in the Ministry of the Interior, in spite of the papal protests that the jurisdiction of the College be limited to merely material affairs. The hierarchy consisted of 15 bishoprics, including the archbishopric of Mogilev with 7 and the archbishopric of Warsaw with 6 suffragan bishoprics. Each bishop took care of a seminary. After the suspension of the Warsaw Academy (1867) there was only one academic institution of university rank, the Roman Catholic Clerical Academy in Saint Petersburg, which earned a reputation through its scholarly and ascetic training of qualified clergymen (53 bishops came from this institution).[12]

The effectiveness of the bishops and the secular and regular clergy in dealing with the faithful entrusted to them and in securing their loyal observance of Catholic traditions was wasted by their defensive stand against state pressures. The Russification measures, which were mostly aimed at the Catholics of Latin and Uniate rites, showed that Catholicism was merely tolerated. Catholicism was exposed to new burdens by the war, the consequences of the October Revolution of 1917 relative to ecclesiastical policies, and the growing independence of Poland and the surrounding Baltic areas after World War I.

The Three Polish Territories

After the fourth division of Poland at the Congress of Vienna, Russia possessed 82 percent, Austria 10 percent, and Prussia 8 percent of the Polish-Lithuanian Empire, which had been dissolved through its partitioning at the end of the eighteenth century. The Polish question kept the European cabinets busy until the Republic of Poland was founded in

[11] W. Gribowski, op. cit., 169.
[12] W. Urban, op. cit., 291.

1918. The passionate determination of the Poles to retain their language and their heritage, the activities of the emigrants, the hope of recovering freedom and unity by being doubly loyal toward the three dividing powers (after the failure of the uprisings in 1831, 1846, 1848, and 1863/64), the dissolution of the Russian Empire, and the defeat of the Central Powers were essential prerequisites for the restoration of the national independence of Poland. During these efforts, the Catholic Church formed a unifying link, transcending political boundaries. In the Resurrectionist Congregation of Priests, whose members were devoted to pastoral work, education, and tutorial activities, faith in the resurrection of Christ mixed in a curious way with belief in the resurrection of Poland.

In Russian territory, after the failure of the uprising of 1863/64 in which several Catholic clergymen had participated, the governor general of the western provinces enforced a rigorous regime, with reprisals against the bishops and priests continuing throughout the next decades: the closing of monasteries, the dissolution of the Uniate bishopric of Chelm (1875), the supervision of pastoral work, and measures aimed at the introduction of the Russian language into the Church. Leo XIII tried to relieve the predicament of the Polish Catholics by direct negotiations with the Tsars Alexander II and III and Nicholas II. The Poles were afraid that their national interests were being threatened by the Pope's agreement with the Russian government. In a public consistory on 19 February 1889, Leo XIII tried to defend himself against these charges. At the same time, through one of his directives, he impressed upon the newly appointed Polish bishops that their mission was to serve the mutual accord and friendly harmony between spiritual and secular powers.[13] The Pope's warnings to the Poles to obey the law and be loyal to the Russian Tsar, and his *epistula encyclica* to the Polish bishops of 19 March 1894,[14] which reminded clergy and laity of their duty as subjects of the Tsar, contributed little to détente. In spite of agreement concerning the appointment of bishops and official willingness to comply with the wishes of the Curia, nothing changed in regard to the curtailment of freedom for Polish Catholics.

In 1886 the regulation requiring that the construction of a church could be allowed only by the minister of the interior, after consultation with the responsible governor and Orthodox bishop, was extended to Polish territory. The regulation was also valid for non-Orthodox religious congregations. The government placed special emphasis on re-

---

[13] E. Winter, *Rußland und das Papsttum* II, 421.
[14] *Acta Leonis* V (1898), 243–54.

ligious instruction conducted in the Russian language. The law of 4 March 1885 regarding the Polish elementary schools left the decision to the curator of the Warsaw school district. He was to share the decision with the governor general whether Catholic religious instruction was to be given in Polish or Russian. In higher schools, the Orthodox teachers taught in Russian, since the Catholic priests refused to abandon their native language. In 1892, all Catholic parochial schools were placed under the supervision of the minister of national education. The result was the founding of secret Catholic parochial schools. To prevent the construction and maintenance of these illegal schools, penal regulations were enacted and again enforced in 1900. The aforementioned instructions of the minister of national education regarding examinations in seminaries were disobeyed, with the result that the governor general in Warsaw did not recognize the examinations and the appointment of newly ordained priests. When Tsar Nicholas II allowed them to reapply for the examination, there was no response. By 1905 the number of unemployed priests had risen to 156, the number of vacant parishes to 263. When, in the same year, the instruction was cancelled, the authorities declared their willingness to confirm even those candidates who had not taken an examination in the Russian language.

Nicholas II's edicts of toleration of April and October 1905 were enthusiastically welcomed by the Poles, since it seemed that the free development of their ecclesiastical life was now guaranteed. On 3 December 1905, the Pope addressed the Polish bishops of the Russian Empire,[15] praising them for their loyalty to the Apostolic See and demanding that they stand up for the preservation of peace, justice, and Christian education. The tensions regarding the language questions were eliminated, as can be deduced from the convention signed in Rome on 22 July 1907.[16] The number of houses of religious, which had rapidly decreased in the first decades and had only slowly risen at the end of the nineteenth century, increased again. Charity centers[17] and social activities commenced, e.g., the circle of young girls which had been organized by Countess Cecylia Plater-Zyberk and published the monthly *Stream* (*Prąd*), in order to waken the population to the social responsibilities of Catholicism. Representatives of the Catholic intelligentsia, such as Wladyslaw Reymont (1869–1925) and Henryk Sienkiewicz (1846–1916), were practicing Catholics.

The majority of the Catholics forced into Orthodoxy and belonging

---

[15] *AAS* XXVIII (1905–06), 321–27.
[16] Mercati I, 1097–98.
[17] K. Górski, *L'Histoire de la spiritualité polonaise: Le millénaire du catholicism en Pologne* (Lublin 1969), 340–42.

to the dissolved (1875) Uniate bishopric of Chelm had to suffer from the Russification measures and wanted to call upon the toleration edict of 1905. Since they were forbidden to return to their faith, about two hundred and thirty thousand converted from the Orthodox Church to Roman Catholicism between 1905 and 1910. In other parts of north-western and southwestern Russia, people who earlier had been force-fully converted to Orthodoxy now rejoined the Catholic Church. The Orthodox bishops, supported by the Holy Synod, organized counter-propaganda. The Orthodox Bishop Evlogi Georgievski of the recently created eparchy of Chelm, a diligent representative of the Russification policy, convinced the Third Duma to create the province of Chelm, a new ecclesiastical entity comprised of parts of the provinces of Lublin and Kielce (1912).[18] The purpose was to halt the expansion of Catholicism. As early as 1908, an Orthodox mission congress in Kiev had demanded the revocation of the toleration edict. The Association of the Russian People of 1906 requested in 1909 that the false interpretation of the Easter manifesto come to an end and that freedom to proselytize be granted only to the Russian State Church. In 1912, the Orthodox Bishop Nikolai of Warsaw declared in the State Council that the historic task of the Russian state used to be and still was the Russification of everything non-Russian and the conversion to Orthodoxy of everyone who was not a member.[19]

The growing pressure against Polish Catholicism was evidenced by the fact, among other things, that foreigners who had established religious orders after 1905 were expelled in 1910, e.g., the Redemptorists of Warsaw and the Franciscan friars of Lódź. When, on 21 January 1911, the priests came to Lublin to take the antimodernist oath, they were forced by police upon their arrival to depart immediately. They were informed that the papal directives were not valid in Russia, since they had not been announced via the proper channels of the state authorities.

In order to weaken Catholicism, the government and the Orthodox Church patronized the Mariavites,[20] who had developed from a society of nuns founded by Felicja Kozlowska (1862–1921) and an association of secular priests founded by Jan Maria Kowalski (1893), which strove for religious renewal among the clergy and people. The Mariavites' Eucharistic and Marian devotion tended toward mysticism and therefore the organization was not approved by Rome. The association of priests was proscribed by the Holy Office in 1904; on 5 December 1906, Jan

---

[18] 476,432 Catholics and 278,311 Orthodox lived in this area in 1913, cf. W. Urban, op. cit., 224.
[19] Ibid., 224.
[20] Ibid., 178–84, 245.

Kowalski, Felicja Kozlowska, and forty priests were excommunicated. As minister general, Kowalski organized a Marian Union, which on 28 November 1906 was recognized by the Russian cabinet council as a special Catholic religious community. In spite of repeated condemnation by the Roman authorities, the Mariavites spread quickly because of their support by the state; in 1909 a law regarding Mariavite parishes secured their position. Negotiations between Kowalski and the Utrecht Union resulted in the acceptance of the union by the Old Catholic churches. Kowalski had the bishop of Utrecht, Gerhard Gul, consecrate him as bishop and he established a new hierarchy with four bishoprics. The number of Mariavites may have reached a maximum of three hundred thousand to four hundred thousand when the Russian government and Orthodox dignitaries was supporting them in any way possible in order to halt the influence of the Roman Catholic Church. Even before World War I, many had left the new church. In spite of decline due to internal and external problems it is still in existence.

In Galicia, one of the Cisleithan crownlands of the Habsburgs, the Catholics were not as defensive as in Russia. In the first half of the nineteenth century, they were exposed to the effects of the state church, Viennese centralism and Germanization. However, they were aided by the self-government which the cities and rural communities had been granted in 1849, by the concordat between Pius IX and Emperor Franz I, concluded in 1855, but annulled in 1870 by Emperor Franz Joseph, and by the constitution of 1867, which favored Polish aspirations toward autonomy. Count Agenor Goluchowski, governor of Galicia, decreed the introduction of the Polish language in the schools, the courts, and civil offices. Numerous Poles were promoted by the Austrian government to the ministerial ranks and two of them to minister president (Count Alfred Potocki in 1870/71 and Count Kazimierz Badeni in 1895/97). They strengthened the special position of Galicia so that it became a "Polish Piedmont."[21] The Polonization of the two national universities in Crakow and Lemberg (which had Catholic theological faculties), the founding of the Crakow Academy for the Sciences (1872), and the collaboration of the conservative Galician aristocracy with the imperial court secured the political superiority of the Poles (about 45 percent of the total population of over 43 percent Ukrainians, 11 percent Jews, and 1 percent Germans).

Polish Catholicism of the Latin rite, which consisted of about 3.5 million faithful in 1910, had a somewhat tense relationship with the approximately 3 million Uniate Ukrainians[22] because of national differ-

---

[21] G. Rhode, op. cit., 413.
[22] Cf. below, pp. 369f.

ences. Even though the solution presented by the Concordat of 1870 resulted in several difficulties within the Catholic educational system and in other areas of the Church's public activity, the ecclesiastical organization of the archbishopric of Lemberg with the suffragan bishoprics of Przemysl and Tarnow and the prince bishopric of Crakow, which was placed under the jurisdiction of the Holy See in 1880 and expanded in 1886 through several deaneries of the diocese of Tarnow, could be enlarged. Outstanding Church politicians, theological writers, and priests were bishops like Cardinal Albin Dunajewski (1879–1914) and Prince Jan Kozielsko-Puzyna (1895–1910) of Cracow,[23] Archbishop Jozef Bielczewski of Lemberg (1900–23), Bishop Leon Walega of Tarnow (1901–33), and Jozef Sebastian Pelczar of Przemysl (died 1924). They were in close contact with the Holy See, as is documented by the letters of congratulation on the occasion of the silver anniversary of Cardinal Puzyna on 4 March 1911[24] and the golden anniversary of Bishop Pelczar's ordination to the priesthood.[25]

The Polish educational system made possible the development of an academic staff in science, art, and journalism. Aside from theological, mostly pastoral publications, the monthly *Przegląd Powszechny* (General Review) appeared in 1883 under the direction of the Jesuits, in which prominent Catholics wrote leading commentaries on fundamental questions of current interest. It became the main publication of Polish Catholicism known beyond the borders of Galicia.

Since Galicia's economic development did not keep pace with its intellectual and spiritual life, and the large increase in population could not be absorbed by industrialization, the peasantry was in danger of progressive deterioration. The Church was aware of its duties in dealing with social problems. In the face of the predominant conservatism of the Polish episcopate, pastor Stanislaw Stojalowski took an interest in the farmers and workers. He struggled against the Conservative Polish People's Party, which he stigmatized as antisocial and, because of its collaboration with the Austrian government, as antinational. He also displayed a socialist attitude and was therefore relieved of his parish and, in 1896, excommunicated and suspended. Both verdicts were lifted shortly afterward. In spite of Leo XIII's ban on his writing and preaching, and in spite of the complaints by Prince-Bishop Puzyna, he remained active on behalf of the Polish Peasants Party until his death in 1911.[26] Other clergymen, such as suffragan Bishop Dr. Josef Weber of

[23] Regarding the veto during papal elections in 1903, see above, p. 53.
[24] *ASS* III (1911), 160.
[25] Ibid. VI (1914), 181.
[26] E. Winter, *Rußland und die slawischen Völker,* 111–16, 159–65; F. Engel-Janosi, op. cit. I, 315–16; E. Winter, *Rußland und das Papsttum* II, 496.

Lemberg, worked in accord with Leo's ecclesiastical policies, which aimed at harmonious cooperation with the state. This is reflected in the address given by the Pope on 21 April 1888 to pilgrims from Galicia and Bukovina.[27] The social encyclical *Rerum novarum* of 15 May 1891 received attention here as well. Bishop Jozef Sebastian Pelczar initiated the founding of a Catholic Social Association in Przemysl in 1906, whose aims were the propagation of Catholic social principles.

Religious life was influenced by representatives of the older orders and younger religious communities. Jesuits who had been expelled from Prussia during the *Kulturkampf* found a new sphere of activity in Galicia. The Pallotines tried to establish a press apostolate in Lemberg in 1908. The Redemptorists formed an independent Polish province in the same year. Several new communities appeared: the male and female Albertines, founded by Adam Chmielowski (1845–1916), who followed the example of the Third Order of Saint Francis; the Sisters of Archangel Michael (*Michaelitki*), founded by Bronislaw Markiewicz (1842–1912); and the Fraternity of the Blessed Virgin Mary, the Queen of the Crown of Poland, inspired by Bishop Pelczar.

In the Prussian territory, the differences between the Protestant government and the Catholics, particularly the Polish-speaking population, had increased through the decades. After settlement of the conflict with Archbishop Martin Dunin of Gnesen-Posen (1831–42), his successor, Archbishop Leo von Przyluski (1845–65) persistently stood up for the restoration of Polish rights. In 1859, in the gardens of Saint Martin's Church in Posen, a memorial was erected for the Polish poet Adam Mickiewicz (1798–1855), a sign of the increase in the Polish national awareness in the ecclesiastical realm. The colonizing and Germanization tendencies of the Prussian state contributed to the growth of the Polish national consciousness. After 1870, the Polish policy of the German Empire created a struggle of nationalities in the eastern German regions, which continued (with few interruptions) until 1918. The school supervision law of 1871 and the decree requiring the use of German in the Polish schools of Silesia (1872), Posen, and West Prussia (1873), the systematic abolition of the Polish language in higher schools (1872–90), the introduction of German as the only official language in all public offices and businesses (1876), the anti-Polish measure during the *Kulturkampf* burdened the situation in regard to Church policy.[28]

[27] *Acta Leonis* III (1893), 61–62.
[28] J. Buzek, *Historya polityki narodowościowej rządu pruskiego wobec Polaków od traktatów wiedeńskich do ustaw wyjątkowych z r 1908* (Lemberg 1909); B. Stasieski, "Zur Geschichte der katholischen Kirche in Posen," *Geschichte der Stadt Posen,* ed. by G. Rhode (Neuendettelsau 1953), 219–21; L. Trzeciakowski, "Stosunki między państwem a koś-

Archbishop Miecislaus Ledóchowski of Gnesen-Posen (1865–86), who endorsed Polish religious instruction in high school classes and paid no attention to the so-called May laws, was the first bishop to be arrested (on 2 February 1874) and to be dismissed by the State Court of Justice in Berlin. In 1875, the time of his imprisonment in Ostrowo, Pius IX created him a cardinal for his courageous defense of the faith. After his expulsion he proceeded to send directives from Rome to his areas of jurisdiction and was subsequently penalized with fines for having usurped episcopal rights. During the negotiations to end the *Kulturkampf,* he was willing to resign. Aside from Ledóchowski, both his suffragan bishops, Janiszewski of Posen and Cybichowski of Gnesen, together with nearly 100 clergymen were arrested during the *Kulturkampf,* so that 97 parishes were vacant and 200,000 Catholics were deprived of proper pastoral care. The diocesan administrative offices were maintained by secret delegates empowered with special plenipotentiary authority. In spite of state pressures, the Polish Catholics were not discouraged by the *Kulturkampf.* They accepted the challenge and intensified their efforts to expand their social, cultural, and ecclesiastical independence.

After Ledóchowski's resignation, Pope Leo XIII made an attempt to eliminate the *Kulturkampf* laws by appointing Pastor Julius Dinder of Königsberg (originally from Ermland), archbishop of Gnesen-Posen (1886–90), and the only German in a long series of bishops who wanted to alleviate nationalism in the controversies regarding ecclesiastical policy. The Pope's attempt failed. He tried in vain to reach an agreement concerning the government's language policies, which were passionately rejected in Poland. Both clergy and diocesan officials ignored his directives and suggestions.

The expulsion of twenty-six thousand foreigners (1885–86) from the eastern provinces,[29] the settlement law of 1886, the East Marches Society of 1894, the fireplace law of 1904 (which was to limit new Polish settlements), the law regarding societies of 1908 (which required that even Polish societies use the German language in their statutes and

---

ciołém katolickim w zaborze pruskim w latach 1871–1914," *Studia i materiały do dziejów Wielkopolski i Pomorza* 9 (1968), 59–80; id., *Kulturkampf w zaborze pruskim* (Poznan 1970); L. Borodziej, *Pruska polityka oświatowa na ziemiach polskich w okresie Kulturkampfu* (Warsaw 1971); T. G. Jackowski, "Samoobrona polaków przed pruską polityką eksterminacyjną w końcu XIX i na początku XX wieku w poznánskiem," *Przegląd Zachodni* 27 (1971), 139–51.

[29] H. Neubach, *Die Ausweisungen russischer und österreichischer Staatsangehöriger aus Preußen in den Jahren 1885/86. Ihre Rolle in der deutschen Polenpolitik and in der Entwicklung des deutsch-polnischen Verhältnisses* (Würzburg 1966).

meetings), and the expropriation law of 1908[30] (which Cardinal Georg Kopp opposed in the House of Lords the same year) intensified the national struggle. During this time, the Poles were able to preserve and strengthen their national characteristics with determined efforts, through parliamentary activities of their factions in the Prussian Provincial Diet and the German *Reichstag,* and through cooperative societies and business organizations. Prelate Piotr Wawrzyniak (from 1892 until his death in 1910 president of the Polish savings bank cooperatives) and other clergymen tried to prevent the purchase of real estate from Polish hands and pursued a successful Polish settlement policy on parcelled latifundias.

Above all, the Poles demanded the reinstatement of Polish as the language of instruction in elementary schools, especially in religious instruction.[31] Their demands for the use of their own language were supported by the Center Party and the German Catholic conventions (1891–92, 1893, 1899, and 1900). Archbishop Florian Oksza-Stablewski of Gnesen-Posen (1891–1906) advocated the preservation of Polish as the language of religious instruction. He also objected to government measures requiring that the twelve- to fourteen-year-old pupils of elementary schools in Wrzesnia speak German during religion classes, which had resulted in the Wrzesnia school strike (1901). He also protested the decree demanding that 20 schools in the administrative district of Posen and 183 schools in the area of Bromberg use German during religious instruction, which had resulted in an extensive school strike in 1906. In a pastoral letter of 8 October 1906,[32] Oksza-Stablewski gave a summary of his efforts toward the protection of Polish religious instruction. He asked parents and clergy to devote more energy to the catechization of the young. He did not witness the end of the school strike, which lasted into 1907. At the beginning of the strike, 90,000 of the 241,000 children received religious instruction in Polish. In 1906, nearly 47,000 Polish children refused to attend 750 schools in

---

[30] This caused international indignation, cf. H. Sienkiewicz, *Prusse et Pologne. Enquête internationale organisée* (Paris 1909). The expropriation law was not applied until 1912 and those four cases received compensation.

[31] T. Grentrup, op. cit., 266–69; J. Chamot, "Rola kleru katolickiego w strajku szkolnym w Wielkopolsce 1906/07," *Studia z dziejów kościoła katolickiego* 1 (1960), 101–12; R. Korth, *Die preußische Schulpolitik und die polnischen Schulstreiks. Ein Beitrag zur preußischen Polenpolitik der Ära Bülow* (Würzburg 1963); M. Pirko, "Stanowisko arcybiskupa Floriana Stablewskiego na tle polityki rządowej w sprawie wrzesińskiej," *Studia z dziejów kościoła katolickiego* 5 (1967), 88–106.

[32] R. Korth, op. cit., 161–62.

the province of Posen. Since the government took rigorous steps against the parents and clergy,[33] the tensions remained.

From 1906 until 1914 the archepiscopal see of Gnesen-Posen remained vacant. At the outbreak of World War I the government approved the nomination of suffragan Bishop Edward Likowski as archbishop (1914/15) in order to appease the Polish population.

In the struggle between German and Polish nationalities, the Polish population succeeded in improving its position. The portion of Germans receded from 41 to 38.4 percent between 1871 and 1905. The Polish Catholics directed their energies toward the preservation of their national identity under the leadership of their archbishops of Gnesen-Posen and prominent prelates within and without ecclesiastical life. In addition to their insistence on the use of the Polish language in schools, they expanded their press.[34] After 1879, they published the *Ecclesiastical Review* (*Przegląd Kościelny*) in place of the outlawed (1874) *Catholic Weekly* (*Tygodnik Katolicki*). In 1895, Archbishop Stablewski provided the initiative for the publication of a weekly paper, the *Catholic Guide* (*Przewodnik Katoliki*). In 1906, at his suggestion, the new *Preacher Library* (*Biblioteka Kaznodziejska*), published between 1872 and 1894, was continued with the publication of the *New Preacher Library* (*Nowa Biblioteka Kaznodziejska*). He placed great emphasis on the training and continuing education of the clergy. The number of clergymen doing pastoral work in the archdiocese of Gnesen-Posen in 1873 amounted to 813; during the *Kulturkampf* it dropped to 513; by 1910 it increased to 821. The old Lubrańsk Academy in Posen had served as a seminary from 1780 to 1896. During the *Kulturkampf* it was forced to close its doors and it was not allowed to open them again until 1889. In 1896, the theology students were provided with a new building, where they attended theological and pastoral lectures after receiving basic philosophical training in Gnesen. In this context it is worth mentioning Polish scholarly societies and their publications, in which clergymen decisively participated. By means of lending libraries and book clubs, the clergy managed the distribution of religious writings.

The monasteries were centers that radiated Polish religiosity. The Community of Servants of the Blessed Virgin Mary, which was founded by Edward Bojanowski (1814–71), a Polish nobleman, and devoted to the care of the sick and the orphans, expanded. After the conclusion of the *Kulturkampf*, the orders and religious communities resumed their dras-

---

[33] Ibid., 165–70: List of penalties from the "documentation of convictions in criminal cases which had to do with the school strike (only convictions for nonattendence of school)."

[34] L. Müller, *Nationalpolnische Presse, Katholizismus und katholischer Klerus* (Breslau 1931).

tically confined activities. In 1895 Maria Karlowska established in Posen a new branch of the Sisters of the Good Shepherd.

The Poles of the German eastern provinces were a source of inspiration for the other Polish territories. Their tightly organized and concentric efforts towards national identity were highly esteemed by the Poles in Russia and Galicia. In view of the different political developments in the three territories, ecclesiastical life contributed to the internal consolidation of Polish Catholicism. Polish self-confidence was strengthened by reports of the activities of the chief pastors and the clergy in numerous parishes,[35] achievements of the orders and other religious communities, and the successes of associations on various levels. Adherence to the Catholic faith and to Polish nationalism merged into one inseparable entity, in spite of all social differences and parties. The Polish Catholics looked toward the popes as advocates of their national interests, even though the popes practised caution in their addresses and letters in order to avoid conflicts with the governments. Cardinal Miecislaus Ledóchowski, who, after 1883, worked in the papal Secreteriat of State (1885 secretary of the papal briefs and 1892 prefect of the Congregation for Propaganda) was their influential spokesman at the Curia.

Austria-Hungary[36]

The dual Habsburg Monarchy of Austria-Hungary, with its many nationalities,[37] harbored numerous internal and external political problems in the decades preceding its decline at the end of World War I. These problems greatly affected the Slavic population in regard to the development of its ecclesiastical history. In 1900 Austria was estimated to have 23 million Roman Catholics, 3 million Uniates, and 600,000 Orthodox.[38] At the same time Hungary was estimated to have 9 million Roman Catholics, 2 million Uniates, and 3 million Orthodox. In addition there were 700,000 Orthodox and 350,000 Catholics in the Turkish provinces of Bosnia and Herzegovina, which had been occupied in 1878 and annexed in 1912. The Orthodox and Uniate Christians belonged to Slavic nationalities. Slavs of the Roman Catholic creed were mainly the Poles in Galicia, the Czechs and Slovaks in Bohemia, and the

---

[35] From 1850 to 1860, the number of parishes in the three parts of Poland increased from 3,007 to 3,154, the number of secular clergy from 4,682 to 5,250, cf. A. Stanowski, "Diocèses et paroisses de Pologne au XIXe et au XXe siècle," Le Millénaire du catholicisme en Pologne (Lublin 1969), 128–29.

[36] Galicia was part of it.

[37] See above, chap. 2.

[38] Including Galicia.

Croatians, Slovenes and some of the Serbs in the south of Austria-Hungary.

The Austro-Hungarian *Ausgleich,* adopted due to pressure by Hungary in 1867, was criticized by Slavic politicans who endeavored to change the Monarchy into a federation of free and equal nations as giving unjustified preference to the Magyars. By 1871 the Czechs voiced their claims against the centralistic German guardianship. In 1880 they effected a language ordinance for Bohemia which required that even in purely German areas each application had to be filled out in the language of the applicant and trials had to be conducted in the language of the accused. In 1882/83, they succeeded in having the University of Prague divided, and after 1891 there existed a German and a Czech Catholic theological faculty with eight professors and one lecturer each. In April 1897 language ordinances for Bohemia and Moravia followed. They decreed dual language usage for all judicial and administrative authorities. Even though the regulations were endorsed by the majority of deputies (comprised of Czechs, Poles, Slovenes, the two conservative groups of the Catholic People's party, and the Center), they had to be suspended under the pressure of the opposition. Not until 1913, under the impact of the impending World War, was the way paved for successful German-Czech negotiations for a compromise in the language question.

In the course of these efforts, the Catholics worked for an expansion of their rights in the following areas: in the archdiocese of Prague, which in 1886 established a Czech seminary for boys in Pribam, in the diocese of Leitmeritz (with 75 percent Germans and 25 percent Czechs), and in the archdiocese of Olmütz, where Czech was spoken exclusively in the east and south. Since the election reform of 1907, Christian forces emerged as rivals of the old national parties (Old and Young Czechs), which formerly claimed exclusive representation, especially among the rural population. From the beginnings of the Czech Christian socialist party formations at the end of the nineteenth century, which took shape in 1904, arose the conservative wing, the People's Party (*Lidová strana*) in Bohemia (1911) and the Catholic National Party (*Katolicko-národní strana*) in Moravia.[39] The Catholic clergyman Jan Šrámek (1870–1953) could consolidate his first success by merging ecclesiastical and national ideas in a true People's Party.[40] In order to alleviate the tensions between the German- and Slavic-speaking clergy,

[39] F. Prinz, op. cit., 118.
[40] Šrámek held several ministerial offices in Czechoslovakia between 1921 and 1938. In 1940–45 he was minister president of the Czech exile government in London.

Leo XIII turned to the bishops of Bohemia and Moravia with his letter of 20 August 1901, asking them to nurture their inherited language, to care for all of the faithful with equal love, to avoid the language controversies, to prevent disagreements in seminaries, and to seek harmony in their dioceses.[41]

Toward the Slovaks, who gradually voiced their claims for autonomy, the government of the Kingdom of Hungary showed no kindness. It oppressed all non-Magyar nationalities and conducted a strict policy of Magyarization, which extended into the ecclesiastical realm. In 1897, Pastor Andrej Hlinka (1864–1939) of Ružomberok founded the *People's Newspaper* (*L'udové Noviny*); the Slovak People's Party, whose goal was political and religious freedom for their own nationality, was formed in 1905. His propaganda on behalf of the Slovaks' national autonomy in Parliament brought him in conflict with state and Church authorities. In 1906, when he supported the opposition in the Hungarian Parliament, where Catholic deputies endorsed the cabinet's bills, he was sentenced to three and one-half years in jail and suspended by his bishop for his political activities. The Council's Congregation annulled the suspension in 1909[42] and Hlinka was allowed to resume his pastoral work. He later cooperated with the Czechs in the formation of the Czechoslovakian Republic.

Like the Slovaks, the Carpathian Ukrainians, Rumanians, and Serbs suffered under the Magyarization process, which also included the educational system under Minister of Religious Affairs Count Albert Apponyi (1906–10) and which made no exception for religious instruction. Not until 1914 did the Hungarian government give in to the pressures of the disadvantaged nationalities. It permitted religious instruction in the respective mother tongues in all elementary and civil schools as well as in teacher seminaries.[43]

In the south of the Dual Monarchy, life for the Slavs was extremely tense. The majority of the Croatians belonged to the Kingdom of Croatia and Slavonia, bound to the Austrian crown; one part belonged to the Cisleithian-Austrian half of the Empire in Istria and Dalmatia, the other to Bosnia-Herzegovina, while the Slovenes belonged to the western part of the Empire in Carnolia, in the south of Styria, and in Carinthia. The Serbs, who had achieved absolute independence at the Congress of Berlin in 1878 and had formed their own kingdom in 1878, tried to attract the minority in the south of the two Austro-Hungarian portions, mainly from Bosnia and Herzegovina, and they propagan-

---

[41] *ASS* XXXII (1900–01), 321–23.
[42] A. Hudal, op. cit., 279.
[43] T. Grentrup, op. cit., 485–86.

dized a Great Serbian South Slavic Empire, which was to include Serbs, Croatians, and Slovenes.

While the Slovenes and Croatians had their roots in Western culture and Roman Catholicism, the Serbs were rooted in the East and in Orthodoxy. After centuries of oppression by the Turks, all three nationalities were filled with a tremendous desire for freedom and left no stone unturned to achieve their political, cultural, and religious independence. Attempts failed to buffer the alternating pressures of the South Slavic question by reorganizing Austria-Hungary along federalistic lines or according to a triadic empire concept in place of the current dualism (Austria-Hungary). The representatives from Croatia, Slovenia, and Dalmatia passed a resolution in Rijeka in 1905 in which they demanded the unification of Croatia and Dalmatia and the triadic organization of the state.

By the beginning of the nineteenth century the Slovenes had created a uniform written language. Their awakening national consciousness is reflected in their societies, cooperatives, and in the Sokol movement. Together with the Croatians, they attempted a solution within the framework of the Habsburg Empire. Under the leadership of the clergyman Dr. Janez Krek, the political and economic organization of the rural population improved. Dr. Anton Korošec (1872–1940) founded the Slovenian Farmers' Party (1907), approved a southern Slavic agreement, and accepted in 1918 the chairmanship of the Slovenian-Croatian National Council.

The Croatians were much more active. They were not satisfied with autonomy in regard to administration, education, and the judiciary, which they had been granted through the Hungarian-Croatian Agreement of 1868.[44] Franjo Rački (1828–94), who was the first president of the Croatian Academy of Sciences in Zagreb (1866–86) and leader of the Croatian People's Party since 1880, and Bishop Josip Jurij Strossmayer (1815–1905)[45] were the spokesmen of their national interests for decades.

The bishopric of Djakovo was headed by Bishop Strossmayer, from 1849/50 until his death, according to his motto "all for faith and country."[46] In 1900, 253,770 Catholics of the Roman rite, 29,000 Uniates, and 169,000 Orthodox lived there. Of ninety parishes, fifty-five were Croatian-speaking and three German; thirty parishes had a mixed Croatian-German population and two a mixed Croatian-Hungarian

---

[44] W. Felczak, *Ugoda Węgiersko-chorwacka 1868* (Wroclaw 1969).
[45] J. Matl, "Josef Georg Stroßmayer," *Neue Österreichische Biographie* IX (1956), sect. 1, 73–83; R. Aubert, *Le pontificat de Pie IX* (Paris² 1962), 409–10.
[46] J. Matl, op. cit., 74.

population. In spite of his political and cultural dedication to his people, Bishop Strossmayer tried to bridge differences for the sake of a union with Rome by demonstrating his loyalty to the Habsburg Monarchy, furthering the Uniates and pursuing the idea of uniting all southern Slavs, even the Orthodox Serbs. In 1872, he retired from active politics. He opposed the Hungarian claims and the hegemony of either Croatians or Serbs, and furthered with his patronage the development of Croatian culture. This can be demonstrated by his donations to the University of Zagreb (1866), the Croatian Academy of Sciences (1867, opened in 1874), and the art gallery in Zagreb. Furthermore, his support was valuable to scholarly publications and instrumental in the construction of a representative cathedral in Djakovo, which was inaugurated in 1882. In view of the concepts of the governments in Vienna and Budapest, his Catholic pan-Slavism brought about conflicts with the national Croatian politician Dr. Ante Starčević (1823–96), who ruthlessly fought the Serbs and demanded a Greater Croatia, which, in addition to its native land, was to include Bosnia, Herzegovina, and Dalmatia. It was to be on an equal footing with Hungary. Strossmayer reestablished the Croatian Institute S. *Girolama dei Schiavoni* in Rome, which Leo XIII, upon a motion by the Croatian episcopate, renamed *Collegium pro gente croatica,*[47] hoping, as did his secretary of state, Rampolla, that it might become a stepping stone for the ecclesiastical unification movement among the Balkan Slavs.

In contrast, Joseph Stadler (1843–1918), after 1881 archbishop of Sarajevo, expected the college to be a nursery for a Catholic Greater Croatia. He carefully pursued the development of the ecclesiastical organization aided by Jesuits, Franciscans, and several religious orders of women. In 1904–11 he wrote a textbook on scholastic philosophy in the Croatian language. During the reorganization of the ecclesiastical arrangement after the occupation of Bosnia and Herzegovina (in 1895 a census counted 675,000 Orthodox, 55,000 Moslems, and 350,000 Catholics), Leo XIII established the archdiocese of Sarajevo with the suffragan bishoprics of Banja Luka and Mostar. During the decades before World War I, the number of Catholics increased to almost 400,000 because of the influx of Catholic civil servants, soldiers, and businessmen. They were cared for by the archbishops of Sarajevo and the bishops of Banja Luka in Bosnia. The bishops of Mostar were the chief pastors in Herzegovina. After 1890, they were simultaneously administrators of the old bishopric of Markana-Trebinje, which had been part of the medieval metropolitan see of Ragusa.

---

[47] This was protested by various people, cf. F. Engel-Janosi, op. cit. I, 318–21, and G. Adriányi, op. cit., 330–33.

The constitutional annexation of Bosnia and Herzegovina in 1908 did not change the ecclesiastical situation, but the resulting international tensions led to World War I, in spite of the agreement between Austria and Turkey concerning the Serbian "Great Power" aspirations and because the European powers were ready for action. During this war, Catholic Slavs fought on both sides. The majority of the Slavic Catholics was supported by Austria-Hungary, while the Orthodox Slavs were protected by Russia.

Southeast Europe

Greece had received its independence in 1830. In the decades between the reorganization of the Balkan states as a result of the Russo-Turkish War (1877–78) and the outbreak of World War I, the following independent principalities became kingdoms: Rumania (1881), Serbia (1882), Bulgaria (1908), and Montenegro (1910). Bulgaria received its independence in 1912. The Ottoman Empire lost one stronghold after another in southeast Europe and had to confine itself to eastern Thrace. In all those states the Catholics were merely a minority of the population.

The ethnographical and religious cohesiveness of the population in Rumania (92 percent Rumanians, 91.5 percent Orthodox) and the long reign of their first king, Charles I (1866–1914) was advantageous for the development of the state. In 1914 there were 100,000 Roman Catholics and 50,000 Uniate Christians among the total population of 6 million. On 23 March 1883 the archbishopric of Bucharest was founded in Wallachia, for which apostolic administrators had been responsible for 150 years. The first bishops were chosen from the congregations of the Passionists, who had taken care of the Catholic immigrants for a long time. They were forbidden, however, to make propaganda among the Orthodox. As for higher education, in five of their houses members of the Congregation of the English Ladies assisted them. For the Catholics in Moldavia, the bishopric of Jassy was established in 1884 and made directly responsible to the Holy See. In Jassy, Conventuals, Jesuits, and the Sisters of Our Lady of Sion were active. It was not easy to train a native clergy because most members of the orders were foreigners.

Neighboring Bulgaria was ruled by Prince Alexander Battenberg (1879–85), who expanded his territory toward the south by incorporating eastern Rumelia, and by Ferdinand I (1887–1918), who adopted the title of tsar in 1908, but had to surrender southern Dobrudja to Rumania and Macedonia to Serbia after the Second Balkan War (1913).

The majority of the population was Orthodox Christian. The Capuchin missionary Andreas Canova, who, as bishop, headed the vicariate apostolic of Plovdiv-Sofia from 1848 to 1868,[48] participated in the Bulgarian unification movement which began in 1859–61 but could not sustain itself. In 1883 the responsibility for the Catholics living in Bulgaria was taken on by the old bishopric of Nicopolis (reinstated in 1648), whose see was transferred to Ruščuk the same year, and the apostolic vicariate of Plovdiv-Sofia with its see in Plovdiv, whose incumbents had been titular bishops since 1885. They cared for about 27,000 Catholics assisted by Capuchins, Conventuals, Jesuits, Assumptionists, Passionists, and nuns of various congregations. When the Catholic Prince Ferdinand had his son and heir to the throne baptized in the Orthodox rite (1895/96), because the Chamber had demanded this, Leo XIII protested. The Pope called it a betrayal of conscience for the sake of politics.[49] In spite of this incident, the Curia hoped that the Bulgarians would join the union. Pius X advised the Habsburg diplomats to closely align with Bulgaria and Rumania. He was concerned that the Slavs could side with the worst enemy of the Church, Russia.[50]

In Serbia, Orthodoxy was the state religion. In spite of the religious freedom guaranteed by the Congress of Berlin in 1878, the Catholics were suppressed by the government and the Orthodox hierarchy. The political uprisings and changes, the Greater Serbian movement, and the antagonism between Austria-Hungary and Russia were also a problem for them. Not until 1855 were they allowed to establish their own parish in Belgrade. The old bishopric of Belgrade existed only as a titular bishopric. In 1728/29 it had been united with the bishopric of Semendria. The Catholics' jurisdiction lay in the hands of neighboring bishops or vicars apostolic. In 1851 Bishop Strossmayer was appointed vicar apostolic for the principality of Serbia. In this capacity he made contact with Serbian government circles during his visitation travels. In 1886 the bishopric of Belgrade was reinstated, incorporated into the new Church province of Scutari, and between 1898 and 1914 placed directly under the Propaganda Fide. It had about 10,000 Catholics and was elevated to an archbishopric by the concordat of 24 June 1914.[51] As the suffragan bishopric of Scoplje, it was to incorporate all areas gained by Serbia after the Balkan Wars. The bishopric was formed from the archbishopric of the same name and included about 15,000 Catholics. The wars delayed the development of a Church organization, which did not develop until 1924 in the Yugoslavian state.

[48] A. Tarnovaliski, op. cit., 47–51.
[49] Schmidlin, PG II, 518.
[50] F. Engel-Janosi, op. cit. II, 125.
[51] Mercati I, 1100–3.

In the principality of Montenegro, where 90 percent of the population were Orthodox, the Catholics were under the archbishopric of Antivari, which, since the concordat with the Curia in 1886, was directly responsible to Rome.[52] In this region, the use of Old Slavic liturgical texts was permitted. They were, to be sure, almost literal translations of the Roman liturgy into modern Church Slavic (*Grajdanka*). When one missal was printed in Cyrillic letters (in Rome, 1893) according to Leo XIII's wish, the archbishop asked for permission to print it in Glagolitic script, so that it might not be mistaken for an Orthodox publication. The number of Catholics increased between 1886 and 1914 from 7,000 to 13,000.

In Albania, which was ruled by the Turks from 1468 until 1912, the majority of the population was Islamic. The southern and eastern areas were populated also with strong Slavic groups which confessed to Orthodoxy and Roman Catholicism. A Turkish-Islamic syncretism had developed, which the archbishops of Durrës and Scutari, the Franciscans who were active as missionaries, and the Jesuits tried to confine. In 1905 the archbishopric of Durrës had about 13,000 Catholics; the archbishopric of Scutari with its bishoprics of Lezhë, Pult, and Sapë had nearly 70,000. Since the Habsburg Monarchy exercised a cultural protectorate in Albania, pursuing political as well as religious goals, and since this area was an intersection of Italian, Croatian, Serbian, and Pan-Slavic interests, conflicts resulted within Catholicism, which was partly inclined toward and partly against Austria-Hungary.[53] Aside from the language problem in schools and seminaries, propaganda in favor of the introduction of Slavic Church texts played a role.

In Greece the majority of the population belonged to the Orthodox. For the small group of Catholics, Pius IX created the archbishopric of Athens (1875) in addition to the existing archbishoprics of Korfu and Naxos. There were few Slavs among the approximately 660,000 Catholics, but their number increased through Greece's expansion toward the north. Because of the Bulgarian claim to all of Macedonia, from which Serbia had received some parts in 1913, a new ecclesiastical organization could not be effected.

The archbishoprics of Scutari and Durrës, located in Turkish territory, and their suffragan bishoprics had been incorporated into the Balkan states. The patriarch vicar of Constantinople was responsible for the

---

[52] Ibid., 1048–50.
[53] F. Engel-Janosi, op. cit. I, 310, and G. Adriányi, op. cit., 279–93.

few Catholics (about 50,000 in 1914), few of whom were Slavs. The Latin patriarch of Constantinople resided in Rome. They were represented at the Sublime Porte by a *vekil*, chief of the chancellory of the Catholic *Reaya*.

The internal complaints of the Slavic peoples and the policies of the great powers, which interfered with the ecclesiastical affairs of the Catholics, prevented any increase in the religious activities of both the Roman Catholics and the Uniates (which were represented in most southeastern European states). The bishops could only maintain the heritage entrusted to them, assisted by the clergy and the religious orders.

The Development of Catholicism
in Modern Society

CHAPTER 12

Catholicism in Society as a Whole

During the pontificate of Leo XIII the Catholic movements arisen from the confrontation with modern society as it evolved from revolution formed themselves into social groups in various countries within society as a whole and thus gave rise to what today is called Catholicism. The idea of restoration had failed; the revolution of the bourgeoisie could not be revoked, having achieved its last victory with the occupation of Rome, which, in conjunction with the commune uprising in Paris, marked the beginning of the revolution against the bourgeoisie. It was an epoch-making turning point in the history of the Catholic Church, representing, at first, a fundamental change in its relation to the "world," touching its very essence and self-awareness. From the time of Constantine the Great until the French Revolution, the Church was able to absorb all political figures into its own organism, duplicating or assimilating them. Indeed, in the early stages of the West, it was even capable of portraying the *imago imperii.* This is no longer true in the age of the liberal and democratic constitutional state and the "growing industrial society with its continuous changes in its stratification." It is no longer true, even though the Church's "lack of social station . . . was still hidden until well into the second half of the nineteenth century."[1]

---

[1] C. Bauer, *Bild der Kirche,* 25f.—The Church's "lack of social station" refers to its position within the total industrial society with its rapid change of economic, social, and intellectual conditions. This is not contradicted by the fact that Catholicism as a special group takes up its position with emphasis, trying to preserve the Church's guidelines since Leo XIII. These guidelines become necessarily more abstract the less the Church is able to "reflect the society" in all its contradictions and the more the differences between the various Catholicisms and the controversies within them have to be considered. The Church has its "social station" within these Catholicisms (as special groups), which can only be termed ideo-typically with the singular "Catholicism" (which will be used in this sense henceforth). Therefore, the history of the Church will from now on be largely the history of Catholicisms, "Church" and "Catholicism" not being identical.— German Catholicism is given preferential treatment in this chapter. The reason is that chapters 1 and 3 concentrate on the *Kulturkampf,* as was planned.

The cultural forms of Catholicism of the various countries took their classical shape during the pontificate of Leo XIII and were typical until the first third of the twentieth century. The multiplicity of denominational associations, especially in Germany, proved statistically to be rather successful. So was the press, ranging from daily papers to intellectual periodicals, whose circulation, with the exception of religious mass literature, was not competitive but did have dedicated readers supporting it. All this was an expression of a strong self-awareness, which, in turn, could affect daily life through solidarity. G. Goyau glorified the *Catholicisme social,* to be understood in a general sense, as a "society of saints" in the midst of the modern world, turning away from the individualism of Châteaubriand toward a *fraternité,* which he said was a definite reaction to the concept of a lay society, and he related his vision of the human society to the *société surnaturelle:* the dream of the old relationship between reality and its image.[2] But he was compelled to bewail the misfortune of the Catholics in his country, who appeared to be the rearguard of society, but were in reality the vanguard.[3] But it is exactly this assessment, be it from the point of view of the liberal bourgeoisie or the Socialists, which defines, if not the "lack of station," a deficient relationship to society as a whole. Even though Catholicism took initiatives, particularly in reference to the social question, it simply used the sociological and political configurations of the postrevolutionary world rather than accepting them from within, at least initially. This is also valid for the popular movements, for the workers' pilgrimages to Rome,[4] for the nonecclesiastical lay societies and their activities,[5] which are, after all, phenomena of an increasingly democratic

[2] G. Goyau I, 69–78, II, 4.

[3] Ibid. I, 211; in regard to a debate in the French Chamber in 1896 about women and child labor where a deputy spoke of the identity of labor potential and worker by referring to Marx: "Ce n'est point le socialisme seulement, c'est le christianisme social, qui s'appuie sur un tel fondement; et l'on pourrait . . . rapprocher Leon XIII non moins aisément que Karl Marx" (I, 234).

[4] W. Schwer, *Leo XIII,* 60: "For years, the princely gate of the Vatican remained closed because the deluded kings of this world were no longer able to find their way to Rome. Then Leo XIII opened it again and in came a workers' pilgrimage which had crossed the Alps in order to take home the blessings of the Pope, just like the sovereigns of days gone by had received their imperial crown." As much as the Pope, after 1887–88, liked to appeal to the people directly over the heads of their governments, and as much as some sort of papal patriotism was able to integrate the minority groups of ecclesiastically minded people—such a rather pathetic picture neither captures the ecclesiastical nor the secular realities.—W. Schwer follows the picture of Melchior de Vogüe, quoted in M. Turmann, *Catholicisme social* (Paris 1901).

[5] At the Catholic Convention of 1881 in Bonn, the lawyer F. Porsch said that the lay activities spurred by the *Kulturkampf* "merely reflected a state of distress," and there was hope for a period of time when "they will be able to practice the guardianship which God provided in order to rule His Holy Church" (Kißling II, 78f).

society. Their tendency toward independence boded conflict with the clerical claim for leadership. The terms in which Catholicism expressed itself were borrowed, and its self-righteous expectations of asserting itself within the total society by means of its re-Christianization had the characteristics of an illusion.

In this context belongs Catholicism's realization of its internationality, which was demonstrated at congresses when foreign guests of the same religion were welcomed.[6] In reality, the national differences were quite substantial, even if one ignores the effects of international political factors, as for instance the Triple Alliance of Germany, Austria, and Italy. Of course, the concept of internationality was realized in the sovereign common to all Catholics and, no matter how controversies about certain issues regarding ecclesiastical policies arose, the authority of the Pope within Catholicism was not questioned during Leo XIII's pontificate. It was intentionally nurtured by observing certain anniversaries and was extensively interpreted by the Pope when he defined the competence of the nuncios,[7] as well as by lay representatives.[8] At major public events such as the Catholic conventions and Eucharistic world congresses (as

---

[6] This is what Windthorst said at the Catholic Convention of 1883 in Düsseldorf about an "international assembly of Catholics" under the leadership of the Pope, similarly in Breslau in 1886 (Kißling II, 86).

[7] See above, p. 22.

[8] Windthorst was upset because of the Vatican's policies in Berlin, which seemed too conciliatory to him. But August Reichensperger told him at the Catholic Convention in Trier in 1887 that one had to serve the Pope, "whose position in the world does not allow him to fulfill our, the Prussian ultramontanes, every whim and wish" (Kißling II, 114).—The celebration of the year 1900, in preparation since 1896, was the subject of controversies because it was not an ecclesiastical affair and because there were reasons to doubt whether Leo XIII would survive the turn of the century. Prince Karl zu Löwenstein wrote about such opinions, toward which Cardinal Mazzella was also inclined: "The Holy Father is not only an infallible teacher, but also the helmsman at the wheel, who is distinguished by special dignity. His judgement about the expediency of a matter is not confirmed by his infallibility, but by the great likelihood of the good, the useful, and God's will speaking through him." K. Buchheim, *Ultramontanismus,* 497, noted in this respect: "The historian has to record the fact that this conviction of faith proved to be correct" because the Pope survived.—Theodor Wacker (cf. chap. 35), at the Catholic Convention in Koblenz in 1890, nurtured illusionary hopes: "Once the social kingdom they mention has taken shape and life, nothing will be more natural than the social Emperor and the social Pope joining hands and staying together" (quoted from Buchheim, 337). Windthorst was more sceptical. One should not overlook the fact that all Catholicisms experienced a certain indifference toward the "Roman question," not only in Germany, where Triple Alliance policies represented an element which even the Center could not ignore. The change in the slogan of protest which was obligatory for every Catholic convention was significant for the Pope: In 1890, in Koblenz (moderately edited by Windthorst), they pleaded "for restoration of the territorial sovereignty of the Holy See"—in 1898, in Neiße, in rather general terms for "sacred rights" referring to Leo's Italian encyclical of 5 August (Kißling II, 281f).

soon as they were fully developed), the idea of the *Ecclesia militans* as the Church of the martyrs took an outspoken militant turn. For example, at a Catholic convention in Trier in 1887, Bishop Korum preached about the *Militia Christi,* and the Porta Nigra was bathed in a sea of flames, above which appeared a cross with the illuminated words: *Stat crux, dum volvitur orbis.*

The forms of Catholicism, to be sure, were not merely at odds with the principles of the liberal bourgeoisie but were also struggling with more or less fierce internal conflicts. These differed according to the specific historic situation and obstructed an international consensus. Attempts were made to divide the Catholicism of the various countries[9] where the pre-revolutionary Church had been the "established Church" (like Spain, Portugal, Latin America, France, Italy, and Austria-Hungary), and the countries whose recent history did not accord the Catholic Church this kind of status and therefore "had fewer difficulties in adjusting to the new political conditions of the nineteenth century."[10] This general typology certainly provides some useful insights, but distinctions must be made. Catholicism in Bismarck's Germany, for instance, where the Church was never "established," significantly differed from Catholicism in the United States. What the different forms of Catholicism had in common in all countries—varied according to their respective social structures—was that they were composed of the same social strata, although less so among the upper classes, as society in general. This posed the problem to what degree Catholicism could act as an integrating force on the conflicting interests of society's subdivisions. The strength of identity of each group depended on the extent to which, in addition to the issue of Church and state, social contrasts could be bridged. A strong, distressed minority could exploit this circumstance, as Windthorst demonstrated brilliantly at the Catholic Convention of 1882 in Frankfurt.[11]

[9] Chaps. 1–11.

[10] J. N. Moody, op. cit., "this dichotomy in the historical experience of modern Catholics in their relation to the modern state is the cause of considerable confusion."

[11] The struggle against defeat (by a majority of votes) "will be even more effective when everyone learns once and for all who we are . . . thus, let us be strong in faith, keep our eyes open, and may we be united, then no one can harm us" (Kißling II, 89).—German Catholicism, however, is different. Unlike any other, it was organized in a political party and it could handle its social heterogeneity. It emerged in the eighties after the upswing of industrialization by making use of the "possibility of balancing the interests in the field of politics" (C. Bauer, *Wandlungen,* 37). It was not easy continuously to restore this balance. The vehement debate over the legally mandatory guilds which the Catholic leaders of trade had demanded at the Catholic Convention in Düsseldorf in 1883 and the social politicians of the Center opposed was concluded by Windthorst with the rhetorical phrase "that we completely agree on all aspects of ecclesiastical and social life" (Kißling II, 165).

Between Total Revision and Reform

It is a characteristic mark of Catholicism that it always saw the "social question," in a narrow sense in the "perspective of the total society" and the labor question as part of the "integral social reform question."[12] This view was only held by some theoreticians in areas where Catholics were in the extreme minority, as in Great Britain and in the United States. Therefore, it is necessary to integrate the Catholic social movements into the concept of the total society. Only then does the dilemma which Catholicism faced wherever it had to strive for more than the civil equality of a small minority become visible. Either it had to inculcate fundamental changes within the total society in which it was embedded (since it was clearly not of the same spiritual descent), or it had to content itself with realizing its principles by way of reforms within the plurality of the total society, foregoing its own concepts and making compromises along the way. This dilemma survived the turn of the century and was resolved, depending on the situation of the individual countries. Even though the differences between the countries have to be considered, the "changes in the socio-political realm of ideas relative to German Catholicism in the nineteenth century," as Clemens Bauer described them, can be regarded as a model case. Change meant primarily Christianization and re-Christianization, which was difficult to equate with charitable activities as proletarization grew in a capitalist society and was increasingly recognized as a general condition that was not absorbed by the "labor problem." When Edmund Jörg termed liberalism the "ruling spirit of our time," and the "natural son of the new national economy," thus closely connecting political and ideological liberalism with the capitalist economy,[13] a "total social reform" could indeed be regarded as the main task of Catholicism, whether "class inspired" in a sentimental social sense or impregnated with socialistic features, whether it was called Christian or not. However one chooses to assess the "newly created socio-economic reality," the desire for fundamental structural alterations of society had to either vanish in utopia or, without admitting it, take on a revolutionary character. How deeply Catholicism was affected by the idea of developing a concept that would

---

[12] C. Bauer, *Wandlungen*, 46.

[13] C. Bauer, *Wandlungen*, 23, 29 (including quotation of E. Jörg), 34, 30.—Of course, there are differences between economic liberalism on the one hand and the not necessarily identical political and ideological liberalism on the other hand (cf. C. Bauer, "Liberalismus," *StL*[6] V, 370–80); but it is probably incorrect to say that the Catholic disputations against liberalism only gathered the "most extreme objects of attack under one overall term" (C. Bauer, *Wandlungen*, 29), since differentiating the liberal segments does not preclude considering liberalism as a total phenomenon.

embrace all of society and putting it in competition with a liberal bourgeois ideology is documented by the encyclical *Rerum novarum.* It was penetrated by only a few ideas about a "total social reform," but was able to revitalize the principal disputes within Catholicism, which had acquiesced to the facts of capitalism under the leadership of the Center Party and followed the path of social reform.[14]

The Problem of Toleration

The "broken relationship" of the Church to the liberal bourgeois society is a phenomenon which is characteristic of all forms of Catholicism, though not so much in the United States during the Gibbons era where the leading segments of the episcopate, although opposed by the Corrigan group, were firmly anchored in the Constitution, i.e., in the principles of human rights. The reasons for this attitude were not merely based on ecclesiastical policy and tactics. In reference to modern society, this is one of the Church's basic dilemmas which the teaching authority had to face in view of internal Catholic tensions as well as the position of the Church in the secular world. Since the opposition put forward by the *Syllabus* was clear, only requiring refined interpretation, was there an alternative? *Tolerantia,* in accordance with the *Syllabus,* was a negative term for Leo XIII and the majority of Catholics (wherever they were not an extreme minority) because it was equated with a concept wherein truth and untruth, morality and amorality are equally valid. The positive term, being alien to the *Syllabus,* is the *patientia* with which the Church is in waiting until mankind discovers the one and only truth, Catholic truth.[15] This principle is applied to religious freedom, which, when indiscriminately granted (*promiscue*), will result in atheism. It applies to the freedom of speech, the press, and education, upon which the state is obligated to place limits,[16] not withstanding the Church's inalienable freedom to teach.[17] All principles of liberalism, which were fundamentally condemned, were banned in the *Syllabus* in the same manner as in the encyclical *Libertas* (1888). However, and this

---

[14] C. Bauer, *Wandlungen,* 41ff.; and therefore it is valid (even in regard to the special conditions in Germany) to say that Catholicism there "had an alienated relationship to what one may call the "bourgeois society" in Germany. Catholicism confronts society with different social ideals and it has a hostile attitude toward the economic system which is perpetuated by this society" (C. Bauer, "Der deutsche Katholizismus . . . ," *Deutscher Katholizismus* [Frankfurt a. M. 1964], 52.

[15] *Libertas* (1888) (*Acta Leonis* VIII, 241): [ecclesia], "quia tam dissolutum flagitiosumque tolerantiae genus constanter, ut debet, repudiat . . ."; he opposes *patientia* to *lenitas,* which the Church practiced generously.

[16] Ibid., 229–34.

[17] Ibid., 235.

is the only difference, the latter speaks of the consideration of "human weaknesses" by the "maternal judgement of the Church," which does not ignore the course of events and therefore does not condemn the state's occasional indifference toward certain events which do not comply with truth and justice in the interest of eventual good and prevention of evil.[18] It is clear that even a liberal who was willing to practice his principles in the face of the Catholic Church[19] was misunderstood as long as his idea of truth was identified with a radical indifferentism and his world view was tolerated by the Catholic Church as the lesser evil. He had to fear that "patience" would only last until an opportunity for the dogmatization of public life arose again.[20] But Leo XIII created a modus vivendi with respect to society's pluralism, and more could not be expected in this particular historical situation. At the same time, he offered a formula for resolving internal Catholic controversies.[21] The test case was Catholicism in the United States. It is indeed understandable that the notion that the American conditions should be considered a model for the Church was discarded as an error. But the limits of an essentially unrealized adjustment were evident in the remark that the Church could reap a rich harvest if it were granted, "aside from freedom," also "the favor of the law" and the "protection (*patrocinium*) of the state."[22] This required the Catholic who adhered to the constitution of the United States to reconcile the irreconcilable. In the papal proclamations on the problem of the relation between truth and freedom there were certain shifts in emphasis,[23] but no essential progress.

The Doctrine of Property

The doctrine of property is of as much importance to liberal bourgeois society as is the principle of toleration. In this respect, however, recent

---

[18] Ibid., [ecclesia] "non recusat, quominus quidpiam a veritate iustitiaque alienum ferat tamen potestas publica, scilicet maius aliquod vel vitandi caussa malum, vel adipiscendi aut conservandi bonum."

[19] Leo XIII criticized the intolerance of the Liberals with Cicero's kind of wit: *Acta Leonis* VIII, 237.

[20] W. Gurian, *Ideen,* 262.

[21] A similar phrase was contained in *Immortale Dei* (1885), where the principle stating that the Church could not concede the existence of non-Catholic religions *eodem iure* was modified in a more pragmatic sense (*Acta Leonis* V, 141). Moreover, in reference to a passage in Saint Augustine's work, it was said that nobody should be forced to convert to the Catholic faith.

[22] *Longinqua Oceani spatia* (1895),—The Weimar constitution contains the separation of Church and state. It calls the churches "religious societies" subject to civil law; this is a compromise which was only possible in this historical context and, moreover, belongs in a later period of time.

[23] For example, in *Annum ingressi* (19 March 1902), which says that this is the correct doctrine, *ut libertas veritate concedat (Acta Leonis* XXII, 67).

research in Neo-Scholastic social philosophy has affirmed that the teaching of Thomas Aquinas regarding personal property was transmitted in a truncated form and eventually fell under the rather strong influence of a liberal economic theory.[24] This is the area where the real theoretical decisions have to be made regarding the question of whether Catholicism should follow its own total conception of social order or whether it should comply and pursue a social reform policy (though, to be sure, in different versions, reflective of its relationship to a capitalist industrial society). It was noted that the individualistic idea of property had its predecessors. Luigi Taparelli (died in 1862) had already presented it in his exemplary work on the Natural Law.[25] He was the teacher of Gioacchino Pecci, who even as Pope remained loyal to his basic concepts, although he did not agree with the reference to the instinct with which the dog will defend its food.[26] "The exaggerated emphasis of the individual side of the concept of property, which neglected the social side . . . , did indeed have an impact on papal documents like *Rerum novarum.*"[27] Nevertheless, in Leo XIII's theoretical writings after 1878, a considerable shift in emphasis can be noted. In the beginning, he discusses the lower classes wanting to occupy the palaces of the rich without thinking about eternal life.[28] The tone of the social encyclical is essentially different, even though Matteo Liberatore (1810–92), the master of Roman Neo-Scholasticism, who placed the natural right to personal property at the center of his social philosophy,[29] had a considerable influence on the history of its creation.[30] Two factors especially seem to have determined the Neo-Scholastic theory of property. Like Leo XIII's encyclical, it basically proceeds from agrarian property: "it is not an exaggeration to maintain that the concept of possession, property as we understand it today, basically was the result of the French Revolution."[31] Perhaps this is why the essentially academic question (in which the Pope remained neutral) of whether personal property, as Suarez claimed, was to be attributed to *ius gentium* is of concrete importance insofar as the historical background of the respective specific property

[24] F. Beutter, with a lot of documentation.

[25] Ibid., 97, following A. F. Utz.

[26] *Rerum novarum,* 5; P. Jostock, op. cit., 15.

[27] O. v. Nell-Breuning, in A. Rauscher (ed.), *Ist die katholische Soziallehre antikapitalistisch?* (Cologne 1968), 15.

[28] *Quod Apostolici muneris* (1878) (*Acta Leonis* I, 171): "Praesentium tandem bonorum illecti cupiditate . . . ius proprietatis naturali lege sanctitum impugnant"; I, 173: Since reward and punishment in the eternal life were forgotten, "mirum non est quod infimae sortis homines, pauperculae domus vel officinae pertaesi, in aedes et fortunas ditiorum involare discupiant."

[29] Quotation in F. Beutter, op. cit., 104.

[30] Antonazzi, 13.

[31] O. v. Nell-Breuning, *Eigentumslehre,* 145f.

law is concerned. If only the "ability to possess property,"[32] thus the fundamental right to have personal property, is determined by Natural Law, then there exists a great deal of leeway in which to regulate property and the proper proportions of personal and community property. In addition, Leo's social encyclical places definite value on the property of the "have-nots." That was "surprising for all those who wanted to secure their monetary interests under the patronage of *Rerum novarum*."[33] Yet Leo XIII "did not distinctly see the two groups of capital and labor as two social classes in the technical sense of the word,"[34] though these groups were of fundamental significance in the formulation of this modern question. Moreover, in spite of the Pope's efforts in terms of social criticism, he did "speak in the tone of a grand seigneur and a patriarch, almost with a voice descending from the realm of eternity, full of fatherly mercy and kindness when addressing his dear children, especially the workers";[35] and, without a doubt, his voice grew more "fatherly" after 1878. It was often noted that Leo XIII did not intend to develop a social theory in his encyclical, but the unquestionably strong systematic elements stem to a great extent from the Neo-Scholastic social philosophy of Liberatores, and this is the point of contact for Catholic moral theology as far as the doctrine of property is concerned.[36]

The other factor which needs to be considered when assessing the Catholic doctrine of property in those decades is the polemical dispute over socialism, that is, socialism as a complex phenomenon with all of its ideological components. Unquestionably the logic in Catholic social theory was to a large degree determined by this confrontation. Never-

---

[32] Ibid., 155.

[33] Ibid., 154.

[34] Id., *Die soziale Enzyklika*, 150.

[35] *Ibid.*, 39. Therefore, one is hesitant to follow Jostock (10) when he declares as "very remarkable" the fact that the encyclical lists among the reasons for social evil the *versi in deteriora mores* last, following the economic and social reasons. He certainly recognized the socio-political tasks. But his emphasis on *cupiditates,* with which the encyclical begins, changes from passage to passage, and one should not project the reform of present conditions from the perspective of Pius XI.

[36] F. Beutter, op. cit., 86f.; see Beutter in regard to the various moral theologians who do not speak in *unisono* (including extensive lit.); also important is the article by G. Gundlach about Theodor Meyer, *StL*[6] V, 695f.; A. Lehmkuhl, ibid., 335f.; H. Pesch, ibid. VI, 226–29. H. Pesch is dealing with the further development of Catholic sociology. Accepting the "historical school," he declares as "good" a regulation of property that follows the law of nature "with proper consideration for the actual conditions, the historical stage of social and economic life" (*Liberalismus* I, 400).—In regard to the Swiss Jesuit V. Cathrein, who endorsed the interdenominational and democratic principles but opposed Socialism and paternalism (according to Soderini, he was one of Leo XIII advisers), see: J. David, *LThK*[2] II, 355ff.

theless, when attempting a historically adequate evaluation of the total situation, one cannot say that the rejection of socialism "from the perspective of the bourgeois society" should be "called a vital error of the theology of the nineteenth century."[37] That, indeed, was precisely the question: Would Catholicism under the given historical conditions of the nineteenth century be able to arrive at a comprehensive concept of society or would it have to assert itself defensively against the mutually contradictory currents of the time, against liberalism as well as socialism, in order to possibly influence reform efforts? Nonetheless, the definite rejection of ideological liberalism did not preclude a more or less strong coloration of the doctrine of property through liberal individualism.[38]

Social Theories

The social theoretical works of the moral theologians often went through numerous editions. But few gained as much international significance for Catholicism as Charles Périn's (1815–1905) *De la richesse dans les sociétés chrétiennes* (first edition 1861).[39] This Catholic economist from Belgium, who also strongly influenced the social activists in France and western Germany, was ideologically and politically a confirmed antiliberalist. But in his principal rejection of state intervention, which was augmented by his opposition to the liberal constitutional state, he acted as representative of economic liberalism. However, he did want this liberalism amended by his concept of "Christian property," meaning the social ties of charity. He accepted the concentration of property in one individual as a result of the progress of civil freedom, but he saw the

---

[37] F. Beutter, op. cit., 149, who does not mean to endorse Socialism.

[38] It was rather the same on all fronts. A. Lehmkuhl, *Die soziale Frage und die staatliche Gewalt* (Freiburg i. Br. ³1896), 75: It cannot be denied that capitalism, "under certain circumstances, possesses some economically good aspects; but without curtailment, it is bad and a source for economic collapse." State Socialism, on the other hand, poses a threat. As far as the "curtailment" is concerned, G. Gundlach notes (in regard to the situation forty years after the issuance of the encyclical) "that the course of the capitalist economic system severely damaged the sociological function of the family as well as private property and the state . . . through paralyzing anonymous power plays"; "Berufsständische Ordnung," *StL*⁶ I, 1127.—To say that Western Europe did not become Marxist because Leo had made the Church "the most formidable foe" is historically wrong and biased. "It becomes evident as the story unfolds that the hand of Leo XIII was one of those strengthening the dike which held back the flood" (L. P. Wallace VII, 408).—The insight that Christ as Christ has only a *norma negativa* in respect to economics, society, and the state could only be gained after many trials and tribulations. This applies to the Conservatives as well as to the Christian Democrats.

[39] F. Beutter, index, esp. 30, 104, 119; Reszohazy (op. cit., chap. 7), index; J. B. Duroselle, *Les débuts,* 470f.

possibility of achieving congruity in respect to self-interests in the sense of sacrifice natural to Christian asceticism. Of course, he deemed the ideal to be moderate wealth, which was most likely to be found among the middle class, and that shows clearly how he underestimated the process of industrialization. The French social scientist Frédéric Le Play (1802–82) had an effect reaching far into the last third of the nineteenth century. Through his sociographical investigations of the family life of workers and craftsmen in France, England, Germany, and Russia, he dealt with an issue that was the central point of Catholic social doctrine.[40] The family is intact when the patriarchal authority of the father is unimpeded. The family is also the model for society as a whole with its "social authorities," including the entrepreneurs. The rejection of liberal human rights and the constitutional state could consistently merge with economic liberalism of a distinctly paternal character, while still implying a serious aspiration toward social justice. The ideas of Le Play were predominant in the *Association des Patrons du Nord.* The antiliberalism of the philosopher and economist Guiseppe Toniolo (1845–1918)[41] had an entirely different background. Professor in Pisa in 1889, Toniolo founded the *Unione cattolica per gli studi sociali in Italia,* which prepared the Catholic social congresses in Italy. In 1891 the *Società operaie cattoliche* included 284 local chapters and was especially popular in northern Italy. The *Rivista internazionale di scienze sociali . . . ,* founded in 1893 in Talamo, obtained a certain official character through Toniolo's consulting activities on behalf of Leo XIII. Thus the Christian social program, designed under the guidance of Franz Schindler (1847–1922),[42] who was a professor of moral theology in Vienna in 1887, was sent not only to Rampolla, but also to Toniolo. In contrast to Rampolla's sober and pragmatic reaction, Toniolo ap-

---

[40] Main work: *Les ouvriers européens* (Paris 1855, ²1877–79); also *La réforme sociale en France,* 2 vols. (Paris 1864, ⁸1901, 3 vols.).—L. Neundörfer, *StL* ⁶ V, 357–60 (lit.); J. B. Duroselle, op. cit., 672–84 (lit.)

[41] F. Marconcini, *Profilo di Giuseppe Toniolo* (Milan 1930); V. Mangano, *L'opera di scientifica di G. Toniolo* (Rome 1940); R. Angeli, *La dottrina sociale di G. Toniolo* (Pinerolo 1956).

[42] The Christian social program was published by F. Funder, op. cit., 132–37; F. Schindler, *Die soziale Frage der Gegenwart* (Vienna 1905), frees Vogelsang's ideas, which the prelate had been exposed to during the "duck evenings," from conservative utopias; there is also a connection to the Swiss K. Decurtins.—Regarding the controversies between the Catholic Conservatives and the Christian Socialists over the Austrian Cardinals Gruscha and Schönborn, cf. chap. 2.—Regarding the champions of the Christian Socialists in Austria, such as J. Scheicher (1842–1924), moral theologian at the Seminary of Saint Pölten, see H. David, *J. Scheicher als Sozialpolitiker* (diss., Vienna 1946), according to which Scheicher was critical of the Christian Socialists' trend toward the middle class (56).

proved, regarding as essential the program of profit-sharing among the workers. He also gave his basic consent to an "organization of society according to occupations," but took exception to the idea of having infinite competition controlled through corporations by arguing that occupational egotism could ruin the consumer.[43] Being strongly influenced by the historical school of German economics, Toniolo is not so much important for the originality of his doctrine as for his influence in Italian Catholicism and with Leo XIII.

Just as Charles Périn's social theory radiated toward the West, so did the influence of the early Viennese school under Vogelsang toward France.[44] Catholics in countries like France, Belgium, and Austria who tried once more to create a universal order of society in the Christian image of man had something in common: they categorically rejected the liberal bourgeois society. This "reactionary" attitude was affected by various political configurations and thus presented one facet during the Third Republic of France, where such social criticism amalgamated more or less by necessity with antirepublicanism. It had a different appearance in the Habsburg Monarchy, where such criticism was suspect with the liberals as well as the conservatives, so that it came to be associated with revolutionary tendencies. This, as well as the East-West gradient in the process of de-Christianization, has to do with the fact that the Christian impetus was more direct, as it were, in France than in Austria, where socio-political objectives were approached in a more direct manner. In Germany, the defense against the *Kulturkampf* absorbed most theoretical and practical interests and the conclusion of the dispute later coincided with the turn toward a social reform concept. However, even here existed an incipient individual program relative to society as a whole. Most of the leading activists and theoreticians belonged to the aristocracy: in France mainly Albert de Mun,[45] and Latour

---

[43] Rampolla's answer in F. Funder, op. cit., 138–41; Toniolo's answer, ibid., 142f.

[44] C. Antoine, S.J., *Cours d'économie sociale* (Paris 1896), 240: "Les catholiques d'Autriche ont cru que le seul moyen de salut pour eux était de confier tout l'ordre économique social aux mains de la dynastie catholique des Habsbourg." The assessment by this author, who was close to A. de Mun, distorts the Viennese ideas through its abridgement.

[45] Impressed by the Commune Uprising in Paris in 1871 (for which he partially blamed the middle class), A. de Mun (1841–1913), a French officer, founded the *Oeuvre des cercles catholiques d'ouvriers* (cf. chap. 13) and the extraparliamentary *Union catholique.* He sacrificed his royalism in obedience to the papal *Ralliement,* was for socio-political reasons in conflict with the Orleanists, and slowly took exception to the theories of Charles Périn. A large part of the French episcopate, headed by Freppel, was disinclined toward the social activities of de Mun, while Mermillod, Doutreloux, and Manning took a positive stand. Nonetheless, in 1885, he began to plan a *parti catholique* according to the Belgian and German model, in which all conservatives were to be united in the

du Pin,[46] in Germany Prince Karl zu Löwenstein,[47] in Austria Count Franz Kuefstein and Counts Revertera and Belcredi, who were mainly interested in politics, and the North German converts Count Blome and Carl von Vogelsang, who during his odyssey had found a protector in Alois zu Liechtenstein,[48] also called the "Red Prince." The background of these men can easily prompt the sweeping conclusion that an attempt was being made to turn back the wheel of history.

In the social theory of Carl von Vogelsang[49] there are elements from the social doctrine of the Romanticists (especially Adam Müller); and

---

spirit of the Christian faith and social action. Leo XIII advised against it (H. Rollet, *A. de Mun et le parti catholique* [Paris ² 1950]; cf. chap. 6). After the failure of the *Ralliement,* he founded the *Action libérale Populaire* in order to fend off anticlericalism, and he worked together with M. Barrès. The funeral of this man, honored as a great Frenchman in spite of all differences, was also attended by Minister President L. Barthou.—J. Piou, *A. de Mun* (Paris 1952; because of his personal acquaintance still important); M. Lynch, *The Organised Social Apostolate of A. de Mun* (diss., Washington 1952); J. N. Moody, op. cit., 146f.; J. Mehling, *Essai sur A. de Mun* (Fribourg 1953); C. Mollet, *A de Mun: Recherches d'histoire religieuse* 1 (Paris 1970), with many new letters.

[46] R. Latour du Pin was de Mun's colleague in the officers' corps, but in contrast to him more interested in theory: *Vers un Ordre social chrètien* (Paris 1907); *Aphorismes de politique sociale,* rev. ed. (Paris 1909). He did not go along with the political turn of the *Ralliement* and rather approached the *Action française.*—E. Borsan de Garagnol, *Le colonel de Latour du Pin d'après lui-même* (Paris 1934); R. Talmy, *Aux sources du catholicisme social. L'École de Latour du Pin* (Paris 1963).

[47] Karl zu Löwenstein (1834–1921), in 1868 president of the *Zentralkomitee der Katholischen Vereine Deutschlands,* founded at the Catholic Convention of Bamberg (four noblemen, three clergymen), 1872–98 (when the central committee was restored after having been dissolved during the *Kulturkampf*) "commissioner" of the Catholic conventions, was accredited with having organized the socio-political conference in the castle of his birth Haid (Bohemia) in 1883 and having founded the *Freie Vereinigung katholischer Sozialpolitiker.* But he was the representative of those Catholics who were not primarily interested in the social question, but rather in the "influences of the revolutionary movement which should be taken advantage of in the interest of the Catholic Church" (P. Siebertz, op. cit., 215, from the Wertheim archive); "one has to mount the horse in order to be able to lead"; "if we cannot prevent the social republic, at least we must be its master" ("confidential" circular, P. Siebertz, op. cit., 215f.). However, he was tolerant enough to invite people of all Catholic persuasions to the conference in Haid. The "Haid theses" and their total revision program were presented to the Catholic Convention in Amberg in 1884 in an abridged version (E. Ritter, op. cit., 83ff.).

[48] Alois Prince Liechtenstein (1846–1920), 1878–89 and 1891–1911: member of the *Reichsrat;* had a conflict with the Austrian Ultra Conservatives; presented in 1888 to the Viennese Catholic Convention the social problems generally ignored there; 1891: elected deputy of the Christian Socialists of the suburb of Hernals. "He introduced to the different antiliberal elements the fundamentally Catholic element" (F. Funder, *StL*⁵ III, 1011ff.).

[49] Carl von Vogelsang (1818–90), son of a major in the Prussian police force, resigned from his position at the district court in Berlin, became a Catholic in 1850 after studying in Munich and Innsbruck, and in 1874 joined the editorial staff of the strictly conserva-

his hypothesis of a "social kingdom" as an alternative to "state socialism" was possible only in the central European regions. However, Gustav Gundlach[50] was justified in observing that the first representatives of a system which later was called "order by occupations" cannot be understood merely on the basis of such deductions. Catholicism produced only one original concept of a constitution embracing all of society. This was intended to be a creative draft of a defense against liberalism as well as socialism. That it later became suspect was due to several reasons which cannot be discussed at this point. It should be noted that only traces of this concept entered into the encyclical *Rerum novarum.* The practical decision to take the path of Catholic cooperation in the social reform of the capitalist society had already been made. Though the successes accomplished were impressive and cannot be disputed, an assessment of this concept regarding society as a whole cannot be reached on this ground alone. In order to confront the real dilemma of Catholicism, one has to consider that the realization of this concept would entail the abolition of the capitalist society and would therefore not have been accomplished without revolutionizing society. Moreover, these strictly antiliberal and thus anticapitalist theoreticians, mainly located in Vienna, knew rather little about economic realities.

What Vogelsang and his friends wanted to achieve (not through upheaval but "through a gradual transformation from within") was the following: the elimination of "exploitation" through capitalism "whose only purpose of economic activity is net profit"; the formation of occu-

---

tive *Vaterland* in Vienna. He created tensions in his relationship to Count Leo Thun, the owner of the newspaper (who otherwise appreciated Vogelsang), when he used phrases in his articles like "the marvelous strike of the railroad employees (in Pittsburgh), in which the disenchanted attacked capitalism with breech loaders and canons." In the *Österreichische Monatsschrift für Gesellschaftswissenschaft und Volkswirtschaft,* which Vogelsang founded in 1879, he published a universal reform plan (C. Allmayer-Beck, 66ff.). The series of articles published after 1883 entitled *Die materielle Lage des Arbeiterstandes* was criticized by the Liberals and Conservatives alike for pouring fuel on the hate of the "present social order." At Prince Liechtenstein's conference in Haid Vogelsang stood on the left. In Vienna, he was supported by Prince Liechtenstein as well as the moral theologian F. M. Schindler, J. Scheicher, and Pastor R. Eichhorn (R. Kuppe, *Eichhorn zur Arbeiterfrage* [diss., Vienna 1926]). In the beginning, A. M. Weiß belonged to this Christian Socialist circle (cf. below). In regard to contacts with the Viennese Socialists, see C. Allmayer-Beck, 90ff., 100f. In contrast to P. Biederlack, S.J., Innsbruck, P. H. Abel, S.J., supported Vogelsang: "In contrast to the un-Christian German and the un-Christian Jewish movements, this Austrian Christian movement in Vienna is indebted to Vogelsang" (C. Allmayer-Beck, 126).—W. Klopp, *Die sozialen Lehren des Freiherrn von Vogelsang* (Saint Pölten 1894; excerpts in French); A. Knoll, *C. v. Vogelsang als Nachfahre der Romantik* (diss., Vienna 1924); C. Allmyer-Beck, *Vogelsang. Vom Feudalismus zur Volksbewegung* (Vienna 1952).

[50] G. Gundlach, "Berufsständische Ordnung," *StL*[6] I, 1124–27.

pational "corporations" in which capital and labor, employer and employee are united, forming a "social institution of society and state"; the replacement of the "horizontal stratification according to class by a vertical one according to occupations, which would be characterized by a "republican cooperative relationship"; elimination of "purely private, absolute, capricious property which is robbing God, society and the state." At the top of such economic and political social order was to reside the "social kingdom" as an integrating element. Vogelsang rejected suffrage by census as asocial and general suffrage as dispersing the "historical and political" individualities into "random sections divided according to external geographical criteria," and he also assigned propaganda to the "corporations." Their structure was certainly conceived from the perspective of the trade guilds, which Vogelsang wanted to modernize and organize into reliable production and sales cooperatives so that they could compete wth industry. He believed that it was possible to transfer this modernized model to industrial enterprises. Austrian anti-Semitism, too, had one of its roots in the Christian social movement because Vogelsang and others saw the Jews as the main perpetrators of the "exploitation of the workers."[51] Vogelsang's social concept solicited a limited amount of attention in other social study groups of Catholicism, particularly through Blome and Kuefstein. Considerable differences existed not only within these circles but also in the individual groups. An example of this is the Dominican Albert Maria Weiß from Upper Bavaria, who was an active apologist in Graz, Vienna, and Fribourg after 1890. To him, the social question was a weapon he employed in his wholesale war against liberalism.[52]

During a social study course of the *Volksverein* in Bamberg in 1893, Franz Hitze[53] called Carl von Vogelsang the kind of "teacher" Germany

[51] W. Klopp, *Lehren,* 65ff.—Aside from being "revolutionary" and "socialistic," anti-Semitism was also charged with being one of the elements with which the Conservatives fought the Christian Socialists in Rome in 1895.

[52] Aside from his apology (chap. biblio.), *Lebens- und Gewissensfragen der Gegenwart,* 2 vols. (Freiburg i. Br. 1911); autobiography of A. M. Weiß (1844–1925): *Lebensweg . . .* (Freiburg i. Br. 1925).—In regard to his action against the Christian Socialists, see F. Funder, op. cit., 144ff.

[53] In 1878, Franz Hitze (1851–1921) went as priest to the Campo Santo in Rome and studied Karl Marx and the works of Vogelsang. His main works are based on these studies (cf. above). After his return in 1880, he became the secretary general of the association *Arbeiterwohl,* which had been founded by the Catholic industrialist F. Brandts, in whose factory he was social adviser. After 1882 deputy in Prussia and later in the *Reichstag,* Hitze became one of the leading and (in opposition to the employers' lobby) most decisive social politicians of the Center Party.—Franz Müller, *F. Hitze und sein Werk* (Hamburg 1928); A. Pieper, "Hitze und die Korporationsidee," *Die soziale Frage . . . ,* ed. J. Strieder et. al. (chap. lit.), 86–98; K. H. Schürmann, *Zur Vorgeschichte der christlichen Gewerkschaften* (Freiburg i. Br. 1958), 53–57; J. Höffner, *StL*[6] IV, 107f.

lacked. The same year, Hitze became professor of Christian sociology in Münster and thus inaugurated the tradition of a new teaching chair in the theology faculty. In that same year, he answered a Social Democrat deputy in the *Reichstag* who had criticized the social politics of the Center Party with reference to Bishop Ketteler: "I still agree absolutely with the opinions Bishop von Ketteler has voiced."[54] These are the reminiscences of a pragmatic politician during a period when he contemplated "a basic transformation of society." Next to Wilhelm Hohoff,[55] he was "the first Catholic sociologist who thoroughly studied Marx and recognized his significance" (J. Höffner). To him it was inevitable that "socialism would come, either the absolute, social-democratic version of the state or the relative, conservative, healthy version of the social classes" (*Quintessenz*, p. 32). Hitze rejected the theory of suplus value, but the criticism of capitalism found in his early writings follows the very phraseology of Karl Marx. Like Vogelsang, he bases his theory on the model of the medieval guilds. But he believes they have to be placed on an "expanded economic and democratic foundation," which meant the evolution of industrial enterprises into productive associations autonomously controlled by all participants. Only in this manner could a situation in which the entrepreneur has the advantage and the employee the disadvantage be changed. Hitze opposed Charles Périn's theory with determination. He also saw danger in the idea of the "company as a family," which, through its social provisions, could adversely tie the worker to his place of work. The fact that during the trade union controversy at the turn of the century some representatives of the Catholic workers' societies criticized his idea of an "organization of society on a Christian basis by occupations" was a bitter pill for Hitze to swallow. For, after divorcing himself from the idea of a reunification of capital and labor and embracing the concept of social reform within a capitalist economy, he advocated the functioning of trade unions as "sales cooperatives" (of labor) and justified striking as a withholding of

[54] Quoted in J. Mundwiler, *Ketteler* (Munich 1927), 145.—Ketteler's impact, even on Leo XIII, who called him his "great predecessor and imitator," was considerable (Schmidlin, *PG* II, 368). In spite of the romantic ideas of his youth, his understanding of "the new socio-economic reality" (C. Bauer, *StL*[6] IV, 953–57) grew.—Since Ketteler offered ideas that aim at structural changes (productive associations with joint ownership of the workers) as well as social reforms, different movements relied on his work.
[55] Wilhelm Hohoff (1848–1923), a Westphalian like Hitze, retired as vicar and led the reclusive life of a scholar, protected by Cardinal Schulte. He tried to combine the scholastic theory of labor with the theory of Karl Marx (*Die Revolutionen seit dem 16. Jh.* [1887]; *Warenwert und Kapitalprofit* [1902]; *Die Bedeutung der Marxschen Kapitalkritik* [1908]).—An evaluation does not exist. E. Alexander, in J. N. Moody, 525, considers him remarkable, even though he rejects other attempts in the German and Austrian Catholicism.

the commodity of labor. The controversy between young Franz Hitze and Georg von Hertling[56] foreshadowed the victory of reform politics with the existing economy over a fundamental rejection of liberal bourgeois capitalism. Abandoned was the "corporative" idea, according to which the relation between capital and labor was not to be determined by the market conditions but by a social contract in the spirit of natural law, because labor was not to be degraded to a form of merchandise. Abandoned also was the conception of the mixed trade unions of "employers" and "employees" as presented mainly by Albert de Mun. The question yet to be answered was how the then clearly weaker partner, labor, could be protected. The following controversy over the state's intervention was dominated by paternalistic ideas (which were particularly persistent in western European Catholicism), but primarily by the relationship to the respective states. In this situation, the Pope, in the encyclical *Rerum novarum,* had to find a moderate position from which to mediate.[57] Now the comprehensive "social question" of Catholicism turned into the more specific question of the workers.

Catholicism had finally evolved into a group within the total liberal bourgeois society and it was responsible for resolving its internal differences over economic interests (the problem of its political parties). The representatives of "Christian Socialism"[58] existed in the background;

[56] In regard to the socio-political stand of the philosopher and statesman Georg v. Hertling (1843–1919), see C. Bauer, *Wandlungen* . . . (1931), 38–41; Schürmann, 53–61; E. Deuerlein, *StL*[6] IV, 61–64; it is significant for the tactical-political differences between Hertling (who was a pragmatist) and Löwenstein that the Catholic convention of 1890 was held in a different location, out of consideration for Prince Regent Luitpold (P. Siebertz, op. cit., 265–71; G. v. Hertling, *Erinnerungen,* 122–26).

[57] *Acta Leonis* XI, 108: "ad eamque rem (workers' question) adhiberi leges ipsas auctoritatemque rei publicae, utique ratione ac modo, putat oportere"—ibid., 121: ". . . in potestate rectorum civitatis est, ut ceteris prodesse ordinibus, sic et proletariosum conditionem iuvare plurimum . . . debet enim respublica ex lege muneris sui in commune consulere." But the intervention, which exceeds the elimination of a situation *rebus extremis,* was rejected, being under suspicion of state socialism; therefore (but also in the interest of the employee's accumulation of assets, not, however, for the purpose of preserving entrepreneural interests), the opposition to "inappropriate" taxes is rejected: "Faciat igitur iniuste atque inhumane, si de bonis privatorum plus aequo, tributorum nomine, detraxerit" (p. 133). The accent is clearly on advocating state intervention, for which the Pope was criticized by the disciples of paternalism.

[58] The early version of Christian Socialism in France disappeared in the face of the radical development of Socialism after 1848. But the idea emerged repeatedly, as in the bishop of Nottingham, E. G. Bagshaw's *Mercy and Justice to the Poor: The True Political Economy* (London 1885). Bagshaw combined his strict anti-Protestantism and anti-individualism with anticapitalism. He felt that the state was obligated to prevent agrarian and industrial accumulation, free enterprise (which he considered devastating), and the exploitation of the tenants. The state was to create revenue through social legislation which would enable it to remedy social abuse (19–21). The rejection of capitalist

but the idea of an "order according to occupations," along with its "revitalization" (Gundlach) in the magnificent encyclical *Quadragesimo anno* (1931), became essentially a theoretical affair.[59]

Catholicism's multiple efforts in the seventies and eighties toward the design of a comprehensive social system were often mutually exclusive, but their fundamental significance could not be erased by mere pragmatism. They were the work of various study circles,[60] whose ideas

---

utilization of rivers and coastal waters has to do with the interests of some Catholics in the land reform program of Henry George (cf. chap. 10). The pragmatist H. E. Manning (cf. chap. 9) advocated in his essay "The Rights and Dignity of Labour" the social priority of labor as compared to capital. He wanted to assure the free distribution of labor (5–14) and believed state interventions to be necessary; but he renounced H. George in his commentary on *Rerum novarum* (in regard to George, see Peter d'A. Jones, *The Christian Socialist Revival* [Princeton 1968]; also V. A. McClelland, *CHR* 58 [1972], 423ff., where the context within Catholicism is lacking).—Abbot Gasquet, O.S.B., opposing the recognition of Anglican orders (cf. chap. 9) at the Conference of Nottingham in 1898: "We all claim to be Socialists of one kind or another" (quoted in Waninger, 98).—Liberal Catholicism is represented by S. Merkle (1914, p. 71) who disdainfully quotes Abbé Pottier of Liège stating that he saw the future of Catholicism in union with the Socialists. He also refers to A. de Mun as an involuntary helper (Merkle relies in this respect on F. X. Kraus). He could have also mentioned the Swiss K. Decurtins (chap. 4). He interprets *Rerum novarum* in the sense of a clearly antisocialist theory of property (O. Schilling, *Staatslehre*, 120). The translation into German and its distortions (Herder edition) are interesting.

[59] H. Pesch, *Liberalismus* I, 567–76, objectively describes the contemporary discussions in the Catholicisms from France to Austria. He himself advocates the need for organizing the "classes as 'organs' of the social body" (556) whose authority would also adjust production to demand (565); but he warns "of a direct projection of purely theoretical constructs to reality" (579) and considers dangerous the idea of installing the classes as "large production and sales cooperatives," arguing that "nowadays the reaction to the liberalism of free enterprise often leads to an exaggeration of the idea of *Gemeinschaft*" (582). In contrast, Scheimpflug demands in his article published in the *Staatslexicon* under the title "Capital and Capitalism" (1894): "The classes are to be dissolved and regrouped"; capitalism evolved out of the "disintegration" of the medieval forms of society and is to be replaced by new "corporations" which would be responsible for "the national management of production."

[60] The *Conseil des études de l'œuvre*, mainly handled by A. de Mun, the founder of the *Cercles catholiques d'ouvriers*, and R. Latour du Pin, began publishing the *Questions sociales* . . . . In Rome, Count Kuefstein, a member of the Vogelsang circle, suggested the founding of the *Circolo dei studi sociali ed economiche*, which was joined by, among others, Liberatore, Mermillod, and Count Soderini. Different groups, predominantly the Viennese (dissolved in 1888), were represented in the *Freie Vereinigung katholischer Sozialpolitiker*, founded in 1883 by Löwenstein. The *Union catholique d'études sociales et économiques à Fribourg* tried to unite these circles internationally; it existed until *Rerum novarum* was issued. The Swiss K. Decurtins, in 1887 invited to Fribourg, was "the democratic element in this highly aristocratic association" (Fry II, 177); he wrote to Segesser: "As different as the representatives of the various ideas—the sovereign and the democrat—may have been, the power of Communion united them all" (Fry II, 179). There is a survey of these circles in A. Knoll, *Der soziale Gedanke*, 116–22.

merged in the *Union catholique* of Fribourg (founded in 1884 by Mermillod). The image of unity which Catholicism presented in its defense toward the "modern world" needs to be modified considerably if one is adequately to appreciate the difficulties which had to be overcome in formulating *Rerum novarum*.[61] The Neo-Scholastic abstract character of many parties has its explanation in the need to cover the rather contradictory concepts within Catholicism itself as they came to light, for example, at the international congresses in Liège, particularly in 1890. Only by placing it in the total historical context of these decades can we comprehend the significance and the limits of this encyclical in historical terms. Perhaps its greatest significance lies in the recognition of the workers' right to organize, along with its cautious affirmation of the state's right and duty of intervention.

Marriage and Family

Although tensions between Catholicism and liberal individualism on the one hand and collective socialism in the economic realm on the other hand were deep, doctrinal authority was united regarding the sovereign origin of the family. In the dispute with socialism, theories which aimed at revolutionizing the traditional concept of the institution of marriage were occasionally offered by bourgeois Catholics and had to be fended off. There was concern that the parents' rights and obligations regarding the care of their children could be diminished or suspended by state measures.[62] The struggle against liberalism in this respect referred to the legalization of divorce, a prerequisite for which was the introduction of civil marriage. Leo XIII pointed out that marriage, insofar as it served the maintenance of human society, created civil correlationships which the state had a right to regulate. But matrimony is primarily a sacrament and as such subject only to ecclesiastical authority. This poses a problem in view of the de-Christianization and the pluralization of society at large. A solution aiming at differentiating the civil contract from the sacrament, which was respected as such, was rejected by the Pope. In respect to the extrasacramental "relation" *(coniunctio)*, he said, avoiding a more pungent expression, that in this manner a "rightful

---

[61] The first draft of the encyclical was probably written by M. Liberatore. The second one was amended by secretaries G. Boccali and A. Volpini, who also used suggestions from Fribourg. Cardinals Zigliara and Mazzella, and again Liberatore, worked on the third version. Schmidlin, *PG* II, 373, critically continues where G. Antonazzi, op. cit., 8–11, 37ff., left off.—The danger of an interpretation by the interested parties prohibited the Pope from "taking an overly concrete and detailed stand" (P. Jostock, op. cit., 11).

[62] *Rerum novarum (Acta Leonis* XI, 106).

marriage" *(iustum matrimonium)* could not be constituted.[63] No less important for the family than the dwindling attitude of society regarding the institutional character of marriage were the changes of the economic conditions resulting from growing industrialization as they affected the family. Leo XIII in *Rerum novarum* spoke only in general terms about a fair wage. He also said that the *pater familias* had to be able to support his family; but aside from the economic problems it was probably the patriarchal concept of the family which prevented the amount of wages from being determined as a "family wage" according to natural law.[64] To be sure, industrial female labor from the perspective of the worker's protection is an important aspect discussed among groups studying the social problem in Catholicism. But this kind of work was basically considered an evil which had to be alleviated.[65] For a long time, the changes in the family structure of the industrial society were ignored and the family of the agrarian society continued to serve as a model.[66] In this context belong representations of the image of the "Holy Family" in Nazareth.[67] Women's emancipation was diagnosed by Christian social doctrine as a symptom of decline.[68]

The School Question

The classical battlefield of the Catholic Church, society, and the modern state is the school and especially the elementary school. This fight is a defense against the state's claim, having come to full force through the French Revolution, to educate its adolescent citizens in accord with its

[63] The encyclical *Arcanum* (1880) *(Acta Leonis* II): against Communist ideas: 19; against divorce: 30ff.; against civil marriage: 21f.; state rights: 34f.; Sacrament and authority of the Church: 23; against the separation of the civil license from the Sacrament: 25f.; extra-Sacramental "union" of Christians: 37.

[64] See O. v. Nell-Breuning, *Eigentum,* 147, with important documentation.

[65] *Rerum novarum (Acta Leonis* XI, 129): "Sic certa quaedam artificia minus apte conveniunt in feminas ad opera domestica natas: quae quidem opera et tuentur magnopere in muliebre genere decus, et liberorum institutioni prosperitatique familiae natura repondent."

[66] O. v. Nell-Breuning, *Eigentum,* 147, calls the "rural family" a family which is closest to nature, to the natural order of things, and thus to the direct application of natural law" (1931); this addresses the problem.

[67] Cf. chap. 16

[68] "The Socialists demanded the absolute equality of the sexes in regard to civil and private law, within and outside of the family. This demand contradicts reason and Christianity" (V. Cathrein, *Sozialismus,* 347).—One reason that the *Katholische Frauenbund* (founded in 1903 in Cologne) encountered conflicts with the Church lies in its trend toward emancipation, moderate as it may have been.—The motion at the Catholic Convention of Düsseldorf in 1908 to admit women as independent members was voted down.

needs and concepts. In the eighteenth century the predominant part of education had still been, at least indirectly, a Church matter. But the purely defensive character of the ecclesiastical school struggle was demonstrated by the fact that it focused principally and, above all, factually on the religious element of instruction. The parents' right and duty to raise their children authoritatively was not defined in general terms but according to Christian mores.[69] The ecclesiastical ideal was a Catholic school financed by the state, which the state had the right to exert influence upon, but only as far as it was congruent with its innate authority. In the sense of choosing the lesser evil, these ideals were infringed upon when non-Catholic schools were also admitted. To tolerate this in the city of Rome was, of course, disagreeable to Leo XIII.[70] Bordering the tolerable was the system wherein only Catholic private schools were allowed, even if, as was the case in the United States, they had the same constitutional status as other schools.[71] The "neutral schools,"[72] which, as a rule, were antiecclesiastical, continued to be principally condemned, even if it was permissible to administer religious instruction within or outside of the school building during the time off. The achievements in the individual countries differed according to the respective political situation[73]: In France, education was largely secularized by the turn of the century after initial favorable interpretation of the law of 1882 by J. Ferry, because Catholic private schools were, in spite of quantitative increases, considerably limited by the laws enacted against the religious orders and congregations. In Italy, the Catholic victories in the local elections slowly counteracted the prohibition of religious instruction in elementary schools. In Belgium, the Liberals were defeated in the school question with their very own political principles. In the Netherlands, the political coalition of Catholics and Protestants prevented a de-Christianization of the schools. In Bismarck's Germany, the school was the responsibility of the *Länder,* and either in practice or through legislation the predominant problem of denominational diversity could be solved while preserving the Christian

[69] *Sapientiae christianae* (1890) (*Acta Leonis* X, 39).

[70] Letter to the cardinal vicar of Rome of 25 March 1879, *Acta Leonis* I, 202–10. The establishment of a Protestant school, *anche sotto gli stessi occhi Nostri, fin presso alle porte del Vaticano* (204), was, naturally, an inappropriate provocation. But Leo XIII rejected (on principle) the attempt to spread *falsi principii del Protestantesimo* in Italy and particularly in Rome.

[71] Cf. chap. 10.—Leo XIII called it unfair to force parents by means of taxes to finance schools which their children could not attend for reasons of conscience: *Quae coniunctim* (*ASS* 24, 656).

[72] *Acta Leonis* II, 118; IV, 15; VI, 154.

[73] Cf. chapters on the individual countries in Pt. I, Sec. I, and Pt. II, Sec. III.

character of the school, even though the school laws were still vehemently debated after the *Kulturkampf*.[74] In Great Britain, the liberal de-Anglicanization of schools gave the Catholics some leeway (which they took advantage of), assisted by state subsidy of private schools. But the rising standards in education here as well as in the United States made it more difficult for the Catholics to remain competitive. This was not only a question of financial means. At the Catholic Convention in Aachen in 1879, Prince Karl Löwenstein presented the motion to form a commission which was to develop learning goals and corresponding teaching plans for universities and all the way down to elementary schools. Though it was modeled after the school of the Middle Ages, it was an outstanding motion, but it faded out after being handed over to the *Görres-Gesellschaft*.[75] The Jesuits, who were especially active in higher education wherever they were admitted, finally adopted *nolens volens* the existing school plans,[76] but they were, except where absolutely necessary, not able to develop their own modern concept. With good reason, the shortcomings of teachers' training were pointed out.[77] In

---

[74] In Prussia, in 1892, a bill of the Center and the Conservatives regarding parochial schools miscarried because of the Liberals' opposition. But the "customary habits in everyday school life, which were moderate and in accord with ecclesiastical desires" (Brück-Kißling IV/2, 314), were finally legalized. In Bavaria, the parochial school became the legally "regular" school in 1883, and the change into nondenominational schools required an ecclesiastical verdict stating "whether or not adequate religious instruction would be impaired" (ibid., 318). In Württemberg, the parochial school had never been questioned. In Baden, there had existed since 1878 the principle of the nondenominational school, but this was practiced in such a way that the teacher of a local school of a certain denomination had to adhere to this creed personally. In mixed schools, the denominational majority determined the teacher, though a constant minority group was also provided with the appropriate teacher (Catholic religious instruction was regulated in 1888 by a "proper episcopal ordinance" (ibid., 318f.). In Hesse, the situation relaxed in a "practical" regard (ibid., 320).

[75] Kißling II, 194, noted that this society of scholars was "strictly speaking" not competent, because at that time such societies did not deal with didactic problems; see G. M. Pachtler, S.J., *Die Reform unserer Gymnasien* (Paderborn 1883), in which he pleaded for a Neo-Scholastic orientation and against the "devastating attitude of a know-it-all!"

[76] H. Becher, *Jesuiten*, 341.

[77] M. Spahn, op. cit., 30.—After the Prussian school law of 1906, this Catholic historian, who favored the state but defended the clerical supervision of schools, asked the question whether Catholic cooperation "in national schools whose legal system they helped create would be more successful" than the achievements of their French fellow believers "in regard to the development of education and their own philosophy" (27). It is interesting that this lecture was presented to the Catholic Teachers' Association. The social difference between the academically trained pastor and the elementary school teacher often effected an opposition which resulted in the de-Christianization of the faculty, especially since even during their training in denominational seminaries resentments were frequently aroused.

Italy, Murri bewailed the traditionalism of Catholic education and the lack of religious instruction.[78] Without a doubt, education in all its stages was one of the most important areas in which to halt the rapid or slow process of de-Christianization. This is why the tensions between Catholicism and society as a whole became most vigorous in this sphere. The dilemma which Catholicism had to face relative to its various relations to the total society became especially apparent: the dilemma of the desire to adapt until a special society could be developed, a desire which arose from the hope for re-Christianization.[79]

Catholic Associations

The history of the Catholic Church since the middle of the nineteenth century is partially, at least in Europe, a history of Catholic associations. Even here national differences are considerable, depending on the political situation.[80] In France, which was not particularly friendly toward associations, the internal political tensions within Catholicism, among other things, impeded a strong development. Aside from the social associations, the *Association catholique de la Jeunesse française* was probably the most important. It was founded in 1886 by Robert du Roquefeuil (headed later by Albert de Mun) and grew considerably after 1899 because the organization reached out toward the social classes as well as to all age groups. The impact of the political problem shows most clearly in the two major movements emerging around the turn of the century: the religiously inspired *Sillon* of Marc Sagnier and the *Action Française*,[81] in which monarchal Catholics and representatives of classical culture in the sense of Maurras joined hands. Whichever concept they followed, the French Catholics were always interested in the whole of France. Germany became primarily the classical land of the Catholic association movement because Catholicism there, in contrast to Anglo-Saxon countries, was such a strong minority that it could organize itself successfully within the general society, especially since it maintained certain regional strongholds in spite of the confessional mixture, and because it could not ignore the historical decisions of 1806, 1866, and 1870, and had to come to grips with the Protestant Hohenzollern Empire. The most famous organization was the *Volksverein für das Catholische Deutschland* [People's Society for Catholic Germany] of 1890, which also impressed many Catholic leaders in France and Italy. It

[78] R. Murri (cf. chap. 15), 117–23.
[79] T. Zeldin, *Conflicts in French Society. Anticlericalism, Education and Morals in the 19th Century* (London 1971); also, A. Daumard, *RH* 148 (1972), 202ff.
[80] Cf. n. 73. Regarding the workers associations, cf. chap. 13.
[81] In this regard, see below, pp. 473–76.

also encountered criticism, but was regarded by many important forces in Switzerland and Austria[82] as a model worth emulating. The founding process involved considerable internal struggles because the conservative agrarian politician Felix von Loë and Bishop Korum of Trier were striving for a society to "teach the German people about the religious and social errors of the present" according to the apologetic of Tilmann Pesch, S. J., who opposed the strongly anti-Catholic *Evangelischer Bund* (Evangelical Union) of 1887. Windthorst saw in it a danger to the Center Party, striving, together with others, for an extensive association for the masses which was to be separate from the Center Party (no election funds, no participation in the election campaign), but was to follow the same goals. This organization succeeded.[83] The association became intensely active with publications, training institutions (for which lecture material was provided), and its "people's offices" (counseling places; after 1900). These activities with their emphasis on reform and decidedly social accent were instrumental in fending off the impact of social democracy on the Catholic workers.[84] Most Catholic employers took a distant or negative stand toward the association, similar to the segment of the episcopate which was suspicious of an association not officially established by the Church, and especially of its democratic concepts.[85] An opponent of the *Volksverein* was also the group around Chaplain Dr. Oberdörffer, who, in 1893, once again took up a "Catholic social program" with an occupational orientation and rejected parliamentarism. The *Volksverein* had, in 1891, nearly 109,000 members, in 1901: 185,000, in 1902: 230,000, and in 1914: 805,000. One should

[82] In Switzerland, in 1904, the *Katholische Volksverein* was founded combining the associations there (chap. 4). It had local chapters, cantonal associations, and a central executive board which elected the central president. The *Schweizerische Kirchenzeitung* in Lucerne had pointed to the German model in 1898, but it was not considered belligerent enough. In regard to its background, see J. Meier, *Der Schweizer Katholische Verein* (Lucerne 1954).—In Austria, the numerous societies combined to form the *Katholische Volksbund* (1909), a central organization which, even in face of the differences between the Conservatives and the Christian Socialists, was strictly apolitical.

[83] E. Ritter, op. cit., 140–44; P. Siebertz, op. cit., 191ff.—Windthorst became honorary president, but died a year later. Upon his initiative, the industrialist Franz Brandts (Mönchen-Gladbach), well-known for his social activities, became the first chairman. It was his wish that the lawyer Karl Trimborn become his deputy. Franz Hitze became secretary (see above). August Pieper (1866–1942; 1889: priest) succeeded Hitze in 1892 and became director general of the *Volksverein* in 1903. In 1905, the *Volksvereinsverlag GmbH* began functioning as the owner of the society (O. v. Nell-Breuning, *StdZ* [1972], 35–50).

[84] The program in A. Pieper (1866–1942), *Sinn und Aufgabe:* "Every Catholic German of age who pays his yearly dues of one mark is a member of this society."

[85] The archbishop of Cologne, F. v. Hartmann (1912–19) disapproved of the introduction of general suffrage in Prussia.

consider that the demands on the members of a mass association are necessarily minor. The association's stronghold was in the Rhineland, while Bavaria kept aloof. There were several conflicts with the many other associations[86] of German Catholicism.[87] The *Volksverein* continued to have one handicap: it was not altogether successful in mobilizing the laymen in the organization itself. The official ecclesiastical suspicion of lay participation should not mislead one to imagine that the activities of the laymen were too intensive. A good part of pastoral work was consumed by care for the associations.[88] But the fact that the associations established without Church direction were a product of the post-revolutionary era, in spite of their significance for the Church in modern society, was not overlooked. Leo XIII emphasized the *summa potestas* of the Pope in his magisterial role even though the laity *(privati)* were allowed *industria nonnulla*. He underscored the fact that they could assume only a "resonance" of the teaching authority.[89] The real reason for this statement was certain tendencies of the *Opera dei congressi,* which was divided after 1884 according to function and placed under strictly hierarchal command despite the lay presidency.[90]

[86] The *Katholische Frauenbund* (1912: 60,000 members), founded in 1903 and addressing mainly the upper class through Trimborn, Bachem-Sieger, and others (the *Katholische Mütterverein,* founded in 1856 in Mainz by Bishop Ketteler and Countess Ida Hahn-Hahn was not organized on a diocesan level until during World War I), rejected the fact that the *Volksverein* was also soliciting membership of women (1914 agreement: the *Volksverein* is to remain an essentially male affair); closely related to the question of the "Christian trade union" was the conflict with the *Katholische Kaufmännische Vereinigung* (1907: 20,125 members, 1912: 35,000), which had members among employers and employees. There were also conflicts of competence with the secretariat general of the Catholic youth organizations in Düsseldorf.

[87] Special emphasis was placed on the development of youth groups. The *Katholische Jungmännerverband* with its 1200 chapters had 140,000 members in 1908 (after 1913, Carl Mosterts, youth vicar, was the president general). The *Zentralverband der Katholischen Jungfrauenvereinigung Deutschlands* was not founded until 1915 (the female organizations usually came later everywhere). The *Gesellenverein* of A. Kolping remained very active (1914: 1,276 local chapters with 86,339 active and 129,714 inactive members (Meister). The Catholic students were organized in three socially and politically different associations: in the fraternity *Cartellverband der katholischen deutschen Studentenverbindungen (CV;* after 1866) and in the *Kartellverband der katholischen Studentenvereine Deutschlands (KV;* after 1866), as well as in the related but more theologically interested *Unitas* society *(UV;* after 1860); the *CV* had 8,966 members in 1910, the *KV* 9,072 in 1912 (including alumni).—The *Katholische Lehrerverband* (after 1889) had 21,000 members in 1912; the female organization 15,000 (after 1885).

[88] M. Faßbender, "Laienapostolat und Volkspflege," *Caritasschriften* 15 (Freiburg i. Br. 1906); he stressed that the main area of activity was not accessible to the priest.

[89] Encyclical *Sapientiae* (1890) *(Acta Leonis* X, 21); "qui, quoties res exigat, commode possunt non sane doctoris sibi partes assumere, sed ea, quae ipsi acceperint, impertire ceteris, magistrorum voci resonantes tamquam imago."

[90] Cf. chap. 5.

The Catholic Press

The daily press was also a child of the Enlightenment and the Revolution. When one pastor spoke of the "authority of the masses" which "threatens to silence the preacher,"[91] he was passing the same judgment that the *Historisch-politischen Blätter* expressed on an elevated level: a "specifically Catholic press" was a "necessary evil," having emerged because Christian society was not "in its normal condition."[92] The remark that Catholics had neither "the writers nor the readers" was valid for some time and with respect to subscribers generally continued to be a problem, especially since this reflected on the revenue from advertisements. But the "evil" increased in terms of necessity. It had another aspect: Catholic journalism reflected and compounded internal strife within the various forms of Catholicism.[93] In this respect, the *Kölnische Volkszeitung*[94] and the Berlin *Germania*[95] in Germany were competitors. The *Kölner Richtung,* to which Julius Bachem contributed (especially political and literary articles such as "Heraus aus dem Turm!" [Leave the Tower!]), joined the dispute that had broken out in 1906, endorsing the principally supradenominational character of the Center Party and its political freedom in the face of direct ecclesiastical instructions. The paper took an analogous position in the controversy over the "Christian trade unions." In Austria, the conservative *Vaterland* (founded in 1860) and the Christian-social *Reichspost* (founded in 1893) opposed each other (the papers united in 1911). A false image of journalism in German Catholicism is created when only the leading organs are considered

[91] Cf. J. Lukas, *Die Presse, ein Stück moderner Versimpelung* (Regensburg 1867).

[92] Quoted according to K. Löffler, op. cit., 57.—Leo XIII's statements to the press, aside from giving general religious and moral advice, request avoiding internal Catholic disputes in the press, (1882) and repeatedly in reference to Spain (*Acta Leonis* III, 178). He deals increasingly with submission to ecclesiastical authority (in regard to France in 1899, see *Acta Leonis* XIX, 208). An instruction by Rampolla in 1902 reads: "Inoltre i giornalisti democratico-cristiani, come tutti i giornalisti cattolici, debbono mettere in pratica i seguenti avvertimenti del Santo Padre" (following a quotation from *Nobilissima Gallorum* of 1884 about ecclesiastical authority); *Acta Leonis* XXII, 12.

[93] In regard to France, see chaps. 6 and 36; Italy: chaps. 5 and 34; the Netherlands: Rogier (1957), 269–75 (quoted in chap. 7).

[94] The title *Kölner Volkszeitung* after 1869 means a change insofar as the conservative patrons who financed the founding of the *Kölnische Blätter* (1860) felt that the word *Volk* sounded too democratic (K. Buchheim). In 1869 Julius Bachem became the head of the editorial staff; editor in chief from 1878 until 1907 was the historian Hermann Cardauns. Copies in 1871: 7,200; in 1874: 8,600; in 1881: 9,000.

[95] In 1871 under the leadership of Councilor F. v. Kehler, the Catholic committee of Berlin founded the *Germania*. Chaplain P. Majunke of Silesia, who maintained that Luther committed suicide, was replaced as editor. During the *Kulturkampf*, the paper was particularly persecuted with prohibitions and penalties; nonetheless, it adhered to its intransigent course.

and not the weeklies and the many small local papers. In 1865, the total number of subscribers was estimated to be about 60,000; in 1890, about one million were reported. Nevertheless, these numbers were relatively low: the *Berliner Tageblatt* alone had 250,000 subscribers.[96] The *Kulturkampf* had effected a significant breakthrough. Of course this was related to the fact that the Catholic daily newspapers after 1870 were practically the mouthpieces of the Center Party.[97] This and the bishops' desire to have a direct impact on the editorial staff resulted in an emphatic recommendation of the Church papers at the Catholic Convention in Metz in 1913.[98] These were a medium of the Church authority itself, but they had to try to address Catholics of all political persuasions and therefore generally refrained from sharp polemics in areas outside of the religious and moral spheres. In the Catholic press which represented intransigent conservative viewpoints—in Belgium *Le Bien Public,* in the Netherlands the *Maasbode,* in Spain the *Siglo futuro,* in Canada the *Vérité* of Tardivel—the French newspaper *La Croix* stands out, not just because of its circulation (in 1897: seven hundred thousand, including the nearly one hundred local editions), but also because of its sometimes almost fanatical attitude.[99] In the realm of journalism, the dilemma between Catholicism as a socially, politically, and philosophically coherent group and the essentially universal orientation of the Catholic Church is also evident.[100]

The Enemy

Even if one were critical of a "world conspiracy," refrained from regarding the Grand Master of the Italian Freemasons, Andriano Lemmi, with

[96] In Germany, there were 221 Catholic newspapers in 1881; 288 in 1890; 378 in 1903; 446 in 1912 (without *Kopfblätter;* 305 were privately owned, 141 the property of a corporation). In the early Weimar Republic, there existed 65 newspapers that had been founded between 1848 and 1871.

[97] K. Bachem, *Julius Bachem* I, p. vii. Earlier, the "political leaning was uncertain, unclear, frequently changing;" K. Bringmann, *Die konfessionell-politische Tagespresse des Niederrheins im 19. Jahrhundert* (Düsseldorf 1938). The *Augustinusverein,* founded in 1878, spoke either of the "Catholic press" or the "Center press" (W. Kisky, op. cit., 77). Now and then there were tensions within the party because it prohibited any kind of criticism (ibid., 167ff.). The temporary presidency of the *Augustinerverein,* consisting of seven members, had only one editor and four clergymen; in 1889 a layman was the president for the first time. There were also disagreements between the publishers and the editors (ibid., 100ff., 148).

[98] A definition was attempted according to which the ecclesiastical papers were "to serve the purpose of pastoral work only" (W. Kisky, op. cit., 154). Cf. chap. 14, n. 19.

[99] Regarding Italy, cf. above, p. 90; regarding *La Croix:* above, p. 105—An international comparative analysis of Catholic journalism according to its tendencies, its quality, and its impact is sorely needed.

[100] Concerning the integralism of the press, see below, p. 473.

his pathological hatred of the Church, as representative of all lodges, and made a distinction between the Roman and all the other organizations, it must be stated that we are dealing here with the intellectual leaders of the time who waged a ruthless war against the Catholic Church, no matter how the humanitarian ideals of that movement are evaluated. This and the successes of the Freemasons within Catholicism itself, especially in Latin America, cannot keep us from considering what impact the intensity of the Catholic struggle against the Freemasons had for the consolidation of group-consciousness in the face of the enemy. Even Leo XIII differentiated in his encyclical *Humanum genus* (20 April 1884) between individual *Sectatores,* who, he said, are not without blame, but do not participate in the malicious actions and do not have a clear picture of the ultimate goals of Freemasonry. But the encyclical begins with a reference to the *Invidia Diaboli,* and it ends with the request to the world episcopate to uproot this "wicked pestilence" (*impuram luem*) because an attack as vicious as theirs requires an equally vicious defense. In the first paragraph, the Pope places God's realm in opposition to that of Satan. The accusations against the "naturalists" are basically the same as those which the Pope had earlier brought against the "socialists and communists" and which he would bring against liberalism a year later, only that he describes it as work in solitary darkness comparable to that of the Manichaeans. Leo XIII reiterates the prohibition of membership under penalty of excommunication which his predecessors had proclaimed.[101]

The positive definition of a Freemasonic lodge led to complications in Canada and the United States.[102] For the Catholic Convention in Amberg in 1885, Prince Löwenstein, according to the account of his biographer, could not find a bishop who was willing to give a speech appropriately warding off the Freemasons. After the papal letter *Praeclara* of 20 June 1894[103] which repeatedly condemned the Freemasons (who had now emerged from the dark into the light), Bishop Korum himself was of the opinion that the leadership of the planned Anti-Freemason Congress in Trent had to be the responsibility of the laity.[104] Gabriel Jogand-Pagés, an ex-Freemason who, with reference to the papal encyclical *Humanum genus,* had been opposing the lodges since 1885, was to

---

[101] *Humanun genus (Acta Leonis* II, 43–70, here: 50, 65, 69, 43, 49).

[102] Cf. chaps. 9 and 10.

[103] *Praeclara (Acta Leonis* XIV, 208f.).

[104] P. Siebertz, op. cit., 478. Löwenstein's biography glorifies its hero, but, in spite of certain naive qualities, it contains a considerable number of facts found in the family archives. Under the pseudonym Ewald, he published articles against the Freemasons, even after the Congress of Trent. They were collected and edited under the title *Die geheime Armee im Kampf gegen Thron und Altar,* but prominent and intelligent Catholics prevented their publication.

appear there. As "Leo Taxil," Jogand-Pagés invented a Miss Diana Vaughan, who had supposedly penetrated the secrets of the Satan cult and since her conversion was forced to live in hiding in order to escape death at the hands of the Freemasons. Jogand-Pagés' accomplice was the physician Charles Hacks who, as Dr. Bataille, published the essay "Le Diable au XIXme siècle." The revelations of one Domenico Margiotta about the Italian Grand Master Andriano Lemmi drew the attention of some French bishops. An excerpt appeared in German translation, as well as the sermons of the Dominican Monsabré who demanded a crusade against the lodges. As president of the "Committee for Roman Affairs," Prince Löwenstein tried at the Catholic Convention to circulate such publications in Germany. But Bishop Korum[105] and others expressed reservations toward such "disclosures" about the Satan cult. Italy initiated the international congress, which took place from 20 September to 30 September 1896 in Trent under the patronage of Cardinal Parocchi. Löwenstein was convinced that in the fight for the Church it was his obligation to take over the chairmanship. Yet some scepticism toward "Leo Taxil" was still brought forward as the result of information which arrived just in time.[106] A Roman investigative committee established in Trent pronounced judgment on 22 January 1897: the existence of Miss Vaughan could neither be proven nor disproven. On 17 April "Taxil" revealed his hoax. It was the general problem which came to light through this affair, rather than the psychology of this man, which is important: large parts of Catholicism found themselves facing a basically anti-Christian and antiecclesiastical world.[107] A difficult path had to be followed between adaptation and absolute resistance.

On another yet not completely separate plain are the anti-Semitic tendencies which permeated various parts of Catholicism, especially in

---

[105] Korum's letter to Löwenstein of 24 August 1896 (after the Bishops' Conference in Fulda): The revelations may be true for France and Italy, but "cannot be proven in regard to Germany;" see P. Siebertz, op. cit., 483.

[106] C. Hacks was a brother-in-law of Julius Bachem. He divulged to him the deception. According to P. Siebertz, Bachem seems to have informed Löwenstein rather superficially; K. Bachem, *Erinnerungen eines alten Publizisten und Politikers* (Cologne 1913), 161ff. In August 1896, the Jesuit H. J. Gruber, who had believed the revelations for a long time, published an article of warning in the *Kölnische Volkszeitung* (initialled H.G.). As H. Gerber he wrote *Taxils Palladismus-Roman,* 3 vols. (Berlin 1897–98); id., *Betrug als Ende eines Betrugs* (Berlin 1897).

[107] A. Boulenger, *Histoire générale de l'Église* III (Paris 1947), 748: It is difficult to believe that Freemasons devised this affair; yet, they derived profit from it. Kißling II, 284–86, tries to diminish the problem and draws attention to Hermann Schell (cf. chap. 29), who has to be given credit for not playing up a marginal event, but rather seeing the affair as a symptom of the internal status of the Church, for which he shows concern.

Austria and France. The reasons are complex: a subcutaneous anti-Semitism in the history of Christianity surfaced due to the animosity of liberal, Jewish writers toward the Church, and this anti-Semitism joined with a general social resentment toward the Jewish world of finance and business. In France, both the right and the left wing of Catholicism were affected.[108] In Austria, a middle-class mentality and Christian social reform ideas joined together. In France, in 1899, Abbé Gayraud called the Jews "la nation malfaisante et parasitaire," and the election slogan of the "Christian-Social Party" in 1903 read: "Catholics and Protestants, unite in brotherly love against Jewish capitalism and the Asian money ethic."[109]

---

[108] G. Hoog, op. cit., 106, is justified in speaking of an "almost international" phenomenon. However, the Congress of Lyon in 1896 did not consider it necessary to be "inspired" by the Viennese anti-Semitism.

[109] K. Rengstorf, *Kirche und Synagoge* II (Stuttgart 1971); P. Sorlin, *La "Croix" et les Juifs* (Paris 1967); P. Pierrard, *Juifs et catholiques français. De Drummont à Jules Isaac* (Paris 1970); I. A. Hellwing, *Der konfessionelle Antisemitismus in Österreich* (Vienna 1972).

CHAPTER 13

The Social Movements

In the second half of the nineteenth century, social organizations emerged from the forms of Catholicism which dealt with the needs and interests of the farmers, the middle-class, and the industrial workers. The attempts to meet these needs were primarily inspired by religious motives. Such a combination of religiously irrelevant economic facts and ecclesiastical attitudes was more in accord with the social awareness of Catholicism than with the self-awareness of Protestantism, in spite of similar and often pioneering events. The activities were actually initiated by the clergy and individual laymen, less so by the workers and farmers concerned. The fact that after the first third of the twentieth century the religious aspects became more or less insignificant in comparison to the economic ones does not allow the original combination to be considered ideologically suspect. Instead, it refers to the problem of the relationship between Church and state in the sense of the image and the model which was discussed earlier. In this context, it is important that the leadership of the organizations was more and more transferred from the clergy to the laity. This process, viewed objectively, was appropriate, but it resulted in the predominance of the representation of economic interests over the initial religious motivations.

Farmers

In Germany, beginning in the sixties, Wilhelm Raiffeisen (1818–88) devoted himself to the development of a rural cooperative system. Raiffeisen was a church-minded Protestant. In 1862 the Catholic aristocrat Burghard von Schorlemer-Alst (1825–95) founded an inter-denominational (according to its statutes) Farmers' Association in Westphalia. It spread so rapidly in the areas with a Catholic population because of its limitation by the *Kulturkampf;*[1] since the social union was impeded by the state, the Catholic farmers became even more active in their local societies.

In Italy the movement began in Venetia, where Cerutti founded a cooperative credit bank in 1880. This institution, (1904: 855 credit institutions) together with the already existing supporting funds of the *Opera dei congressi,* became the foundation for the development of the farmers' associations. In accord with the agrarian condition in Italy, there were societies for farm laborers and for farmers (in 1904: 33 and 43 respectively).[2] In Belgium, the *Boerenbond,* founded in 1889 by G. Helleputte[3] and the priest Mellaerts, achieved considerable significance (1902: 359 local "guilds"). In 1896, a Catholic farmers' union was founded in the Netherlands. In France, in 1892, E. Duport and L. Durand created a rural system of cooperatives in the vicinity of Lyon, and rural youth groups were active. From these activities emerged the *Ligue agricole chrétienne.* Its goal, formulated in the statutes of the Farmers' Society of Schorlemer-Alst, was "to further the members in religious, moral, intellectual, social and material respects." It was applied in all rural organizations and, in its universal formulation, was especially pertinent in areas where de-Christianization had already early affected large parts of the rural population, mostly in western Europe. The organization of the credit system, buying, and selling played a special role in the Christian farmers' movement. This was a result of modern economic exigencies which also affected the agrarian sector. However, after World War I, the religious character of the farmers' societies survived only in Belgium and in the Netherlands. Consequently, economic interests were intensified.[4]

---

[1] F. Jacobs, *B. Freiherr von Schorlemer-Alst* (Hiltrup i. W. 1953).—In Bavaria, where the societies formed a special association, Georg Heim was later the initiator (1865–1938).

[2] A. Gambasin, *Il movimento sociale* . . . (biblio., chap. 5).

[3] Cf. chap. 7.

[4] An early example of this problem is the Catholic Convention in Aachen in 1879. In the previous year, Bebel had had a surprising electoral victory in this city. At the convention of the *Piusverein,* taking place at the same time in Aachen, Schorlemer-Alst defended the strongly agrarian protective tariffs policy which was supported by the Center against the Liberals' opposition, and which also encountered the disapproval of the

The "Middle Class"

The term "middle class"[5] needs to be defined in generous terms, because the ecclesiastically active industrial entrepreneurs and businessmen (the denominational statistics themselves mean little) were running only medium or small businesses, and with regard to their social policies they stood isolated from their colleagues, especially from those in higher ranks.[6] This explains, aside from socio-theoretical questions, why the idea of the mixed trade unions and paternalistic ideas dominated Catholicism for a long time. The entrepreneur regarded his small business (in which he knew everyone) as sort of an extended family. Since there were only minor economic differences, it was possible for employers and employees alike to belong to the Catholic organizations of this social stratum. (While farmers were among the self-employed, they constituted a separate category.) The journeymen's union of Adolf Kolping followed the tradition of the class of craftsmen, and the journeymen who were promoted to masters continued to be special members of the union. A similar situation existed in the mercantile associations within Catholicism. In 1884, an association of Catholic entrepreneurs emerged in the north of France, and in 1889, Léon Harmel and the priest Alet founded the *Union fraternelle du Commerce et de l'Industrie,* which consisted mainly of shopkeepers and small manufacturers who, because of their religious affiliation, also wanted to help each other economically. The members of such associations were largely paternalistic, and entrepreneurs who liked to experiment incurred displeasure.[7]

Catholic workers. Schorlemer-Alst also tried to promote solidarity with his slogan of the "poor man," who, together with the other classes, had defended the Church during the *Kulturkampf* (Kißling II, 65f).

[5] Regarding this concept, see O.v. Nell-Breuning, *StL*[6] V, 783–90.

[6] Regarding Germany, cf. C. Bauer, *Deutscher Katholizismus* (Frankfurt a. M. 1964), 32–42. It is especially significant that the main areas of industrialization, the Rhineland and Upper Silesia, were rather uniformly Catholic regions, which changed their denominational structure little, in spite of mobility. However, there was "hardly any Catholic participation in the leadership of industrialization," but rather a "completely disproportionate participation in the enterprises of industrial entrepreneurs" (38).— Denominationally homogeneous countries can only be assessed adequately if one can look beyond the more or less active participation in Church life and include the factual religious attitude.—The isolated social activities in the companies owned by religiously and morally responsible entrepreneurs brought these companies into a disadvantageous competitive situation.

[7] H. Rollet, op. cit., (1947 ed.), describes the resistance the entrepreneur C. Feron-Vrau encountered at the Congress of Mouvaux in 1895 because he had allowed a works council to be elected, even though he had added that it was necessary "to accustom the worker to respect the areas of business which are the responsibility of the entrepreneur."

Since the interests were different in the various economic sectors, a central federation with various special sections was founded in 1901. Abbé Puppey-Girard had suggested this federation, and in 1892 he also initiated the union of young engineers, the *Union sociale des ingénieurs catholiques,* which became a trade union in 1902. In the Netherlands, at the beginning of the twentieth century, Catholic employers' combines emerged in the tobacco and mechanical engineering industries. In Belgium and Germany, given the political partisanship, there was no need for such organizations. In Austria, in the nineties, the Christian Socialists emerged in opposition to the Conservatives. They were interested in the labor question, but they themselves were a decidedly middle-class movement, in which many employed and independent people of the petite bourgeoisie gathered.[8]

At the beginning of World War I, the two Catholic indistrialists Léon Harmel (1829–1915)[9] and Franz Brandts (1834–1914)[10] died. As heads of their own companies and in their capacity as organizers they had tried to find a solution to the labor question. They both used a patriarchal style, though it was different in each case because of the situation in their respective countries and their personal way of thinking; and they were both from the textile industry. These men are not at all representative of their colleagues of the same denomination, but they document what was a serious paternalistic reform. Harmel, *le bon pére,* was theoretically indoctrinated by Le Play,[11] and he endorsed and practiced himself a certain form of workers' participation in company policies (the *Conseil professionel* of 1888 changed to the more precise term *Conseil d'usine* in 1891). Harmel also tended to induce the workers to execute their own

[8] F. Funder, op. cit., 82–155.

[9] In the seventies, L. Harmel was a disciple of the Bourbon Monarchists, a supporter of the Count of Chambord, a grandson of Charles X who was loyal to the fleur-de-lis. He was strictly ultramontane and supported the *Syllabus.* He divorced himself from antirepublican tendencies. His main estate was located in Val des Bois near Rheims (G. Guitton, *Léon Harmel,* 2 vols. [Paris 1925, ²1930]; id., *L. Harmel et l'initiative ouvrière* [Paris 1938]; H. Rollet, op. cit., index).

[10] F. Brandts was the son of a wealthy textile merchant (*Verlagssystem*). During his stay of several months in England in the sixties, he learned about industrial weaving and equipped his mill in Mönchen-Gladbach accordingly ("How can one be afraid of becoming too rich, we are only beginning," according to Hohn, 25). He was an energetic and self-conscious man, who occasionally quarrelled with his later collaborator F. Hitze (when Brandts pleaded for harmony in the Center and made reference to his relation to Hitze, Windthorst said: "Yes, this is what your wife does!" Schwer-Müller [biblio., chap. 12], 59)—W. Hohn, ed., *F. Brandts* (M.-Gladbach 1914, ²1920), Brandts's quotations, memorial addresses by A. Pieper and C. Sonnenschein; E. Ritter, *Volksverein* (biblio., chap. 12), index.

[11] Buchheim, *Ultramontanismus,* 327; cf. chap. 12.

initiatives. His distant goal was a corporation of employers and employees, but, in contrast to Albert de Mun, he believed that it could only be accomplished if the idea of trade unions was accepted. He was critical of state intervention, but also of his colleagues, whom he charged with being idle in terms of the workers' question, except for their customary charitable activities. He formulated his principles in the *Catéchisme au patron* (Paris 1889). Harmel was one of the main organizers of the French workers' pilgrimages to Rome, and after 1895 he was the president of the *Oeuvres des cercles catholiques d'ouvriers,* which he wanted to lead out of the conservative conception of de Mun in order to win the workers themselves. Through F. Brandts's recommendation he served as consultant during the founding of the *Arbeiterwohl* in Mönchen-Gladbach, an association of "Catholic industrialists and friends of the workers" (1879). Through this association and its publication, the German textile entrepreneurs wanted to propagate their socio-political ideas. Members of the executive board were Georg von Hertling and Prelate F. C. Moufang of Mainz, who brought with him the traditions of Ketteler. In 1880 Hitze, who had just returned from Campo Santo, joined the group as its secretary. Hitze had great impact on the social policies of the Center Party and was able to carry through the "Mönchen-Gladbach concept" over the Viennese Vogelsang school and the clerical "Berlin concept" (in 1890, Brandts became the chairman of the *Volksverein*).[12] Brandts was also a patriarch,[13] and as such, in 1886, he moved with his family to the Saint Joseph's House, in whose original structure he had accommodated the welfare institutions of his company in 1878. He was well aware that all the social works of the company would not suffice. He was a decisive representative of the state's right and duty to intervene, and, after initial reservation toward his resistant colleagues, he finally pulled his weight to grant the workers the same right to form coalitions in the trade unions that the employers enjoyed. However, the legal reform was needed to assure that "the activities of the trade unions would be restricted once the fight was launched."[14]

---

[12] Cf. chap. 12.—In 1892 F. Hitze invited Father August Pieper (1866–1942) to join the group; in 1903, he became director general of the *Volksverein* (A. Rhode, "Die sozialpolitischen Ideen A. Piepers" (diss., Cologne 1950).

[13] In 1890: "Alongside the absolute recognition of the worker as an equal human being (as head of a family and as a 'voting member of society') . . . the feeling of the old patriarchal relationship between worker and employer, the feeling of belonging together should not disappear" (W. Hohn, op. cit., 109). Brandts considered his factory an "extended family" (ibid., 23).

[14] W. Hohn, op. cit., 81, 111–17; Brandts planned workers' councils in which both partners would be represented.

The Socio-ethical Justification
of the Workers' Movement

In regard to this topic, concepts were being formulated which emerged from the socio-theoretical debates within Catholicism, and, in spite of continued differences, found a magisterial basis in the encyclical *Rerum novarum* (1891). The endorsement of state intervention in this document[15] represented a fundamental decision toward the liberal capitalist society and now left it up to the Catholics to act within the political parties of the constitutional state according to the principles of ecclesiastical sociology. How this was reflected in specific individual decisions (for instance, when designing a social insurance plan, or in parliamentary coalitions) is a matter of general history and belongs to Church history only insofar as it resulted in conflicts with the hierarchical claim to a magisterial role.[16] The other, equally important directive of this encyclical, the recognition of the workers' right to form coalitions, had a direct effect on the social structure of Catholicism and had to go through a process of critical assessment. In this respect, the Pope elaborated on the title of the encyclical (*De conditione opificum*) by turning to the workers themselves. In the paragraph on the "workers' associations" (*sodalitia artificum*), Leo XIII dealt with the discussions of the medieval guilds, but he also stressed the necessity of adapting to modern conditions. This was of pressing importance at the time and had practical implications because it expressly left unsaid whether the societies were to be exclusively composed of workers or were to be mixed organizations. Since the formation of such associations is justified on the basis of the natural law, the state has no right to forbid them, and the state is warned not to misuse its right to justified intervention under the mere pretext of public interest.[17] Leo XIII considered a strike categorically evil because it harms the employer and the employee as well as the public welfare (*mercaturae, rei publicae utilitates*), especially since strikes usually entail violence. It is the duty of legislation to eliminate the causes of such conflicts. The subsequent discussion of Catholic social theoreticians proceeded from the paragraph on employees, who are to

---

[15] Cf. chap. 12, n. 57. This encyclical can only be assessed fairly if it is placed into the historical context of the traditional sociology of the Catholic Church. It was certainly not innovative within the general socio-historical development, but it was significant as the word of an outstanding conservative power, and it contributed considerably to alleviating conservative as well as liberal opposition toward a decisive social policy.—A good study in terms of the history of the papal social doctrine up to Pius XI in particular and of the history of social theory in general: A. Simon (Brussels): H. Scholl (ed.), 13–49.
[16] Regarding the Center controversy in 1906, cf. chap. 35; regarding the special problems in Italy, cf. chaps. 5 and 34.
[17] *Acta Leonis* XI, 133–35.

fulfill absolutely the work contract which they signed voluntarily and under the conditions of equity (*libere et cum aequitate*).[18] At this point, the encyclical clearly expressed that the wealthy do not require the protection of the state to the extent that the *miserum vulgus* does, and there was no doubt that work contracts had to be consented to which were anything but voluntary and fair. Moreover, the encyclical could and did deal with the question of fair wages only in very general terms.[19] The problem of strikes, to be sure, touched on a fundamental aspect of a stratified society.[20] With which *ordo* could this phenomenon of antagonism be met?

Leo XIII strongly emphasized that the fostering of piety was to be the priority of the workers' associations and that, in the name of episcopal authority, the clergymen, in regard to the associations, were responsible

---

[18] Regarding the strike, see ibid., 126; regarding *pactum operae,* see 110.

[19] I. Healy, *The Just Wage, 1750–1890* (The Hague 1966).

[20] The problem of strikes became increasingly more urgent with the formation of "Christian trade unions." The moral theologian A. Lehmkuhl declared in his book *Arbeitsvertrag und Streikrecht* (Freiburg 1899, [4]1904), that the immediate "defense strike" for the purpose of self-defense was permissible when the workers were forced into an "unfair" contract; the employer is at fault if, despite profits, he does not pay the kind of wage which would "suffice for the livelihood of the worker and his family" (and is difficult to establish, of course [55–59]). An organized strike is permissible if it is not a question of a "fair" but a higher wage, whose proper increase is naturally not as clearly defined as its decrease" (59ff.). Canonist A. Vermeersch from Louvain expressed a similar idea (*Quaestiones de iustitia* [[2]1904], 627). I. Treitz, secretary general of the Catholic workers' societies in the diocese of Trier, published in opposition to the *Christlichen Gewerkschaften* a pamphlet entitled *Kann ich, werde ich für eine Arbeiterbewegung auf katholischer Grundlage eintreten?* ("Can I, will I support a workers' movement based on Catholic principles?") (Trier 1904). Treitz, in his article *Der moderne Gewerkschaftsgedanke vom Standpunkt der Vernunft und Moral* ("The modern idea of trade unions from the perspective of reason and morality") (Trier 1909), rejected the idea of a strike and granted to the state only the right of arbitration, as did Secretary General Fournelle of Berlin. The statutes of the "special sections" of the Catholic workers' societies of Berlin, which were directed by clergymen, read: "The clergymen cannot find a place in belligerent organizations, only in organizations dedicated to reconciliation, law, and peace" (quoted according to H. Brauns, *Christliche Gewerkschaften oder Fachabteilungen* [1904], 50). The answer of J. Biederlack ("Die Frage der sittlichen Erlaubtheit der Arbeiterausstände," *ZKTh* 34 [1910], 302): Who would be optimistic enough "to dare hope that our present day rulers would end the economic struggle only having in mind the well-being of their state and their people." H. Pesch ("Streik und Lockout," *Stimmen aus Maria Laach* 77 [1909], 1–12, 142–54) is critical of the "infamous freedom of contract" and believes that a strike is a great evil but "does not necessarily need to be condemned." He expresses the most significant opinion, stating that, today, it is still a matter of "groups" (and not "organized professions") that should be subject to civil law and, once they are established, to society and not to the state (148).—For a moderate concept of the Christian social doctrine, see O. v. Nell-Breuning, "Streik," *LThK*[2] IX, 1111f.; id., Festschrift für E. Liefmann-Keil (in prep.).

for everything that had to do with pastoral work.[21] For the early Catholic workers' movement, this was hardly a problem, since many socially concerned clergymen devoted their energy to the workers' questions in a comprehensive sense, even though they did not always meet with the approval of their superiors. However, the rural and middle-class organizations of Catholicism practiced religious solidarity primarily in regard to economic questions. Their mutual assistance in economic distress strengthened the religious solidarity of the Catholic special groups within the de-Christianization of the society at large. Therefore, the workers' movement, whether it was Marxist or not, was on the whole an anti-middle-class bellicose movement. Is it true that the more the Catholic workers' movement was religiously determined, the less it was a workers' movement according to the above definition? On the other hand, was its religious character as a *Catholic* workers' movement less pertinent when it was more belligerent, as in the "Christian trade unions"? This touches on the key question of the Catholic workers' movement, the only one, incidentally, Leo XIII spoke about. Were its religious character and the character of a necessarily belligerent movement compatible? In case of a possible conflict, was it not necessary to separate the representation of interests from the Catholic workers' societies and transfer it to the trade unions? What reason was there for representing economic interests in religious form? The "Christian trade unions" wanted to distinguish themselves through this particular name from then mostly atheistic socialism without giving expression to a strongly religious motivation in regard to their concrete goals. The subsequent controversy about the "Christian trade unions," above and beyond the denominational issue, had its basis in the lack of such differentiation and also partially in the rejection of the idea of trade unions per se.

Industrial Workers

If one were to superimpose the European map which delineates the industrial centers developed after the second half of the century onto the map of the Catholic denomination, one would find that the following areas coincide: Upper Silesia, the plains of the Po river around Milan and Turin, the areas around Barcelona, Bilbao, and Oviedo as well as the southern regions from Hamm to Dunkirk. In Upper Silesia, associations emerged in whose publication *Robotnik* purely pastoral goals were pursued; and in Spain, there were no or only very insignificant Catholic workers' organizations (Barcelona became a showplace of horror). In Italy, the institutions of the *Opera dei congressi* concen-

[21] *Acta Leonis* XI, 138f. Supporters of *Rerum novarum* as integralists: cf. below, p. 472.

trated in Venetia and Lombardy (1904: 1,339 out of 2,432) and, around this time, 170 workers' associations were counted. The ecclesiastical conflicts were kindled by the question of leadership and the character of the organizations.[22] The stage of the Catholic workers' movement during Leo XIII's pontificate was essentially the Rhenish-Westphalian, the Belgian, and the northern French industrial areas.

Around 1880, the *Cercles catholiques d'ouvriers,* founded in 1871 by de Mun, had about 40,000 members. They declined as a result of the political differences within Catholicism in France and revived slightly in 1892 through the *Ralliement.* In 1906, there were about 60,000 members in 418 workers' societies. The relatively small numbers are not as decisive as the social status of the members. In a speech before the then entirely bourgeois Catholic youth association, de Mun said: "The simple folk, gentlemen, the workers in the cities, the factories, and the fields— this is the great problem which you should keep in mind!"[23] But this appeal found little response except with the interested Catholics of the landed gentry and the upper middle class. Moreover, it did not succeed in "taking root in the world of the workers"; it continued to be "agir de l'extérieur."[24] The reasons were partly of a political and partly of a specifically French nature. Even when de Mun, in 1885, in response to the Pope's wish relinquished the idea of founding a Catholic party, and

[22] Carl Sonnenschein (biblio., chap. 15), 8–12, in regard to the social question, differentiates five social groups: 1) the Rosminian liberal Catholics, who deal almost exclusively with the social question; 2) the intransigents, "men with the exclusive loyalty of a praetorian group"; a member of this group was the priest and journalist Davide Albertario (1846–1902), who, after the general strike in Milan between 6 and 9 May 1898 (suppression of the strike left over one hundred dead), was sentenced to prison along with the Socialist Filippo Furati (Magri [biblio., chap. 5] I, 216ff.; E. Nolte in: T. Schieder [ed.], *Handbuch der europäischen Geschichte* 6 [1968], 415f.); 3) the Curia in a city without industry; 4) the feudal south where Freemasons and clergymen lived in harmony; 5) the *Opera dei congressi,* which was conducted according to hierarchical principles, but fell under the influence of landed proprietors and industrialists and was known for a "formalism of immense proportions, a few Catholic conventions without people and a surfeit of Byzantine protests."—This is the picture that was so vividly drawn by Sonnenschein, pastor in Berlin, in 1900: priest in Rome, in 1906: counciior of the *Volksverein* in Mönchen-Gladbach (cf. chap. 34; A. Gambasin, also in S. H. Scholl [ed.], 214–42). In 1902, the controversy in the *Opera dei congressi* over purely occupational societies (usually attempting to be transformed into trade unions) increased, resulting in a crisis and the suspension of the *Opera.* In 1907, the first general congress of the *Unione economica-sociale* took place in Bergamo. Its president pleaded with Pius X in vain to put more emphasis on the economic character of the struggle. Nevertheless, the religious demands were actually very tolerant. In 1919, there were (including rural laborers) 104,614 Catholic ("white") trade unionists out of a total of 817,034 trade unionists in Italy (out of 9 million employees) (cf. chap. 34).
[23] Quoted according to M. P. Fogarty, op. cit., 309.
[24] H. Rollet, op. cit. II, 372–74.

even though he had sacrificed his political convictions during the *Rallie-ment,* the following goal remained decisive: to unite the Catholics in the "défense religieuse" and the "action sociale."[25] Indeed, it was a question of a "religious, social, and political counterrevolution" which could not, however, break the economic liberalism predominant in the upper ranks and was therefore not approved by the antibourgeois working class.[26] But the incorrect assessment of working class political psychology[27] was compounded by the problematic question of which way the bourgeois spirituality (aside from its political implications) could match the mentality of the working class. The symbol of the *cercles* was a combination of the cross and the Sacred Heart.[28] But even such a movement was much too revolutionary for Bishop C.-E. Freppel of Angers (1827–91).[29] In 1911, toward the end of his life, de Mun admitted the failure: It had been almost impossible to touch the workers, let alone impress them.[30] This was the candid word of a candid man, and he should not be blamed for the fact that for many of the northern-French patrons[31] this religious activity was only an escape from the social question. The first beginning of a Christian trade-union movement was the *Syndicat des Employés du Commerce et de l'Industrie* of 1887, whose executive board, in 1891, rejected a protective committee of Catholic employers,[32] as well as a clerical advisory body. From this and similar organizations emerged the *Confédération Française des Travailleurs Chrétiens* (CFTC).

[25] H. Rollet, *A. de Mun* . . . , 118f.

[26] W. Gurian, 278 (biblio., chap. 12).

[27] "This renascent social movement . . . imagined a working class hostile to the Revolution and missed totally the workers psychology" (J. N. Moody, op. cit., 146f.).

[28] Lynch, 187. The society's anthem had the following text: "Quand Jésus vint sur la terre ce fut pour y travailler / Il voulut, touchant mystère, Comme nous être ouvrier / Espérance / De la France, / Ouvriers, soyez chrétiens: Que votre âme / Soit de flamme / Pour l'auteur de tous les biens."

[29] Until his death (1891), he was an opponent of state intervention (for instance, at the Congress of Liège in 1890) because it infringed upon individual freedom and was Socialism (Terrien II, 696). He wanted to "restaurer la société "chrétienne par l'affirmation de la doctrine catholique contre la Révolution, qui a détruit l'ordre social, où régnait le Christ" (ibid. II, 204).

[30] Combats VI, 194: "Il faut bien dire la vérité. Nous avons des œuvres nombreuses, souvent florissantes, cercles, patronages, associations. Cependant, nous n'avons pas entraîné la classe ouvrière, je dirais presque que nous ne l'avons pas atteinte, du moins que nous ne l'avons pas pénétrée."

[31] H. Rollet, op. cit. II, 322: "The entrepreneur's wife coming into the firm and firing non-Catholic women; the chaplain of Fourmiers preaching in the works council about the peace of the Holy Scriptures; the entrepreneur of Roubaix forbidding a visit to the local pub instead of raising wages."

[32] The proposal came from L. Harmel, who gave the movement of Count A. de Mun a more realistic basis and organized the workers' congresses in Rheims after 1893. After 1901, the movement joined the *Sillon.*

In Belgium, the meeting place of the international Catholic social conferences, Bishop Doutreloux of Liège with his charitable activities and the establishment of the *Aumôniers du travail* (1895), the political Professor G. Helleputte with his workers' guilds, the social priest Pottier in Liège, and Fr. Rutten initiated a Catholic workers' movement which was not concerned with the political problems of the French and was much more pragmatic, but which could only assert itself against the supremacy of the conservatives through the increasing influence of the *Ligue démocratique belge* (since 1891). But here as well, the de-Christianization of the working class spread more and more. In the Netherlands, two movements developed: the one of Leiden, which was oriented toward trade unions, and the one of Limburg, which pursued a religious-social program.[33]

"During this trip through Belgium, my sojourn in Aachen and the tour up the Rhine river I have come to the conviction that we have to combat the clerics vigorously, especially in the Catholic areas . . . . The scoundrels are flirting with the workers' question whenever it seems appropriate (e.g., Bishop Ketteler in Mainz, the priests at the Congress of Düsseldorf, etc.)." Karl Marx wrote this to Friedrich Engels on 25 September 1869.[34] This observation about the enemy is also a warning against underestimating the efficiency of the Catholic workers' movement in the northwestern corner of the European continent. So was Bismarck's remark condemning the numerous "so-called Catholic local newspapers," which were often edited by chaplains and mocked the state measures against the "workers' intrigues" even though the uprising of the Commune in Paris should have opened their eyes.[35] The "Congress of Düsseldorf" that Karl Marx wrote about was the Catholic Convention of 1869, during which—after previous individual foundings—the ques-

---

[33] See the contribution by S. Hermann Scholl, 52–77, who set an excellent example when he placed the Catholic workers' movement in Belgium into the general socio-economic history, avoiding a distortion of perspective often unintentionally caused by Catholic literature. Scholl differentiates between "social Catholicism" from 1789 until 1886 and "Christian democracy" from 1886 until 1914 (which concerns the era discussed here). In 1891, Helleputte founded the Belgian People's Association at the Congress of Louvain. It was to unite the various efforts of the Catholic workers' movement, which was rarely led by workers, neither in Belgium nor in other countries. At the annual convention in 1901, Father Rutten gave his first lecture on the Christian trade unions, which had 11,000 members at that time. In 1909, there were 40,521 and 142,035 Socialists.—Regarding the Netherlands, see P. H. Winkelmann: Scholl (ed.), 255–286, also presented in context.

[34] *Correspondence between Marx and Engels* IV (ed. Berlin 1950), 272.

[35] H. Rothfels, *Bismarck und der Staat. Ausgewählte Dokumente* (Stuttgart 1958), 235.— In a letter addressed to Viennese Legate von Schweinitz of 27 January 1873, Bismarck mentions the *Christlich-sozialen Blätter* of Aachen in order to prove the "merging" of clerical and socialist tendencies (*Gesammelte Werke* VIc, 31f.).

tion of workers' organizations was discussed, but with utmost restraint relative to independent associations (or sections in Catholic male associations). In 1869, Chaplain E. Cronenberg of Aachen working together with Chaplain Dr. Litzinger, who had been transferred from Essen (Chaplain Laaf had been called from Aachen to Essen), founded the *Arbeiterverein vom heiligen Paulus* [Workers' Society of Saint Paul]. Litzinger was an intellectual among the "social chaplains," who could be quite disagreeable among themselves. Thus, Cronenberg carried on a controversy in his *Christian Social Voices* against the *Christian Social Newspaper* in Aachen, edited since 1869 by Chaplain Joseph Schings.[36] Cronenberg was of the opinion that "the Christian workers should take the workers' question into their own hands" and that, in spite of their Christian affiliation, the social problems should be considered relatively independently. He went bankrupt with his building society (in 1878, he was sentenced for forgery of his accounts). Around 1875, the *Paulusverein* in Aachen had a considerable reputation with its approximately five thousand members. That is when the battle began over the nomination of a Center Party candidate, which, at first, was won by the middle class; in 1877, in Essen, the worker J. Stötzel won and was elected to Parliament by a great majority.[37] The final breakthrough of an independent Catholic workers' movement did not occur until 1884, at the Catholic Convention of Amberg (thanks to Hitze's efforts). The unification into regional associations was accomplished between 1892 and 1910 (at the Catholic Convention in Mainz, a cartel association was formed in 1911).[38] This development already stood under the sign of the struggle over the "Christian trade unions."

The trade unions were the problem of the religious workers' associations and these, in turn, were the problem of the trade unions. This was not primarily a question of belief, which was only pertinent in Germany. It was also not just a question of the direct ecclesiastical leadership which was claimed by the integralistic concept during Pius X's pontifi-

[36] Schwer-Müller, 187f.; E. Naujoks, op. cit., 101–16, offers much material, however, he exaggerates the differences between the protagonists due to his anticlerical leaning; H. Lepper, "Kaplan F. E. Cronenberg . . . ," *ZAGV* 79 (1968), 57–148; J. Thielmann, *Die Presse der katholischan Arbeitervereine Westdeutschlands* (diss., Munich 1935).

[37] A "bourgeois" reaction, also to be seen in the context of the difficult situation during the *Kulturkampf,* can be documented in the seventies with the changes in names. The publication of the *Gesellenverein* in Munich called *Arbeiterfreund* (1873) called itself *Arbeitsfreund,* and the *Christlich-soziale Arbeiterverein* (1874) in Augsburg dropped the word "social" in 1876 (Naujoks, op. cit., 81).

[38] The number of members in 1914 in western Germany: 203,000, in eastern Germany: 132,000, in southern Germany: 122,000 (Kißling II, 376).

cate in Germany as well as in other countries.[39] The key issue becomes clear when considering the disputes which were carried on during the organizational period of the "Christian trade unions" and when assessing the situation after the first third of the twentieth century. During the general meeting of the leaders of the German workers' associations in 1892 in Mainz (Hitze's participation had considerable impact), it became obvious that religious education was to remain a priority, that occupational questions were to be dealt with separately, and finally that the struggle was part of the essence of a true workers' organization. The "individual trade sections" within the Catholic workers' associations differed from the "individual trade sections" in Berlin during the subsequent trade union controversy. This is substantiated by the fact that the participants in Mainz accepted a strike as the inevitable "last resort,"[40] but they believed strikes not to be feasible under "local and denominational limitations" (of the workers' associations). At the Catholic Convention in Cologne in 1895 they spoke about the "individual trade sections" as being the first step toward the "professional organization of the industrial worker on a Christian foundation" (H. Brauns). But this was the opinion of a minority. At the Catholic Convention in Bonn in 1900 it was difficult to arrive at a compromise: "Catholic workers' associations and Christian occupational organizations," avoiding the term "trade union," intended to include "the entire economic life."[41] Yet, in 1899 the first congress of the *Christliche Gewerkvereine Deutschlands* [Christian Trade Unions of Germany] had taken place in Mainz, which later caused the reaction in Berlin. The men initially involved in the Christian trade union movement showed "true denominational courage" in the struggle with atheistic socialism on the one hand and the (mostly Catholic) employers on the other hand—not to mention the opposition of bishops Korum and Kopp.[42] But did Brauns not imply more than just the German denominational problems when he differentiated between the "spiritual attitude" in the "Christian trade union" and the "moral-religious attitude" in the workers' association?[43] In other countries such as in Belgium and Holland, one followed the path discussed in Mainz in

---

[39] Regarding the "trade union controversy," cf. chap. 35.—The manner in which it was conducted can be partially deduced from a letter by Prince-Bishop G. v. Kopp addressed to August Pieper: "I only need to say one word and you will be condemned, as was Marc Sangnier in Paris" (Ritter, 327).

[40] H. Brauns, *Christliche Gewerkschaften oder Fachabteilungen in katholischen Arbeitervereinen?* (Cologne 1904), 5–13, in retrospect.

[41] Kißling II, 373.

[42] O. v. Nell-Breuning, *LThK*² IV, 857.

[43] H. Brauns, *Die Wahrheit über den Gewerkschaftsstreit* . . . (Mönchen-Gladbach 1912), 11.

1892, differentiating between "league" and trade union within one and the same Catholic workers' organization (in the trade union, the clerical leader was merely a "councilor"). In 1921, Cardinal Gasparri remarked that the Catholic workers' movement in Holland, Belgium, and Switzerland[44] had sensed more acutely than elsewhere "that the personal development (the foundation of a Christian class movement) would be subjugated more and more to the predominant economic activities if there were no common authority to keep the balance."[45] But whichever path was taken, the Belgian, the German, the French (which only led to a Christian trade union in the broadest sense) or the Italian (where the *Associazioni Cristiane Lavoratori Italiani* remained a purely educational movement) the historical result was basically the same everywhere. The Christian trade unions remained in the minority as compared to the others, and on the battlefield of labor they were in competition with them, which made it more difficult to assert their own principles. Within Catholicism itself, the Christianity of the trade unions only rarely permitted the antagonism of the class society to take on a different appearance; the religious "personal development" became insignificant in comparison to the fight for labor, or it was limited to a small circle, and this happened even more where the general development of trade unions took its own course.[46]

The fact was often discussed that industrial workers especially were becoming alienated from the Church, and with good reason. The apathy of bourgeois Catholicism was deplored, clearly recognizable in the opposition which the Catholic workers' movement had to overcome within the ranks of its own fellow believers. But two points have to be made: The process of de-Christianization extended over all of society, but appeared more pronounced among the industrial workers because here, instead of a "fourth class," a new class, which essentially differed from the agrarian bourgeois society, was emerging. Therefore, it was unable to relate to the Church traditions through which a conventional form of Christianity could yet survive for decades. Above all, the industrial workers were earlier and more directly than any other class affected by technology and thus by the epoch-making break with tradition[47] which affected all of society.

---

[44] Following the denominational attempt of Vicar J.-B. Jung in Saint Gall (cf. chap. 4), the Christian trade unions were organized interdenominationally (in 1907 in Winterthur), but they were practically dominated by Catholics.

[45] Quoted according to Fogarty, 237.

[46] A survey of the general history of the trade unions and the specific position of the Christian unions (Catholic) can be found in O. v. Nell-Breuning, op. cit., 853–58.

[47] The Swiss Capuchin Father Theodosius Florentini was applauded at the Catholic Convention in Frankfurt in 1863 for his thesis: "The factories need to become monas-

This explains why the general problems entailed in the relationship of Catholicism to modern society as a whole so oddly climaxed in the Catholic workers' movement. Its religious urge to exceed the goals of the trade unions[48] caused it to be felt as a foreign body within the general workers' movement, even in the non-Marxist movement. Its efficiency, to be sure, was not the showpiece of Catholicism. But it represented Catholicism's utmost effort to reconcile tradition with a radically secularized world, or at least to demonstrate the feasibility of such reconciliation. The question remains whether an independent Catholic workers' movement that was able to combine religious education and the inevitable belligerent goals regarding labor was indeed possible. In a similar situation, the socialist movement was able to combine the party and its trade union. However, it also remains to be noted that, varying from country to country, Catholic workers' movements significantly contributed to counteracting the de-Christianization[49] and social radicalization within society at large.

---

teries!" (J. Höffner, 33f. [chap. 12]), but in the literature he was ridiculed. In 1859, he acquired a textile mill in Obersleutensdorf (Bohemia); in 1862, he opened a paper mill in Thal (Saint Gall). His experiments there would probably have failed had he not died in 1865, because the nuns, whom he sent because the "directors of factories" are expensive people, were indeed cheap, but they did not appear trustworthy to the moneylenders, who canceled their loans. The often quoted example puzzles us today because the serious attempt to extend the monastic *ora et labora* into the age of technology by pretending nothing had happened and technology was merely an improved form of trade clarifies in its utopian absoluteness what had really happened to the essence of work.

[48] The treatment of M. Berger, outstanding in its descriptive parts, prohibits a historically adequate interpretation because the criteria are not derived from the object itself (the Catholic workers' movement in Wilhelminian Germany and its inherent problems), but from the "democratization of society" as a normative goal. This does deny that the political Christian Democrats overcame the paternalism, which, by the way, should also be understood and appreciated historically, and that they were successful with certain reforms. That the Catholic workers' societies were "multi-purpose organizations, typical for a transitory society" (215), characterizes the facts precisely. What else could they have been?

[49] M. Schmidt, "Die Entchristlichung . . . im deutschsprachigen Gebiet," *ZKG* 79 (1968), 342–57.

CHAPTER 14

The Relationship to the State and the Parties

The encyclical *Graves de communi* of 18 January 1901, which does not contain a trace of the political meaning implicit in the term "Christian democracy," is often assessed as a document of the later period of Leo XIII's pontificate demonstrating a departure from the initial program. Indeed, in those years the style, the climate, and the emphasis changed in nearly all aspects of ecclesiastical leadership. But when the pragmatic conciliatory attitude in the Pope's earlier statements regarding the democratic form of government is carefully interpreted, a change of course in the true sense can hardly be found. Yet it is misleading to systematize the didactic statements which Leo XIII made throughout his pontificate in regard to the various questions of politics and social life, especially if one consequently neglects to differentiate between principles and the respective pragmatic adaptations to situations in individual countries.[1] Above all, however, the exceedingly vague term *Démocratie chrétienne*[2] could simultaneously have different, even contradictory implications at different times and in different countries. It could be taken religiously, in the sense of social reform, or even from the perspective of constitutional politics (from the constitutional and parliamentary monarchy to the republic); in short, it covered a highly diffused area of meanings. Subsequent to the encyclical *Rerum novarum,* the usage of the term (it had been used in connection with the revolutionary events of 1830 and 1848) considerably expanded, because it had become a verbal signal in the Catholic social movements of the various countries, often interchangeable with *Catholicisme social* or "Christian social." It was also significant that this development coincided with the Pope's *Ralliement* policy regarding the French Republic. A fundamental interpretation of this policy was able to raise the value of the political content of the term "Christian democracy" to the point that it caused considerable complications.[3] The Pope himself never made official use of the term (after its circumscriptive usage in the address of 1898) except in *Graves de communi;* and Rampolla's instructio *De Actione populari christiana seu democratico-christiana* of 27 January 1902 not only underlines the papal confinement of "Christian democracy" to Christian charity, but also emphasizes that this was not at all a *cosa nuova.*[4] What

[1] This is particularly prevalent in the works of O. Schilling (biblio., chap. 12).
[2] Concerning the history of this term, see H. Maier, op. cit., 303ff.; concerning the history of ideas, see 227–43; at the time of Leo XIII: 259–71.
[3] At the Catholic Convention in Osnabrück (1901), E. M. Lieber said, subsequent to quoting the Pope, who confined the term to Christian activities benefitting the people: "In this sense, we are all democrats"; Kißling, 307.
[4] *Acta Leonis* XXII, 8–28: *"L'azione democratico-cristiana non è da ritenersi come cosa nuova; essa è antica quanto i precetti e gli insegnamenti evangelici."*—The remark (H. Maier, op. cit., 277) that "the Pope's effort (*Ralliement*) had introduced an extensive rehabilitation of the Christian democratic movement" can only be applied to the concrete tactical goal which the Pope was pursuing with his French policies (cf. the introduction), or it may be referred to the consequences which the active French pioneers of the *Ralliement* experienced as a result of the papal policies.

had started out as an attempt to interpret the democratic ideals of equality and freedom (in accord with political theology) as the realization of the gospel[5] ended here with the observation (which was meant to define the conflicts within the *Opera dei congressi*[6] in Italy but was more encompassing), that a relationship between Church and democracy is not possible in the same manner as it had existed between the Church and the sacred monarchy.

Nonetheless, there existed in Leo XIII's pontificate a certain *cosa nuova*, but it had already taken place twenty years earlier and was anything but a way toward "Christian democracy." The encyclical *Diuturnum illud* of 29 June 1881 mentions the *cupiditates populares* which had emerged from the unfortunate doctrine of the people's sovereignty; and according to this encyclical, the patriarchal monarchy is unquestionably the ideal form of government, perfected at the time of the *imperium sacrum*, when the popes consecrated political power in a unique way.[7] But it does not contradict the Catholic doctrine stating that in certain cases the principal representative of civil authority can be elected "according to the desire and the judgment of the masses," whereby power is not transferred, but rather it is determined who will execute it.[8] With this contrivance, democracy is introduced as an ecclesiastically tolerable form of government. But at the same time it is deprived of its historical essence; that is, its revolutionary character is eliminated. It should be noted (and this is true for all encyclicals which attempt an accommodation with the modern era) that this piece of text is short and enclosed in a voluminous traditional text. The polemics against the social contract and the people's sovereignty clearly have priority.

More so than the encyclical of 1881, the encyclical *Immortale Dei* of 1 November 1885 is composed, with respect to France, in order to avoid at least an intensification of the situation regarding Church policies and to prevent the separation of Church and state. In fact, its aim is to find a

---

[5] K. Buchheim, *Ultramontanismus,* 516: "The problem of democracy was present from the beginning, because the ideals of freedom, equality, brotherhood are rooted in Natural Law and especially in the Gospel."—In regard to the "sacred democracy" which was to replace the "sacred monarchy," see H. Maier, op. cit., 276.

[6] Cf. chaps. 5 (p. 94) and 34.

[7] *Acta Leonis* II, 269–87; concerning the people's sovereignty (*imperium populare*) which Leo XIII attributes (as can be seen again and again) to the Reformation, like all other modern evils: 282.—In regard to the monarchy: there is no society "in qua non aliquis temperet singulorum voluntates ut velut unum fiat ex pluribus" (274); analogy to the one and only divine legislator and judge and to fatherhood: "isto autem modo diversa genera potestatis miras inter se habent similitudines" (275).—With respect to the medieval empire in which power reached "the climax of its dignity": 282 (by using the term *instituto imperio sacro,* Leo XIII avoids the theories of translation).

[8] Ibid., 271f.; it seems remarkable that he uses *popularis* in a negative sense and that he speaks of *iudicium multitudinis.*

way of reaching an agreement which would lead toward Leo XIII's ultimate goal: re-Christianization of the modern, democratic world.[9] Also in this encyclical, the paragraphs in which the democratic form of government is recognized as equal to the other systems stand isolated within the main theme "Church and State" (*utraque* [*potestas*] *est in suo genere maxima*), and the doctrine that the elected official need only execute the will of the people is rejected. But these paragraphs are rather positively flavored, for instance when the Pope says that it is not worth a reprimand per se if the people (*populos,* not *multitudo*) more or less take part in the government. In fact, "at certain times" and "under certain laws" it may not only be useful but also the duty of the citizen to do so. This argument was used to justify the opposition toward the founding of an antirepublican party.[10] This attitude is called an expression of ecclesiastical *lenitas* and *facilitas.* Also the encyclical *Libertas* of 20 June 1888, in which liberal human rights are condemned, concedes at the end that is not per se a violation of one's duty to prefer a democratic system of state.[11]

[9] Cf. chap. 6.—A perfect example of the confusion that the abstract language of doctrine can create is the controversy between Bishop Freppel of Angers and Archbishop Thomas of Rouen breaking out as a consequence of this encyclical. Thomas had interpreted it in the vein of Lacordaire and had been so careless as to differentiate it from the *Syllabus* of Pius IX. Freppel called this heresy. He was supported by Oreglia, cardinal of the Curia, who said that the abuse of *Immortale Dei* only served *de dénaturer le Syllabus*). Leo XIII criticized the comparison of his encyclical to the *Syllabus;* however, he finally sent a letter of praise to Thomas, who was more useful to his French policies. Subsequently, Cardinal Pitra tried to console the Bishop of Angers, saying that he was living in "abnormal times," the repetition of which was a banality (tendentiously described in Terrien II, 517–28, 541–47).

[10] *Acta Leonis* V, 118–50: "Immo neque illud per se reprehenditur, participem plus minus esse populum rei publicae: quod ipsum certis in temporibus certisque legibus potest non solum ad utilitatem, sed etiam ad officium pertinere civium." In October 1885, the Pope had inhibited A. de Mun's plan to found a Catholic party (cf. chap. 6).—It is significant for the situation of the Church as a whole that F. Hettinger, in the Herder edition (2nd collection, 1887), translated *participem . . . esse populum rei publicae,* adapting it to the German situation, into: ". . . *Anteil empfängt* [*sic*] *am öffentlichen Leben"* (to participate [*sic*] in public life); P. Tischleder, *Staatslehre,* 249, in his battle against the legitimists of the Weimar Republic, interpreted these words: "a constitution designed to be democratic and moderate."—The following passage has to be seen in the context of the development of the *Kulturkampf* in Germany (chap. 3). It states that the Church does not condemn those governments that, "in accordance with traditions and customs, tolerate *divini cultus varia genera* in their state for reasons of considerable public advantages or in order to avoid calamities," even though the Church does not permit these *varia genera* to have equal rights (cf. chap. 12).

[11] *Acta Leonis* VIII, 245: "malle rei publicae statum populari temperatum genere, non est per se contra officium"—the rejection of the people's sovereignty is conditional.— The following remark stating that it is honorable to participate in public life is specifically in regard to Italy: "nisi alicubi ob singularem rerum temporumque conditionem aliter caveatur."

The contemporary disciples of a politically understood "Christian democracy" did not sufficiently consider in their interpretations (or perhaps they wanted to overlook it) that the Pope indeed accepted the democratic form of government (among others), but in spite of differentiations, he recognized it merely as a fait accompli. Leo XIII had always imagined that democracy was the result of revolution. In the encyclical *Quod Apostolici muneris* of 28 December 1878, which primarily turned against socialism and preached obedience toward the state's authority, the Pope brought to mind that the Church, even if the princes did not execute their authority *ultra modum,* refused to tolerate an autonomous rebellion against them (*proprio marte*). Even if the situation were hopeless, there is only Christian patience and prayer available to expedite rescue. Obedience can only be refused if the demand contradicts the law of God and nature.[12] The encyclical *Libertas* (1888) exceeds the admonition for patience. It speaks of the "unfair power" which oppresses the citizens or denies freedom to the Church, and it calls lawful (*fas*) the request (*quaerere*) for "another constitution" which would permit action "in freedom."[13] It is not said in this context how this *quaerere* is to occur, since unfair regimes are not in the habit of resigning voluntarily. At the same time, the violent resistance of the oppressed Irish is condemned. But the encyclical letter to the French episcopate, the clergy, and all French Catholics, *Au milieu des sollicitudes* of 16 February 1892 and the letter to the French cardinals *Notre consolation* of 3 May 1892,[14] which inaugurated the *Ralliement,* cannot speak in such general terms to the land of obviously irreversible revolution, especially since it requests loyalty to the French Republic "comme representant le pouvoir venu de Dieu." Of what was called "venu de Dieu," the sons and grandsons of the age of the "great Revolution"—however they felt about it—had very precise memories. The questions in regard to the *Diuturnum illud* (1881) whether the rejection of the people's sovereignty only meant to condemn Rousseau or also the theory of Suarez, was answered rather cautiously by Rome.[15] However, now it was stated that all authority emanated from God, though this was not to be taken to mean that the divine designation defines "always and directly the way power is transferred, nor the contingent forms and personalities." The *modes de transmission* were naturally the decisive element. Who affects them? "Time, this great transformer of everything

---

[12] *Acta Leonis* I, 170–83.—Similarly, *Diuturnum illud.*

[13] *Acta Leonis* VIII, 245.

[14] *Acta Leonis* XII, 19–41, 107–16.

[15] Feret was informed by Billot that only Rousseau was meant and that the Pope had deliberately excluded Suárez's differentiation of the direct or indirect transferral of power (L. Feret, *Le pouvoir civil devant l'enseignement catholique* [Paris ²1888]; also P. Tischleder, *Staatslehre,* 216f.).

which exists here below." This is probably the only place in the encyclicals of Leo XIII where he does not refer exclusively to history, be it to bring to mind the achievements of the papacy for the benefit of the West and specifically for Italy, or to characterize the devastating consequences of the Reformation. He also invokes history to facilitate an understanding of his request to accept this Republic "comme venu de Dieu." Compared to this, the Neo-Scholastic remark about the "pouvoir considéré en lui même," not touched by the "innovation," appears weak and abstract. The most remarkable statement by the Pope with respect to the Revolution as such is the one maintaining that the *changements* of the era—Leo XIII refers to the Eastern Empire of antiquity—are far from ever having been legitimate. Indeed, it is difficult to say that they are legitimate ("il est même difficile qu'ils le soient"). Not one word is said to restrict the doctrine of the Church which states that the Church does not permit rebellion against the authority in power; instead, the actual power having emerged from the Revolution is to be accepted for the sake of the general welfare ("le pouvoir civil dans la forme où, de fait, il existe").[16]

Leo XIII noted that internal pacification in France was not only in the interest of the Catholics but in the interest of the entire country, even though the religious goal was not only the ultimate but also the only sufficient motive. Of course, this raised the question of whether the acceptance of the Republic as a mere fact still allowed the traditional conception of the relations between Church and state. In his political encyclicals, the Pope repeatedly evoked the medieval image of the relationship of body and soul, though he did refrain from mentioning the papal theories of the late Middle Ages. In *Au milieu des sollicitudes* he happens to mention that form of separation of Church and state in which the Church is reduced "to the freedom to live according to the common law of all citizens." What was apparently practiced in "some countries"—he obviously meant the United States—implied great "inconveniences," but it also offered some advantages, especially if the legislation allowed itself to be inspired by Christian principles due to a "fortunate inconsistency." The principle of separation continued to be false even though the aforementioned situation "was not the worst of all." But France, a "nation catholique par ses traditions et par la foi

---

[16] *Acta Leonis* XII, 112, 31, 32, 113, 111.—P. Tischleder, *Staatslehre,* 233, wants to distinguish the practical situation in Ireland and the question of whether Leo XIII "expressly and on principle intended to reject the right of a people to practice resistance because it disagrees with Catholic doctrine." Actually, in his dispute with the Bavarian legitimist F. X. Kiefl, Leo XIII's only argument was the recognition of political facts, notwithstanding the question of when the "changing times" had solidified them sufficiently.—In regard to the principles of the *Ralliement,* cf. the introduction.

présente de la grande majorité de ses fils," was not to be brought into this "precarious situation."[17] In spite of the somewhat relatively favorable results recorded by an investigation of the ecclesiastical and religious attitudes conducted by the state in the years between 1879 and 1888 in France,[18] the question needs to be asked whether a country which, at the end of the nineteenth century, according to denominational statistics, was nearly homogeneous can really be called a "Catholic nation." The term *grande majorité* stems from the preamble of the Concordat of 1801, while the term *nation catholique* ignores the fact that almost one hundred years earlier other sects had been provided with equality before the law. Meanwhile, the process of de-Christianization continued. This did not necessarily result in the separation of Church and state, and certainly not in hostility. But the old image of the correlation between body and soul—no matter how much Leo XIII stressed that each power was the highest in its area of competence—was a contrivance which clouded an essential condition of the constitutional state, namely, that the position of the Church had become dependent on the majority standing of the political parties in a pluralistic society and was not dependent on the degree to which the constitution pronounced the Catholic faith to be the state religion or not. This is closely related to the complex problem of the Catholic parties in a democracy which is partly determined by the alternation of position and opposition and by the relations of the substantially differently structured Catholic Church to such political entities.

In 1885, Leo XIII inhibited the founding of a Catholic Party in France through Albert de Mun, and on 12 May 1892, a few days after the papal letter *Notre consolation,* the anti-republican *Union de la France Chrétienne"* was dissolved. Both incidents should initially be seen from the perspective of the papal *Ralliement* policy and the attempt to close the cleft in French Catholicism between republicans and monarchists. But it contradicted Leo XIII's principles to involve the Church in the battles of the political parties (*Ecclesiam trahere in partes*) because he presumed that religion (i.e., the Catholic faith) had to be sacred and inviolable to everyone. There is no doubt that on purely political grounds (*in genere politico*), the Christians can fight for the success of their respective opinions (*opiniones*), "given the observation of truth and justice." But the Church cannot become a party because it is common to every one.[19] This is applicable to the differences within Catholicism in

---

[17] *Acta Leonis* XII, 39.

[18] Cf. chap. 6.

[19] Encyclical *Sapientiae christianae* of 10 January 1890; *Acta Leonis* X, 28f.—The Pope raised an issue which was a problem everywhere, even in Germany, where *Rechtskatholiken* (Catholics of the right) protested against "political Catholicism," for instance F. X.

France, Spain, and Italy, where each group operated under the assumption that it alone represented the rights of the Church; and to the papal admonition aimed at furthering the unity of the Catholics so that they could form a phalanx against the enemies of the Church. But his goal was the universal re-Christianization of state and society, where religion will be sacred to every one and the Church does not have to be represented by a party. There is a close connection between the tactical viewpoint that political party formations entangle Catholicism in internal strife and the principle that religion is not a matter of parties at all, because it has priority for all citizens.[20]

An equally important problem in the relationship between the Church and the Christian parties was the concept of the hierarchical authority of giving directives. The Vatican's attempt to comply with Bismarck's wish and exert influence on the Center Party relative to the antisocialist law and the question of the septennate failed[21] because of the polical self-awareness of this party, which surpassed all other political entities of Catholicism in its cohesiveness. But this attempt was characteristic of Leo XIII's idea about the universal responsibility of the papacy. Ferrata's ecclesiastical internal policies exceeded such intervention. He was not content with prohibiting the French monarchists from a religious and ecclesiastical argumentation; rather he demanded the sacrifice of a fundamental political conviction. It was in accord with the character and range of this problem that the Pope in Italy reserved the right to make the decision in the question of the *Non expedit* and its exegesis to himself and to censor all special actions. But it was also in keeping with this policy that the movement of the *Opera dei congressi,* which was strictly organized in 1884, became the battlefield for all political questions whose resolution was therefore subject to hierarchical directives. In comparison to other countries, the interpretation of the competence of the nunciatures practically resulted in a *potestas directa* over political matters which had been rejected in Leo XIII's theory concerning the relationship between Church and state.

Kraus (cf. chap. 29), especially rejecting the Center party as the only representative of German Catholic interests and often forming their own lobby within this party (I. Schauff, *Die deutschen Katholiken und die Zentrumspartei* [Cologne 1928]; W. Ferber, "Der Weg Martin Spahns," *Hochland* 62 [1970], 218–29; id., "R. Baumstark," *Anregung* [Cologne October 1970], 333–35; id., "Fred Graf Frankenberg," *Deutsche Tagespost* [7 May 1971], 11).

[20] Schmidlin, *PG* II, 365: "Initially pursuing the formation of Catholic parties, Leo XIII, after 1885, energetically proceeded to disapprove a purely denominational or clerical organization of the Catholics and to recommend their assimilation into the national entity." Such a disapproval, however, is not documented anywhere.

[21] Cf. chap. 3.

Since the Church had to deal with very different political constitutions, only the recognition of all forms of government could be decreed didactically, given the known conditions. On the other hand, if, on the basis of the historical situation, Christian motives regarding the transformation of social conditions should coincide with political convictions, then both the French and Italian "Christian democrats" and—though in a different manner—that part of the episcopate which did not merely respect the constitution of the United States but also on principle accepted it, faced a dilemma between the necessarily abstract ecclesiastical political doctrine and their concrete political conviction. The term "Christian democracy" grew enriched in content when the paternalistic social practice flowing from top to bottom was replaced or at least supplemented by a social reform movement from below, conducted by the disadvantaged themselves. This enrichment essentially meant that the term also gained a political profile. This did not necessarily affect the form of government as such.[22] But the state itself changed when the "self-liberation of the classes"[23] began. The Christian republican, in turn, derived a good deal of his political convictions from the view that the paternalistically oriented social activities of the monarchists missed their target, and a real social reform was only possible in a democracy.[24] A de-politicization of the term "Christian democracy" did not merely affect the form of government, but also the concept of politics in general.

However, wherever Catholics gathered in parties, as in Belgium, the Netherlands, Germany, Switzerland, and Austria, they were confronted with the task of balancing the various social interests if they wanted to gain political weight as a "people's party." This difficult process was only successful when the common Christian belief became the catalyst of the development of a political will. One can certainly say that in France "the *Démocratie chrétienne,* in turn, repeated the mistake of the monarchists when it entered the political arena and turned the problem of the form

---

[22] "Dans la monarchie italienne comme dans la république française la Démocratie chrétienne pouvait donc présenter le même visage économique et social: ce n'était pas une question de régime politique" (G. Hoog, 120).

[23] R. Murri (op. cit., 32) calls this process "logical in its true essence, human, and quite Christian" and he is unhappy that it occurs "in an anti-Christian party"; in his opinion, the Conservatives, "separating the religious cause from that of democracy," are solely guided by political interests of power and they do not want to be disturbed by a religious movement.

[24] "Il ne s'agit pas seulement d'enraciner les ouvriers dans de ravissants petits jardins, de leur offrir de petites habitations tandis que le le patron se dira en se frottant les mains: maintenant, mes ouvriers seront bons, ils seront sages car il ont un joli joujou. Non il faut que les citoyens soient eux-mêmes responsable de ce qu'ils font" (M. Sangnier, in Rollet II, 26f.).

of government into a question of religious principle."[25] It must be added that most of the Christian democratic parties of the twentieth century have their antecedents in those which made this mistake.

The first time Leo XIII discussed the problem of "Christian democracy" was in his address on the occasion of a French workers' pilgrimage on 8 October 1898, wherein he was apparently responding to an "allusion à la démocratie." If democracy would be inspired by a belief in enlightened reason, if it accepted in "religious humility" and as a necessary fact ("comme un fait nécessaire") the difference between classes and living conditions, if when seeking a solution for the social problems, it would never lose sight of the superhuman love ("charité surhumaine") that Christ held to be a sign of his followers, then if democracy wanted to be a Christian democracy ("si la démocratie veut être chrétienne"), it would bring France peace, well-being, and fortune.[26] The dangerous evil, from which this "democracy" is distinct, is socialism. In March 1896 Rampolla had still supported the abbés and laymen in France who were political believers in democracy. But since they failed to make Catholic voters agree upon promising candidates, the election of May 1898 was not successful. The *Ralliement* policy had failed and, in the address of 8 October 1898, no longer played a role.[27] The tone in the socio-political questions also was quite different from that in *Rerum novarum*. The de-politicization in the sense of *religieuse résignation* was extensive. The speech reminds one of the encyclical *Quod Apostolici muneris* of 1878, which was subsequently quoted (before *Rerum novarum*) in the introduction to the *Graves de communi* of 18 January 1901. This letter was actually occasioned by the tensions in the *Opera dei congressi,* but the key sentences have a general character. The differentiation of the terminology is interesting: the Pope states that the term "Christian Socialism" was rightfully abandoned; *Actio christiana popularis* is evaluated positively; it is used in the Italian "Congressi" organizations for which episcopal leadership authority is emphasized. Of the two terms "Christian Socialism" and "Christian Democracy," the second one, "not so much" the first one,[28] is said to have caused displea-

---

[25] H. Maier, op. cit., 268.—Goyau II, 16f. (1901) differs: The time when attempts were made to combine Catholicism and democracy has passed; both are *faits* and "Des faits ne se concilient pas, ils se constatent."

[26] *Acta Leonis* XVIII, 223.

[27] In the Catholic debate about democracy of that time, in which especially Tischleder referred to Leo XIII, O. Schilling (*Staatslehre* 43 and 148) said about this speech, and rightfully so: "Since the list of demands apply to any form of government and the term Christian democracy is not to be understood in a political sense, a political interpretation totally contradicts Leo's intentions."

[28] The *non adeo* is an allusion to the resistance which the Christian Social party encountered in Austria from the Conservatives and especially from Cardinal Gruscha (cf. chap.

sure *apud bonos plures* because of its "ambiguity" and its "danger." One fears that it could "favor the people's state" (*popularis civitas foveatur*) and that it could be preferred to other forms of government. After the encyclical had emphatically differentiated between the *democratia socialis* ("social democracy") and the *democratia christiana,* it clearly rejects "the distortion" of the latter "into a political term" (*ad politica detorqueri*).[29] "Democracy," in contrast to the general usage, could in connection with "Christian" only mean "beneficial Christian action for the people" (*beneficam in populum actionem christianam*). The earlier statements that democratic constitutions are just as feasible as any others are amended with the negative statement that the Natural Law and the Gospel are not dependent on any constitution. In this respect, none of the basic teachings of the Church are changed. But it is added that the Catholics would neither theoretically nor practically want to prefer one form of government to another or introduce a new one (*catholicorum mens atque actio*).[30] With respect to social politics, the climate had changed even more compared to the address to the French pilgrimage of 1898. The Pope not only emphasized that the Church has to be available to all classes and may not prefer the lower, but also stated that in spite of shorter working hours[31] and higher wages the workers' life is "crowded and miserable" (*anguste et misere*), which does not indicate an intensification of social reform but means that the workers still live with "rotten morals" and

---

2; H.-D. Wendland, *Der Begriff "Christlich-sozial"* [Cologne 1962]; R. Knoll, *Zur Tradition der christlichsozialen Partei [Österreichs]* [Cologne 1972]).

[29] Interestingly, the Herder edition (1901) 8, translated *democratia christiana* with "Christian social democracy," even though the encyclical itself differentiated between the two terms.

[30] The encyclical: *Acta Leonis* XVI, 3–20; in regard to *Acta christiana popularis,* 14f. (whether one chooses this term or "Christian democracy" is irrelevant; also important is: "si quidem impertita a Nobis documenta, quo par est obsequio, integra custodiatur); cf. also 17.—The abstract expression *Catholicorum mens atque actio* is not quite clear. It can mean one should not introduce in the name of the faith and Catholic Action, or Catholics should not introduce another form of government. In 1888, this had been generally approved (n. 13, above).—The first draft of *Graves de communi* was written by Cardinal (1901) F. Cavagnis and was more pointed than the encyclical (G. Martina, *RSTI* 16 [1962], 492–50; R. Lill, *Der Kampf . . .* [biblio., chap. 24], 110).

[31] The success, partially achieved through strikes, partially through the active initiatives of the legislation pertaining to worker protection (which was promoted by the Catholic lobbyists and parties in Parliament) was of historical significance: in 1877, France still permitted children between the ages of twelve and fourteen to work twelve hours (in Switzerland and in the Netherlands, child labor was forbidden), in Germany (1878), six hours were allowed (under certain conditions). Around 1910, most members of the labor force in most of the industries worked from nine to ten hours (cf. R. Kuczynski, *Arbeitslohn und Arbeitszeit in Europa, 1870/1909* [Berlin 1913]; a survey in A. Knoll, 143–52).

without religion.[32] The fight against socialism dominated the intention of the encyclical.

If the principal statements in all of Leo XIII's magisterial writings are distinguished from the modifications incited by the given situations,[33] the following transpires: democracy is a result of the "transformer time" with which one can and has to come to grips for the sake of ecclesiastical goals if the hierarchical leaders deem it opportune. Also the Christian social reform policies are less interested in the economic conditions of the working class than in a defense against atheistic socialism, which includes the elimination of social misery. These, in fact, are also the essential goals to be pursued by the official teaching of the Church. In the framework of his splendid universal program, aimed at presenting the papacy to the world as a moral, spiritual, and clerical authority and freeing this institution from the negative aspects of the *Syllabus,* Leo XIII had to confront the actual problems of his time, and he had to do so in the face of a society which was involved in a continuous dialectical process, oscillating between political parties and economic classes, and in the face of a Catholicism struggling with its own internal differences. The French monarchists were reported to be closer to his own political-clerical persuasion than the Catholic supporters of the Republic.[34] But Leo XIII expected that they, as he had done, would sacrifice their conviction for the sake of a higher goal and that they would accept the democratic constitution, which he had officially only tolerated (along with others), restricting it by adding "per se."

In Neo-Scholastic social philosophy the Pope believed to have found a generally binding synthesis based on Natural Law which could confront the antagonisms of the time.[35] In reality, however, Catholicism represented special groups within the general, increasingly secularized society, and it had its own problems of integration, with or without identifying with a political party. Since the religious aspects were decisive in this respect, a dilemma regarding the universality of the Church could possibly emerge if the religious motives were combined with certain social and political goals whose actuality could only coincide very generally with the Neo-Scholastic social philosophy. The dilemma increased the more Christian faith and social political convictions were tied to-

---

[32] *Acta Leonis* XXI, 10.

[33] P. Tischleder, *Staatsgewalt,* 61, tried to interpret the *Graves de communi* against the background of Marxism and the Italian situation, which is not possible.

[34] Cf. Introduction.

[35] A thorough, critical assessment of this social philosophy and Neo-Scholasticism as a whole is desirable (it should outline its limits, but also its generally accepted achievements). This is especially necessary since the subsequent development of the "Christian social doctrine" after Pius XI is almost forgotten by the Catholics and since the "critical theory" contains a lot of ideas that cannot be found elsewhere.

gether and the more they were simultaneously intent on changing inherited conditions. Each in his own way, Leo XIII and the political "Christian democrats," were unable to see that the old relationship between Church and world, that is, the world as a duplicate of the Church, was not real any longer. This is the ultimate reason for the conflict which resulted from the subsequent pontificate's interpretation of hierarchical magisterial directives in political questions. This conflict was already on the horizon in Leo XIII's pontificate.[36]

[36] Cf. chap. 35.

CHAPTER 15

*The Position of Catholicism in the Culture
at the Turn of the Century*

The relationship of Catholicism to its various national cultures in the last third of the nineteenth century and at the beginning of the twentieth century varies greatly. What was classified as cultural "ghetto-Catholicism" existed only in Germany, because there the confessional minority was strong enough to develop a sound self-consciousness, and its social structure was considerably different from that of the society at large. For Irish Catholicism in England, constituting a majority, the Anglo-Saxon culture was foreign for religious reasons; moreover, in its social isolation it did not even have a chance to deal with this culture. In Ireland itself, the "revival" around the turn of the century clearly documents that the affiliated writers were born Catholics, but the movement, spiritually indebted to France, divorced itself from Irish traditionalism by emancipating itself from the Church. The two smaller Catholic groups in England, the Old-English Catholics and the converts, belonged to the Anglo-Saxon culture, conducted their intellectual disputes in the English language, and the significant poets were immersed in the tradition of English poetry. Catholicism in the United States, itself culturally scarcely creative, tried to adapt to society as a whole.

In the Catholic countries of France, Spain, Italy, Austria, and Poland it is difficult (regardless of the intensive national Christian traditions) to determine which phenomena should be viewed as Catholic in an ecclesiastical sense and what distinguishes those who cannot be understood outside general Catholicity from those who are almost or completely alienated from the Christian tradition.

This is especially true of France. The poet Charles Baudelaire (1821–67) with whom modern French poetry begins stands at the beginning of the epoch treated here. This man whose career ended so early dominated the field for generations to come. He is certainly not to be reckoned in the same category as Chateaubriand as representative of the Christianity of the restoration. Yet it cannot be denied that the author of the *Fleurs du Mal* which he originally called *Limbes* and who saw abandonment of the idea of original sin as the basic evil of the age[1] was at heart a Catholic, yet no one would ascribe *catholicisme* to him. At the end of our era stands Charles Maurras (1868–1952), who was entirely different from Baudelaire (even though he also hated the eighteenth century). But he is an example of how wide the borders of French Catholicism range. Working for conservative newspapers in his early years, he lost his faith in Catholicism, but not in the monarchy or classical literature. He was an opponent of Romanticism and democracy and, in 1899, founded the *Action française,* which raised the hopes of many conservative Catholics in France and not just *their* hopes. He confessed to having lost the Christian faith, but he belonged to a *catholicisme,* which (he said) had saved mankind.[2] The condemnation of some of his works in 1914 was not publicized by the Church until 1926. But even if one proceeds from such marginal personalities into the middle of the cultural life of French Catholics at that time, one does not find an extraneous group, but members of the *Littérature française:* converts, not in the usual sense of the word, but men who had experienced their *conversio,* and this in the middle of their engagement in one of the literary trends which they shared with other Frenchmen. In this respect, the *Renouveau catholique*[3] differs essentially from the literary

---

[1] A. Thibaudet, *Histoire de la Littérature Française de 1789 à nos jours* (Paris 1936, Freiburg i. B. 1953 [Germ.]), 340–43; J. Pommier, *La mystique de Baudelaire* (Strasbourg 1932).

[2] *La politique religieuse* (Paris 1914), 23.—That he died reconciled with the Church (in 1937 he had written a submissive letter to Pius XI from Lisieux) is a phenomenon to be assessed differently than the will of the positivist historian Fustel de Coulenges: "I demand a burial according to French customs" (during the funeral of Victor Hugo in 1885 in the Pantheon, the city council of Paris had removed the cross). Even though C. Maurras, who died in 1952, had a long and hard life, the possibility of such an end should not be dismissed, especially in view of the situation around the turn of the century (A. Cormier, *La vie intérieure de Ch. Maurras* [Paris 1956]).

[3] The poet F. Coppée (1842–1908), very popular in France around the turn of the century, had achieved success as one of the *Parnassiens* with his book *Intimités* (1868). He was the poet of the lower class and small things. In the wake of his religious conversion, he wrote *La bonne souffrance* (1898) (P. Le Meur, *F. Coppée* [Paris 1932]).— G. Huysmans (1848–1907) was one of the great representatives of naturalism, equal to É. Zola, a pioneer (*En route,* 1895). In his autobiographical novel *L'oblat* (1903), he describes his return to the Catholic Church (G. Chastel, *Huysmans et ses amis* [Paris 1957]).—The poetry of F. Jammes (1868–1938) can be compared to another representative of Flemish culture, the priest and poet Guido Gezelle. Jammes returned to the

movement in German Catholicism. But an apologist writer such as Paul Bourget (1852–1935), who from the start wanted to describe the demoralization of the middle class of the French Republic, the adultery, the hypocrisy of the anticlerics, and the asocial individualism of the liberal bourgeoisie; even he was considered "for thirty years an original representative, as it were, of the French novel as created by Balzac and George Sand."[4] Just as much a part of the *Littérature française* was his spiritual friend Ferdinand Brunetière (1849–1906), who, after his visit to Leo XIII in 1894, published the *Visite au Vatican* and who appeared as a polemical Catholic.[5] With his critical essays, which he published in the *Revue des Deux Mondes,* he had quite an impact on the *Académie Française,* which he joined in 1893, and his public turn toward Catholicism was the result of his basic attitude, which prompted him to place the seventeenth century, the century of French classicism, in opposition to the century of enlightenment, romanticism, and the resignation of the fin du siècle, which was entirely in the spirit of French rationalism. Incurring the ridicule of the leftist intellectuals, the former disciple of Comte spoke of the "faillites partielles de la science." The conservative Brunetière pilloried contemporary pessimism, attacking the "believers in the Great Revolution and the legitimate, though perhaps decadent heirs of Voltaire and Rousseau" who are nurtured more by their anticlericalism than by their own tradition.[6] But despite whatever hypocrisy his adversaries charged him with, nobody could dispute that Brunetière had a brilliant French style. G.-P. Fonsegrive-Lespinasse (1852–1917) (philosopher and writer, editor of the publication *Quinzaine* [1896–

---

faith of his youth through symbolism (*De l'Angélus de l'aube à l'Angélus du soir,* 1898) (J. P. Inda, *Du faune au patriarche* [Paris 1952]).—Each belonging to one of the "two Frances," the author and poet C. Péguy (1873–1914, died in the battle of the Marne River) and the writer of pamphlets, L. Bloy (1846–1917), were political enemies. Péguy, siding with Dreyfus, joined the Socialists, posed as a mouthpiece of the different opponents of the Combe regime in his *Cahiers de la Quinzaine* (1900–14), and wrote *Mystères* and especially *Ève* (1914), great religious works, even though he could never be an "ecclesiastical" Catholic (R. Lauth, *Lexikon der Weltliteratur im 20. Jh.* II [Freiburg i. Br. 1961], 610–15).—Bloy belonged to the "reactionaries," yet, in his passionate struggle against the disciples of the *Ralliement* policy of Leo XIII, against the anticlerical and the conservative armchair Catholics, he found himself in "splendid isolation." Nevertheless, in France he is still considered "one of the greatest prose writers of his century" (A. Thibaudet, op. cit., 406; J. Bollery, *Léon Bloy,* 3 vols. [Paris 1949–54]).—The religious experience that eighteen-year-old P. Claudel underwent in 1886 in the church of Notre Dame in Paris and that was to be the foundation for his creative work concurred with his discovery of the symbolist A. Rimbaud.

[4] A. Thibaudet, op. cit., 453.
[5] Cf. chap. biblio.—V. Giraud, *De Chateaubriand à Brunetière* (Paris 1936); J. G. Clark, *La pensée de F. Brunetière* (diss., Paris 1954); A. Thibaudet, op. cit., 480–84 and passim.
[6] *Discours de combat* III (1903), 142f.

1907]), who had to be protected by Leo XIII against his conservative critics, said toward the end of his life that "thirty years ago one could barely detect in the French public the kind of interest in spiritual questions that has surfaced now" (in the *Renouveau catholique*).[7] The Jesuits also saw in the *Études* of French cultural Catholicism a form of new ecclesiasticality, though L. Laberthonnière, a strict disciple of Blondel, appeared very sceptical. As in the case of all cultural forms of Catholicism, one would have to distinguish between the profit gained from making Catholic existence possible in the modern world and the effect it would have on general society, which had abandoned its aggressive anticlericalism only because its apathy had become too great.[8]

M. de Vogüé, in the *Revue des Deux Mondes* (1901), described the "two contradictory concepts of national history" in France. This does not apply to Spain of that same time period. Even the famous "Generation of 98" does not permit overt discussion of "two Spains."[9] Therefore, the appeal of the politician Joaquín Costa (died in 1911) "Lock the grave of El Cid with three keys!" was immediately opposed by the true representatives of this generation, even though they were open to modern currents. Above all, it was rejected by Miguel de Unamuno, a Spanish Catholic who did not agree with Church dogma but had nothing in common with the Catholicism of Charles Maurras ("El Cristo de Velázquez", 1920). The Civil War of the twentieth century destroyed the unity of the spirit of the *Hispanidad*. In comparison, Italy was split so deeply because of the Roman question that even Dante's greatness as reflected in the various interpretations by national writers was no longer a unifying element. The intransigent Pope-supporting Catholics had become homeless in their national culture because they had nothing to counteract the positivism invading Italy from France as well as Hegelianism, and they had to stand by and watch while the Tuscan Giosuè Carducci, a fanatical anticlerical, was celebrated as the poet of the new Italy. Alessandro Manzoni (died in 1873) had overcome the Enlightenment, had confessed his Catholic belief in fiery language in the *Inni sacri* (1812–22), and had written the Italian national novel, *I Promessi Sposi* (1827). His heirs could not understand the *Non expedit* for the same reasons which compelled Manzoni, the great pioneer of the religious-national unification of Italy, to become silent. Antonio Fogaz-

---

[7] *L'évolution des idées*, 228.—P. Archambault, *P. Fonsegrive* (Paris 1932).

[8] W. Gurian (biblio., chap. 12), 300: "They love everything about Catholicism, but dogma is only beautiful metaphysics to them and the Church a brilliant organization"; this is the argument of H. Bremond, *Vingt cinq ans de vie littéraire* (Paris 1908), 70, especially in view of the *Action française*.

[9] Cf. chap. 8.

zaro (1842–1911),[10] the most outstanding of them all, in his main work *Piccolo mondo antico* (1895) described the Italian fight for freedom against Austria with as much national as religious enthusiasm. His novel *Il Santo* (1905), equally filled with deep religious sentiment, was condemned because of the four evils of the Church described therein. In 1887, during the critical year of Leo XIII's pontificate, forty sentences from the work of the famous theologian and philosopher A. Rosmini-Serbati, to whom Fogazzaro was very much indebted, were extracted and censored.[11] Thus, cultural life in Italy was dominated by verism, G. d'Annunzio (the successor of G. Carducci), and the neo-Hegelians.

In Poland, after the failure of the uprising of 1863, the identity of creed and nation had become stronger, but the disappointment created a mood which was a fertile ground for western European positivism (Comte, Taine, Darwin), which seized "Young Poland." Thus emerged a fierce opposition between the leftist liberals and the conservatives. Their most eminent representative was H. Sienkiewicz (1846–1916), the author of historical novels about the era of Polish wars in the seventeenth century and of the internationally famous novel on the early Christian period, *Quo Vadis* (1896). A Polish example of *conversio* is the important poet Jan Kasprowicz (1860–1926), who was persecuted in the Prussian province of Posen because of his nationalistic attitude. From the atheism of his early socio-critical writings he proceeded to religious hymns, rooted in his native peasantry.

In Austria, the names Grillparzer and Stifter characterize the tradition of the kind of Catholicity which, in spite of its liberal and at times even anticlerical features, derives from a Catholic spirit. This spirit, to be sure, was watered down by anticlerical tendencies in the plays of Ludwig Anzengruber (1839–89) and in the folk tales of the Styrian Peter Rosegger (1843–1918), who was influenced by Anzengruber. Catholicity is most strongly represented in the writings of Hugo von Hofmannsthal (1874–1929), who, in the spirit of Grillparzer and Calderon renounced the "magical power over the word" in symbolization and returned from his areligiosity to the great tradition of the West, whose historic tragedy he witnessed in the decline of the Habsburg Empire.[12] This can be compared to the unfortunate poet Georg Trakl of Salzburg (1887–1914), who wanted to find the world's secret harmony in the language of the symbolists. A contemporary of these non-ecclesiastical poets was the convent-bred Enrica von Handel-Mazzetti

[10] Cf. chap. 32, n. 18.
[11] Cf. chap. 5 and p. 312 below; in chap. 32, the religious situation in Italy.
[12] K. Lazarowicz, *LThK²* V, 426f.

(1871–1955). Her novel *Jesse und Maria* (1906), dealing with the era of the Counter-Reformation, incited after its serial publication in the *Hochland* (1904) of Carl Muth a "literary controversy" because in this novel the Catholics as well as the Protestants are guilty. The novel was written with deep Catholic conviction, but it broke with the tendentious literature which had become popular in German Catholicism after the Romantic period.[13]

At the general meeting of the *Görres Gesellschaft* in Constance in 1896, its president, G. v. Hertling, said: "But what we need now are not so much apologists but rather real scholars."[14] Until Carl Muth, this was true not just for scholarship but for literature in general. When Hermann von Grauert, at the Catholic Convention in Munich in 1895, expressed his envy of French Catholicism of Brunetière (while Germany was dominated by Nietzsche[15]), he referred to the wide public reputation which the French literary critic had acquired. What was later called the "educational deficit" in German Catholicism of that time had several causes. Lessing, Schiller, Goethe, Kant and the philosophy of idealism, J. G. Herder and Humboldt, the representatives of the German spirit, were Protestant. The significance of Catholic features in Romanticism is not easily assessed. Its Catholic spokesman, the convert Friedrich Schlegel was a protean figure, who turned to gnosticism in the last phase of his life in Dresden and died in 1829. In this movement, the Catholics had been as much a part of German literature as the ecclesiastical Catholics had been of French literature. Not just converts, but also born Catholics such as Clemens Brentano and Eichendorff participated. In his later years, the Silesian poet wrote about the "event in Cologne" (1837): here emerged what "the Romanticists had dreamt of and did not possess themselves: a Catholic spirit." But prophetically he had also warned of the "rigors of ecclesiastical restrictiveness," which, of course, was to some extent unavoidable in the belligerent position which German Catholicism as a minority group was forced into by a largely Protestant society, and which it brought upon itself by its awareness of being a strong minority. This is another point which explains the isolation of German Catholicism after the second third of the nineteenth century.

---

[13] W. Grenzmann, *Lexikon der Weltliteratur im 20. Jh.* I (Freiburg i. B. 1960), 850ff.; cf. chaps. 2 and 35, and p. 427 below; cf. F. Fuchs and P. Funk (cit. chap. 29, n. 1).

[14] *Erinnerungen* II, 168; in regard to Hertling's pamphlet (biblio., chap. 15), Brück-Kißling VI², 329, maintains that the mistrust of Catholics "was mostly justified: many Catholics, who had been able through considerable sacrifices by the clergy and generous laymen to obtain a higher education, turned against their faith later." F. X. Kraus (*Dt. Lit. Ztg.* 21 [1900], 12–19) is critical of the fact that Hertling's principles were denounced de facto.

[15] Kißling II, 270.

This was the price that Catholicism paid for being able, unlike other sects, to structure itself within society. The German Catholics were underrepresented in higher education and especially at the universities (particularly, if one ignores theology). This was the result of cultural and historical development and at the same time the cause of its intensification, especially if the socio-cultural and the socio-economic facts are combined.[16] It was correctly pointed out then (1803) that secularization was a catastrophe for Catholic education;[17] the academic career of Catholics at universities was, even after the *Kulturkampf,* greatly impaired by the intolerance of the Liberals. But one has to see the whole complex situation at once if one is to understand the reaction of Catholics in the overall cultural world during these decades. One has to isolate the key issue from the polemical global reproach of "inferiority." German Catholicism had at its disposal pertinent means of communication, and it was an internal matter when the "calendar for time and eternity," published by the Alemannian priest Alban Stolz (1808–83), and his own strongly autobiographical essays, which contain more than the usual polemics against liberalism, were pushed aside by a sort of literature of which *Das Opfer eines Beichtgeheimnisses (The Sacrifice of a Confession)* by J. Spillmann is an example (Spillmann's novels appeared between 1882 and 1903 and were a great success). It is Friedrich Wilhelm Weber's (died in 1894) *Dreizehnlinden* (1878), rather than Heinrich Hansjakob's true-to-life folk story *Der Vogt auf Mühlstein* (1895), which is representative. This work, written in concise language that was meant to satisfy sophisticated demands, could be found into the twentieth century in the bookcases of Catholics who had to live in the limited circumstances for which history had destined them.[18] Yet the

---

[16] Utilizing the census of 1907, H. Rost found that the Catholics (36.5 percent) had a share of 44.2 percent in agriculture, 29.9 percent in business, 18.5 percent among the mining entrepreneurs. At the same time, in the county of Koblenz, the Protestants (33 percent), had a share of 50 percent of the tax yield, in Cologne (14 percent) a share of 25 percent. Regarding the problems of statistical studies, see C. Bauer, *Deutscher Katholizismus* (biblio., chap. 12), 33.—In 1886, in Prussia, the Catholics (approx. 35 percent) had a share of 21.3 percent of the students in *Gymnasien* (a share that is proportionate to the population average of 1910 in the Prussian school district); in the *Realschulen,* the share went down from 16.7 to 14.5 percent between 1886 and 1910. At Prussian universities, 13 percent of the students were Catholic (1885–97); W. Lossen, *Der Anteil der Katholiken am akademischen Lehramt in Preußen* (Cologne 1901), 1.

[17] See G. v. Hertling, *Kleine Schriften,* 569.

[18] P. L. Haffner (philosophy professor at the seminary of Mainz, from 1879 until 1886 editor of the apologetic *Frankfurter zeitgemäße Broschüren,* later bishop of Mainz) said at the Catholic Convention of Amberg in 1884 that even "harmless" novels had a devastating influence; F. Hülskamp made a similar statement in Trier in 1887 when talking about the metrical language of the *Dreizehnlinden.* This evaluates the novel as being the literary genre of the bourgeoisie that emerged from the Revolution.

situation is not so much characterized by clumsy attempts such as that of Weber, but rather by the respectable effort, as it were, to offer a decent selection in the "library of German classical writers for school and home," for which the inclusion of Lessing's *Nathan* must have been a difficult decision. The belligerent Swiss Jesuit Alexander Baumgartner laid bare in his three volume work *Göthe* (1879–86) the "dirty love novels" of his idol and called the humanity of *Iphigenie* a "Trojan horse," whose content he wanted to expose.[19] The breakthrough brought about by Muth in *Hochland* resulted in conditions much like those in France: the works of these writers ceased to appear in Catholic publishing houses because the authors—once again to a large extent converts—wanted to be part of the general German literature.

The scholarly works in Catholicism gravitated naturally toward theology, philosophy, and (Church) history.[20] Here, tradition provided a starting point and Neo-Scholasticism, which had become official through Leo XIII's Thomas encyclical, offered not only an international basis but also the possibility of developing, beyond the disputations and apologetics over the zeitgeist, an independent and even partially creative system and of giving the retarding forces a positive orientation. Also, the old and the new universities, founded during Leo XIII's pontificate, made attempts toward a comprehensive modern curriculum. Louvain distinguished itself in Near Eastern studies as well as in biology; Fribourg (1889) had started a philosophy and a law faculty and, in 1896, established a mathematics and natural science faculty; Washington (1889) developed its sociological emphasis, which was also pursued in Louvain. In France, the Catholic universities in Paris, Angers, Lille, Lyon, and Toulouse, founded around 1875, had to change their name to *Institut catholique* following the law of 1880, according to which the title *université* was reserved for state institutions. But with imperturbable enthusiasm they held on to their academic programs; and the plan also to establish schools of medicine was not a symptom of ambition but of the realization that intellectual decisions were particularly at stake in this field. Of course, grave technical difficulties stood in the way. That the establishment of theological faculties occurred subsequently is primarily a result of their problematic relationship to the diocesan seminaries. The names of the scholars affiliated with the individual institutions represented the rather different spirit of each institution.[21]

[19] O. Köhler, *Bücher als Wegmarken . . . ,* 46–49; J. Antz, *Der Katholizismus . . . ,* 173–81.
[20] Cf. chaps. 21 and 22.
[21] In regard to the focal points (with the exception of theology and philosophy): Angers began with law, literature, and natural sciences (the Thomist L. Billot, S.J.); Lille developed the social sciences (also the technical fields) and he was able to establish a medical

In 1810, the University of Salzburg was closed, and attempts to expand the theology department, installed in 1851, into a full university were not successful, in spite of Leo XIII's encouragement through briefs in 1890, 1900, and 1902. During the Catholic Convention in Aachen in 1879, the decision of 1862 to create a Catholic university in Germany was reiterated; but in 1882, there were no more than three hundred thousand marks in the budget, and too many serious arguments were blocking the plan. However, the *Görres-Gesellschaft,* founded in 1876, the year of Joseph Görres's one hundredth birthday, may be called one of the most significant societies of Catholic scholars. The initiative had come from Georg v. Hertling (1843–1919)[22], in 1867 lecturer of philosophy in Bonn, in 1882 professor at the University of Munich. With his Neo-Scholastic philosophy of law, politics, and society and as a Center Party politician (in 1875–90 and 1896–1912 member of the *Reichstag),* he was one of the most intelligent leaders of German Catholicism, a man who knew how to combine determination and restraint. The *Görres-Gesellschaft* enjoyed the ecclesiastical patronage of the incumbent of the diocese of Cologne, but it was founded as a private society. It renounced a theological section, although theologians formed a great part of its membership. The original four sections were devoted to philosophy, history, law, sociology, and natural science.[23] The Austrian *Leo Gesellschaft,* founded in 1891 by J. A. Helfert and named after the ruling Pope, published mainly studies of the general and ecclesiastical history of Austria.[24] In Germany and Austria it was of special significance that the theology faculties had remained in the academic structure of the universities. Thus, they were in a better position than the diocesan seminaries to preserve for Catholic theology a place in the general

---

school.—Lyon, where only a few medical disciplines and a department for natural sciences could be developed, had a law school and a college for social sciences (after 1898, theology was headed by Tixeront, professor in patrology, after 1906 by Podechard, Old Testament scholar from the seminary).—Paris offered law, Far Eastern studies, natural sciences. Famous rectors were M. d'Hulst (until 1896) and Baudrillart. Among the faculty in theology were the Church historian Duchesne, in canon law Gasparri, in apologetics A.-T.-P. de Broglie, in philosophy Sertillanges (after 1900) and later Maritain.—Church historian Batiffol (1898–1907, rector) taught in Toulouse.

[22] Cf. chaps. 1, 3, 12, 21 and 35.

[23] These focal points were adopted from the most important publications of this time period: *HJ* (since 1880), *PhJ* (since 1888), *Staatslexikon* ([1] 1887, [2] 1901–04), publications of the Council of Trent (after 1901). In 1888, the Roman Institute was founded. It was supported by the rector of Campo Santo, A. de Waal.—W. Spael, *Görres-Gesellschaft, 1876–1941* (Paderborn 1957).

[24] F. Schindler, *Die Leo-Gesellschaft 1891–1901* (Vienna 1902); A. Dörrer, *LThK*[2] VI, 959.

scholarly and scientific public.[25] In spite of the conflicts within "reform Catholicism" and "modernism," into which theologians such as H. Schell, A. Ehrhard, F. X. Kraus, F. M. Schindler, and L. Wahrmund were drawn, there was rarely a real schism (contrary to the time of Döllinger).[26]

The numerous scholarly publications in all forms of Catholicism, which received fresh impulses and were newly founded,[27] document that Catholicism had defined its self-concept more in the realm of scholarship than anywhere else, even though the natural sciences came up for discussion more indirectly in the apologetic literature. There were a few exceptions, such as at the University of Louvain (the only Catholic institution which was a full university), the research on ants by the Jesuit E. Wasmann (published in the nineties), and the astronomical works of the Jesuits Hagen, Kugler, and others. Wasmann's studies of Haeckel's monism was based on his own scientific research. Tilmann Pesch approached the same problem on the basis of his natural philosophy (*Die großen Welträtsel*, 1883–84). Although the questions posed by the natural sciences were taken quite seriously, the many French Catholic scientists were more directly affected by the discussion taking place in Bible exegesis, which, since the nineteenth century, had resulted in more and more radical interpretations within liberal Protestant theology.[28] It is understandable that they did not succeed in carrying out their intention to exclude this complex of questions at the international congresses of Catholic scholars and scientists in the last decade of the nineteenth century. This failure, in conjunction with the crisis of modernism and integralism, ended an attempt which could have become quite significant for the development of a common Catholic intellectuality able to confront modern problems decisively. The idea had emanated from the future president (1894) of the *Institut catholique* in Toulouse, Duilhé de Saint-Projet (1822–97), who in 1875 had been one of the men instrumental in the founding of the Catholic universities in France. In his *Apologie scientifique du christianisme* (Toulouse 1885) he

---

[25] Regarding Würzburg, see *Festschrift zum 350 jährigen Bestehen der Universität Würzburg* (1932), essays by S. Merkle, A. Bigelmair, etc. Regarding Innsbruck, see "100 Jahre Theologische Fakultät Innsbruck," *ZKTh* 80 (1958), 1–235; E. Kleindam, *Die kath. theol. Fakultät Breslau, 1811–1945* (Cologne 1961); E. Hegel, *Gesch. der kath. theol. Fakultät Münster, 1773–1966* 2 (Münster 1971). Regarding Tübingen, see *ThQ* (1970; anniversary ed.). Regarding Bonn, see *150 Jahre Rhein. Friedrich Wilhelm Universität zu Bonn, 1818–1968*. (Bonn 1968). A systematic continuation of these histories is desirable.

[26] Cf. chaps. 2 and 29. Concerning the problem of the modernist oath, see chap. 33.

[27] Cf. biblio., chap. 15.

[28] Cf. chaps. 23, 30, 31, 32.

developed a program for international congresses, which was worked out in detail in conversations with the first president of the *Institut catholique* in Paris, Maurice d'Hulst. This man, who represented such a remarkable combination of views[29] and was actually the personification of arbitration, seemed to be the suitable promoter of the congress idea. Of course, he encountered strong reservations, because there was fear that at such congresses nontheologian participants would ask questions about dogma and exegesis and thus create great confusion. As always in such cases, Leo XIII was optimistic and asked Maurice d'Hulst for his expert opinion. D'Hulst suggested excluding the treatment of all questions concerning ecclesiastical teachings, but he emphasized the necessity of discussing the contemporary status quo of the sciences. In a letter of 1887, the Pope approved the plan.

The first congress in Paris in 1888 proceeded to everyone's satisfaction, even though its international makeup was limited, as was the second one, which took place in 1894 (also in Paris) under the presidency of Bishop Freppel.[30] During the third congress in Brussels in 1894, when university President Abbeloos of Louvain was honorary president, a paper by M. d'Hulst attacked the theologically controversial material which had accumulated. He warned against minimizing dogmatic statements of the Church. He strenuously advised against exaggerating them and suspecting everyone of rationalism who did not share one's own opinions. During the fourth congress in 1897 (in Fribourg), which was able to attract three thousand participants under the presidency of G. v. Hertling, the participants had the courage to form, aside from newly founded sections, a special group in which "exegesis and related disciplines" were to be discussed. What the *Görres-Gesellschaft* had avoided when it renounced the creation of a theological section happened here. The Dominican A.-M. Lagrange was the leader in the group concerned with exegesis and would later insist in vain that the group had approved his principles.[31] The convention in Munich in 1900, which attracted even more participants, parted with the expectation of convening again in Rome in 1903. This was an illu-

[29] Cf. chap. 23, n. 15.

[30] In 1888, the Görres Society as a whole did not participate. Only individual members were on the list of participants. An embarrassing incident took place at the congress of 1891: The echelon of the Görres Society, G. v. Hertling, H. v. Grauert, and H. Hüffner, had appeared. While the congress was going on, the German version of a letter that Freppel had written to the French correspondent of the *Berliner Lokalanzeiger* on 17 March 1891 was published. In it, the Alsatian demanded the return of Alsace-Lorraine to France. The German congress participants cancelled their attendance of the dinner given in honor of Bishop Freppel (G. v. Hertling, *Erinnerungen* II, 133).

[31] Cf. chap. 23.

sion.[32] The *Istituto cattolico internazionale per il progresso delle scienze,* which had been announced in the encyclical *Pascendi* for 1907 and for which Pius X had appointed Ludwig Pastor secretary general, failed to survive the initial stages. At that time, Albert Ehrhard had been deprived of his title as prelate; G. von Hertling was only going to be accepted because he could not be ignored in his capacity as president of the *Görres Gesellschaft;* the Church historian Duchesne was rejected by the Pope. In spite of Rampolla's misgivings, Pastor succeeded in winning the Pope's support for men like the radical apologist A. M. Weiß and the historian E. Michael, S.J. of Innsbruck.[33] Rampolla asked the Pope on 13 February 1909 to relieve him of the chairmanship of the commission. The institute did not materialize. Most likely it would not have represented the kind of Catholicity which unfolded after World War I in the cultural life of the Church.

[32] Hocedez III, 93–96. Very critical in regard to Munich: G. P. (F. X.) Kraus, *Allg. Zeitung,* 4 October 1900.
[33] Pastor, *Tagebücher,* 482–96, 499–502, 511.

Forms of Piety

CHAPTER 16

Externalization and Internalization of Nineteenth-Century Spirituality
Beginnings of the Eucharistic Congress Movement
Veneration of Saint Thérèse of Lisieux

The forms of piety which had developed in the second third of the nineteenth century grew in scope during Leo XIII's pontificate. They were invigorated through demonstrative gestures in ceremonies of consecration, through liturgical festivities, and through the confirmation of congregations and fraternities. They were valued as socially integrating factors in the forms of Catholicism taking shape within the various countries. And yet their significance cannot be recognized unless they are valued as the daily religious nourishment of the faithful who were living in a strange or hostile environment and who, in those pious exercises, found the strength to remain loyal to a faith which was finding less and less support in the secular world. Depending on the country, the situation was quite different, of course, and cannot generally be differentiated according to urban and rural areas. There were rural areas in France where de-Christianization had progressed far,[1] and the development during the course of the Third Republic was characterized by juxtaposing the "déchristianisation du peuple" and the "rechristianisation de la bourgeoisie."[2] Agrarian concentrations in southern Spain resulted in the rural proletariat's alienation from the faith. In the German-speaking area, the Catholic rural population remained untouched by the modern spirit; to the right and to the left of the cross in the reliquary they hung a picture of the Sacred Heart and the Virgin Mary, as the pastor had recommended, without their religious attitude changing in essence. The rosary, lead by the head of the family in the livingroom, continued to be popular as part of the deeply ingrained veneration of the Virgin Mary. The political development in France toward the end of the nineteenth century contributed to the revitaliza-

---

[1] Chap. 6.—The missionary J.-B. Berthier (1840–1908) was successful among all classes.
[2] A. Dansette, op. cit., 30–51; cf. chaps. 15 and 36.

tion of the consciousness of faith. However, during the same period in Germany, a partial paralysis could be detected, because the stimuli of the *Kulturkampf* were missing.[3]

Contemporary observations regarding the significance of the political battle (including its national variations) are applicable to the style of religiosity in all forms of Catholicism, whereby we have to consider that the conservative group consciousness in religious life was accompanied by a subjectivism which, on the one hand, was generally embedded in the spiritual trend of the outgoing nineteenth century after the disappointments of the bourgeois revolutions, and which, on the other hand, was consciously nurtured by the pastors as a defense against the materialistic-collectivistic spirit of the time.[4] This juxtaposition of sociality and subjectivity is one of the reasons for the late emergence of the liturgical restoration. Also significant is the positivistic concept of the "sanctity of the Church,"[5] which was believed verified through reference to the catalog of beatification and canonization examinations conducted by the Congregation of Rites of 1901. Moreover, since for the most part religious orders and congregations promoted the canonization of members and since they predominated among the Latin peoples, the picture was distorted. Reflected in this naive quantitative interpretation is the idea of the Catholic "membership" movement, which was necessary for the development of Catholicism and represented the result of often tremendous efforts as well as a mere reaction to processes in the secular society. The contemporary *Geschichte der katholischen Kirche in Deutschland* by Brück-Kißling, with its (for that time) pertinent two volumes of altogether 1,014 pages, is characteristic of that movement in that it devoted 55 pages to the inner life of the Church, more specifically to organizations of this kind. That the organizational element remained

---

[3] J. C. Schulte, *Die Kirche und die Gebildeten* (Freiburg i. Br. 1912, [3] 1919), 12.— Another phenomenon, popular at that time, but nevertheless rather unpleasant, was the mutual assessments of religiosity among the French and the German Catholics. G. Goyau, *Les catholiques allemands et l'Empire évangélique* (1916) was countered by H. Schrörs, *Deutscher und französischer Katholizismus in den letzten Jahrzehnten* (Freiburg i. Br. 1917). If one disregards the polemical aspects, then one discovers that the two authors are sophisticated enough to make correct points in spite of their animosity.— Regarding the problems of urban pastoral work, see H. Swoboda (Regensburg 1911).

[4] Anton L. Mayer, op. cit., 49f.

[5] K. Kempf, introduction: M. Scheeben already described the divine mark of the sanctity of the Church, "however, he could not furnish the kind of documentation available now." Kempf then describes the "first steps" toward Pius IX's canonization. He lists the saints (or those nominated for canonization) according to their hierarchal position (bishops: 24–49, secular priests: 50–78, members of orders: 79–265, laymen: 266–334, including relatively extensive biographies). He indicates the various stages in the canonization process regarding J. B. Vianney, Klemens M. Hofbauer, Konrad von Parzham, G. Bosco. V. Pallotti, Bernadette Soubirous, and Contardo Ferrini.

"fashionable" to the extent "that the inner life, the grace, the mystery were frightened away"[6] also had an effect on the organization of devotional practices. One of the examples of this is the manner in which First Communicants were now brought into the old Corpus Christi fraternities in groups and forced to sing hymns of Eucharistic theology,[7] which were difficult to comprehend even for adult Christians. Religious devotional art was quite popular at that time and is a difficult phenomenon to assess. In its precise meaning, this kind of popular devotional art appears for the first time in the late nineteenth century as the result of certain cultural and historical conditions. Favored by the possibility of reproduction, popular devotional art demanded and furthered participation in conventional art which was simultaneously isolating itself from society. These demands could not be satisfied. Therefore, they were appeased by elevating popular devotional art one step above banality—a phenomenon which cannot be compared to the disintegration of high art, sustained by an elite, into handicraft.[8] Upon investigation of the mystical essence underlying Eucharistic piety and the Sacred Heart devotion of that time, it becomes clear that the faithful were overtaxed by this bid for sophistication. It is also evident that they were given an acceptable version with the best of intentions and thereby possessed an adequate means of expression in the art forms of the Nazarenes,[9] who had fallen below their original level of quality. These conclusions are comparable to the analysis of secular popular art. Notwithstanding the nationalistic aversion to "the French," the fact remains that these expressions of piety, stemming from the Latin mentality, could only be transferred with difficulty to Germanic countries. The close relationship between art and religion is unquestionable; yet drawing conclusions from this assumption alone would result in a simplified judgment about the religiosity of that period: the faithful of the middle and lower classes were pious in regard to traditional forms of expression. An assessment of the religious quality itself escapes historic evaluation.

The considerable increase of charitable activities in all countries, flourishing in individual parishes, in diocesan societies and (especially in

---

[6] A. Mayer-Pfannholz, op. cit., 129.

[7] *In der Monstranz/Ist Christus ganz/Nicht Brot-Substanz/Ave Jesu/Wahres Man-hu.*

[8] R. Egenter, *Kirsch und Christenleben* (Etal² 1958; biblio.). It is possible to follow the ethical assessment and to see the function of kitsch, an apparent satisfaction of the senses, as a religious variable without considering the problem of the relation between the shortcomings or elimination of the muses and the quality of religious life to be solved. Nonetheless, the exis :nce of this problem, naturally, reveals something about the situation of the religious experience in the society of the late nineteenth century.

[9] Cf. chap. 19.

France, Italy, and Germany) in national organizations, can be measured by the number of institutions and participants.[10] Lorenz Werthmann (1858–1921) received encouragement from France and the organizational forms of the Protestant "Home Mission" when, in 1897, he founded the *Deutscher Caritas-Verband* and propagated its goals in the publication *Caritas* (since 1896). He had to defend himself against the often-heard reproach that Christian charity had to take place without fanfare,[11] and he had to fend off the envy of the episcopate, which did not recognize the organization until the conference of Fulda (1915) and Freising (1916). This placed it under episcopal supervision and suggested the formation of diocesan branch organizations. The organizational amalgamation of the many charitable institutions did not only aim at the concentration of the various enterprises, but proceeded from the assumption that in the age of industrialism the initiative to help your fellow men was by no means dispensable. However, in the interests of maximal effectiveness, a theoretical investigation of the economic conditions was unavoidable. The *Dictionnaire d'économie* was a model for Werthmann, the first president of the association, whose headquarters he moved to Freiburg in Breisgau, where his bishop had released him for charitable tasks.

How vital it is not to interpret the organizational features of piety as mere externalizations is documented by the emergence of the Eucharistic congress movement. E. Marie Tamisier (born in 1834 in Tours) was one of those restless religious personalities who could not easily be pressed into institutional molds. After having had first a gentle and then a rather rigorous pastor, she was finally fortunate to meet Gaston de Ségur, who assigned to her Eucharistic youthful piety the proper area of activity. Ségur designed a plan of operations entitled "France at the feet of the Most Holy Sacrament," in which he listed the locations of Eucharistic miracles. But we should not forget that he is also the author of *Jésu vivant en nous,* which was condemned because of pantheism and quietism.[12] Upon the industrialist Philibert Vrau's suggestion, a central pilgrimage to Douai was decided on at Lille in 1874. The site of miracles, Avignon became in 1876 the stage for the first Eucharistic mass demonstration (the study conference in connection with this seems to go

---

[10] Regarding the centennial of the *Société de S. Vincent de Paul: Livre du Centenaire,* 2 vols. (Paris 1935); *Manuel de la Société . . .* (Paris 1958).—Cf. biblio., chap. 16.

[11] L. Werthmann, op. cit., 7. The founding of the *Caritas Verband* contributed greatly to the needed variety of general charitable activities.

[12] Illustrative purposes were served by places such as Bourges, where a Eucharistic miracle had proven the Albigensians wrong in 1224; Paris, where one of the countless demonstrations of anti-Semitism (1290) took place; Pozilla (Perpignan), where the atrocities of the Revolution were remembered.

back to Mermillod, whom Marie Tamisier had encountered earlier in Rome). During an event in Favernay, Besançon in 1878, the first beginnings of the movement's internationalization emerged. Due to the unfavorable political circumstances in France, E. M. Tamisier traveled to see Cardinal Dechamps, who was indeed benevolent, but had misgivings about the Belgian government's reaction and therefore recommended the Netherlands. The archbishop of Utrecht was equally amicable, but advised a talk with Bishop Snikers because Amsterdam had been mentioned as the place for the congress. His hesitant attitude was like a cold shower for the Eucharistic enthusiasm of Tamisier. Finally, on 17 January 1881 in Paris, at the deathbed of Ségur (the Jesuit Verbeker, a Belgian enthusiast for the cause, had come for the occasion), it was decided to organize the congress in France after all, that is in Lille. On several occasions, Leo XIII had given his blessing, but not until 16 May 1881, scarcely one month after the date was announced internationally, did he give his approval.[13] Ségur, who in the face of these difficulties had intended to cancel the congress, did not live to experience it. Three hundred sixty-three clergy and representatives of the laity came, yet the French were in the great majority, in spite of participants from Belgium, Holland, Austria, Switzerland, and Italy. The opening address was entitled "The Social Kingdom of Jesus Christ." The concluding procession was accompanied by about four thousand of the faithful from Lille. Upon Cardinal Dechamps's invitation, Avignon was followed by Liège in 1883, where E. M. Tamisier had had a patron in Bishop Doutreloux for a long time. The congress in Fribourg in 1885 was presided over by Mermillod, who had meanwhile become president of the congress movement. This event for the first time included the entire public. The movement's center of gravity remained for the time being in France (in 1888 in Paris) and in Belgium (in 1898 in Brussels with Cardinal Goossens). National congresses took place in Italy (1891: Naples, 1896: Orvieto, under Cardinal Parocchi, 1897: Venice, under the chairmanship of Patriarch Sarto). The first event to be attended by a papal legate was the congress of Jerusalem in May 1893 under the leadership of Cardinal Langénieux. This congress was characterized by the efforts of the Pope regarding the Near Eastern Churches (fifty Latin bishops in contrast to eighteen Uniate Eastern bishops).[14] At the regional Congress of Washington, Protestants were admitted for the first time. The inter-

---

[13] P. Vrau, the superior general of the Assumptionists Picard, and the Vicomte de Damas had traveled to Rome for that reason. In addition to these men, the following became important for the movement: Msgr. de la Bouillerie, M. de Benque, and Comte de Nicolay. They were indicative of the "atmosphere of the *Vieille France,* where the enterprise had found its first disciples" (R. Aubert, op. cit., 62).

[14] Cf. chaps. 25–27.

national congresses in London (1908) and in Amsterdam (1924) resulted in vehement anti-Catholic reactions.[15]

These boisterous events were in curious contrast[16] to the old and now rejuvenated idea of Perpetual Adoration. But in this form of piety, which happens in complete quietude, the idea of religious reparation was coupled with something like a silent protest. In Rome, in 1883, the "Society of Reparation of the Catholic Nations" was founded, which allotted to individual countries certain weekdays for worship in order to unite the whole world in support of the "imprisoned" Pope. The principal fraternity of daily "Perpetual Adoration," founded in 1890 in the Franciscan church of Turin, was extended in 1893 to all of Italy and in 1909 to include the Catholic world. More congregations and fraternities in the same vein emerged. Among them were the Sisters of Perpetual Adoration, which had branched off in 1893 from the *Steyler Missionsschwestern.* They observed enclosure and spread especially in the United States. Other societies, generally devoted to the worship of the Eucharist, such as the *Sacerdotes Sanctissimi Sacramenti* (S.S.S.), which had been founded in 1856 in Paris and held its communal prayer before the exposed Sacrament, radiated beyond their places of origin during this time. In Rome, in 1902, the "Society of the Acolytes of the Holy Sacrament" was organized for children from five to fifteen years of age. The Eucharistic encyclical of 28 May 1902, *Mirae caritatis*[17] places the institution of the Last Supper at the end of Christ's life in curious analogy to the impending end of the author's life. The encyclical points to the papal approval in regard to Eucharistic institutions and confines itself in other respects essentially to general practices. A few paragraphs, however, point into the future: Mass, though somewhat set off, is placed in line with the other traditional forms of Eucharistic worship, but it is also indicated that it had been the Church's wish all along "that at every Mass the attending faithful should go to the table of the Lord."[18] Three years earlier, in his encyclical *Annum Sacrum* of 25 May 1899,[19] Leo XIII had ordered the consecration of all mankind to the Sacred Heart (after elevating it in 1889 to the liturgical rank of a feast day). This encyclical hardly suggests the mystical love between the Lord

---

[15] Regarding the congress movement after Pius X, see R. Aubert, *op. cit.,* 63–66; here: 419f.

[16] The itinerary of the *Benediktinerinnen von der ewigen Anbetung* (1909) includes the French motto: "In isolation, the Eucharistic Savior shall speak, heart to heart, with the one who prays" (quot. in Anton L. Mayer, op. cit., 26).

[17] *ASS,* 34, 641–54; German in Rohrbasser, 106–25.

[18] Rohrbasser, 109, 119, 121.—Cf. chap. 27.

[19] *ASS,* 31, 646–51; Rohrbasser, 77–84. Concerning the spirit of the time, see L. Chasle, L. Sattler, *M. Droste zu Vischering* (Freiburg 1906), 362–67.

and his own because the nonbaptized are "still sitting as the unfortunate ones in the shadow of death," so that only the power of the sovereign and the law can be applied to them. In this respect, the Pope adhered, with Thomas Aquinas, to the medieval conception of the pagan world. Also characteristic is his mention of the cross as the Constantinian sign of victory, replacing it with the "Most Sacred Heart, transcended by the cross surrounded by the splendid halo of a fiery wreath."[20] In 1891 the church of Sacré Cœur on Montmartre in Paris was completed. The restraint with which Pius IX had reacted to the desire for a wordly dedication had been abandoned, and Leo XII, in the conclusion of his letter, supplemented the new motives with a "purely personal, yet noteworthy and valid reason," namely that God had just recently delivered him from a serious illness. The number of Sacred Heart societies founded or confirmed under this pontificate does not fall short of those of Pius IX's era: five societies of priests, twenty-four women's communities, and two brotherhoods.[21] Societies that had an impact on both Americas were favored. The Jesuits were especially involved in the propagation of this form of piety. In 1872, they had consecrated all provinces of their society to the Sacred Heart.[22] Unquestionably, the demonstrative and seigneurial character of this worship under Leo XIII's pontificate intensified; but no one can determine in which way it was the source of true piety for each individual.

Leo XIII had devoted nine encyclicals and seven apostolic letters to the rosary. Their individual tones were rather different. A great portion of the letters deals with the spiritual guidelines for this prayer and only occasionally contains polemic passages. The encyclical *Octobri mense* of 22 September 1891,[23] introducing the daily rosary for the month of October, recalls the "murders and outbursts of hatred" of the Albigensians, who could only be conquered through the power of the rosary; similar incidents are called to mind as well (such as the victory of Lepanto). The Albigensian *impii* were none other than the Freemasons. An interesting token of social criticism is contained in the *Laetitiae sanctae* of 8 September 1893: previously, "the undisturbed security of life was considered the reward for one's toils; today, the masses are only interested in filling this life with a maximum of pleasures, laboring under the illusion that the government system could be perfected to the

---

[20] Rohrbasser, 80, 81, 82, 83f.

[21] Cf. K. Hofmann, *LThK*² V, 294–99.

[22] In all areas of the Church, countless small papers appeared with Sacred Heart titles or signets (in 1894: B. E. Bougaud, *Histoire de la Bienheureuse Marguérite Marie et les origines de la dévotion du Cœur de Jésus*).

[23] *ASS*, 24, 193–203; Rohrbasser, 669f. (excerpt).

extent that everything unpleasant would be eliminated."[24] While the October encyclical limited an extreme Mariology through a *fere*,[25] this period, as did others before and after, witnessed extremes regarding Marian worship (e.g., when the rosary became an independent cult).[26] The entreaty *Regina sacratissimi Rosarii,* introduced in 1883 to the Litany of the Blessed Virgin, referred directly to Mary herself. In 1891, Leo XIII approved the Festival of the Appearance of the Virgin for the Church Province of Auch (Pius X did the same for the Church at large in 1907); in addition to the church situated above the grotto (dedicated in 1876), the Church of the Rosary was built between 1883 and 1901 just 20 meters below. Particular attention was given to the Marian Congregation, which had grown a great deal after the rejuvenation of the Society of Jesus. In addition to the Eucharistic congresses, there were now also Marian congresses, such as in Livorno in 1895, in Turin in 1898, in Lyon in 1898, and in Fribourg in 1902 with international attendance. At the same time, along with the consecration to the Virgin of individual nations, the movement beginning with Pius IX to dedicate the whole world to the Heart of the Virgin grew stronger, intensifying at the congresses between 1908 and 1914. Throughout the nineteenth century, many ecclesiastical societies were founded and dedicated to the Virgin. One of the more outstanding ones, because of its practical work, was the *Societas Mariae,* founded in 1871 by Chaminade. Its statutes were approved in 1891 and it did a great service for the educational system in the United States: the *Marianistes de Sainte-Croix* (founded in 1841), taking care of the girls' schools in North America (1883, an independent branch in Canada); the *Missionaires de Notre-Dame de La Salette* (founded in 1852), expanding beyond the diocese of Grenoble; the Sons of the Immaculate Heart of Mary (founded in Spain in 1849 by A. M. Claret y Clará [canonized in 1950]),[27] who gradually spread all over the world, devoting themselves to domestic and foreign missions. There is no question that the increasing Marian devotion entailed abuses far into the twentieth century, particularly sentimentalizing prayers and

[24] *ASS,* 26, 193–99; Rohrbasser, 678–85 (excerpt).
[25] ". . . ut, quo modo ad summum Patrem, nisi per Filium, nemo potest accedere, ita fere, nisi per Matrem, accedere nemo possit ad Christum" (*ASS* 24, 196).
[26] In the *Annuaire de la Très Sainte Vierge* . . . (1887): "O mon Rosaire chéri, o ma couronne des roses, je vous offrirai tous les jours . . ." (quot. by Anton L. Mayer, op. cit., 52); one needs to consider that this is recited in connection with the Marian interpretation of each day of the year.—Officially banned from the Church were the sisterhood founded in 1888 in Plock (Poland) by Felicja Kozłowska and the Mariavites, a society of priests founded in 1893 by Vicar J. Kowalski, after they were refused recognition by Rome in 1904.
[27] Biography by C. Fernández, 2 vols. (Madrid 1946).

hymns;[28] but even though the longing for motherly warmth expressed therein could tempt one to withdraw into insular illusion,[29] this form of piety has to be understood in its historical context.

The fact that the figure of Saint Joseph played a role in the education of workers, especially in France, was the reason for French postulates under Leo XIII to enter his name in the *Confiteor, Suscipe,* etc.[30] This circumstance was also mentioned in the encyclical *Quamquam plures* of 15 August 1889, where Saint Joseph, after 1870 the patron of the whole Church, was labeled the model of a good husband and father and a consolation to "the proletariat, the workers, and all people in modest circumstances." The Pope emphasized that they had the right "to strive for an improvement of their situation with all legitimate means," but they had no right "to overturn the order ordained by divine providence."[31] As popular as the devotion to Saint Joseph (one of the most frequent patron names) was in all levels of society, this manual laborer of a patriarchal period of history could not be made a model to be realized in an industrial society; neither could the image of the "Holy Family,"[32] as numerous as the foundings of religious societies named "Holy Family" may have been at that time.[33]

The Catholic enlightenment did not just reduce the multiplicity of forms of piety, it often eliminated them entirely. The reaction to this in the Catholic restoration created even more institutions to practice the numerous new forms of worship whose style was often an expression of the contemporary popular taste, but which differed markedly from the Baroque because they were isolated from the culture as a whole. It is equally significant that while in the wake of the French Revolution class differences between the hierarchy and the people had been eliminated, the clericalism of the nineteenth century established new barriers. This is demonstrated clearly in the focal point of Catholic piety, the Mass. The prologue of H. Bone's *Cantate* (Mainz 1847) says that the "quietly praying congregation" derived "benefit" from being able to participate,

---

[28] The collection of songs devoted to the Virgin Mary by D. Delama (1898) also contains: "O bella mia speranza, Dolce amor mio, Maria, / Tu sei la vita mia / La pace mia sei Tu." But unless one has joined Italians in the singing of this almost classic sentimental song, he does not know anything about the vitality contained therein, amalgamated as it may be.

[29] A. Mayer-Pfannenholz, op. cit., 128, points to this element in connection with the relationship to the Church.

[30] Jungmann, *MS* I, 221.

[31] *Acta Leonis* IX, 175–82; Rohrbasser, 1110–16 (excerpt).

[32] Brief *Neminem fugit* of 14 June 1892 (*ASS* 25, 8–10), Rohrbasser, 1103ff. (excerpt). In *Graves de communi* (*Acta Leonis* XXI, 18), the Holy Family is an example of poverty leading to virtue.

[33] K. Hofmann, *LThK²* V, 94f.

from being permitted to "repeat the words."[34] The political implications were expressed by the fact that the liturgical indications of enlightenment are called "communion of the divine service" and furthermore by the statement that the "Catholic temple" would maintain its eminence even if the congregation would never gather there, "because it is not the congregation that is the inspirational principle of the Catholic temple, but rather the indwelling of the All Holy and the sacrifice of the priest."[35] The polemical mentality, which was implicit in the expiatory sacrifice, is documented by the fact that Leo XIII added the prayer of St. Michael to the Marian prayer, which Pius IX had introduced as the conclusion of the Mass.[36] Part of the Catholic restoration were Prosper Guéranger's[37] efforts in Solesmes to restore the liturgical text, to eliminate Gallicisms and to return to the Roman liturgy—efforts which had very fertile effects in later years. They aimed primarily toward a renovation of monastic life, similar to the efforts of the Benedictines, inspired by Solesmes,[38] in their new monastery at Beuron. The distance between the officiating priest and the people, which had a history of a thousand years, was confirmed by the prohibition against translating the text of the Mass. This was renewed once again in 1857 by Pius IX, but violations were not seriously prosecuted any longer.[39] The prohibition was quietly dropped when Leo XIII did not mention it again in the revision of the Index of Forbidden Books in 1897. But the translation of the canon of Holy Scriptures and even more so that of the consecration text was postponed until the twentieth century. By then, however, translations appeared whose subsequent significance could hardly be anticipated at that time. In 1878, the *missel des fidèles* by Gérard van Caloen was published in Maredsous, where, among others, the Beuron monk Anselm Schott resided during the time of the *Kulturkampf*. His *Meßbuch der heiligen Kirche,* published in 1884, had already sold one hundred thousand copies by 1906.[40] It took a long time, however, until the "Mass devotions" in the prayer books were supplemented by liturgical texts. Diocesan prayer books multiplied in Germany during the nineteenth century, but they were only very slowly introduced to the public because of the Holy See's regulations. They contained a wide variety of Mass devotions for special occasions, which were often far removed from the liturgical process itself, even in regard to their psy-

---

[34] Introduction, VII; cf. Trapp, 278.

[35] Jungmann, op. cit., 206.

[36] ". . . worried by the devilish spoof created by Leo Taxil": T. Klauser, op. cit., 58.

[37] Jungmann, op. cit., 210.

[38] Cf. chap. 17.

[39] Jungmann, op. cit., 214.

[40] D. Zähringer, *75 Jahre Schott* (Freiburg i. Br. 1959).

chological interpretation.[41] A German specialty was the "sung Mass," which had been compiled during the period of Enlightenment and now had a very subjective flavor, especially the songs for Communion. Even though Leo XIII pointed out that Communion was a part of the sacrifice of the Mass,[42] "spiritual communion" continued to be recommended. The separation of special prayers of preparation and thanksgiving at the Communion remained the custom until far into the twentieth century.[43] In view of the hectic economic, social, and spiritual developments, one was, as in all areas of ecclesiastical life, intent on devotional writings, which were often carried so far that a differentiation between essential and incidental issues was said to be a "deeply devastating illusion."[44] But in retrospect, even progressive ideas can be discovered. For example, in the case of ritual books, it was recommended that Hosts be offered which were consecrated during Mass itself, because "in this manner, the essence of the Eucharist as consecrated bread and wine and the community of the worshippers . . . is so much more prominent."[45] But such rare pastoral thought remained, for the time being, the privilege of the theologians who were in fact the real pioneers, especially in regard to the significant scholarship in liturgical history.[46]

Even though the statistics of canonizations do not constitute a "century of saints" like the seventeenth century, the very few outstanding spiritual personalities constituted, together with the great number of anonymous devotees, a historical "balance," without which a period cannot be understood. Charles de Foucauld (1858–1916) was one of them, no matter whether the impending beatification process will be

---

[41] J. Hacker, op. cit., 132ff.; Anton L. Mayer, op. cit., 61. In the "Mass in honor of the sufferings and death of Jesus Christ," the prayer in intervals reminds one of the olive grove, the kiss at the altar, the kiss of Judas, etc. Similar features in *Livre de piété de la jeune fille* (1885).

[42] Concerning the debates before Pius X, see chap. 27.

[43] Well-known examples are also: C. Fievet, *Formulaire de prières pour les enfants de Marie* (1904); J. Millner, *The Key of Heaven* (1891); cf. J. Hacker, op. cit., 68, Anton L. Mayer, op. cit., 63ff.

[44] F. Hettinger, *Aphorismen über Predigt und Prediger* (Freiburg i. B. 1888), 276. According to Hettinger, the liturgy, like the *Biblia pauperum,* includes all the secrets of faith and the whole of Christian ethics. In his work about the liturgy and the Latin language (1856) he had said that the liturgy carried "the mark of constancy . . . like faith itself" (16) and any kind of variation should be rejected (36) (cf. Trapp, 277; Jungmann, op. cit., 210).

[45] A. Gaßner, *Pastoral* . . . (Salzburg 1881), 997.—Concerning Pius X, see 426.

[46] Anton L. Mayer, op. cit., 75ff.—V. Thalhofer, *Liturgik,* 2 vols. (Freiburg i. Br. 1883–93), I, 246, welcomes "the most recent custom" of letting the people at least sing the responsory. He saw in the liturgy a "constant order" (Trapp, 277) and not the genetic element; however, this is true for most historiographic theologians who limited change to the adiaphora (cf. chap. 22).

finalized or not. After his conversion in 1886, the officer lived at first as a Trappist in France and Syria (1890–96), then, until 1900, as a hermit in Nazareth. In 1901, he was ordained priest.[47] His idea of realizing Jesus' message entirely through the example of his own life without any physical protection in the midst of a Moslem world (which remained closed to all missions from the beginning to the present day) can be seen as a prophecy of the conditions of Christian life in the future, despite—or because of—the fact that Foucauld died in absolute solitude (he was shot by Tuaregs).

In contrast, Thérèse Martin, the saint of Lisieux (1873–97), was completely a witness of her own time, in spite of her effect on the twentieth century. This statement, to be sure, requires that her recent reassessment as an existentialist be regarded sceptically. It is probably no exaggeration to say that Thérèse of Lisieux[48] embodied the entire struc-

---

[47] Ed.: *Oeuvres spirituelles* (Paris 1958); M. Carrouges, *Ch. de Foucauld* (Fribourg[2] 1958); J.-F. Six, *Itinéraire spirituel de Ch. de Foucauld* (Paris 1958, biblio.); R. Aubert, *DHGE* 17, 1394–1402.

[48] Thérèse Martin was the fifth surviving daughter of a French middle class family that conducted a successful lace business in Normandy (Alençon) thanks to the mother's energy. Her father was a watchmaker and jeweler. The atmosphere in the home was determined by strict piety and scorn of the modern "world"—even though the family participated in its economy. All the daughters joined the Carmelites of Lisieux (Normandy, where the father had moved to settle in his house in the country after the mother's early death). The last of them to join (after Thérèse's death), Léonie, was a difficult child and probably not quite understood by Thérèse. When her mother died, Thérèse was barely four years old and was raised by her sister Pauline (later Mère Agnès), who later, against the will of the spiritual director and the bishop, instigated Thésèse's admission to the convent when she was fifteen. Pauline herself had been a member since 1882. During the years until 1886, which were the most painful years of her life, according to her own testimony, she was torn away from her childhood amidst a happy family. She suffered periodically from a severe mental illness, including tremendous scruples and unusual, frightening visions. The crisis resulted in the awareness "que j'étais née pour la gloire," and she felt destined to be "a great [stricken in the precritical edition] saint," but not in the eyes of man. At a pilgrimage to Rome in 1887, she asked Leo XIII to grant her an audience. She did this according to the plan of her prioress, Marie de Gonzague, and her sister Pauline-Agnès, but in disobedience to the episcopal representative. However, the Pope sent her in a friendly, but correct manner to the proper Church authorities (more in chap. 6 of the *Histoire d'une Âme;* I. F. Görres [n. 56], 198–208). On 9 April 1888, Thésèse received the bishop's permission to enter the Carmelite order. In 1893, under Prioress Agnès, it had twenty members, four of them Martin sisters. They formed a special group within the spiritually average community. Even when disregarding the sisters' criticism of Marie de Gonzague, who was again elected prioress in 1896, as several times before, it is clear that the aristocratic nun was not equal to her task, which, indeed, was particularly difficult in this group (I. F. Görres, 258–88, practices more restraint than most biographers). "Most of all, today I had nothing but bitter dryness for the daily bread of my soul" (chap. 8 of *Histoire d'une Âme*): This word [dryness], which is not literary but original (Juan de la Cruz, whom she used to read later, left her "cold"), is the motto of her monastic life. Moreover, her four

ture of piety as it had developed since the second third of the nineteenth century. This piety was propagated by the *milieu* Catholicism which was to be ridiculed later, at a time devoid of understanding. It was expressed in the tasteless pictures of her time, embedded in the clan spirit and subsequent exuberant sentimentality of a devout French family. The extraordinary feature of this saint was her conventionality, which caused her to take the "narrow path" of mystical love for God, like Teresa of Avila, who remained a stranger to Thérèse and her friends. Though remaining in the Carmelite tradition, Thérèse activated it, however, when she recognized that the clergy, revered "like gods," required intercession. But in spite of her submersion in the New Testament, she did not depart from the contemporary image of Jesus. The revision of her literary remains[49] by the Carmelite order and the significance of the critical edition has been overestimated as well as underestimated. However, and this is crucial, there is no difference between Thérèse Martin's influence, which was quickly felt all over the Catholic world, and her own religious existence.[50]

---

sisters, though dear to her, were one of her main problems. The "dryness" increased until God was totally absent, even at the hour of her death (she died of tuberculosis, twenty-four years old). Her last words, spoken while looking at her small cross, are preserved: "O, I love Him. My God, I love you."

[49] Ed.: Her literary legacy, published in 1898 under the title *Histoire d'une Âme*, contains her memoirs, which she recorded between January 1895 and January 1896 at the instigation of her real sister Agnès, at that time prioress. It also includes the letter to her sister (in both senses of the word) Marie written in September 1896, writings instigated by Prioress Marie Gonzague in June 1897, letter fragments, notes of conversations, and poems added by Agnès. The critical facsimile edition, edited by the Carmelite François de Sainte-Marie in 1956, demonstrates that a lot of essential material had been changed stylistically or eliminated. Moreover, the edition of 1898 contains considerable additions. The correspondence edition by A. Combes (Lisieux 1948) was followed by editions of notes, poetry, and prayers (cf. A. Combes, *LThK*[2] X, 102ff.).—For decades, the edition of 1898 determined the image of Thérèse; but it is, in her own words, a "synthesis of the best expressive elements from different photographs" (François de Sainte-Marie, *Visage de Thérèse de Lisieux. Portrait* [Lisieux 1961]).—Biblio.: After her canonization in 1925: A.-P. Laveille, *Sainte Thérèse . . . d'après les documents officiels du Carmel de Lisieux* (ibid., 1926).—After the beginning of the critical eds.: A. Combes, *Introduction à la spiritualité de Ste. Thérèse* (Paris 1948, Trier 1951 [German]); H. Urs v. Balthasar, *Thérèse de Lisieux* (Cologne 1950); G. Bernoville, *Ste. Thérèse . . .* (Paris 1954); I. F. Görres, *Das Senfkorn von Lisieux* (Freiburg i. Br. 1958), revised edition of *Das verborgene Antlitz* (Freiburg i. Br. 1944); St. J. Piat, *Ste. Thérèse à la découverte de la voie d'enfance* (Paris 1964); J. F. Sise, *La véritable enfance de Th. de Lisieux* (Paris 1972); *Th. de Lisieux au Carmel* (Lisieux 1973); R. Laurentin, *Th. de Lisieux. Mythes et réalités* (Paris 1972).

[50] The *Histoire . . .* of 1898 sold 700,000 copies in France within three decades. A popular edition sold 2.5 million copies. By 1925, the book had been translated into thirty-five languages.—From 1897 until her canonization, 30.5 million pictures of the saint were sold and 17.5 million sent off as souvenirs (A.-P. Laveille, op. cit., 455).

CHAPTER 17

The Organization in the Old and New Orders
Inner Reform and the Power of Attraction

Even though Pius IX had repeatedly interfered in the reorganization of
the Franciscan order (O.F.M.), it was not possible to bring about the
necessary revision of the statutes in view of the more or less anachronistic discussions within the order. At the general chapter of 1862, one
proposal received a great majority, but appeared in 1882 only as a
draft.[1] A memorandum presented at this chapter, according to which
the Observants, Reformed, Discalced, and Recollects were to unite
under the name "Franciscans," was rejected as inopportune. Only at the
general chapter in 1889, which took place in the new Collegium S.
Antonii in Rome, were uniform constitutions passed. They were not,
however, accepted by the Reformed, who were allowed to keep their
special statutes and who consequently began a lively propaganda campaign against the union despite the prevalent opinion among the Reformed that the monastic discipline of the Observants was no less strict
than theirs. But even now, the new constitutions were only practiced in
the numerous provinces in different versions. Leo XIII made Cardinal
Mauri, a Dominican, president of the General Chapter of Assisi in
1895, and he announced that the union of the different branches of the
orders was to be the main topic of the Chapter. The draft contained the
demand that the statutes be applicable to all, that they determine the
customs in the territorial divisions of the provinces, and that the order
not have, as heretofore, only one general, but also one procurator. At
the voting, which took place separately in each of the four orders, the
Observants voted almost unanimously in favor of the bill, the Reformed
and the Discalced voted against it. After the interpretation of the order's
poverty was accepted by the Recollects, a general secret vote turned out
in favor of the union by 77 to 31 votes, a result which changed considerably after subsequent "yes" votes (8 no, 100 yes). Leo XIII ratified
the resolutions on 15 May 1897, and he issued the constitution *Felicitate
quadam.* Friars who were conscientious objectors were delegated to
special houses. The Spanish provinces, however, insisted on their privileges, recognizing the constitutions, but continuing to refuse submission
to the order's general. In the eighties, the order counted only 14,000
friars; by 1907 there were 17,092 (8,152 were priests) in 1,460 houses.
Pius IX's plan to unite the Conventuals and the Capuchins failed. The
Conventuals still had 1,481 members in 1893 (in 1884, they succeeded

[1] H. Holzapfel, op. cit., 371–79.

270

in uniting with the Spaniards). In 1907 the nuns of the Order of Saint Clare (Poor Clares), which was mostly destroyed after the French Revolution, numbered 10,204 sisters in 518 cloisters. The Third Order developed remarkably after 1883, when Leo XIII had modernized the rules, reducing, on the one hand, the regulations for prayer exercises and fasting, on the other hand, requiring monthly confessions (previously only three per year). It is estimated that around the turn of the century 2.5 million belonged to the order, which tried to differ from the activities of other orders primarily by intensifying religious life.[2]

"The day we become centralized will be the day when a reform will be impossible. The lively spontaneity will be eliminated and replaced by bureaucracy, which may be very well, but it imitates life and is not life itself;" this idea, attributed to Prosper Guéranger, the founder of the Abbey of Solesmes (1837),[3] is more than a social theory of the constitution of the Benedictine order. It is the expression of a spirituality of contemplation, which is impossible without spontaneity. Conversely, the spirituality of activism requires organizational concentration. Significantly, the following sentence belongs in the context of this statement: "What is strength for the Jesuits, is a danger for us." In 1862, Prior Maurus (Rudolf) Wolter was in Solesmes for three months, where he was deeply moved by the spirit of Guéranger. Wolter had just negotiated with the royal court of the Prince von Hohenzollern-Sigmaringen to transfer the secularized Augustinian Beuron monastery to his as yet very small community of monks.[4] After the catastrophes of the Revolution and the secularizations, and for internal reasons also, the Benedictine order had difficulties recovering. This is evidenced by the efforts both in France, where Solesmes certainly inspired new foundations, and especially in Bavaria, where Ludwig I encountered little re-

---

[2] H. Holzapfel, op. cit., 671.—In 1909, this historian of the order assumed "that in more than one respect the author's opinions were not shared by the order's leadership" (foreword, VII). This should prove to be correct, but with certain consequences; the criticism of the order's legalism had caused dismay (cf. K.-V. Selge in the review of K. Eßer and E. Grau, "Franziskanisches Leben [Werl 1968]," *ZKG* 82 [1971], 133f.).

[3] In P. Delatte, *Dom Guéranger*, 2 vols. (Paris 1909), II, 344.—Regarding the expansion of Solesmes until the turn of the century, see Schmitz IV, 165; P. Weißenberger, *Das Benediktinische Mönchtum im 19. u. 20. Jh.* (Beuron 1953).

[4] Maurus (Rudolf) Wolter (1825–90), after 1850 priest and high school teacher in the Rhineland, followed his brother Placidus (Ernst) as a novice into the Benedictine monastery of *S. Paolo fuori le mura* in Rome (1856). There, the brothers made the acquaintance of the widowed Princess Katharina von Hohenzollern-Sigmaringen (née Hohenlohe-Schillingsfürst). An admirer of the Benectine monks, she had negotiated with Pius IX a new monastery in Germany and, with her stepson, a settlement in Beuron after an attempt in Cleve had failed (U. Engelmann, *LThK*[2] X, 1220f., including biblio., also about the connection with Guntherianism).

sponse to his desire to revive the Benedictine order (1830: reopening of Metten Abbey, beginning of the Bavarian congregation, which flourished in the course of the nineteenth century).[5] Here, it was a question of revitalizing old monasteries; Solesmes and Beuron in form and concept were new foundations. The theoretical and practical inclination to the liturgy as the focal point of spirituality[6] was at first an internal monastic affair; but finally, this renascence was to penetrate the public life of the Church. In view of the small number of order members,[7] the tendency to found more and more filial monasteries and to achieve the status of a congregation is striking. In the newly reopened Metten Abbey, Fr. Bonifaz Wimmer strove to expand to the United States, where the bishop of Pittsburgh gave him the community of Saint Vincent in Latrobe (1846). But the bishop vehemently resisted its elevation to an abbey, particularly since the Irishman did not wish the pastoral work of the Germans to become even more independent.[8] Fr. Wimmer succeeded in Rome with the assistance of the Bavarian delegation, and the monastery became the pioneer foundation of the American Cassinese Congregation. While the Propaganda Fide had reservations about Metten's activity, the Swiss monks from Einsiedeln were welcomed in Indiana, where, from the Abbey of Saint Meinrad (1871), they devoted themselves to the mission of the Sioux Indians. In 1884, this abbey joined, within the Swiss-American Congregation, the Swiss branch of the Engelberg monastery in Missouri, which had likewise been elevated to an abbey. One of the motives for these Swiss activities had been the concern that the radical Liberals could abolish the monasteries in their homeland. The eagerness of the young Beuron Abbey[9] to found more branches was given ample opportunity in Maredsous in 1878, where (in the same year) Placidus Wolter became the first abbot. The abbey owed this opportunity to the initiative of the Desclée family. The monastery, in which a flourishing abbey school was established in 1881, had a gifted journalist in the monk van Caloen, who, in 1884, founded the periodical *Messager des fidèles* (since 1890: *Revue bénédictine*). In Anselm Schott of Beuron they had a mediator of the liturgy for the lay world and later the reorganizer of the Brazilian Benedictines. At the

---

[5] Schmitz IV, 171ff.

[6] Cf. chaps. 16 and 18.

[7] Heimbucher I, 173, reports for 1896 the "approximate sum" of 2,000 *patres* in approx. 120 monasteries, organized into 14 congregations. Statistics of 1929 in S. Hilpisch, op. cit., 390–95; id., for 1958; more than 12,000 friars in more than 200 monasteries (*LThK*² II, 192).

[8] S. Hilpisch, op. cit., 274ff.; the bishop is said to have "undermined" his elevation (cf. chap. 10). Saint Vincent became an archabbey in 1892.

[9] V. Fiala, *Ein Jahrhundert Beuroner Geschichte. 1863–1963* (Beuron 1963).

suggestion of Bishop Ullathorne, O.S.B. (Birmingham),[10] Maredsous initially branched out into Erdington, which became an abbey in 1896 but disappeared in 1922. Another branch, founded by Bishop Ullathorne, the Priory of Fort Augustus (Scotland), which was established in 1878 from Downside, was elevated in 1882 by Leo XIII to an abbey and placed under direct jurisdiction of Rome. After a visitation by Placidus Wolter and Leo Linse, prior of Erdington, undertaken by order of Rome, the latter was appointed adviser of Prior Kentiger-Milne, who *ad nutum Sanctae sedis* had to resign for Linse's benefit in 1887 (Linse became abbot in 1888). The closing of Beuron in 1875 during the *Kulturkampf*[11] turned Maurus Wolter's attention toward Austria. After an unsuccessful attempt in the Tyrol, through Cardinal Schwarzenberg's mediation, Wolter was given the almost empty Emaus monastery in Prague by Emperor Franz Joseph. Emaus, in turn, sent monks to the former canonry of Seckau (Styria; 1887 abbey). After Placidus Wolter had taken two trips to Rome (1882–83) and had brought about the approval of the constitutions of the Beuron congregation, Maurus Wolter became archabbot of Beuron (1885).[12] Like Fr. Wimmer of Metten, Fr. A. Amrhein turned to the Propaganda Fide (1882),[13] where he was exclaustrated by the Pope in 1884. The mission monastery of Reichenbach (Upper Palatinate), under episcopal jurisdiction, was transferred in 1887 to Saint Ottilien (near the Ammersee) and elevated to independent priory (1902 abbey) by the Propaganda Fide after some controversy (1897).[14] Thanks to the transferral of the apostolic prefecture, which, upon Bismarck's suggestion, was established in Zanzibar (German East Africa), it became the starting point of the *Kongregation von Sankt Ottilien,* which developed world-wide missionary activities.[15] The first archabbot of Saint Ottilien, which became the largest abbey of the order, was Norbert Weber (1902–1930). The plan, favored by Bishop Korum, to settle the former Abbey of Saint Matthias in Trier in 1888–91 with monks from Beuron failed, because the diocesan clergy did not want to relinquish a parish.

The historian of the Dominican order rightly remarked that Leo XIII

---

[10] Schmitz IV, 168f.; cf. chap. 7.

[11] Concerning the development of Beuron, see Schmitz IV, 174f. and V. Fiala (see n. 9).

[12] Concerning art in Beuron, cf. chap. 19.

[13] Abbot Maurus Wolter permitted Fr. Amrhein to join a missionary society, but in such a manner that the Beuron congregation could "profit from your apostolic activities" (P. Weissenberger, op. cit., 36).

[14] In 1896, Abbot J. Schober of Seckau visited Saint Ottilien by order of the archabbot and "as the representative of the archabbot of Beuron" (Weissenberger, op. cit., 55). In November, Schober became the superior general and inspector in Saint Ottilien by order of the Pope "to overcome internal difficulties" (Weissenberger, op. cit., 56).

[15] F. Renner, ed., *Der fünfarmige Leuchter,* 2 vols. (Sankt Ottilien 1971).

involved himself in the affairs of the Franciscans (1892) and the Benedictines (1893) much "deeper" than in those of his own order.[16] The papal plan in regard to the Benedictines had been prepared for some time after the congregations had negotiated in vain. In 1886, a congress of the abbots of the Monte Cassino congregation took place in Rome. After separating from the congregation of Subiaco (1871) in order to realize a stricter observance under Abbott Casaretto,[17] this congregation had gone through a process of rejuvenation. The main issue was the renewal of the College of Saint Anselmo as a Benedictine world center. It opened in 1888 temporarily in the *Palazzo dei Convertendi* under the leadership of Archbishop J. Dusmet, O.S.B. (born in Palermo), to whom Leo XIII had explained his ideas of a totally Benedictine college in 1887 (Dusmet was elevated to cardinal in 1889). The next step was the ordination of Hildebrand de Hemptinne[18] in Monte Cassino as abbot of Maredsous, after Placidus Wolter had become archabbot of Beuron and thus successor to his brother, who had died in 1890. A brief of 9 December 1892 called all Benedictine abbots of the world to convene for the occasion of laying the foundation stone of Saint Anselmo on the Aventine in Rome in April of the following year. During a trip in 1887 by order of the Pope for the purpose of preparing the congress, O'Gorman, prefect of the English Benedictine congregation, encountered considerable resistance from the Benedictine abbots. In spite of that, Leo XIII decided to act. In a speech on 20 April 1893, Cardinal Dusmet interpreted the intentions of the Pope, stating that the *Societas quaedam* should not abolish the individual characteristics of the congregations.[19] The abbots were to make a decision on the following points: the election of an abbot primate to represent the entire order in Rome (after consultation with the abbots; election of a *repraesentans* [rather than a primate] with a two-thirds majority [however, in accordance with Leo XIII's wish the first primate was appointed by the Pope]); the abbot primate to reside in the College of Saint Anselmo,

---

[16] A. Walz, *Frühwirt,* 166.

[17] Regarding the internal tensions because of the new constitutions, see Schmitz IV, 184.

[18] Hildebrand de Hemptinne (1849, Geneva; 1913, Beuron) was sixteen years old when he became a *Zuave* (member of the papal body guard created in 1860), and in 1870 he became a novice in Beuron (H. de Moreau, *H. de Hemptinne* [Paris 1930; Germ., 1938]; Schmitz IV, 168–246f.

[19] "Advertendum interea existimo verba Summi Pontificis . . . ita accipienda esse et intelligenda, uti si ex foederatis familiis Societas quaedam formetur et stet, quae uniuscuiusque familiae specialem ac nationalem characterem ac propria statuta revereatur et servet"; S. Hilpisch, op. cit., 386ff.; S. Mayer, *Die benediktinische Konföderation* (Beuron 1957); Schmitz IV, 244–47, also regarding the discussion about a confederation within the order in 1868–69.

which does not belong to any congregation and represents its own community, composed of various congregations (consultation with the abbots: the confederation should not imply dependence on a certain congregation); the primate's term of office to be twelve years (the term of the abbot prefect heading a congregation: six years). On 12 July, the "confederation" was confirmed by the papal brief *Summum semper*. The confederation meant a deep invasion of the old structure of the Benedictine monastic life and certainly did not correspond to Prosper Guéranger's ideal. Whether this ideal could generally be realized and whatever the confederation really meant, is equally debated. Even Pius XII had to deal with the constitution of the confederation.[20]

After the Beuron congregation had sent at first only a few monks to the desolate Brazilian abbeys, van Caloen made two inspection tours in 1894/95, reporting about them to the Beuron general convention in Maredsous. Olinda, where van Caloen became abbot,[21] was the point of departure for the rejuvenation of the Brazilian congregation, whose headquarters was the abbey of Saint Benedict in Rio de Janeiro. The Portuguese monasteries of Cucujaes and Singeverga, which were integrated into the Beuron congregation and visited in 1894 by the abbot of Seckau, became victims of the political development. The archabbey of Beuron, which was chosen by the abbot primate in 1896 as the place for a convention of the abbots, initiated the establishment of Maria Laach, whose church Emperor Wilhelm II gave to the Beuron monks in 1892 after an audience with Placidus Wolter (1893 papal erection of the abbey, W. Benzler first abbot).[22]

Shortly before his death in 1872, the master general of the Dominicans, V. A. Jandel, witnessed the reincorporation of the Spanish provinces which had been separated in 1804. After the interim of the vicariate general under J. M. Sanvito, the provincial of the Roman province, Jandel was succeeded by J. M. Larroca (elected by mail), who had been the vicar general in Manila and contributed to the restoration of the order's unity in Spain. In spite of Jandel's efforts, the membership of the order had diminished under his office, even by 1910 it had barely

[20] Concerning centralization, see Hostie, 239f.
[21] Chap. 8, n. 36; also: M. E. Scherrer, "Fin großer Benediktiner, Abt Michael Kruse von São Paulo, 1864–1929," *SM* 17, suppl. (1963); id., "Beuron und die Restauration der Abteien in Brasilien," V. Fiala, *Beuron 1863–1963* (Beuron 1963); J. Jongmans, "A Restauração da Congregação beneditina brasileira. Papel de Gerad van Caloen," *Revista eclesiast, brasileira* 32 (1972), 640–54.
[22] Wilhelm II demonstrated his benevolence with his visits in 1897 and 1901. Beuron entertained him in 1910. S. Merkle, 66 (biblio., introduction), remarked in 1914 during a presentation in honor of Wilhelm II that the Benedictines "were the least involved in the quarrels of this world."

reached the status of 1844.[23] The general chapter of 1885 in Louvain decided to purchase a new residence for the general in Rome in the Via San Sebastiano. Shortly before his death, Larroca became "somehow"[24] entangled in the controversy regarding papal politics toward the Italian state, having made some positive statements about Bonomelli's (bishop of Cremona)[25] translation of the *Homiliae* by Monsabré, who had been the preacher of Notre Dame until 1890. As with the Franciscans and Benedictines, Leo XIII had also directed his attention to the rearrangement of the Dominicans, and in a letter of 31 May 1889 he impressed upon them the observance of the *vita communis*. After Larroca's death on 8 January 1891, the Pope wanted to appoint a vicar general. However, J. A. Laboré, the provincial of Lyon, presented himself. The general chapter, whose residence determines the office of the vicariate general, was convening in Lyon.[26] At the general chapter, the greatest majority of votes went to Andreas Frühwirth, who had just been made provincial of the Austrian imperial province for the second time; the intransigent Laboré was nominated as the second candidate. The Styrian Andreas Frühwirth (1845–1933) had joined the order in 1863, had studied in Graz and Rome, and became provincial of the imperial province for the first time in 1880–84. Until 1904 he was to the Dominicans an equally energetic and diplomatically adroit general, who prevented the order from showing any signs of weakness, and who was eager, primarily, to make himself indispensable for Neo-Thomism. With amazing energy he visited province after province[27] and regularly conducted general chapters (1895 in Avila, 1898 in Vienna, 1901 in Ghent, 1904 in Viterbo).[28] Frühwirth devoted himself with special passion to the establishment of colleges.[29] In a letter of 4 October 1893,

[23] 1844: 4,562 members; 1876: 3,341; 1910: 4,472 (A. Walz, *Compendium*, paragraph 20).

[24] A. Walz, *Frühwirth*, 166; according to Walz, Larroca destroyed all documents related to this context.

[25] Chap. 5.

[26] A. Walz, *Frühwirth*, 166: "It was unfortunate that the Pope was initially informed incorrectly about the general vicariate of the order after Larroca's death. It seemed as if the Pope was to appont him." When Laboré appeared in Rome, the Pope is supposed to have said: "Why does one not simply follow the constitutions?"

[27] On 23 April 1895, the German order province was restored (Albert Trapp: first father superior).

[28] A. Walz, *Frühwirth*, 167, noted that the voters of the general were careful not "to dissatisfy the great patron of the order, Leo XIII." Pius X must have been more to Frühwirth's liking, according to the Dominican writer Walz, who knew him personally. Pius showed the general "sympathy in the handling of individual problems, while Leo XIII was balancing on the high wire of general benevolence . . . . More could be achieved with Pius X in one year than with Leo XIII in one decade" (272).

[29] List in A. Walz, *Frühwirth*, 241–43.

Leo XIII made the Dominican order solely responsible for the edition of Thomas Aquinas.[30] After three years, in 1882, the commission of cardinals appointed for this edition had published the first volume, and by 1892 seven volumes (Cardinal Giuseppe Pecci, the Pope's brother, headed the commission of the cardinals for the edition). In April 1903 the Pope received volume XI from the Dominicans.

During the generalship of Frühwirth there occurred the initial controversies regarding the Dominican M.-J. Lagrange. His first attempts to develop a "critical method" for interpreting the Pentateuch produced often crude suspicions after the Congress of Fribourg in 1897. Frühwirth, who had given Lagrange the title of "Master of Theology" in 1901, provided his research with some protection in his capacity as general of the order (until 1903).[31] However, Pius X assigned the leadership of the new Biblical Institute not to the Dominicans, but to the Jesuits.[32] In terms of spirituality, the order went along with the consecration to the Sacred Heart and the pledge to recite the rosary as was the general trend of the time.

After the death of the general of the Jesuits, P.-J. Beckx (1795–1887), during whose long term in office (since 1853) the number of members had increased remarkably (in spite of the prohibitions),[33] the Swiss A. M. Anderledy, assistant for German-speaking provinces, took office. His predecessor had generally practiced moderation, but under Anderledy, who, as head of the German province, had emphatically supported the *Syllabus* (1864), those indiscriminate polemics against everything modern broke through, polemics which clouded the apostolic goals of the Society of Jesus. It is significant for the new general that he neglected the Fathers and the religious authors in his writings and that he preferred to rely on papal letters addressed to the society and on selected quotations from general congregations and generals.[34] His successor, the Spaniard Luis Martín (general 1892–1906), deserves credit for the history of the order, and he assigned the edition of the *Monumenta Historica Societatis Jesu* to the Spanish provinces. After his election he was greeted warmly by Leo XIII.[35] The Society of Jesus still

---

[30] A. Walz, *Compendium,* 527, 616f.; cf. chap. 20.

[31] Cf. chap. 23.

[32] A. Walz, *Frühwirth,* 216f.; "the courageous Dominican pioneer of a reasonable and progressive exegesis . . . should expect new trials." Regarding the further development of the Bible Institute and the nunciature of Frühwirth in Munich (1907–15), cf. chaps. 33 and 35.

[33] 1838: 3,067; 1850: 1,874; 1874: 9,260; 1900: 15,073; 1914: 16,894 (1950: 30,579).

[34] "He stressed more the "old intrinsic values" of the order . . . rather than demanding to look for the positive aspects in our modern time" (H. Becher, *LThK²* I, 507); id., *Jesuiten,* 370.

[35] Schmidlin, *PG* II, 567.

preferred to think of philosophy as *ancilla theologiae* rather than theology itself, which theme the Jesuits concentrated on in terms of the question of grace and an ecclesiology oriented toward the papacy. During Leo XIII's pontificate, however, the tendency of the Gregoriana toward postive theology, and against speculative theology, was corrected, and as a result the Pope's brother, Giuseppe Pecci, left the Jesuits (he was reinstated shortly before his death). The general congregation of 1883 decided to choose the encyclical on Aquinas, *Aeterni Patris,* as its guideline, and in 1886 Leo XIII confirmed the privileges of the society. The traditional emphasis on moral theology proved fruitful in dealing with the problems of modern society, with Jesuit authors providing important contributions.[36] To the influential publications of the order were added the *Przeglad Powszechny* (in Cracow since 1884), *Razón y Fé* (Madrid since 1901), *America* (New York since 1909). Wherever Jesuits were allowed to be active in schools, especially in the United States, lively discussions were held about curricula, primarily the relationship of humanism to the exact sciences. These debates essentially ended in 1906 with an adaptation to the secular schools.[37]

It is a remarkable phenomenon that the Jesuits continued to have relatively large numbers of new recruits in spite of the prohibitions. In Portugal (which refused admission of Jesuits in 1814, accepted them in 1829, and retracted admission again in 1834), the Jesuits had only a short period of activity from 1880 until 1908. In France, schools had to be closed in 1880, because the order could not accept the school laws. In Italy, where the general of the order had been expelled from the professed house al Gesù, and had to settle in Fiesole (1895, Curia transferred back to Rome), the Jesuits were prohibited or at least inhibited from living together. New members were scarce, in contrast to Austria, Germany, and Switzerland, where the order obtained many new members for its activities in foreign countries, particularly in the United States.[38] A majority resolution of the German *Reichstag* (168 to 145) for reinstatement was voted down in the *Bundesrat.* However, the Redemptorists, who had turned to Latin America after their suppression in Europe, were not considered an illegal organization any longer. Rather unencumbered, the Jesuits were able to develop in Austria-Hungary after 1820. There they had high schools, and also the college *Stella matutina* (since 1856) in Feldkirch and the theological faculty of the University of Innsbruck,[39] centers of learning that influenced Ger-

---

[36] Cf. chaps. 21, 12, and 13.

[37] Cf. chaps. 10 and 12.

[38] With 1,167 members around the turn of the century, the German province was the strongest among the twenty-three provinces; Heimbucher (1897) II, 135.

[39] The anti-Jesuit activities of the Liberals in Vienna during the seventies failed, last but not least, because of the opposition of the Tyrolese provincial diet.

many also. In the province of England, which was combined with Ireland, Maryland, New York, and Missouri through a vice-province, conflicts arose concerning pastoral work, which were intensified when the College of Chelsea was established through direct papal authority over the heads of the episcopate; consequently the Jesuits did not have Cardinal Manning as a friend. After his death, the celebration of the hundredth anniversary of the College of Stonyhurst in 1894 served as a kind of conciliatory event. Conflicts between the German-speaking Jesuits in the United States were emotionalized by the question of nationalities.

Since the Cistercians of the Strict Observance and the Reform congregations could not come to an agreement, the Reformed Cistercians (Trappists) separated in 1892, a separation which Leo XIII confirmed in his brief of 17 March 1893 and the decree of 1902, including the privileges of the old order. In 1898 they were able to obtain the original monastery of Cîteaux. The Cistercians of the old observance still possessed at the end of the nineteenth century thirty-two monasteries, most of them in Austria-Hungary (Mehrerau on Lake Constance was the only Swiss-German congregation). Papal unification tactics, successful with the Franciscans, would have been out of the question in this case.[40]

Another reform attempt at this time failed and ended in the isolation of the initiator. Mère Marie du Sacré-Cœur (died in 1901) had intended to improve the training of the *Filles de Notre-Dame* according to the model of Bruges, but she had encountered the resistance of the bishop of Clermont. Even though she had gained the support of Monsignor d'Hulst in 1895 and finally the partial assistance of the French episcopate, she was sent back to her old convent, which, however, did not accept her.[41]

The extraordinary activity regarding the new establishment of congregations had peaked by the middle of the century. Most congregations were unable to extend their local impact. The Christian Brothers, one of the older congregations, achieved significant success and could be found all over the world toward the end of the century. The Redemptorists experienced a similar upswing. By 1900 they had 132 foundations, 30 of them in Italy, and after 1894 they were also admitted in Germany. The Salesians of Don Bosco, who counted 774 members in 57 foundations in 1888 at the death of their founder, expanded also outside of

[40] A. Wulf, *Compendium of the History of the Cistercian Order* (Milwaukee 1944); C. Grolleau and G. Chastel, *L'ordre de Cîteau. La Trappe* (Paris ²1954).

[41] Dansette (biblio., chap. 16), 26f. Msgr. Sueur, the bishop of Avignon, had allowed her book *Les religieuses enseignantes* to be printed. The chief opponent was the archbishop of Aix. It was a question of adopting the curriculum of the *écoles normales* in order to prepare the students properly for their teaching duties.

Italy, and by 1900 they had gained about 2,000 members in 300 houses (since 1903 also in Austria). They intensified their activities, begun in 1875, in the foreign mission.[42] The Pallotines (finally confirmed in 1904) experienced a more rapid development only after World War I. In terms of members, the Sisters of Charity (Vincentians) were leading all female congregations. They suffered civil restrictions relatively rarely and in general only for short periods of time, because everyone was dependent on their hospital care. At the end of the century, they counted approximately thirty thousand sisters in 2,500 houses. The Sisters of the Sacred Heart, founded in Paris, began in 1879 the beatification process of their founder Sophie Barat.

It was a character trait of the activities of the Dominican general Andreas Frühwirth that he paid special attention to the financial situation of the provinces of his order and the office of the general. Economic foundations had always played a significant role in the history of the orders and the congregations, but it was only natural that the conditions of the industrial age had an impact in this area as well. A good example was the founding by the Assumptionists of their publishing house *Bonne Presse.*[43] The political circumstances in Europe (less so in the Near East) were rather unfavorable for the congregation. However, two other enterprises were able to develop unencumbered by political factors, even though they were not confirmed by the Church until the beginning of the twentieth century: the *Societas Divini Salvatoris* (S.D.S., Salvatorians) and the *Societas Verbi Divini* (S.V.D., Society of the Divine Word). Even through the hagiographical style of the biographies of the societies' founders one can sense that genuine religious engagement was combined with the virtues of an industrial manager.

The founder of the Salvatorians, Johann Baptist Jordan,[44] was an ornamental painter, who had privately obtained a high school education and in 1878, as a priest, received through his pastor a stipend in Rome. The Alemannian, born on the Rhine River near Baden (1848–1918), got an audience with Leo XIII in 1880 (arranged by Cardinal Bilio). He extensively expounded the papal blessing of the founding of his *Apostolische Lehrgesellschaft* in Rome. He secured his position through recommendations by Cardinals Hergenröther and Parocchi. With the help of his publication *Der Missionär,* which he managed and which was approved by the bishop of Linz but directed from Rome, he wanted to

[42] A. Schmitt, *LThK*² IX, 263f.

[43] J. Monval, *Les Assomptionistes* (Paris 1939); concerning their role in France, see chap. 6; in the Middle East: chap. 25.

[44] P. Pfeiffer, *J.-B- Jordan und seine Gründung* (Rome 1930; the author is the second superior general of the congregation); E. Federici, *G.-B. Jordan* (Rome 1948); concerning the early stages, see B. Lüthen, *Die Gesellschaft des Göttlichen Heilandes* (1911).

establish an "association" whose program was to show no clear contours, but which was to have a diverse membership.[45] His main problem was to find trained priests, and he therefore wanted to educate young people speedily, using his own career as an example. In spite of considerable difficulties, including financial ones,[46] he was able to establish one foundation after another after obtaining a mission in Assam: 1890 in Tivoli, 1892 in Vienna, then in North and South America, 1898 in Meran, then in Rumania, Belgium, and Brazil (1902), for the most part developed from modest beginnings. It was with reservations that he finally decided to convene a general chapter in 1902, and the chapter's criticism, presented in 1906, of the extremely self-willed general superior is rather understandable.[47] Under Jordan's successor, his biographer P. Pfeiffer (died 1945), began the great expansion of this society.

Arnold Janssen (1837–1909), founder of the Society of the Divine Word,[48] was the son of a transport business owner on the Lower Rhine River. In 1861 he became a priest and a high school teacher and began his activity by also founding a publication called *Kleiner Herz-Jesu-Bote* (1874). After a fund-raising trip through Germany and Austria in 1875, Janssen purchased a piece of property with an old inn in Steyl, a town in the Netherlands near the border. Together with a carpentry apprentice, a Franciscan brother, and his real brother (a Capuchin from Münster), he founded a society here. His plan encountered great scepticism among the clergy and bishops, and with his autocratic style he caused most of his fellow members to leave in 1876.[49] The same year, Janssen

---

[45] Three categories were planned: (1) full members (priests and laymen); (2) permanent, academically educated "staff"; (3) the readers of the journal, which was to appeal to all classes from the clergy to the maid (P. Pfeiffer, op. cit., 71f.).

[46] In 1882, the Curia forced him to change the name of his society and erase the word "apostolic"; in 1886, he had difficulties because the words "approved by the Church" were not set off clearly enough; in 1892, a Carmelite came to inspect him, "a heavy cross to bear" for Jordan (P. Pfeiffer, op. cit., 260), but probably also for the inspector.

[47] P. Pfeiffer, op. cit., 336–339; the priest B. Lüthen of Westphalia was a loyal assistant.

[48] H. Fischer, S.V.D., *Arnold Janssen, der Gründer des Steyler Missionswerkes* (Steyl 1919).

[49] Vaughan's assessment was very negative. Later, he became an English cardinal who founded the Mill Hill mission and visited Janssen; his evaluation: he was insufficiently educated in theology and not practical. Indeed, Janssen's interests in theology were probably rather limited, which was the reason for his break with Dr. v. Essen, towards whom Archbishop Melchers had wanted to direct Janssen's activities (H. Fischer, op. cit., 382: Janssen did not think much of "educated professors"). He was not an "impractical" organizer, but rather a quite daring manager. However, his leadership style was somewhat unpleasant (e.g., a conflict over who should officiate at what time), yet he was supported by the bishop of Roermond, who called the opponents "social democrats" (H. Fischer, op. cit., 155). H. Fischer, op. cit., 436, quotes a characteristic statement made by Janssen in 1900: "As far as the brothers are concerned, they shouldn't read but the Sunday paper, this is certainly sufficient." Regarding the support Janssen received from the German Catholic convention, see Kißling II, 126–30.

found a capable economist, the future superior general Nikolaus Blum, and so he began the construction of Steyl, even though he had only one tenth of the construction funds at his disposal. Within a few years he had accumulated three hundred thousand marks worth of debts. When the construction of Saint Michael's with its double church was completed in 1886, his debts were repaid. To the publication of the *Herz-Jesu-Bote* he added the magazine *Die heilige Stadt Gottes* and a calendar, printed in his own press, for which the lay brothers provided cheap labor. In 1888, he founded Saint Raphael's in Rome, 1889 Saint Gabriel's in Vienna, 1892 Heiligkreuz near Neisse,[50] 1898 Saint Wendel's in the Rhineland, 1904 Saint Rupert's near Bischofshofen. Janssen acted according to the principle that it is not a question of the availability of funds, but of the necessity of the building.[51] Regarding the general chapter, Janssen followed J.-B. Jordan's attitude: he procrastinated as long as possible (1884 the first chapter with four priests, 1885 with twelve priests, the only ones eligible to vote). The constitutions were designed in a centralistic fashion (instead of provinces only "regions"), approved (with reservations) in 1901, and after some dispute regarding the general chapter's competence, they were confirmed in 1905 (not finalized until 1910).[52]

Because the congregations for women were, aside from education, primarily active in charity and hospital care, they were, as a rule, less touched by state laws. Because of that, and thanks to their active religious willingness to make sacrifices, they were able to develop under the pontificate of Leo XIII. The Sisters of Mercy of Saint Charles Borromeo had founded, via their original congregation in Nancy, new congregations in Germany, Austria, and the Netherlands, which developed considerable activities (the Saint Hedwig hospital, founded in 1846 in Berlin, took care of 5,500 patients in 1895). Aside from the largest female society, the Sisters of Charity (Vincentians), smaller societies like the Niederbronn Sisters (1880 the general mother house in Oberbronn/Alsace) and the Ingenbohl Sisters (1894 confirmed by the Pope) also had an excellent reputation across religious borders.[53]

---

[50] Heiligkreuz became the subject of political favoritism. Bismarck preferred the Steyl missionaries to the Jesuits. Heiligkreuz was involved in the question of the protectorate of South Shantung, where Anzer from Steyl was missionary bishop. The Prussian government did not want Steyl to become a papal congregation. This conflicted with Janssen's plans, but was acceptable to Prince-Bishop Kopp. The Silesian Janssen did not like the new settlement any more than the Salzburg authorities liked theirs; financial problems were feared.

[51] H. Fischer, op. cit., 188f.

[52] Regarding the missionary activities of this and other congregations, cf. P. III.

[53] W. Hohn, *Die Barmherzigen Schwestern vom hl. K. Borromäus* (Trier 1900); id., *300 Jahre Barmherzige Schwestern vom hl. Vinzenz von Paul* (Munich 1933); H. C. Wendlandt,

Looking at the history of the older religious societies and the new foundations during the pontificate of Leo XIII as a whole, one cannot ignore the desire for an internal rejuvenation of the Church (not least in the foreign mission) and for a social impact upon education, hospital care, and social action. There was also the amazing attraction of the religious life for a considerable part of the youth in the Catholic Church in spite of the political tactics of suppression, the general attitude of the time, the continuously increasing resignation and scepticism, and the way of thinking which resulted from the growing role of technology in life. But the religious societies found in Catholicism, which had meanwhile reached self-awareness, a resonance of resistance to the secularization of life and a religiously motivated willingness to devotion which bore witness to the vitality of the Catholic Church. This vitality is particularly obvious in the societies with "simple vows," which by now found full recognition. To gather these impulses, to eliminate or prevent sterile divisions, and to make use of these societies for the ideals of his pointificate were the goals of Leo XIII's ecclesiastical legislation, whose most significant feature was the concentration of orders and congregations in Rome. It is historically understandable that such efforts were most difficult in regard to the oldest order of the West, the Benedictines. Its decentralized structure had corresponded to the specific liberties of a feudal society. The principle of centralization was the principle of a growing highly industrial society—and it was also the principle of Leo XIII and his successors in the sense of an economy of spiritual powers. Most religious societies were induced to transfer their headquarters to Rome. In 1908 Pius X established the *Sacra congregatio negotiis religiosorum sodalium praeposita* as the highest authority for orders of the Latin Church, to whom the religious of both sexes were subordinated.

Die weiblichen Orden und Kongregationen der kath. Kirche und ihre Wirksamkeit in Preußen. 1816–1918 (Paderborn 1924); A. Sinningen, *Kath. Frauengenossenschaften Deutschlands* (Düsseldorf ²1944, biblio.).

CHAPTER 18

The Dispute over Church Music

Since church music is directly connected with the liturgical action, the question of how musical forms of expression of the zeitgeist can be incorporated in the Church service is much more crucial than in regard to the fine arts.[1] Indeed, the religious subjectivity of the sacred music of a Franz Schubert does correspond to the subjectivity of general piety;[2] however, it is certain that as the representative musical creations of Classicism and Romanticism emerged from the modern spirit born in the Revolution, frequently Christianity was simply the occasion for their creation. In France, the interest in the Gregorian chant of the Benedictines at Solesmes was primarily an esoteric and historical matter, and the *Schola cantorum,* which had just been introduced in all Romance countries according to the model of the Lateran Church (1868), lived in harmony with the well-known plain-chant, a popularization of the chorale. Even Charles Gounod's *Cecilia Mass* (1882) or the romantic harmony of César Franck, (died in 1890) did not give offense. However, in German Catholicism, a movement developed which wanted to restore the "pure" sacred music, believing that a musical reform, which was unquestionably necessary, could only be achieved by turning away from modern developments. The German example found an echo in many other forms of Catholicism (the Netherlands, Belgium, Ireland, North America), but not in Austria, where attempts were made to apply contemporary forms to the ecclesiastical spirit. Pierluigi da Palestrina (died 1594 in Rome) was for the revival of church music in the nineteenth century what Thomas Aquinas had been for philosophy and theology.[3] Composition and declamation of the "Palestrina style" were renewed in the first half of the nineteenth century. Regensburg, the episcopal see of Michael Sailer, was the leading center, a city from which spread the tradition which Karl Proske (died 1861) started with his editions from the sixteenth and seventeenth centuries. That musicians who composed in the "Palestrina style" (such as M. Haller [died 1915 in Regensburg], who was called the Palestrina of the twentieth century) were unable to produce important works is due to the process of superficial imitation. It is more important that, through the efforts of the highest church authorities, the *a capella* music of vocal polyphony was canonized, which was equally a historic misunderstanding of the great master Palestrina and a disregarding of artistic originality.

At first, there was criticism of the church music which was composed of elements of the symphony and the opera.[4] Now, by separating the *musica sacra* from the *musica profana,* the church was separated from the world. In regard to instrumental music, as it was then composed by the church music directors, and which continued to be played, though not

---

[1] Cf. chap. 19.
[2] Cf. chap. 16.
[3] Fellerer, *Geschichte,* 148, 150; *LThK*[2] VIII, 3.
[4] F. Krieg, op. cit., 129.

as often, the Belgian Edgar Tinel (died 1912[5]) stands out, because he refused to follow this separation. Of course, he was not played very often. During the Catholic Convention in Bamberg in 1868, the priest F. X. Witt (1834–88) founded the *Allgemeinen Cäcilienverband für die Länder der deutschen Sprache,* which Pius IX confirmed in 1870 as an organization under papal law with a cardinal protector. The brief contains the society's statutes as presented. Its first and foremost obligation is: "Gregorian chant (*cantus planus*) is to be cultivated intensively everywhere. Polyphonic arrangements for several voices (*cantus figuralis*) of older or newer compositions are to be furthered, as long as they comply with church regulations." Palestrina was not mentioned in this document, but he was the idol of the Cecilian movement.[6] The society was thus authorized to determine in its catalog what sacred music was.[7] The struggle over true Catholic church music was considered one of the most important ones in the battle with the zeitgeist.[8] Deviations were condemned with extreme intolerance and with reference to the Church.[9] Even the German Catholic church hymn, which

[5] K. Weinmann, op. cit., 249–54; following J. S. Bach, Tinel placed "active devotion and piety in his work," in opposition to formalism, which guided the church music organizations (Fellerer, *Geschichte,* 148).

[6] In regard to the brief *Multum ad movendos animos* of 16 December 1870, see H. Hucke, op. cit., 164ff.—It is characteristic for F. X. Witt to write: ". . . the better works in the 'Witt style' embrace the chorale more so than many works in the Palestrina style, at least in regard to the main point, i.e., the elucidation of the sacred melody and the text" (quoted ibid., 172). Fellerer, *Grundlagen,* 34, is justified in placing him in the historical situation, but that does not make reading H. Hucke superfluous.

[7] The neo-Cecilian K. Weinmann (op. cit., 189–204) considers the judgment regarding "liturgical usefulness" justified; he was critical, however, of the fact that it was also evaluated from an artistic point of view. O. Ursprung (op. cit., 280) feels that the development was hindered by the society's expert advisers in charge of the catalog because now either "a style reduced to *Gebrauchsmusik*" or the historic fixation on Palestrina, who was, after all, very contemporary even in the sixteenth century, became the accepted standard. Fellerer, (*MGG* II, 623f.) calls the catalog the "official recognition of the infinite number of sacred compositions which are devoid of any artistic significance and often not even technically well executed . . . ." Krieg, who endeavors to honor from a historical perspective F. X. Witt's "cleansing fiery spirit" (op. cit., 137), speaks of the "devotional harmony" (op. cit., 134) of the society's catalog.—F. X. Haberl, the father of the Regensburg chorale edition, originally intended to compile an index of music forbidden in church (H. Hucke, op. cit., 171). Everyone is in agreement about the society's catalog (cf. Fellerer, *Geschichte,* 155).

[8] F. J. Selbst, *Der katholische Kirchengesang* (Regensburg 1880), 133: "What terror, what mockery of our progressive century! The Cecilian movement is a return to the dark Middle Ages . . . ."

[9] P. Krutschek, *Die Kirchenmusik nach dem Willen der Kirche. Eine Instruktion* (Regensburg 1891): Not everyone has to be a member of the Cecilian society, but everyone has to follow its guidelines, "otherwise he would be resisting the Church itself" (240f.).

treasure had been rediscovered by the Romanticists, partly fell under the influence of Cecilianism,[10] and especially the convents of women added popular, sentimental songs. F. X. Witt, who, in spite of his aggressiveness, was one of the more forward-looking minds in the movement, did not want to see instrumental music excluded and hoped for "a Palestrina of modern orchestral music." He probably had Franz Liszt in mind,[11] who respected him. The great value and impact of Cecilianism consists of the fact that it recognized the problematic relation of Classical and Romantic music to the liturgical ceremony. Its attempts to solve the problem, which should be seen in the historical and ecclesiastical perspective of that time, were inadequate. This is nowhere more obvious than in the fact that Anton Bruckner (1824–96), who as a Romanticist created his sacred music with liturgical objectivity,[12] was not accepted by the movement.

Supported by papal authority,[13] Cecilianism spread in the last third of the nineteenth century through most countries, after the Gregorian Society had been founded in the Netherlands in 1868. Its impact was particularly strong in Ireland. In the country of Giuseppe Verdi (1813–1901), where the influence of the national opera was especially problematic, the *Regolamento per la Musica sacra in Italia* of 1884 ruled: Except for the organ, only trombones, flutes, and drums and "similar instruments popular with the Israelite people" were permitted. They concentrated on cultivating the chorale, which was supported by ecclesiastical decrees. Cecilianism also exerted a certain influence.

Those who charged him with fanaticism were told: "You see, I call the devil devil and Christ my God and Master."

[10] W. Bäumker, *Das katholische deutsche Kirchenlied in seinen Singweisen,* 4 vols. (Freiburg i. Br. 1886–1911).—The statutes of the Cecilian society, which were contained in the papal brief, discuss the toleration of the hymn in devotion; the German practice of using songs during Mass is ignored (H. Hucke, op. cit., 168f.).

[11] Ursprung, 280.—Franz Liszt (1811–86), who had been ordained in Rome in 1865, attempted in his sacred music a blending of Gregorian elements, vocal polyphony, and modern orchestration (Fellerer, *Geschichte,* 146).

[12] F. Krieg, op. cit., 146f.: "Bruckner's personal emancipation (as a Romantic) serves this community (the Church) better than the orthographical imitation of old styles." Fellerer, *Geschichte,* 147: "Through Bruckner, the symphonic art has taken church music to new heights, comparable to Palestrina in the sixteenth century, when polyphony reached a climax in ecclesiastical expression."—Naturally, the difficulties of performance play a big role.

[13] F. X. Witt reached the limit of his purism when he wrote a letter to Leo XIII, accusing the prefect of the Congregation of Rites, Cardinal Bartolini, of having called Haydn, Mozart, and Cherubini "select and sincere" in a letter to the founder of the *Associazione di S. Cecilia.* Bartolini took revenge when he was appointed cardinal protector of the Cecilian society (H. Hucke, op. cit. 173f.).

Almost two decades after Palestrina's death, the Stamperia Medicaea in Rome, a printing office founded by Cardinal Fernando Medici and G. B. Raimundi, published an edition of the Roman gradual in which Gregorian melodies had been adapted to contemporary principles.[14] This little-known publication was adopted in Mechelen in 1848, but it did not have any historical significance for the Church until after 1871, when the publishing house of Pustet in Regensburg prepared reprints. The inspiring and driving force was the priest F. X. Haberl (1840–1910) who, after sojourns in Rome, became cathedral conductor in Regensburg, where he founded a church music school in 1874.[15] The Congregation of Rites offered Pustet a thirty-year imprimatur, even though the historical validity of the *Medicaea* was already being questioned at that time.[16] A decree of the Congregation of Rites of 14 April 1877 bestowed upon the edition a somewhat official character.

In the meantime, the Benedictine J. Pothier (1835–1923)[17] had conducted his research on chorales in Solesmes by order of his abbot, Prosper Guéranger, intending to do away with Gallicism and to restore tradition. After the publication of the principles of Solesmes, a congress was organized in Arezzo in 1882, to which the Congregation of Rites reacted on 10 April 1883 with a reiteration of the legitimization of the Regensburg edition. This was expressly confirmed by Leo XIII with the statement that papal directives be taken as mandates. In Regensburg, Witt and particularly Haberl fought passionately for their concept, and they did not fail to refer to the Roman authority.[18] But after the termination of the imprimatur, Leo XIII seized the opportunity and found a way out of the dilemma with his brief *Nos quidem* of 17 May 1901, addressed to the abbot of Solesmes. The motu proprio *Inter*

---

[14] L. Kunz, "Medicaea," *LThK*[2] VII, 230. The edition appeared in 1614–15.

[15] F. X. Haberl deserves credit for editions of Palestrina and Orlando di Lasso.

[16] A memorandum to the German bishops' conference by R. Schlecht and others in 1869 (quoted in Ursprung, op. cit., 269). L. Kunz (*LThK*[2] VII, 230) speaks of a "Roman contract" for Pustet; Ursprung: "It may be that the Roman Chorale Commission had already decided on a revised edition of the *Medicaea* or that the Pustet publishing house in Regensburg had proceeded accordingly with a petition." F. Krieg (op. cit., 53): The people in Regensburg are accomplishing "a liturgical work of pioneers" with "complete trust" in the *Medicaea*.

[17] In 1880, *Les mélodies grégoriennes d'après la tradition* appeared (after 1883, the chorale edition). Regarding the battle between Regensburg and Solesmes, see P. Combe, op. cit. 209.

[18] P. Krutschek: "In view of the official announcements of Leo XIII and the Congregation of Rites, it is incomprehensible how one can still maintain that I recommend the wrong chorale, and further retorts are wasted" (op. cit., [n. 9], preface to the second ed., XXI).

pastoralis officii (1903) of Pius X introduced a new phase in the under-standing of the Gregorian chorale.[19]

[19] P. Krieg, 139f.: F. X. Haberl "suffered this hard fate, which destroyed his life's work on the chorale, with dignity and humility."—In regard to his reaction to Leo XIII's brief of 1901, see his essay "Geschichte und Wert der offiziellen Choralbücher," *Kirchen-musikalisches Jahrbuch* (1902).—For criticism in Germany regarding the Regensburg chorale edition, see R. Molitor, O.S.B., *Die nachtridentinische Choral-Reform in Rom* (Beuron 1902).—The breakthrough in Rome followed in 1893 through a vote by the Congregation of Rites, which was initiated by A. De Santi, S.J., and Solesmes. The Latin-German text of Pius X's motu proprio in Krieg, op. cit., appendix.—Cf. chap. 27, also in regard to De Santi.

CHAPTER 19

Church Art in the Nineteenth and Twentieth Centuries

Since the beginning of Church history, ecclesiastical art has carried the hallmark of the contemporary relation between the Church and the world and of the different forms of the notion of salvation, according to their epochal and ethnic background. In that respect, a work of art preserves in visualized form something from a past situation and can therefore serve, provided it is interpreted correctly, as a source for Church history. Art is particularly informative when it reports incidents that were not considered worthy of literary treatment or remained in the subconscious.

There is good reason that Church art should be chosen as a topic of investigation in the part of this series that deals with the nineteenth and twentieth centuries. The previous, almost naive function of Christian art has become more and more the object of serious study and decrees and is thus a special section of Church history.

Architecture

After the Council of Trent, the Church developed an awareness of the specific character of its artistic activities, especially in the countries north of the Alps, which, having been effected by the Reformation, externalized its forms of expression. Stained glass and ribbed vaults continued to be considered "ecclesiastical," even though they were not customary any longer in secular architecture. In those areas in which the Reformation had left its mark, but which had been recovered by the Catholic Church, clear relapses into medieval architecture can be observed. The result is a "sacral style" with historical dimensions.[1] However, Church art in consistently Catholic countries generally runs parallel to the contemporary development of style. It also does not lose touch with aesthetics, which grows more and more independent, even though the concept of beauty is no longer a theological one as in the Middle Ages.[2] But since 1588, beginning with the activities of the Congregation of Rites, the Church in these countries felt compelled to publish papal and episcopal decrees, edicts, and recommendations on artistic activities in order to draw the line against Protestantism and the secular areas which were in the process of emancipation.[3] The demands relate essentially to preservation of or connection to the Christian tradition, to avoidance of offensive presentations or recommendation of instructive ones, and to the observance of ethnographic customs (*usus*), provided they do not contradict liturgical regulations. The interpretation of these regulations and recommendations leaves a great deal of latitude and allows strict traditionalism as well as the recently increasing influence of the individual artist. The artistic context in general was thus able to be preserved by the Church throughout the Baroque and Roccoco eras, and during the secular Classicism of the end of the eighteenth century, in which the Enlightenment erected or at least designed its own edifices of art for the "Supreme Being" or the gods of "nature" and "reason."[4]

Corresponding to the turn toward Greek art within the context of Classicism,[5] churches, like palaces, theaters, and museums, decorated

[1] E. Kirschbaum, *Deutsche Nachgotik. Ein Beitrag zur Geschichte der kirchlichen Architektur von 1550–1800* (Augsburg 1930).

[2] In regard to medieval aesthetics, see E. de Bruyne, *Études d'Esthétique médiévale* I–III (Bruges 1946); in regard to architectural aesthetics of modern times, see R. Wittkower, *Architectural Principles in the Age of Humanism* (London ³1962).

[3] The papal resolutions can be found in *CICfontes*, ed. by P. Gasparri and J. Serédi (Rome 1923–39), and in *AAS* (Rome 1909ff.). A selective synopsis in C. Gurlitt, "Kirchen." *Handbuch der Architektur* IV, 8, 1 (Stuttgart 1906), 63ff., 176–81; R. B. Witte, *Das katholische Gotteshaus* (Mainz ²1951), 2ff., and *LThK*² VI, 199–205 (A. Fuchs) and 682–87 (W. Braunfels). The resolutions were often interpreted by provincial councils. For example, the papal request to adhere to tradition (*CIC fontes*, 1164) was interpreted to mean the use of Old Christian, Romanesque, or Gothic styles only, and the cross-shaped ground plan was especially recommended. The last papal instructions are found in the seventh and last chapter of the liturgy constitution of the Second Vatican Council of 1963 and in the subsequent directives and amendments (cf. H. Schnell, "Der neue Kirchenbau und die Konzilsberatungen," *ThG1* 53 [1963] and U. Rapp, O.S.B., *Konzil, Kunst und Künstler. Zum VII. Kapitel der Kiturgiekonstitution* [Frankfurt a. M. 1966]).

[4] E. Kaufmann, *Architecture in the Age of Reason. Baroque and Post-Baroque in England, Italy and France* (Cambridge, Mass. 1955); K. Lankheit, *Der Tempel der Vernunft. Unveröffentlichte Zeichnungen von Étienne-Louis Boullée* (Basel, Stuttgart 1968).

[5] D. Wiebenson, *Sources of Greek Revival Architecture* (London 1969).

their entrances with a Greek temple facade in the form of a portal of columns with a pediment. In Classicism this mixture threatened to obscure the borders of profane architecture and to cloud the sacred purpose.[6] But it also offers the opportunity to find from this vantage point the transition to early Christian architecture.[7]

While the Classicism of the Enlightenment was understandably unable to influence Church art deeply, the sympathy for the Middle Ages emerging from the Romantic countermovement succeeded in defining the sacred art of the entire nineteenth century. This enthusiasm for the Middle Ages, furthered by the corresponding belles lettres,[8] was almost from the start determined by Christianity. But the first beginnings of art are rooted in the secular realm, in the Gothic ruins of the eighteenth century erected in English gardens as symbols of *vanitas* to inspire meditation,[9] or in the Gothicized garden houses which served as temporary shelter for Romantic poets.[10] Wherever enthusiasm for Gothic elements in church buildings was aroused, it was devoid of insight into the sacred character of this architecture. Goethe[11] discovered in 1772 in the facade of the Strasbourg Cathedral a "Babel-thought" of the Promethean architect Erwin von Steinbach, with which the human genius may win his freedom "on the confined and dismal clerics' stage of the *medii aevi.*" The Gothic architecture, once mocked by Vasari as *maniera tedesca,* is now in a positive sense celebrated as German or Germanic architecture, determined by the forces of natural growth and striving to illustrate the majestic and infinite. At first, interpretations of the Gothic

[6] Sainte-Geneviève in Paris, begun in 1764 by Soufflot and completed in 1790 and displaying the facade of a temple, changed its function without special renovations several times. In 1791, the Pantheon was constructed for the great freedom fighters (Mirabeau, Marat, Voltaire, etc.). In 1809 it became a church again, 1830: Pantheon, under Napoleon III: *Basilique Nationale* (1852). After Victor Hugo's death (1885) it again became the Pantheon (M. Petzet, *Soufflots Saint-Geneviève und der französische Kirchenbau des 18. Jahrhunderts* [Berlin 1961]).

[7] Saint-Vincent-de-Paul in Paris (1824–44), by Jakob Ignaz Hittorf, combines a Greek temple facade with a five-nave basilica and straight beams of a Constantine type.

[8] W. H. Wackenroder, *Herzensergießungen eines kunstliebenden Klosterbruders* (Berlin 1997); J. L. Tieck, *Franz Sternbalds Wanderungen* (Berlin 1798); cf. A. Addison, *Romanticism and the Gothic Revival* (Philadelphia 1938); K. Clark, *The Gothic Revival* (London ²1950).

[9] H. Vogel, *Die Ruine in der Darstellung der abendländischen Kunst* (Kassel 1948); A. Kamphausen, *Gotik ohne Gott. Ein Beitrag zur Deutung der Neugotik und des 19. Jahrhunderts* (Tübingen 1952).

[10] P. Cleman, "Strawberry Hill und Wörlitz. Von den Anfängen der Neugotik," *Neue Beiträge deutscher Forschung. Wilhelm Worringer zum 60. Geburtstag,* ed. by E. Fidder (Königsberg 1943), 37–60.

[11] E. Beutler, *Von deutscher Baukunst. Goethes Hymnus auf Erwin von Steinbach. Seine Entstehung und Wirkung* (Munich 1943).

church in a historically adequate and theologically symbolic sense are the exception.[12]

An exemplar of the diverging motives in evaluating Gothic architecture is the story of the restoration of the Cologne Cathedral, which had been in a state of incompletion since the beginning of the sixteenth century. The motives for its completion were very different.[13] The choir, completed in 1322, is seen as an intense image of the forest, which as an element of nature bears witness to the direct manifestation of God,[14] but at the same time is also a reminder of the prehistory of man, who built himself his first hut out of branches and tree trunks, thus creating the Gothic style.[15] Moreover, the cathedral is the "most elevating symbol of eternity,"[16] whereby the term eternity is to be understood in a general philosophical, not in a specific Christian sense. Primarily, however, the cathedral is a document of German history, striving again for national unity after its decline at the end of the Middle Ages and after its wars of independence. In the proclamation inspired by Sulpiz Boisserée and written by Joseph Görres, which appeared on 26 November 1814 in the *Rheinische Merkur,* the Cathedral is seen as "a symbol of the new Empire that we want to build." When the foundation stone was laid in 1842, Friedrich Wilhelm IV celebrated the planned completion as the "work of brotherhood among all Germans and all creeds," and the art historian Franz Kugler saw in it "a unifying sign for all people of the German tongue to gather around."[17] In resuming medieval architecture and in view of Classicism, there is a feeling of progress from heathenism to Christianity, from things Hellenic to things German.[18] Occasionally, the national impulse dominated the

---

[12] F. von Schlegel in his essay "Grundzüge der gotischen Baukunst" of 1804–05, *Sämtliche Werke* VI (Vienna 1846), 182f.

[13] H. Lützeler, *Der Kölner Dom in der deutschen Geistesgeschichte* (Bonn 1948).

[14] G. Forster in his *Ansichten vom Niederrhein u.s.w. 1790* (Berlin 1791); the cathedral as a "work of nature" also in Schelling; H. Lützeler, op. cit., 17.—Concerning nature as a manifestation of God and the most worthy object of Christian art, see H. Schrade, "Die romantische Idee von der Landschaft als höchstem Gegenstande der christlichen Kunst," *Neue Heidelberger Jahrbücher* (1931).

[15] J. Hall, *Essay on the Origin, History, and Principles of Gothic Architecture* (London 1813); cf. also J. Gaus, "Die Urhütte. Über ein Modell in der Baukunst und ein Motiv in der bildenden Kunst," *Wallraf-Richartz-Jahrbuch* 32 (1971), 7–70; Interest in the history of mankind, rather than an aesthetical assessment is the main motive of Seroux d'Agincourt, *Histoire de l'art par les monuments etc.,* 6 vols. (Paris 1812–23).

[16] A. Reichensperger, "Einige Worte über den Dombau von Köln," *Vermischte Schriften über christliche Kunst* (Leipzig 1856), 90.

[17] F. Kugler, *Kleine Schriften* II (Stuttgart 1854), 41. The cathedral in Speyer, restored by King Ludwig of Bavaria, is a national monument.

[18] A. Reichensperger, *Die christlich-germanische Baukunst und ihr Verhältnis zur Gegenwart* (Trier 1852), 56.

Christian medieval spirit to such a degree that there was talk about the victory of the Reformation, especially in view of the active participation of the Protestant Prussian government. One also bewailed as a contradiction the fact that the "slaves of Rome" were permitted to turn the edifice into a "place of Jesuit stupefaction and mendacity." Because of these and similar opinions, the Catholic population of Cologne remained demonstratively absent from the final celebration on 15 August 1880, at the time of the *Kulturkampf*.[19] The first railroad bridge across the Rhine River, built between 1855 and 1859 at the King's wish as a continuation of the cathedral's axis and as a symbol of the new time connecting medieval history and technological progress, was inaugurated by the equestrian statues of Friedrich Wilhelm IV (1861–1862) and Wilhelm I (1867). Through the demolition of two churches and sixty-nine houses, free space was created around the cathedral.

Even though it had been shown in 1830 that Gothic architecture did not originate in Germany but in France,[20] and though it was recognized shortly after that the Cologne Cathedral had been constructed according to the Cathedral of Amiens, Gothic architecture continued to be considered German for some time.[21]

More enduring than the national motive proved to be the perception of the Gothic as a specifically Christian sacral style suited for the construction of churches. Sulpiz Boisserée, Joseph Görres, and August Reichensperger in Germany, A. W. N. Pugin in England,[22] Viollet-le-Duc in France,[23] and many others laid the foundation for the many churches in neo-Gothic style which had to be built to meet the demands

---

[19] H. Lützeler, op. cit., 75.

[20] F. Kugler, *Handbuch der Kunstgeschichte* (Stuttgart ⁵1872).

[21] Georg Dehio's question, whether the German architect of the choir of the Cologne Cathedral also designed the choir of Amiens, demonstrates how scholarly judgements can be obscured by the idea of national rivalries (G. Dehio and H. von Bezold, *Die kirchliche Baukunst des Abendlandes* II [Stuttgart 1901], 276). On the other hand, there is Émile Mâle's statement that all the better parts of the Cologne Cathedral are French, the tasteless parts German ("Studien über die deutsche Kunst," *Monatshefte für Kunstwissenschaft* 10 [1917], 55).

[22] Pugin (1812–52) built more than sixty neo-Gothic churches. Converted in 1834, architect Pugin also wrote theoretical works like *True Principles of Pointed or Christian Architecture* (London 1853) and *An Apology for the Revival of Christian Architecture in England* (London 1843).

[23] Viollet-le-Duc (1814–79) was commissioned to restore many important churches (Notre-Dame and Sainte-Chapelle in Paris, Vézelay, etc.). His ten-volume *Dictionnaire raisonné de l'architecture française du XIᵉ siècle* (Paris 1854–68) was indispensable for a precise knowledge of Gothic construction principles. It was followed by a similar dictionary concerning the interior design of medievel structures. Viollet-de-Duc justified the "progressive character" of the Gothic style, explaining that technically trained laymen (*Hochbauingenieure*), rather than monks trained as craftsmen designed the cathedrals. Therefore his suggestion to call Gothicism *style laïque* (*Dictionnaire raisonné* I, 114).

of a rapidly increasing population. The Cologne Cathedral construction office, managed after 1833 by Ernst Friedrich Zwirner (1802–1861), sent out numerous architects now familiar with Gothic construction principles, who renovated old churches and erected new ones in the Rhineland[24] and elsewhere, and who went to revive construction offices in Strasbourg, Vienna, and elsewhere, or who were appointed to teaching chairs at technical colleges. However, the orthodox neo-Gothic generated by these activities in the second half of the nineteenth century encompassed a certain variety, since the respective geographical situation was more and more taken into consideration. Consequently the French neo-Gothic churches were modeled after the cathedral Gothic of the Île-de-France, such as Saint-Clothilde in Paris, while in Germany, according to native medieval tradition, brick buildings were also customary;[25] and in the Rhineland the so-called transition style of the late Hohenstaufen period was taken into account.

In Italy, the revival of the Gothic was sporadic. The Florentine Cathedral was adorned with a new facade in the style of the fourteenth century (1875–1887); but the Nordic Gothic of the Milan Cathedral was rejected on the grounds of Vasari's negative verdict and particularly because in the Middle Ages numerous German (in the nineteenth century also Austrian) architects were involved in the construction.[26] In 1859 a competition was announced for the modern *Galleria* to be built on the cathedral grounds and dedicated to King Vittorio Emmanuele II. One of the suggestions was to tear down part of the cathedral in order to obtain decent building materials.[27]

For a very long time, the Gothic style was *en vogue* in America. Actually, it was not used until around 1900, and only receded in church construction in the fourth decade of our century. There, as in Germany and England during the Romantic period, many Protestant artists converted for aesthetic reasons. The architect Crom, who, like Pugin in England earlier, wrote many books praising the Gothic, induced the bishop of New York in 1911 to renovate and complete the Cathedral of Saint John the Divine in the Gothic style, even though it was begun in the Romanesque style. Upon Crom's death in 1942, it was not yet completed. The Washington Cathedral did not get its Gothic central cupola until 1963.[28]

---

[24] W. Weyres and A. Mann, *Handbuch zur rheinischen Baukunst des 19. Jahrhunderts, 1800–80* (Cologne 1968).

[25] For example, neo-Gothic brick churches by Conrad Wilhelm Hase of Hannover (1818–1902).

[26] C. Boito, *Il Duomo di Milano e i disegni per la sua facciata* (Milan 1889).

[27] P. Mezzanotte: *Storia di Milano* XV (Milan 1962), 398.

[28] In regard to American neo-Gothic in the twentieth century, see J. Paul, "Chartres in Amerika. Ein Beitrag zur mittelalterlichen Ikonographie der Neuzeit," *Kunstgeschichtliche Studien für Kurt Bauch* (Munich, Berlin 1967), 287–300.

In view of the freedom that church regulations offered by recommending that only the form handed down by Christian tradition be followed,[29] an extensive, partly polemical dispute about the choice of proper style evolved. Reichensperger and many others advocated Gothic because they considered it progressive in contrast to the old Christian and Roman architecture, and they rejected the Renaissance because it was based on heathenism.[30] Others recommended the architecture of the Italian Renaissance, since this era was not a Protestant one and had produced, moreover, outstanding saints.[31] The popular handbook of liturgy by Franz Xaver Thalhofer[32] preferred the Gothic because the German Renaissance was not of sufficient quality. This demonstrates once again how independent of each other art and worship had grown, and how the blending of the two had moved into the realm of the aesthetic and the arbitrary.[33] The question posed by Hübsch in 1837 "In which style shall we build?"[34] was still being asked in 1899.[35]

In Protestantism, the connection to Gothic style was even more definite, having nothing but Gothic examples in mind since the Eisenach Regulations of 1856 had recommended the model of a "historically evolved Christian architecture." But in the first half of the century, the Protestants also used Classical elements and toward the end of the century they built structures copying the Baroque.[36] The Eisenach Regulations of 1908 finally did away with recommendations of a certain style and simply suggested "sincere and noble simplicity in form and color."[37]

In spite of this change around the turn of the century, there is no doubt that, even after a definite rejection of historicism, the Gothic and its elements remained effective in the construction of churches in the twentieth century, not only during the time of Expressionism in Germany, as in the case of Dominikus Böhm,[38] but also in the numerous

[29] At the Fulda Bishops' Conference of 1923, R. B. Witte, op. cit., 6.

[30] A. Reichensperger, "Zur Kennzeichnung der Renaissance," *ZChK* (1890), no. 1.

[31] J. Graus, *Die katholische Kirche und die Renaissance* (Graz 1888).

[32] I (1883), 741ff.

[33] The title of a small book by C. Meyer is significant: *Über das Verhältnis von der Kunst zum Kultus. Ein Wort an alle gebildeten Verehrer der Religion und der Kunst* (Zurich 1837).

[34] Cf. G. Palm, *Von welchen Prinzipien soll die Wahl des Baustyls, insbesondere des Kirchenbaustyls geleitet werden?* (Hamburg 1845).

[35] O. Prill, "In welchem Stile sollen wir bauen?" *ZChK* (1898), 246, 267; (1899), 83, 247.

[36] The conventions of the Protestant Church on church architecture and art taking place regularly from 1896 until today are presented clearly in G. Langmaack, *Evangelischer Kirchenbau im 19. und 20. Jahrhundert* (Kassel 1971), 270ff.

[37] G. Langmaack, op. cit., 290f.

[38] See the large pointed arches in the church of Frielingsdorf of 1927. The designs of A. Bartning for a "star church" (1922) have elements of expressive Gothicism.

Gothic structures after 1950 which incorporated versions of ribbed vaults,[39] rose windows with tracery, and, above all, extensive stained glass.[40]

The definitions of the Christian sacral style of the nineteenth century included, aside from the Gothic and old Christian, Romanesque and, last but not least, Byzantine architecture. Classicism provided a natural transition from old Christian to modern architecture;[41] Romanesque architecture was given attention predominantly in the Rhineland with its many structures from the Hohenstaufen period;[42] Byzantine elements are occasionally found in France.[43] Since historicism was a frequent topic of contemplation in the nineteenth century and since antiquity and medieval Christianity were not always considered opposites, it occasionally happened that one artist would make proposals using both styles for one and the same church.[44] There were also attempts to harmonize the principles of several styles, as was the case in Schinkel's hotly debated but never-realized plans of 1815 for a cathedral commemorating the wars of independence. He designed "this church in the impressive style of old German architecture, whose ultimate perfection is the task of the future after the peak of its development has been interrupted for centuries by a wonderful and benevolent glance back at antiquity, whereby, it seems, the world will be enabled to instill into this art the element which it is lacking for its perfection."[45] In other words, he demanded that the Gothic, which was interrupted by the Renaissance, be improved through the insights into antiquity gained during that period; that a progressive architecture be created.

This eclectic principle had a unique kind of ethos, which became especially effective in the second half of the century. The blending of several styles in ecclesiastical architecture was seen as a simile for Chris-

---

[39] Indicated with tubing in the Liebfrauen Church in Cologne-Mühlheim by Rudolf Schwarz (1955).

[40] W. Weyres and O. Bartning, *Kirchen, Handbuch für den Kirchenbau* (Munich 1959), passim. Indications of Old Christian and Romanesque church architecture remain alive in modern times in the form of semicircular apses, naves arranged in basilical fashion, and free-standing belltowers.

[41] See Saint-Vincent-de-Paul church in Paris, mentioned in n. 7. In Munich the Bonifatius Church of 1835.

[42] A. Mann, *Die Neuromantik* (Cologne 1966).

[43] For instance, Sacre-Cœur in Paris, 1876–1919 (C. Gurlitt, op. cit., 167).

[44] Like Schinkel for the church of Werder in Berlin. In 1818 an English church building society offered (for churches of suburban communities) plans for one and the same spatial layout in Classical, Gothic, and Baroque styles (H. G. Evers, "Kann die historische Kirchenbaukunst des 19. Jahrhunderts als Trivialkunst verstanden werden?" *Triviale Zonen in der religiösen Kunst des 19. Jahrhunderts. Studien zur Philosophie und Literatur des 19. Jahrhunderts,* 15 [Frankfurt a. M. 1971], 196).

[45] P. O. Rave, "Karl Friedrich Schinkel," *Berlin,* part I (Berlin 1939), 196.

tianity, embracing time and space.[46] In secular architecture, it was considered an expression of the cosmopolitan tendency of the nineteenth century with its tremendous progress in the area of technology and with its radiant expansion in all scientific and humanistic disciplines, especially history. Thus, the *Giornale dell'Ingegnere architetto e agronome* of 1853 demanded that all known styles be combined, since only an *architettura composita* as *architettura cosmopolita* could equal the spirit of the new times.[47]

Church Interiors

Similar tendencies can be observed in regard to church interiors of the nineteenth century which conformed to the liberal ecclesiastical regulations. An attempt was made to match the furnishings of the church with the historical style of the architecture. But in the first half of the century, contemporary art concepts were applied, for instance in the use of large frescoes that did not exist in the Nordic medieval Gothic. In this case, the insufficient archeological knowledge of the immobile and mobile furnishings of medieval churches as well as the intention to combine elements of the north and south may have played a role.[48]

In the second half of the century, when architecture also began to copy old plans, the interior design appeared more and more orthodox, thanks to the old book collections and drawings published in the meantime.[49] Numerous collections of medieval ecclesiastical treasures, obtained since the secularization, were created with the express goal of offering adequate models to the artisans. This was the foundation for many of our craft museums.[50] One even began to follow the instructions of medieval treatises in order to make utensils and tools in the proper style.[51]

In architecture, Romantic enthusiasm for the Middle Ages responded to secular and rational Classicism with a revival of the Gothic. Likewise, young painters from various countries reacted with new concepts to the

[46] The critique of the French Academy of 1845 regarding the use of the Gothic style for Saint-Clothilde church in Paris (H. G. Evers, op. cit., 183–90).

[47] P. Mezzanotte, op. cit., 367.

[48] Cf. Schinkel's statement, n. 5.

[49] A noteworthy collection is, besides Seroux d'Agincourt (see n. 15), Viollet-le-Duc, *Dictionnaire raisonné du mobibilier français de l'époque carolingienne à la renaissance,* 6 vols. (Paris 1858–75).

[50] A late example is the collection begun in 1867 by Prebendary Professor Dr. Alexander Schnütgen (1843–1918), the basis of today's Schnütgen Museum in Cologne. These projects kept the craftsmen as well as the pastors who commissioned them in mind (A. Thomas, "Die liturgische Erneuerungsbewegung im Bistum Trier unter Bischof von Hommer," *Archiv für mittelalterliche Kirchengeschichte* 15 [1961], 208–38).

[51] Viollet-le-Duc, "Le grand encensoir de Théophile," *Annales archéologiques* VIII (1848), 95–104.

aesthetic dogmas originating in antiquity which they had learned at the academies. They turned to the "divine" Raphael and the older Italian paintings of the quattrocento and trecento, to the Germans Dürer and Holbein, and to old German paintings. Subsequently, Johann Friedrich Overbeck (1789–1869) and similarly minded people founded a Saint Luke Fraternity (1809) in Vienna in opposition to the local academy. The society soon moved to Rome and settled in the isolated monastery Sant'Isidoro in voluntary monastic communion. They wanted to rejuvenate painting on the basis of religion. Because of their beards and long hair they were known in Rome as "Nazarenes." Like the poets and architects, many of them converted. Franz Pforr, Ludwig Richter, Schnorr von Carolsfeld, Johann Führich, Philipp Veith (the stepson of Friedrich Schlegel) and the most important among them, Peter von Cornelius (1783–1867), took up the themes of Christian iconography, whose biblical stories and medieval legends matched the newly awakened sense of history.[52] Especially popular were motives in which medieval piety and the new concept of nature as a divine manifestation could be combined, like the legend of Saint Genevieve, who, according to the tragedy which Tieck had devoted to her in 1799, was illustrated in numerous pictures, graphic series, and, most elaborately, in frescoes by Puvis de Chavannes (1874–1878) in the church in Paris dedicated to her. The popular hermit theme of Caspar David Friedrich's gloomy pictures with monks and ruins, down to the last pictures at the end of the century combined nature and religion, historical contemplation and private worship.[53] It should not be ignored that the general trend toward genre in the art of the nineteenth century included religious art. In spite of its sentimental or even trivial effect, it created a type of picture which, according to its function, can indeed be compared with the devotional paintings of the fourteenth century. Theological didacticism in church art was less prominent than sensitive private piety. The Nazarenes placed figurative Christian stories in the foreground, while in the Protestant north nature inspired religious devotion.[54]

---

[52] Raphael's work inspired great allegorical compositions. Secular themes featured national history and material from rediscovered medieval epics. A first great commission of this kind was the painting of the Casino Massimo in Rome (1819–30). Goethe opposed the combination of religious and national elements in his essay "Neu-deutsche religiös-patriotische Kunst," which was largely written by Heinrich Meyer in 1817.

[53] H. Ost, "Einsiedler und Mönche in der deutschen Malerei des 19. Jahrhunderts," *Bonner Beiträge zur Kunstwissenschaft,* ed. by H. von Einem and H. Lützeler, vol. 11 (Düsseldorf 1971).

[54] Of interest are *Der Mönch am Meer* and the altar in Tetschen by C. D. Friedrich (both 1808). In regard to landscapes in religious concepts, see the essay mentioned in n. 14 by H. Schrade and H. von Einem, "Die Symbollandschaft der deutschen Romantik," *Katalog Klassizismus und Romantik,* Nürnberg, Germanisches Nationalmuseum (1966), 28–38.

Not only thematic-iconographic preferences, but also those for a particular genre became recognizable. The monumental art of mural painting, which had disappeared from the churches during the period of Classicism, was revived again. They wanted to "fill the lonely chapels and high cathedrals with life" and so designed large sequences of frescoes with pictures of biblical stories. Worth mentioning are those frescoes that Peter von Cornelius painted after 1840 in the Ludwig Church in Munich, the murals by Johann Schraudolph in the Cathedral of Speyer (1845–1853)[55] and the frescoes by students of Wilhelm von Schadow in the Appolinaris Church in Remagen (1843–1854).[56]

The paintings of the Nazarenes soon fell below their original level of quality due to their increasing popularity. The impersonal schematicism of their composition and the flat brush technique conquered some of the art academies in Germany, but in view of the new movement of Realism around the middle of the century and later Impressionism, the Nazarenes found their art more and more limited to the often trivial problems of Christian utilitarian art. Likewise, in Italy, the *puristi,* comparable to the Nazarenes, had become academic and could not endure the new trends.[57]

To be mentioned in France are the early Ingres, Hippolyte Flandrin (1809–1864),[58] and Pierre Cecil Puvis de Chavannes (1824–1889), who painted the great Genevieve series in the Pantheon in Paris (1874–1878). Puvis de Chavannes started a new style, which had an effect on the church art of the twentieth century via French post-Impressionism and Symbolism, represented primarily by Maurice Denis (1870–1943).[59] There are connections between Maurice Denis and Father Desiderius Lenz (1832–1928), the founder of the art school in Beuron,[60] and the two symbolists Jan Toorop (1858–1928) and Jan Thorn-Prikker (1868–1932), whose frescoes, mosaics, and glass paintings laid an im-

---

[55] There are 123 paintings with 470 more than life-size figures; two thirds fell victim to the "restoration" of the following years (A. Verbeek, "900 Jahre Speyrer Dom," *Festschrift zum Jahrestage der Domweihe 1061* [Speyer 1961], 138–64).

[56] The Apollinaris Church, erected between 1839 and 1843 by cathedral architect Ernst Friedrich Zwirner on a wooded hill near the Rhine River, enjoyed the highest reputation in the nineteenth century, because as a neo-Gothic structure with large mural paintings and as a memorial fitting the surrounding landscape, it fulfilled the art ideals of the time.—There is a drawing by Schinkel (Berlin), in which he had transferred the Milan Cathedral to hills close to Trieste.

[57] G. Brundu, "Preraffaelismo e Purismo," *Enciclopedia universale dell'Arte* X, 943–48.

[58] He did the paintings in the church of Saint-Vincent-de-Paul and in the church of Saint-Germain-des-Prés in Paris (1854–63).

[59] P. Jamot, *Maurice Denis* (Paris 1945).

[60] See below.

portant foundation, in connection with a new church architecture, for the religious art of Expressionism.[61]

The relationship between nineteenth century art and the new styles after 1900 in France can also be found in England, where Edward Burnes-Jones (1833–1898) founded the Society of the Pre-Raphaelites, following the model of the Saint Luke Fraternity of the Nazarenes and adopting many of their religious and moral principles as well.[62] But in contrast to the Nazarenes, this community of artists, including Millais, Hunt, Rossetti, and others, kept in touch with the progressive forces of its time. They also adhered to the Nazarenes' ideals of national and religious restoration and often made use of sentimental and symbolic genre painting, but at the same time they demanded "truth to nature" and were thus able to keep contact with the basically secular Realism of the middle of the century.[63] It became customary to paint outdoors and even in religious paintings precision of archeological detail was demanded. William Holman Hunt (1827–1910), the most important among the artists, went to Palestine for several years in order to familiarize himself with the location for his biblical pictures. The century of the exact sciences, photography, and historical "truth" also challenged religious historical painting to provide reliable information.[64] "Not Christ, the supreme judge, but Jesus, the son of the Jewess Maria" was to be represented.[65] Even in the progressive nineteenth century, the traces of the Pre-Raphaelites did not fade, in spite of the early dissolution of the Society, because at the same time their patrons John Ruskin and William Morris pioneered the great art revolution of 1900 and ushered some of the principles of the Pre-Raphaelite artists, such as craftsmanship and teamwork, into the new era.

In Germany in the second half of the century, an area of church art arose that was to have an effect in the future. Not unimpressed by the art of the Nazarenes, but keeping an apparent distance, Desiderius Lenz

---

[61] M. Janssen, *Schets over het Leven en enkele Werken von Jan Toorop* (Amsterdam 1928); A. Hoff, *Thorn-Prikker und die neuere Glasmalerei* (Essen 1925).

[62] N. Pevsner, "Gemeinschaftsideale unter den bildenden Künstlern des 19. Jahrhunderts," *Deutsche Vierteljahresschrift für Literaturwissenschaft und Geistesgeschichte* 9 (1931), 125–54; W. E. Fredeman, *Pre-Raphaelism. A bibliocritical study* (Cambridge, Mass. 1965).

[63] In Germany realism took effect in regard to religious art only in Protestant painting (e.g. Fritz von Uhde, 1848 to 1911, and Eduard von Gebhardt, 1838 to 1925).

[64] St. Waetzoldt, "Bemerkungen zur christlich-religiösen Malerei in der zweiten Hälfte des 19. Jahrhunderts," *Triviale Zonen in der religiösen Kunst des 19. Jahrhunderts. Studien zur Philosophie und Literatur des 19. Jahrhunderts* 15 (Frankfurt a. M. 1971), 30–91.

[65] C. Gurlitt, *Die deutsche Kunst des 19. Jahrhunderts* (Berlin 1900), 545.

had founded an art school in the Benedictine monastery of Beuron. This school was intent on creating in the monastic realm the liturgical unity of an artistically designed space, of music regenerated through the study of Gregorian sources, and of the devotional ceremony. They wanted to replace the contemporary principle of *l'art pour l'art* with the humble *l'art pour Dieux*.[66] They were convinced that the stylization of artwork (primarily in abstract art, using "universal shapes" like the equilateral triangle) gave the composition an air of sacred solemnity and quiet by suppressing the individual and allowing man to submerge himself in God. Intending to create "timeless" art, they used elements from Byzantine art, from the mosaics of Ravenna, and from Egyptian murals to produce the Maurus Chapel near Beuron (1868–1870), the furnishings of the Emmaus monastery in Prague (since 1880), the furnishings of the abbey of Maria Laach, populated again by Beuron in 1892, and the grave of Saint Benedict and Saint Scholastica in the vault of Monte Cassino (1899–1913).[67] The contemporary interest in Art Nouveau, and also in the beginnings of the liturgical movement, the intense encounter of Maurice Denis and Desiderius Lenz, and their collaboration with Paul Verkade (1868–1946),[68] as well as the last vestiges of the Pre-Raphaelites and the Dutch and Belgian symbolists created an art circle between 1880 and 1910 that was to become the basis for an artistic renewal in the twentieth century. The significance of the art school in Beuron lies, last but not least, in the fact that the church interior was not exclusively determined any longer by murals and glass paintings, as was the case in the previous century, where any other kind of design was considered a "craft" and entrusted to craftsmen's skills. This school subjected everything, even textiles, paraments, liturgical utensils, and furniture to one unifying design concept. This was a direction which the church art of the twentieth century carried on, paying particular attention to the vessel, which is so important for the liturgy.

With his strict rejection of all art in the style of Giotto, his rejection of all expressive phenomena of the past (El Greco), and of the present,[69] Desiderius Lenz overextended himself, causing his former disciples in the twenties to disperse. Subsequently, polemical treatises appeared (as in the nineteenth century) which, in view of the broad framework of

---

[66] D. Lenz, O.S.B., *Zur Ästhetik der Beuroner Schule* (Vienna 1912).

[67] J. Kreitmaier, S.J., *Beuroner Kunst. Eine Ausdrucksform der christlichen Mystik* (Freiburg i. Br. 1923).

[68] W. Verkade, *Die Unruhe zu Gott* (Freiburg i. Br. ²1923). Verkade, born in the Netherlands, felt close to Gauguin, Sérusier, and Vuillard and joined Beuron in 1894 after his conversion.

[69] For example, Jan Thorn-Prikker (1868–1932) and Ludwig Gies (1887–1966).

ecclesiastical regulations, turned against Expressionism in general and demanded a harmonic Naturalism,[70] or accepted certain elements of the art form called "expressive,"[71] but which would not permit anything unusual or shocking.[72] Finally, there were several advocates of absolute Expressionism[73] who originated, in connection with the simultaneous renovation of church architecture, the truly modern features of church art. They made possible the appreciation of religious works created outside the area of church art, like paintings by Georges Rouault, Emil Nolde, or Schmidt-Rottluff. The appreciation of individual creative achievements provided the chance to entrust even non-Catholic artists with tasks related to church art.[74]

In regard to sculpture and plastic art of the time in question, we have to say that it was bound to play a more important role than painting and that the creations of Thorwaldsen (1786–1844) and Dannecker (1758–1841) largely determined the conceptions of Christ. Through Neo-Gothic, the cathedral construction offices inspired a more thorough study of medieval sculpture of the thirteenth and fourteenth centuries, since the Cologne Cathedral, for example, required a number of new figures for its completion. The historical assessment of these masters, who also created tomb art, has not progressed very far due to the fact that they had to subject their work to the unity of the entire structure. Iconographically significant for furnishing Neo-Gothic churches in the nineteenth century with sculptures is the solution offered in the typological programs of the Middle Ages. Aside from characters of the Old Testament,[75] those figures of the Passion and Salvation of Christ are preferred who impress in a special way through their human fate.[76] Remarkable in regard to church sculpture is a certain phenomenon that occurs rarely in older art after the sixteenth century: large groups of several figures on an altar without any retable

---

[70] P. R. Boving, O.F.M., *Kirche und moderne Kunst* (Bonn 1922).

[71] Like medieval book design, Grünewald, El Greco, Gauguin.

[72] J. Kreitmaier, S.J., *Von Kunst und Künstlern* (Freiburg i. Br. 1926). The contemporary artists recommended in this book usually combine expressionist elements and features of the Nazarenes.

[73] For example, August Hoff with his support of Ludwig Gies and Thorn-Prikker.

[74] Cf. P. Regamey, *Kirche und Kunst im 20. Jahrhundert* (Graz, Vienna, Cologne 1954; French 1923). Le Corbusier, though not Catholic, was commissioned to build the pilgrimage church of Notre-Dame-du-Haut in Ronchamp (1950–55).

[75] Like the relief figures of Johannes Benk in the Votive Church in Vienna (1873).

[76] Goethe's suggestion of 1830 for a series of sculptures including Christ and twelve figures from the Old and the New Testament is not based on theological meaning but on human ethics (manuscript from his literary legacy [1830], printed in vol. 13 of the Artemis edition of 1954, 1066–72)

or frame, giving expression to the idea of the memorial, which was preferred by and characteristic of the nineteenth century.[77]

New Art Forms

Around the turn of the century, an art revolution caused the rejection of historicism because not the traditional, but the "living" form was deemed more effective.[78] This change occurred in church construction later than in secular architecture, because ecclesiastical resolutions and recommendations were continuing obstacles.[79] Moreover, many worthy forms of past church architecture—like the semicircular apse, the basilican succession of steps, and extensive glass paintings—retained their fascination and continued to be frequent design elements.

A first indication of the change in attitude is the fact that the utility of the space used for the purposes of liturgy—for the celebration of the Eucharist for administering the sacraments and for preaching—always having been required by ecclesiastical decrees, was put more and more into the foreground after 1900. The statement, made frequently after 1896 by Cornelius Gurlitt, that the liturgy is the architect of the church,[80] was taken up by the Protestants at the Second Church Architecture Convention (1906) in Dresden, which was connected with an exhibition of appropriate liturgical utensils.[81] Gurlitt's idea also became the main motto of the simultaneous liturgical movement, which intended to increase the congregation's active participation in the liturgy. The consequences for church construction, especially for the spatial arrangement, were impressive, particularly since the new structures were usually community churches, while medieval church construction (a model for historicism) was essentially determined by monastic churches, in which the needs of the choir service prevailed and the question of the congregation's ability to see the ceremony (around the

---

[77] For example, the group of Mary Magdalene with angels of 1841 by Carlo de Marochetti, which is located on the high altar of the Sainte-Madeleine church in Paris (R. Zeitler, "Die Kunst des 19. Jahrhunderts," *Propyläen-Kunstgeschichte* 11 [Berlin 1966], ill. 333b).

[78] "The most essential, most indispensable requirement to assure the beauty of an art work is the life which radiates from the material in which it is created" (H. van de Velde, *Die Belebung des Stoffes als Prinzip der Schönheit* [1910] reprinted in H. van de Velde, *Zum neuen Stil. Aus seinen Schriften ausgewählt und eingeleitet von H. Curjel* [Munich 1955], 175).

[79] See *CICfontes*, 1164, ART. 1: "The ordinaries need to take care that in church construction those forms are preserved which are part of the Christian tradition." A decree of the archdiocese of Cologne recommended in 1912 to use the "Romanesque, Gothic transition-style."

[80] C. Gurlitt, *Kirchen*, 83.

[81] W. Weyres, O. Bartning, *Kirchen*, 209f.

altar) and hear the oral part of the service, was never taken into consideration. However, the exclusive purpose of the church as a church for the community as well as for the emancipation of the middle class and the democritization of political life has strengthened the urgency of the new demands.[82]

In accord with these tendencies of the liturgical movement was the simultaneous general architectural theory whose highest maxim required that justice be done to function, material, and construction.[83] The same perspective of religious and artistic reform around the turn of the century evolved from the ability to understand and appreciate any kind of form, including the liturgy, as an organic entity; an ability that was furthered by the development of sensitivity and perceptual psychology in the second half of the nineteenth century.[84] In regard to church architecture, the new maxims meant that quality and effectiveness of the final creation were no longer considered dependent on their approval by history. At first, the fixation on the Gothic style[85] was criticized; later on, the slightest historical reminiscence fell victim to objection. The goal and the basis for evaluation are not the precise correspondence with the architectural model but, on the contrary, the impact of the new building materials of the advancing technological age on form and construction. Thus, the use of iron for support beams and ribbed vaults in the Church of Saint Eugene in Paris (1854–1855)[86] or the use of a reinforced concrete framework in the Church of Saint Jean de Montmartre (begun 1894)[87] were praised as progressive accomplishments, even though the innovations in these basically Neo-Gothic churches came about principally for practical and financial reasons. Nevertheless, the abandonment of the exclusive use of raw stones was

---

[82] Ibid., 95ff. Regarding the influence of the liturgical movement, see W. Braunfels, *LThK²* VI, 682–87, and A. Fuchs, ibid., 199–205. Epoch-making for understanding the new liturgy: R. Guardini, *Vom Geist der Liturgie* (Freiburg i. Br. 1922); cf. also R. Schwarz, *Vom Bau der Kirche* (Würzburg 1938, Heidelberg 1947) and T. Klauser, *Richtlinien für die Gestaltung des Gotteshauses aus dem Geist der römischen Liturgie* (Münster i. W. 1955). In Protestantism: O. Bartning, *Vom neuen Kirchenbau* (Berlin 1919).

[83] N. Pevsner, *Wegbereiter moderner Formgebung* (Hamburg 1957; Engl. 1946); S. Giedion, *Raum, Zeit, Architektur. Die Entstehung einer neuen Tradition* (Ravensburg 1964; Engl. 1941); G. Bandmann, "Der Wandel in der Materialbewertung in der Kunsttheorie des 19. Jahrhunderts," *Beiträge zur Theorie der Künste im 19. Jahrhundert,* ed. by H. Koopmann, J. A. Schmoll (Eisenwerth) (Frankfurt a. M. 1971), 129–60.

[84] Aloys Goergen speaks of "devotional form" (in W. Weyres, O. Bartning, *Kirchen,* 14ff.).

[85] When Gothic construction principles were demanded for the construction of the cathedral of Liverpool, there was opposition against this narrow-mindedness (C. Gurlitt, *Kirchen,* 66ff.).

[86] By L. A. Boileau (1812–96); N. Pevsner, *Wegbereiter,* 81.

[87] By A. de Baudot; N. Pevsner, *Wegbereiter,* 85.

regretted. However, the church of Notre-Dame de Raincy, built by Auguste Perret (1874–1954) in 1923 with visible ferroconcrete, was intended to show off its innovations, and the contractor, Abbé Nègre, decided: "A paroisse jeune édifice d'esprit neuf!"

This process of emancipation of formerly profane materials and related construction principles, which may no longer be obscured by traditional decorations, has not ceased yet,[88] even though, as mentioned above, the aftereffects of individual historical forms and formulas can still be observed. These allusions and reminders, however, turn into pliable elements in the hands of the individual architect who does not feel obligated any longer to the theological symbolism of the structure and its parts, but tries to transcend the material composition of the church by means of the individually designed form and to instill it with "sacred poetry."[89] The sacred character of the edifice is, therefore, created by the individual's sensitive interpretation of form. The natural conflict between ecclesiastical traditionalism, which does not allow, for example, "unusual" pictures and demands consideration of the *formae a traditione christiana receptae et artis sacrae leges,*[90] and the individuality of the artist are thus resolved in favor of the artist, at least as long as his creation complies with the demands of the liturgy. Naturally, the new demands of the liturgy (in regard to church architecture: abolition of the choir rails and altar pieces, new seating arrangements for the congregation and relatively free ground plans, abolition of the multiplicity of altars and much more)[91] was subject to the changes in theological concepts, which, in turn, are not independent of the general tendencies of the time. This opened up welcome opportunities for change to contemporary church architecture. However, this change, no longer encumbered by traditionalism, according to which the church structure belonged to the external aspects of the liturgy,"[92] entailed threatening consequences for churches of the past which are still in use today and stand in high esteem as art works.[93] Thus, according to a report in 1963

---

[88] F. Pfammater, *Betonkirchen* (Zurich 1948).

[89] R. Schwarz, *Vom Bau der Kirche,* passim.

[90] *CICfontes* ART. 1279, 1164.

[91] T. Klauser, op. cit.; W. Weyres, O. Bartning, op. cit.; U. Rapp, op. cit. It has been noted occasionally that these demands can be compared to those during the period of the Enlightenment (W. Weyres. O. Bartning, op. cit., 88ff.) and that church architecture thus began to approach Protestant styles; for the Protestants, traditions are of less importance, but they have always kept the needs of the congregation in regard to the liturgy's visibility and audibility in mind.

[92] Thus, in ART. 128 of the resolutions regarding chapter VII of the liturgy constitution of the Second Vatican Council of 1963 (U. Rapp, op. cit., 83).

[93] G. Bandmann, "Der Kirchenbau der Gegenwart und die Vergangenheit," *Kunst und Kirche* XXIX (1966), 51–56, 122–25.

on the previous decade by the state curator of Westphalia, Hermann Busen, the congregation of an important Gothic Catholic church in Westphalia proposed in 1953 to lift the choir by seven steps, "in order to do justice to the newest liturgical insights regarding the idea of Christ the King," and in 1962, the same congregation requested that the choir "be dropped by seven steps, and to move the altar forward by fifteen meters in order to follow the newest liturgical understanding of the concept of the circumstance."[94]

In church architecture, the new principles of architectural theory, as aforementioned, succeeded less swiftly than in secular architecture. An early example of the attempt to bring form "to life" is the continuing construction of a church in Barcelona which was begun in 1867 and was dedicated to the Holy Family. The project was carried out by Antonio Gaudí (1852–1926), who used a Neo-Gothic ground plan and stylized the historical elements according to Art Nouveau, taking them to new heights of expression.[95]

Only after 1920 did Germany and France build churches that corresponded to the altered demands. The early churches of Dominikus Böhm,[96] the Antonius Church of Karl Moser in Basel (1927), the Corpus Christi Church of Rudolf Schwarz in Aachen (1930), and the aforementioned Notre Dame de Raincy were the models for the many new structures after World War II,[97] which the original artists of the twenties helped to a large extent to build.[98]

Since about 1960, new architects took their place who were likewise disciples of the aesthetic maxims of modern times, but who were not compelled by the same need for expression as were their predecessors, who had been imprinted with the spirit of the youth movement of 1919–1933. Moreover, the need and the capability for worship seem to have diminished as well.[99]

---

[94] H. Busen, *Westphalen* 41 (1963), 21.

[95] J. Bergós, *Antoni Gaudí, l'hombre i l'obra* (Barcelona 1954); H. G. Evers, *Vom Historismus zum Funktionalismus* (Baden-Baden 1967), 61f. He realized in the building his own symbolism, hardly based on tradition. The west side was to be dedicated to Christ's majesty, the north side to his passion, the south side to his youth. The middle tower and the four surrounding towers were to mean Christ and the Evangelists, the choir tower the Virgin Mary. Only the south side was completed when Gaudí died.

[96] Neu-Ulm, 1925–26; Frielingsdorf, 1927; Saint Engelbert in Cologne-Riehl, 1933.

[97] W. Weyres, O. Bartning, *Kirchen,* passim.

[98] Good summaries in W. Weyres, O. Bartning, *Kirchen;* J. Pichard, *Les églises nouvelles à travers le monde* (Paris 1960).

[99] H. Schnell, "Kirchenbau im Wandel. 'Was ist eine Kirche?'," *Das Münster* 25 (1972), 2. The book by H. Schnell, *Der Kirchenbau des 20. Jahrhunderts in Deutschland* (Munich, Zurich 1973) is in the process of publication and could not be studied, though it covers many issues presented here.

The resolutions of the Second Vatican Council regarding Chapter VII of the liturgical constitution of 4 December 1963, which refrained from dependence on a certain historical sacred style (ARTICLE 123) and desired the structure to be an "external aspect of the liturgy," "dignified and functional" (ART. 128), confirm what has been in existence for a long time and is possibly facing another change even now.

Teaching and Theology

CHAPTER 20

The Encyclical Aeterni Patris

The encyclical *Aeterni Patris* of 4 August 1879[1] was not just a specific doctrine about the philosophical and theological orientation of Catholic schools, but also the foundation of the entire program that Leo XII wanted to pursue in his pontificate. One can easily refer all subsequent doctrines and activities to this document. Otto Willmann called this encyclical the "ripe fruit of spontaneous regeneration attempts";[2] it reiterated earlier efforts to continue not just any form of medieval scholasticism, but specifically revive the philosophy of Thomas Aquinas.[3] At first, the program concerned the Catholic Church only, and Franz Erhle prognosticated correctly when he remarked that for those "who renounced Christ and his Church the word of Christ's deputy would fade away like the voice of one crying in the wilderness."[4] However, the encyclical did, indeed, initiate a philosophical movement whose most important representatives were able to revive Aquinas as one of the greatest thinkers of Hellenic-Occidental philosophy. To follow the encyclical and refer to Thomas Aquinas himself required tedious historical research. But philosophical thought itself also had to internalize the true work of Aquinas, that is, to include it in the philosophical process. Thus, the encyclical *Aeterni Patris* contains two aspects: It speaks from tradition, but this tradition must be revived in order to be able to do justice to the problems of the modern world.[5]

The heading of the encyclical reads: *De philosophia christiana ad mentem sancti Thomae Aquinatis Doctoris angelici in scholis catholicis instauranda.* Of this "Christian philosophy" and its creator, Thomas Aquinas (died 1274), Pope Innocent VI, six hundred years later, is

---

[1] *Acta Leonis* I, 255–84.

[2] *Geschichte des Idealismus* (Braunschweig ²1907), 908.

[3] In Perugia, Cardinal G. Pecci, his brother Giuseppe (Jesuit), and several Dominicans founded the Accademia San Tommaso.

[4] In F. Pelster, op. cit., 38.

[5] ". . . encyclique, traditionaliste en un sens mais assez révolutionaire par rapport aux routines antérieures": R. Aubert, *Nouvelle Histoire de l'Église* (in preparation).

quoted as having said: Aside from its "canonical doctrine," this philoso-phy distinguished itself from all others by its peculiar vocabulary, its *modus docendi,* and its truthfulness, so that those who followed it never left the path of truth, and those who rejected it became suspect (*de veritate suspectus*). Thomas alone (*unus*) succeeded in overcoming all er-rors of previous times and in providing "invincible weapons" to combat future ones. This school was replaced by the method of a "a certain new way of philosophy" (*nova quaedam philosophiae ratio*), which, however, did not have the desired effect. Instead, philosophical directions have increased to a large extent, causing doubt and finally errors. Even Catholic philosophers, eager to imitate, have fallen victim to this revival mania, instead of replenishing the "inheritance of ancient wisdoms." This does not exclude making use of the treasure of new thoughts in order to perfect this philosophy (*novorum inventorum opes ad excolendam philosophiam*). Later, in regard to natural sciences, Innocent VI said that the Scholastics had learned that human intelligence could only be ele-vated to the capacity of knowing spiritual beings by way of the sensible world; they had also studied nature with great interest, as Albertus Magnus proved. This and statements by natural scientists themselves allow the conclusion that Scholastic philosophy has nothing to counter it. The *artes belles* and the *artes liberales* also are at home in this philoso-phy.[6]

By reviving the philosophy of Thomas Aquinas, the encyclical claims to offer a universal solution to all problems of the modern world, last but not least for social problems: Whatever Thomas Aquinas taught concerning the true nature of freedom and the divine origin of authority possessed an "invincible power" to overcome those principles of the "new law" (i.e., revolution) which harm order and public welfare. Scholastic philosophy could be the remedy because Thomas Aquinas differentiated properly between reason and faith and, at the same time, combined the two in "friendship" and because he perfected reason to the utmost degree, so that it could not easily be improved. From this, the encyclical concludes, the rationalists could be led to faith against their resistance, provided they were taught the highest rationality of Thomistic philosophy. "Aside from the supernatural assistance of God," nothing is as effective against error as this philosophy.[7]

The encyclical clearly differentiates between the philosophy of Thomas Aquinas and that phase of Scholasticism in which the philoso-phers proceeded *nimia subtilitate,* referring to the period of decline of the *disputatio.* The encyclical suggests that the wisdom of Thomas

---

[6] *Acta Leonis* I, 273f., 276, 277f., 280ff.
[7] Ibid., 274, 279.

Aquinas be drawn from other sources. But the development of Thomistic philosophy is described as a totally continuous process, leading smoothly from the old Christian apologists via Augustine to culmination in Aquinas, to whom we must return. Modern questions should be incorporated and the doctrine should be refined, but the intellectual world was perfected in the thirteenth century (in a classical sense). *Aeterni Patris* refers to everything, to society and politics, to the natural sciences and aesthetics; however, it leaves out the problem of history, as contemporary Neo-Scholasticism generally continued to do.[8] It is remarkable that the famous historian of Scholasticism, Franz Ehrle, in his commentary on *Aeterni Patris* (his first great work), should present the historical development toward Thomas Aquinas as uninterrupted progress (in accord with the encyclical); later, however, when dealing with the subsequent fate of Thomas's work and the history of Scholasticism, he expressed his historical appreciation for the pro and con of the struggle, no matter how Thomas, as the *princeps,* is evaluated. Ehrle emphasized most of all that the older Spanish scholastics of the sixteenth century were "for the most part intelligent, independent scholars, not inclined for reasons of mere piety to close themselves to the challenges of good arguments, and far removed from the kind of devotion which was to become characteristic of the newer Dominican school after Báñez." It should be noted that the interests of the order were involved in this matter; yet this commentary from 1880 shows that the Thomistic renascence was interpreted as a historical, creative process, not as a classical copy.[9] By commissioning the edition of St. Thomas (*Editio Leonina*), appearing since 1882, Leo XIII earned significant and everlasting credit in the field of historical Thomas scholarship.[10] Unfortunately, understanding Thomas as an entity removed from his historical context (which later led to canonical regulation regarding the instruction in Catholic schools) partly prohibited a philosophical and thus a real acquisition of Aquinas.[11]

---

[8] The philosophical pioneers in Italy were the Jesuits Taparelli d'Azeglio (died 1862) and mainly M. Liberatore (died 1892; his chief work 1840/42), who also dealt with social philosophy. That "its position is weakened by a (subconscious) rationalistic tint" (O. H. Pesch, *LThK*[2] X, 160) continues to be a basic problem in Neo-Scholasticism (P. Dezza, *All'origini del Neotomismo* [Milan 1940], 65–73).

[9] In F. Pelster, op. cit., 63–89.—A biographical sketch of F. Ehrle: 191–202.

[10] The weaknesses which resulted from the speed with which the edition of the first volumes was prepared were avoided by the Dutch C. Suermondt, O.P., who collaborated after 1919 (G. F. Rossi, *Il 4° pioniere della commissione leonina, C. S.* [Piacenza 1954]).

[11] *CICfontes,* 1366, ART. 2, requires that philosophy and theology are to be taught "according to the method, doctrine, and principles" of Thomas Aquinas. The definition of Aquinas's historical position was not facilitated by this requirement. "Research on the

Following the *Constitutio de fide catholica* of the First Vatican Council, the significance of true philosophy for theology was strongly emphasized. This is evident in the title of the encyclycal *De philosophia christiana*. Quoting Clement of Alexandria, the encyclical states that the doctrine of the Savior, being God's wisdom and in and of itself perfect, can not acquire more force through Greek philosophy, but by means of the proper philosophy the truth of the revelation could be defended. Moreover, it maintains that the use of philosophy compelled theology to attain the character, the appearance, and the spirit of a true science (*requiritur philosophiae usus, ut sacra Theologia naturam, habitum, ingeniumque verae scientiae suscipiat atque induat*).[12] This feature of theology is based mainly on the fact that the Neo-Scholasticism of the period when the encyclical was written arrived at theology via philosophy,[13] causing Neo-Scholastic theology to be largely characterized by the application of the terminological tools of the Neo-Scholastic philosophy,[14] at least until Biblical theology forced its way in the course of the twentieth century.

Stubbornly and energetically, Leo XIII implemented his encyclical. On 18 January 1880, he ordered Cardinals A. de Luca, Simeoni, and Zigliara, O.P., to undertake the editing of the works of Aquinas, as well as the commentaries by Cajetan (1507–22), who was (even by Neo-Scholastics) considered the definite expositor of Thomas, thus making it difficult to dispute his authority by using Thomas himself. In May of the same year, under the presidency of Giuseppe Pecci, the Pope's brother, the Accademia Romana di San Tommaso was opened and well funded in order to enable it to educate the next generation. The foundation became the model for the Catholic world. Leo XIII emphatically supported the theologians of his program: in 1880 he appointed his former student Francesco Satolli professor of dogmatics at the Pontifical Urban College of the Propagation of the Faith; G. Cornoldi, S.J., was called by the Pope from Bologna to help found the Academy; after 1881 S.

---

historical context of Aquinas's work begins at the end of the nineteenth century and soon . . . makes tremendous progress; however, for decades it remains, amazingly, without any influence on the systematic interpretation of Aquinas, especially when it threatens to question the absolute value of Aquinas and the presumed total identity of his doctrine with Church doctrine" (O. H. Pesch, ibid. [op. cit. in n. 8]).

[12] *Acta Leonis* I, 262, 263.

[13] Leo XIII himself had studied philosophy and theology with G. Perrone and F. Patrizi at the Roman College. Perrone (1794–1876) was friends with H. Newman and influenced by Möhler in his doctrine of tradition. He was less inclined toward theological speculation than toward the positive, apologetic method and belongs among the founders of Neo-Scholasticism with his *Praelectiones theologicae* (1835–42) (W. Kasper, *Die Lehre von der Tradition in der Römischen Schule* [Freiburg i. Br. 1962], 29–181).

[14] G. Söhngen, *LThK²* VII, 923.

Schiffini, S.J., taught mainly philosophy at the Gregoriana; after 1885 L. Billot, S.J., taught theology; in 1886 C. Mazzella, S.J., from 1878 dogmatist at the Gregoriana, was appointed cardinal. In 1884, at papal request, the University of Louvain established a teaching chair for Thomistic philosophy, which was first occupied by D. Mercier, and developed one of the most important centers of creative Neo-Scholasticism. However, D. Palmieri, S.J., after 1867 professor for dogmatics at the Gregoriana and critic of hylomorphism, was dismissed in 1879 because he was unable to comply with the philosophical program of the Pope and preferred to keep silent rather than speak out against his convictions.[15] In Piacenza in 1880, the periodical *Divus Thomas* began a series of new Thomistic publications: the *Philosophisches Jahrbuch der Görres-Gesellschaft* (1888), *Pastor Bonus* (Trier 1888), *Revue Thomiste* (Paris 1893), *Revue néo-scolastique de philosophie* (Louvain 1894), *Rivista di filosofia neo-scolastica* (Milan 1909). There were plenty of channels for a Thomas renascence.

---

[15] Hocedez III, 48, 371f. But Leo XIII was considerate enough to agree to transfer Palmieri as exegete to Maastricht, where Palmieri represented a conservative standpoint until 1894. Other professors at the Gregoriana had to go, too (R. Aubert, *Aspects,* 159ff.).

CHAPTER 21

Neo-Thomism, Neo-Scholasticism, and the "New Philosophers"

The necessary conceptual differentiation between "Neo-Scholasticism" and "Neo-Thomism"[1] indicates that scholastic-systematic philosophy and theology in the Catholic Church of the nineteenth century and also during Leo XIII's pontificate do not represent a monolith, as most of the publications[2] seem to suggest. However, they often simply claim to be written *ad mentem S. Thomae Aquinatis.* But the traditions of Duns Scotus (especially with the Franciscans) and of Suárez (especially with

---

[1] "Neo-Scholasticism" refers to the Scholasticism of the nineteenth century, including the Scholastic traditions which continue to survive in spite of Thomas Aquinas's official preferential position since 1879, traditions which particularly follow Duns Scotus and Suárez; "Neo-Thomism" begins in the middle of the nineteenth century (after a few predecessors) and is the renascence of Aquinas's philosophy and theology, proceeding without direct relation to academic tradition. However, most Neo-Thomist philosophers and historians are not pure Thomists.

[2] The Thomist bibliography (1920) contains 2,219 entries for the period from 1800 to 1920; F. van Steenberghen, op. cit., 352.

the Jesuits) continue to thrive. There is also a difference between the often sterile letter-bound Neo-Thomism ("Paleothomism" [Steenbergen]) and the attempts of those, in the minority though they were, to proceed not formally from Thomas and thereby deduce the actualizing conclusions but rather to reverse the process and return to the great tradition of a real live questioning of contemporary problems. The picture becomes much more variegated if one considers that the other great (and older) tradition of Catholic thought, leading from Augustine via Bonaventura to Pascal, had not died out, even though those men who lived in it, as for example Maurice Blondel, could cause conflicts if they were not willing to subordinate the great father of the Church Augustine to the now dominant doctrine by quoting him occasionally. The Jesuit Franz Ehrle, who began his scholarly career with commentaries on *Aeterni Patris*,[3] proved, as one of the great scholars of medieval Scholasticism, what the "Augustinianism" of the thirteenth century, existing alongside and in harmony with Aristotelianism, had meant. However, it took time to recover the entire wealth of tradition and thus the freedom to philosophize in the Catholic Church.

In Rome itself, the encyclical was unable to give rise to a Neo-Thomism which could be compared to the significance of Matteo Liberatore. This is partially due to the difficulties of changing the current school traditions, partially to the tendency of formally arguing with Aquinas' authority, and to not taking modern philosophy and science seriously. The influential Jesuit Camillo Mazzella[4] advocated in his extensive treatise a Suarezian Scholasticism (Grabmann). Its most important representative was the Jesuit Louis Billot of Lorraine, who regularly taught theology at the Gregoriana from 1885 until 1911. He was a "Thomist totally adhering to Thomas and the older Thomists" (S. Tromp) defending the *immutabilitas* of tradition against all historical thought, which he equated with heretical evolutionism (rejection of a history of dogma).[5] G. Cornoldi, who participated in the founding of the Accademia Romana di San Tommaso, fought against the disciples of Rosmini, charging them with a "synthesis of ontologism and pantheism," a dispute which, in 1887, in conjunction with the political problem of the "Roman question," brought about the ecclesiastical censure of forty of Rosmini's propositions.[6] Two years before the encyclical on Thomas, the Collegio di S. Bonaventura was established in Quaracchi (Florence). There, the works of the Franciscan Doctor of the Church (since 1588) were published and an international research center was

---

[3] Cf. chap. 20.
[4] Cf. below, p. 315.
[5] H. Le Floche, *Le cardinal Billot* (Paris 1947).
[6] Cf. chap. 15.—P. Dezza, *I neotomisti italiani del secolo XIX,* 2 vols. (Milan 1942–44).

developed.[7] This did more to overcome a stagnation of philosophical-theological tradition than narrow-minded anti-Thomist polemics.

In Germany and Austria, Neo-Thomism also had numerous, often rather belligerent representatives who continued the tradition of Jakob Clemens and Constantin von Schäzler (died 1880) and contributed a great deal to the failure of the intention underlying Leo XIII's encyclical.[8] Matthias Joseph Scheeben (1835–88), by far superior to the theologians of his generation, was an unusually open-minded spirit and a deeply devout dogmatist from the Rhineland. He left a gap in this period in Germany which will never be closed. It is questionable whether Scheeben, who incorporated post-Tridentine theology and the Tübingen school as well as Neo-Thomism into his creative, original, and modern work, should be included in "Neo-Scholasticism." But excluding him from this category would mean isolating him in a manner which is not in accord with the movement as a whole. It would mean presenting "the theology of the past as a multiplicity of efforts exerted by

---

[7] The first assistant prefect was Fidelis a Fanna (1838–81), who searched five hundred libraries for manuscripts. His successor was the Westphalian I. Jeiler (1832–1904), after 1879 in Quaracchi; J. Reinhold, *AFrH* 47 (1954), 1–44.—Since 1885 publication of *Analecta Franciscana,* since 1903 the *Bibliotheca Franciscana Scholastica mediiaevi.*

[8] Especially polemical was E. Commer (1847–1928, born in Berlin), who founded in 1886 the *Jahrbuch für Philosophie und spekulative Theologie* (after 1914 *Divus Thomas*), author of *Immerwährende Philosophie* (1899), 1900–11 professor of dogmatics in Vienna; regarding his fight against H. Schell, cf. chap. 29.—As a result of the conflict with the rector of the Catholic University in Washington, J. Keane, J. Pohle returned to Germany in 1894 (cf. chap. 10), thereafter professor of dogmatics in Münster; in 1888, he and K. Gutberlet (1837–1928) founded the *Philosophische Jahrbuch* of the Görres-Society; concerning Gutberlet, see E. Hartman, *PhJ* 41 (1928), 261–66; P. Simon, *Hochland* 25 (1927), 437ff.—As a politician, as well as in his few philosophical works, G. von Hertling (cf. chap. 15) pursued an objective presentation of Neo-Scholastic principles; C. Baeumker, *DLZ* 39 (1918), 3–7, 35–40.—The apologist from Würzburg, F. Hettinger (1819–90), derived his criticism of the period from his profound knowledge, while A. M. Weiß, O.P., from Upper Bavaria, after 1890 professor in Fribourg, fought a very unsophisticated battle against Liberalism.—Leading away from a very narrow-minded opposition, the moral theologian from Münster, J. Mausbach (1861–1931), was able to combine Thomism with the Augustinian tradition; G. Schreiber, *J. Mausbach* (Münster 1931).—Regarding the Jesuit moral theologians, cf. chaps. 12 and 13.—Dogmatist J. B. Heinrich (1816–91) was known as the "head of the second Mainz circle" (L. Lenhart). He was a cofounder of the Görres-Society, like P. L. Haffner (1829–99; 1886: bishop of Mainz), whom he influenced greatly and who became the first chairman of the philosophical section; H. Lenhart, *Die philosophische-theologische Fakultät des Mainzer Priesterseminars* (Mainz 1946); Grabmann G., 230–36.—Since the faculty of theology at the University of Fribourg was entrusted to the Dominicans, Neo-Thomism ruled supreme. T. Coconnier (1846–1908; 1875: student of Zigliara in Rome, 1890: dogmatist at the Institut catholique in Toulouse), J.-J. Berthier (1847–1924, after 1905 mostly in Rome) and P. Mandonnet (1858–1936) founded the *Revue Thomiste* (1893).

devout thinkers" (J. Höfer). Many of Scheeben's main works had already been published long before *Aeterni Patris,*[9] penetrating an area of action that had been inspired by the encyclical among groups who did not interpret the letter as a request for 'repristination.' When Scheeben was completely himself, "he thought, like no other Neo-Scholastic, purely from faith and 'unapologetically,' "[10] from the "childlike faith" (Scheeben) which was to him the perfection of religious belief. This, of course, did not comply with the kind of conclusion theology which dominated Neo-Scholasticism. The "double form" of theology—devotion and intellectual agreement—remained a problem for Scheeben, which he faced through the influence of Kleutgen and Schäzler.

With the exception of Scheeben, all German Neo-Scholastics of that period are outranked in significance by the scholars of medieval Scholasticism (Franz Ehrle, Heinrich Denifle, Clemens Baeumker, and Martin Grabmann), whose early activities still belong in this period. The Dominican Denifle from Tyrol (1844–1905) and the Jesuit Ehrle from the Allgäu (1845–1934) collaborated (after 1880 in Rome) in the publication of the *Archiv für Literatur und Kirchengeschichte des Mittelalters:* from 1885 until 1900 seven volumes of "eternal value" (Grabmann). Denifle deserves special credit regarding mysticism (Eckhart, Tauler, Suso), and Ehrle demonstrated with his scholarship and editions the variety of Scholastic thought.[11] The historian of philosophy Baeumker (1853–1924; following his professorship in Breslau, Bonn, and Strasbourg, he succeeded Georg von Hertling in Munich in 1912) showed the connection between Scholasticism and Moslem philosophy and called attention to the continued existence of Platonism, which he demonstrated in his main work on Witelo (1908) and his metaphysics of light in the thirteenth century. Now the stage was set for an extensive study of the Scholastic method, which was presented by Grabmann (1875–1945).[12] Included in this group of scholars is the Belgian

---

[9] *Natur und Gnade* I (Mainz 1861); *Mysterien des Christentums* (Freiburg i. Br. 1865); *Handbuch der katholischen Dogmatik* I and II (Freiburg i. Br. 1874–75), III–VI (1880–87), incomplete; new edition by J. Höfer and others, 7 vols. (Freiburg 1941–57).

[10] K. Eschweiler, *Die zwei Wege der neueren Theologie. G. Hermes—M. J. Scheeben* (Augsburg 1926), 183; biblio. in regard to Scheeben until 1957 in the new edition (cf. n. 9). In that regard, see F. S. Pancheri, *Il pensiero teologico di M. Scheeben e S. Tommaso* (Padua 1956).

[11] M. Grabmann, *H. S. Denifle* (Mainz 1905); A. Walz, *Studi storiografici* (Rome 1949), 28–33; id. *Analecta Denifleana* (Rome 1955); A. Redigonda, *H. S. Denifle* (Florence 1953). Regarding F. Ehrle, 1895–1941 prefect of the Vatican Library, cf. chap. 20.

[12] C. Baeumker founded the *Beiträge zur Geschichte der Philosophie des Mittelalters* (1891). The title of one of his main works, *Die europäische Philosophie des Mittelalters* (Leipzig 1909), was changed for its second edition in 1913 to *Die christliche Philosophie des Mittelalters.* In regard to his audience with Pius X on 2 March 1908 in connection

Maurice De Wulf (1867–1947), a pupil of Désiré Mercier, who founded the collection *Les Philosophes belges* (Louvain 1901ff).[13] Even though the Neo-Scholastic systematists initially ignored these efforts, they kept the Thomistic renascence from stagnating into a classicism.

In France, most of the Neo-Thomists, strictly following the Gregoriana, did not go beyond their sterile disputations. An exception was the *Institut catholique* in Paris where Maurice d'Hulst seized upon Duilhé's idea of trying to avoid spiritual provincialism and to prove the productiveness of the Neo-Thomist method by holding international congresses for Catholic scholars.[14] In this respect, the spirit of the center took effect where this particular period succeeded in an actual encounter with Thomas Aquinas: the spirit of the University of Louvain and Mercier (1851–1926). This scholar from Brabant, after studying philosophy and theology, became interested in psychiatry, which had an impact on the curriculum which Mercier taught after 1882 in his position as professor of Thomist philosophy, which had been created by the Belgian episcopate at Leo XIII's request. The thirty-one-year-old professor fascinated his students, including nontheologians, with the decisiveness with which he responded to the ultimate questions posed by the natural sciences, and with his efforts to "philosophize for one's contemporaries." Of course, his extensive use of psychology raises the question whether this approach is appropriate for Thomist ontology. However, Mercier tried most of all to come to terms with Positivism, so popular those days, and he was just as interested in it as he was in Kant's philosophy. He was intent, however, on preserving theology's independence relative to philosophy. The *Institut supérieur de philosophie,* established in 1889, was the result of a proposal by Mercier to Leo XIII in 1887. Mercier was also its first president. The *Revue néo-scolastique,* founded in 1894, achieved international repute. The success created enemies, at first in Belgium, later in Rome, where the new prefect of the Congregation of Studies, Cardinal Mazella, S.J., considered theologians'

---

with the founding of an international society for scholars (cf. chap. 15) L. Pastor (*Tagebücher,* 490) writes: the Pope said that, "in agreement with Cardinal Rampolla and Merry del Val, it is out of the question that M. Spahn and C. Baeumker be accepted" (M. Grabmann, "C. Baeumker und die Erforschung der Geschichte der mittelalterlichen Philosophie," *BGPhMA* 25 [1927], 1–38).—M. Grabmann conducted his manuscript studies in Rome after 1900, supported by Ehrle and Denifle (L. Ott, *M. Grabmann zum Gedächtnis* [Munich 1949]).

[13] The *Histoire de la philosophie médiévale* (Louvain ¹1940) deals with the question of what Scholastics have in common; the revision of the 6th edition (1934ff.) shows with which problems a universal presentation has to deal; F. van Steenberghen, *RPhL* 46 (1948), 421–47.

[14] Cf. chap. 15.

intensive occupation with natural sciences a waste of time. Of equal importance was the objection that the lectures in French were jeopardizing not only Scholastic terminology, but also the theological correctness of the doctrine. Since Mazzella succeeded in persuading the Pope in favor of his reservations, Latin was decreed as the language of instruction for some time after 1895. Mazella's succession by Cardinal (after 1895) Satolli, who respected Mercier, brought about the conclusion of the affair in 1898.[15]

The picture of a united front does not entirely match the reality of Neo-Scholasticism. This is evidenced by the effort in regard to Bonaventure, the rather aggressively defended positions of Suarezianism[16] which the Jesuits (often somewhat artificially) tried to coordinate with Thomism, and Scotism to which the Franciscans were devoted.[17] Such differences were still confined to Neo-Scholasticism. However, within the tradition of occidental thinking, attempts were made by individuals (consequently isolated people) to break, so to speak, the anthropocentric concept of the world from the inside and to prove the terminologically absolute opposite of immanence and transcendence to be an apparent opposite by using the argument of concrete existence. This resulted in a dispute with strangely inverted fronts: These philosophical theorems are based on the Christian mystery of Incarnation and on the belief in the support of the Holy Spirit, even though they were clearly philosophical or, at least, intended to be. They were rejected by the Neo-Scholastics as "modernistic" and categorized under different, hostile "isms." Neo-Scholastic philosophy and theology, on the other hand, often contained a goodly measure of rationalism, which could only seemingly be brought in tune with the Christian belief in revealed religion. These disputations often entailed quite subjective assessments of Neo-Scholastic efforts. The German theologian and religious philosopher Herman Schell taught that "in the acknowledgement of the Holy Spirit as the essential manifestation of Deity the principle of immanence and the idea of transcendence are intimately linked and the intrinsic worldliness of action is combined in superior harmony with the nontemporal power of creation." Reject-

---

[15] Some of D. Mercier's most important works are: *Psychologie* (Paris 1892); *Logique* (Paris 1894); *Métaphysique générale ou Ontologie* (Paris 1894).—M. De Wulf et al., *RNPh* 28 (1926), 5–22, 99–249; J. Pirlot, *L'enseignement de la métaphysique. Critique et Suggestions* (Louvain 1950), 33–59; L. de Raeymaeker, *Le card. Mercier et l'Institut supérieur de philosophie de Louvain* (Louvain 1952); A. Simon, *D. Mercier* (Brussels 1960).

[16] For example, by the Spaniard J. J. Urráburu, S.J. (1844–1904), (Eguía Ruiz, *EE* 4 [1945], 45–59) and by the French P. Descoqs, S.J. (1877–1946).

[17] For example Déodat de Basly (1863–1937), especially in regard to Christology; R. Haubst, *ThRv* (1956), 145–62.

ing any form of pantheism, Schell developed an image of God as "being completely in Himself and of Himself." He did not believe that the dynamics of this image could be grasped by the terminology of academic tradition. Thus he conceived the term God as *causa sui,* which he later (after being put on the Index) replaced with "self-reality," without terminologically relinquishing the actuality of God and His being-active-in Himself. This concept of God was the foundation of Schell's personalism: In God's living personality rests all human personality.[18] This Augustinian tradition was transmitted by German Idealism, while the philosophy of Maurice Blondel (1861–1949) was supported by Blaise Pascal, who survived in the background of French philosophical life, and by Nicolas de Malebranche, who influenced Leibniz. One of Leibniz's key problems was the topic of Blondel's first and fundamental work: the *Vinculum substantiale.* Blondel's basic philosophical theme dealt with the attempt "to overcome the static and concrete concept of substance and to define substance both as a unifying force and as a metaphysical entity, thus evading Idealism as well as the all too material Realism. Blondel's philosophy tried to solve the problem of transcendence by integrating the triple reality of life, of thought, and of being in existence.[19] In contrast to objectivism, Blondel believes knowledge and existential revelation to be tied to subjectivity. He does not accept the opposition of immanence and transcendence, but rather finds them unified in "action" (existential realization), from which immanence automatically reaches out toward transcendence. This is the basis for the famous *Lettre sur les exigences de la pensée contemporaine en matière d'apologétique et sur la méthode de la philosophie dans l'étude du problème religieux* (1896): The "supernatural" in the Christian message is not an *extrinsécism,* something which approaches human reality like a stranger from the outside, rather it corresponds to reality, and is thus logically necessary, even if this logic does not say anything about the freedom of divine revelation and the freedom of human acceptance of it.[20]

[18] Regarding H. Schell, cf. chap 29. Quotations from: *Türmer Jahrbuch* (1906), 194; *Dogmatik* IV (1893), x; O. Schröder (op. cit., biblio. chap. 29), 370–91.

[19] R. Scherer, *Einführung zu: M. Blondel, Das Denken* (Freiburg i. Br. 1953), viii–xxxii; U. Hommes, *Transzendenz und Personalität. Zum Begriff der Action bei M. Blondel* (Frankfurt 1972).

[20] R. Scherer, *LThK*[2] II, 533.—Preceding the *Lettre, L'Action. Essai d'une critique de la vie et d'une science de la pratique* was published in 1893 (Paris); in contrast to the volumes of 1936–37, it was called "first action." The period covered here includes the following works by Blondel: *Histoire de dogme. Les lacunes philosophiques de l'exégèse moderne* (La Chapelle-Montligeon 1904), a critical study of historicism.—Basic literature regarding the *Lettre:* R. Aubert, *Le problème de l'acte de foi, données traditionelles et résultats des controverses récentes* (Louvain 1945).—A. Hayen, *Bibliographie blondélienne* (Messina

Blondel's teacher was L. Ollé-Laprune (1839–1898), professor in Aix-en-Provence from 1896 to his death, who from 1875 on had taught philosophy at the École normale supérieure in Paris as a disciple of Malebranche: The conflict between faith and knowledge can only be overcome in personal experience, which is inaccessible to dialectic analysis.[21] This was also the basis for the philosophy of Lucien Laberthonnière (1860–1932), who became an Oratorian in 1886. In the *Annales de Philosophie chrétienne,* which he edited between 1905 and 1913, he campaigned passionately for Blondel's work and against Neo-Scholasticism.[22] When (in 1913) the Holy Office prohibited him from publishing, his loyalty to the Church remained unshaken.

Both the initiative to revive the Thomism that was inspired by Leo XIII and that was productive in significant ways, as well as the efforts of these "new philosophers" have to be seen in context, in spite of their opposition to Neo-Scholasticism, if one intends to obtain a historically adequate picture of the sincerity of the philosophers and theologians of those decades and of their efforts regarding the intellectual conditions under which the Christian faith can be experienced and justified in the modern world.

1953); J.-P. Golinas, *La restauration du Thomisme sous Léon XIII et les philosophes nouvelles. Études de la pensée de M. Blondel et du Père Laberthonnière* (Washington 1959); O. Schröder (op. cit., biblio., chap. 29), 255–71.

[21] R. Crippa, *Il pensiero di L. Ollé-Laprune* (Brescia 1947).

[22] M.-M. d'Hendecourt, *Essai sur la philosophie du Pere Laberthonnière* (Paris 1947); J.-P. Golinas, op. cit.

CHAPTER 22

The Theory of Church History

The "almost turbulent expansion and specialization of Church history" (H. Jedin) corresponds to the general interest in history, developing in the last third of the nineteenth century and continuing into the twentieth. Prerequisite for research was the publication of new sources of Church history in which secular institutes participated. Following the extensive editions of A. Theiner of Silesia[1] (1855–70 prefect of the Vatican Archives), and after Leo XIII opened the Archives to scholars in general in 1881, a new era began. The prefect at the time, Cardinal (after 1879) J. Hergenröther, had considerable difficulties solving the

[1] H. Jedin, "A. Theiner. Zum 100. Jahrestag seines Todes (4 August 1974)," *ArSKG* 31 (1973).

technical problems of using the Archives.[2] The rules of 1878 and 1888 regarding the use of the Vatican Library were helpful, as was its significant expansion after 1890 through the Borghese and the Barberini Libraries. In 1895 the medievalist Franz Ehrle (1922 cardinal) was appointed prefect. The opening of the Vatican Archives, which was followed by the founding of a series of national historical institutes in Rome—1881: the Austrian Institute (first director: the Protestant T. von Sickel; after 1901: L. von Pastor), 1888: the Prussian Institute (director after 1903: P. F. Kehr), later the *École française de Rome* (director after 1895: L. Duchesne)—was one of the most important moments for the rich deployment of editions and books on Church history. They have been described extensively in the first volume of this series[3] and are of interest here only in so far as we are dealing with the theoretical notion of Church history during Leo XIII's pontificate.

As is the case in all aspects of life, history has to inquire about the relationship which Catholicism had established in regard to this academic discipline since its introduction to the modern world during Leo XIII's pontificate. The superficial debate concerning historical "objectivity," which many Catholic authors at that time felt compelled to discuss in their forewords, had no theoretical basis after G. Droysen's

---

[2] An advocate of this decision was, among others, L. Pastor, whom Hergenröther asked to write a memorial (*Tagebücher*, 128–32). A glance into the situation at that time is provided by Pastor's statement explaining that his abstracts of the archives, which he was able to prepare by special permission, were shortened by the keeper of the archives (K. A. Fink, "Das Vatikanische Archiv," *Bibliothek des Deutschen Historischen Instituts in Rom* [Rome ²1951], 155–67).

[3] Regarding the strong development of the history of the orders, see M. Heimbucher, *Orden und Kongregationen der katholischen Kirche* (Paderborn 1896–97, ³1933–34); regarding the *Benedictines* in France, see J.-J. Bourasse (Tours 1900); in England: E. L. Taunton (London 1898); in Maredsous, U. Berlière and others deserve credit for the publication of the *Monasticon belge* (after 1890); the *Revue bénédictine* (Maredsous, after 1884, at first a general spiritual publication) was joined in 1903 by the *Bulletin d'histoire monastique;* in Munich, the *Studien und Mitteilungen aus dem Benediktiner- und Zisterzienserorden* was published after 1880.—Concerning the *Dominicans,* see B. M. Reichert (ed.), *M.O.P.* (Rome after 1896); A. Mortier, *Histoire des maîtres généreaux de l'ordre des frères prêcheurs* (Paris 1903).—Regarding the Franciscans, see AFrH (Florence after 1908); H. Holzapfel's handbook (Freiburg i. Br. 1909) is still indispensable.—Concerning the Jesuits, see *MHSI* (Rome, after 1894), also: P. de Leturia, "Geschichte und Inhalt der Monumenta. . . ," *HJ* 72 (1953), 585–604; *Bibliothèque de la Compagnie de Jésus* (Brussels, Paris after 1890); A. Astraín, *Historia de la Compañía de Jésus en la Asistencia de España* (Madrid 1902; up to 1773); P. Tacchi-Venturi (inspired by Cardinal Ehrle), *Storia della Compagnia di Gesù in Italia* (Rome 1910); St. Zaleski, *Jezuici w Polsce* (Lemberg 1900–06); T. Hughes, *The History of the Society of Jesus in North America* (London, New York 1907–17); B. Duhr, *Geschichte der Jesuiten in den Ländern deutscher Zunge* (Freiburg i. Br. 1907), especially apologetic; C. Sommervogel, *Bibliothèque de la Compagnie de Jésus,* 9 vols. (Brussels 1890–1900).

Historik, which in the meantime was rendered obsolete especially since its advocates from the nineteenth century could be proven guilty of a natural subjectivity of their own. But just how problematic the Catholic study of history could be is shown by a remark made in 1889 by the influencial apologist A. M. Weiß, O.P. He justified the fact that the textbooks of Church history still constituted an extreme minority compared to the systematic theological textbooks by asserting that "this fact is in accord with the nature of this matter. For us, exegesis and the description of the traditional doctrines of faith and morals are the essential elements in theology. History can only be granted the rank of an ancillary science."[4] The historical-theological thought of the Tübingen school was replaced by the essentially ahistorical Neo-Scholasticism. Even though the numerous and productive Catholic historians of those decades did not consider themselves representatives of an ancillary discipline, the question remains whether and in what respect "the world" could be conceived "as history." The dispute over Johannes Janssen's (1829–91) *Geschichte des deutschen Volkes seit dem Ausgang des Mittelalters*[5] largely missed the point that it was not a question of selecting the documents, which Janssen had done with utmost conscientiousness, but rather of the futility of letting the sources themselves speak. "Historical understanding" was the new hallmark of historical studies. Janssen had a better comprehension of this understanding than the otherwise much more important papal historian Ludwig Pastor (1854–1928), who was "seized by the material aspect to such an extent that he continued to work"[6] on his sixteen-volume *Geschichte der Päpste seit dem Ausgang des Mittelalters* (first volume 1886) "undisturbed by all intellectual developments around him, and unconcerned about the changes in historical theories." "Negating the historical development, he unfolded a detailed concept of the centralistic Church and papacy and projected it on the past." This endeavor separated him later in Innsbruck from the general development of German Catholicism,[7] but it endeared him to the Rome

---

[4] In O. Köhler, *Der Katholizismus in Deutschland und der Verlag Herder* (Freiburg i. Br. 1951), 130.

[5] J. Janssen, *An meine Kritiker* (Freiburg i. Br. 1882); id., *Zweites Wort an meine Kritiker* (Freiburg i. Br. 1883).—L. von Pastor, *Joh. Janssen* (Freiburg i. Br. [2]1894); id., *J. Janssens Briefe,* 2 vols. (Freiburg i. Br. 1920). Regarding the difference between Pastor and the basically irenic Janssen, see W. Baum, "J. Janssen, Persönlichkeit, Leben und Werke," (diss., Innsbruck 1971).

[6] C. Bauer about L. Pastor, *Hochland* 26 (1928–29), 578–88 (reprint in: *Gesammelte Aufsätze* [Freiburg i. Br. 1965], 466–75).—Characteristic is Pastor's strict opposition to the title of the *Reformationsgeschichtliche Studien,* ed. by J. Greving (after 1906) (H. Jedin, *J. Greving* [Münster 1954]).

[7] Interesting in this respect is the conflict developing since 1891 between Pastor and the medievalist from Munich, H. von Grauert (1850–1924), in the editorial office of the

of Pius X (less that of Leo XIII), where he exerted considerable influence on the ecclesiastical personnel policy in Germany and Austria. Pastor's spirit permeated Cardinal J. Hergenröther's *Handbuch der allgemeinen Kirchengeschichte* (1876/80, three volumes). It preserved this orientation throughout the revisions.

Leo XIII did not grow tired of including in his letters and encyclicals rather lengthy passages about Church history and especially the history of his predecessors and their service to the Western World. In the brief *Saepenumero* of 18 August 1883, addressed to Cardinals A. de Luca, J. B. Pitra and J. Hergenröther, he explained what he expected from the historians: a defense against accounts of the papacy written in *mendaci colore*. He trusted that the *incorrupta rerum gestarum monumenta,* if studied without prejudice, would successfully defend the Church and the papacy *per se ipsa.* With special regard to Italy, he called to mind the papacy's achievements during the time of the barbarian migrations, in the struggle against the medieval Emperors, and in the Turkish Wars. He also mentioned the preservation of Roman and Greek literature by the popes and the clergy.[8] The Pope spoke with conviction when he said in 1884 "Non abbiamo paura della pubblicità dei documenti,"[9] scornfully calling the sceptics around him "small minds." But, as a sharp observer noticed, Leo XIII could only say this because he did not understand the "historical method."[10] It is completely erroneous to judge this as a "gap" in Leo XIII's education. In spite of the complex quality of his personality, there was no room for historical thinking. This should not be understood to mean that the Pope was unable to follow Pastor's description of Alexander VI;[11] the history of the institution was not

---

Historisches Jahrbuch. Pastor (*Tagebücher,* 244, 270, 288); "in Munich, Grauert and Hertling developed a new point of departure toward a liberal Catholicism" (28 December 1895). The conflict caused a critical revision of the "Geschichte des deutschen Volkes" by the Church historian Emil Michael in *Historisches Jahrbuch.* Consequently, in July 1901, Pastor resigned his position in the editorial office (*Tagebücher,* 193). However, cf. the letters addressed to F. X. Kraus (H. Schiel, *Rheinische Vierteljahresblätter* 19 [1954], 191–233). Regarding E. Michael, see W. Baum, *ZKTh* 93 (Innsbruck 1971), 182–99.

[8] *Acta Leonis* III, 259–73.

[9] Schmidlin, *PG* II, 400, maintains that this was addressed to the "German circle of historians in Rome." Pastor (*Tagebücher*) noted the reception of the "historian of Campo Santa," commenting: "Which secular sovereign could say this?" According to Pastor, Anton de Waal (1837–1917; 1873: rector at Campo Santo) was willing to "work in full force for the honor and glory of the Church and the defense of the Holy See."

[10] P. M. Baumgarten, quoted in Schmidlin, *PG* II, 399; he means "historical sense."

[11] L. Pastor (*Tagebücher,* 309) noted one of Leo XIII's statements to Boyer d'Agen in 1897: "If you want to write about Alexander VI, you have to read the third volume of Pastor's book first."

thereby touched. In Leo XIII's opinion, the first law for writing history demands that nothing false be said, furthermore, that the truth not be hidden, and, lastly, that any suspicion of either favoritism or hostility be avoided.[12] But in view of indeed widespread hostility toward the Church and particularly the papacy, he presented these principles in an apologetic context which permeated all of *Saepenumero.*

German Catholicism lost its edge in the area of critical historical method after the conflict with Ignaz von Döllinger,[13] even though certain scholars tried to continue the historical method, such as: Franz Xaver Kraus, one of the founders of Christian archeology, who had already offended the sensibilities of tradition with his early work on blood ampuls found in Roman catacombs and on the Holy Nail in the Cathedral of Trier (both: 1868); K. J. Hefele's successor in Tübingen, Franz Xaver Funk, who, in his textbook of 1886, tried to overcome the static condition of Neo-Scholasticism with his concept of "development";[14] and Albert Ehrhard, who did not join the battle until 1901, and whose unpretentious scholarship was reflected in his research on the hagiography in the Greek Church.[15] The fundamental deliberation of these issues took place in France, because there the problem of the relation between revelation and history was debated by including the "Biblical question" and the history of dogma.

Charles de Smedt, S.J. (1864–76 professor of Church history at the Jesuit College in Louvain, 1882–1911 president of the Bollandists), developed certain principles of philological criticism which were used by his tremendously successful collaborator (after 1891) H. Delehaye, S.J. Per se, these principles were not problematic, even though de Smedt had to defend them, presenting them in his work *Principes de la critique historique* (Liège 1883) in the perspective of the total problem. However, Louis Duchesne (1843–1922), the famous Church historian and professor at the Institut Catholique in Paris from 1877 to 1885, got

---

[12] *Acta Leonis* III, 268.

[13] Concerning the headstart of the "Munich School" relative to France, see Hocedez III, 56.

[14] This theory derived one of its arguments from the fact that the Vatican Council used Vinzenz von Lérins's image of the seed for the defense against theological evolutionism. An older and more historical attempt was the essay by H. Newman "On the Development of Christian Doctrine" (London 1845), which caused a serious controversy around the eighties (cf. the following). Regarding the problem of the relationship between "development" and "tradition", see O. Köhler, *Mysterium salutis,* n. 24 with text.

[15] Regarding F. X. Kraus and A. Ehrhard, cf. chap. 29. A. Ehrhard, in connection with the antimodernist oath, was deprived of his title as prelate (1908), which hurt him deeply. He was reinstated by Pius XI in 1922 (K. Baus, *Bonner Gelehrte, Katholische Theologie* [Bonn 1968], 114–22).

into a critical situation with his lectures on the history of dogma, creating debate and painful consequences.[16] In 1895, he became the director of the École française de Rome.[17] In 1882, Abbé Rambouillet attacked Duchesne for his theory of the development of the dogma.[18] Duchesne's response was supported by Maurice d'Hulst. While universal inerrancy was the issue of the "biblical question," historical change was the problem in regard to the history of dogma. Billot rejected even the term itself.[19] The debate, which continued into the crisis of Modernism, included in its arguments the famous essay by John Henry Newman dealing with the personal tradition of faith in history,[20] in contrast to the unfortunate concept of Vincent of Lérins, which is purely biological and develops an "unhistorical theory of tradition" (J. Ratzinger). Joseph Tixeront, after 1881 professor of the seminary of Lyon, carefully furthered the method of his teacher Duchesne. Pierre Batiffol (1861–1929), a friend of Albert Lagrange and patronized by Duchesne, studied early Christian history in Rome and became rector of the Institut Catholique in Toulouse in 1898, a position which he had to relinquish in 1907 after his book about the Eucharist (1905) was put on the Index. In his *Études d'histoire et de théologie positive* (1902), he had attempted a theoretical solution to the problem. In 1892, the historian of dogma J. Turmel was dismissed from the seminary in Rennes. His own crisis

---

[16] With his study about the "Holy Nail" (Trier), L. Duchesne wounded sensitivities regarding tradition even more than F. X. Kraus, because he destroyed the legend of the apostolic origin of the old French dioceses; his research, conducted since 1881, is contained in the three volumes of *Les fastes épiscopaux de l'ancienne Gaule* (Paris 1894, 1900, 1915); A. Houtin, *La controverse de l'apostolicité des Églises de France au XIXᵉ siècle* (Paris 1903). Between 1886 and 1892, his critical edition of the *Liber pontificalis* appeared. The *Histoire ancienne de l'Église*, 3 vols. (Paris 1906–10) was put on the Index in 1912.—The *Bulletin critique*, which Duchesne published for twenty years, trained a critical and quite ecclesiastically minded generation of historians.

[17] F. X. Kraus (*Tagebücher*, 461f., in March 1883), about a visit in Paris: Duchesne, "who is indeed even more liberal than I am and who hates the ultramontane bunch at least as much if not more, is also *aux peines* regarding the Index . . . , he wants to resign from teaching"; in November 1895 (p. 630): "D. is very happy in his position; but he seems to lean more and more toward ultramontanism . . ."; in 1898 (p. 698): ". . . now, he is obviously through with the Curia." L. Pastor (*Tagebücher*, 309, in 1897): Duchesne "expressed rather liberal and in part even strange opinions" (referring to Leo XIII's politics); in 1902 (p. 385): statement by Duchesne about T. Mommsen, who "overreacts in his hatred of Christianity" and would probably exaggerate even more if he would not have to fear criticism in "progressive Berlin."

[18] In *Revue des sciences ecclésiastiques* (Lille 1882). It is understandable that Cardinal Franzelin rejected d'Hulst's attempt to present himself as in agreement with Duchesne (Hocedez III, 162).

[19] Hocedez III, 84; regarding the whole controversy: 161–172; regarding Billot: 322, 337.

[20] He was not touched by the controversy.—Cf. n. 14.

occurred in the period of Modernism.[21] In Germany, the problem was ignored. The convert Constantin von Schäzler, after 1874 consultant to the Holy Office, advocated an ahistorical position in his book *Die Bedeutung der Dogmengeschichte vom katholischen Standpunkt aus* (1884), as did J. Schwane in his four-volume history of dogma (Münster 1862/90).

Because of the methodological specialization, several disciplines were singled out from general Church history, such as patrology,[22] a large area which, after the Vatican Council, was put aside for the time being along with the history of councils.[23] However, with few exceptions, the history of dogma within Catholic theology was unable to divorce itself from dogmatics.[24] This circumstance is significant for the condition of Church history as a whole. The fundamental problem was, on the one hand, to overcome an ahistorical concept of tradition implying a Church historiographical positivism, and on the other hand, to avoid falling victim to relativistic historicism. The largely methodical critical work of Church historians regarding editions and research during Leo XIII's pontificate set the scene for a theoretical solution of the problem of Church history.

[21] Cf. chap. 33, n. 28.

[22] The controversy developing around the turn of the century over this term is related to the problem of the history of dogma. O. Bardenhewer (1851–1935) rejected the theory according to which patrology is the literary history of Church Fathers, including the heretics. He advocated relying closely on the history of dogmatic definitions.

[23] K. J. von Hefele's *Conciliengeschichte* I–VII (1855–74) was continued by J. Hergenröther in volumes VIII and IX (1887, 1890). In Hefele's estate (died 1893), nothing was found because the noble bishop destroyed almost all his papers before he died (R. Reinhardt, "Der Nachlaß . . . ," *ZKG* 82 [1971], 261–72; letters addressed to F. X. Kraus: H. Schiel, *ThQ* 168 [1957], 178–86).

[24] Cf. in this regard the thorough work of J. Ratzinger (1966; biblio., chap. 22).

CHAPTER 23

The Question of the Bible

While the Protestant Bible societies in Germany, England, and the United States developed with increased activity at the beginning of the nineteenth century, the efforts toward a Catholic biblical movement were suppressed and pastoral use of Holy Scripture fell behind the scholastic question-and-answer catechism. Readings of the Epistle and Gospel during Sunday Mass were generally bilingual, which was of less significance if they were considered part of the "pre-Mass" and had no relation to the sermon. "Biblical history," which was introduced to religious instruction in Germany[1] and generated a great deal of familiarity with the Holy Scriptures, had a continuing impact in that country.

Both the position of Holy Scripture in everyday religious and pastoral life and the position of biblical studies in Catholic theology have the same origin: "Since the Reformation, Catholic theology in general and biblical studies in particular considered their foremost task to be confrontation with Protestant theology."[2] This resulted in the dilemma of whether biblical studies, in accord with the Catholic idea of the Church, were "to play a role inferior to" that of theology. It is part of the Catholic self-awareness that the First Vatican Council reiterated the Tridentine decree regarding the use of the Holy Scriptures, requiring that the ecclesiastical teaching authority had the exclusive right to decide on the "true meaning" and interpretation. However, this purely negative definition did not exactly encourage the desire for biblical research, regardless of conflicts. This is demonstrated by a glance at the bibliographies relating to biblical studies at that time, when Catholic works represented a clear minority, not to mention their quality. This situation intensified in proportion to the phase difference between the defensive attitude of the teaching authority (which was understandable in view of the radical biblical criticism of David Friedrich Strauß (died 1874), Bruno Bauer (died 1882), Ernest Renan (died 1892), and others) as contrasted to the development of biblical studies according to principles about which everyone is in agreement nowadays.

Among the Bible translations in German-speaking countries, Joseph Franz von Allioli's, published between 1830 and 1832, was able to maintain its leading position throughout the nineteenth century and beyond. It follows the Vulgate "with reference to the basic text." The French translation by Jean-Baptiste Glaire was also based on the Vulgate. It was later incorporated by Fulcrain Vigouroux (1837–1915) into his *Bible polyglotte* (Paris 1897–1909). The translation of the original texts by C. Crampon gained in significance (NT 1885, OT 1894–1904). The efforts to approach the original texts by using handwritten manuscripts, i.e., philological-critical Bible editions, causing research to progress swiftly in the last third of the nineteenth century, were made almost exclusively by Protestant scholars.[3] A "decisive impact"[4] on the

---

[1] Regarding M. Sailer, ibid., 436.—Regarding the *Biblische Geschichte* by Christoph von Schmid and by Ignaz Schuster, see G. Mey: ibid., 435. Regarding the catechetical problem, see B. Dreher and H. Kreutzwald (biblio., chap. 28).

[2] A. Wikenhauser, J. Schmid, op. cit., 8.

[3] The New Testament text by Anglicans B. F. Westcott and F. J. A. Hort (Cambridge, London 1881) was, at first, considered the final version; later, H. von Soden (New Testament 1913) offered a wealth of variances, but his theses were rejected. Research

stimulation of biblical studies in France was accredited to the Sulpician Vigouroux, whose *Manuel Biblique* appeared between 1879 and 1890. His *Bible polyglotte* (8 volumes, in Hebrew, Greek, Latin Vulgate, and French) is derived from the Protestant *Bielefelder Polyglotte*.[5] Vigouroux was totally occupied with the battle against biblical criticism and he fought it in every way possible. In that respect he is like T.-J. Lamy (1827–1907), an exegete from Louvain, who is somewhat more moderate, however. As a Hebraist and Syriologist, he is important for the development of Eastern studies.[6] Of prominent influence in German-speaking areas was the exegete F. P. Kaulen from Bonn (1827–1907). He served as the editor of the second edition of *Wetzer und Welte's Kirchenlexikon* (Freiburg 1882–1903, 13 vols.). In 1903 he became a member of the Pontifical Biblical Commission. He was especially interested in the history of the Vulgate (1868), emphasizing this text as the "valid expression of biblical revelation" and describing the edition of the Benedictines of Tournai (1885) as "almost without errors." Like Kaulen, almost all exegetical collaborators of the Church lexicon took an extremely conservative viewpoint, which explains why, for instance, the biblical information about the patriarchs' ages was considered "historical data."[7]

The participation of Catholic exegetes in historical-literary biblical criticism was closely related to the concept of inspiration. Lenormant's attempt to limit the correctness of the Bible to dogmatic and moral statements failed, as did the complex undertaking of Salvatore di Bartolo to differentiate between facts, which are an integral part of dogma and ethics, and incidental, possibly erroneous data.[8] Statements of "pro-

---

regarding the Hebrew text of the Old Testament reached a climax with R. Kittel's work (1905–06).

[4] Hocedez III, 80.—The *Manuel Biblique* appeared in many editions. Because of additions in the fourteenth edition it was put on the Index. Vigouroux became professor of exegesis at the Institut catholique in Paris (1890) and (between 1903 and 1913) was secretary of the Pontifical Biblical Commission. Between 1895 and 1912 the five-volume *Dictionnaire Biblique* appeared, which was continued in supplements.—E. Levesque, *RB* 24 (1915), 183–216.

[5] J. Ziegler, "Polyglotten," *LThK*[2] VIII, 596.

[6] R. Aubert, *LThK*[2] VI, 770f.

[7] F. P. Kaulen, "Vulgata," *Wetzer-Welte* XII (1901), 1140; regarding the further history of the Vulgate edition, see K. T. Schäfer, *LThK*[2] II, 383, and ibid., X, 901f.—F. P. Kaulen ("Patriarchen," *Wetzer Welte* IX, 1603) maintains that "scholars searched, partly out of incredulous opposition, partly for cowardly consideration, for means to circumvent the literal acceptance of this information. However, this information can be explained by the fact that "the transmission of the unabridged revealed truth is guaranteed by the phenomenon of three generations embracing two millenia."

[8] F. Lenormant, *Les origines de l'histoire et les traditions des peuples orientaux* (1880), put

fane truth" in the Bible were usually considered nonerroneous, even though, in regard to the six-day creation, it was conceded that there was "no need for clinging anxiously to the letter of the text." However, in cases where an undeniable error could be noted in regard to "perfectly certain facts of natural history, geology, and chronology," the explanation had to suffice that the inspired original text had been perverted in the course of tradition.[9] A fundamental problem existed in the Holy Scriptures regarding the relationship between God, the inspiring "author," and the human author. The Neo-Scholastic theologian Johann Baptist Franzelin, S.J.[10], in his *De divina traditione et scriptura* (1870) defined the term "inspiration" so broadly that in fact, in accord with tradition, only the verbal inspiration was excluded. This theory dominated the textbooks to the end of the nineteenth century. In the middle of the nineties began the kind of criticism that was especially advocated by the Dominicans with reference to Thomas Aquinas. To avoid mixing revelation itself with the process of inspiration, there were attempts to define the latter as a *motion inspiratrice,* thus expanding the freedom of the writer.[11] But the Jesuit theologians continued to adhere to their theory of inspiration. The work *De inspiratione* (Rome 1903) by Louis Billot, S.J., one of the most influential theologians (from 1885 to 1911 professor at the Gregoriana),[12] opposed the modernistic exegesis, but also the efforts of scholarly biblical studies by authors who stayed within the ecclesiastical tradition. However, it was precisely the inspiration of the Bible on the whole that motivated critical Catholic exegetes to discover the "true 'literal meaning'" of the Bible.[13] This, however, put them for a long time in the extremely difficult position of vacillating between liberal biblical criticism and general ecclesiastical traditionalism.

The defense of Alfred Loisy's[14] first writings by Maurice d'Hulst

---

on the Index; Salvatore di Bartolo, *I criteri teologici* (1886), put on the Index in 1891. In this context belongs Newman's attempt (retracted later) to introduce the term *obiter dicta* (Hocedez III, 126).

[9] This general procedure was used in "Inspiration," *Wetzer-Welte* VI, 806.

[10] Franzelin taught from 1850 until 1876 at the Gregoriana. Later, as cardinal, he was very influential in the Roman congregations. Regarding Franzelin's important contribution about the relationship between the written word, tradition, and the Church, see W. Kasper, *Die Lehre von der Tradition in der Römischen Schule* (Freiburg 1962), 397–401, 406ff.

[11] The discussion in Hocedez III, 133–40. One of the most important books written in this Dominican vein is: C. Gonzáles y Días Tuñón, *La Biblia y la Ciencia,* 2 vols. (Madrid 1891, ²1894).

[12] Cf. pp. 312, 323, 458, 470.

[13] J. Schmid, "Bibelkritik," *LThK*² II, 366.

[14] Cf. pp. 432–38.

(1841–96),[15] rector of the Institut catholique in Paris, where Loisy was a member of the faculty, in his article "La question biblique," which appeared in 1893 in *Correspondant,* caused a severe controversy, which was also carried on by the daily press. D'Hulst tried, according to his character—he was a monarchist, opponent of the *Ralliement* and in terms of church policy a liberal—to bridge the differences and to define in regard to the Bible question a "middle-of-the-road school," from where he was trying to mediate between the *école étroite* (the thesis of the equal inspiration of the Bible) and the *école large,* which he defined similarly to the attempts by Salvatore di Bartolo. Opposition came from all sides.

In November of the same year, the encyclical *Providentissimus Deus* appeared,[16] stating that the defense against the rationalistic enemies of Holy Scripture, the "sons and heirs" of the Reformation, was especially urgent, since there are some men among them who want to be known as Christian theologians. It is an unreliable approach to overcome "difficulties" by admitting that the inspiration only referred to questions of faith and morals; such interpretations originate from the erroneous opinion that the primary goal is the discovery of why God said a certain thing. Referring to the Council of Trent and the Vatican Council the encyclical states that the "authentic parts" (*locis authenticis*) of the Bible do not contain any errors. Positively, the letter demands that biblical studies, *ad temporum necessitates congruentius,* be furthered carefully but decisively. The improvement of the Vulgate is encouraged by a quotation from Augustine. To determine the meaning, the encyclical suggests consulting, aside from parallel passages, the findings of related sciences (*externa quoque appositae eruditionis illustratio*); Eastern studies are to be strengthened. The exegeses of the Church Fathers, including the allegorical ones, are to be respected, which does not exclude *ultra procedere.* It is wrong to prefer the studies of "heterodox scholars," even though they may be useful at times; however, the untainted meaning cannot be found outside of the Church. The *Critica sublimior,* which judges parts of the Scriptures according to "internal motives" is rejected; only the *historiae testimonia* is important. One passage of the encyclical was particularly interesting to those who interpreted it for the purpose of finding assistance. Here, a quotation of Thomas's regarding questions of natural science serves to express the idea that the sacred author followed physical phenomena, similar to popular speech (*ea secutus est, quae sensibiliter apparent*). In regard to historical problems, the

---

[15] A. Baudrillart, *Vie de M gr. d'Hulst,* 2 vols. (Paris 1912–14); Aubert, *LThK²* V, 524; cf. above, p. 255.
[16] *Acta Leonis* XIII, 326–64;

encyclical reiterates the thesis that errors are the fault of the copyists; moreover, the original meaning of a passage (*germana alicuius loci sententia*) could remain ambiguous (*anceps*). Also, the phrase stating that the Holy Spirit inspired and motivated (*excitavit et movit*) the biblical writer was interpreted to indicate a theory of inspiration which favors the human collaborator.[17]

The encyclical found practically no opposition among Catholic theologians, but it was still short of solving the problems.[18] The necessary effort made to agree with the encyclical resulted in artistic interpretations. The quotation of Thomas's regarding the physical phenomena in biblical texts inspired Albert Lagrange to write his famous study *La méthode historique sourtout à propos de l'Ancien Testament* (1903), which outlined the thesis of the *apparences historiques*. But this raised the decisive question: What was the historical place and time when inspiration struck the biblical authors? This was the point of departure from which the historical positivism in the arguments of the "error debate" had to be overcome. It was unfortunate that the term *vérité relative*, which can be correctly understood and was used to replace the term historical or scientific "error," met with the twilight of modern relativism. In this regard, the "quotation theory,"[19] according to which a biblical author sums up other texts, was an expedient in view of the unsolved question of inspiration. This and other theories, also used by Lagrange and Hummelauer, were solidified into a system by the French Jesuit Ferdinand Prat (1857–1938).[20] The Jesuits Delattre and Fonck, who rejected this theory, pursued with particular vehemence the Dominican Lagrange, who had studied Eastern cultures in Vienna from 1888 until 1890 and had founded the *École Biblique* in Jerusalem by request of his order. Lagrange planned to make his series of monographs, the *Revue Biblique* (1892) and the *Études Bibliques* (1903), to be scholarly-critical as well as Church-minded.[21] A fateful trial for Lagrange was his occupation with chapters 1–6 of Genesis (published in manuscript form, Paris 1906) and especially the Pentateuch. He followed his principles of the "historical method" and was convinced that it was no longer possible to

[17] Ibid., 339f., 357f., 327f., 342f., 346f., 348, 353, 355, 357, 358.
[18] Schmidlin, *PG* II, 398: The encyclical encouraged the studies, "however, even most of the scholars with good intentions were unable to find the necessary means to solve the questions or to reconcile the truth of the texts with modern accomplishments."
[19] About the usage of this term, see Hocedez III, 129f. Representatives of the "quotation theory": ibid., 131.
[20] In 1903, appointed consultant to the Biblical Commission (1907 dismissed), devoting his time to Pauline theology (J. Calès, *Ferdinand Prat* [Paris 1942]).
[21] In 1903, J. Goettsberger and J. Sickenberger founded the *Biblische Zeitschrift*. Sickenberger introduced the "two sources theory," developed by K. Lachmann, to the Catholic exegesis of the Evangelists Matthew and Luke.

hold the opinion that Moses had composed the whole Pentateuch, as we know it; that while the antiquity of the Ten Commandments in their substance and their proclamation by Moses be adhered to, the Pentateuch be differentiated according to various editorial levels, of which a large part is younger than Moses.[22] Lagrange's importance is substantiated by the fact that he is one of the few older exegetes who is still quoted in basic scholarship. However, at that time he encountered the bitter animosities of the Jesuits, and even the Dominican order no longer authorized his refutation, written in defense against the attacks by A. Delattre, S.J., *Éclaircissement sur la Méthode historique* (1905, only published in manuscript form). He suffered the most painful blow when his order requested his withdrawal from the exegesis of the Old Testament.[23] Another important center for similar efforts was the University of Louvain, where the Old Testament scholar A. van Hoonacker had started a course in 1889 called "Histoire critique l'Ancien Testament." His significant book *Le sacerdoce lévitique dans la Loi et dans l'histoire* (1899) won him European recognition. His work about the Hexateuch, written in Latin, was not published (Bruges 1949) until after the encyclical *Divino afflante Spiritu* (1943). Among the founders of the *Cursus scripturae sanctae,* a collection of commentaries published after 1888 and not finished, were R. Cornely, S.J., and J. Knabenbauer, S.J.; but the most outstanding of them was the Jesuit Franz von Hummelauer (1842–1914), who deserves special recognition for his serious definition of literary genres and who proceeded from the conviction that "every (literary) genre possesses its very own unique truth, which is the only thing we are justified in demanding from it."[24] Like most critical scholars of the Old Testament, E. Podechard, after 1892 professor at the seminary in Lyon, published very little; he was the teacher of J. Chaine.

When revising the regulations of the Index, the apostolic constitution *Officiorum ac munerum* of 25 January 1897 declared that, according to experience, translations of Holy Scripture edited by Catholics in the

[22] J. Chaine, 27f.
[23] In 1909, L. Fonck, S.J., who had spoken of the pernicious spirit permeating the École Biblique, became rector of the Pontifical Biblical Institute. On 29 June 1912, *scripta plura* of P. Lagrange were put on the Index. In his letter to Pope Pius X, Lagrange amended his words of submission imploring: "However, just because I feel I am a most loyal son, may I be permitted to speak to a father, the most illustrious of all fathers but nevertheless a father, concerning my anxiety over the motives which caused the total censorship of most of my work." Lagrange was willing to admit that his works contained errors. However, he made an appropriate, but clear protest against the charge that he wrote them in the "spirit of disobedience" (Vincent, 348f.). On 4 September 1912, the order recalled him from Jerusalem.
[24] Quoted according to V. Hamp, *LThK*[2] IV, 688. Hummelauer was appointed consultant to the Biblical Commission in 1903 and dismissed in 1908.

language of the people usually do more damage than good, as long as distinctions were not made (*sine discrimine*). Therefore it was decreed that these Bibles contain *adnotationes* from the Fathers or Catholic scholars.[25] In 1902, the Society of Saint Jerome for the Propagation of the Holy Gospel was founded. Its chairman, Giacomo della Chiesa, was a member of the Curia from 1887 to 1907 and later became Pope Benedict XV. In the first year, one hundred eighty thousand copies of the New Testament were sold in Italy. On 30 October 1902, the apostolic letter *Vigilantiae* was issued,[26] on the basis of which the Pontifical Biblical Commission was established, so that the studies might be conducted *auspicio ductuque Sedis Apostolicae* and new problems, not covered by doctrine, be solved according to ecclesiastical norms. The intention to safeguard during disputes the "limits of mutual love" could be sufficiently realized. Members of the Commission were the Cardinals Rampolla, Parocchi, Satolli, Segna, and Vives y Tutó. Two of the secretaries were the very conservative Vigouroux and the Franciscan Fleming, who had an open mind for exegetical problems. Leo's plan was oriented toward mediation, which is shown by the fact that the *Revue biblique* was originally intended to be the organ of the Commission. The forty consultants comprised an international committee, to which men like Lagrange, Prat, and Hummelauer were appointed. The intention of the founders was supervision (to preserve the faith) but also the support of truly scholarly studies. However, the question was whether the optimistic words which the Pope addressed to d'Hulst and which were recorded by Baudrillart[27] would have an impact.

[25] *Acta Leonis* XVII, 24f.

[26] *Acta Leonis* XXII, 232–38.

[27] "Il y a des esprits inquiets et chagrins qui pressent les congrégtions romaines de se prononcer sur des question encore douteuses. Je m'y oppose, je les arrête: car il ne faut pas empêcher les savants de travailler. Il faut leur laisser le loisir d'hésiter et même d'errer. La vérité ne peut qu'y gagner. L'Église arrivera toujours à temps pour les remettre dans le droit chemin" (A. Baudrillart, op. cit. I, 456).—Regarding Catholic exegesis from 1880 to 1914, Leo XIII's "more constructive than repressive initiative" at the founding of the Biblical Commission, and the measures taken after 1903, see J. Levie, *La Bible. Parole humaine et message de Dieu* (Paris, Louvain 1958), 46–88; cf. chap. 30.

CHAPTER 24

The Condemnation of "Americanism"

The term and theory of "Americanism" originated in French academic circles. This is the reason for the content of the papal letter *Testem benevolentiae* of 22 January 1899, addressed to Cardinal Gibbons, which condemned "opinions, the sum of which some call 'Americanism.'"[1] In 1897, Walter Elliot's biography of the founder of the Paulists, Isaac Hecker (1819–88), which appeared in the United States of America in 1891, was published in France in a shortened version prepared by the author himself from the French text. It was made "more attractive" (T. T. McAvoy, C.S.C.) by Abbé Félix Klein (1862–1953), who was professor at the Institut catholique in Paris from 1893 to 1907. The original edition had been given a special importance because the introduction was written by Archbishop Ireland, but it had not received particular attention. However, by calling Hecker the "priest of the future" and thus presenting the "American Way" of Catholicism as a model for the French traditionalists, Abbé Klein, in his foreword, gave a signal which aroused the indignation of the conservatives, who were already deeply wounded by the papal *Ralliement* policy. The book soon went through six editions. The same year, Denis O'Connell gave a lecture at the Congress for Catholic Scholars in Fribourg on Hecker and the advantages of American democracy. He encountered the strong opposition of the bishop of Nancy, Charles François.[2] In the spring of 1892, Ireland, who spoke fluent French since his youth,[3] was invited by the advocates of the current *Ralliement* policy in France to speak. He impressed Abbé Klein, who, in 1894, published a selection of his lectures under the title *L'Église et le Siècle*. Finally, he was contacted by those forces in French and American Catholicism which hoped to find the remedy for Church life by opening up toward the modern spirit that had arisen from the Revolution.[4] This contact was expedient, if only because the Gibbons-Ireland group had been in trouble since 1895.[5] In 1897, Ireland tried in his speeches to fend off the "retractors," charging them with rebelling against the Pope in conservative disguise.

The term "Americanism" was not defined by those who tried to follow the "American Way" in practice more than in theory, but rather by the French ultraconservatives. It began with a series of articles on *Amér-*

---

[1] *Acta Leonis* XIX, 5–20.

[2] F. X. Kraus (*Tagebücher,* 719) notes his agreement with L. Duchesne about Bishop Turinaz being a leader of the *rétrécissements.*—O'Connell's lecture: *Compte-rendu du IVe congrès* . . . (Fribourg 1898), 74–81.

[3] In 1899, he preached as guest of the French government on the occasion of the anniversary of Joan of Arc.

[4] F. X. Kraus (*Tagebücher,* 720) notes in April 1899 the plan of "a meeting of equal-minded men" in Freiburg i. Br., expecting, among others, Denis O'Connell, Loisy, Abbé Klein, and "maybe even" H. Schell: "They will negotiate a uniform attitude toward the Curia." At the end of 1898, O'Connell had visited Abbé Klein to discuss the impending papal condemnation. One has to consider, however, the notable differences between these "equal-minded men."

[5] Cf. chap. 10.

icanisme mystique by Charles Maignen, an opponent of the *Ralliement,* published under the pseudonym "Martel" in the conservative Paris paper *Vérité Française.* In a course of sermons, the Jesuits of Paris warned of the danger of "Hecker's Americanism" threatening the Church. In 1898, Maignen published his newspaper articles and other essays under the title *Études sur l'américanisme. Le Père Hecker, est-il un Saint?* Since Cardinal Richard refused the imprimatur, Maignen obtained approval from the *Magister Palatii,* the Dominican A. Lepidi in Rome, which was interpreted as papal sanction. Gibbons, Ireland, and Keane protested to Rome against the book, considering it a defamation of the American Catholicism they represented, while Archbishop Corrigan welcomed it. The controversies reached Belgium, Germany, and Italy and compounded the respective territorial tensions. The most vehement opponents of Hecker's friends were, among others, the Jesuit A. Delattre, who also sharply condemned the moderate biblical criticism of Lagrange; the Belgian Benedictine L. Jannsens at the Anselmianum in Rome; Merry del Val, who was promoted by Leo XIII and had been consulted in the battle against the validity of the Anglican ordinations; and especially Cardinals F. Satolli and Camillo Mazzella, S.J. (1833–1900), who taught dogmatics in Georgetown and Woodstock (after 1868) and at the Gregoriana (after 1878).[6]

The Pope rejected the request to put the Hecker biography on the Index and he appointed a Commission of Cardinals; representatives of the American episcopate were not included. The text of *Testem benevolentiae* was mainly written by Mazzela. The Pope changed the beginning and the end of the letter in order to avoid the impression of condemning the Gibbons group and the American situation. Whether Gibbons's telegram and Ireland's trip to Rome came "too late" (T. T. McAvoy C.S.C.) or whether the letter could not be retracted by any means cannot be determined.

Leo XIII's letter to Gibbons began with a few words about the Hecker biography, especially its translation, noting that it had caused innumerable controversies because of certain opinions about the Christian way of life; these problems the Pope would treat extensively later (*de re universa fusiori sermone*).[7] He condemned the following views: dogmas that are incomprehensible to contemporaries should not be denied, but rather be emphasized less or ignored; the ecclesiastical office is to refrain from authoritative statements to ensure the freedom of the individual through whom the Holy Spirit speaks more distinctly today than ever; natural virtues which promote activity are more impor-

---

[6] Regarding Satolli, see chap. 10; regarding Mazzella, see chap. 21.
[7] *Acta Leonis* XIX, 6.

tant than supernatural ones; contemplative orders used to be justified, however, today, active virtues are needed; vows in the older religious orders kill the freedom to make decisions, which are so necessary today; the apostolate has to relinquish the old methods if operating among non-Catholics.

None of the suspects identified with these condemned opinions. But it wounded them deeply that the *cavenda et corrigenda,* though in a quotation, was cited *Americanismi nomine.* On 27 February the tactful Ireland wrote to the Pope that all "misunderstandings" had been cleared away and "true Americanism" was only "what was so called by the Americans."[8] The letter by Cardinal Gibbons to the Pope was published *post festum:*[9] "I do not believe that there is a bishop, a priest, or even a layman in this country who knows his religion and utters such enormities. No, this is not, has never been, and will never be our Americanism." The opponents of the Gibbons group, however, among them the German Archbishop Katzer of Milwaukee, who compared the "Americanists" with the Jansenists, thanked the Pope for having saved the Church in America from a great danger. Even though it was not put on the Index, the Paulists took the Hecker biography off the book market.

A distinction was drawn between "dogmatic" and "historical" Americanism, the latter being defined in Abbé Klein's words as *une hérésie fantôme.*[10] However, one may question whether it was proper to extract papal doctrinal authority in this manner from its exceedingly complicated context; after all, the letter was addressed to Cardinal Gibbons. It is also questionable whether one could speak of a connection with modernism;[11] this depends entirely on the definition of "modernism" and the customary terminological distinctions. In the perspective of the Roman procedure, it was noted that the "basic tendency and method of defense against modernism had largely been anticipated."[12]

---

[8] It does not quite make sense that L. Hertling, S.J., 238f., should call this an "unfair" departure from the "friends in France," because not "friends" such as Abbé Klein, but C. Maignen and his followers were meant by Ireland when he wrote: "We can be upset about such insults inflicted upon us, the bishops, the faithful, and the nation."

[9] J. T. Ellis, *Gibbons* II (1952), 71.

[10] G. Weigel, *LThK*[2] I, 434f.—F. Klein, "Une hérésie fantôme: l'Américanisme," *Souvenirs* IV (Paris 1949).

[11] L. Hertling (op. cit., 232), not very friendly toward Gibbons: "Even the most fanatic Americanists did not consider for a moment loosening the ties which bound them to the Church and its center"; 243: it was "true injustice" that prompted A. Gisler to write that Americanism was the pioneer of modernism.—A. Houton, *L'Américanisme* (Paris 1903), was put on the Index; regarding A. Houtin, cf. chap. 30, n. 13.

[12] R. Lill, "Der Kampf der römischen Kurie gegen das 'praktischen' Modernismus," *Die päpstliche Autorität im Selbstverständnis des 19. und 20. Jahrhunderts,* ed. by E. Weinzierl; *Internationales Forschungszentrum . . . in Salzburg,* Discussion 11 (1970), 110.

Chapter 25

Papal Hopes for Unification
The Independent Eastern Churches and the Uniates

Papal Hopes for Unification

The unions formed with Eastern Churches by the Popes of modern times were felt by most Eastern Christians to be violations of their traditions, which go back to the first centuries. The Holy See recognized the dignity of the old liturgies, but its efforts toward unification were based too strictly on the Tridentine concept of the unified Church and did not consider sufficiently the evolutionary character of the national churches of the East, thus creating a "Uniatism" which was an obstacle to the organic unification of the independent Eastern Churches separated from the universal Church. The unionist initiatives which had arisen in the middle of the nineteenth century and had been partially adopted by the Propaganda Fide failed to develop.

Pius IX's proclamation of unification of 6 January 1848 in his encyclical *In suprema Petri Apostoli Sede* was harshly rejected by the four Orthodox patriarchs for its authoritarian tone. His brief *Arcano Divinae Providentiae consilio* of 8 September 1868, addressed to all Orthodox bishops, suggesting a return to Catholic unity and participation in the council, also failed; the Patriarch of Constantinople Gregorios (1867–71) bemoaned, for instance, the lack of respect for apostolic equality and brotherhood. Cardinal Alessandro Barnabò, prefect of the Congregation for the Propagation of the Faith, presided over the Commission for Missions and Churches of the Eastern Rites, one of the five subcommissions for the preparation of the First Vatican Council. This commission convened thirty-seven plenary sessions between 29 September 1867 and 9 May 1870.[1] At the first working session, Barnabò declared that the negotiations were to avoid everything that could possibly injure the feelings of the Orthodox. However, the topic, debated by the seventeen consultors for months concerned the possibility of applying the disciplinary canons of the Council of Trent to the Uniate Church and was therefore little suited to pay tribute to the spiritual heritage of the Christian Middle East. The commission's task, to deal simultaneously with problems of missions and the Uniate Churches, must have been shocking to the Eastern Churches. The Latin patriarch of Jerusalem, Archbishop Giuseppe Valerga (1813–72), participated energetically in the formulation of the mission plan, which had been prepared by the

---

[1] "Acta commissionis super missionibus et ecclesiis ritus orientalis," *Mansi* XLIX (1923), 985–1162.

commission and, after several revisions, on 26 June 1870, was extensively debated by the Council's fathers. More than half of the text (forty-four folio-size pages) dealt with the Uniate Churches, the rest (thirty-five pages) with the Latin mission in the Middle East. Valerga was intent on equating the Uniates with the Latin Church as far as canon law is concerned, but he wanted to let them retain their liturgical customs. At the request of the cardinals' commission, Valerga wrote a report on the manner in which the upcoming council was to handle questions regarding the Eastern Churches. At the council itself, the Uniate hierarchs were not united. The Melchite patriarch, Gregory II Jussef Sayyur (1864–97), the Chaldean patriarch, Joseph II Audo (1848–78), and the Syrian patriarch, Philip Argus (1866–74), left Rome before the final voting on the dogmatic constitution *Pastor aeternus* of 18 July 1870. Later, they agreed to it, but they remained indignant because of insufficient consideration of the patriarchs' traditional rights and privileges.

The pontificate of Leo XIII, who pursued liberal conciliatory policies in the political and social arena and hoped for reconciliation with the Anglicans and independent Eastern Churches, began a new phase in the relations between Rome and the Eastern Christians,[2] reflecting the results of scholarly research and productive dialogues between open-minded experts. The reunification of those separated from the Church by belief and obedience was one of the Pope's main objectives, which he advocated in 6 encyclicals, 7 apostolic briefs, 14 pronouncements, and 5 addresses.[3] Reunification was an integral part of his mission as peacemaker. In his encyclical *Grande munus christiani nominis propagandi* of 30 September 1880, on the Apostles of the Slavs, Cyril and Methodius,[4] the Pope drew attention to the close relationship between those two men and the Holy See and to the Pope's interest in the Slavic peoples. He had special concern for the Eastern Churches and his most ardent wish was for them to unite with "Us and be committed to the eternal bond of unity (*concordia*)."[5] The Uniates welcomed the encyclical with enthusiasm, for instance at the pilgrimage of fourteen Slavs on 5 July 1881 in Rome. It was led by Bishop Josip Jurij Stroßmayer of

---

[2] L. Berg, "La réunion des églises orientales avec l'église catholique romaine au cours des siècles," *Ex Oriente,* op. cit., 115–17; A. S. Hernández, op. cit., 413–17; J. Alameda, op. cit., 91–99; R. F. Esposito, op. cit., 687–701; W. de Vries, *Orthodoxie,* 127–34; J. Hajjar, op. cit., 243–51.

[3] R. F. Esposito, op. cit., 412. According to his estimate, Leo XIII discussed the Christian East in thirty-two important documents and in more than two hundred paragraphs. He lists 248 significant papal statements (ibid., 702–12, appendix 1: *I documenti Leoniani interessanti l'Oriente*).

[4] *ASS* XIII (1880), 145–53.

[5] Ibid., 152.

Djakovo,[6] who had impressed the Pope with his ideas on ways of uniting with Russia and the Slavic faithful. Catholic Panslavism, which Stroßmayer supported and which originated in the Brotherhood of Saints Cyril and Methodius (in existence since the middle of the nineteenth century), encountered resistance in Russia, where it was feared its influence on the Slavs in the Habsburg Monarchy and on the Balkans would suffer a setback.

England's occupation of Egypt in 1882 and the Russian Orthodox Imperial Society of Palestine, founded the same year, turned Leo XIII's attention to the Near East. The Greek government asked that the Pope no longer appoint bishops *in partibus infidelium* for vacant episcopal sees in the Greek territories. The Pope granted the wish on 10 June 1882, using the term *episcopus titularis* in his apostolic letter *In suprema*.[7]

In 1883, he received two extensive reports concerning the resumption of contacts with the Orthodox Churches. One was written by the apostolic delegate of Constantinople, Serafino Vannutelli. His motion regarding "the best available means to lead the dissidents back to the Catholic Church"[8] demonstrated the failure of the Latin missionaries in the Near East and criticized their Latinization measures. The other report was written by Carlo Gallien, the Turkish consul general in Rome. He suggested sending new missionary societies into the respective areas, once their members had been made aware of the basic problems. The papal brief *Abbiamo appreso* of 4 January 1887,[9] addressed to Giuseppe Benedetto Cardinal Dusmet, O.S.B., archbishop of Catania, seemed to be the first to be inspired by this proposal. In this brief, the Pope congratulated Dusmet, praising him for reopening the College of Saint Anselmo and including it in plans for the Christian Near East.

New ideas came from the Eucharistic Congress in Jerusalem of 14 to 21 May 1893.[10] Bishop Victor Doutreloux of Liège (president of the Permanent Committee for Eucharistic Congresses, which prepared the Jerusalem Congress together with the Superior General of the Assumptionists, François Picard), expected the participation of representatives of the Eastern Churches paying homage to the Eucharist, and hoped for the return of the separated brethren to the great Catholic family. Leo XIII avoided expected diplomatic complications by informing Sultan Abdul Hamid (1876–1909) and Emperor Alexander III of Russia (1881–94) (via a French mediator) about the planned congress

[6] See chap. 11, p. 184.
[7] *Acta Leonis* I (1887), 277–85, especially 283f.
[8] J. Hajjar, op. cit., 243.
[9] *Acta Leonis* II (1887), 250–53, especially 252f.
[10] *Irénikon* 1 (1926), 353–57; A. S. Hernández, op. cit., 414–17; O. Rousseau, op. cit., 370–71; R. F. Esposito, op. cit., 367–84; C. Soetens, op. cit., 107–15.

and by assuring the governments in Berlin, Vienna, and London that the meeting had a strictly religious purpose. He appointed Cardinal Benedict Maria Langénieux, archbishop of Rheims, his legate and president of the congress, which was attended by thousands of Catholic pilgrims, several cardinals, fifteen dignitaries of the Roman Catholic Church, eighteen representatives of the Uniate Churches, and twenty priests of the independent Eastern Churches. In his opening address, the cardinal legate emphasized the fact that his mission was marked by the sign of love and piety, implying an invitation to unite in faith. The congress submitted to the Pope eight desiderata, including Eucharistic prayers of Eastern liturgies in manuals of Roman Catholics, the encouragement of studies on the religious problems of the Eastern Churches with a view to church union; and the strengthening of relations between the faithful of the East and West and their clergy.

The Pope had ordered Cardinal Langénieux to inquire into the situation of the Uniates, the impact of the Latinization measures, and ways and means of overcoming the separation of the Eastern Churches from Rome. On 23 May, the Melchite Patriarch Gregory II Jussef Sayyur delivered a complaint concerning the Latinization measures, claiming they hindered the task and mission of the Uniate Churches. On 2 July, the cardinal of Lourdes sent a secret report to Rome on his investigations.[11] Remembering the consequences of the Crusades, which are still felt today, he mentioned the Eastern Christians' mistrust of private interests and political goals. He also reprimanded Latin missionaries, whose behavior often contradicted apostolic directives, and expressed regret over the predominance of the Latin rites over the Uniate rites. He described the lack of authority and power of the Uniate Churches, which suffered from a lack of support and whose clergy was insufficiently trained. He reiterated the objections and opinions voiced by Latin missionaries, claiming that the theory of the apostolate of Uniate Christians in the Eastern Churches was a utopia. He was convinced of the future of the Uniate Churches, hoping that their revival could overcome their inferiority and link the Roman Catholics with the Eastern Orthodox. To disperse the prejudice of the schismatics and to strengthen the Uniates, he stressed the publication of an encyclical that would clarify papal principles regarding Eastern Christianity.

The apostolic brief *Praeclara gratulationis* of 20 June 1894,[12] which Leo XIII addressed to all sovereigns and peoples on occasion of the 50th anniversary of his consecration as bishop, clearly reflects the ideas that were inspired by the Jerusalem Congress. He recalled the original

[11] J. Hajjar, op. cit., 246–48.
[12] *ASS* XXVI (1893–94), 705–17; cf. R. F. Esposito, op. cit., 385–90.

unity of the Church, challenging the Eastern Christians to restore it. All Christians in the East and West, he said, recognized the Roman bishop, the successor to Saint Peter, before their separation. He promised that he and his successors would not touch their rights, the privileges of the patriarchs, their rites and customs. The Pope devoted one paragraph to the Slavic peoples, pointing out that the papacy had supported them since the time of Cyril and Methodius, but that a great segment had been alienated from the Roman belief; he therefore challenged them to unite. As far as the Eastern Churches were concerned, this programmatic letter contained the "first appeal for ecclesiastical unity with acceptable arguments."[13]

To use the results of the Congress in Jerusalem to strengthen further the Uniate Churches and reunite with the Eastern Churches, Leo XIII organized and chaired several conferences with Uniate patriarchs (24–28 November). In attendance were the Melchite Patriarch, Gregory II Jussef Sayyur, the Syrian Patriarch, Cyril Behnam Benni (1893–97), the patriarchal vicar, Archbishop Elias Huayek (replacing the aging Maronite Patriarch, John Hagg [1890–98, born 1817]),[14] Cardinal Secretary of State Rampolla, the Cardinals Galimberti, Langénieux, Ledóchowski, and Vincenzo Vannutelli, who had been sent as papal legate to Saint Petersburg in 1882 on the occasion of Tsar Alexander III's coronation. These patriarchal conferences clearly defined the competencies of Latin missionaries and the rights of Uniate dignitaries. They also prepared the papal brief *Orientalium dignitas* of 30 November 1894,[15] which relinquished the adaptation of rites and disciplines to Latin. "The preservation of the Eastern rites is more important than one is led to believe. The honorable age which distinguishes the various rites dignifies the entire Church and confirms the divine unity of Catholic belief."[16] In thirteen theses, the Pope gave guidelines for the preservation of the old liturgies. He strengthened his intention to expand the Uniate seminaries and colleges for the native clergy.

In his letter *Christi nomen* of 24 December 1894,[17] Leo XIII referred to his expositions in the apostolic brief *Praeclara gratulationis* of 20 June, stressing his efforts toward unity with the Eastern Churches and asking for support and training of a qualified Uniate clergy. In the motu

---

[13] J. Hajjar, op. cit., 248.
[14] Armenian Patriarch Stefan Peter X Azarian (1881–99), residing in Constantinople, did not receive permission from the sultan to leave the country. The Chaldean patriarchate was vacant after the death of Patriarch Elias XII Abolionan (1879–94).
[15] *ASS* XXVII (1894–95), 257–64: *De disciplina orientalium conservanda et tuenda.*
[16] Ibid., 258.
[17] Ibid., 385–87.

proprio *Optatissimae* of 19 March 1895,[18] he decreed that a permanent cardinals' commission for Uniate rites and reunification, chaired by Cardinal Ledóchowski, continue the deliberations of the patriarchal conferences of the fall of 1894. The brief *Provida matris* of 5 May 1895,[19] on preparation for Pentecost, the extensive encyclicals *Satis cognitum* of 29 June 1896,[20] dealing with the unity of the Church, and *Divinum illud munus* of 9 May 1897,[21] concerning the Holy Spirit, elaborated his theological thoughts and practical suggestions pertaining to the union. On the occasion of the publication of the encyclical of 29 June 1896, Leo XIII had a medal struck, the front of which displayed his image with the inscription *Pontifex maximus* and the year of his pontificate (*anno XIX*) while the reverse side showed an allegory of Church unity with the words: "May there be one fold and one shepherd."[22]

All these pronouncements differed from earlier papal utterances in their tone and their expression of sympathy for the Eastern Christians. They avoided terms like "schismatics" and "heretics," instead using words like *fratelli separati* or *dissidenti;* they distinguished themselves by respect for the rites and ecclesiastical laws of the East and prepared the climate for reconciliation. These papal efforts of appeasement were supported by Catholic diplomats (the Belgian Baron d'Erp),[23] princes of the Church (Cardinals Langénieux and Vincenzo Vannutelli), bishops (Doutreloux of Liège and Stroßmayer of Djakovo) and theologians (Abbé Fernand Portal),[24] who passionately pleaded for closer relations between the Catholic Church and the Anglicans as well as the Eastern Christians. Portal was a friend of Lord Halifax's and was inspired by the ideas of Russian religious philosophers, especially those of Vladimir Soloviev (1853–1900),[25] who, as an Orthodox Christian, recognized the

---

[18] *ASS* XXVIII (1895–96), 323–24: *De commissione pontificia ad reconciliationem dissidentium cum Ecclesia fovendam.*

[19] *ASS* XXVII (1894–95), 646–47.

[20] *ASS* XXVIII (1895–96), 708–39; also cf. R. F. Esposito, op. cit., 420–56.

[21] *ASS* XXIX (1896–97), 644–58; also cf. R. F. Esposito, op. cit., 462–67.

[22] *Fiet. Unum. Ovile. Et. Unus. Pastor. MDCCCXCVI*, cf. L. K. Goetz, op. cit., 233–34.

[23] R. Aubert, *Un document*, 429–35.

[24] F. Portal. op. cit., 5–8; also cf. A. Gratieux, op. cit.

[25] V. Solovjev, *La Russie et l'Église universelle* (Paris 1889); id., *Monarchia Sancti Petri. Die kirchliche Monarchie des heiligen Petrus als freie und universelle Theokratie im Lichte der Weisheit. Aus den Hauptwerken von Wladimir Solowjew systematisch gesammelt, übersetzt und erklärt*, ed. by L. Kobilinski-Ellis (Mainz, Wiesbaden 1929); id., *Una Sancta. Schriften zur Vereinigung der Kirchen und zur Grundlegung der universalen Theokratie*, 2 vols. (Freiburg i. Br. 1954–57); cf. T. G. Masaryk, *Zur russischen Geschichts- und Religionsphilosophie. Soziologische Skizzen* II (Jena 1913), 225–77; L. Kobilinski-Ellis, "Die freie Theokratie nach der Lehre von Wladimir Solowjew," *Ex Oriente*, op. cit., 278–86; T. Grivec, "L'Indépendance et originalité de Wladimir Solowjew," ibid., 298–305; *Un*

Pope and supported unification with Rome, the traditional center of the Christian world. For Soloviev, the papacy was a *mysterium unitatis,* the center of apostolicity, universality, and ecumenicity, the temporal manifestation and metaphor of the great secret of *Sophia.* In his philosophical works he strove to make his doctrine of the sophic world-soul agree with Christian theology.[26] His convictions regarding the Russian Church's mission to unify all the churches evoked no response in the Eastern Churches during his lifetime, but his writings have had an ecumenical impact to the present day.

Leo XIII's intentions were published in numerous theological periodicals: the *L'Œuvre d'Orient* (published since 1857 in Paris), the *Revue de l'Orient chrétien* (Paris 1896), *Échos d'Orient* (since 1897, the quarterly published by the Assumptionists' Central Institute for Eastern Studies), and the *Oriens Christianus* (Rome, after 1901, for the study of the Christian East). These and other periodicals, such as *Bessarione, pubblicazione periodica di Studi Orientali,* published in Rome since 1896, provided a wealth of information, documentation, historical and theological research. By virtue of their scholarly integrity and theological sensitivity they rendered a clear picture of the history and the current situation of Eastern Christianity.

Generously, Leo XIII supported the Assumptionists, Benedictines, Dominicans, Jesuits, Capuchins, Carmelites, Lazarists, Lyon Missionaries, Redemptorists, Salesians, Christian Brothers, and White Fathers, who actively advocated the union in their pastoral work. The Pope also founded or restored colleges in Rome to train the Uniate clergy, such as the Armenian College (1883) and the Maronite College (1891). He carefully placed suitable candidates in the Propaganda College and in the international academies of orders, such as the pontifical Benedictine academy, the Anselmianum. He established Uniate seminaries and schools for the Copts in Cairo, for the Melchites in Jerusalem, for the Bulgarians in Plovdiv and Adrianople, for the Syrians and Chaldeans in Mosul, for the Greeks in Constantinople, Kadikoy (formerly Chalcedon), and in Athens. He willingly donated considerable funds for the development of these educational institutions.

Even though the Uniate Churches did not increase in their membership to any considerable extent in the last decades of the nineteenth

---

moine de l'Église d'Orient, La signification de Soloviev: 1054–1954. L'Église et les églises, neuf siècles de douloureuse séparation entre l'Orient et l'Occident II, ed. by L. Beauduin (Chevetogne 1955), 369–79; G. Florowski, op. cit., 295–96; St. Napierała, "Wizja jedności kościoła w 'wielkim sporze' Włodzimierza Sołowjewa," *Collectanea Theologica* 40 (1970), 49–62.

[26] B. Schultze, "Probleme der orthodoxen Theologie," *Handbuch der Ostkirchenkunde,* op. cit., 144–55.

century, the Pope emphasized their unique value within Catholicism as a whole. In his encyclicals and many other writings, Leo XIII traced their historical descent from early Christianity and the first Christian centuries to the missionary popes of the early Middle Ages who assured the Slavs their own ecclesiastical language, to the re-union councils of the early and high Middle Ages, the Second Council of Lyon in 1274 and the Council of Basel-Ferrara-Florence-Rome in 1431–45, and to the popes of modern times who struggled for union, especially Benedict XIV. These references alleviated the Uniates' inferiority complex; they no longer felt isolated, but were confirmed in their conviction of being recognized members of the universal Catholic Church, and entrusted with the task of building a bridge to the separated Eastern Christians. Their patriarchs, who had suffered under the Latinization measures instituted by Rome and under disciplinary regulations, were relieved and, because of the papal kindness and its accompanying proclamations, they felt themselves to be on equal footing with the Roman Catholic episcopate.

The Pope expected his unification program, his personal involvement on behalf of reunification with the separated Eastern Churches, and the expansion of the Uniate Churches to be successful. But many external and internal difficulties obstructed the realization of his ambitions. Turkish, French, Austro-Hungarian, and Russian interests clashed in the Balkans and in the Middle East. The cultural protectorate,[27] which had developed from an institution of international law into a protectorate of foreign countries over Christians living in Turkey, enabled France (since the sixteenth century) and Austria (since the end of the eighteenth century) to obtain certain privileges, particularly since numerous churches were under their protection and financed by them. The attempt to win over the Orthodox Slavs had to take Russia into consideration. When favoring the Uniate Slavs in Austria-Hungary, the delicate situation in this multi-national state could not be ignored. By order of their governments, diplomats intervened and expressed their anxieties over possible conflicts, as did, for instance, the Russian representative at the Vatican, Alexander Izvolsky (1888–96), and the Austro-Hungarian ambassador to the Vatican, Duke Friedrich Revertera-Salandra (1888–1901).[28]

At the Curia, Leo XIII encountered resistance to his unification efforts and rejection of his personally benevolent attitude toward the Eastern Churches. He was unable to transfer his hopes to his immediate environment and the lower levels of his administration. Also, the penal

[27] J. Lammeyer, op. cit., 57–82, 84–88, M. Lehmann, op. cit., 37–44.
[28] A. Hudal, op. cit., 236–54; G. Adrianyi, op. cit., 241–339.

regulations regarding Latinizing missionaries contained in his encyclical *Orientalium dignitas*[29] were not very successful because they were not obeyed by the order members who devoted their efforts to traditional Latinization.[30] Yet the Pope adhered to his ideas. According to Revertera's notes of New Year's Day 1897, Leo XIII desired to attempt the ecclesiastical unification with the Christian nations outside of the Church. This, Revertera said, would be very difficult in Russia: "He could not hope to witness more than the first dawn of a future which he so ardently desired."[31]

Leo XIII had no illusions about the impending reunification with the Eastern Churches. Yet he strove for the unity of all Christians in the one and only Church, a characteristic of all his ecclesiological thoughts, which were the focal point of his theological concepts.[32] When he died in 1903, the Uniates lost in him a pioneer and protector. His initiative prepared an ecumenical foundation which led to détente between Rome and the separated Eastern Churches, was continued by his successors, was reinforced by Pope John XXIII, and is still in effect.

His successor, Pius X (1903–14) proved to be primarily a pragmatic spiritual adviser. As patriarch of Venice (1894–1903), he had learned about the Slavic liturgy and the interests of the union through the Mechitharists, the Armenian Uniate monks, whose monastery on the island of San Lazzaro near Venice had been the center of religious and scholarly work since 1717. As Pope, he renewed the unification efforts of Leo XIII. He put the Roman churches San Lorenzo ai Monti and San Salvatore alle Capelle at the disposal of the Uniate Russians and Rumanians. He personally took charge of the protectorate over the Greek abbey of Grottaferrata near Rome, for which his predecessor, in 1881 had decreed the use of the original Greek-Byzantine rite. In 1904 he attended the celebration of the nine hundredth anniversary of the abbey, and he supported it throughout his pontificate. He anxiously observed the situation of the Uniates in Galicia and the propaganda of Russian missionaries in favor of unification with the Orthodox Church. For the Uniate Ruthenians, who had emigrated to the United States of America from Galicia and Hungary, he issued the bull *Ea semper* of 14 June 1907;[33] that year, he appointed Vicar Apostolic Stephan Soter

---

[29] See above, n. 15.

[30] W. de Vries, *Orthodoxie,* 128: "In 1920, the Oriental Congregation had to resign itself to the fact that Latinization continued after *Orientalum dignitas* and that penalties were not enforced and could not be enforced."

[31] F. Engel-Janosi, op. cit. I, 322.

[32] E. Hocedez, *Histoire de la théologie au XIXe siècle* III (Brussels, Paris 1947), 387–91; R. F. Esposito, op. cit., 409–97.

[33] *ASS* XLI (1908), 1–12.

Ortynski and (in 1912) he sent, on behalf of the Ruthenians in Canada, Niceta Budka[34] to be the bishop of Winnipeg. In his letter *Quidquid consilii* of 8 June 1908, addressed to Uniate Archbishop Andreas Szepticki of Lemberg (1900–44), he recognized the unification efforts of the separated Eastern Churches and praised him in his capacity as president of the Union Congresses in Welehrade.[35]

By order of the Pope, Cardinal Vannutelli prepared festivities in Rome to honor the fifteen hundredth anniversary of the death of the patriarch of Constantinople, John Chrysostom,[36] who was venerated by Christians in both the East and West. On 12 February 1908, in Saint Peter's Cathedral, Melchite Patriarch Cyril VIII Geha (1903–16) and his bishops and archimandrites celebrated the liturgy in the presence of the Pope, who sang the benediction, which according to their rite was to be delivered in the Greek language by the highest dignitary present. The next day he spoke to the numerous Uniates who had come to Rome of the Holy See's respect for the dignity and glory of the Eastern rites; he assured them that the Pope would guard the preservation of their national customs, that the congregation for the Propagation of the Faith would annually send a number of native priests to the East with the message to remain loyal to national rites and to avoid conversion to the Latin rite, and that he admired the accomplishments of great Eastern men and intended to make efforts to revive their heritage.[37]

In his apostolic letter *Ex quo* of 26 December 1910,[38] the Pope declared that the interest of the Holy See in the problems of the Eastern Churches had not ceased, that his predecessors had passionately desired the end of the separation, and that all Catholics were obligated to support the reunification. In 1910 he approved the world prayer octave for the unification of the separated Christians, which was to last from 18 to 25 January and had been initiated by the Anglican clergyman Paul J. Francis Wattson (1863–1940), who had converted in 1909 to the Catholic Church together with the Brother- and Sisterhood of the Reconciliation, which he had founded. The octave was observed after 1908

---

[34] *AAS* IV (1912), 531, 555–56.

[35] *Acta Pii* V (1971), 287–88.

[36] *ÉO* 11 (1908), 131–46; C. Charam, *Le quinzième centenaire de Jean Chrysostome* (Rome 1909); B. Arens, *Papst Pius X und die Weltmission* (Aachen 1919), 16–18.

[37] *ASS* XLI (1908), 130–34; *Allocutio, quam die 13 Februarii 1908 Pius X habuit ad Orientales.*

[38] *AAS* III (1911), 117–21.—This letter was addressed to all apostolic delegates in the East and took issue with an article published in *Roma e l'Oriente* (see n. 40). Its dogmatic and historical errors were criticized and corrected (also cf. "*Roma e l'Oriente* pensieri sull'unione delle chiese," *CivCatt,* 62 [1911], I, 64–78, and "La parola del papa intorno all'unione delle chiese," ibid., 129–34).

by the Anglican and Catholic congregations in the United States and spread in the next decades to most of the Christian Churches.[39]

After 1910 the monks of Grottaferrata published the periodical *Roma e l'Oriente,* which proselytized for the union of the Eastern Churches with Rome and was subsidized actively by the Pope. He was not always in agreement with all its articles, especially not with the essay "Thoughts about the Question of the Reunification of the Churches," which was written by Prince Maximilian of Saxony, a professor who had done respectable studies on Eastern liturgies.[40] In this article Prince Maximilian spoke of the Roman lust for power. Yet in 1914 the Pope wrote to the editor: "Continue with your work on behalf of a difficult and frustrating cause and always apply the necessary wisdom."[41]

In 1912 he established for the Hungarian Uniates the diocese of Hajdudorog.[42] On 14 September of the same year, in connection with his liturgical reforms which earned him the sobriquet "Pope of the Liturgy," Pius X published the apostolic constitution *Tradita ab antiquis,*[43] dealing with the receiver and administrator of Holy Communion. He gave the faithful the choice whether they wanted to receive the Eucharist in the form of leavened or unleavened bread, and, if possible, they were to receive Communion according to their own rites during Easter and the last viaticum.[44]

Under Pius X's pontificate, the interest in the independent churches and those united with Rome was not as pronounced as under the pontificate of his predecessor; yet the papal hopes for reunification did not cease.[45] The Pope assessed the possibilities of realizing his ambitions more sceptically and more realistically than Leo XIII. He did not share the optimism which had permeated Leo's proclamations. He was worried about the division of the Uniates into smaller churches where the lay element exerted great influence. He carefully observed the political development in Galicia and Southeastern Europe, and the attempts of the Orthodox Church to convert the Slavs of Dalmatia. He doubted

---

[39] R. Aubert, *La semaine de prières pour l'unité chrétien* (Louvain 1950); A. S. Hernández, op. cit., 417–19.

[40] Max Prince de Saxe, "Pensées sur la question de l'union des églises," *Roma e l'Oriente* 1 (1910–1911), 13–29; cf. Schmidlin, *PG* III, 129, n. 4.

[41] "Pio X e le chiese orientali," *Roma e l'Oriente* 8 (1914), 70.

[42] *AAS* IV (1912), 429–35.

[43] Ibid., 609–17.

[44] J. Hajjar (op. cit., 251–52) assesses this constitution, which was dictated by motives of spiritual guidance in order to facilitate a more frequent Communion recommended by Pius X. Hajjar considers it to be an "anti-Oriental reaction" and "a step backward under Pius X."

[45] B. Arens, op. cit., 5–18; A. S. Hernández, op. cit., 417–19; J. Alameda, op. cit., 101–05.

whether Austria-Hungary would be able to preserve its cultural protectorate in the Balkans and feared the annexation of the Slavs to Russia, which he considered the greatest enemy of the Church.[46] Therefore, he urged that the Uniates be bound closer to the Holy See and that they strengthen their religious life.

It was Benedict XV who finally created institutions which, taking Leo XIII's appeals seriously, could reliably carry out papal unification policies in the twentieth century. These institutions were the *Sacra Congregatio pro Ecclesia Orientali* (the result of the motu proprio *Dei providentis* of 1 May 1917)[47] in which the Uniate Churches were freed from the union with other Roman congregations and placed under their own cardinals' congregation; and the Pontifical Institute of Oriental Studies (the result of the motu proprio Orientis Catholici of 15 October 1917),[48] which was devoted to the study and teaching of all Eastern Churches and trained men to serve the reconciliation of the churches.

The Independent Eastern Churches

To facilitate an understanding of the papal unification efforts and the development of Church history at the end of the nineteenth and the beginning of the twentieth century, we insert a brief summary of the situation of the Eastern Churches separated from Rome, which can be divided into five groups: 1) the Orthodox Church in Russia (100 million), which had assumed jurisdiction over the Georgian Church in the nineteenth century; 2) three Orthodox Churches in Austria-Hungary: the Serbian Church of Karlowitz (800,000), the Church of Bukovina and of Dalmatia (550,000), the Church of Sibiu for the Rumanians living in Hungary (220,000); 3) five national Orthodox Churches in Southeastern Europe: the Church in Rumania (5 million), in Bulgaria (3.5 million), in Serbia (2.5 million), in Greece (2 million), in Montenegro (150,000); 4) the four old Orthodox patriarchates of Constantinople, Alexandria, Antioch, and Jerusalem (8.5 million); 5) the National Church of the Syrian Nestorians (80,000), the Monophysite Churches of the West Syrian Jacobites (100,000), the Thomist Christians in Southern India (450,000) the Copts in Egypt (800,000), the Ethiopians (3.5 million), and the Armenians (4 million).[49]

---

[46] L. v. Pastor, *Tagebücher—Briefe—Erinnerungen,* ed. by W. Wühr (Heidelberg 1950), 584–85; F. Engel-Janosi, op. cit. II, 122–25.

[47] *AAS* IX (1917), 529–31.

[48] Ibid., 531–33.

[49] Cf. N. Zernow, op. cit., 314–320. The numbers of faithful he lists for the year 1910 need to be corrected in some cases, especially regarding the Orthodox in Austria-Hungary (see n. 69) and the four old patriarchal churches: Constantinople: 3 million, Alexandria: 50,000, Antioch: 250,000, and Jerusalem: 20,000.

The Orthodox Church in Russia

The largest and most influential Orthodox Church was the Russian State Church, which was ruled by the Holy Synod. Since the dissolution of the first Muscovite patriarchate at the beginning of the eighteenth century, the State Church was more than ever subject to the monarchs who called themselves autonomous rulers by the grace of God. The Holy Synod was considered an administrative organ of the state, and it felt its subordination to be submission to the ruler himself. The Synod was chaired by the metropolitan of Moscow, but he was completely dependent on the representatives of the Tsar and on the chief procurator, whom Peter I had appointed as the chief secretary of the chancellory and called "our eye and administrator of state affairs." He received ministerial rank and was empowered with unlimited authority over the Church, which reached its peak in the second half of the nineteenth century.

Chief Procurator Count Dmitri Tolstoy (1865–80) was a dry bureaucrat who wanted to pursue reforms in the Church similar to those in the state. He abolished the division of the bishoprics into three categories and regulated the salaries of the secular clergy in detail. He had little interest in matters of faith and extended the liberal reforms of Alexander II to the seminaries (1867) and academies (1869). His plan to reform clerical jurisdiction was never completed. He was extraordinarily critical of the Catholic Church, as is proven both by his two-volume work about the Catholics in Russia,[50] which he had written as a civil servant in the Department for Spiritual Affairs and Foreign Creeds in the Ministry of the Interior, and by his strict incorporation of the faithful of the Uniate bishopric of Chelm (1875) into the Russian State Church.

His successor, Constantin Petrovich Pobedonostsev (1880–1905),[51] an outstanding lawyer and jurist, was a devout and pious Orthodox Christian. He grew up with the ideals of Muscovite Russia: Church and state, the faithful, and the tsar all form a unity according to the example of the Byzantine State Church. He considered people's sovereignty, parliamentarism, and democracy to be the great falsehoods of the time. He rejected liberal innovations and believed that a powerful authority headed by the patriarchal autocrat, preservation of the traditional faith,

[50] D. A. Tolstoj, *Le catholicisme romain en Russie*, 2 vols. (Paris 1863–64).
[51] F. Steinmann, E. Hurwicz, *Konstantin Petrowitsch Pobjedonoscew, der Staatsmann der Reaktion unter Alexander III.* (Königsberg 1933); R. F. Byrnes, *Pobedonostsev. His Life and Thought* (London 1968); G. Simon, *Konstantin Petrovič Pobedonoscev und die Kirchenpolitik des Heiligen Synod* 1880–1905 (Göttingen 1969); F. Jockwig, *Der Weg der Laien auf das Landeskonzil der Russischen Orthodoxen Kirche, Moskau 1917/18. Werden und Verwirklichung einer demokratischen Idee in der Russischen Kirche* (Würzburg 1971), 42–55.

encouragement of the liturgy and worship of icons, and reinforcement and strengthening of monarchism would protect Russia from revolutionary threats. Under Tsars Alexander II, Alexander III, and Nicholas II he conducted the affairs of the Russian State Church. He supervised the election of the bishops, allowed them little independence, and systematically expanded the administrative body of the Holy Synod to supervise the Church. He felt responsible for state and Church, wanting to protect the latter against fads and to strengthen it for its providential task of preserving the state. He provided the clerical schools, seminaries, and academies with new statutes in order to purge them of liberal infiltration. He reorganized parochial schools, demanding considerable state funds for their development. He intensified the Orthodox mission among the Old Believers, fought against the sectarian groups of the Dukobors, Molokans, Chilysty, and Skoptsy, and opposed all non-Orthodox religious congregations in Russia, such as the Catholic Church, the Evangelical Lutheran Church, Evangelical sects like the Stundists, and the Muslims.

On the occasion of the nine hundredth anniversary of the Christianization of Russia by Grand Duke Vladimir I of Kiev (979–1015) on 15 July 1888, Pobedonostsev delivered a speech in which he pointed out that Russia had risen to its present height because of Christianity and under the flag of the autocracy of the tsar.[52] True Orthodox religiosity, Russian Church policy, and Russian Panslavism converged in the secular and ecclesiastical meetings that were attended by the Orthodox metropolitans of Serbia and Montenegro, by a Greek archimandrite, Serbian and Rumanian delegations, and Abyssinians. Ruthenians and Slovacs from Galicia and Hungary also assembled, in spite of their governments' prohibition against travel outside the country. The historical significance of this anniversary, which extended beyond the Russian borders, was characterized by, among other things, a telegram, sent by Bishop Stroßmayer of Djakovo to Tsar Alexander III.[53]

The chief procurator asserted his leading position in Church and state administration during the first years of Nicholas II's government, so that one can speak of the age of Pobedonostsev. It ended with the Revolution of 1905, the collapse of autocracy, the toleration edict of Nicholas

[52] F. Steinmann, E. Hurwicz, op. cit., 208: "We are standing under this flag, under it we form a united entity with a united will, and in it we see the future guarantee of truth, order, and the welfare of our country."

[53] J. Matl, "Josef Georg Stroßmayer," *Neue Österreichische Biographie* sect. i, IX (Vienna 1956), 76: "I have the honor and sincere pleasure of participating in this festivity. . . . May God bless Russia and help her to fulfill in true faith with God's help and with Christian courage this great world mission which God assigned to her in spite of all her other duties."

II of 17 April and his manifesto of 30 October, in which he promised the introduction of civil liberties and general suffrage. Without success, Pobedonostsev protested against the toleration edict, which annulled the restrictions he had imposed for decades. In vain he worked on a project for the Duma, whose members were only entitled to propose legislative bills to the Council of State. The project was announced on 6 August, but was neither accepted by the liberal nor by the revolutionary critics. As he had done throughout the last few years, he bemoaned the fact that there was no longer an authority that was ready to fight. Because of questions pertaining to Church reforms and a council, which the patriarchate of the Russian Orthodox Church was to restore (questions which were debated in ecclesiastical circles and in the press), Pobedonostsev resigned two days after the publication of the October manifesto, twenty-five years after taking office. After his resignation, he wrote to Bishop Eulogi Georgievski (1868–1946), who was at that time bishop of Lublin and later, in the emigration, metropolitan of Paris: "The situation has become intolerable. . . . In the church itself wolves appeared who did not spare the sheep."[54] A time of gloom and the power of darkness had arrived, he wrote, it was time to go.

The protests against the power of bureaucracy in the Church were continued by the first constitutional prime minister, Duke Serge Witte (1905–6) and Metropolitan Antoni Wadkovski (1898–1912) from Saint Petersburg. Nicholas II ordered the metropolitans of Saint Petersburg, Moscow, and Kiev to convene a national council in order to "change the structure of our national Church on the solid basis of the ecumenical canon for the purpose of consolidating Orthodoxy."[55] A precouncil committee met from 8 March to 15 December 1906,[56] working as seven commissions, whose minutes were published. The deliberations were based on responses to a questionnaire which the Holy Synod had sent to the bishops on 29 July 1905. They dealt with the upper Church leadership, diocesan administration, parishes, and the principle of councils; and they contained extensive proposals for the council, e.g., the participation of laymen in the council's proceedings. In six plenary meetings, the resolutions of the commissions were voted on.[57] The votes were unanimously in favor of rejuvenating the patriarchate, on limiting the authority of the chief procurator to a mere controlling function, and

---

[54] I. Smolitsch, op. cit., 213f. n. 8.—After his dismissal, Pobedonostsev wrote several essays expressing his protest against state and Church reforms. He died on 10 March 1907.

[55] Ibid., 320.

[56] F. Jockwig, op. cit., 101–32.

[57] Ibid., 164–81.

on appointing laymen to the council. There was disagreement about the clergy and laity's right to vote, about standing orders, and other questions of formalities. Nicholas II, after dissolving the Second Duma on 8 July 1906, once again ruled autocratically. He suspended the precouncil committee and assigned the preparations for the National Council to the Holy Synod, which presented him with a comprehensive report. After a few changes, he approved it, but postponed the council indefinitely.

Four insignificant men[58] held the office of the chief procurator between 1905 and 1911. Then, in May, it was occupied by C. V. Sabler (1911–15), who had been Pobedonostsev's closest adviser from 1892 until 1905. He rose to the leadership of the Holy Synod, limited the religious freedom of non-Orthodox Churches through special regulations which were enacted by the Ministry of the Interior, and treated the proposals of the precouncil committee dilatorily, although he established, in 1912, a precouncil commission at the Holy Synod. He was intent on restoring the harmony between Church and state and initiated appropriate declarations on the occasion of the three hundredth anniversary of the ruling Romanov family (1913) and on the occasion of the outbreak of World War I.

In spite of the submission of the Russian Church to the state, those internal forces which are evidence of a deeply rooted religious life should not be ignored.[59] The official statistics of the Holy Synod for 1914 offer the following numbers,[60] allowing a glance into the organization and institutions of its 100 million faithful: 73 dioceses, 163 bishops, 51,105 clergymen, 1,025 monasteries, with 94,629 monks and nuns, 54,174 churches, 25,593 chapels, 4 clerical academies, 57 seminaries, 185 boys' seminaries, 37,528 parochial schools, 291 hospitals, 1,113 nursing homes, and 34,497 parish libraries. The growth rate of the

---

[58] Prince A. D. Obolenskij (1905–06), Prince A. A. Schirinskij-Schichmatov (1906), P. P. Izwolskij (1906–09), S. M. Lukianov (1909–11).

[59] I. Peresvetov, "Zur Geschichte der caritativen Tätigkeit in der Ostkirche, mit besonderer Berücksichtigung der russischen Kirche," *Das diakonische Amt der Kirche,* ed. by H. Krimm (Stuttgart ²1953), 242–68; P. Hauptmann, "Die ekklesiologische Neubesinnung in der russischen Theologie des 20. Jahrhunderts," *Kyrios* 10 (1970), 225–34; F. Jockwig, "Kirche und Staatsduma. Zur politischen Aktivität der Russisch-Orthodoxen Kirche am Vorabend der Revolution," *Wegzeichen. Festgabe zum 60. Geburtstag von Hermenegild M. Biedermann,* ed. by E. C. Suttner, C. Patock (Würzburg 1971), 437–50; G. Simon, *Kirche, Staat und Gesellschaft,* 199–233; P. Hauptmann, *Die Katechismen der Russisch- Orthodoxen Kirche. Entstehungsgeschichte und Lehrgehalt* (Göttingen 1971); K. C. Felmy, *Predigt im orthodoxen Rußland. Untersuchungen zu Inhalt und Eigenart der russischen Predigt in der zweiten Hälfte des 19. Jahrhunderts* (Göttingen 1972).

[60] M. Lacko, P. Chrysostomus, "Geschichte und jetziger Stand der orthodoxen Kirchen," K. Algermissen, *Konfessionskunde,* 185.

monasteries is remarkable (1865: 587, 1894: 774, 1914: 1,025). Before the outbreak of World War I, the 550 monasteries housed 11,845 monks, 9,485 novices; the 475 convents had 70,283 nuns and 56,026 novices.[61] The monasteries were centers of charity. Strong influence on the public was exerted by the starets, the ordained or nonordained hermits or monks who had matured through renunciation and contemplation and worked as fathers confessor or spiritual advisers among the common people and the educated, and by the attractiveness of the places of pilgrimage, such as the cavern monastery of Kiev, the island monasteries of Valamo on Lake Ladoga, and Solovki on Onega Bay on the White Sea.

The training of the clergy emphasized the study of liturgy and homiletics. Almost all branches of theology were represented by outstanding experts, for example (in Church history), E. E. Golubinsky (1834–1932), N. N. Glubovski (1863–1932), and N. F. Kapterev (1847–1917). The four clerical academies in Saint Petersburg, Moscow, Kiev, and Kazan educated respectable scholars. The episcopate consisted largely of the so-called educated monks who did not feel obligated to monastic life. Most of the eparchs stood the test as lecturers in seminaries and academies. The Russian Orthodox Church received new impetus from lay theologians, such as the landowner and private scholar Alexei Chomjakov (1804–60), the religious philosopher Vladimir Soloviev (1853–1900), and the social philosophers Sergei Bulgakov (1871–1944) and Nicolas Berdyaev (1874–1948), who were later both ordained as priests. Chomjakov developed the idea of the Church offering unity, freedom, and love. In his opinion, Orthodoxy combined unity and freedom, while Catholicism offered unity without freedom and Protestantism freedom without unity. His ideas gave rise to the much-debated doctrine of Sobornost,[62] according to which the entire community of bishops, priests, and laymen are the pillars of faith and doctrine and are thus infallible.

In the wake of ecclesiological reassessment, priests and laymen stood up for the renovation and revival of the Church. They participated in the preparations of the National Council and in the debates of the four Dumas.[63] Priests and bishops served as deputies of various parties; the 440 deputies of the third Duma included 49 representatives of the clergy. Since governmental pressures did not allow a development of

---

[61] I. Smolitsch, op. cit., 713.

[62] B. Plank, *Katholizität und Sobornost'. Ein Beitrag zum Verständnis der Katholizität der Kirche bei den russischen Theologen in der zweiten Hälfte des 19. Jahrhunderts* (Würzburg 1960); cf. B. Schultze, op. cit., 109–21.

[63] F. Jockwig, *Kirche und Staatsduma*, 437–50.

parliamentary life, the ecclesiastical demands for easing dependence on the state could not be attained.

Not until a provisional government had been formed on 12 March and Tsar Nicholas II had resigned on 15 March 1917, were the plans for a National Council dealing with the reform of the Church realized. The Council convened on 15 August in Moscow and lasted until September 1918. The 586 participants were composed of the bishops from the 65 dioceses (which included 115 million faithful), 5 delegates, 2 clergymen, and 3 laymen from each bishopric. Twenty commissions deliberated an extensive reform program, based on the material prepared by the precouncil committee. The discussions about restructuring the upper Church administration took place in the turbulent days of the October Revolution, when the Bolsheviks seized power in Russia. The most important accomplishment was the restoration of the patriarchate.[64] The patriarch was to be the first among equal bishops and to cooperate with the authorities of the Church administration regarding reports to the National Council. On 5 November Muscovite Metropolitan Tychon (1865–1925) was elected patriarch of Moscow and Russia. On 21 November he was solemnly enthroned in the Cathedral of the Assumption of the Blessed Virgin. Two hundred seventeen years after the death of the last patriarch, Adrian (1700), the Russian Orthodox Church was once again headed by a patriarch. The Church had entered into a new period of its history. It had shaken the shackles of the Russian State Church system, but in the following years it was systematically suppressed by Soviet Church policies, which forced its representatives to make declarations of loyalty and limited its activities to a large extent.

The political annexation of Georgia by Russia in 1811 was followed by the suspension of the independent Orthodox Georgian (Grozny) Catholics and their subjugation to the Holy Synod. A Russian exarch with his see in Tiflis received the order to incorporate the Georgian Church into the Russian State Church. In 1886, the Byzantine liturgy and preaching in the Georgian language were forbidden. On 12 March 1917, after the collapse of the Russian regime and the formation of a provisional government in Saint Petersburg, a synod granted autocephaly to the Georgian Church.[65] With its 2.5 million faithful, it became

---

[64] A. Herman, op. cit., 92–93; K. Onasch, op. cit., 127–28; J. Chrysostomus, *Kirchengeschichte in der neuesten Zeit* I (Munich, Salzburg 1965), 92–101.

[65] M. Tamarati, *L-Église Géorgienne. Des origines jusqu'à nos jours* (Rome 1910); R. Iwanitsky-Ingilo, "Lose Blätter aus der Geschichte der georgischen Kirche," *Ex Oriente,* op. cit., 133–51; M. Tarchnišvili, "Die Entstehung und Entwicklung der kirchlichen Autokephalie Georgiens," *Kyrios* 5 (1940–41), 177–93; D. M. Lang, *A Modern History of Georgia* (London 1962).

independent again, reorganized its catholicate with four bishoprics, elected Bishop Kyrion patriarch of Georgia and introduced the Georgian language into the church service.

The Orthodox Churches in Austria-Hungary

In the middle of the nineteenth century, the Serbian metropolitan of Karlowitz became the head of all the Orthodox in Austria. His patriarchal title was approved in 1848 by Emperor Joseph I. In 1864, the bishopric of Sibiu (Hermannstadt) was taken out of the Karlowitz system and was made a metropolitan see for the Rumanians in Transylvania. After the Austro-Hungarian agreement of 1867, both Orthodox metropolitan sees were located in the Hungarian section of the Empire. Therefore, Chernovtsy in northern Bukovina was elevated to metropolis for the Cisleithan half of the Empire (1873) and also received two bishoprics in Dalmatia. The patriarch of Constantinople recognized the autocephaly of those three Churches. After their election by the appropriate Church congresses, the bishops were confirmed by the Austrian Emperor. They were controlled by the Austro-Hungarian bureaucracy, which limited them severely, because they were suspected of being potential allies of the neighboring Orthodox states. The upper Church echelon and the congresses tried to solidify their legal position in the Monarchy, which had been decreed in Austria and Hungary through imperial documents.[66]

The Church of Karlowitz took care of the Serbs in Hungary. The metropolitan, who carried the title of patriarch, and the six bishops were assisted by an episcopal synod and a national Church congress with twenty-five clergymen and fifty laymen. Both institutions also supervised the numerous Basilian monasteries. The patriarchal church had its own printing press and a theological school in Karlowitz, which was elevated to a theological faculty in 1906.

For the Orthodox Rumanians in Hungary and Transylvania, the Emperor established the Orthodox Church in Sibiu. Its metropolitan and his administration were supported by two suffragan bishops, one epis-

---

[66] Regarding the Eastern Churches in Austria-Hungary, cf. A. Ratel, "L'Église orthodoxe de Bukovine," *ÉO* 5 (1902), 225–36; M. Théarvic, "L'Eglise serbe orthodoxe de Hongrie," ibid. 5 (1902), 164–73; I. Silbernagl, J. Schnitzer, op. cit., 63–65, 180–214; K. Lübeck, op. cit., 88–90; A. Hudal, *Die serbisch-orthodoxe Nationalkirche*, 38–61; M. Lehmann, op. cit., 26–35. The literature gives different numbers of believers: N. Zernow (op. cit., 319) lists 800,000 for the Church of Karlowitz, 220,000 for Sibiu, and 550,000 for Bukovina-Dalmatia. K. Lübeck (op. cit., 88–90) gives much higher numbers for the first two churches: 1,063,000, 1,075,000, and 528,000. According to M. Lehman (op. cit., 66), Austria had 666,458 Orthodox, Hungary 2,799,846, Bosnia-Herzegovina 826,338 (1 January 1913).

copal synod and a national Church congress (thirty clergymen, sixty laymen).

The Orthodox Church of Chernovtsy included a metropolis of the same name in Bukovina with Slavic and Rumanian nationalities, two dioceses in Dalmatia, mainly populated by Serbs, the Orthodox congregation in Trieste, and the Serbian-Orthodox parish of St. Sava in Vienna. The metropolitan synod took place once a year in Vienna. The differences between the Rumanian and Slavic population caused conflicts between the considerable number of Rumanians, the Ukrainians, and Russophile groups. After 1909 the Austrian administration employed strict means of defense to counteract the propaganda of Russian Orthodoxy, which reached into parts of Galicia and northern Hungary.[67] The controversies climaxed in the first half of 1914 with three high treason trials.

The Austro-Hungarian government did not suggest making the four Serbian Orthodox exarchates in Bosnia and Herzegovina, whose bishops carried the metropolitan title, independent areas of jurisdiction. They remained formally subject to the patriarch of Constantinople after the occupation (1878), as well as after the annexation (1908). A seminary in Sarajevo took care of the training of prospective priests. Around the end of the nineteenth century, the Orthodox population launched a protest against the dependence of the metropolitan on the Austro-Hungarian government. This caused priests in the Bosnian eparchy of Mostar to refuse to baptize and conduct funerals (1898).

The Orthodox Churches in Southeast Europe

The struggles for freedom launched by the Balkan peoples against Turkish rule occasioned the creation of new states in Southeast Europe, whose Orthodox population was struggling for ecclesiastical independence. Five independent churches emerged in Greece, Bulgaria, Rumania, Serbia, and Montenegro.[68] After the Balkan Wars and the founding of the Albanian state in 1914, the Orthodox Albanians also tried to form an autocephalous Church. The five or six new churches were filled with belligerent nationalism and quickly consolidated themselves.

The Orthodox faithful in the principalities of Moldavia and Wallachia had preserved their customs in spite of foreign rulers and Hellenization

[67] R. Kißling, "Die russische Orthodoxie und der Nordosten des ehemaligan Habsburgerreiches 1908–1914," *Ostdeutsche Wissenschaft* 9 (1962), 287–300.
[68] The patriarch of Constantinople recognized the autocephaly for those churches in Greece in 1856, Montenegro in 1878, Serbia in 1879, and Rumania in 1873. He denied it to Bulgaria in 1872.

measures by the patriarchs of Constantinople. Their monasteries, which had received generous donations, were centers of religious and cultural life. When the principality of Rumania became politically independent, the two metropolitan sees joined to form the Rumanian National Church.[69] Its independence was proclaimed in 1865 by a national synod and a national congress. The Rumanian language, which had been customary after the seventeenth century next to Old Church Slavonic but was replaced by Greek at the initiative of Constantinople, was decreed to be the liturgical language in 1862. The Holy Synod was headed by the metropolitan of Bucharest. It included 2 metropolitans, 6 eparchal bishops and 8 vicar bishops. Even though (in 1863) the estates of the patriarch of Constantinople and some Greek monasteries were confiscated and their funds deposited in a state-owned church account, the monastic system was successfully restored. In 1902 there were 22 monasteries with 709 monks and 19 convents with 1,742 nuns. In 1884 the University of Bucharest opened a theology faculty, which was in charge of two seminaries and also tried to provide a solid theological and pastoral education for the secular clergy. Its influence was felt in independent Rumanian Churches outside of Rumania: in Sibiu, Chernovtsy, and, among the Rumanians living under Russian rule, in Bessarabia. The eparchs resisted the intervention attempts of liberal ministers. Metropolitan Athanasios Mironescu had to resign in 1910.

In Bulgaria, desire for a national Orthodox Church emerged after 1860. By order of the sultan, an independent exarchate was established on 27 February 1870,[70] which was to include all Orthodox Bulgarians in one Church, in order to eliminate Russian intervention in Bulgarian Church affairs. Since Turkish and Greek groups suppressed the Bulgarians, the forces striving for freedom came together in the Bulgarian National Church, which took the lead in the struggle for freedom. The patriarchs of Constantinople refused to grant the Church independence because the expansion of the Bulgarian Church into Macedonia, then part of the Ottoman Empire, did not conform with the principle of territorial unity held by the Orthodox National Churches. Thus the patriarchs declared the Bulgarians to be schismatics.[71] In 1872 the National Assembly sanctioned an exarchal statute which had been designed

[69] S. Pétridès, "Les séminaires orthodoxes in Roumainie," *ÉO* 6 (1903), 191–98; I. Silbernagl, J. Schnitzer, op. cit., 147–62; R. Janin, op. cit. (1957), 522–24.

[70] X. Véren, "Choses de Bulgarie," *ÉO* 6 (1903), 328–36; S. S. Bobtchev, *La lutte du peuple bulgare pour une église nationale indépendante* (Sofia 1938), 1–19; S. Zankow, "Die Bulgarische Orthodoxe Kirche in Geschichte und Gegenwart," *IKZ* 48 (1958), 189–208; W. de Vries, *Der christliche Osten,* 137–41.

[71] On 22 February 1945, Patriarch Benjamin (1936–46) declared the end of the schism and recognized the autocephaly of the Bulgarian Church.

by a synod in 1871. The administration of the Church was entrusted to the Holy Synod, to which the exarch in his capacity as chairman appointed 4 bishops, and to the exarchal council, composed of the exarch himself and 6 laymen. The exarchate included 32 eparchies, 11 of them located in the principality of Bulgaria, 21 in Thrace and Macedonia. Exarch Joseph (1877–1915) initially resided in Constantinople, from where he directed the eparchies in and outside of Bulgaria. After the Balkan Wars he transferred his see to Sofia (1913). He also supervised the monastery of Rila, which had been restored after a fire (1833–47) and had preserved its reputation as a national shrine. Aside from this, there were 78 monasteries with 193 monks and 14 convents with 348 nuns. In 1912 the Holy Synod complained to the government about the inadequate administration of religious instruction, which was given by liberal, often atheistic teachers. The Synod was worried about the future.

After the political recognition of Serbia's autonomy within Turkey (1830), the patriarch of Constantinople had granted the metropolitan of Belgrade some independence in a concordat concluded in 1832, which had been amended in 1835/36 by a consistorial statute.[72] Immediately after Serbia's declaration of independence at the Congress of Berlin (1878), Patriarch Joachim III granted the Serbian Orthodox Church its autocephaly (1879).[73] After Serbia was elevated to a kingdom (1882), the government enacted a law regarding the Church administration, which caused a conflict with Metropolitan Michael (Mihailo), who had stood up for the rights of the Church since 1859, and resulted in his dismissal in 1881. The ecclesiastical constitution of 1890 eliminated the tensions and solidified the cooperation between state and Church. It regulated the competencies of the episcopal synod, the metropolitans, and the four eparchal bishops. After the second Balkan War, the territories taken by Serbia in Macedonia and Albania were incorporated into the metropolis of Belgrade and divided into two metropolitan sees and one bishopric. The monastic system (44 monasteries with 118 monks) was still in its infancy. Aside from the theological seminary in Belgrade, a second one was opened in Prizren in 1872. The efforts exerted after the end of the nineteenth century to restore the medieval Serbian patriarchate, which had been renewed in 1557 and dissolved in 1766, failed, since the consolidation of the Serbian Churches of Belgrade, Montenegro, Karlowitz, Bosnia, Herzegovina, and Dalmatia into one patriarchate could not be realized in view of the differences between Russia and Austria-Hungary regarding Church policies.

[72] J. Mousset, op. cit., 54–106.
[73] I. Silbernagl, J. Schnitzer, op. cit., 162–75; N. Djordjević, *Die Selbständigkeit der serbischen Kirche* (Berne 1922); J. Mousset, op. cit., 301–31.

After the suspension of the Serbian patriarchate, the Orthodox Church in Montenegro was de facto independent. The metropolitan of Cetinje combined in his office spiritual and secular power. Since Danilo I (1697–1737), this double office was inherited within his family according to the custom of the Nestorian Church, a nephew always succeeding his uncle. The ecclesiastical prince entrusted the secular government to a civil governor. After the death of Metropolitan Peter III (1830–51), his nephew Danilo renounced his ordination as bishop and as Danilo II (1851–60) founded the secular principality of Montenegro, with the aid of Russia, which, since Peter I, had sent financial and diplomatic aid to the little mountainous country and succeeded in making it the base for its Balkan policy. Danilo's successor Nikita (1860–1918), after successful battles with Turkey, achieved the recognition of his country's independence (1878), including his territorial acquisitions. In 1910 he accepted the title of King. The Orthodox Church, which, since 1878, had been officially autocephalous, included, aside from its metropolis, two bishoprics, which were established in 1876 and 1913.[74] The efforts of the bishops to elevate the clerical ranks and to renovate monasticism (at the beginning of the twentieth century not more than fifteen monks each lived in the eleven monasteries) were not very successful.

After Otto I, son of King Ludwig I of Bavaria, had been elected King of Greece (1832–62), the Greek Orthodox Church,[75] which had declared its independence in 1833, organized itself as a National Church with the King as head, according to the model of the Evangelical Church of Bavaria. It was administered by a permanent Holy Synod with five active and four attending members appointed by the Minister of Religious Affairs. It was chaired by the current archbishop of Athens. In 1850 Constantinople confirmed the autocephaly of the Holy Synod, preserving the honorary primacy of the ecumenical patriarch. Through the territorial expansion of Greece in the second half of the nineteenth century, the number of eparchs rose to thirty-two. According to the constitution of 1852 the Holy Synod was independent of political authority, yet, through the royal commissioner (procurator) who was assigned to the Synod according to the Russian model and who was empowered with unlimited veto rights, it became rather dependent on the government. This was reflected, for instance, in the decline of monasteries, whose rich estates were often confiscated; nevertheless, around 1900, there were 169 monasteries and 9 convents, with almost 2,000 monks and 152 nuns. Most clergymen had nothing but an elementary school education. There were some clerical schools. Only a few priests

---

[74] I. Silbernagl, J. Schnitzer, op. cit., 175–79; A. Hudal, *Die serbisch-orthodoxe Nationalkirche,* 31–38.

[75] I. Silbernagl, J. Schnitzer, op. cit., 66–85; R. Janin, op. cit. (1957), 501–03.

came from the Rizarios School in Athens, which was turned into a religious teachers' seminary in 1911. Archimandrite Chrysostomos Papadopulos, later archbishop of Athens (1923–39), finally initiated the founding of several qualified seminaries for priests. In addition, there was a theological faculty in the University of Athens which had been established in 1837.

The Orthodox in Albania (180,000) belonged (after 1767) to the patriarchate of Constantinople. Before Albania became a principality (1913), efforts to form a separate church where Albanian was spoken during the service rather than Greek had already begun.[76]

The Four Old Orthodox Patriarchal Churches

The patriarchates of Constantinople, Alexandria, Antioch, and Jerusalem, which had developed during Christian antiquity, suffered under Turkish rule. The Orthodox population, like all non-Islamic groups, was treated as second-class citizens, even though its spiritual advisers were granted certain administrative autonomy. The Ottoman Empire, organized according to the Koran as a theocratic monarchy, gave the patriarch of Constantinople certain rights and recognized him as ethnarch, bearing the responsibility for the subjects of his nation not only in ecclesiastical, but also in secular areas (Millet system). This strengthened the Greek hegemony which had impaired the independence of the other three patriarchs in the Near East since the Middle Ages, at the same time transferring power to the Serbian, Bulgarian, and Rumanian eparchies. The trend toward independence within the Orthodox Churches of Southeast Europe, the growth of a middle class, and the influence of Anglican and Catholic missionaries had aided in weakening the domination of the patriarch of Constantinople over the other three patriarchates.

The ecumenical patriarchate of Constantinople[77], which comprised in the early Middle Ages the entire territory of the Byzantine Empire (624 episcopal sees), shrank more and more during the course of the nineteenth century and included at the beginning of the twentieth century only the rest of European Turkey and the coastal areas of Asia

[76] In 1922, these efforts led to the creation of an autocephalous Albanian Orthodox Church, recognized in 1937 by the ecumenical patriarch.
[77] I. Silbernagl, J. Schnitzer, op. cit., 3–23; K. Lübeck, op. cit., 58–74; G. M. Drabadjeglon, "Geschichte und Verfassung des Ökumenischen Patriarchats," Ekklesia X (1941), 27–61; G. Every, The Byzantine Patriarchate (London 1947); G. Zananiri, Histoire de l'Église byzantine (Paris 1954); R. Janin, op. cit. (⁴1955), 114–23; id., op. cit. (1957), 498–501; I. Totzke, Die alten Patriarchate (1959), 204–07; F. W. Fernau, op. cit., 78–81; R. Potz, op. cit., 86–98.

Minor that had been settled by Greeks. Easing of the Millet system undermined the secular rights of the patriarch. The relationship between state and Church was fundamentally regulated through a law in 1856. The so-called statutes of 1860 defined the competencies of the patriarchal synod, which was composed of twelve metropolitans under the chairmanship of the patriarch and the newly created mixed council of four bishops and eight laymen. The constitution of 1876 guaranteed the freedom of the sects existing in the Ottoman Empire and assured the privileges granted them; however, under Sultan Abdul-Hamid II (1876–1909), a judicial reform (suspending, among other things, the privilege of immunity of the Greek clergy), limitation of the patriarchal rights, and interventions in ecclesiastical life (such as in schools), finally led to a *Kulturkampf* between 1884 and 1890. The constitution of 1908, secured by the Young Turks, changed the Ottoman Empire into a constitutional monarchy. The ecumenical patriarch lost his right to represent Greeks and other ethnic groups under Turkish rule before the sultan, since elected deputies were now responsible for the people's representation. A law of 1910 regarding schools and churches in Macedonia interfered with the property rights of the patriarchate. The Balkan Wars in 1912/13 brought fear of losing the metropolitan sees in northern Greece. Patriarch Joachim III (1878–84, 1901–12) defended himself heroically against the tutelage of the state. He expanded the academy existing since 1844 on the island of Chalki, which was also attended by candidates of the other Orthodox Churches. He founded the periodical *Ecclesiastical Truth* (Ἐκκλησιαστικὴ ἀλήθεια), improved relations with other Orthodox Churches, and cultivated contacts with the Anglican Church, the Old Catholics and Protestantism. His successor Germanos V (1913–18) initially fended off the restrictions placed on the patriarchate by the Young Turks, but he finally abandoned the search for a modus vivendi with the new rulers.

The unification efforts of Leo XIII and Pius X were rejected by the patriarchs. Anthimos VII (1895–97), in his synodal encyclical of 1895, spoke of the introduction of "countless impious innovations" through the bishops of Rome[78] and protested against the activities of Uniate priests. Joachim III disputed the Assumptionists' support of the union in an encyclical of 1907.[79]

In 1901, official statistics listed 78 metropolitan sees in the ecumenical patriarchate: 42 were located in the European section of Turkey, 20 in Asia Minor, 12 on the Turkish islands of the Aegean Sea and the Sea of Marmara, 4 in Bosnia-Herzegovina, including altogether 3 million faith-

---

[78] Schmidlin, *PG* II, 518–19; W. de Vries, *Orthodoxie,* 134.
[79] Schmidlin, *PG* III, 129.

ful. The patriarchate was responsible for some monasteries on the Turkish islands and the Athos monasteries[80] in the Asian part of Turkey, which (in 1913) housed 6,345 monks in twenty large monasteries, twelve sketes, and numerous hermitages.[81]

The other three old patriarchal churches existed in the shadow of Constantinople. The patriarchate of Alexandria[82] had lost its significance in the early Middle Ages when the majority of the Orthodox converted to Monophysitism. The members who had remained loyal to the Byzantine Imperial Church were called Melchites by the Copts. The Melchite patriarch transferred his residence to Constantinople at the end of the sixteenth century because of the despotism of the Turkish conquerors. The number of his followers decreased rapidly and did not increase again until the nineteenth century (through the immigration of Greeks who were supported by Orthodox dignitaries in countries around the Danube River and Russia). General Muhammad Ali (1806–49), the almost autocratically ruling Turkish governor, made sure that the patriarch was elected by the native clergy (1846) and established residence in Cairo and also in Alexandria. In the middle of the nineteenth century, the patriarchal church had only ten old churches and two monasteries. Patriarch Hierotheos II (1846–58) established a council ($\sigma\nu\mu\beta o\acute{\nu}\lambda\iota o\nu$) to which he assigned the execution of secular and miscellaneous affairs. He and his successors succeeded in easing the tensions between the Greek and Arabic faithful, to fend off partially the intervention attempts of the patriarch of Constantinople, and to initiate an upsurge in religious life. Nikanor (1866–69) created a Holy Synod according to the Russian model. Sophronios IV (1870–99) restored both monasteries and initiated the construction of churches, schools, and charity centers. Photios (1900–25) furthered these efforts and founded a patriarchal printing press which published two theological periodicals after 1908. The four metropolitian sees of this patriarchate slowly developed into ecclesiastical centers.

---

[80] I. Silbernagl, J. Schnitzer, op. cit., 52–59; *Le millénaire du Mont Athos 963–1963, études et mélanges*, 2 vols. (Chevetogne 1964); P. Huber, *Athos. Leben, Glaube, Kunst* (Zurich 1969); P. M. Mylonas, *Der heilige Berg Athos: Alte Kirchen und Klöster Griechenlands. Ein Begleiter zu den byzantinischen Stätten*, ed. and transl. by E. Melas (Cologne 1972), 93–119.

[81] 3,243 Greeks, 1,914 Russians, 706 Bulgarians, 379 Rumanians, 89 Serbs and Montenegrins, 14 Georgians.

[82] I. Silbernagl, J. Schnitzer, op. cit., 36; J. Lacombe, "Patriarcat grec orthodoxe d'Alexandrie," *ÉO* 38 (1939), 174–81; E. Michailides, "Geschichte, Verfassung und Statistik des Patriarchats von Alexandrien," *Ekklesia* X (1941), 71–79; R. Janin, op. cit. (⁴1955), 161–69; id., op. cit. (1957), 508–09; T. Mosconas, "Das griechisch-orthodoxe Patriarchat von Alexandrian *Kyrios* 1, rev. ed. (1960–61), 129–39; I. I. Totzke, *Die alten Patriarchate* (1959), 301–07.

From 1724 to 1851, the patriarchate of Antioch[83] was staffed by Constantinople with Greek prelates. They were met with scepticism by the majority of the Orthodox believers who were Arabic-speaking Syrians. In addition to these internal tensions, ecclesiastical life was hampered by political unrest, e.g., the attacks by Muslim fanatics under the leadership of the Druses (members of an Islamic sect), which were directed against all Christians in Lebanon and Syria. The patriarchal church in Damascus, its treasures, and its library burned down in 1860. The Holy Synod and an ecclesiastical national council including 4 metropolitans and 8 laymen tried to curtail the progress of the Uniate Melchites and to preserve the 15 dioceses, the 14 monasteries (with a small number of monks), and the seminary of the monastery of Belement, which existed since the middle of the nineteenth century. With the support of Russia, the Syrian Meletios II Doûmanî (1899–1906) was elected patriarch. He was not recognized by the other three Old Christian patriarchs. The resulting schism was only ended under his successor Gregory IV (1906–28). Since then, the Antioch patriarchate has called itself "Syrian Orthodox." The first two Syrian patriarchs used Russian funds to renovate the seminary in Belement, increased the parishes to 68, and made possible the publication of the periodical *Mercy*. The ruthless attacks of the Turks on the Orthodox population at the beginning of World War I threatened all ecclesiastical activities. Only the numerous congregations composed of members who had emigrated to North and South America were able to develop without interference.

The church of Cyprus, originally under the patriarchate of Antioch,[84] became autocephalous after the Council of Ephesus. Following the Turkish conquest of 1571, it began to approach the patriarch of Antioch again. It owed him new appointments to the episcopal see of Nicosia and to the five sees whose incumbents had been executed for their participation in the Greek uprising (1821–25). Archbishop Makarios I (1854–66) emphasized the expansion of parochial schools, their network being expanded even further under the English dominion (1878–1935). Archbishops Sophronios (1865–1900) and Cyril II (1909–16) were not spared conflicts with the occupational forces, but they succeeded in ensuring the independence of their Church and in blocking the attempts by the patriarchs of Constantinople and Antioch to restore their jurisdiction. In 1910 a seminary was established in Saint

---

[83] G. Bardy, *L'Église d'Antioche* (Paris 1918); Alexandros, "Das Patriarchat von Antiochien," *Ekklesia* X (1941), 80–92; I. Totzke, *Die alten Patriarchate* (1960) 203–12.

[84] J. Hackett, *A History of the Orthodox Church of Cyprus* (London 1901); Hippolytos, "Die Autokephale Apostolische Orthodoxe Kirche Cyperns," *Ekklesia* X (1941), 117–29; R. Janin, op. cit. (⁴1955), 139–44.

George's monastery at Larnaca and a bimonthly, *Ecclesiastical Messenger,* was published. The Church constitution of 1914 regulated the duties and tasks of the Holy Synod, of the 4 bishops, the clergy, the monks (about one hundred in seven monasteries), and of the faithful (200,000).

The patriarchate of Jerusalem,[85] with several titular archbishops, was completely dependent on the patriarchate of Constantinople until 1860, and it was only able to survive through the financial support of the Russian Church. The Brotherhood of the Holy Sepulcher, which took care of the holy places in Jerusalem and the thirty-five monasteries (seventeen in Jerusalem), had to deal with the claims of other Christian congregations. Patriarch Cyril (1842–72) restored the patriarchal school of the monastery of the Holy Cross in Jerusalem (founded in 1736), and constructed churches and schools in various cities and towns in Palestine. In 1875 a patriarchal statute concerning the rights of the patriarch and the Holy Synod was passed. The differences between the Greek hierarchy and the largely Arabic-speaking faithful required two elections. Patriarch Damianos (1897–1931), himself a Greek but favorably inclined toward Arab demands, was temporarily suspended from office by the synod due to the pressure of Greek diocesan members (1908/09). The mixed council, created in 1911 through Arab pressures, was unable to eliminate the tensions.

The small church on Mount Sinai[86] directed by the abbot of the Saint Catherine monastery, had been autocephalous since 1575. Its archbishop, consecrated since 1782 by the patriarch of Jerusalem, was responsible for thirty monks and thirty Bedouins.

The Near Eastern National Churches

Aside from the Orthodox Churches, the Eastern Churches of the Nestorians and the Monophysites (Jacobites, Thomas Christians, Copts, Ethiopians, and Armenians), independent since Christian antiquity, must be mentioned.

Of the Nestorian Church, a missionary Church which had spread during the Middle Ages into Central Asia and the coast of Malabar in India, only a few faithful had survived through modern times in Northern Mesopotamia, in the area of Lake Urmia, and in the mountains of

[85] T. E. Dowling, *The Orthodox Greek Patriarchate of Jerusalem* (London ²1913); K. Meliaras, "Die Kirche von Jerusalem," *Ekklesia* X (1941), 95–114; R. Janin, op. cit. (⁴1955), 153–61.
[86] H. L. Rabino, *Le monastère de Saint-Catherine du Mont Sinaï* (Cairo 1938); H. Skrobucha, *Sinai* (Olten, Lausanne 1959).

Kurdistan north of Mosul.[87] Its members, also called Assyrians, a term
which derived from a truncation of the words Syrian Church, were
suppressed by the Muslims and cruelly persecuted by Kurdish tribes,
who reduced the hierarchy decade by decade. Around 1900, the
Church consisted of eight metropolitans and several suffragan bishops.
Their head was the patriarch or catholicos, as he was called in the
Middle Ages; he resided in Kochânes. After 1450 the Mama family
furnished this highest Nestorian dignitary, an uncle always succeeded
by a nephew. The patriarchs tried to curtail the missionary successes of
the Chaldeans,[88] the Presbyterians, the Anglicans, and the Orthodox
Russians. In 1838 3,000 faithful converted to Orthodoxy and settled in
Transcaucasia. In 1898 Bishop Mar Jonah of Sunurgan and Urmia converted to Orthodoxy together with his diocesan subjects, after which
the Russian Church operated an Orthodox mission in Persia and intensified its propaganda. Catholicos Simon IX Benjamin (1903–17) in
1914 considered the conversion of all Nestorians to Orthodoxy. When
the faithful hoped for liberation from Muslim pressures by Russia during World War I, they were persecuted by the Turks and Kurds as
traitors. Almost half of the Nestorians died trying to migrate to Persia
and defending themselves in the highlands; the catholicos was murdered
by a Kurd. Even his successor, Simon XX Paul (1918–20) died a violent
death. The Nestorian Church witnessed one of the most difficult periods in its history.

Nor could the decline of the Jacobite Church,[89] beginning in the late
Middle Ages, be stopped.[90] Its hierarchy, which had included 20 metropolitan sees and 103 dioceses in the twelfth century, was composed of
8 metropolitian sees and 3 bishoprics at the beginning of the twentieth
century. The patriarchs residing in Mardin or Diarbekr repeatedly
asked the Russian Church for help and carried on unification negotiations which failed because of controversies over dogma. They could not
prevent the victories of the unification movement and the effectiveness
of Anglican missionaries. Patriarch Ignatius XXXIV Peter III (1872–
94) turned to the Coptic Church in order to overcome the isolation. In

---

[87] I. Silbernagl, J. Schnitzer, op. cit., 245–73; P. Kawerau, "Die Nestorianischen Patriarchate in der neueren Zeit," *ZKG* 67 (1955–56), 119–31; R. Janin, op. cit. (1957),
536–37; B. Spuler, "Die nestorianische Kirche," *Handbuch der Orientalistik,* op. cit.,
163–69; A. S. Atiya, op. cit., 282–88.

[88] See p. 375.

[89] The name of the Jacobites was derived from James Baradai (490–578) who was
ordained as bishop of Syria and Asia Minor by Monophysite Patriarch Theodosios of
Alexandria and laid the foundation for an independent ecclesiastical organization.

[90] I. Silbernagl. J. Schnitzer, op. cit., 302–16; B. Spuler, "Die westsyrische
(monophysitische/jakobitische) Kirche," *Handbuch der Orientalistik,* op cit., 213–16;
A. S. Atiya, op. cit., 212–18.

1882 he succeeded in being recognized by the Turkish government as the spiritual and temporal head of the Jacobites, which theretofore had been a function of the Armenian patriarch of Constantinople. The ecclesiastical constitution of 1913/14 granted laymen the right to participate in the Church administration. In spite of all external pressures and internal difficulties, some monasteries were able to survive. The political reorganizations in the Near East after World War I, which incorporated West Syrian believers into various states, and the movement toward autonomy of the Indian branch church created new burdens.

The Thomas Christians of Malabar,[91] on the Southwest coast of India, witnessed both unions and separations throughout their colorful history.[92] The series of metropolitans who submitted to the Jacobite patriarch can be dated back to the middle of the seventeenth century. Their goal of uniting all Thomas Christians under their tutelage failed because the Uniate Syrian Church of Malabar was able to consolidate its position, because the Anglican Church Missionary Society accomplished conversions after the beginning of the English dominion (1795), and because a large part of its members left under the leadership of Bishop Mar Athanasios (1843–77). They formed the Mar Thoma Church, which preserved the organization and the customs of the Monophysites, but changed internally by adopting Anglican doctrines. Pressured by the Metropolitan Mar Dionysius V (1865/66–1909), the Jacobite Patriarch Ignatius XXXIV Peter III came to Malabar and excommunicated Bishop Athanasios and his followers in 1876. At a synod he divided the metropolis into six dioceses and ordained several bishops as metropolitans. The Church constitution, adopted at the same time, normalized relations with the patriarchate. After Metropolitan Dionysius V's death, the patriarchal and the metropolitan party launched a feud. They were striving for a separation from the mother Church and for the establishment of their own catholicate. Patriarch Ignatius XXXVI Ebd' Allah III (1906–15) tried in vain to settle the dispute. In 1911, he excommunicated the Indian Metropolitan Dionysius VI (1908–34) and his followers, appointing Metropolitan Cyril Mar Curilos (1909–11) head of the Jacobite Thomas Christians. In 1912 the metropolitan party pro-

---

[91] I. Silbernagl, J. Schnitzer, op. cit., 317–21; E. Tisserant, *Eastern Christianity in India. A History of the Syro-Malabar Church from the Earliest Time to the Present Day* (London, New York, Toronto 1957), 147–57; B. Spuler, "Die Thomas-Christen in Süd-Indien," *Handbuch der Orientalistik,* op. cit., 231–39; P. J. Podipara, *Die Thomas-Christen* (Würzburg 1966); N. J. Thomas, *Die Syrisch-Orthodoxe Kirche der Südindischen Thomas-Christen. Geschichte - Kirchenverfassung - Lehre* (Würzburg 1967); E. R. Hambye, J. Madey, *1900 Jahre Thomas-Christen in Indien* (Freiburg i. Ue. 1972), 45–50.
[92] Cf. B. Spuler, "Die Thomas-Christen in Süd-Indien," *Handbuch der Orientalistik,* op. cit., after 238, table: Thomaean groups.

nounced Mar Ivanios (as Basileios I) the catholicos of India and the East, with his seat in Kottayam. The catholicos was responsible for the ordination of the bishops and the chrism, while Metropolitan Dionysius VI was entrusted with the administration of Church estates. Next to this independent Syrian Orthodox Church of the Thomas Christians, which granted the Jacobite patriarch an honorary primate, existed the church which was directly subordinate to the Jacobite patriarch.[93] Both were divided into seven dioceses, had one seminary each, and took care of the same number of the faithful, about 250,000.

The Coptic Church[94] became stable in the first half of the nineteenth century, when the Turkish governor Muhammad Ali (1806–49) ensured an orderly administration in Egypt and did not put any obstacles in the way of the development of the Christian community. Energetically the patriarchs continued the ecclesiastical renovation that had begun under Mark VIII (1796–1809). Peter VIII (1809–52) ordained a bishop for the Sudan and increased the dioceses to thirteen. Cyril IV (1854–61) contributed to the reform of the Church by founding schools, establishing printing presses and constructing churches. Under Demetrios II (1862–75) and Cyril V (1854–1927), a new self-awareness and internal consolidation of the Copts was demonstrated in the new editions of old Coptic works and in theological publications which dealt with dogmatic, historical, and canon law questions. Conflicts arose between the conservative forces, represented by the influential monks and Patriarch Cyril V, and the Coptic National Council of 1874, in which the laymen had participatory rights regarding Church administration. Efforts toward a better training of the clergy in two seminaries and at the theological faculty in Cairo, expansion of the dioceses, missionary victories among the Muslims, and the cooperation of eager laymen assured the Copts (in terms of numbers the strongest Christian sect in Egypt) a respectable position within the Monophysite Churches in the twentieth century.

The Ethiopian Church[95] was dependent on the Coptic patriarchate.

---

[93] For decades, there were trials concerning Church property and controversies about the legality of excommunications declared by the Jacobite patriarch. Not until 1958–59 did the two Churches come to terms and unite. Catholicos Mar Basileios III George II (1929–64) headed the "Orthodox Church of the South Indian Thomaeans" after 1959.

[94] I. Silbernagl. J. Schnitzer, op. cit., 274–93; J. G. zu Sachsen, *Neue Streifzüge durch die Kirchen und Klöster Ägyptens* (Leipzig, Berlin 1930); R. Strothmann, *Die koptische Kirche in der Neuzeit* (Tübingen 1932); R. Janin, op. cit. (1957), 532–34; M. Cramer, *Das christlich-koptische Ägypten einst und heute. Eine Orientierung* (Wiesbaden 1959); S. Chauleur, *Histoire des Coptes d'Égypte* (Paris 1960), 147–63; B. Spuler, "Die koptische Kirche," *Handbuch der Orientalistik,* op. cit., 299–308.

[95] I. Silbernagl. J. Schnitzer, op. cit., 294–301; H. M. Hyatt, *The Church of Abbyssinia* (London 1928); J. B. Coulbeaux, *Histoire politique et religieuse d'Abyssinie depuis les temps*

Its only metropolitan, the Abuna (our father), was appointed by the Coptic patriarch from the ranks of monks around him, ordained bishop, and placed at the head of the native, uneducated, numerous clergy, who considered him an intruder. Next to him, the native abbot of the monastery of Dabra Lebanos played an important role. He carried the honorary title *Etschege* (the one standing next to the throne). He directed the extensive monastic system and administered the estates. The spiritual adviser Abuna Salama (1841–67) was known for his infamous life style and his simony. He and his successors had little freedom within the State Church, which had been involved in the struggles of the small princes fighting for ultimate power. Not until the domestic political situation was cleared under Emperors John IV (1872–89) and Menelik II (1889–1909), did state initiatives bring about renewal within the Church. In 1881 Emperor John IV asked the patriarch for four bishops and assigned them to certain territories. One of them, Matthew, later rose to Abuna (1889–1926) and transferred his see, according to Menelik II's wish, from Gondar to the imperial residence of Addis Ababa (1893). After his death, the monarch succeeded in reforming the Ethiopian Church and separating it from the mother church.[96]

Since the Middle Ages, the Armenian catholicate had been divided into five branch churches,[97] whose catholicates, or rather patriarchates, were Echmiadzin, Constantinople, Agthamar, Cilicia, and Jerusalem. The catholicos of Echmiadzin was the head and representative of all Armenians, and the other high dignitaries recognized his honorary primacy. The Armenian monks obeyed the rules of Saint Basil. The bishops, supported in their diocesan administration by a council composed of clergy and laymen, ordained priests, deacons, and "vardapets" (preachers and teachers). In 1828 the main area of Armenia (Greater

---

les plus reculés jusqu'à l'avènement de Ménélik II, 2 vols. (Paris 1929); R. Janin, op. cit. (1957), 534–36; B. Spuler, "Die äthiopische Kirche," *Handbuch der Orientalistik,* op. cit., 314–18; E. Hammerschmidt, *Äthiopien. Christliches Reich zwischen gestern und morgen* (Wiesbaden 1967); F. Heyer, *Die Kirche Äthiopiens. Eine Bestandsaufnahme* (Berlin, New York 1971).

[96] Under Haile Selassie (after 1928 negus, after 1930 emperor), four native bishops were ordained in 1929. Cyril (1929–50) was the last Coptic abuna. After the death of Coptic Patriarch Cyril VI (1959), the Ethiopian Church was declared an independent patriarchal church, granting the head of the mother church only an honorary rank.

[97] I. Silbernagl, J. Schnitzer, op. cit., 214–44; M. Ormanian, *The Church of Armenia. Her History, Rule, Discipline, Liturgy, Literature, and Existing Condition* (London ²1955); R. Janin, op. cit. (⁴1955), 345–52; id., op. cit. (1957), 528–31; B. Spuler, "Die armenische Kirche," *Handuch der Orientalistik,* op. cit., 259–68; J. Mécérian, *Histoire et institutions de l'Église arménienne. Évolution nationale et doctrinale, spiritualité - monachisme* (Beirut 1965); A. K. Sanjian, *The Armenian Communities in Syria under Ottoman Dominion* (London 1965).

Armenia, Yerevan) was incorporated into the Russian Empire, which had previously intervened in the election of the catholicos of Echmiadzin. A basic law, enacted by Nicholas I in 1836, subjected the Armenian Church to his control. A synodal council, an imperial commissioner, and an administrative adviser for secular affairs exercised the same funtions as the Holy Synod and the chief procurator in the Russian Church. Nicholas II in 1896 and 1903 nationalized the entire Church property, which was partially restored in 1905. Catholicos Georg V Surenian (1911–30), who was responsible for seven dioceses in Russia and two in Persia, achieved the independence of the Armenian Church when the Russian Revolution enabled the formation of the Soviet Republic of Armenia.[98]

The sultan had assigned the supervision of all Armenians in his Empire to the Armenian patriarchate of Constantinople (Millet system), making it responsible for the three areas of jurisdiction in Aghtamar, Cilicia, and Jerusalem. Regarding the administration, he was assisted by three councils (one clerical, one secular, and one mixed council), whose competencies were precisely defined in a national statute of 1860. Through the formation of new Southeastern European states in the second half of the nineteenth and in the beginning of the twentieth century, the patriarchate lost several dioceses; in 1914, it still included 12 archbishoprics, 27 bishoprics, and 6 monasteries. Thousands of people lost their lives when, in 1894/96 and 1909, fanatical Turks ruthlessly threatened the Armenians because of their language and religion, charging them with Russophilia at the beginning of World War I. Mass deportations, forced conversions to the Muslim religion, and emigrations weakened the patriarchate tremendously.

Even the small catholicate of Aghtamar on Lake Van suffered from such persecutions. Catholicos Katchadar Chirojan (1864–95) had no successors. The last vestiges of his area of jurisdiction were taken over in 1895 by the patriarchate of Constantinople and in 1915 by the catholicate of Echmiadzin.

The catholicate, or rather patriarchate of Cilicia in Little Armenia (2 archbishoprics, 10 dioceses, and 2 monasteries) was incorporated into the patriarchate of Constantinople according to the national statute of 1860; it was able, however, to preserve a certain measure of autonomy in spite of pressures by the Turkish government.

The patriarchate of Jerusalem, which took care of the Armenians in Palestine, Syria, and on the island of Cyprus, was divided into 5 dio-

---

[98] After a short time, the successful reconstruction of the Church was threatened by persecutions, which all religious communities in the Soviet Union had to suffer. They did not cease until the catholicos was willing to declare his loyalty toward the regime and to serve Soviet foreign policies.

ceses. When the patriarchate of Constantinople took power, it was limited to the administration of the diocese of Jerusalem, whose spiritual center was the Jacob Monastery.[99]

This summary of the internal and external situation of the independent Eastern Churches shows what paralyzing effect the pressures by Russia, Turkey, and other states had on Church organization and the life of the believers. Reform movements can be found among the Orthodox, e.g., in Russia and on Cyprus, and among the Monophysites, e.g., in southern India and Egypt. However, they did not have the strength to break the shackles imposed on them by the states. Therefore their efforts toward mutual communication and collaboration in the ecumenical movement remained futile.[100] Some Church dignitaries cultivated contacts with the Anglican and Old Catholic bishops; however, the centuries-old prejudices and dogmatic differences disclosed deep rifts. Church historians and liturgical scholars of Eastern and Western Christianity studied its past, so rich in traditions, and recognized the value of preserving Old Christian treasures. However, the desire for closer relations between the Orthodox, Nestorian, and Monophysite congregations and for contact with the separated Christians of the West did not emerge until after World War I and after the breakthrough of the ecumenical movement in the following decades.

The Uniate Eastern Churches

In spite of all the schisms between the Eastern and Western hemispheres of Christianity, the Popes tried to restore unity. When they finally succeeded in concluding union treaties with the Orthodox Churches in Eastern Europe at the end of the sixteenth and in the seventeenth century, they expected to reduce the hardened barriers between the papacy and the Christian East, and unions with the Near East, Ethiopia, and India were established.[101] But in spite of some success they had to endure backlashes. The pontificate of Leo XIII, oriented toward the future, opened new perspectives toward unifica-

---

[99] Regarding the present day jurisdiction of the Armenians, cf. M. Krikorian, J. Madey, "The Armenian Church. Extension, Hierarchy, Statistics," *OstkSt* 21 (1972), 323–25.
[100] K. Lübeck, op. cit., 193–206; C. Lialine, *La position spéciale de l'Orthodoxie dans le problème œcuménique: 1054–1954. L'Église et les églises,* op. cit. II, 389–413; G. Florowski, op. cit., 231–96; N. Zernow, op. cit., 317–58; F. Heiler, op. cit., 402–05.
[101] Cf. G. Zananiri, *Catholicisme orientale* (Paris 1966), 241–50: chronology; *Atlas zur Kirchengeschichte. Die christlichen Kirchen in Geschichte und Gegenwart,* ed. by H. Jedin, K. S. Latourette, J. Martin (Freiburg, Basel, Vienna 1970), 132: the development of the Catholic Eastern Churches and the most important unification efforts.

tion.[102] Around 1900, approximately 8 million believers[103] were jurisdictionally assigned to the Armenian patriarchate of Cilicia, the Maronite, Melchite, and Syrian patriarchates of Antioch, the Chaldean patriarchate of Babylon, the Uniate Coptic patriarchate of Alexandria, and to several archbishoprics and bishoprics in eastern and southern Europe, in Lower Italy and in southern India.[104] On the basis of their liturgical languages they were divided into five groups: the Byzantine, Alexandrian, Antiochic (West Syrian), Chaldean (East Syrian), and Armenian rite. They were defined by the liturgies within and without the Byzantine Imperial Church in Christian antiquity.

The Byzantine Rite

The different versions of the Byzantine rite, also called Greek rite, were most popular among the Ruthenians, Russians, Rumanians, Hungarians, Serbs, Bulgarians, Greeks, Melchites, and Georgians.

The inclusion of the Orthodox metropolis of Kiev and all of Ruthenia into the Catholic Church through the Union of Brest in 1595/96 was the foundation for the reunification of the Ruthenians (Ukrainians) with the Roman center. The efforts in this respect were continued in Uzhgorod (1646), including the Carpatho-Ruthenians, Slovaks, Hungarians, and Rumanians.

Russia, penetrating into eastern central Europe in the eighteenth and nineteenth century, forced the Ruthenians living under its rule to convert to the Orthodox Church. In 1875 the only remaining diocese, Chelm, was dissolved.[105] In spite of ruthless persecutions, 50,000 believers remained loyal to the union and in 1904 sent a delegation to Pius X. Their expectation that Nicholas II's edict of toleration would be applied to them was not fulfilled. They were only allowed to convert to Roman Catholicism.

In the Habsburg Monarchy, in Galicia, in Hungary, and in Transylvania, the Ruthenians were able to develop their Church organization. In the archbishopric of Lemberg (Lvov), a second bishopric (Stanislav)

---

[102] See above, pp. 336–43.

[103] *Atlas zur Kirchengeschichte*, 138–39.

[104] Basic information about the history of the unions, cf., in addition to the chapter bibliography, A. Ehrhard, op. cit., 24–45; I. Silbernagl, J. Schnitzer, op. cit., 325–85; K. Lübeck, op. cit., 30–39; P. Werhun, "Die orientalischen Riten und kirchlichen Gemeinschaften," *Der christliche Osten*, op. cit., 350–68; W. de Vries, *Der christliche Osten;* R. Janin, op. cit. (1957), 538–44; C. Korolevskij, *Liturgie in lebender Sprache. Orient und Okzident* (Klosterneuburg near Vienna 1958); R. F. Esposito, op. cit., 42–361; P. Hofmeister, "Die Kultsprachen der Ostkirchen," *OstkSt* 11 (1962), 196–203; A. Brunello, op. cit., 499–521; F. Heiler, op. cit., 406–14.

[105] See above, p. 172.

was formed within the suffragan bishopric of Przemyśl. The reform of the Basilian order, the Provincial Synod of Lemberg of 1891, the founding of the Ruthenian College in Rome in 1897, the two archbishops Sylvester Cardinal Sembratovitch (1882–98) and Duke Andreas Szepticki (1900–44) led to the golden age of their Church[106] (counting over 3 million believers within its three dioceses). The golden age was documented by the establishment of new orders (the Studites, an eastern branch of the Redemptorists, the female Basilians, the female Studites, the congregation of the Servants of the Immaculate Virgin Mary), new theological institutions, periodicals, schools, and charity centers. Basilian Archbishop Szepticki[107] was known beyond Galicia's borders for his pastoral and missionary ambitions, his patronage, and primarily for his efforts regarding unification. His pastoral letters of 1907 and 1908 dealt with the theme of unity, which he tried to realize in the spirit of tolerance and love. After 1910 he was president of the Welehrade Union Congress.[108] He became one of the outstanding figures of the union movement and was admired as the patriarch of the Ruthenians.

Szepticki supported White Russian students in order to restore the torn ties between the Ukrainian and White Russian people. In 1907 he traveled incognito to White Ruthenia, to the Russian Ukraine, and to Moscow. Through talks and negotiations, he initiated a new union movement of the Byzantine Slavic rite, which was expressly approved by Pius X the next year. Centers for the Russian Uniates[109] were Saint Petersburg and Moscow.

As in Galicia, the Uniate Ruthenians in Hungary's bishoprics of Munkács (Slovak: Mukachëvo) and Eperjes (Slovak: Prešov) enjoyed

---

[106] A. Korczok, *Die griechisch-katholische Kirche in Galizien* (Leipzig, Berlin 1921); T. Halusczynskyj, "Die gegenwärtige Lage der katholischen Kirche (ukrainisch-katholischer Ritus)," *Ex Oriente,* op. cit., 90–101; *Die Kirche und das östliche Christentum. Ukraine und die kirchliche Union,* ed. by the Catholic *Emigrantenfürsorge* Berlin (Berlin 1930); *Documenta Pontificum Romanorum historiam Ucrainae illustrantia (1075–1953)* II, ed. by A. G. Welykyj (Rome 1954), 453–515; L. Nemec, "The Rutheninan Uniate Church in its Historical Perspective," *CH* 37 (1968), 365–88; J. Madey, *Le Patriarcat Ukrainien vers la perfection de l'état juridique actuel* (Rome 1971).

[107] A. Szepticky, "Das russische katholische Exarchat," *Ex Oriente,* op. cit., 78–89; J. Drozd, "Andreas Šeptyckyj, metropolita Leopoliensis, praeses Academiae Velehradensis 1910–1939," *Acta Academiae Velehradensis* 18 (Olmütz 1947), 92–102; G. Prokotschuk, *Der Metropolit. Leben und Wirken des großen Förderers der Kirchenunion Graf Andreas Scheptytzkyj* (Munich 1955); J. Madey, *Kirche zwischen Ost und West,* 174–99.

[108] See above, p. 344.

[109] See chap. 11, above, p. 170.—In 1917, Szepticki convened the first synod for the Uniate Russians in Saint Petersburg, after three years of captivity. By authority of Pius X, he appointed Leonid Feodorov exarch for Russia. The new government recognized the new exarch at first, but later dismissed him from office and sent him to Siberia, where he died in 1935.

an upswing through their own initiative and state aid. In the small bishopric of Kreutz (Croatian: Krizevci), established in 1777 for the Uniates of Croatia, Slavonia, and Batschka, almost half of the faithful were Ruthenians who had emigrated from Galicia and Carpatho-Russia to the south of Hungary.

In Transylvania, in the church province of Alba Julia-Făgăras, with its suffragan bishoprics of Oradea Mare, Lugoj and Szamos Ujvár, the Rumanian Byzantine rite was used. Like the Uniate Ruthenians, the Rumanians expanded their educational system, their press, and their charity. But while trying to preserve their national identity, they had to struggle with the Magyarization measures of the administration.

The Uniate Hungarians,[110] belonging partly to the Ruthenian dioceses, partly to the Rumanian dioceses, after 1868 demanded their own ecclesiastical jurisdiction and introduction of Hungarian as the liturgical language. In 1873 the vicariate of Hadjudorog, composed of thirty-three congregations, was established for the Hungarian Uniates. Pressured by the Hungarian faithful and the government, Pius X through the bull *Christi fideles Graeci ritus* (1912) created the diocese of the same name[111] and demanded that it use Old Greek as the liturgical language. He approved Hungarian only for extraliturgical functions. Nevertheless, the liturgy was celebrated in the people's language. After World War I, the diocese was reduced by turning seventy-seven parishes over to the Uniate Church in Rumania, which also incorporated the archbishopric of Fogarasch and parts of the Slovak bishopric of Mukachëvo. The rest of this diocese and the bishopric of Prešov were given to Czechoslovakia.[112] After the end of the nineteenth century, many Uniate Ruthenians and Rumanians emigrated to South and North America, where they created their own hierarchy.

Bishop Josip Jurij Stroßmayer of Djakovo helped the Uniate Serbs and stood up for them even outside of his bishopric.

According to the census of 1910, the number of Uniates in Austria

---

[110] *AAS* IV (1912), 429–35; G. Patacsi, "Die ungarischen Ostchristen," *OstkST* 11 (1962), 273–305; I. Žeguc, *Die nationalpolitischen Bestrebungen der Karpato-Ruthenen 1848–1914* (Wiesbaden 1965), 113–16; G. Adrianyi, *Friedrich Graf Revertera*, 216–66, 310–12; id., "Die Bestrebungen der ungarischen Katholiken des byzantinischen Ritus um eigene Liturgie und Kirchenorganisation um 1900," *OstkSt* 21 (1972), 116–31; E. Weinzierl, *Spannungen in der österreichisch-ungarischen Monarchie 1878–1914*, see above, chap. 2.

[111] See above, p. 345.

[112] Immediately after World War II, the unions of eastern Central Europe were dissolved under Soviet pressure (1946 in western Ukraine, 1948 in Rumania, 1949 in Slovakia). Only the two dioceses of Hajdudorog in Hungary and Kreutz in Yugoslavia survived.

was 3.5 million, in Hungary 1.9 million, and in Bosnia-Herzegovina 8,000.

In Bulgaria the union movement, initiated by Titular Archbishop Joseph Sokolski (1860–61), could not develop because of Russian intervention. Under Raphael Popoff (1865–76), the movement took hold in Macedonia and Thrace, assisted by the Assumptionists, Lazarists and Resurrectionists. In 1883 Leo XIII established an Apostolic Administration in Constantinople, which was responsible for two vicariates apostolic in Macedonia and Thrace. The approximately 15,000 faithful suffered from the pressures of the Bulgarian exarch, the Orthodox bishops, and the Turkish government.

The Uniate Greeks had even less of a chance to expand. They owed their internal organization to Hyacinth Marango's efforts, who founded a periodical in Constantinople in 1865 and established two congregations. The Assumptionists continued his work in the seminary of Kadikoy and through the periodical *Échos d'Orient.* In 1909 John Papadopulos was appointed vicar general of the Apostolic Delegates of Constantinople for the Uniate Greeks. In 1911 he was ordained bishop and entrusted with the independent administration of the small congregations. Hyacinth Marango also made propaganda for the Uniates in the Kingdom of Greece, but because of the anti-Catholic animosities of the Orthodox population he was only moderately successful. Leo XIII's efforts regarding the educational institute in Athens patronized by him and the work of several orders essentially failed. The Catholic archbishop of Athens was responsible for 2,000 Uniate Greeks in his capacity as apostolic delegate.

The Italo-Greeks and the Italo-Albanians, centered in the Basilian abbey of Grottaferrata near Rome, in Calabria, and Sicily, were threatened by Latinization measures or mixtures of Latin and Byzantine liturgies, but their independence was supported by Leo XIII. He decreed the elimination of any liturgical additions which did not agree with the Byzantine rite.

The Melchites were headed by the patriarch of Antioch.[113] Maximos III Mazlum (1833–55) after 1838 also was the incumbent of the two Uniate patriarchal sees of Alexandria and Antioch. Gregory II Jussef Sayyur, whose jurisdiction over all Melchites was expressly recognized by Leo XIII in 1894, Peter IV Geraigiry (1898–1903), and Cyril VIII Geha (1903–16) improved the organization of the four archbishoprics and eight bishoprics with the help of the patriarchal vicars of Alexandria and Jerusalem. They provided a good education for the secular clergy in

[113] Silbernagl, J. Schnitzer, op. cit., 334–41; R. Janin, op. cit. (⁴1955), 275–87; R. F. Esposito, op. cit., 61–78.

the Seminary of Saint Anna in Jerusalem and made sure that the orders could expand. Among others, the three Basilian congregations and the congregation of the Paulinists, founded by Archbishop Germanos Moakkad of Baalbek (died in 1912), excelled in their educational, charitable, and missionary activities. They succeeded in bringing together all the faithful scattered throughout the Near East and Egypt (1907: 140,000) and to affirm their loyalty to the Apostolic See, in spite of the social differences among the believers and demands from the laity for more participation, according to the Orthodox model. The Synod of Aïn-Traz in Lebanon (4 April to 8 July 1909) dealt with dogmatic and pastoral questions in order to improve religious life. The results of the thorough deliberations were defined in 1,017 articles,[114] which were sent to Rome in a Latin translation, but failed to be approved because of some questionable points. The Synod favored the further development of the Melchites in organizational and spiritual respects. The Arab paper *The Good Will,* whose publication was decided at the Synod, carried the basic concepts to the public.

In Georgia, Theatines (after 1629) and Capuchins (after 1662) had solicited support for the union. In 1848, the 50,000 Georgian Catholics were subordinated to the bishop of Tiraspol. Ten thousand of them were Uniates, mostly Armenians, and only a small portion adhered to the Byzantine liturgy.[115] In 1886 the Russian government forbade this liturgy as well as the use of the Georgian language in sermons and public church service. After World War I, some priests took care of these faithful, who subsequently suffered the reprisals of the Soviet government.

The Alexandrian Rite

This group of liturgies includes the Uniate Copts and the Egyptians. The union of the Copts, initiated in the eighteenth century by the Franciscan Friars,[116] progressed when Leo XIII supported the union in his apostolic letter of 11 July 1895,[117] and when he responded to the request of a delegation under the leadership of Cyril Makarios of 26 November by restoring the Alexandrian patriarchate.[118] Aside from the

---

[114] C. de Clercq, op. cit., 790–831. These articles deal with worship (nos. 1–110), the hierarchy (nos. 111–546), the Sacraments (nos. 547–875), and problems of canon law (nos. 876–1017).

[115] S. Bathmanschwili, "L'Église catholique en Géorgie," *Ex Oriente,* op. cit., 152–58; R. Janin, op. cit. (⁴1955), 320–21.

[116] R. Janin, op. cit. (⁴1955), 490–92; S. Chauleur, op. cit., 163–66; R. F. Esposito, op. cit., 327–49.

[117] *ASS* XXVII (1894–95), 705–09.

[118] *ASS* XXVIII (1895–96), 257–60.

patriarchal bishopric, he established the dioceses of Hermopolis and Thebes. In 1899 he made Cyril Makarios patriarch. With resolutions regarding the faith, liturgy, and hierarchy, the Synod of Cairo of 1898 laid the foundation for the organization of the Church.[119] Its reconstruction was interrupted when the ambitious patriarch resigned in 1908 and converted to Orthodoxy.[120] He was replaced by an apostolic administrator. The number of Uniate Copts increased from 4,630 (1897) to 14,576 (1907).

For the Uniate Ethiopians, who were cared for since the middle of the nineteenth century by French Lazarists and Italian Capuchins, Leo XIII, in addition to the two existing vicariates apostolic, created an apostolic prefecture for the area of Eritrea (1894), which had become an Italian colony in 1890. In 1896 he sent Cyril Makarios to Addis Ababa, who asked in his behalf for the release of Italian prisoners. In his correspondence with Emperor Menelik II (1889–1909) he tried to improve the situation of the Uniates which, for political reasons, was difficult. Pius X also appealed to him in 1906. In 1910, by order of the Pope, the first native Ethiopian, Abuna Kidana Maryam Kassa, was ordained as bishop of Asmara. After 1911 he headed the vicariate apostolic of Asmara for the 4,000 Uniate Ethiopians.

The Antioch Rite

This group of rites included the Uniate Jacobites and Maronites. After 1783 these Syrians (West Syrians)[121] from Syria, Mesopotamia, and Egypt had been subject to the patriarch of Antioch, who resided in Mardin after 1854. After the settlement of internal disputes at the Synod of Scharfa,[122] where the ecclesiastical situation was newly regulated, the patriarchs gave their Church a clearer profile. With the help of four metropolitans, six bishops, and foreign and native orders, they improved the training and material security of the clergy and expanded the educational system. Aside from Patriarch Cyril Behnam Benni (1893–97), Ignatius Ephraim II Rachmani (1898–1929) also contributed to the stabilization of the union through his historical and liturgical

---

[119] C. de Clercq, op. cit., 759–80.

[120] In 1912, in Rome, he was restored to communion. He died in Beirut in 1921.

[121] R. Janin, op. cit. (⁴1955), 387–393; W. de Vries, "Dreihundert Jahre syrisch-katholische Hierarchie," *OsthSt* 5 (1956), 137–57.—The West Syrian Rite was also used by a group of Thomaeans, who had separated from the Monophysite Church of the Jacobites in Southern India in 1930. For the Uniate Malankars, the archbishopric of Trivandrum was established (1933). Its faithful increased rapidly in the next decades (60,000).

[122] C. de Clercq, op. cit., 599–628.

studies as well as the addition of a Syrian ritual. When the faithful in Turkey (80,000) were threatened by persecutions during World War I, their number decreased, and dwindled further through emigrations. The patriarchal see was moved from Mardin in Turkey to Beirut.

The Maronites,[123] in the only patriarchal Uniate Church without a parallel separated Eastern Church, had strongly increased in the eighteenth century. But in 1861/62 many of them fell victim to the terror of the Druses. In 1885 there were 1,050 secular clergymen, 800 monks in 45 monasteries, and 8 convents. Around 1900 there existed 9 dioceses, 3 patriarchal seminaries, 6 diocesan seminaries, and a flourishing native order system, following the rules of Saint Anthony. Under Patriarch Paul Masad (1854–90) and Patriarch Elias Peter Huayek (1899–1931) the religious life of the Maronites improved (1913: 250,000), and was further strengthened by the Maronite College in Rome, which had been founded in 1584 and renewed by Leo XIII in 1891.

The Chaldean Rite

The Chaldean and Maronite rites belong to the East Syrian group of liturgies. The center of the Chaldeans[124] (Uniate Nestorians) was located in Mesopotamia. Under their Patriarch Joseph II Audo (1848–78), residing in Mosul, an internal crisis broke out. It began with the patriarch's attempt to extend his jurisdiction over the Uniate Malabars, and the crisis was intensified through the Holy See's interventions in the administration of the Chaldean Church, reaching its climax in 1869 when Joseph II Audo refused to ordain two bishops appointed in Rome. In 1870 Pius X offered him the alternatives of either consecrating the bishops or resigning. Even though he yielded in this matter and in regard to controversies about the wisdom of the definition of infallibility, new tensions developed pertaining to the Uniate Malabars. These tensions first decreased under Elias XII Abolionan (1879–94) and Joseph Emanuel II Thomas (1900–47), when Leo XIII assured them of his benevolence. Under those two patriarchs, many Nestorians found

---

[123] I. Silbernagl, J. Schnitzer, op. cit., 361–385; K. Friz, "Die christlichen Minderheiten im Vorderen Orient," *Kyrios* 3 (1938), 208–23; R. Janin, op. cit.(⁴1955), 457–62; R. F. Esposito, op. cit., 268–84; B. Spuler, "Die Maroniten," *Handbuch der Orientalistik,* op. cit., 217–25; P. Dib, *Histoire de l'église Maronite,* 2 vols. (Beirut 1962); A. S. Atiya, op. cit. 389–423.

[124] I. Silbernagl, J. Schnitzer, op. cit., 350–57; W. de Vries, "Nel quarto centenario della chiesa cattolica caldea," *Civ Catt* 103 (1952), 236–52; R. Janin, op. cit. (⁴1955), 422–29; R. F. Esposito, op. cit., 287–308; H. Schulte, *Der Beginn. Eine Hilfsaktion für den christlichen Orient* (Limburg 1966).

their way to the union, so that in 1914 100,000 believers belonged to the Chaldean Church in four archbishoprics and eight bishoprics. Aside from Dominicans, Capuchina, Lazarists, Carmelites, and Pallottines, two native congregations intensified the internal life of the Church.

The Malabars had difficulty[125] disassociating themselves from their dependence on the Latin hierarchy. Patriarch Joseph II Audo's efforts to replace the Latin Carmelite missionaries with Bishop Mar Rocco as head of the Malabar Church failed. In 1874–76 about 24,000 believers assembled around Chaldean Bishop Elias Mellus of Accra, whom his patriarch had sent to Southern India. They separated from the union[126] and joined the Nestorian Catholicate in 1907 (neo-Nestorian Church; 1914: 14,000 members). In 1887 Leo XIII withdrew the Uniates from the supervision of the Latin bishops and created for them the two vicariates apostolic of Trichur and Kottayam, which were at first entrusted to Latin prelates until, in 1897, the Pope filled three independent vicariates apostolic with native bishops. Their rites were cleansed from Latin additions. In the following years, their numbers rose from 200,000 (around 1900) to 300,000 (1914).[127]

The Armenian Rite

In 1867, when Pius IX combined the two Uniate Churches of Constantinople and Cilicia, a crisis broke out among the Uniate Armenians,[128] causing the nomination of a competing patriarchal candidate after the First Vatican Council and the conversion of numerous Uniates to Monophysitism. The crisis was finally settled when Leo XIII appointed Patriarch Anthony Peter IX Hassan (1867–80) cardinal of the Curia and Stephen Peter X Azarian (1881–99) his successor. At a synod in 1890 dogmatic, ritual, and organizational matters were discussed.[129] The Pope supported the reconstruction of the patriarchate (2 archbishoprics, 13 bishoprics) by erecting the Armenian College in Rome (1883), which had already been planned in 1584 by Gregory XIII, and by approving the constitutions of the Viennese Mechitarists (1885). He

---

[125] I. Silbernagl, J. Schnitzer, op. cit., 357–58; E. Tisserant, op. cit., 108–20; R. F. Esposito, op. cit., 309–26; E. R. Hambye, J. Madey, op. cit., 55–58.

[126] Elias Mellus joined the union again in 1889 and became bishop of Mardin (1893–1908).

[127] Finally, in 1923, a Church province was established for the Uniate Malabars, which has two archbishoprics and five bishoprics today with 1.5 million believers.

[128] C. de Clercq, op. cit., 719–52.

[129] I. Silbernagl, J. Schnitzer, op. cit., 342–49; R. Janin, op. cit. (⁴1955), 355–64; R. F. Esposito, op. cit., 213–18; B. Spuler, "Die armenische Kirche," 264–66; A. K. Sanjian, op. cit.; P. Krüger, "Die armenischen Mechitharisten und ihre Bedeutung," OstkSt 16 (1967), 3–14.

also helped those Armenians who were threatened by the Turks (1894–96). In 1911 new controversies erupted, ignited by the differences between Patriarch Paul V Peter XIII (1910–31) and the laity in the Church administration who demanded more participatory rights. The patriarch was expelled by the Turkish authorities. In 1911 he held a synod in Rome, which was unable, however, to settle the internal difficulties. The atrocities inflicted upon the Armenians during World War I, killing about 50 percent of their clergy, paralyzed the further development of the 100,000 believers in the Armenian patriarchal Church.[130] More favorable was their situation in the Armenian archbishopric of Lemberg (2,500), in Rumania (30,000), and in Russia (40,000).[131] After World War II, however, they succumbed to Soviet ecclesiastical policies.

The spiritual Latinization of the Eastern Churches was finally stopped by Leo XIII after the First Vatican Council.[132] He had recognized the unique qualities of the Uniates beyond their liturgical customs. The strengthening expected by the Pope, however, was hampered by internal and external difficulties. The superimposition of the Latin liturgy on the Syrians, Malabars, and Maronites continued to exist. The lay portion of the Church administration, customary in the independent Eastern Churches, caused tensions (e.g., among the Armenians). The possibilities of growth were curtailed by continuous state pressures, especially in Russia and Turkey, and by the persecutions of the Armenians, Chaldeans, Georgians, Maronites, and Syrians. Only the Ruthenians and Rumanians in Austria-Hungary, as well as the Malabars in Southern India improved their Church organization. All Uniate dignitaries tried to elevate the educational level of their clergy, to return to the original liturgy of their Churches and to devise contemporary spiritual care. The help they received from Leo XIII and Pius X had positive effect on their initiatives and defined the position of the patriarchs, bishops, and secular and regular clergy.[133]

[130] After World War I, the number decreased to 60,000 people who lived in Egypt, Lebanon, Persia, Syria, Turkey, and, after the emigration, especially in France. In 1928, an Armenian episcopal conference was held in Rome which reorganized the bishoprics and devised new guidelines for pastoral work in the diaspora. Regarding the current hierarchy of the Uniate Armenian Church, cf. M. Krikorian, J. Madey, op. cit., 325.
[131] A. M. Ammann, op. cit., 517–18, 535–36, 581–82.
[132] W. de Vries, in collaboration with O. Bârlea, J. Gill, M. Lacko, *Rom und die Patriarchate des Ostens* (Freiburg, Munich 1963), 232–37, 318–27; J. Hajjar, "L'Épiscopat catholique oriental et le Ier Concil du Vatican d'après la correspondance diplomatique française," *RHE* 65 (1970), 423–55, 737–88; id., *Zwischen Rom und Byzanz*, 221–52.
[133] C. de Clercq, op. cit., 1007–20.

PART TWO

Defensive Concentration of Forces

INTRODUCTION

Pius X, a Conservative Reform Pope

When the conclave which was to elect Leo XIII's successor opened, the Sacred College faced a situation much more complex than in 1878. A significant group of cardinals was convinced that the *Pontifex Maximus*, who had improved the reputation of the papacy to a great extent, was best replaced by electing his secretary of state, Cardinal Rampolla. They considered him to be intimately familiar with his thoughts; also he had collaborated in all prominent plans and activities of the last fifteen years. This was the opinion of those Church dignitaries who desired a continuation of the conciliatory policies which the deceased Pope had exercised toward contemporary philosophy and modern institutions; this was also the conviction of one segment of the intransigents who held Rampolla in esteem for being a relentless opponent of the Italian government. But the failure of Rampolla's French policy was not in his favor. Many cardinals thought it necessary to take an entirely different path, though they were not always in agreement as to the direction. Some, likewise contemplating political expedience, wished the Holy See to take a less rigid stance toward Italy because they considered it idle to speculate on its impending collapse. They also preferred the Church to rely on the assistance of Catholic Austria and the German Center Party rather than on Orthodox Russia, whose increasing influence in the Near East they feared; instead, they suggested taking a chance on anticlerical France. Others, who were more concerned with the principle at stake, worried about the liberal trends in exegesis and theology, about the danger of democratic ideas as propagated by the secretary of state threatening the principle of authority, and about the extent of the concessions he was ready to make to governmental authority in order to solicit its support or at least its neutrality. Therefore, they demanded a return to intransigence, the hallmark of Pius IX's pontificate. Still others, conservatives as well as reformists, believed that after so many years of giving preference to the "Ministry of Foreign Affairs" it was high time to think of the "Ministry of the Interior." Therefore they desired a pope who had matured in the office of bishop and would be most interested in pastoral questions, in a better administration of the dioceses, and in the improvement of ecclesiastical works.

Of the candidates nominated by Rampolla's opponents, Cardinal Serafino Vannutelli was mentioned frequently. For years, Austria's friends had assembled around him, and he was, as everyone knew, well disposed to the Quirinal. Named most often was Cardinal Gotti, prefect of the Propaganda, a Carmelite who was conservative in regard to doctrine, yet liberal in respect to Church policy and a very able administrator. Some, however, spoke of the saintly patriarch of Venice, Cardinal Sarto, who was not well known to the public and the foreign cardinals, but had been discreetly and repeatedly named by Leo XIII as his successor. He was also supported by those Italian cardinals who did not belong to the Curia, especially since they knew that the government approved his candidacy and considered him the "the more pliable of the inflexible candidates."

The problem was further complicated by the significant role which the diplomatic factor played. In 1878 the great powers arrived at the conviction that the Pope's function in the European political configuration had ceased to be significant since the Papal State had been dissolved. Therefore, they limited themselves to the request that a man be chosen who was moderate and committed to conciliatory settlements of the conflicts between Church and state. However, due to Leo XIII's intelligent policies, the great powers had to admit once again that the moral support of the Pope, meaning the Vatican, was still potentially of great value. Consequently they were not as indifferent toward the election of the new Pope as they had been twenty-five years ago. The French, of course, preferred Rampolla as Pope, since he had always supported, possibly even advanced the Francophile policies of Leo XIII. Likewise, the Spaniards fondly remembered the time when he was nuncio in Spain. The government in Vienna was less favorably disposed to him and criticized him for insufficient sympathy toward the Triple Alliance, for his pro-Slavic Balkan policy, and the support he had given the opposition of the Christian Socialists in Austria and Hungary. The Viennese hesitated to use their ancient right of veto. Finally, however, the Emperor decided to take this step, pressured by Cardinal Puzyna, the archbishop of Cracow, who maintained that the election of Rampolla would have negative effects on the Church and charged him with having sacrificed Polish interests for the sake of his pro-Russian policies.[1] The influential Cardinal Prince-Bishop Kopp of Breslau, who was informed about Puzyna's mission, preferred that the veto not be used. Therefore he tried to arrive at a compromise with Rampolla and come to an agreement concerning an acceptable candidate, but Rampolla eluded his efforts. Kopp thereupon tried to persuade the French and Spanish cardinals to withdraw Rampolla's nomination, even though they

---

[1] Aside from F. Engel-Janosi, *Revue belge de philosophie et histoire* 29 (1951), 1135, n. 1, and 1137, see Z. Obertyński, op. cit., especially 183–84. Among other things, he quotes the cardinal's statement: "Austria did not use me, I used Austria" (p. 188); cf. chaps. 2 and 11.

had unanimously decided to give him their vote. But Kopp was not successful.

Such was the situation when the cardinals—38 Italians and 24 foreigners[2]—entered the conclave. At the first ballot, on 1 August, 62 votes were cast; 12 went to 9 different candidates, 24 to Rampollo, 17 to Gotti, 5 to Sarto and only 4 to Vannutelli, whose chances had been diminished by the indiscreet campaign his brother had conducted on his behalf. In the afternoon, the distribution of votes changed: Rampolla's rose to 29 and Sarto's to 10, while Gotti only received 16. The Germans and the Austrians, who had hesitated a long time before they supported Gotti's Roman followers, were convinced that Gotti had lost his chance and they decided to follow Agliardi's advice to vote for Sarto. On the other hand, they considered it prudent to officially announce Vienna's veto against Rampolla. This was a totally futile gesture, since the former secretary of state had obviously received the highest number of votes he could expect. His followers were able, if they held together, to block any other candidature, but they had to give up all hope for his election. On the morning of 2 August, Puzyna fulfilled his mission and voiced his veto, even though Rampolla still had 29 votes, while Sarto's increased to 21. The papal cardinal chamberlain and even Rampolla himself protested immediately, and at the next ballot the victim of the veto received even one more vote. Numerous cardinals wanted to prove in this manner that they would not make allowances for such secular interference in the papal election. But this was no more than a token demonstration, because, as of the next morning, the number of votes cast for Rampolla decreased to that of the first ballot. His supporters suggested he choose the candidate to whom they could give their votes. He declined, explaining that he could not relinquish his candidacy because this would give the appearance of yielding to Austria. Without a doubt, however, he himself felt that he was in no position to turn the election in the direction he deemed desirable.

While Rampolla's followers made such futile efforts, the votes cast for Sarto rose from 21 to 24, and on the morning of 3 August increased to 27, surpassing Rampolla and practically eliminating Gotti. For a while, the cardinals feared Sarto would refuse to accept the responsibility which he himself felt exceeded his strength, but he could, in the end, be persuaded, and, on the morning of 4 August, he was elected, receiving 50 votes to the 10 cast by those who had remained loyal to Rampolla. Sarto declared that he would choose the name Pius X in memory of the

[2] 7 Frenchmen, 5 Spaniards, 5 Austrians, 3 Germans, 1 Portuguese, 1 Belgian, 1 Irishman, and 1 American. This was the first time Americans were represented in the conclave.

Popes of the same name "who, in past centuries, had courageously fought against sects and rampant errors." This indicated the direction he intended to take in his pontificate.

The new Pope was born in 1835 in a village of Venetia, the son of a simple family. He rapidly climbed the ladder of a pastoral career. He was coadjutor priest in a rural parish, pastor in a larger town, chancellor of the diocese of Treviso and at the same time spiritual director in the local seminary, and bishop of Mantua, an ailing diocese which he was able to restore within a few years to a model diocese, proving his pastoral strength. Finally, in 1893, he became patriarch of Venice and cardinal. Wherever he was active, he left the impression of a virtuous and diligent spiritual adviser, indeed, almost of a holy man of great benevolence; yet at the same time he was energetic, moved by a strong sense of duty, and highly intelligent. He did not think much of innovations, such as the new trends in the area of exegesis and apologetics originating in France, as well as the program of the young Italian Christian Democrats who had assembled around Murri. As bishop he tried to inspire his priests, especially in regard to instruction in the catechism, preaching, and frequent Communion, and he encouraged the laity to get involved as much as possible in ecclesiastical activities, insisting, however, that this collaboration was subject to the strict control of the clergy. From the clergy, in turn, he demanded absolute obedience, even toward the minor directives of their bishops. A devoted reader of Cardinal Pie's works, who branded the liberal Catholics "wolves in sheepskin" in his pastoral letters, Sarto was intensely interested in socialist charges against the traditional religious foundations of society and did not hesitate to descend to the level of city politics and demand an alliance between the Catholics and the moderate liberals in Venice in order to erect a dam against the rising flood of radicals.

This course of action gave rise to the expectation that the new Pope would take a more conciliatory stance toward the new Italy than his predecessor. And indeed, his pontificate inaugurated a slow but gradual improvement of the relations between the Vatican and the Quirinal. The question which attitude the Pope would adopt in regard to the Roman question was highly interesting to the Italian journalists and politicians. However, this aspect was only secondary in the spiritual orientation of the Pope because the concepts which guided his pontificate differed drastically from those of this predecessor. While Leo XIII derived pleasure from the delicate games of diplomacy and politics, Pius X did not enjoy them at all and was not willing to succumb to the compromises which are part of the game. In his estimation, Leo XIII's policy of reconciliation with the governments and royal courts had generally failed, and he was determined to concentrate on the problems of the Christian apostolate and religious life. Moreover, there was a glaring difference between the new Pope and his predecessor in all other respects, even physically, but particularly in essential matters. Leo XIII was known as the "Pope of the royal courts, the chancellories, the bishops"; his successor, in contrast, would prove to be the "Pope of theology and canon law, of the simple folk and the pastors" (J. Fèvre). Leo XIII was an intellectual with a thorough education and a speculative spirit, finding pleasure in synthetical constructs with broad perspectives. Pius X was a pragmatic spirit, deeming a bird in the hand worth two in the bush and having a good sense for detail. A comparison between his and Leo XIII's encyclicals is revealing: Pius's theoretical part is shorter, but he elaborates in detail passages dealing with advice and practical experiences. However, one should not be deceived. Pius X liked to portray himself as the "good rural pastor" and his opponents were quick to take him at his word. Unquestionably, he lacked a university education, which would have allowed him to be more receptive to the critical method in the crisis of modernism and to be more independent of the narrow-minded opinions of his informants. But everyone who had contact with him was astonished at his intelligence, certainly a "rather more robust than subtle intelligence" (Baudrillart), but one which functioned clearly and precisely, grasping the essential point of a problem and supported by "a healthy common sense, almost a man of genius" (Briand). Prince Bernhard von Bülow declared that he rarely encountered such penetrating insight into human nature and into those forces which dominate the world and modern society.

No less remarkable were his moral qualifications. Many of the characteristics reported by eye witnesses leave the compelling impression that this man possessed a wealth of virtues ranging all the way to heroism. Thus, the ceremony of his canonization in 1954 merely officially confirmed what many of his contemporaries had felt spontaneously. One point above all must be emphasized: the deep commitment he felt toward his responsibility as spiritual director enabled him to become a man of prayer as well as of action, a man of relentless will, ready to bear the criticism of the public if he felt the interests of the Church to be at stake. He carried this so far that some asked whether he was not excelling by virtue of strength rather than by virtue of intelligence, and often his energy could have been enhanced by a good measure of flexibility.[3] The often rather pressing awareness of his responsibility may explain the rather authoritarian government of this otherwise friendly and social

---

[3] "The persecution does not bother him. The supernatural element in his personality is confusing. I have seen an honest, strong, and beautiful holiness," Lemire wrote after an audience (J. M. Mayeur, *L'abbé Lemire* [Paris, Tournai 1968], 318).

man,[4] who "prepared the dictatorship that would save the Church," as one adviser of Cardinal Mathieu said.[5] Indeed, Pius X was firmly convinced that the service of God and the salvation of the faithful required a serious change in many areas.

Pius X instinctively mistrusted progressive endeavors. It was clear to him that the liberal policies of his predecessor regarding the modern world should not be condemned in principle, but these seemed to him to have been conducted with insufficient precautions and to have run risks which would shortly incur regrettable consequences. Thus he considered a certain reactionary policy absolutely necessary, giving his pontificate from the start the hallmark of retreat into "wholesome isolation" and a "Catholic defensive," which was reflected mainly in relations with various governments, in the attitude toward the Christian Democrats, and in the suppression of modernism.

Regarding the governments, with the exception of Italy Pius X returned to a rigid and inflexible stance. Relentlessly and without consideration of political expedience or eventual, direct, and harmful consequences, he insisted on the rights of the Church. This was most apparent in the case of France: with regard to the separation of Church and state, he prohibited any settlement via negotiations or arbitration, in spite of the opposing views of a considerable segment of the episcopate and the public. Also in Spain and Portugal, his policies of decisiveness and inflexibility prevailed. In both countries, he risked an actual break in relations. Even communication with England and Russia took a turn for the worse. That this did not result in an open quarrel was due to the fact that the Vatican supported the demands of the Catholic minorities in Ireland and Poland, which Leo XIII had sacrificed more than once to the necessities of his policy. In a similar refusal to submit to any kind of negotiations and compromises when he thought truth to be at stake was rooted the serious incident with Germany caused in 1910 by the encyclical released on the occasion of the three hundredth anniversary of the canonization of Charles Borromeo, the pioneer of the Counter Reformation, in which the Pope elaborated on Luther and Protestantism using vocabulary which was anything but ecumenical.[6] In spite of his sym-

---

[4] He was able to listen patiently to his assistants, but he demanded above all that they be loyal executives. In the Vatican, he was said to have made the following remark: "Basta che la testa l'abbia il Papa," quoted in C. Confaloniere, *Pio XI visto da vicino* (Turin 1957, German: Aschaffenburg 1958), 172.

[5] E. Renard, *Le cardinal Mathieu* (Paris 1952), 411.

[6] The intransigence toward Protestantism caused another incident (in 1910) with the former president of the United States, Theodore Roosevelt, who was informed that the Pope would only grant him an audience if he would abandon a visit of the Methodist congregation in Rome. Naturally, Roosevelt declined (cf. F. Zwierlein, *Th. Roosevelt and*

pathy for the old Emperor Franz Joseph, Pius X was at one time on the verge of breaking off diplomatic relations with Austria because the government in Vienna hesitated to suspend from office a professor of canon law in Innsbruck who openly sympathized with modernistic trends. This again confirms how far the Pope was willing to remain inflexible if matters of religion seemed to be at stake.[7]

At first glance, the Pope's reaction to the Christian Democrats was even more puzzling. After all, he had sprung from the common people and had always been a friend to the poor. He found it simply impossible to accept the fact that there were Catholics who wanted their social action to be more independent of the hierarchy and more self-reliant, or that some priests tried to orient social action more and more toward the political arena. Here lie the reasons for the fundamental reorganization which the Pope forced upon the *Opera dei congressi* at the beginning of his pontificate, for his disapproval of Romolo Murri's *Azione popolare*, followed by a formal condemnation, and later for the rejection of the new trends perpetuated by the *Sillon* group in France. Compromises with both the modernistic movement in Italy and proclamations in France, too undefined and doctrinaire, partly justify the interventions of ecclesiastical authority. However, the formulation of various papal acts regarding these questions and problems, and the more flexible attitude toward the *Action française* unquestionably demonstrate the Vatican's temporary devaluation of democratic ideas in favor of a paternalistic solution to social problems. The Pope also expressed preference for a hierarchal conception of society and at the same time demanded intensified attempts to keep the professional organizations of workers under the strict control of the clergy. All these aspects are rather characteristic of the ecclesiastical climate in Venetia, which Pius had never left before his election.[8]

In regard to the suppression of modernism, it is unquestionable that there are troublesome aspects to the various reform movements at the beginning of the twentieth century and that the dishonest action of many a pioneer of these movements forced the Pope to call to mind certain principles and warn of blunders. However, one has to admit that

---

Catholics [St. Louis 1956], 343–50). Typical of the anti-Protestant attitude of the Vatican under Pius X was a remark made by an Austrian diplomat after a conversation with the secretary of state regarding the candidate for the throne of Albania in 1913: "Finally, the cardinal slipped in a remark which one would have to interpret to mean the following: 'Rather another Muslim than a Protestant!' " (*Österreich-Ungarns Außenpolitik* V [Vienna 1930], 468).

[7] Concerning L. Wahrmund, see chap. 2, n. 61 and above.

[8] R. Colapietra spoke about a "venetismo ammodernato, mento temporalista ma più pugnacemente confessionale" (*RStRis* 55 [1968], 328).

the various measures employed to hold back the tide of modernism must be assessed negatively. Many men loyal to the Church were mercilessly banned and only few were relatively quickly rehabilitated, such as Father Lagrange. But more serious than these personal fates were other facts: for a long time the undifferentiated suppression of modernism kept the majority of the clergy from pursuing intellectual investigations. This prevented a gradual clarification of the intellectual processes taking place in the Catholic intelligentsia until around 1900 and kept them from learning to differentiate the constructive from exaggerations or even errors. The gap between Church and modern culture widened. The solution of fundamental problems was postponed, and by simply ignoring them nothing was won, but, on the contrary, harm was done.

The way in which Pius X pursued his main interest, that is, concentrating on the internal affairs of the Church, and the way in which he insisted under any circumstance on "demanding for God's sake omnipotent power over man and beast" (inaugural encyclical), disregarding political or diplomatic contexts, and primarily the spirit of the methods with which he pursued this program, especially in the last years of his pontificate, caused and are still causing rather different assessments. Some critics praise the saintly Pope as the fearless defender of orthodoxy and of ecclesiastical rights. Others, in contrast, sharply criticize the stubborn intransigence and narrow-mindedness of the Pope, claiming that he did not know how to treat the grave problems confronting the Church from a new perspective; instead he tried, using more and more authoritarian methods, to preserve the Church's reactionary and clerical concepts, which were in flagrant contrast to the historical development. Whatever the future judgment of Pius X's defensive actions may be, it would be historically incorrect if the meaning of this pontificate were limited to this hotly disputed aspect.

No matter how often the fact is emphasized that Pius X did not think much of the rules of politics and diplomacy so dear to his predecessor, one must not forget that he was by no means disinterested in the political dimension of these problems and that he even presented certain ideas in this regard which make him appear to be a forerunner. For Pius X, spirituality determined policies, and they had to be Christian policies Thus, he declared in his first consistorial address: "We are forced to deal with politics because the *Pontifex Maximus,* invested by God with this highest of offices, does not have the right to divorce politics from the realm of faith and morals."[9] With this decisive resolution toward a political theology, he rejected, on the one hand, the pretenses of the lay

[9] Address of 9 November 1903 (*ASS* 36 [1903–04] 195).

liberalism of the nineteenth century; on the other hand, because of his extraordinary restraint toward the tendencies of "political Catholicism," he was in agreement with many justified trends of that same liberalism. Not only did he have grave reservations toward the politically engaged priests, but he believed even less than Leo XIII[10] in the usefulness of denominational parties. He felt that they harbored the risk of compromising religion in purely secular conflicts in which, according to his opinion, the Church had no business getting involved. Thus, it is typical that a sharp critic such as Falconi should praise him, claiming "he was the first in history to practice an *idealismo antitemporalistico,* even after the memory of such idealism had gotten lost in the first centuries of the Church."[11]

However, more significant and of fundamental importance is the fact that Pius X appeared to his contemporaries as not very modern and rather conservative, which indeed he was in many respects; yet in reality he was one of the great reform Popes of history. This explains, by the way, why he was enthusiastically welcomed by a great number of people who strove for religious renewal, at least during the first months of his pontificate. Their first impression was one of religious resurrection rather than return to obscurantism.[12] The motto of this Pope was *instaurare omnia in Christo;* and the restoration of the Christian community—this was the point in question[13]—included, in his opinion, a rigorous defense of the rights of Christ and the Church as well as positive reform activity and initiatives with essentially pastoral goals, intensifying the communities' internal life and ensuring a more effective utilization of its potential. To this end, he issued the decrees regarding frequent Communion and the Communion of children, measures to improve the instruction of the catechism and the sermon, reform of Church music and revision of the missal and the breviary, and reorganization of seminaries to improve the training of the clergy. Though inspired by an obsolete conception of the lay world, many guidelines and directives made Pius X a pioneer of Catholic Action in the modern sense of the word. In this context belong the adaptation and codification of canon law and the reorganization of the Roman Curia, intended to enable the central administration of the Church better to fulfill the more and more difficult tasks imposed on it by the development of ecclesiastical centralization. Pius X dealt with all these different problems utilizing forty years of practical experience in multiple areas of pastoral work far

[10] Cf. above, p. 239.
[11] *I papi del ventesimo secolo* (*Milan 1967*), 89; also 91–92.
[12] Cf. P. Scoppola, *Crisi modernista e rinnovamento cattolico in Italia* (Bologna 1961), 113–15, and L. Bedeschi, op. cit., 45–49.
[13] Cf. É. Poulat, *Intégrisme et catholicisme intégral* (Paris, 1969), 171–72, n. 164.

away from the Curia, a background that is rare for a Pope. Thus he was able to apply to his new office the experience and energy which he had already displayed as head of the dioceses of Mantua and Venice. He could not be held back by bureaucratic routine; rather, with authority he enacted reforms within a few years which had been requested for centuries or were considered almost revolutionary in his time.

According to the unanimous testimony of all his advisers, Pius X played an important role in the design of such plans and in their rapid execution. Naturally, like every Pope, he had to rely on assistants. He made sure that they shared his ideal of religious renewal and therefore recruited them preferably from among the orders (but not only from the ranks of the Jesuits, as his opponents like to maintain). Consequently, the portion of religious priests increased in the Roman congregations. From among the bishops he chose co-workers whom he had known for a long time[14] to be opponents of liberalism of whatever version. They were virtuous and diligent men, but often narrow-minded. They were completely devoted to the Holy See, but their ambitions sometimes lacked the proper insight, and their understanding of the real situation of the Church and the intellectual processes beyond the horizon of the small Italian ecclesiastical world was small. Naturally, there were exceptions, one of them being Pietro Gasparri.[15]

Among the Pope's men, the four personal secretaries[16] deserve special credit. They enjoyed his full trust and, driven by "somewhat exaggerated ambitions" (Della Torre), they reinforced more than once the intransigent orientation of the papal decisions. In addition, several particularly influential cardinals played a great role: Francesco Segna, after 1908 prefect of the Congregation of the Index; Oreglia, dean of the Holy College had a vigorous opponent of Christian democracy; Benedetto Lorenzelli, a strict Thomist, and extraordinarily active in the Holy Office.

Of greatest influence, however, was the severely criticized triad of Vives y Tutó, Gaetano De Lai, and Merry del Val. First place must go to the Capuchin Vives y Tutó,[17] of the group of Spanish integralism which

---

[14] The fact that some of them came from Venetia caused Msgr. Duchesne to remark that the Pope had changed the boat of Saint Peter into a gondola.

[15] L. Bedeschi, op. cit., 115, also mentions Talamo, Faberi, Battandier, P. Lepidi, and others.

[16] Msgr. Bressan, supported by Pescini, Bianchi, and Gasoni. Since they made preparations with the proper authorities, they often caused short circuits in the Secretariate of State. This is the reason for their nickname *La Segretariola*. In regard to them, see: *Disquisitio circa quasdam obiectiones*, 25 and 51–52.

[17] In regard to Joseph Calasanz Vives y Tutó (1854–1913), who was given the nickname "Vives fa tutto" in Rome, see Antonio de Barcelona, *El cardenal Vives y Tutó* (Barcelona

produced the book *El liberalismo es pecado*. In 1884 he was assigned to the Roman Curia and, during the crisis of the Italian Catholic Action, he supported the campaign of Paganuzzi. He was a hard-working man of outstanding knowledge, a favorite adviser of the Holy Office, and prefect of the Congregation of Orders from 1908 until 1912. One of his followers was the feared creator of the reform of the Curia, Cardinal De Lai,[18] an energetic and tireless organizer, who succeeded in concentrating in his hands a power unequalled in the history of the Curia. Since the time the Pope had been bishop of Mantua, De Lai had been his friend and he used this friendship to extend his already considerable power as prefect of the Consistorial Congregation by invading the authority of the Congregation of the Council. He dictatorially controlled the appointments of bishops and supervised the dioceses and seminaries. His principle was to proceed rigorously rather than softly when evil was to be eliminated. The third man in the triad was Cardinal Merry del Val,[19] secretary of state at thirty-seven years of age. He occupied this office throughout the pontificate and was envied by the Holy Office for having been assigned to this office at such a young age, particularly as a foreigner, which was something unheard-of. In contrast to the secretaries of state of the last two centuries, he was much more involved in the religious policies of the pontificate. Merry del Val was a devout and moralistic priest, a distinguished and polite aristocrat, and totally devoted to the Holy See. He faced the modernistic tendencies with an untroubled but rigid intransigence. According to D. Secco Suardo, he possessed the "positive and negative characteristics" of a Spaniard, which caused him at times to be carried away by his eagerness

---

1916), and *Estudios franciscanos* 55 (1954), 531–34; 56 (1955), 5–42, 179–214; 57 (1956), 113–30, 161–81; 60 (1959), 247–66. Also L. Bedeschi, op. cit., 104–07, and D. Secco Suardo, *Da Leone XIII a Pio X* (Rome 1967), passim (see index).

[18] About Gaetano De Lai (1853–1928), see F. Crispolti, *Corone e porpore* (Milan 1934), 221–26, and L. Bedeschi, op. cit., 53, 94–95, 99–104.

[19] There are only biographies of a hagiographical nature regarding Raphael Merry del Val (1865–1930). Fairly acceptable is the one by P. Cenci (Rome 1933) and the one by J. M. Javierre (Barcelona ²1966). Numerous documents and testimonies can be found in *Romana beatificationis et canonisationis Servi Dei Raphaelis card. Merry del Val informatio* (Vatican City 1957). See also A. C. Jemolo, *Chiesa e Stato in Italia negli ultimi cento anni* (Turin 1948), 483–562; and L. Bedeschi, op. cit., passim, especially 88–94. He was the son of a Spanish diplomat and an Irish woman, raised in England and Belgium. He was still very young when he gained Leo XIII's favor. From 1900 until 1903, he expertly directed the *Accademia dei nobili ecclesiastici,* where prospective nuncios were trained. Pius X had chosen him for good reasons, that is for his outstanding intellectual qualities, his knowledge of many languages, and his diplomatic capabilities (which were more theoretical than practical, however), as well as for his greater independence, which he expected because Merry del Val had no ties to Italy.

to defend orthodoxy and to cover up denunciations which did not redound to the honor of the secretariat.[20] He was more familiar with abstract principles than with the complex conditions of reality and, moreover, fairly isolated within the boundaries of the Curia. Thus he often gave the impression that he was unable to keep up with the times.[21] However, Pius X respected this diligent, unconditionally loyal co-worker, who was from the start receptive to his own ideal of Catholic renewal and shared his conception of an authoritarian Church government. Thanks to his intimate relationship with the Pope, Merry del Val possessed immense power, which assisted him in extending the Secretariat of State's rights of intervention, which in turn resulted in more incisive reforms of the Curia. This created many enemies for him, even in Rome. He was charged with being a tool in the hands of the omnipotent *Societas Jesu,* which is exaggerated, even though his relations to the general of the Jesuits and the leaders of the *Civiltà Cattolica* were very close.[22] He was further accused of having intensified the Pope's rigoristic inclinations when executing practical measures, forcing "an old man of angelic gentleness" to violent actions "worthy of the Spanish Inquisition." This requires a correction, however. One should not give in to the temptation of a hagiographer to justify Pius X in a generalizing fashion or to make excuses for him by blaming all unfavorable aspects of his pontificate on his surroundings. One should not forget that Merry del Val kept Giacomo della Chiesa as substitute of the Secretariat of State for four years, gladly relying on his judgment in matters of diplomacy, even though Della Chiesa continued to get advise from his former chief Rampolla. However, above all, É. Poulat's[23] publication of the dossier of the *Sodalitium Pianum* showed that Benigni, at least after 1911, constantly charged Merry del Val with undue restraint when applying papal directives and with a diplomatic temperament that was always willing only partially to execute a tough decision in the face of the resistance it caused.

These texts and various documents collected during the process of beatification contradict the "legend of the secretary of state who brainwashed a benevolent and pious Pope with intransigence, the same Pope who had entrusted him with the reins of government." Yet this does not

---

[20] An example illustrating this can be found in *Les fiches pontificales* by Msgr. Montagnini (Paris 1908).

[21] The Austrian Ambassador Prince Schönburg-Hartenstein made the remark: "The cardinal knows how to centralize, but not how to be a center himself" (Engel-Janosi II, 130).

[22] Concerning the real influence of the Jesuits in the Roman Curia under Pius X, see the detailed presentation of L. Bedeschi, op. cit., 66–74.

[23] *Intégrisme et catholicisme intégral* (Paris, Tournai 1969), especially 76–77.

mean that Pius X was not at all directed by his environment or that he was solely responsible for all measures taken, even the most draconic ones which accompanied the antiliberal reaction so characteristic of his pontificate. He was justified when he turned indignantly against everyone who quietly maintained that the Church was led by "three cardinals," and he repeatedly asserted his complete independence. However, these protestations only prove his good faith, as G. Martina observed;[24] they leave the problem of the real responsibility completely open. Today it cannot be disputed that many of his assistants were carried away by misguided ambitions, exceeding the Pope's intentions when applying certain decisions and using certain methods. On the other hand, it should be clear that the Pope based his decisions in more than one case on biased and tendentious information given to him by men in his trust. Holiness is no guarantee of the best ecclesiastical policies, and a Pope who thinks he has to make decisions for the Church single-handedly is unfortunately the prisoner of his informants and the executive body, loyal and devoted as they may be. An additional observation should be made: Many an assistant of Pius X may have exceeded his intentions; yet there were others who often countered his impulses with passive resistance or at least somewhat softened his intolerant directives. In the last months of his life, Pius X complained about this, especially when the antiintegralistic reaction became apparent even in Vatican circles. But at the beginning of his pontificate, several of his reform measures had encountered the passive resistance of the conservatives, who were just as opposed to the changes demanded by the highest authority as they were to the reformism of the progressives. In view of such cases, impressively illuminating Pius X's occasional difficulties in moving even those men toward obedience who considered themselves the pioneers of the defense against democratic anarchy, É. Poulat spoke of this Pope as having a "strong will and weak authority."[25] Even though this may be exaggerated, the wording shows that the problem of relations between the Pope and his assistants is much more complex than most of his admirers and his slanderers—each in the opposite sense—would care to admit.

[24] *RSTI* 23 (1969), 232.
[25] *Archives de sociologie des religions* 29 (1970), 201.

The Reform Work of Pius X

Immediately following the death of Pius X, the London *Times* wrote: "It is not an exaggeration to say that J. Sarto instituted more changes in the administration of the Catholic Church than any of his predecessors since the Council of Trent." Even if one must note that most of the significant decisions of this Pope date from the first five years of his pontificate and that his reform program was slowed down by his excruciating efforts effectively to fend off the threat of modernism, it is nevertheless clear that he took numerous and versatile initiatives and even realized many of the relevant goals. Immediately after his election, he had taken several steps to attain the reorganization of the diocese of Rome and to eliminate the many abuses committed by the clergy of Rome.[1] However, this is merely an indication of the more general and urgent matters which he openly professed and which caused, initially, a great wave of hope among those who, after Leo XIII's "political" pontificate, expected a renovation of the Church in a more religious direction. These first decisions explain the initial confidence with which those who later on sharply criticized the reactionary stance of the Vatican could say: "Il papa farà eccelenti riforme." In the course of 1905, however, in this optimistic atmosphere, an entire series of pro-reform pamphlets appeared in close succession (Bedeschi only just recently pointed them out).[2] The exaggerated expectations of pro-reform groups, however, were disillusioned to such an extent that they often completely lost sight of the positive impact, by no means insignificant in spite of limitations, especially at the pastoral and institutional level.

[1] Cf. Fernessole II, 29–47. Throughout the whole pontificate, he observed the situation closely (cf. Schmidlin, *PG* III 38–39).
[2] L. Beschi, *Riforma a religiosa e Curia all'inizio del secolo* (Milan 1968); see especially 27–30.

CHAPTER 26

Reorganization of the Roman Curia and Codification of Canon Law

As pastor and bishop, Pius X often had occasion to discover that a reorganization of ecclesiastical institutions was urgently needed in order to better enable the clergy at all levels, from the top to the bottom, to fulfill their tasks. Thus, without much ado, he proceeded with this task, making good use of his organizational talent and the administrative experiences he had acquired in eighteen years as chancellor of the diocese of Treviso.

There is no need to list all the individual measures Pius X took in the course of his pontificate, even though they often had significant consequences.[1] Only two undertakings of great impact shall be treated in depth: the reform of the papal administration and the reform of canon law.

The organization of the Roman Curia, essentially instituted by Sixtus V, was in dire need of change.[2] In the course of three hundred years, it had turned into a heterogeneous assemblage of thirty-seven agencies whose rights and responsibilities were often totally undefined and who were constantly in conflict with each other, because each one dealt individually with administrative and judicial problems and controversies of the administration, and their areas of jurisdiction were often incompatible. Moreover, the elimination of temporal authority rendered some of these agencies totally superfluous. Pius IX and his successor had limited themselves simply to isolated reforms. On the other hand, however, the progressing Roman centralization in the course of the nineteenth century and the expansion and improvement of the possibilities of communication had essentially strengthened the contacts between the center and the periphery, making the development of certain offices desirable. Furthermore, the administrative methods were completely obsolete, inflexible, out-of-date, and quite costly, in spite of Leo XIII's modest attempts to lower the expenses of the Holy See. Moreover, many did not consider work within the Curia a challenging and demanding ecclesiastical pastorate conducted in the service of God's people, but rather a career promising the cardinal's hat, provided everything went well.

The idea of reform was in the air and not only in progressive circles, as was recently proven by a newly discovered plan which had been devised in the Vatican a year before Leo XIII died. However, this reform idea offended the principle *Quieta non movere,* honored by all administrations of the world, and it was rejected by all who saw their interests

---

[1] It should suffice to mention two: the constitution *Vacante Sede Apostolica* (25 December 1904) regarding the Pope's election (cf. M. Scaduto, "I precedenti di una reform e le leggi di Pio X sul Conclave," *CivCatt* V [1944] 6–20); the change of the *Acta Sanctae Sedis* into the official publication of the Holy See (23 May 1904), and later its replacement with the *Acta Apostolicae Sedis* (cf. *AAS* 1 [1909], 5–6, and N. Hilling, op. cit. I, 33–34).

[2] Cf. F. Roberti, "De Curia Romana ante pianam reformationem," *Rom. Curia,* 13–34.

threatened. Facing a difficult financial situation,[3] Pius X hurried to remedy the most glaring abuses, but that was not all. He began with several partial reforms which seemed especially urgent. On 17 September 1903 he suspended the obsolete special congregation *De eligendis episcopis,* founded by Benedict XIV and renewed in 1878 by Leo XIII. The Holy Office became responsible for the appointment of bishops in those countries which were not dependent on the Congregation for the Propagation of the Faith (the Propaganda) or subject to the regulations of a concordat. On 26 May 1906 he also suspended the two relatively new congregations *Super disciplina regulari* and *De statu regularium,* with the result that everything concerning the members of religious orders was concentrated in the Congregation of Bishops and Regulars. But he had already planned a much more extensive reform, as was requested by several prelates who had assembled around Cardinal Agliardi. His intentions were probably impelled by the idea of stopping the criticism of the radical front by taking the wind out of its sails. The radicals had begun to question the insufficient functioning of the Curia as well as its fundamental right of existence because they saw it as an obstacle between the Pope and the bishops. In the early summer of 1907 he decided to take steps which introduced a rapid development of the matters at hand.

A commission of cardinals was to be created to which Gaetano De Lai, secretary of the Congregation of the Council was assigned; De Lai was the chief supporter of this reform from the beginning to the end. According to the directives personally drafted by the Pope, the commission pursued the following goals:[4] the abolition of superfluous offices and agencies and the creation of appropriate new ones as necessitated by the development of the situation; the separation of administrative and judical responsibilities; the absolutely clear and rational definition of the responsibilities of each dicastery (assigning to one single organ all affairs pertaining, among others, to the bishops, the clergy, the orders, the sacraments, the missions, the simplification and thus the efficiency of the activities of individual offices; the assignment of a certain number of consultants to prepare resolutions; the coordination of criteria needed to come to a unanimous conclusion, and, finally, the standardization of fees and salaries of officials, which had been different depending on the individual functionary. The first plan drawn up by the Pope himself was presented to the commission in November. Concerning the Roman

---

[3] Cf. P. Scoppola, *Crisi modernista e rinnovamento cattolico in Italia* (Bologna 1961), 120, n. 126.

[4] Text: *Rom. Curia,* 38–42.

congregations, he relied extensively on a draft by Monsignor De Lai.[5] In regard to the Secretariat of State, he followed Cardinal Merry del Val's standpoint: On the one hand, several countries were incorporated into the area of responsibility which had been subject to the Propaganda, even though they were no longer mission countries (Great Britain, the Netherlands, the United States, Canada); on the other hand, the Secretariat of State was assigned two previously independent agencies: the Congregation for Extraordinary Ecclesiastical Affairs and the Secretariat of Briefs. These expansions increased the significance of the Secretariat of State considerably. Finally, in order to separate the administration and the judiciary, the Pope revived the old medieval jurisdiction of the *Rota Romana,* which had been hobbled through the proliferation of the congregations equipped with judicial power to such an extent that its responsibility had been confined to liturgical questions (since 1870). In the course of the next months, the basic draft was repeatedly revised, but the changes did not impair the economy of the original plan: The Congregation of Matrimony became the Congregation of the Sacraments; the section of the former Congregation of Bishops and Regulars which had charge of the bishops was incorporated into the Congregation of the Consistory, so that all questions pertaining to the members of religious orders were now handled by a special congregation (the case of the Congregation of the Missions caused debates); the Congregation of the Index, at Pius X's request, was separated from the Holy Office "in view of the great number of books to be examined";[6] the Congregation of Rites and the Congregation of the Canonization of Saints were combined in one congregation.

On 29 June 1906 the constitution *Sapiento consilio*[7] was published. The experts admired the "constructive and simplifying genius of Pius X" reflected in it (Torquebiau). From now on, the Curia was to include a triad of agencies: eleven congregations, three tribunals, and five offices. Within the area of congregations, the Congregation of the Sacraments was completely new. The former Congregation of the Council had been remodeled so drastically that it was also practically new; at the time of

---

[5] De Lai's plan reduced the congregations from eighteen to eleven, even though he proposed the creation of a new congregation *De re matrimoniali* and the separation of the old Congregation of Bishops and Regulars into two different dicasteries. In addition, he suggested to change the "old and despised" name of the Inquisition (which he compared to the Congregation of the Index) to *Congregation de fide tuenda.* Pius X preferred to keep the traditional name.

[6] Cf. *Rom. Curia,* 58, 67. Benedict XV returned to the original idea and changed the Index into a special section of the Holy Office (*AAS* 9 [1917], 161–66).

[7] Text: *AAS* 1 (1909), 7–19.

its establishment, it was to supervise the execution and interpretation of the decrees of the Council of Trent; but in the future it was to be in charge of the general discipline of the clergy and the faithful. The consistorial congregation's functions were considerably extended; it was even assigned the supervision of seminaries (in 1915, Benedict XV entrusted this function to the Congregation of Studies, whose only responsibility had been universities). The competence of the Propaganda was now limited to the mission countries in the true sense of the word;[8] moreover, it had to relinquish all matters regarding marriage to the Rota and problems pertaining to sacraments to the Congregation of the Sacraments. For jurisdiction there were to be three responsible agencies: the Rota and the Apostolic Signature (as court of appeal) were to deal with the external forum, which had gradually been taken on by the Sacred Penitentiary; the internal forum was to be the responsibility of the Penitentiary. The five offices included the Apostolic Chancery, the Apostolic Datary, the Apostolic Camera (with very limited responsibilities), the Secretariat of Briefs, and the Secretariat of State as the most important. The constitution, which was amended by a detailed *Ordo servandus*[9] (all together about eighty pages of small print), outlined precisely the functions of the new organs: appointments to the respective offices, schedules and statutes, the specific dispositions of the many subdivisions, and frequent reports, which often had to be presented to the Pope himself before a decision would be made. In order to facilitate the speedy preparation and execution of matters it was required that only the most important problems were to be submitted to the plenary session of the respective congregation. Other affairs were to be handled by the *Congresso,* a committee limited in number and consisting of high officials and the cardinal prefect of the congregation.

The practical application of the new regulations began immediately and was closely observed by the Pope himself. The fact that De Lai, who was created cardinal in December 1907, was given responsibility for the reorganization in a special commission was received with some amazement. Though many believed that the conservative Pius X proved to be rather revolutionary, the reform was generally received with satisfaction. Of course, the desire for a clear separation of administrative responsibilities and judicial functions was only partially fulfilled. The court of the Rota, indeed, confined itself to matters of matrimony; however, the congregations continued to handle controversies in other

[8] There was talk about removing the apostolic vicariates located in the areas of common law; however, the urgent intervention of Cardinal Gasparri, the leading authority in canon law, resulted in the relinquishing of this plan (cf. *Rom. Curia,* 66–67).
[9] This *Ordo servandus* was published in two parts on 29 June and on 29 September 1909 (text: *AAS* 1 [1909], 36–108).

areas and issue penalties via administrative channels. Unquestionably, the basic structure of Sixtus V's organization was not as decisively changed as would be the case half a century later under Paul VI on the occasion of the reform of the Curia. For Genocchi rightfully complained that the spirit of the "old machine" had not been trenchantly altered, and the men who were asked to set this machine in motion and to keep it running were essentially bureaucrats without pastoral experience, isolated from the world outside and its problems. Among other things, there was no mention of giving bishops who actually responsibly managed a diocese a position in the sections of the congregations dealing with practical matters. But even considering these obvious limits and shortcomings of Pius X's reform, the point must be clearly made that for the first time since the sixteenth century the entire Curia was reorganized according to, all in all, truly rational criteria.

These measures did not only possess a unique character, they were also of symbolic significance. They appeared to anticipate another highly crucial undertaking, the general reorganization of ecclesiastical law, in preparation since the beginning of Pius X's pontificate.[10]

For several centuries, the idea prevailed of revising canon law and formulating a code that would systematically compile the entire body of law adapted to the contemporary situation. This code was to replace the immense, often inaccessible and obsolete collections of papal decrees. At the Vatican Council, a number of bishops had made certain requests in this respect; and shortly before this council convened, Pope Pius IX had issued the constitution *Apostolicae Sedis* (12 October 1869), thoroughly revising the legislation regarding ecclesiastical censures. Leo XIII[11] had annulled or amended numerous obsolete regulations and even undertaken some partial codifications, using certain schemes prepared in view of the upcoming Vatican Council. His changes primarily affected the constitution *Officiorum ac munerum* (25 January 1897), codified and moderated in the legislation regarding censorship of books, and the constitution *Conditae a Christo* (8 October 1900), which finally afforded the religious congregations with simple vows a precise legal statute. Private canonists[12] had made several attempts: G. de Luise in

---

[10] In his first instructions in the beginning of the summer of 1907, Pius X expressly specified: "Questa riforma deve farsi *subito* per essere messa in esecuzione al più presto in via di esperimento, onde colle eventuali mutazioni, che seranno suggerite dalla pratica, venga definitivamente pubblicata nel nuovo Codice," (quoted in *Rom. Curia*, 41).

[11] Cf. N. Hilling, "Die Gesetzgebung Leos XIII. auf dem Gebiet des Kirchenrechts," *AkathKR* 93 (1913), 8–31, 254–76, 460–83, 623–37; 94 (1914), 75–95, 252–64; Cf. here, p. 292.

[12] *DDC* III, 915–17.

1873, E. Colomiatti in 1888, H. M. Pezzani in 1893, F. Deshayes in 1895, and mainly A. Pillet, whose *Ius canonicum generale distributum in articulos* (1890) had proposed legal regulations according to the model of the civil code of law, proving that a complete codification of canon law is indeed possible. Even though German canonists kept quiet on this matter, the international Catholic congresses after 1891 constantly received reports suggesting that the Church legislation be revised and codified.

"Two or three days after his election" (Merry del Val), Pius X was already expressing a desire to follow this path of reform.

He was strongly encouraged by Monsignor Gasparri, one of the best canonists of his time, and by Cardinal Gennari.[13] On 19 March 1904 the Pope announced through his motu proprio *Arduum sane munus* the formation of a commission of cardinals, to be aided by a certain number of consultors, which was to adjust ecclesiastical legislation to the present circumstances and to codify it. In the following week, a letter was sent to all archbishops asking them to consult with their suffragan bishops regarding the main changes which were to amend the present law and to send their recommendations to Rome, including additional nominations for consultors. A few days later, he also solicited the cooperation of Catholic universities throughout the world.

The announcement of this plan caused totally different reactions: satisfaction from those who witnessed in daily life the many-sided disadvantages of the present system; scepticism from the many scholars, mainly in Rome and Germany, who had better insight into the difficulties and thus predicted failure. The latter were supported by the famous editor of the *Corpus Iuris Canonici,* the Protestant Emil Friedberg, who charged the Pope with (among other things) attempting to extend in this way his power even further.[14] Others feared that the sections dealing with ecclesiastical civil law and with the relations between Church and state could appear in a new edition of the *Syllabus* and lead to new confrontations with governments. Other Catholic groups, e.g., in Spain, criticized the project for attempting to copy the Napoleonic codes of law, which were considered an expression of liberal individualism.[15] But Pius X remained unperturbed and made sure that everyone set to work at once.

From the very start, the chief promoter of this undertaking was Mon-

---

[13] Cf. N. Hilling, "Von wem ist der Plan der Abfassung des Codex iuris canonici zuerst ausgegangen?," *AkathKR* 116 (1936), 88–91.

[14] *DZKR* 18 (1904), 1–74.

[15] Cf. L. de Echeverría, *Miscellanea in memoriam Petri card. Gasparri* (Rome 1960), 327–41.

signor Gasparri,[16] secretary of the Congregation for Extraordinary Affairs. The Pope appointed him secretary of the papal commission and president of the College of Consultors, and he was the heart and soul of the project until its conclusion.

To speed up the work, the consultors were divided into two commissions working next to each other. One was led by Gasparri with Eugenio Pacelli as secretary; the other one was headed by Cardinal De Lai with F. A. Sapieha as secretary. As of 13 November these commissions met weekly, comparing and discussing the editorial drafts for each chapter, which were presented by two, sometimes even three or four consultors working completely independently of each other. Proceeding from the different texts and opinions voiced, the president wrote a new draft, which was again discussed and reworked. Usually, this procedure was repeated at least three or four times, occasionally even ten or twelve times. To save time, the texts were first sent to the consultors for their critical examination and written comments. When they finally agreed on one version, Gasparri presented it to the commission of cardinals, which did not reveal its comment until after it had studied the text twice.[17] The entire process took place in strict secrecy. One or two chapters or paragraphs, however, were published in the form of a papal constitution or a decree of a congregation either because the Pope considered the matter urgent or because he wanted to test the effectiveness in real life, trying to find out how the texts were received. For instance, among others this was the case with the constitution *Sapienti consilio,* through which the Curia was reorganized, and with the following decrees: the Eucharistic decrees *Ne temere* (2 August 1907), which cancelled the exemptions of the Tridentine legislation regarding matrimony in force since the sixteenth century (can. 1094–1103); *A remotissima* (31 December 1909), regarding the *Visitatio liminum* (can. 340–342a); *Maxima quidem* (29 August 1910), regarding the transfer of pastors (can. 2147–2167); and *Cum singulae* (16 October 1911), regarding the dismissal of members of religious orders (can. 646–672).

By 1912 many parts had been amended to the point that Gasparri

---

[16] Pietro Gasparri (1852–1934) was a man of amazing energy, "another, but more active and effective Raymund de Peñaforte." Concerning him see: *Il card. Pietro Gasparri* (Rome 1960); J. Denis, *Actes du congrès de Droit canonique. Cinquantenaire de la Faculté de droit canonique* (Paris 1950), 239–45; H. Tüchle, *Die Außenminister der Päpste,* ed. by W. Sandfuchs (Munich 1962), 94–108; G. Spadolini, *Il card. Gasparri e la Questione Romana* (Florence 1973). Concerning his activities as secretary of state under Benedict XV and Pius XI, see Pt. III.

[17] The successive plans remained inaccessible in the dark corners of the archives, with one exception: F. Roberti, *Codicis Juris canonici schemata Lib IV De processibus, I De judiciis in genere* (Vatican City 1940).

was able to propose sending them to the bishops and heads of the orders asking them for their comments. In spite of the resistance of several cardinals fearing new delays, the Pope agreed. This consultation, where the bishops, in turn, could confidentially consult with two or three men in their trust, proved to be very useful. On 20 March 1912 Books I and II were delivered; on 1 April 1913 Book III; on 1 July Book V; and finally on 15 November 1914 Book IV. At that time Pius X had already been dead for three months. The final, conclusive version would take two more years. However, at the time of Pius X's death, the major work had already been accomplished, consistently inspired by the Pope who had personally followed its progress step by step. Therefore, according to Gasparri, he deserves a great deal of credit for this work.

Doubtless this project had its limits. Today, we see it as a new step in the direction of centralization and extreme uniformity of the Latin Church.[18] Some, however, regret that it fails to make reference to the Holy Scriptures or the Church Fathers, in contrast to the ancient canonical collections. Even from a strictly juridical standpoint, a threatening insecurity in the terminology itself can be found, even regarding concepts which are expressly defined" (G. Schwaiger), in spite of abundant discussions and subsequent revisions. Concerning the main content, a more radical further questioning of certain positions inherited from medieval law or from modern absolutism would have been desirable.[19] However, one must admire the extent of a task executed in record time. After all, this work represents a well-structured summa, including the entire legislation of the Latin Church, excepting a portion of the liturgical material and excluding the particularly delicate problem of the relations between the Church and the respective state. It distinguishes itself through clarity and precision of style and seems to be inspired by civil codes of law rather than imitation of the rhythmic phraseology and rhetorical verbosity characteristic of the previous texts, including those of Leo XIII. It reveals the attempt (proving that Pius X was not antimodern on principle) to synchronize the various segments of canon law with the demands of modern times and to give it the benefit of achievements in the field of learning and of the accomplishments of contemporary juridical practice. One must also praise Pius's interest in cooperating, from the beginning to the end, with the episcopate throughout the world and with the non-Roman canonists. Proof of his

---

[18] The code is not valid for the Eastern churches united with Rome.
[19] U. Stutz introduces his chapter about the "New Elements in the Code" with the following words: "The code has basically few new elements" (op. cit., 57). Cf. H. E. Feiner, op. cit., 707: "The character of the work is rather conservative. The real innovations are limited to the most essential issues." Regarding these innovations, which should not be underestimated, cf. ibid., 709–19.

realism and moderation are the decisions made between the overly specialized position of the theoreticians and the extreme pragmatism of many a practitioner. Along these lines, one must not forget the absolutely pertinent observation of the Protestants Stutz and Feine, who saw in the new code the expression of "the progressive and increasing spiritualization of the Roman Catholic Church," which had become more and more apparent during the pontificates of Pius IX and Leo XIII. Thus the two authors, who certainly were not admirers of Pius X, agree that the code was an epoch in the history of ecclesiastical law.

CHAPTER 27

Eucharistic Decrees and Liturgical Renewal

At the beginning of the twentieth century, a clearer perspective in favor of frequent Communion had been conceived. Yet the disputes between its advocates and opponents continued. Even Leo XIII's encyclical *Mirae caritatis* (1902),[1] encouraging the "frequent use of the Eucharist" and protesting against the "contrived reasons for relinquishing Communion," did not succeed in settling the controversy, which was especially intense in France and Belgium. Following the moral theologian E. Génicot, S.J., and the canonist Gasparri, Abbé F. Chatel and the Redemptorist Godts stressed the absolute necessity of doing away with premeditated venial sin before one could expect to be admitted to frequent Communion. Others advocated the concept of Monsignor de Ségur, according to which the Eucharist is not "a reward for achieved virtue, but on the contrary, the means of achieving virtue." From this perspective, they strictly distinguished between the absolutely necessary and the desirable spiritual disposition. They were supported by Cardinal Gennari in Rome and Monsignor Heylen, the Bishop of Namur and new president of the Eucharistic congresses; and they could refer to several responses in their favor by the Roman congregations (mainly to the decree *Quemadmodum* of the Holy Office of 17 December 1890 for the benefit of nuns). Thus their number was especially great in Italy, where the rigoristic tradition never had had a strong impact; but they also had followers north of the Alps, above all among the Jesuits.[2]

---

[1] *ASS* 34 (1901–02), 641–44.

[2] Among others, the French Jesuit P. L. Cros, who had settled in Spain. Disregarding the objections of the hierarchy, he enthusiastically developed a program including four points: *comulgar* (communicate), *cada día* (daily), *sin confesarse* (without confessing), *hasta la muerte* (until death).

As an admirer of Don Bosco, who had been an enthusiastic defender of the frequent and early Communion of children, Giuseppe Sarto had made the development of the celebration of the Eucharist the key issue of his program as bishop. Thus it was not surprising that as Pope he tried to realize this program for the Church at large. In a period of only two years, between 30 May 1905 and 14 July 1907, he issued twelve interventions in this regard (decrees, letters, or addresses). On the occasion of the international Eucharistic Congress, convened in Rome in June 1905, he approved a prayer "for the propagation of the pious custom of daily Communion," bringing to mind that "Jesus meant to be the daily remedy and the daily food for our daily shortcomings." The most decisive act, however, was the decree of the Congregation of the Council of 20 December 1905, *De quotidiana SS. Eucharistiae sumptione,*[3] which provided the appropriate settlement of the impending controversy, specifying that two conditions for receiving Holy Communion be sufficient: the state of grace and the proper intention. At the same time, the faithful were asked to communicate "frequently and even daily." By order of the Pope, this decree was sent to all bishops and heads of orders, instructing them to "send it to their seminaries, parishes, religious institutions, and priests and to let the Holy See know what they had done to assure its execution." In the course of the next few months, other decrees encouraged the communicants by granting absolution (14 February 1906), by dispensing the sick confined to bed for more than one month from the Eucharistic rule of fast (7 December 1906 and 6 March 1907) and by defining the term "all faithful" used in the decree to include the children who had attended First Communion (13 September 1906).

The "age of reason" required for First Communion continued to be controversial. Frequently consulted about this disputed question, the Congregation of the Sacrament prepared a decree for which the Pope showed great interest, even though he anticipated strong resistance. After discussing the problem from a historical, dogmatic, and practical point of view, the decree *Quam singulari* (8 October 1910)[4] declared that it is sufficient for children to be able "to recognize the difference between the Eucharistic Bread and common bread, and that it is unnecessary to postpone First Communion until the age of ten or twelve or even fourteen, as was done frequently at that time. This meant the new application of a principle on which all Eucharistic reforms of Pius X were based: Communion is not the reward for virtuous living, but the

[3] *AAS* 2 (1910), 894–98. See the comments of E. Barbe (Rheims 1905) and J.-B. Ferreres (Paris 1909).
[4] *AAS* 2 (1910), 577–83.

food to effect virtuous living according to the theological maxim *ex opere operato.*

Issuing appropriate decrees was not enough. It was necessary to apply this legislation to practical life. By the way, the new regulations were not at all as revolutionary as they seemed to be at first glance. Nevertheless, they turned many old customs upside down and encountered definite resistance in many countries.[5]

Instigated by the Fathers of the Blessed Sacrament, a league of priests was founded in April 1905 for the purpose of enforcing the application of the decree about frequent Communion. Six years later, more than 50,000 priests had joined this league. Furthermore, immediately after the issuance of the decree *Quam singulari,* a Pious Union for the Communion of Children was founded in Rome, soon joined by many other national organizations (Italy, Spain, Belgium, South America, the United States, Canada). As of 1907 the Pope demanded the annual convention of a Eucharistic triduum in each diocese and if possible even in every parish. This was to draw the attention of the clergy and the faithful to the significance of the decree of 1905. In Belgium, in response to this triduum, the Jesuit Lintelo,[6] one of the most ardent apostles of frequent Communion, started Leagues of the Most Sacred Heart, whose members pledged regularly to receive Communion.[7] Similar leagues were founded in other countries under different conditions, for example in France by Father Bessière and in England by Father Leister.

Pius X also used the international Eucharistic congresses to promote the acceptance and propagation of the Roman decrees. Originally these congresses were meant to be public manifestations[8] to inspire the enthusiasm of the Catholics for all versions of the veneration of the Most Holy Sacrament and to liberate them from their fear of public judgment through clear and official testimony of Christ's Kingdom embracing all mankind (which was rejected by the followers of laicism). Typical manifestations of such triumphant posture were primarily the con-

---

[5] After Cardinal De Lai, many would have wanted to appeal to the Holy Office (*Disquisitio circa quasdam objectiones . . .* [Vatican City 1950], 129); Pius X was charged with having made a decision regarding the Communion of children without consulting the episcopate.

[6] Regarding Jules Lintelo (1862–1919), see J. Severin, *Vie du P. Lintelo, de la Compagnie de Jésus, apôtre de la communion quotidienne, membre du bureau des congrès eucharistiques* (Toulouse, Brussels 1921).

[7] Some numbers may serve to illustrate the results of these efforts: the diocese of Mechelen, where the average number of Communions per inhabitant and per year fluctuated around 2.7 between 1870 and 1900, reached around 5.1 in 1911 and even 7.6 in 1912 (F. Houtart, *Collectanea Mechliniensia* 42 [1957], 595).

[8] Cf. above, pp. 260ff.

gresses of Montreal, Madrid, and especially Vienna, where the Emperor and the Archdukes marched in the procession wearing gala uniforms, surrounded by several thousand participants. Since the beginning of Pius X's pontificate, however, another aspect came to the foreground, which had been only faintly present under Leo XIII: the desire to encourage the faithful to receive Communion frequently, even daily. This was especially pertinent at the Congress of Metz in 1907, where Father Lintelo spoke about the duties of the preacher in regard to the decree. Reflecting certain reservations expressed by the bishop of Châlon, Father Lintelo was officially congratulated in the name of the cardinal legate. He confirmed that the "ideas and wishes of the Holy Father were most clearly reflected in his [Lintelo's] writings." From now on, congresses were unthought of without Father Lintelo's speeches. Based on rich personal experience, his report on the catechism and frequent Communion at the Congress of Madrid (1911), immediately following the decree *Quam singulari,* inspired the Eucharistic Children's Crusade, which was founded officially in 1914 on the occasion of the Congress of Lourdes and had already taken root two years later in fifty-four countries. Thus, all those were brilliantly refuted who had believed or sometimes even hoped that Pius X's death would ensure a relaxation of the decrees. On the contrary, their main content was even incorporated in the new code of canon law.

The utilization of the Eucharistic congresses bore increasingly rich fruit because their effect on the public grew considerably during the pontificate;[9] the number of participants, their reputation and influence rose tremendously: in 1914, no less than six cardinals and two hundred bishops came to Lourdes, which approached the total number of participants of the first congress in 1881. Above all, the congresses became more and more international in character; of the first fifteen congresses, nine had taken place in France, four in Belgium, and one in Switzerland, areas which were generally considered an extension of France. To be sure, the Congress of Jerusalem in 1893 had been an exception, but one must not forget to what degree France had felt at home in the Levant. Nevertheless, Pius X, always very interested in the program of the congress, decided to hold it in 1905, the year of its twenty-fifth anniversary, in Rome. The next meeting places of the congress were determined: Metz (1907, German at that time), London (1908), Cologne (1909), Montreal (1910), Madrid (1911), Vienna (1912), and Malta (1913). Not until 1914 did the congress return to France, to Lourdes.

---

[9] Cf. L. de Paladini, *Die eucharistischen Kongresse. Ursprung und Geschichte* (Paderborn 1912), and E. Lesne, *Cinquantenaire des congrès eucharistiques internationaux* (Lille 1931).

Similarly, the significance of the foreign delegations attending the respective congresses increased. This expansion was needed in view of the fact that efforts had been made for several years (a direct result of the systematic propaganda activities) also to organize national Eucharistic congresses almost everywhere. Therefore the international congresses were forced to emphasize their difference from the national congresses more clearly and to obtain a higher degree of internationality.

The Eucharistic decrees of Pius X, independent of their liturgical context, interpret Communion mainly as food for the individual Christian. On the other hand, Pius X played an important role in the rediscovery of the real position that the liturgy should take in Catholic life. Monsignor Wagner and Monsignor Jounel agreed that the first significant reforms in the area of liturgy since the Council of Trent were owed to Pius X. Under his pontificate and partially under his influence, the so-called "liturgical movement," so far limited to a small elite and developing in the confinements of Benedictine abbeys, began to invade parishes.

One of the first acts of the pontificate of Pius X was the motu proprio *Tra le sollecitudini* of 22 November 1903,[10] on the subject of Church music. However, its significance by far extended this area so that it is justified to speak of it as being the "charter of the liturgical movement." As bishop, the future Pope Pius X tried to combat "orchestral opera music," which had infiltrated Church music (more so in Italy than elsewhere), replacing it with classical polyphony and mainly with Gregorian chants, that is, the traditional chorale of the Church, whose true character the monks of Solesmes had gradually retrieved from the numerous changes they underwent in the course of the centuries.[11] But he was not satisfied with such reforms instituted with the help of his conductor Perosi in his dioceses of Mantua and Venice. Thus in 1893 he proposed to the Congregation of Rites a motion about the reform of Church music, which text had been prepared (with the help of some monks from Solesmes) by Father A. De Santi, a Jesuit with connections with the *Civiltà Cattolica;* De Santi became more and more the "mover of the Gregorian reform" under Leo XIII's and Pius X's pontificates. Following the advice of Santi and with his assistance, a motu proprio was drafted in November 1903 which reiterated the text of the motion. It defined the true essence of Church music, its sources of inspiration, its exterior form, and its execution, and it banned from the ceremonies of

---

[10] *ASS* 36 (1904), 329–32.

[11] Concerning the work done in Solesmes regarding the revival of the Gregorian chant and the controversies resulting from the so-called "Medicean edition" of the Pustet publishing house in Regensburg, see chap. 18. See also chap. 18 regarding "Cecilianism."

worship everything that did not conform to these principles. Gregorian chant in "its original and pure form, to which it has been appropriately restored by recent efforts" was presented as the "perfect model of Church music": A church composition is more ecclesiastical and liturgical when it approaches Gegorian chant in its composition, its spirit, and its inner attitude; on the other hand, the more it deviates from this model, the less it is worthy of the house of God." However, even though Gregorian chant was propagated as the norm, Pius X inhibited its exclusive use, in contrast to many of the executors of his will who kindled illusions about the possibility of turning the monodic church chant into song truly accessible to the people, as subsequent experience was to show. Merry del Val's testimony belongs in this context: "He certainly did not simply push aside the local or national customs, provided the basic principle of preserving the religious and artistic character of Church music was conscientiously adhered to. Pius X did not want to ban polyphonic music from the Church; rather he accepted the works of modern composers with benevolence, demanding, however, that they strictly obey the prescribed rules, making their compositions as much as possible echos and extensions of the chorale. He certainly did not agree with the actions of some fanatics who went so far as to ban from our churches all music that was not compatible with Gregorian music. He declared this to be extremism."[12]

Through a second motu proprio of 25 April 1904,[13] likewise inspired by Father De Santi,[14] Pius X entrusted the Benedictines of Solesmes with the preparation of an authentic Vatican edition of the Gregorian melodies, under the control of a special Roman commission led by Dom J. Pothier, who had become abbot of Saint Wandrille in 1898. He requested that the melodies "be restored in their integrity and purity according to the oldest manuscripts, but also with special consideration of the legitimate tradition which had permeated the manuscripts in the course of time and of the practical use in present liturgies." This statement, inspired by Dom Pothier, caused endless debates in the commission. As a matter of fact, there were two camps, and not only within the ranks of the theoreticians (there was a disagreement between Dom Pothier and his student Dom Mocquereau)[15], but mainly on the practical

[12] *Impressioni e ricordi* (Padua 1949).
[13] *ASS* 36 (1904), 586.
[14] Cf. J. M. Bauduccio (biblio., chap. 18).
[15] The author, who had outlined his theory in vol. VII of his *Paléographie musicale* (1901), offered a detailed exposé in *Le nombre musical*, 2 vols. (Toulouse 1908–27). Concerning the more eclectic opinions of Dom Pothier offered in his *Revue Chant Grégorien* (Grenoble 1892ff.). see *LThK*² VII, 648–49, and U. Bomm, *Festschrift Th. Schrems* (Regensburg 1963), 63–75.

and pastoral level: Should one demand, as Dom Mocquereau and most of his fellow brothers of Solesmes did, literal adoption of the oldest manuscripts for an edition to be used in liturgy, even if these manuscripts did not agree with modern sensitivities, or should one request, as did Dom Pothier and the Germans (mostly Father Wagner), acceptance of the modifications and moderations later introduced by "living traditions"? The disagreements between the members of the commission were intensified by personal conflicts. Moreover, the question of whether the systematic study of the old manuscripts would not necessitate many years of scholarly research, thus postponing the publication of the official edition, which, according to the Pope's intentions, was to standardize the practice of Church music in the entire Catholic Church, was legitimate. In order to solve this problem, the Pope, actually favoring the second solution, decided to proceed from the edition published in 1895 by Dom Pothier. In 1905 Pothier was asked to take charge of the final preparation and completion of the new edition. The Vatican commission ceased its work. In October 1905, the *Kyriale* was published, followed in 1908 by the *Graduale* and in 1912 by the *Antiphonarium.* Several decrees of the Congregation of Rites reinforced the order to observe the regulations carefully,[16] and the bishops were forbidden to allow future editions whose melodies did not conform with the Vatican edition. The opponents of Solesmes believed it could be concluded from this that those editions would be prohibited which had been provided with rhythmic signs according to Dom Mocquereau's method. But in spite of often rather annoying intrigues, the Holy See rejected taking this step. Instead, the Pope took up a suggestion by Father De Santi and recognized the legitimacy of these editions as "private editions."

The significance that the Pope attributed to the restoration of Church music does not only have aesthetic reasons—"provide a prayer with a beautiful background," he said—but rests mainly in the desire to awake in the faithful love for the liturgy and for solemn Church prayer, which the Pope considered "the first and irreplaceable source of Christian strength," according to the wording of the motu proprio of 1903. This intention compelled Pius X, who had been a man of the Church all his life, to institute several liturgical reforms. From the perspective of the second Vatican Council, they may seem rather modest, but they required a certain measure of courage and, in any case, provided the first, not insignificant guideline for the great liturgical awakening of the twentieth century.

---

[16] A letter of 18 February 1910, addressed to Msgr. Haberl, president of the Cecilia Society of Germany, criticized the so-called mensuralism in the execution of the Gregorian chant.

The expedience of certain liturgical reforms or at least their revision had been in the air since the Vatican Council, which had offered the opportunity of a series of *vota* regarding the reform of the breviary.[17] This matter, frequently discussed in professional journals, was brought up again by the publication of the *Geschichten des Breviers* by Father Batiffol (1893) and Suitbert Bäumer (1895). Furthermore, the progress of historical studies in Catholic circles during the last decades suggested a revision of the martyrology and certain readings of Matins. For this purpose, Leo XIII had founded a Historical-Liturgical Commission (1902), whose membership was composed of L. Duchesne, J. Wilpert, F. Ehrle, G. Mercati,[18] and others. Pius X was not indifferent to this problem, and the benevolence with which he treated the school of Solesmes was partly due to the fact that this school endeavored to restore the purity of the old Roman music on the basis of thorough studies of the manuscripts. His interest in the liturgical discipline, however, was primarily of a pastoral nature. This can be demonstrated by the solution, for example, in favor of which he had decided in the controversy between Dom Mocquereau and Dom Pothier. Moreover, the reform, which he began after successfully concluding the restoration of Church music, was not primarily designed to eliminate the historical errors contained in the breviary, but rather to upgrade the prayer of the weekly psalter and to restore Sunday to its rightful place in the liturgical cycle.

The festivals of saints or other more recent feasts with their own unique attributes had increased to such an extent that the Sunday or ferial office was rarely celebrated, consequently, numerous psalms were not recited any longer. Recently, Leo XIII had made the situation worse by conceding the votive office *ad libitum,*[19] practically destroying the liturgical yearly cycle. Various undertakings led to the establishment of a papal commission to reform the psalter (July 1911): two brochures by Monsignor Isoard,[20] published at the instigation of Rome in 1900 and 1901; several articles appearing in the following years in the German journals *Pastor Bonus, Theologie und Glaube,* and *Der Katholik,* and an

---

[17] Mansi XLIX, 446–48, L, 602, 626–27, 636–38, 652, 669–70, 679, LIII, 331–52, 466, 470. The commissions were of the opinion that the question belonged in the personal area of papal responsibility (ibid., L 930–31, LIII, 674, 687). Cf. J. W. Corcoran, *Meinrad Essays* 12 (1961), 4, 33–41.

[18] Cf. A. P. Frutaz, *La sezione storica della S. Congr. dei Riti* (Vatican City 1963), 9–10, 33–35.

[19] Decree of the Congregation of Rites of 5 July 1883 (*Decreta authentica C.S.R.* [Rome 1898ff], no. 3581); cf. H. Vinck, op. cit., 52–54.

[20] "Le saint Bréviaire et son avenir" and "Nouvelles observations sur le saint Bréviaire."

essay by the Benedictine Abbot Dom Guépin in 1908[21]; the urgent necessity of a new edition of the breviary; but primarily, however, several interventions addressed directly to the Pope by the liturgy professor Father Piacenza, whose ideas on liturgy were progressive and liberal. This commission was ordered to work independently of the Congregation of Rites, whose tendency to cling to tradition would have made any serious reform impossible. The commission was also to work independently of the historical-liturgical commission which Leo XII had established. This documented the wish not to let objections by the historians get in the way. The commission was chaired by the new secretary of the Congregation of Rites, C. La Fontaine, a pastor who was intimately familiar with the liturgy but not with its history. The commission went to work at once. Working according to his own unique method, only assisted by a few advisers (in this case Monsignor Piacenza[22]), Pius X was able after several months to publish the bull *Divino afflatu* (1 November 1911).[23] It not only undertook the restructuring of the Divine Office in the spirit of tradition, but it also paid attention to the reasonable request to ease the burden of the breviary for the priest serving a parish. Matins was shortened from eighteen psalms on Sunday and twelve on weekdays to nine psalms or pieces of psalms. No holy days were suspended, but Sundays took a special place from now on; on most holy days, the ferial office was to be used along with the hymn of Matins, the lessons, and the concluding prayers. The *Proprium de Tempore* was restored to significance, readings of the Holy Scriptures were allotted more time, and the entire Office became more varied, even though it was considerably shortened and simplified, unfortunately sacrificing many traditional elements.

However, this was only the beginning. Despite the opposition of Monsignor La Fontaine, who claimed that an incisive reform required the consultation of the episcopate, Pius X adopted the more far-reaching concept of Piacenza and extended the duties of the commission to include a complete reform of the breviary and the missal. The execution of such an extensive program required thorough studies. The pressures by the publishers anxious to publish the new model edition

[21] "De ratione breviarii romani-monastici eiusque emendatione Commentarium"; cf. *NRTh* 76 (1954), 413.

[22] His role, for a long time insufficiently assessed, was represented correctly by H. Vinck, thanks to unpublished documents (op. cit.). He shows primarily—as opposed to O. Rousseau (*Miscellanea liturgica in onore card. Lercaro* I, 525–50)—"that it was thanks to him and not to Beauduin that Sunday came back to favor again (1913)."

[23] *AAS* 3 (1911), 631–36; cf. P. Piacenza, *In constitutionem "Divino afflatu"* . . . *commentarium* (Rome 1912), and F. Cabrol, *La réforme du bréviaire et du calendrier* (Paris 1912).

of the breviary as soon as possible finally forced the Pope to find a temporary solution which emphasized the Sunday and ferial office, especially during Lent (motu proprio *Abhinc duos annos* of 23 October 1913). In the beginning of 1914, the reform of the missal was begun; however, the death of the Pope brought everything to a standstill, especially after the commission was strongly criticized for its working habits. The liturgical historians charged that it had sacrificed many time-honored values, for example, the prayer of Psalms 148–150, recited every morning at dawn.[24] The pragmatists thought that the revisions, forced upon the concerned groups without consulting them, had been made "hastily" (Della Chiesa), without paying sufficient attention to the difficulties of application.

The role Pius X played in the restoration of the liturgy is not confined to his legislative work, as significant as this may have been for the reevaluation of the celebration of the Christian mysteries in the context of the annual cycle. In his motu proprio of 1903, regarding Church music, the Pope said that the first source to feed the Christian life of the faithful was to be found in "active participation in the mystery of worship and in the common and solemn prayers of the Church."[25] From this statement the Belgian Benedictine Lambert Beauduin derived the inspiration and the foundation for founding the liturgical movement of Mont-César (Louvain) on the occasion of the Congress of Mechelen around 1909. He was supported by Cardinal Mercier. Since Beauduin possessed remarkable organizational talents and a contagious optimism, he succeeded (in his own special way) in interesting the parishes in the liturgical life. He distributed among the masses tens of thousands of pamphlets containing the translation of all Sunday Masses and their annotations. At the same time, he trained the pastors with both a journal, doctrinal in character, and the *Questions liturgiques.* He also organized yearly liturgical conventions, which grew more and more successful until the outbreak of the war. These meetings contributed a great deal to the spread of the movement for the liturgical pastoral outside of Belgium. It was to reach its peak in the course of the next quarter of the century.[26]

---

[24] See mainly the essays by A. Baumstark, *Roma e l'oriente* 3 (1911–12), 217–28, 289–302; 4 (1912), 93–96. F. Cabrol is more positive, in spite of some regrets.

[25] The official Latin translation of this passage of the Italian original is not quite correct; cf. *QLP* 32 (1952), 161.

[26] The strength of the movement started by Dom Lambert Beauduin was partly due to his sensitivity for pastoral realities, and partly to his efforts of basing his pastoral work on a solid doctrinal and historical foundation. He collected his thoughts in the classical little book, *La piété de l'Église* (Louvain 1914).

CHAPTER 28

Concern for Pastoral Improvements: Seminaries, Catechetical Instruction, Catholic Action

All popes of the nineteenth and twentieth centuries were intensely interested in improving the spiritual and moral level of the clergy and inspiring their pastoral enthusiasm. No pope was more systematically devoted to this task than Pius X. He continuously issued new memorandums and offered advice in this matter and again and again took new practical measures.

In March 1904, on the occasion of the thirteen hundredth anniversary of the death of Gregory the Great, he defined in an encyclical "the ideal of the true priest," as Gregory had described it in his *Regula pastoralis;* and he ordered for all of Italy apostolic visitations which were to bring to light the shortcomings of the clergy in order to eliminate them.[1] A few months earlier, he had recommended to the priests joining the *Unio apostolica,* a fraternity of priests "whose usefulness and excellence he had tested himself." The questionnaire, prepared in 1909 by the consistorial congregation under his direction, focused on the clergy's observance of their duties and the situation in the seminaries.[2] The bishops were to answer this questionnaire during their *visitatio liminum.* In view of the reaction of the national episcopate, Pius X did not make the wearing of the cassock mandatory all over the world, and he did not introduce everywhere the Italian custom of prohibiting the seminarians from returning to their families during vacation (in order to better protect them from worldly indoctrination). But he constantly reminded the bishops to use stricter standards when recruiting priests and to expel those young seminary candidates whose spirit of obedience gave cause for serious doubts.[3] He urgently wanted the priests to concentrate

[1] Encyclical *Iucunda sane* (1 March 1904); *ASS* 36 (1903–04); brief of 11 February and 7 March 1904: ibid., 532–43. The *Regolamento personale e questionario del visitatore apostolico* (26 pages) is very important. It was published by L. Bedeschi, *Lineamenti dell'Antimodernismo* (Parma 1970), 145–62.

[2] *AAS* 2 (1910), 21–22, 26–28.

[3] On the other hand, it should be noted that Pius X, prompted by disputes over the book *La vocation sacerdotale* (Paris 1909) by the French seminary professor J. Lahitton, appointed a commission of cardinals, which approved his essential theses on 2 July 1912: (1) Nobody has the right to ordination before the free nomination by the bishop; (2) the appointment as priest is not "necessarily and usually" based on inner leanings; (3) the only indispensable requirements are honest intention, capability, purity of life and doctrine, justifying the hope that the candidate will be able to perform his office as priest and to do his duty (cf. *AAS,* 4 [1912], 485; also 5 [1913], 290). About Lahitton, see *Catholicisme,* V, 1626.

on their ultimate religious task, and he took several measures for the purpose of releasing them and preventing them from participating in all activities of an economic or political nature. In order to improve the spiritual guidance of the clergy, he did not hesitate to ease the traditional rules regarding the tenure of the pastors.[4]

Several of these measures may give the impression of a sort of police system of surveillance and espionage, and of an overestimation of obedience at the cost of a free exchange of opinions. However, in spite of these weak points, to which we are especially sensitive today, we must not forget that Pius X was always guided by a very high, positive ideal. This ideal found an especially remarkable and eloquent expression in *Haerent animo* (4 August 1908),[5] an urgent reminder to the clergy, representing the true spiritual charter of the priesthood and remaining authoritative for a long time to come. It was written entirely by the Pope himself on the occasion of the fiftieth anniversary of his ordination as priest, and it took only "about fourteen days of the few moments of free time at his disposal" (Merry del Val). He drew a truly traditional picture of the priesthood; but he incorporated the rules of the priest's office which evolved in the course of the nineteenth century, challenging the clergy to follow them zealously. This does not change the fact that this saintly Pope, with his totally unique flair for challenges, instilled in the pastoral ministry a new spirit, the effects of which could be felt long after his death.

Impelled by the desire to improve the quality of the clergy, Pius X dealt particularly with the question of the seminaries, including the preparatory seminaries; except in German-speaking countries and in Belgium, they trained most candidates for the priesthood from ages twelve to thirteen. The instruction offered in these seminaries was completely antiquated. The situation was worsened by the fact that most teachers were autodidacts. They were in no position to prepare future priests for coping with the problems of the modern world. These grievances had been pointed out for several years by various people. For example, the superior of the seminary of Boston, Father John Hogan, discussed them in his book *Clerical Studies* (1898), which was translated into French in 1901 and inspired the archbishop of Albi, Monsignor Mignot, when he wrote his sensational *"Lettres sur les études ecclésiastiques"* (1900–01). Especially in Italy reforms were urgently needed, because the great number of small dioceses made the situation worse. Many bishops of this country faced the dilemmas of financing and recruiting the faculty. Shortly before his death, Leo XIII discussed this problem

[4] Decree *Maxima cura* of 20 August 1910: *AAS*, 2 (1910), 636–648.
[5] *ASS* 41 (1908), 555–77.

before the episcopate in a motu proprio of 8 December 1902;[6] Pius X was completely open-minded toward these problems; after all, in Treviso and as bishop of Mantua he had tried hard to improve the diocesan seminaries. He may also have been influenced by the measures taken by a former German Franciscan, Monsignor Döbbing, in his dioceses of Nepi and Sutri.[7] During the apostolic visitation ordered for March 1904, the real circumstances in the diocesan seminaries were to be uncovered. According to the judgment of a biographer who can hardly be charged with prejudice toward the Curia, even in Rome itself "everything was in need of repair or restoration, materially and spiritually, in terms of staff and education."[8] In the rest of Italy, conditions were no better. In January of 1905 the bishops were asked to think about the interdiocesan reorganization of the seminaries, and a papal commission was ordered to prepare reform plans analyzing and utilizing the reports of the inspectors. The papal adviser responsible for this project was Father Pietro Benedetti.[9]

After three years of work carefully observed by the Pope, a program of studies was published (10 May 1907), followed by norms for the organization of the seminaries in regard to education and discipline (1 January 1908).[10] It paid attention to minute details. All in all, the proposed reforms were too weak and increased the shortcomings of an educational system leading a ghetto life without contact with the outside world. Eventually some improvements were made. Among them were: the consolidation of smaller institutions, adaptation of the high school curriculum to that of state institutions, introduction of a preparatory year at the beginning of theological studies, emphasis on the significance of a spiritual adviser and on the genuineness of vocations (especially urgent in countries where the clerical profession often meant social advancement). A new group of apostolic visitors was ordered to supervise the consequent execution of the Roman regulations. Unfortunately, the reform did not produce the results expected, especially in southern Italy. Qualified staffs were lacking, and the radical purge in reaction to modernism reduced the number of suitable men. The establishment of regional seminaries proved to be more difficult than had been expected,

---

[6] *ASS* 35 (1902–03), 257–65.

[7] Cf. L. Hardick, "Bischof Bernhard Döbbing (1855–1916). Ein deutscher Bischof in Italien, seine innerkirchliche Reformtätigkeit," *WZ* 109 (1959), 142–95. He was appointed bishop in 1900 and Pius X called him "the pearl of the Italian episcopate."

[8] P. Fernessole, *Pie X* II (Paris 1953), 45.

[9] G. Gremigni, *Cuore e testa. Mgr. Pietro Benedetti, missionario del S. Cuore* (Rome 1939), 193–200. Regarding the archives of the commission, see M. Guasco, op. cit., n. 32.

[10] *ASS* 40 (1907), 336–43, 41 (1908), 212–42.

even though the Holy See financially assisted many bishops who did not have the necessary means at their disposal.

All these measures pertained only to Italy, but in the opinion of the Pope they could be taken as models elsewhere. All instructions received by the congregation entrusted with the control of the seminaries required that the regulations initially issued for Italy also be applied worldwide. Certain explanations in this regard specified the Pope's intentions. For example, when the archbishop of Rouen was widely criticized for having applied to his diocese the regulations intended for the Italian bishops "regarding books to be handed to the seminary students," he was praised in a Roman document "for having understood that these regulations were also valid for the seminaries in other countries."[11]

Pius X's restoration efforts regarding a more effective pastoral extended over other areas as well. Holding the conviction that good bishops are a must if one wants good priests, he did not confine himself to pious reprimands, as contained in the encyclical *Communium rerum* (21 April 1909), in which he represents Saint Anselm of Canterbury as a model pastor, fervently drawing the picture of the ideal bishop.[12] He also tried to improve the recruitment of the episcopate by revising the methods of appointments. He issued precise directives for the maintenance of the candidates' personal file, studying each one personally before making a decision. On the other hand in order to increase his control over the activities of his bishops he tightened not only the rule on the periodical *visitatio liminum* whereby every bishop was obliged, according to a strictly determined alternating schedule, to appear at the Vatican every five years. The bishop was now obliged to present a detailed report on the conditions in his diocese based upon a minutely detailed questionnaire.[13]

Instruction in the catechism was also one of Pius X's concerns. Clearly recognizing the situation, the Pope drew attention to the fact "that it is much easier to find a brilliant speaker than a catechist who is an excellent teacher." He did not grow tired of reminding the priests to present Christian doctrine clearly and simply, and to deal thoroughly with the catechesis for adults, which had been greatly neglected in the nineteenth century because the instruction of children took precedence. As always, he did not confine himself to issuing a solemn encyclical regarding this problem,[14] rather, he devised a series of measures,

[11] C. Cordonnier, *Mgr. Fuzet* (Paris 1950), II, 330.
[12] *AAS* 1 (1909), 333–88.
[13] *AAS* 2 (1910), 13–34.
[14] Encyclical *Acerbo nimis* (15 April 1905): *ASS* 37 (1904–05), 613–25.

demanding, among other things, the more frequent employment of lay catechists, a novelty at this time. His words were followed by his example and, as he used to do, he personally explained the catechism every Sunday. Listeners came by the thousands wanting to hear the Pope who had not forgotten that he was also the bishop of the diocese of Rome.

Pius X also instigated the preparation of a new catechism, pointing out the elements which were to be considered. After examining the draft personally and correcting it with care, he introduced this catechism as the required text in the ecclesiastical province of Rome. At the same time, he expressed a wish to adopt it in all dioceses,[15] because he was interested in fulfilling the desire for a universal standardized catechism which had been repeatedly voiced after the First Vatican Council.

The interest in catechismal instruction, which Pius X had displayed continuously as a young priest and in later life, was in line with contemporary concerns. In 1889 the first Italian catechetical congress had taken place in Piacenza. But it was primarily in German-speaking countries that an active movement in search of new directions emerged. In 1875 a journal called *Katechetische Blätter* had been founded in Munich. This was followed in 1878 by the *Christlich-Pädagogische Blätter* in Vienna and in 1888 by the *Katechetische Monatsschrift* in Münster. These journals, especially the first two, found good response even in non-German-speaking countries and the catechetical societies, whose mouthpiece they were, organized important congresses in Munich (1906) and in Vienna (1912). Gradually, under the influence of H. Stieglitz, a new method was developed which had been inspired by the Protestant pedagogue Johann Friedrich Herbart and was known as the Munich catechetical method: an inductive method no longer proceeding from the text, which is explained, but from what the child knows already or perhaps (but at that time rarely) from a story of the Bible[16] that was to be added to the text of the catechism. However, some time passed before the majority of catechists adopted the new ideas, and it took even more time before interest in the pedagogical problems related to the method were replaced by the more fundamental question of

---

[15] *AAS* 4 (1912), 690–92. Regarding this catechism, see in C. Bellò (*Geremia Bonomelli* [Brescia 1961], 180) the critical comments of the bishop of Cremona, who charged him, for instance, with maintaining a scholastic vocabulary and, in regard to morals, neglecting love of his fellow man. It should be noted that all catechisms since Deharbe had deviated from the traditional sequence. They had inserted the morals in between the exposé about the credo and the Sacraments. Pius X returned to the sequence outlined by the Council of Trent.

[16] Of all the men who helped to restore the significance of the "Salvation and Passion of Christ" in religious instruction F. J. Knecht needs to be mentioned. His *Kommentar zur biblischen Geschichte* (1882) reached its twenty-fifth edition in 1925 (Cf. H. Kreutzwald, *Zur Geschichte des biblischen Unterrichts* [Freiburg i. Br. 1957], 161–62).

the content to be taught: What should really be taught, a religious knowledge verbalized in scholastic terms or a message of salvation in Christ as presented in the Holy Scriptures?

It has already been pointed out that Pius X requested the frequent employment of lay catechists. But instruction in the catechism was not the only area in which he appealed to the laity. A conversation which Monsignor de Bazelaire reported is frequently mentioned: Speaking with some cardinals, the Pope asked the question: "What is most essential for the salvation of society?" "The construction of schools," said one cardinal. "No! Build more churches!" answered another. "No! To activate the recruitment of priests," suggested a third. "No! No!" declared the Pope. "Today, it is most important that every parish have at its disposal a group of enlightened, virtuous, decisive, and truly apostolic laymen." As a priest and bishop, Pius X knew from experience what effective help laymen, aware of their Christian responsibility, could provide the clergy regarding the vitalization of a parish and the modification of society. He did not neglect repeatedly to solicit this assistance from the laity, for example in the encyclical *Il fermo proposito* (11 June 1905).[17] It would not be difficult to find those passages in this encyclical which could be discarded as obsolete according to today's standards. Nevertheless, this encyclical can be accepted as the charter of the organized Catholic Action as well; because it did not just challenge the Catholics to practice their personal virtues, but also appealed to them to "pool all their vital forces in order to reinstate Jesus Christ to his position in the family, the school, and the society."

Emphasizing the importance of the organized lay apostolate, Pius X may indeed appear to be a forerunner. Yet he proved to be conservative in the way he tried to implement this idea. "The activities assisting the spiritual and pastoral office of the Church . . . must be subject to Church authority in every detail. . . . But even the other works undertaken to restore the true Christian civilization in Christ and forming Catholic Action in its aforementioned significance cannot be understood without the counsel and the high leadership of the ecclesiastical authority." This passage from the encyclical *Il fermo proposito* is characteristic of Pius X's viewpoint: he was aware of the indispensable effort of the laity to instill Christian principles into secular life; but he did not yet realize the specific character of the action of the Catholics within society, seeing

[17] *ASS* 37 (1904–05), 740–67. The encyclical had been edited by the Jesuits of the *Civiltà cattolica* (L. Bedeschi, *La Curia Romana*, 68). It has the title *De actione cattolica*, a phrase, more or less technical in meaning, which had emerged in Italy during Leo XIII's pontificate and was usually applied to the Action in the social area. This phrase was not used on the other side of the Alps until after World War I.

it almost exclusively as an expansion and extension of the action of the clergy. He was inspired by certain formulas which had been successful during his time in Venetia, and he propagated an organization of Catholic Action according to a more or less uniform model which did not grant the laymen more than the role of an executor under the very strict control of the bishops. The Catholics were to join in certain groups in order to begin their various activities not only in the area of the religious apostolate, but also in the area of the social organizations, the press, or even political elections. But those were always strictly denominational organizations, incorporated into the framework of the parishes and the dioceses and dependent on the episcopate, which, in turn, was subject to the directives from Rome. By necessity, such a clerical conception of Catholic Action was bound to encounter clandestine or open resistance almost everywhere, depending on the situation. The most sensational oppositions of this kind were the crisis of the *Opera dei congressi* in Italy, breaking out in the first months of his pontificate, the affair concerning *Le Sillon* in France a few years later, and finally the conflict pertaining to the Christian trade unions in Germany.

The Modernist Crisis

It is increasingly clear that the definition of modernism in the encyclical *Pascendi* offers in abstract terms a uniform system which is rightfully declared to be in conflict with the Catholic faith, offering the historian nothing but a somewhat inadequate framework, because, while the theologian assesses documents and formulas from an absolute perspective, the historian has to make an attempt to understand mankind in its actual multifariousness, its deeper aspirations, and its spiritual concerns. However, there is another reason: The Jansenism of the seventeenth century was nothing more than the marginal phenomenon of an often absolutely orthodox, but sometimes simply anachronistic Augustinian movement. Likewise, the restoration movement, developing within the Church at the turn of the nineteenth century, showed rather different kinds of tendencies: Some of them were certainly legitimate, even though they may have confused people moving along in traditional ways; but other tendencies were dangerous because of their lack of proper distinctions, even though they may have had sound principles. Others were extremely heretical and in some cases completely lacking in Christian content.

The term "New Catholicism" (later "modernism")[1] embraced a series of concepts reflecting, in the opinion of contemporaries, the liberalism of the nineteenth century: renewed questioning of the traditional conception the Church had of the political and social order; the *aggiornamento* of the ecclesiastical institutions, the forms of the pastoral and the life style of the Christians living in and committed to this modern world; and the restoration of exegesis, theology, and religious philosophy. In this very general sense, modernism could be defined as "the meeting and confrontation of a long religious past with a present which found the vital sources of its inspiration in anything but this past" (É. Poulat). In this respect, the effects of modernism could be seen in Christian socialism and even in Christian democracy, in Sillonism, in

---

[1] Regarding the origin and the history of the term "modernism," confirmed by the encyclical *Pascendi,* see A. Houtin, op. cit., 81–95, and J. Rivière, op. cit., 13–34. In the same strict sense in which the encyclical uses the term, it appears again in Italy around 1904, at first used by journalists (the first one may have been G. Sacchetti in his disputation against Murri), later by the theologians.

Americanism (at least in the French version),[2] and in the many different, often independent currents of an ecclesiastical reform movement as it appeared around 1900 in Germany, Italy, and France. Several of these efforts and their effects have been discussed elsewhere in this volume. One chapter in this section is entirely devoted to German Reform Catholicism, because in this area, especially at the beginning of the twentieth century, tendencies came to light originating in the confrontation of Catholicism with the currents of a changing society. Most of all we must investigate the religious and cultural crises transpiring primarily in France, occasionally in Italy, and in some Catholic groups in England, caused by the unexpected collision of traditional Church doctrine with modern religious studies that had developed independently of and often even in opposition to the control of the churches.

The crisis with which we must deal at this point is comparable to the one that broke out half a century earlier in the churches of the Reformation under the name of "liberal Protestantism." However, this crisis was on a much larger scale. While certain groups, often called "Progressives," confined themselves to placing the newest discoveries of religious studies into the service of the traditional faith, other, more radical groups (the modernists in the true sense of the word) considered it necessary to give this faith a new form of expression, which was to do justice to the changes of the human mind, whose symptom and driving force was precisely the very development of these new studies. Such attempts were considered by certain adventurous minds as the dawn of a new era. To others, especially to most of the ecclesiastical authorities, they appeared to be the beginning of an impending catastrophe.

Here are the roots of the bitter antimodernistic reaction which will be the subject of the last chapter in this section. This bitterness cannot be solely explained by the methods of Church leadership and the delight of the contemporary press in sharp polemics. It was also caused by the realization that the Church felt deeply shaken and that, aside from some particularly acute men, no one could anticipate, sixty years before the Second Vatican Council, that the outcome of this renewed questioning, induced by a collective change of mind, would not necessarily lead to a total elimination of the essence of the Christian faith.

[2] Regarding the Americanist crisis, which was but a tempest in a teacup in the United States and in France, on the whole, nothing but a *hérésie fantôme* (F. Klein), see above, chap. 24.

CHAPTER 29

Reform Catholicism in Germany

Since the German clergy received a much more thorough training than the clergy in Latin or Anglo-Saxon countries, Germany was practically untouched by the phenomenon of modernism in the true sense of the word. However, in the two decades preceding the outbreak of World War I, the Catholic intellectuals were seized by a liberal current and a reform movement which wanted to reverse German Catholicism's trend of retreating within its own confines. This isolationism, the consequence of resistance to the *Kulturkampf,* had resulted in a kind of reaction that was inimical to the modern spirit and especially to its manifestation in German national liberalism.[1] But these movements also wanted to combat clerical and authoritarian tendencies which had permeated the Church since the victory of ultramontanism under Pius IX's pontificate, and they planned to be more open-minded toward the modern world and its aspirations. Also called "present-day Catholicism" or "critical Catholicism," (in contrast to a blind submission to Church authorities), these reform efforts in the German Catholic Church toward the end of the nineteenth century and throughout the first half of the twentieth century were usually described by the term "Reform Catholicism," coined by Josef Müller in his publication of 1899, even though Müller, a priest in Bamberg and editor of the journal *Renaissance,* was not representative of the phenomenon at large. It was precisely this term, by the way, which contributed to its ill repute among those who were intent on emphasizing the differences between the Catholic Church and the Evangelical Reformation.

It is true that the term "Reform Catholicism" is a "collective name for many diverse, mostly unrelated tendencies" (Hagen), including: liberal elements who wanted to instill Christianity with the rationale of the natural sciences or strove for a diminution of authoritative dependence in theological research; theologians and philosophers who were interested in an exchange with modern thought and therefore disapproved of the pressure Rome exercised in favor of Neo-Scholasticism; historians who were sensitive to the evolutionary aspect of things, thus

---

[1] Concerning this situation, see F. Fuchs, "Die deutschen Katholiken und die deutsche Kultur im 19. Jahrhundert," *Wiederbegegnung und Kultur in Deutschland* (Munich 1927), 9–58, and P. Funk, "Der Gang des geistigen Lebens im katholischen Deutschland unserer Generation," ibid., 77–126. Also O. Köhler, "Bücher als Wegmarken des deutschen Katholizismus," *Der katholische Buchhandel Deutschlands. Seine Geschichte bis zum Jahre 1967* (Frankfurt a. M. 1967), 11–90.

provoking the majority of the ultramontanes, who wanted to keep the thought and life of the Church prisoner of the norms which had been determined in the Middle Ages or at the time of the Counter Reformation; opponents of the centralistic Church regime who had not followed the Old Catholics in their schism with Rome but agreed with many of their demands; heirs of the reform movements in the area of the liturgy (use of the German language), of Church discipline (among other things, the question of clerical celibacy), of the training of future priests, heirs, therefore, of ideas which had been posed and supported by followers of the earlier ecclesiastical enlightenment and, in the course of the first half of the century, by men like Hirscher; laymen who had involved themselves in the life of the Church and wished for more independence, especially in regard to social and cultural affairs and decisions, often also in regard to the organization of life in the parish or in the selection of pastors; patriots who were proud of the growing power of the new German Empire and wanted to reintroduce to the Church the rich heritage of German cultural and intellectual life, seemingly alienated from German Catholicism since the middle of the nineteenth century; religious men, partially rooted in the tradition of German Romanticism, who wanted to replace the legalistic Church, mired in organizational matters and Church politics, with the apostolic Church of love or the Church of the spirit, as they called it. All of them shared a certain anti-Roman, especially anti-Jesuit attitude, often even an animosity to the "political Catholicism" organized in the Center Party, and furthermore a "naive overestimation of the scholarly characteristics of the nineteenth century."[2] They also shared their loyalty to the Catholic Church and, in contrast to the modernists in the true sense of the word, the intent to respect unconditionally the basic structures of the faith and the Church. Some aspects of their demands and efforts were unquestionably narrow-minded and dictated by the circumstances of the time, but they "were loyal to the revelation and the Church, even though they dealt with the problems of the time more decisively and sometimes more obstreperously than their contemporaries."[3]

In all these efforts, certain parallels can be detected to the demands voiced by men such as Monsignor Ireland or Father Hecker in the

---

[2] J. Spörl, *HJ* 57 (1937), 5; F. Heiler judges from his perspective: "Like the earlier efforts of the theology of enlightenment and of Old Catholicism, these reforms were often too rationalistic and doctrinal; they did not emerge from the religious center of the Catholic Church, the mystery of Christ, and the desire for holiness" (*RGG*[2] IV [1800]).

[3] G. Schwaiger, *Geschichte der Päpste im 20. Jahrhundert* (Munich 1968), 64. See also J. Spörl, op. cit., 6: "Many things that have now become the common property of the German Catholics thanks to the Catholic youth movement had to be fought for fervently at that time."

United States, the disciples of Americanism, some Sillonists in France, F. von Hügel in England, Monsignor Bonomelli, the followers of Rosmini or the Milan group of the *Rinnovamento* in Italy whose work had some response in Germany. All in all, German Reform Catholicism developed rather independently of the foreign reform movements of that time. It was oriented toward the tradition of German Catholicism, its own situation after the *Kulturkampf,* and its subsequent problems.

In view of the multiplicity of phenomena, the polemical terminology was especially disastrous. Thus, Ludwig Pastor recorded in his diary in 1895: "In Munich a new liberal Catholicism began to emerge around Grauert and Hertling."[4] That was the language of Pastor, for Grauert and Hertling can hardly be called "liberal." In the course of the following years these undefined efforts gained ground, but they were confined to certain academic circles, mainly in southern Germany, and they were usually unrelated. They were represented by three outstanding personalities: F. X. Kraus, H. Schell (above all) and later A. Ehrhard.

Franz Xaver Kraus,[5] a brilliant professor of Church history and essayist, was at that time "the head and soul of the theology faculty in Freiburg" (H. Schiel) and one of the respected informants of the government in Berlin as far as Church policy was concerned. With unending loyalty he stood by the Church, no matter what his opponents maintained; but he was unable to understand the viewpoints of those who did not adhere to his ideas. He judged the general policies of the Church on the basis of his personally inimical sentiments. He was con-

---

[4] *Tagebücher,* ed. by W. Wühr, 288. The historian H. Grauert (cf. *HJ* 44 [1924], 169–96) was responsible for the *Historische Jahrbuch* after 1884. Pastor charged him with systematically denouncing the Catholic historians of ultramontane leanings (see, for instance, *Tagebücher,* 244). G. von Hertling, philosophy professor and one of the main leaders of the Center Party, was the president of the Görres Society. At the Congress of Constance the following year, he warned the participants of the German Catholics lagging behind regarding the sciences.

[5] Regarding Franz Xaver Kraus (1840–1901), Church historian and pioneer in the field of archeology and in Christian art, professor in Freiburg after 1878, author of an extensive work about Dante (1897), for a long time considered an authority in Germany, see, in addition to his diaries (ed. by H. Schiel, [Cologne 1957]) revealing, as expected, his deeply religious soul: H. Schiel, *Im Spannungsfeld von Kirche und Politik, F. X. Kraus* (Trier 1951); id., *F. X. Kraus und die Tübinger Katholische Schule* (Ellwangen 1958); id., *TThZ* 61 (1952), 5–20; id., *AMrhKG* 3 (1951), 218–39; C. Bauer, *Deutscher Katholizismus* (Frankfurt 1964), 93–136; H. Tritz, *Spicilegium hist. congr. SS. Redemptoris* 11 (1963), 182–232; also O. Köhler, *Bewußtseinsstörungen im Katholizismus* (Frankfurt a. M. 1972), 225–38. The author of the article "In Canossa," signed "v. S.," published in the *Allgemeine Zeitung* on 3 August 1881, could only be identified after Kraus's literary estate had been released. Interested in the episcopal see of Trier, Kraus had agitated in this article against M. F. Korum: see H. Schiel, *Die Trierer Bischofskandidatur . . .* (Trier 1955).

vinced that the future of the Church was threatened by the narrow-minded attitude and the fanaticism of the ultramontanes, and he branded them the Pharisees of our time, who "placed the Church before religion and were willing to sacrifice a clear decision of their conscience in favor of the decisions of an external authority." As a "liberal" in the sense that the word had in the nineteenth century" (C. Bauer) and with the Dantean distinction between "religious" and "political" Catholicism, he sharply opposed the policies of the Roman Curia and the Center Party, not only in numerous anonymous articles, but also in his ecclesiastical-political "Spectator Letters," which appeared from 1896 until 1900 in the *Allgemeine Zeitung.*

Even though Kraus moved away from the Reform Catholicism J. Müller had praised as the "religion of the future,"[6] and even though "his own ecclesiastical-political principles and concerns dealt principally with questions other than the struggle of the antimodernists,"[7] his dissatisfaction with the existing situation and his sharp criticism of ultramontanism earned him the honor of carrying the banner for those liberal Bavarian Catholics who had founded, in 1904, under the name *Krausgesellschaft,* a "society for the advancement of religion and culture," which combined a naive admiration of "independent scholarship'" with strong anti-Roman accusations and prejudices.[8]

Herman Schell,[9] after 1884 professor of apologetics, Christian art history, and comparative religious studies in Würzburg, attracted many enthusiastic admirers. He was an outstanding intellectual of tireless energy, anything but a polemicist, but a sincere and original philosopher and theologian, who has been discovered today as a forerunner of Christian existentialism because he emphasized the personal and vital aspect and the inwardness of Catholicism without in the least denying the visible and hierarchical aspects of the Church. He developed theories

---

[6] The pamphlet, published in 1898 under this title, was expanded in the following year to two volumes dealing with the topics: "Die wissenschaftliche Reform" and "Die praktischen Reformen." The author made demands in favor of the synods, proposed plans for the training and organization of the clergy and for a greater participation of the laity in ecclesiastical life, criticized Church intervention in the political arena, the work of the Congregation of the Index, and Neo-Scholasticism, concluding with a charge against the Jesuits (II, 101–54). The little work was put on the Index on 7 June 1901.
[7] H. Schiel, *Tagebücher,* xix.
[8] A record of its activities can be found in *Das Neue Jahrhundert* 6 (1914), 265–71.
[9] Concerning Herman Schell (1850–1906), see H. Hasenfuß, *H. Schell als existentieller Denker und Theologe* (Würzburg 1956); id., *LThK²* IX, 384–85; V. Berning, *Das Denken H. Schells* (Essen 1964); id., *MThZ* 19 (1968), 102–20; P. Wacker, *Glaube und Wissen bei H. Schell* (Paderborn 1961); id., *Theologie als ökumenischer Dialog* (Paderborn 1965); O. Schröder, op. cit., 370–92. His main works: *Katholische Dogmatik* (4 vols. 1889–93); *Gott und Geist* (2 vols., 1895–96); *Apologie des Christentums* (2 vols., 1901–05); *Christus* (1903).

which were somewhat unfamiliar to the theology of his time, for example, about religious freedom, the apologetics of immanence, the role of the Holy Spirit, and the position of the laity in the Church; and he introduced religious studies to the ecclesiastical disciplines. Within a few years, he published amazingly varied and voluminous works, whose audacious constructs were often subject to justified criticism, but it was to his credit that he presented the traditional doctrine in personalistic categories, and that he was inspired by the continuous desire to "baptize" modern philosophy and science and to prove that they were by no means incompatible with Catholic belief. From this perspective he published in 1897 a pamphlet with the title *Katholizismus als Prinzip des Fortschritts,* in which he declared that the Church had to ally itself with progress in whatever form, requesting that Catholics not be forced to behave like "mental eunuchs." These sensational declarations were made in the name of an "ideal Catholicism" and supplemented by a program for applying his theses to the areas of religious, intellectual, and political activities. Schell had not received sizable public attention so far, but this pamphlet unleashed a storm of indignation. He responded to the criticism with a second publication, entitled *Die neue Zeit und der alte Glaube.* In it he criticized the methods of the Church government even more directly, and he expressed his conviction that the Church, provided its core was unchangeable, must rejuvenate itself continuously through dialogue with the world. On 15 December 1898 both pamphlets and his most important works were put on the Index.[10] Schell submitted, and he was allowed to continue teaching. His prestige grew. However, the bitter polemics against him continued in an "unworthy manner" (Schwaiger), his loyalty and his fatith were doubted, and as a matter of fact, he was charged with planning "to revolutionize the clergy." According to his doctor, all these intrigues impaired his health, and he died in 1906, only fifty-six years old. At the academic obsequies, S. Merkle delivered the funeral oration. He also organized a committee, joined by the representatives of Reform Catholicism, which was responsible for erecting a tombstone.

In the meantime, other progressive voices were making themselves heard. There were even attempts made to organize the liberal forces. In 1901 a former colleague of Schell's, patrologist Albert Ehrhard,[11] pub-

---

[10] The official report was published by K. Hennemann, *Widerrufe H. Schells?* (Würzburg 1908), 82–86.

[11] Regarding Albert Ehrhard (1862–1940), professor of Church history in Würzburg (1892–98), Vienna (1898–1902), Strasbourg (1903–18), and Bonn (1920–27), specialist for Old Christian literature, see A. Dempf, *A. Ehrhard. Der Mann und das Werk* (Colmar 1944); K. Baus, *Bonner Gelehrte. Kath. Theologie* (Bonn 1968), 114–22; *NDB* IV, 357; *DHGE* XV, 62–65; O. Schröder, op. cit., 392–407.

lished not just a pamphlet, but a larger, scholarly work with the significant title *Der Katholizismus und das 20. Jahrhundert im Licht der kirchlichen Entwicklung der Neuzeit.* Based on his solid knowledge of the past, this work attempted to prove the thesis that it is possible to overcome the conflict unquestionably present between Catholicism and the modern world of thought, provided that, on the one hand, modern thought relinquish its anti-Christian prejudices, and that, on the other hand, the Church cease to conceptualize the Middle Ages in absolute terms. In Ehrhard's opinion, the Middle Ages do not represent the climax of Christianity's development. Its religious institutions had only relative value, and Neo-Scholasticism would have to fail if it was conceived merely as an unqualified restoration of the past. He also had reservations about the Society of Jesus and had several desires; for example, he wished to give the national languages an appropriate place in the liturgy. His work was very successful (twelve editions in one year), but almost the entire Catholic press in Germany and Austria criticized Ehrhard. He was especially vehemently opposed by the Redemptorist A. Rössler (supported by Cardinal Archbishop Gruscha of Vienna), who called him an "anti-Catholic." Albert Ehrhard, not faced with any critics of his caliber, responded harshly with his new ingenious work: *Liberaler Katholizismus? Ein Wort an meine Kritiker* (1902).

Several other less prominent professors joined in the controversy in the following years, taking Ehrhard's side: O. Sickenberger published several belligerent writings between 1902 and 1904, charging the Catholics mainly with their extreme anti-Protestantism (however, his authority was somewhat impaired by his notorious resistance to the celibacy of the clergy); a colleague of Schell's, F. X. Kiefl, a man of speculative talent and very pugnacious, who, between 1904 and 1905, repeatedly opposed the vehement criticism of Schell voiced by the Jesuit Stufler; M. Spahn, history professor in Strasbourg and brilliant essayist, who was concerned with rescuing the Catholics from their ghetto existence, whose often rather discerning, yet too severe biography of Leo XIII was considered a manifesto.

After 1901 the avant-garde gathered around several journals: *Renaissance* (1901–7), published by the aforementioned, not very talented J. Müller; *Zwanzigstes Jahrhundert* (1902–9), whose motto was: "religion, Germany, culture," perpetuated by an active minority of young Bavarians. *Hochland* had an entirely different format (1903–71; forbidden in 1941, continued in 1946). This journal, published by C. Muth, opposed the criticism which, thanks to the powerful organization of the Borromeo Society, dominated most of the Catholic literary productions and was perpetuated by the clergy. Instead, *Hochland* advocated a literary evaluation, which emphasized aesthetic aspects over moralizing concerns.[12] This journal greatly benefitted the alleviation of the ghetto mentality of German Catholicism, aside from its contributions to good literature.

The reactions of the hierarchy toward reforms were mostly of a negative nature. The hierarchy, interested in preserving its structures and strict orthodoxy and fearing the religious confusion of the masses, resisted change as such. This was also true in view of Reform Catholicism at the beginning of the twentieth century. The problem was aggravated by the fact that the latter, aside from justified demands and healthy efforts, succumbed to ill-advised or vague proposals and exaggerated criticism. This gave rise to the occasional, but usually completely unjustified question of whether these men, if only de facto, worked hand in glove with the Away-from-Rome movement raging through Austria at that time, and whether they were not striving for a Christianity practically independent of Rome. Even Bishop P. W. Keppler of Rottenburg, a prelate who was certainly not considered a reactionary (formerly professor in Freiburg) and who had approved, though with reservation, the publication of Ehrhard's disputed work, thought it necessary to intervene in the controversies with a public lecture "About the True and False Reform" (1 December 1902). He conceded that certain things in the Church needed improvement. However, his sharp, barely disguised criticism of men such as Kraus, Schell, and Ehrhard was astonishing. This lecture was fatefully influenced by the very successful writer Julius Langbehn (the "Rembrandt German"), an anti-Semitic forerunner of the "conservative revolution."[13] To the dismay of the ultramontanes, Rome kept quiet for a long period of time. However, Pius X was more and more disturbed by the developments in Germany,[14] especially by indications that the reform efforts were gaining ground. One such symptom was the founding of a society in Münster in the spring of 1906 which was joined by an elite of Catholic laymen (such as several leaders of the Center Party) and pursued the goal of prompting the Holy See to

---

[12] The "literature controversy," as it was termed at that time, began with the pamphlet by C. Muth (1867–1944): "Steht die katholische Belletristik auf der Höhe der Zeit?" (1898). The main opponent in the other camp was the Austrian journal *Der Gral* (1906ff.), managed by R. von Kralik. Concerning the "literary controversy," see F. Rappmannsberger, "C. Muth und seine Zeitschrift Hochland als Vorkämpfer für die innere Erneuerung Deutschlands," (diss., Munich 1952); A. W. Hüffler, *C. Muth als Literaturkritiker* (Münster 1959); *LThK*² V, 399–400, and VI, 1082; *StL*⁶ IV, 112–14.
[13] Regarding this lecture, see A. Gisler, op. cit., 150–53; H. Schiel, *ThQ* 137 (1957), 296–98; A. Donders, *Bischof Keppler* (Freiburg i. Br. 1935); Keppler's introduction to: M. Nissen, *Der Rembrandtdeutsche* (Freiburg 1926), 1–6, where Keppler speaks of terms coined by Langbehn "which I prefer not to see in our language today."
[14] Cf. below, pp. 477–79, and 500–7.

change the Index procedures.[15] Another symptom was the support given to two bishops, about thirty seminary professors, and prominent laymen by a committee established for the purpose of erecting a memorial for Schell. After the Austrian theologian E. Commer had published an extremely aggressive book against Schell following his death, the Pope sent him a brief on 14 June 1907, praising him for the great service he had done for the Church. In this same brief, he charged the advocates of this memorial with "laboring under a misapprehension of the Catholic truth" and "resisting the authority of the Holy See."[16] The appointment of the former Dominican General Frühwirth as nuncio in Munich at the end of 1907 was to serve both as a bulwark against the feared progressing decline of Catholic Germany toward liberalism and as an introduction to a reevaluation of the situation.[17]

However, the turbulence and polemical controversies did not cease. They were even reignited through the disputes over the encyclical *Pascendi* and later over the antimodernist oath.[18] In 1909 the *Zwanzigstes Jahrhundert* was renamed *Das neue Jahrhundert* with the significant subtitle: *Organ der deutschen Modernisten*. After a few months, however, a change occurred under the leadership of Philipp Funk,[19] an idealistic

[15] Concerning this Society for Christian Culture, whose arguments against the Index coincided with those that Cardinal Frings had carried through at the Second Vatican Council, see K. Bachem, *Vorgeschichte, Geschichte und Politik der deutschen Zentrumspartei* VII (Cologne 1930), 187ff; A. ten Hompel, *Indexbewegung und Kulturgesellschaft* (Bonn 1908).

[16] Texts in A. Michelitsch, *Der neue Syllabus* (Graz 1908), 53–55. L. Pastor went so far as to say that the dedication of the memorial could become an occasion to convene a "council of reformers" (cf. *Tagebücher,* 461). Aside from Merkle, the members of the committee were, among others: Julius Bachem, H. C. Cardauns, A. Dyroff, E. Eichmann, H. Finke, F. X. Funk, H. Grauert, F. von Hügel, C. Muth, J. Sauer, J. Sickenberger, M. Spahn. The memorial is a marble bust with the inscription: *Vivas in Deo* (cf. K. Hennemann, *H. Schell im Lichte zeitgenössischer Urteile* [Paderborn 1909]).

[17] *Tagebücher* by L. von Pastor, 482 and 485. See also A. Walz, *Andreas Kardinal Frühwirth* (Vienna 1950), 304–05.

[18] Of the few Germans who openly professed Modernism, the following should be mentioned: J. Schnitzer (1859–1939), professor in Munich and author of remarkable works about Savonarola (cf. F. Heiler, "J. Schnitzer, ein Vorkämpfer des deutschen Reformkatholizismus," *Eine heilige Kirche* 21 [1939], 297–313); K. Gebert (1860–1910), a Neo-Kantian, president of the *Krausgesellschaft;* H. Koch (1869–1940), who rejected the dogma regarding the pope on the basis of his studies concerning Saint Cyprian (cf. *RGG*³ III, 1687); and mainly T. Engert (1875–1945), an exegete and student of Schell, who was in charge of the *Zwanzigste Jahrhundert;* in 1910, he converted to Protestantism (see *Gesammelte modernistische Vorträge* [Würzburg 1909–10]; cf. *DHGE* XV, 492–93).

[19] Regarding Philipp Funk, a former seminarian of the diocese of Rottenburg, after World War I member of the *Hochland* group and after 1926 professor of history at the University of Freiburg, see J. Spörl, *HJ* 57 (1937), 1–15, and A. Hagen, *Gestalten aus*

young layman from the Catholic youth movement who was characterized by "a mixture of belligerence and religious inwardness" (Spörl).
He turned away from the purely negative and polemical tendency of the
journal, differentiating it sharply from French modernism and the Austrian Away-from-Rome movement and declaring that Reform Catholicism had to remain "a matter disputed *within the confines* of the
Church."

Of all the personalities involved in Reform Catholicism around 1910,
one man stands out for his energetic, unique character and his fearless
and unconditional advocacy of the truth: S. Merkle,[20] professor of
Church history in Würzburg, whose lectures had incited conflicts between the boards of seminaries and the episcopal administration. In
1902 Cardinal Steinhuber had complained that most of the Munich
"reformists" came from the ranks of Merkle's students.[21] Merkle was
the pioneer of a new, more positive Catholic evaluation of Luther and
the ecclesiastical enlightenment. His viewpoints had not been accepted
amicably in ultramontane circles whose dismay climaxed in 1912 when
he opposed their plans for an exclusively Catholic university, instead
defending theological faculties incorporated into the state universities.
One of his chief arguments for maintaining the faculties was that they
contributed greatly to the preservation of religious peace in Germany,
but the effect of the indignation stored up during the *Kulturkampf* intensified the denominational differences among the heirs of the Mainz
faction. They felt strengthened in their convictions by the support
Pius X had given the opponents of the interdenominational trade
unions during the trade union controversy. Thus the political and social
conflicts in Germany on the eve of World War I intersected with the
controversies over Reform Catholicism, as had been the case several
years before in France in the course of the modernist controversy.

---

dem *Schwäbischen Katholizismus* III (Stuttgart 1954), 244–83. He described his reform
program in: *Das geistige Erbe von F. X. Kraus* (1912); *Von der Kirche des Geistes* (1913); *Der
religiöse Schell* (1916). New subtitle of the journal: *Wochenschrift für religiöse Kultur.*
[20] Concerning Sebastian Merkle (1862–1945), who had gained prominence in the world
of scholars through his edition of the records of the Council of Trent (I, 1901; II, 1911),
cf. also H. Jedin, *ThQ* 130 (1950), 1–20, and A. Bigelmair, *Lebensläufe aus Franken* VI
(Würzburg 1960), 418–35.
[21] *Tagebücher* of L. Pastor, 396.

CHAPTER 30

The Beginning of the Crisis in France

With justification Loisy wrote: "The *Histoire du modernisme* by Houtin rests on fiction: on the agreement of Duchesne's ideas about the early history of the Church conceived between 1881 and 1889 with my thoughts on the history of the Bible and Hébert's concepts of philosophy."[1] It is a matter of fact that there was initially no concentrated action, even on a purely national level. Rather, there existed various concepts that had spontaneously developed during the last years of Leo XIII's pontificate and were favored by the general atmosphere of reconciliation between the Church and modern society, a climate seemingly confirmed by several papal initiatives. The controversy over Americanism[2] had been in this respect symptomatic.

Influenced by Neo-Kantianism and believing to have found their ultimate master in Maurice Blondel, whose ideas were often falsified, philosophers strove to replace scholastic intellectualism with a doctrine that would include the forces of the heart and the actual processes of life. Some of them remained under the vague influence of a religious symbolism based on Schleiermacher, combined with the evolutionism of Hegelian or Spencerian inspiration. They declared that theology has to relinquish unalterable concepts and devise new interpretations in order to preserve contact with steadily progressing life. Philosopher Marcel Hébert,[3] priest and director of a large Paris college, joined this movement, which was strongly affected by A. Sabatier's work *Esquisse d'une philosophie de la religion d'àpres la psychologie et l'histoire* (1897), a book disseminating the concepts of German liberal Protestantism even in France.[4]

Parallel to this philosophical movement, publicized through the *Annales de philosophie chrétienne,* young theologians, familiarized by Duchesne with historical criticism, discovered that German non-Catholic scholars, applying the principles of historical criticism to the documents and history of the beginnings of Christianity, had called in question certain traditional interpretations, such as those pertaining to Moses' work, to the history of Israel's religion, to the teachings of

---

[1] *Mémoires* I, 535.—Regarding Duchesne, see chap. 22, n. 17.
[2] See above, chap. 24.
[3] Concerning Marcel Hébert (1851–1916), see A. Houtin, *M. Hébert* (Paris 1925), and A. Vidler, *A Variety . . . ,* 63–75.
[4] See some of the data provided in J. Fontaine, *Les infiltrations kantiennes et protestantes et le clergé française* (Paris 1902). The book is lacking in details.

Christ, and to life among the first Christian generations. From this arose the problem of the compatibility of Catholic belief with the results of modern exegetic scholarship. The encyclical *Providentissimus,* issued by Leo XIII in 1893,[5] had provided several principles for solving these problems, but certainly not all of them. The Pope's warnings against exaggerated criticism encouraged even the conservative forces to brand all attempts to apply the critical methods to inspired texts as thoroughly infested with rationalistic prejudices. Yet more and more exegetes upheld the conviction that the application of the critical method to this field was not sacrilege. On the contrary, intellectual righteousness and honesty demanded the application of the tested principles of historical method to studies of the Holy Scriptures, even at the risk of consequently having to change traditional postures in the controversies between believers and rationalists by making new fundamental distinctions between the (sometimes acceptable) literary and historical results of critical investigations and a conception of Israel's history and the origins of Christianity that would systematically erase the supernatural aspect.

From this perspective, Duchesne's student Alfred Loisy (1857–1940) devoted himself after 1883 to the study of the Old Testament and then the gospels, and M.-J. Lagrange founded in 1890 the École Biblique in Jerusalem, publishing two years later the *Revue biblique.* Lagrange confined himself to the world of experts and was intent on demonstrating the identity of his research results with the official doctrine of the Church (which did not prevent his critical appraisal by the conservatives and denunciation in Rome). Loisy and several of his collaborators, on the other hand, were less cautious. Convinced that Catholic apologetics, in view of the progress made by so-called "independent" criticism, had to completely revise its concepts, they did not hesitate to abrogate, even in popular journals, a great number of traditional doctrines. That even in 1896 an open-minded man such as Batiffol would speak of "superfluous intrepidities" and later of "intellectual anarchy," "agitating at this very moment the philosophical and scholarly elite of the French clergy,"[6] explains the anxiety of the ecclesiastical authorities, who, unfortunately, were hardly able to deal competently with the problems at

---

[5] Regarding this document, the circumstances inititating it, and the reactions it caused, see chap. 23.

[6] Letter addressed to P. Lagrange, quoted in P. Fernessole, *Pie X* II (Paris 1953), 171; letter addressed to Chanoine of January 1901, quoted in *BLE* 67 (1966), 271. He added: "Like you, I have no sympathies for the curialists, the Mazzellas and *tutti quanti;* but don't Loisy and his friends, without intending to, work in the interest of those very same curialists?"

hand.[7] In spite of his efforts not to impede the progress of the investigations, Leo XIII deemed it necessary to send a letter to the bishops of France warning them, among other things, of "the alarming tendencies attempting to invade the exegesis of the Bible."[8] This document incited the French Jesuit J. Fontaine to rebuke the "Protestant infiltrations" of the French clergy in a series of articles. He turned mainly against the *Revue d'histoire et de littérature religieuse,* founded in 1896 by Loisy, and against Loisy's articles concerning original revelation, the development of Israel's religion, or the development of dogma, published for the general public in the *Revue du clergé français.* Both the death of Cardinal Mazzella (1900), prefect of the Congregation of the Index and revered by the conservatives who were especially numerous and active in the Society of Jesus, and several interventions by the Pope (such as the one in favor of the bishop of Albi, Monsignor Mignot) caused a certain détente. This was shown through the creation of the Pontifical Biblical Commission at the end of the summer of 1901 (officially constituted in October 1902).[9] The appointment of the Franciscan Fr. Fleming as secretary of the commission, the first consultants, largely chosen from the ranks of the progressive exegetes, and the original plan to make the *Revue biblique* the public relations channel of the commission illustrate the constructive rather than repressive character of this initiative. However, this was merely the calm before the storm. Several weeks later a new intervention by Loisy rekindled the controversy even more violently.

Loisy was a scholar of extraordinary intellectual prominence. Thoroughly informed and endowed with a penetrating critical mind, he was also a talented writer, possessing a very unique gift for words. Because of the encyclical *Providentissimus* he was forced to relinquish his chair at the Institut Catholique in Paris. He utilized the time afforded him through this suspension from office in transferring his research from technical exegesis to the more general problems posed by Holy Scriptures, investigating the divine truth and the value of the Church expressed and preserved therein. The French translation of Adolf Har-

---

[7] The decree of the Holy Office of 13 January 1897 regarding the authenticity of the *Comma johanneum* (ASS 29 [1896–97], 637), which wanted to authoritively explain a question of text criticism, is a typical example of the attitude in the Roman circles.

[8] Encyclical *Depuis le jour* of 8 September 1899 (ASS 32 [1899–1900], 193–213). The year before, in the letter addressed to the general of the *Minderbrüder* on 25 November 1898 (ASS 31 [1898–99], 264–67), he expressed regret over "a daring and far too liberal form of interpretation" in the area of exegesis.

[9] See A. Loisy, *Mémoires* II, 84–90, and M.-J. Lagrange, *M. Loisy et le modernisme,* 119–35.

nack's lectures on "The Essence of Christianity," published in 1902, gave him the opportunity to present a synthesis of the systems of Catholic apologetics that he had prepared shortly before. He promulgated this in a small book entitled *L'Évangile et l'Église* in November 1902; it caused more sensation and excitement in the world of religion than all but a few other books (F. Klein).

Like the famous Protestant historian Harnack, Loisy was convinced that the content of a critically interpreted Gospel and the various forms of historical Christianity were not necessarily identical. However, he wanted to prove that this disagreement was not a distortion, as claimed by the Protestants. Quite the contrary, the evolution of Catholicism, showed in three respects (institution, dogma, and cult), based inextricably in the authentic message of Jesus Christ, how this identity could be restored through history. However, this continuity differed fundamentally from that upheld by traditional apologetics.

Loisy was inspired by the thinking of the German eschatological school, revising their arguments in a novel way and declaring at length that it was not Jesus' intent to organize a new religious community to continue his work on this earth; rather, he endeavored to proclaim the impending establishment of the kingdom of heaven. However, things turned out differently than planned: "Jesus announced the coming of the kingdom and what transpired was the Church." Yet the Church sustained messianic hope, assuming the responsibility of nurturing and organizing this expectation, since the hour of salvation was a long time coming. From this adaptation of the term "kingdom" to the variable conditions of time and place, Loisy said, arose the successive formulations of Church dogmas, the development of its hierarchical institutions and the deployment of its sacramental rites. These experiences of the past show, Loisy added, that the essence of Christianity had to be seen in its evolution, not in a rigid core, as Harnack proposed. Consequently the future harbored the possibility, even the likelihood of new discoveries. Since the dogmas of the Church reflected "the general state of the knowledge of the times and the people who devised them," the conclusion was justified that a profound change in the state of scholarship could necessitate "a new interpretation of old rules," especially since it was obvious that "dogmas are not truths descending from heaven" but merely symbols of the eternal truth.

Those who were familiar with the difficulties which Loisy wanted to solve generally reacted positively to his theses: finally, here was someone to prove, on the basis of a strictly scientific method and in the face of the arrogant appraisals of liberal Protestants, that the Catholic Church was indeed the only legitimate fruit of the Gospel. Other readers objected primarily to the nonconformism of this new branch of apologetics, raising the question to what extent it was compatible with Catholic orthodoxy. They objected to many of his constructs, in spite of the various precautions which the author took to indicate rather than clearly define them. Thus praise was quickly infused with criticism and rejection, voiced not only by the conservatives, whose "strong language often concealed complete *ignoratio elenchi,*"[10] but also by open-minded experts such as Lagrange and especially Batiffol, who turned his Institut Catholique of Toulouse into a "stronghold of the struggle against modernism," contributing to the embitterment of this struggle for reasons as yet indiscernible.[11]

On 17 January 1903, pressured by Cardinal Perraud, Cardinal Richard, archbishop of Paris, condemned Loisy's work, claiming that it threatened "to confuse seriously the faithful's belief in the fundamental dogmas of the Catholic Church." However, the episcopate at large preferred, with four or five exceptions, not to take issue; so did Leo XIII. The atmosphere in Rome changed during the summer after the election of Pius X, who had anxiously observed the theological and exegetical dissent in France for a long time.

The controversy flared up again even more seriously in the fall, when Loisy published a new volume justifying the first book: *Autour d'un petit livre.* Loisy's main concern in this book was the liberation of Catholic historians from a tutelage that he called anachronistic, expressly confirming the autonomy of biblical criticism of theological doctrine. But this was not all. He stated with even more precision, contradicting the pretentions of classical apologetics, that Christ's divinity evades history; so does his resurrection, his conception by the Virgin, or any other personal intervention of God in the course of human affairs. According to Loisy, the subject of history is not the existence of the resurrected Christ, but solely the disciples' belief therein, a belief undergoing progressively precise definition. While suggesting differentiation between the Christ of history and the Christ of faith, he did not declare, in contrast to the assertions of his Catholic opponents, that faith deemed true what seemed to be false to the historian. Though he believed, on the one hand, that the impact of faith acting in Christian consciousness did not just mean a development of ecclesiastical institutions, but also an idealization of the person of Jesus Christ, he also held the notion, on

---

[10] J. Rivière, op. cit., 169. To be noted is the statement of É. Poulat, *Histoire, dogme et critique,* 291: "Though scientifically they were not prepared to solve the existing problems, theologically they were sufficiently informed to pinpoint them and to emphasize the seriousness of the differences of opinion."

[11] É. Poulat, op. cit., 363–92. Poulat even asked the question: "What part had the progressivist school [that is, the school of Batiffol and Lagrange] in the condemnation of Modernism?" (p. 366).

the other hand, that this phenomenon of a collective consciousness and its objective basis are commensurable.

However, these declarations did not alleviate the anxieties; on the contrary, they intensified them; and this time, the little book encountered the almost unanimous opposition of the theologians and the episcopate. On the other hand, interventions in favor of Loisy were offered in Rome by Baron von Hügel, a long-time admirer, and by Monsignor Mignot, one of the few French prelates who conceded that it was absolutely essential to make room for these new critical methods in the framework of eccesiastical studies.[12] Nevertheless, on 16 December 1903, the Holy Office condemned Loisy's works, but used rather ambivalent terms apparently indicating that the Vatican still hesitated to get seriously involved. Shortly afterward, Loisy made known that he would submit. For three years, he held aloof from the controversies he had incited, but, in seclusion, he devoted himself to the preparation of his great commentary on the Synoptic Gospels (1907–8).

Later he declared repeatedly that he had lost faith in the divinity of Christ and even in the existence of a personal God long before the publication of *L'Évangile et L'Église,* but he had preferred to conceal his true opinions, hoping to initiate more successfully a reform of the Church from within, deeming it useful for humanity. His biography by Houtin,[13] who knew him well, seems to confirm his declaration at first glance. Houtin's text, unpublished for a long time, was edited by É. Poulat, some of whose discerning statements suggest that it was precisely the existence of this manuscript (of which Loisy knew more or less without ever having seen it) that partially explains the reconstruction of his religious development, which he wanted to promulgate a posteriori, after having abdicated all positive faith. This impairs the trustworthiness of the exegete's statements about the exact date when he ceased to believe, and it proves that many people were only too eager to believe his own explanations. In any case, the fragments of letters and his memoirs, published by R. de Boyer de Sainte-Suzanne under the title

---

[12] Concerning Friedrich Baron von Hügel, see chap. 31. Regarding Msgr. Mignot (1842–1918), see L. de Lacger, *Mgr. Mignot* (Paris 1933), to be supplemented by É. Poulat, *Histoire, dogme et critique,* 448–84, and by the letters recently published by M. Becamel in *BLE* 67 (1966), 3–44, 81–114, 170–94, 257–86; 69 (1968), 241–68; 71 (1970), 262–73.

[13] Concerning Albert Houtin (1867–1926), a priest and historian, progressively turning away from the Church and the Christian faith, who had published (in 1902) an ironical report entitled *La question biblique chez les catholiques de France au XIXe siècle,* mercilessly exposing the weakness of the answers that rationalistic exegesis had been faced with before the appearance of Loisy and his school, see É. Poulat, op. cit., 332–63.— Regarding the question of the Bible under the pontificate of Leo XIII, cf. chap. 23.

Loisy entre la foi et l'incroyance, confirm his distance from Renan, whose scientistic rationalism he despised, or from Houtin, who was an evil spirit in many respects.[14] In 1900 Loisy already differentiated clearly between *foi* and *croyance,* between faith and belief. But today, progress in the sociology of religious cognition, in the theology of faith, and in hermeneutics enables us to understand the complex psychology of the modernists better than at the beginning of the century.

Whatever Loisy's personal opinions may have entailed, it is a matter of fact that he became the catalyst of the anxiety spreading among the Catholic intelligentsia and that his two "little books" and their condemnation incited a dispute which rippled outward after 1908 and extended far beyond France's borders. To the conservative theologians, Loisy appeared as a new Renan, perhaps worse; but his defenders called to mind the trial against Galileo, charging that a "Dreyfus Affair of the clergy" was in progress.

These revolutionary ideas found a resounding echo in certain intellectual groups, especially among the young clergy. They were fascinated by these suggestive concepts, fundamentally differing through their sensitivity toward the diversity of historical truths from the superficial character and the naivete of the "Lives of Jesus" and the stories about early Christianity available to the Catholic public. The (often misunderstood) thoughts of Newman concerning the development of the Christian doctrine and on the relationship between faith and reason, propagated at that time by Bremond[15] in France, seemed to them a guarantee—the guarantee of a cardinal—for the new apologetic path Loisy had described and for his less abstract conception of revelation. In addition, they had a presentiment of the entire terrifying implication of the assurance that the Gospel was no historical scripture in the true

---

[14] Cf. É. Poulat, *Une œuvre clandestine d'H. Bremond,* 21–22: "In reality, Modernism was in the center of tendencies, the rights of which were represented by the progressivism of Msgr. Batiffol, P. Lagrange, P. Grandmaison, etc., and which encountered on the left the rationalism of men such as Turmel, Houtin, and Sartiaux. The continuous communication with Loisy of the latter two and the undifferentiated opposition of the former could cloak the depth and the significance of their differences, which were not always a matter of temperament."

[15] Between 1904 and 1906, he published three volumes of translated excerpts about the development of the dogma and the psychology of faith and *Newman, essai de biographie psychologique.* Concerning Henri Bremond (1865–1933), see *DSAM* I, 1928–38 *Entretiens sur H. Bremond,* ed. by J. Dagens, M. Nédoncelle (Paris, The Hague 1967), esp. 43–98; É. Poulat, *Une œuvre clandestine d'H. Bremond* (Rome 1972). Regarding his relations to the modernist movement, in addition to this last work, Loisy's opinion should be noted: "Bremond was not closely involved in the modernist struggle. He rather joined in the service of the Red Cross: he collected the dead bodies and attended to the wounded."

sense, but a document of a catechetic nature expressing the belief of the first Christian generations as it was trying to formulate itself. Their misgivings were compounded by the realization of some Christian democrats that, on the one hand, their efforts to integrate the Church into modern society were comparable to Loisy's work of restoration on the theological level, and that, on the other hand, his demands for the autonomy of the exegete or the historian of dogma from the ecclesiastical teachings paralleled their own demands for the autonomy of the laity and bourgeois society from the clerical autocracy. Symptomatic of this attitude was the weekly paper *Demain* of Lyon (1905/07), managed by two young laymen.

Many of Loisy's enthusiastic admirers thought like Bremond, who responded to the deluge of rationalistic criticism with the following words: "He is a true Noah, and the Church should be happy to possess his ark."[16] However, many were worried, and not only in the conservative camp, as was proven by the volume of letters compiled by R. Marlé. Many a progressive agreed with Loisy as to the need for an incisive revision of traditional Catholic apologetics and to a series of his critical conclusions. Yet they refused to agree to his radical idea of the total autonomy of criticism from ecclesiastical teachings and to question, as he did, the basic concept of orthodoxy. This was the case with Batiffol, for instance, who apparently just wanted to restore his reputation in Rome, and with Blondel, whose articles entitled *Histoire et dogme* emphasized the true concept of tradition in the Catholic system and still appear to be especially acute, even though Blondel shared the philosophers' usual difficulties of comprehending the problems of the historians and did not always understand the extent of the difficulties exposed by Loisy.

Even though Loisy was the focal point of the controversy animating the world of Catholic intellectuals in the first decades of the twentieth century, and even though it may be justified to call him "the father of modernism" (Heiler), the question of the Bible and dogmatic history were not the only areas at that time to incite fundamental controversies, which some considered indispensable to rescue what could be rescued of Christianity, while others believed that they would destroy the essence of the Christian faith as they understood it.

---

[16] H. Bremond, M. Blondel, *Correspondance* I, 494 (23 May 1904). Concerning this enthusiasm among the youth, see É. Poulat, *Histoire, dogme et critique*, 270–315, quoting the testimony of Msgr. E. Amann, etc.: *RevSR* 10(1930), 676–93, esp. 685. See also the report by M. Rifaux of 1906 about *Les conditions du retour au catholicisme* (Paris 1907); concerning this, see J. Rivière, op. cit., 258–61.

The controversies over Blondel's proposals at the end of the nineties regarding a renovation of apologetics by using the philosophical method of immanence (immanence apologetics) gradually subsided. One of his students, Lucien Laberthonnière,[17] revived these disputes and extended them to include the entire complex of the problem of religious cognition. In two collections of articles entitled *Essais de philosophie religieuse* (1903) and *Le réalisme chrétien et l'idéalisme grec* (1904), which Loisy called a work by "Maurice Blondel translated into French," Laberthonnière criticized the philosophy of "essences," intending to replace them in the name of a moral dogmatism with a philosophy of action and personal inspiration. At this point, he also discussed one of the fundamental questions raised by the modernists: the question regarding the originality and character of Christianity as a revealed historical religion. However, his conception of philosophy compelled him to subject Thomism, which he hardly knew, to a radical appraisal and to correlate the natural order and the supernatural so closely that it appeared as if he wanted to fuse them. He was also inspired by Blondel's critique of "extrinsicism," charging the Church with proceeding in too authoritarian a manner. He gave theologians adhering to tradition good reason to oppose him, especially when his influence began to grow (around 1905) after he had accepted the management (together with Blondel) of the *Annales de philosophie chrétienne*[18] and founded the *Association d'études religieuses,* an association which regularly brought together Christian philosophers and scholars open toward modern thought.

A member of this very group, Édouard Le Roy,[19] a mathematician, philosopher, and a student of Bergson, preoccupied with religious problems, incited one of the most passionate disputes of these troubled years between Catholic theologians and philosophers, "a real turmoil," according to Rivière. At the beginning of 1905, he published an article entitled "Qu'est-ce qu'un dogme?"[20] challenging philosophers and theologians to think about the impact that the dogmatic rules offered to

---

[17] Concerning Lucien Laberthonnière (1860–1932), Oratorian, see E. Castelli, *Laberthonnière* (Paris 1931); L. Passaglia, *Educazione religiosa e libertà umana in Laberthonnière. La formazione di un pensiero* (Milan 1967); T. Perrin, Le P. "Laberthonnière" (diss., Paris 1970); A. Ngindu, "Le problème de la connaissance religieuse dans la crise moderniste. L. Laberthonnière" (diss., Kinshasa 1972); *Laberthonnière. L'homme et l'œuvre,* ed. by P. Beillevert (Paris 1972).

[18] See the first article of the new series entitled *Notre programme* (vol. 151, 5–31).

[19] Concerning Edouard Le Roy (1870–1954), see *Études philosophiques* 10 (1955), 161–210, and T. Tshibangu, *Théologie positive et théologie spéculative* (Louvain, Léopoldville 1965), 250–67.

[20] In *La Quinzaine* 63 (1905), 495–526; resumed with significant additions in his book *Dogme et critique* (1907), providing a bibliography about the disputes caused by the article (pp. 359–63).

the faithful by the Church may have on a modern scholarly mind. Once again he questioned the classical conception of the dogma, which he felt was related to the Scholastic philosophy inherited from the Middle Ages and to its static concept of an eternal truth. He stressed the radical incommensurability of the mysteries and the human spirit and suggested assigning to dogmas an essentially pragmatic significance. Consequently it would no longer be a matter of speculative conceptions to be forced upon us, but one of rules pertaining to ethical and religious actions. Presenting us with such dogmas, the Church would merely ask us to believe that the religious reality indeed contained the arguments for justifying the obligatory mental attitude. Outstanding thinkers such as the Jesuit de Grandmaison or the Dominicans Sertillanges and Allo showed understanding; but most theologians reacted adversely to this "pragmatism," taking it, in ignorance of Le Roy's constructs, merely as profound agnosticism. Therefore they vehemently opposed this trend, particularly since Le Roy did not conceal the fact that he considered a series of Loisy's conclusions to be certain, and moreover, since he did not hesitate, once again in the name of the demands posed by a modern attitude, to bring the traditional concept of the miracle and its apologetic significance up for debate.[21]

Thus within a few years, "the Tridentine peace of an entire Church world" (A. Dupront) was suddenly and almost simultaneously shaken in regard to a whole series of essential issues: the nature of revelation, the inspiration of the Holy Scriptures and religious cognition, the person of Christ and his true role in the birth of the Church and its sacraments, the nature and role of oral tradition within the Catholic system, the limits of dogmatic development, the authority of ecclesiastical teachings and the true meaning of the term "orthodoxy," and the value of classical apologetics. Those were indeed serious questions calling for an answer. The answers provided by Loisy, Laberthonnière, and Le Roy contained acceptable and often leading elements, as was proven through the subsequent development of theology and certain initiatives taken by the Second Vatican Council. But these positive elements were not sufficiently thought through and often presented without the imperative detailed differentiations or with inappropriate vocabulary, causing the nonconformists to be confused and bewildered. Moreover, (especially in Loisy's case) sometimes truly ambiguous affirmations had to be dealt with, which could either be interpreted as erroneous and, in the final analysis, destructive to any Christian belief, or as being concerned with innovations, yet basically orthodox and really liberating in view of rather pertinent difficulties caused by the progress of religious studies. Those

[21] *Annales de philosophie chrétienne* 153 (1906–07), 5–33, 166–91, 225–59.

men defending the innovators believed that the latter had paved a promising path through obscurity, notwithstanding their rashness and their insufficient clarifications. Their opponents saw only the first possibility of interpretation and presumed that the ambiguous wording corresponded to the true thoughts of the authors. Their battle against these tendencies became increasingly fierce because the initial confusion turned more and more into blind panic. This panic had its origin in the ambiguous literature which was carrying the existing controversies (without clearly defined positions) into wider and wider circles. The consequences were devastating, especially among the clergy, who, because of very superficial training in the seminaries, were ill prepared to remain cool and whose increasing "outbursts" pleased the observers.[22] Considering that Church authorities at that time had to fend off particularly vehement anticlerical offensives and that the emergence of socialism gave impetus to the right wing to resist any kind of innovation, the almost all-embracing confusion of responsible Catholics can be better understood, especially since the opposition took on progressively international dimensions.

[22] Above all, A. Houtin, whose book *La crise du clergé* (Paris 1907) was successful, as demonstrated by new editions and translations.

CHAPTER 31

The Crisis in England

In contrast to its manifestations in France and Italy, modernism in England displayed some unique characteristics. Even when the movement had reached its peak, the modernists there comprised a modest group;[1] this is also true if the term "modernism" is defined in the sense of abstract immanentist heresy used in the encyclical *Pascendi.* Such a condition was to be anticipated in a country where Catholics were in the minority, including, in turn, a small minority of intellectuals. Yet on the continent and particularly in Italy, British modernism, by virtue of its

[1] This does not mean that one should confine the movement to two or three people, which was often the case. M. Petre's remark (*Congrès d'histoire du christianisme* III, 233) is correct: "One must not believe that the faithful, who do not specifically deal with history and other disciplines, are always completely satisfied with the theological doctrine presented to them. Many secret struggles take place in their simple hearts. The doctrine and the Sacraments of the Church are indispensable means of spiritual life; yet, some find elements in this doctrine which offend their most noble feelings. These are the unassuming modernists."

quality, exerted an influence disproportionate to its numerical strength.[2] If Loisy, on the one hand, deserves to be called the "father of Catholic modernism" due to his accomplishments in the area of exegesis and dogmatic history, the question arises whether Tyrrell does not deserve this title for his achievements in the area of fundamental theology and religious philosophy. On the other hand, all historians agree that von Hügel is the most prominent link between the modernists and the progressives of various countries and, at least at the beginning of the crisis, between the progressives and the ecclesiastical authorities. After all, again in contrast to French and, to a lesser extent, Italian modernism, no respected British modernist leaned toward an agnostic rationalism. The British modernists affirmed to the very end the definition Tyrrell, who has been more accurately appraised by recent scholars than by those of previous generations, had espoused in *Christianity at the Cross-Road:* "I understand a modernist to be a Christian of any denomination who is convinced that the essential truths of his religion and the essential truths of modern society can enter into a synthesis." At this point, the definition formulated by Maud Petre may be added: "Modernism is not only searching for a synthesis of modernity and religion, but also of modern religion and the Church."

The struggle for a synthesis between loyalty to the Catholic Church on the one hand, and the affirmation of modern culture and academic freedom on the other hand, had already in the sixties of the past century caused tensions within the core of British Catholicism, the so-called *Rambler* group; tensions that relaxed rather quickly, however. After a recess of about two decades, religious liberalism awakened again to new life under the pontificate of Leo XIII. In 1892 the Catholic journalist E. J. Dillon had begun to criticize the policies of the Roman Curia in the *Contemporary Review.* In 1896 Wilfrid Ward,[3] son of the pioneer of the strictest ultramontane movement, had founded the Synthetic Society in reaction to the ghetto mentality of his religious brothers, a society in which Catholics joined with Anglicans and Protestants. In 1897 F. von Hügel, highly respected in the British Catholic world, had presented to the international congress of scholars in Fribourg a report concerning the sources of the Hexateuch, essentially following Wellhausen's viewpoints. In the course of the next years, he succeeded in soliciting within his circle more and more disciples of Loisy,[4] with whom he communi-

---

[2] In addition, he had a rather remarkable influence on certain Anglican circles.

[3] Cf. above, p. 142.

[4] In 1903, "L'Évangile et l'Église" by P. Lucas, published in the Jesuit journal *The Month,* and W. Ward and Dom C. Butler in *The Tablet* were assessed positively. See also "Voces catholicae, The Abbé Loisy and the Catholic Reform Movement," *Contemporary Review* 83 (1903), 385–412.

cated regularly by mail. The disputes over Americanism and later, at the beginning of 1900, the abdication of the Old-Catholic scholar St. George Mivart,[5] representing a moderate transformism within "Mivart-ism," and, finally, the turbulence created by all of this in the press were new indications of the emergence of a pro-reform attitude among certain Catholic circles. Hoping to seize control again, the bishops issued a joint pastoral letter dealing with "The Church and Catholic liberalism,"[6] proclaiming the defense of the Roman congregations and emphasizing the difference between the "teaching Church" and the "learning Church." The predominantly negative character of this document only increased anxieties,[7] in spite of an affirmative brief by the Pope.

A prominent figure among the progressive Catholics in England at the beginning of the twentieth century was Friedrich Baron von Hügel (1852–1925), about whom Maud Petre wrote: "He was not only a modernist, but an arch-modernist, and since he was certainly the pioneer of modernism in England . . . , he was the teacher of us all."[8] For a long time, Baron von Hügel was quite critically appraised by the Catholic historians for his unquestionable sympathy toward the fundamental tendencies of the emerging modernism and for the devoted support he gave for many years to its most prominent leaders, even the most compromised ones. For these efforts, Paul Sabatier called him "the lay bishop of the modernists." In the meantime, his well-deserved rehabilitation was in progress, and more and more he appeared to be one of the most illustrious religious personalities of his time. He always stood apart from the religious subjectivism of several of his friends and from their efforts to reduce religion to the human problem of the inner self.[9] He described his own ideal in a letter of May 1903: "Not only as simple a thing as honest scholarship, but also as complex, costly, and consoling a thing as honest scholarship must be lived and created in and with a sincere religion deeply anchored in history, and in and with a living Catholicism."[10] More understanding than original, he felt better

---

[5] Concerning this affair, see J. W. Gruber, *A Conscience in Conflict, the Life of St. G. J. Mivart* (New York 1960).

[6] Text of this "Joint Pastoral" of 22 December 1900: *The Tablet* 97 (1901), 8–12, 50–52.

[7] Regarding the reaction to the "Joint Pastoral," see M. Ward, op. cit., 134–43; M. Petre, *Autobiography and Life of G. Tyrrell* II, 146–61, and L. Barmann, op. cit., 149–53.

[8] *Congrès d'histoire du christianisme* III (Paris 1926), 227, 233.

[9] The best proof of this is his main work, *The Mystical Element of Religion as Studied in St. Catherine of Genova and her Friends* (1908), which was written during the climax of the modernist crisis. It must be noted that W. Temple, in 1925, declared that this work "could be considered the most significant theological work written in the English language during the last half century" (quoted by M. de la Bedoyère, op. cit., 223).

[10] *Selected Letters*, 123.

than most how important it is to remain equally loyal to the demands of a tradition embodied in an ecclesiastical community and to the demands of a thoroughly honest rational criticism, knowing at the same time how necessary it is to witness in the depths of one's personality as a human being and as a devout Christian the tension between those two aspects, instead of striving for a close balance of the two. This openness toward all true values may have been the most characteristic feature of Baron von Hügel's rich personality. His concern not to lose any of these values explains his will never to destroy the bridges to and to preserve the bonds with even those who were in error, in his opinion, for their exclusive claims, but who deserved credit for having drawn attention to an aspect of reality or a real problem that should not be ignored.[11]

Friedrich von Hügel was the son of an Austrian diplomat and a Scottish mother who lived in London after 1871. In his youth he overcame a severe spiritual crisis thanks to the aid of Abbé Huvelin, who gave him the guideline: "For you, nothing but the truth, never orthodoxy." Therefore, he was deeply concerned throughout his life with preserving the independence of scholarly research within the Church. This rationality did not prevent him from being deeply pious and invincibly loyal to the Church, because he believed life in the Church, administering the sacraments, to be an indispensable source of any truly religious life.[12] He was an autodidact, like many aristocrats of his generation. His religious education exceeded that of many clergymen. He combined German thoroughness with the English empirical method, thus becoming a forerunner of the "existentialist" thinkers of the following generation. He was no expert in any special field, but, rare at that time, he was equally competent in the area of biblical criticism, religious philosophy, and the history of spirituality. He also possessed the very special talent of shaking up spirits and souls, stimulating people, through restraining criticism as well as inspiring exhortation, to search sincerely for the truth. It is even more remarkable that he was able to utilize his complete fluency in the major international languages in the service of establishing constructive relations between exegetes, theologians, and phi-

[11] A letter, written after the crisis, reveals the intent of these efforts: "I try to do everything I can to make my old Church intellectually as acceptable as possible, not because reason is the most important thing in religion, but rather because my old Church already possesses all the knowledge necessary to guide spiritual life; while, for reasons that would fill a whole volume, it is less equipped to deal with the needs, the rights, and the duties of rational life. This second aspect of my ambition includes the ardent desire and sincere hope to serve the wounded and embittered Catholics who have fallen or are about to fall away from the faith, to dress their wounds and return them to the fold of the Church" (*Letters to a Niece*, no. 60, of 9 December 1921).

[12] "No book is worthy of such a sacrifice as that of the Sacraments of the Church," he told Miss Petre one day.

losophers searching for such truth in France, England, Germany, and Italy. For this purpose, he carried on an extensive correspondence and made frequent journeys to foreign countries. Many of these men stimulated von Hügel's thinking and became his best friends, while he, in turn, tried to help them with unequalled understanding, perspicacity, and sensitivity. He was not as erratic as many of them, looking for balance and rejecting radical concepts on principle. Thus he succeeded in evading condemnation,[13] probably assisted by his social rank. He did his best to defend his friends to the bitter end; he rejected the improper and often superficial criticism that some of his friends were exposed to by the conservative wing, and he felt the Vatican's authoritarian methods to be shocking to a religious person of the twentieth century.

George Tyrrell (1861–1909) was a respected preacher and spiritual leader, author of devotional books of rare sensitivity and writer of apologetic essays reflecting in a remarkable way the attitude of his contemporaries; perhaps he would have adhered to this line of activities throughout his life had he not met von Hügel. Mainly through his influence he became familiar with biblical criticism and Neo-Kantian philosophy. Having turned to these pursuits, he began questioning a series of essential theses of fundamental theology. In this regard, as Bremond perceived correctly, one must not overlook the influence that was exerted upon Tyrrell by the English liberal Protestants of the nineteenth century, particularly by M. Arnold. Tyrrell was of Irish descent. To his Celtic temperament he owed the critical spirit that occasionally played tricks on him, but also endowed him with the astonishing capability of investigating the secret depths of the suprarational forces nurturing religious experience. At the age of eighteen he converted from the Anglican to the Catholic Church, joined the Society of Jesus, and, in 1896, was assigned to the editorial staff of *The Month*. Soon he was one of the best-known collaborators of this journal.[14] Two prayer books, *Nova et Vetera* (1897) and *Hard Sayings* (1898), establishing his friendship with Baron von Hügel, and a collection of spiritual lectures given to the students of Oxford, "External Religion, its Use and Abuse" (1899), established him as a writer. But precisely at that time he encountered difficulties with ecclesiastical censorship. Tyrrell, overly

---

[13] Except for an indirect reprimand for a secondary affair, which was not justified, (cf. M. de la Bedoyere, op. cit., 191). Regarding von Hügel's attitude toward the ecclesiastical authorities on the eve of *Pascendi*, see his letters to Tyrrell and Loisy, analyzed in ibid., 188–89. Concerning his attitude in 1907, see L. Barmann, op. cit., 183–209.

[14] In *The Month* he published thirty-nine articles in seven years. Some of them are compiled in a book entitled *The Faith of the Millions* (2 vols., 1901). The title refers to Tyrrell's concern not to confine himself to the problems of an intellectual elite, as did the modernists in many cases, but rather to reevaluate the problem of faith, facing the masses of the Christian population.

sensitive and irritable by nature, even more irritable because of the first symptoms of Bright's disease, of which he eventually died, was highly incensed by the narrow-minded limitations imposed upon his intellectual pursuits. Consequently, he began to doubt the authority of the ecclesiastical hierarchy. The extensive reform movement developing on the continent inspired him in his questioning. At the same time, other matters entered into his awareness: the all-too-frequent identification of the Catholic faith with its medieval forms of expression, the unique character of the individual's approach to truth, including religious truth, and, finally, the contrast between the static conception of dogma espoused by the Scholastics and the significance of the development of Christian doctrine in the context of history, all of which he had been exposed to through new books. From then on he was of the opinion that the classical concepts of the *depositum fidei,* the inspiration of the Bible, and revelation had to be analysed from an entirely new perspective, placing emphasis on the mystical element of religion. With moderate restraint, he tried to prove that Christ did not appear as a teacher of orthodoxy and that Catholic theologians were mistaken when they considered faith to be a spiritual affirmation of the historical and metaphysical assurances given by a theology that was apparently revealed and miraculously saved from error; dogma was merely a human attempt to express the divine force within man in intellectual formulations. Under the pseudonym E. Engel, he promulgated these ideas in a brochure entitled *Religion as a Factor of Life* (1902), dedicating it to a friend with the words: "Something that preserves the strength of my faith under the rubble of my orthodoxy."[15] A year later, under another pseudonym (Hilaire Bourdon), he published a more extensive book, the most radical of all his works, *The Church and the Future.* In it he opposed the system of despotic authority concentrated in the Roman Curia and the conception of the Church as an official institute of truth; according to him, the Church must be seen as nothing more than a "school of divine love on this earth" and its only task is continually to translate the inspirations, which the divine life effects in the hearts of its members, into new temporary rules. These publications found wide response in the modernist circles of France and Italy. At first, Tyrrell was left alone. However, one day in 1906, when it became known through the indiscretion of the press that he was also the author of an anonymous brochure in which he had espoused similar ideas,[16] he was expelled from the Jesuits. *Lex credendi* (1906) and *Through Scylla and Charybdis*

---

[15] *Lettres de G. Tyrrell à H. Bremond,* 129.
[16] *A Letter to a University Professor* (1904), reprinted by Tyrrell in 1906 under the title *A Much-Abused Letter,* with an introduction and footnotes.

(1907), two works which he published in the following months in an effort to find a middle way between the extreme dogmaticism of the theologians and the all-too-human pragmatism of certain philosophers, did not contain anything particularly subversive; in fact, the former was praised in a review in the *Month*. His vehement protests against the encyclical *Pascendi*, published in the national press, and his opposition to the inquisitorial attitude expressed therein resulted directly in his excommunication. A few months later, Cardinal Mercier called him the typical representative of philosophical and theological modernism branded in the encyclical. Tyrrell responded with a small book entitled *Medievalism* (1908), sharply criticizing papal absolutism and traditional Catholicism.[17] At the same time, he intensified his communication with the modernists of the continent, above all in Italy, where he had numerous admirers, trying to organize a "strong force of excommunicants who were to form a living protest against the papacy."[18] But the submission of the majority and the inclination of most others toward a socialist humanitarianism or toward an immanentist rationalism were bitter disappointments to him. Moreover, his progressing disease deprived him of the ability to continue to play an active role. On 15 July 1909, death prematurely concluded the tragic career of a man who was for many years one of the most promising figures of British Catholicism.[19]

In spite of his narrow-mindedness toward spiritual problems, Cardinal Bourne (after 1903 bishop of Westminster) avoided dramatizing the modernist danger. For a long time he declined to oppose Tyrrell. He supported the modern orientation that Wilfrid Ward tried to give the *Dublin Review*, protected several Catholic thinkers who had been denounced by people suspecting heretics in every corner, and helped prevent a condemnation of von Hügel. As was mentioned at the beginning of this chapter, modernism in England involved but a small seg-

---

[17] Regarding the emotions under the influence of which he wrote this work in only a few weeks (it had a sensational success: four editions and one translation into French), see G. Daly, *The Month* 228 (1969), 15–22. His less aggressive work, completed shortly before his death (*Christianity at the Cross-Road*), seems to confirm, no matter what Rivière may say about it, that he remained closer to Catholicism (particularly from the perspective of the Second Vatican Council) than was often declared (see, for example, M. Nédoncelle, op. cit., 22–23). Regarding the book and its modernist leaning, see, in opposition, A. Kolping, *ThRv* 59 (1963), 1–8.

[18] Letter to Buonaiuti of 23 April 1908, quoted in id., *Le modernisme catholique*, 144.

[19] His funeral caused an incident that has become famous in the history of antimodernist reaction. After his friend, Abbé Bremond, said a liturgical prayer at his grave site, he was immediately punished with a *suspension a divinis*, which was not annulled until after exhaustive negotiations (see M. Petre, *Autobiography and Life* II, 420–46; M. de la Bedoyère, op. cit., 231–33; *Lettres de G. Tyrrell à H. Bremond*, 302–15; *Correspondence Blondel-Valensin* II, 73–92; A. Loisy, *G. Tyrrell et H. Bremond* [Paris 1936], 1–46).

ment of the Catholic public. This is proven, for instance, by the lack of journals modernistic in nature or at least somewhat open to modernist interests. There is no reason to believe that modernism in Britain died with Tyrrell. Maud Petre,[20] devotedly caring for Tyrrell in the last years of his life, was not the only one to refuse to take the antimodernist oath demanded by the bishop and continued her opposition, even though she was denied the sacraments in her diocese. How important the number of allies was is demonstrated by the fact that A. Vidler was capable of devoting a whole chapter of his book on the modernists to the "Lesser Lights and Fellow Travellers."[21] He drew attention to the generally little-known case of the famous scholar Edmund Bishop,[22] who, like von Hügel, always remained a loyal and devout Catholic. But in 1908 he wrote to von Hügel: "I was a modernist even before modernism," confirming once again how historically ill-defined the concept of modernism really is.

[20] Concerning Maud Petre (1861–1942), see J. A. Walker, *The Hibbert Journal* 41 (1943), 340–46, and *Lettres de G. Tyrrell à H. Bremond* (index).
[21] *A Variety* . . . , 153–90.
[22] Regarding Edmund Bishop (1846–1917), see N. Abercrombie, *The Life and Work of E. Bishop* (London 1959), and A. Vidler, *A Variety* . . . , 134–52.

CHAPTER 32

The Crisis in Italy

The restoration of the world of Catholic intellectuals in Italy around the beginning of the twentieth century proved to be more urgent than the one in France. Caused by the timid, negative attitude of the intransigents toward the liberal revolution, the cultural stagnation had left a void; on the other hand, a longing for greater intellectual freedom that gradually developed in the course of two generations could be felt among those persuaded to defend the new cause. The first indications of such awakening became visible during the last few years of Leo XIII's pontificate. This awakening was accelerated by various foreign influences: by exegetical publications in France and through Tyrrell's works, whose impact in Italy was much stronger than that of Loisy; by the personal impact of Monsignor Duchesne, who had settled in Rome in 1895; and above all by Baron von Hügel, who often sojourned in Italy. For too long the originality of this restoration movement, contemptuously called a "by-product" by Rivière, was belittled. The conclusions of recent research and the publication of documents, both of which greatly increased in the last decade, have illuminated the unique characteristics of Italian modernism. Firstly: this modernism rested in a long tradition which followed the *risorgimento* and stood for political liberation and religious reform. Two aspects of this tradition have particular significance: the desire for liberation from ecclesiastical tutelage, felt to be more oppressive in Italy than elsewhere, and an effort to present the Church as a community of the faithful, replacing the traditional concept that was oriented toward the hierarchy. Secondly: the French modernists were mainly interested in bringing ecclesiastical studies up to par by attempting to find solutions to the new problems that had emerged from the development of religious studies. Italian modernism, however, was characterized by extensive efforts to propagate the new discoveries among the masses, which partially explains why the contacts between the modernists and the Christian Democrats were closer there than in France. There is another difference: while the French modernists put the emphasis on reason, serving as a guideline for the modern academic culture, many Italian modernists were rather fascinated by the mystery of the charismatic Church and inspired by the ardent desire to return to original Christianity.

Within the Italian reform movement, developing in the first years of the twentieth century, roughly three tendencies can be distinguished: 1) young priests and friars, especially numerous in central Italy, tried to bring ecclesiastical studies up to date: 2) fanatics trained in the ranks of the intransigent *Opera dei congressi* realized the practical shortcomings of this movement and its ideological limits and tried to overcome them by developing the cultural foundations of a true Christian democracy; 3) against this movement, several young laymen, mainly from Lombardy, joined the liberal and national trends, trying to forge a link between Catholicism and the tendencies of the modern world.

Within the first group, scriptural studies were (for the most part) represented by three individuals: Giovanni Genocchi[1] and Umberto Fracassini,[2] two brilliant Catholic scholars, whose great intellectual open-mindedness was coupled with strict loyalty to the Church, and

---

[1] Regarding Giovanni Genocchi (1860–1926) of Ravenna, superior of the Roman procurature of the Missionaries of the Most Sacred Heart of Jesus, in spite of his progressive viewpoints in the field of exegetics highly respected by Pius X, see V. Ceresi, *Padre Genocchi* (Vatican City 1934).

[2] Regarding Umberto Fracassini (1862–1950), superior of the Seminary of Perugia, from which he was recalled in 1907 under suspicion of dangerous doctrinary attitudes (after he had been appointed consultant of the Bible Commission in 1903), see *DHGE* XVII, 1367–69, and C. Pizzoni, *Vangelo, Chiesa, Civiltà nel pensiero di Mons. U. Fracassini* (Perugia 1963).

Salvatore Minocchi,[3] a young, courageous priest, who did not intend, however, a reform to exceed the framework of the Catholic system. One of his contemporaries said about him: "This man has something of Danton within him, moderated through ecclesiastical expedience and Italian smoothness." In 1901, in Florence, Minocchi had founded a journal entitled *Studi religiosi,* whose subtitle precisely defined the program: *Rivista critica e storica promotrice della cultura religiosa.* This journal offered space to all ecclesiastical studies, including religious philosophy, but the main portion was reserved for scriptural studies. Without question, the journal often merely translated eloquently the thoughts of Loisy, Lagrange, von Harnack, Houtin, Tyrrell, Blondel, Laberthonnière, and Le Roy, sometimes elaborating upon them. However, Minocchi possessed the art of indulgently making allowances for the sensitivities of the guardians of orthodoxy, while also stressing that readers of his reviews of new books contemplate the insufficient solidity of numerous traditional positions. In spite of the criticism voiced by the *Civiltà cattolica,* Minocchi's journal soon became the center of the enlightened and progressive young priests.

One of them was Ernesto Buonaiuti,[4] a brilliant mind, endowed with extensive knowledge and possessing an extraordinary gift for assimilation besides. He was to become the most outstanding figure of Italian modernism.[5] In 1905, Buonaiuti published, directly in Rome, a similar journal, the *Rivista storico-critica delle scienze teologiche.* Apparently, its purpose was to take a *via media,* a middle-of-the-road between the

---

[3] Regarding Salvatore Minocchi (1869–1943), professor of Hebrew language and literature at the universities of Florence (1901–9) and Pisa, who left the Church in 1908, see A. Agnoletto, *S. Minocchi. Vita e opera* (Brescia 1964).

[4] Regarding Ernesto Buonaiuti (1881–1946), professor of Church history at the Roman Seminary, from which he was recalled in 1906, leader of the resistance against antimodernism, due to his diplomatic skills able to remain in the Church until 1926 (in spite of two excommunications in 1921 and 1924), held the chair for the history of Christianity at the University of Rome from 1915 until 1926, see, in addition to his autobiography entitled *Pellegrino di Roma* (1945), the two studies by V. Vinay, *E. Buonaiuti e l'Italia religiosa del suo tempo* (Rome 1956; amicable; biblio.), and D. Grasso, *Il cristianesimo di E. Buonaiuti* (Brescia 1953; hostile), to be supplemented by P. Scoppola, op. cit. See also M. Ravà, *Bibliografia degli scritti di E. Buonaiuti* (Florence 1951); E. Buonaiuti, *Die exkommunizierte Kirche,* ed. and introduced by E. Benz (Zurich 1966), esp. about the relation to the *Eranos* circle, 43–52; F. Parente, *E. Buonaiuti* (Rome 1971; biblio.); F. Margiotta, Broglio, "E. Buonaiuti," *Storia contemporanea* 2 (1971), 803–23.

[5] The most prominent, but not the most typical figure of modernism after P. Scoppola, who (op. cit., chap. 6) expressly mentions the fact that Buonaiuti found himself quickly isolated in the modernist movement due to his leaning toward radicalism. The main advocates of modernism were reformists with often quite independent attitudes, who considered a denial of their affirmation of the Catholic dogma out of the question.

progressivism of the *Studi religiosi* and the conservatism of the *Civiltà cattolica,* providing more room for scholarly erudition. However, in reality, the young, eminently dynamic editor strove for leadership of the entire Italian reform movement. Emphasis was primarily placed on the history of dogma and of the Church, rather than the question of Scripture.

One of the leading collaborators of Minocchi and Buonaiuti deserves mention: Giovanni Semeria,[6] an extraordinarily gifted friar, whom Cardinal Siri today considers the "best instrument to preserve the faith in the bourgeoisie of Genoa," even though Semeria was branded by his contemporaries as one of the leaders of Italian modernism.[7] Close to Baron von Hügel and several personalities of the academic world in foreign countries, he played an important mediating role in the field of the early history of Christianity as well as in religious philosophy, since he was more successful than most in assimilating the results of contemporary research and in presenting them in a series of brilliant lectures, immediately published in book form, to the general public.

Disregarding the different viewpoints and levels of education, we surprisingly find in all these agents of the intellectual renewal of Italian Catholicism one common and apostolic concern, which distinguished them from similarly inclined Frenchmen, who appeared rather to be bookworms. The Italian modernists were less interested in competing with Protestant or rationalistic scholarship, but rather in improving the religious education of the average Catholic, knowing full well that the lack of religious education was the cause of the superficiality of Italian religiosity.

Similar concerns of a cultural nature are visible in one of the most prominent figures of Italian modernism, in the young democratic priest

---

[6] Regarding Giovanni Semeria (1867–1931), Barnabite, talented apologist, famous preacher and speaker, received in Belgium by Cardinal Mercier in 1912 when the antimodernist reaction forced him to leave Italy, who devoted the last part of his life to the care of war orphans, see, in addition to his memoirs (above), E. Vercesi, *Padre Semeria servo degli orfani* (Amatrice 1932); F. Sala, *Padre Semeria, barnabita* (Turin 1941); A. Schenardi, "Un orateur sacré au XXe siècle, le P. Semeria" (unpubl. diss., Paris 1957); V. Lupo, "L'itinerario spirituale di P. Semeria," *Humanitas* 23 (1968), 610–34, 702–32; E. Passerin d'Entrèves, *Storia contemporanea* 2 (1971), 825–42; the extensive introduction by A. Gambro in his *Saggi clandestini,* ed. by C. Argenta (Alba 1967), and the bio-bibliography by V. Colciago, ibid. II, 371–500.

[7] One day, Pius X charged him with having abused his outstanding talents "by writing books that do not agree with the doctrine of the Church." When he responded that he did so in order to make religion more accessible, the Pope replied: "You enlarge the gates in order to bring in those who are outside, driving out those who are inside" (*Positio super virtutibus* [Vatican City 1949], 256.)

Romolo Murri.[8] He joined the modernist movement rather late, and his membership was simply a transitional episode in his stormy career.[9] He started in the *Opera dei congressi,* where those antiliberal Catholics assembled who longed for a society of theocratic character. Murri was not very interested in the tendencies that inspired Minocchi, Buonaiuti, and their friends; however, he was convinced that the lack of intellectual maturity disabled the Italian Catholics and, above all, the members of the clergy in dealing effectively with the problems confronting the Christian in regard to the activities of his public life. In his journal published after 1898, pretentiously entitled *Cultura sociale,* he was already extending the democratic movement to all areas of thought. He also adopted the premature conclusions of religious criticism in order to be able to preach, surrounded by the halo of a prophetic message, the spiritual and religious renovation of a Catholicism reconciled with the modern world in the worship of freedom.[10] In a famous lecture, given on 24 August 1902 in San Marino, he treated the topic "Freedom and Christianity," invoking the work of Tyrrell, Ehrhard, and Mignot, as well as the rejuvenation of exegesis and historical research, dreaming of a "great liberation." By "returning to the Gospel," Catholicism was to be liberated from all its obsolete elements: "from the warmed-over semiheathen customs, from the juridic concepts derived from Roman Law, from the decadent monastic institutions that are incapable of rejuvenation, and from the abstract categories that kill like the letter of the law."[11] Thus, his orientation intensified in proportion to the development of his social and political activities and gradually merged with an atmosphere of total intellectual and disciplinary freedom outside of the control of the hierarchical authority. His ideas attracted a number of priests who demanded more or less radical reforms in the Church, e.g., reduction of the number of dioceses, modification of the Index procedures, reform of the seminaries and traditional apostolate methods, suspension of sacerdotal celibacy, etc.[12] The progressing development

---

[8] Concerning him, see chaps. 5 and 34. Regarding his relations to the modernist movement, see the two works (biblio., chap. 32) by Guasco and Bedeschi, in addition P. Scoppola, op. cit., 133–62, 249–60.

[9] This point was clearly made by M. Guasco, op. cit.

[10] His most outstanding articles were published in book form: *Battaglie d'oggi,* 4 vols. (Rome 1901–04). Above all, see vol. II.

[11] Text in *Il Domani d'Italia,* no. 35 (31 August 1902), and in F. Magri, *L'azione cattolica in Italia* I (Milan 1953), 184–90. It should be noted that Murri adhered to Thomism throughout his development. Thomism was brought into discredit by all those who more or less professed the modernist movement (this was emphasized by P. Scoppola, op. cit., 155–62).

[12] For example, D. Battaini, who published for the German-speaking part of Switzerland a pioneering paper: *Cultura moderna.* This reformist trend can also be found among

of a simple reform movement in the direction of a so-called "social modernism" finally compelled many to proclaim, at first rather awkwardly, the "autonomy of the temporal realm," as it is called today. Yet they later considered religion a problem of the inner self, so to speak, and the Church a civilizing and morally progressive factor rather than an institution of supranatural salvation. These ideas were also espoused by the group of the *Socialismo cattolico,* founded by G. Quadrotta and F. Perroni, to whom Buonaiuti lent his support after the promulgation of the encyclical *Pascendi.*[13]

Fundamentally different in origin was the group of reformists from Lombardy, the heirs of liberal Catholicism from the period of the *risorgimento.* Among them were men of action, such as the promoters of the *Opera Bonomelli,* a charitable institution for Italian emigrant workers. These men did not exercise as much restraint as the old bishop whose patronage they enjoyed. But most of the disciples of this group were intellectual laymen, passionately interested in religious problems, rare in Italy at that time. Most attractive to the general public was Antonio Fogazzaro,[14] a brilliant writer full of mystical idealism, who stood in close contact with Semeria, Genocchi, and von Hügel, and was a great admirer of Loisy, Blondel, and Tyrrell, but also strongly influenced by Rosmini and his ideals of a religious reform movement as described in his book *Cinque piaghe della Chiesa.* Fogazzaro was also interested in coordinating Darwin's theory of evolution with Catholic dogma. In 1905 he published the novel *Il Santo,* whose hero appointed himself the apostle of a reform based on the spirit of love, love that was to permeate all areas of religious and social life. This novel contains numerous remarks about the nature of religious feeling, about the role of the priest, about the true Christian spirit, and the formalism of Catholic worship. However, the climax of this work is a long discourse on reform, addressed to the Pope, in which the four evil spirits, having invaded the Church, were branded: the spirit of dishonesty, closing his eyes to the light of modern scholarship and indicting the best defenders of the truth; the spirit of omnipotent power, changing paternal authority into a

---

some laymen; e.g., in the Neapolitan lawyer G. Avolia, director of the journal *Battaglie d'oggi,* who finally preached a "lay priesthood" in the perspective of Christian socialism (cf. É. Poulat, *Journal d'un prêtre d'après-demain* [Tournai, Paris 1961], 131–37).

[13] Regarding this group, the mouthpieces of which were the journals *Nova et Vetera* (1908) and *Cultura contemporanea* (1909–13), see P. Scoppola, op. cit., 261–326.

[14] Regarding Antonio Fogazzaro (1842–1911), poet and writer, who, in 1873, reading Gratrys, converted, and was senator after 1896 (in spite of the *non expedit*), see, in addition to the work by O. Morra, op. cit., T. Gallarati-Scotti, *La vita di A. Fogazzaro* (Milan 1920, [3]1963); P. Nardi, *A. Fogazzaro* (Milan 1938); L. M. Personè, *Nuova antologia* 481 (1961), 327–44; *DHGE* XVII, 696–700.

terrible dictatorship; the spirit of avarice, a mockery of evangelical poverty; and, finally, the spirit of rigid adherence to tradition, fearing any kind of progress and driving the Jewish rabbis to reject and condemn Jesus. (This comparison was made by Tyrrell.) The novel became a great success and was translated into several languages. However, it also led to violent controversies.

Less spectacular, but more profound, was the effect of the journal *Il Rinnovamento.* It was founded at the beginning of 1907 by a few young Milanese encouraged by Fogazzaro and Semeria.[15] One of its main patrons, Stefano Jacini, was in close contact with the forerunners of German Reform Catholicism. He was especially interested in liberal Protestantism, particularly in Eucken and Troeltsch. The journal emphasized the primacy of conscience over external authority, without negating the rights of the latter.[16] In addition, it promoted freedom of scholarly research and the position of the laity in the life of the Church. Following post-Kantian philosophy, it stressed the significance of subjectivity, which was badly neglected by Scholastic thinking. True to liberal traditions, it espoused a new conception of the relations between Church and state in reaction to the "confusionism" of the previous centuries. The staff of the journal tried to extricate the values of secular education from all areas and to give them practical applications in the fields of philosophy, history, research methods, and law. At the same time, its publishers attempted to awaken interest in religious problem, since most intellectuals of that time found religious indifferentism to be a matter of course. Though being as open-minded as possible toward the contemporary trends and the solid accomplishments of religious studies, these intellectuals were nonetheless to remain loyal sons of the Roman Catholic Church, forming, so to speak, a "third" party, that felt its way around between the incomprehension of the integralists and the exaggerations of the radicals. As part of the latter, the group of young idealistic philosophers from Lugano, led by G. Rensi, deserves special mention. Their journal was the *Coenobium,* founded in 1906.

As in France, the ideas proclaimed by the leaders of the movement to renovate ecclesiastical studies found a positive response among the young clergy in Italy. Around 1906 it often happened in central Italian seminaries that when a priest was ordained, not only were works by Semeria and Lagrange chosen as gifts, but also those of Loisy and Tyr-

---

[15] Regarding this amicable and at the same time reserved attitude of Msgr. Bonomelli, see F. Fonzi, *RStRis* 56 (1969), 188–92, 220–22.

[16] The subsequent behavior of the editorial staff on the occasion of the strict disapproval of the prefect of the Congregation of the Index in May 1907 is typical. See the commentary by P. Scoppola, op. cit., 212–20.

rell.[17] Since the hierarchy in Italy was even less equipped than that in France to effectively deal with contemporary problems (in Italy, there was not a single prelate who could be compared to Mignot), their confusion was even greater. And as always in such cases, reaction raged against everything that deviated in the slightest from the traditional paths, that is, against the moderates as well as against the radicals. Even a man so above suspicion as Francesco Lanzoni[18] became the target of allegations and denunciations simply because he wanted to apply the principles of historical criticism to the study of hagiography. The moderates, mostly loyal followers of the Church, submitted quietly; the more progressive, however, tried to organize resistance. To that end, they attempted to unify, both outwardly and inwardly, the movement that aimed at cultural and religious renovation, to give it a unity it was largely lacking, as we have already seen. For the purpose of such unification, Murri, Buonaiuti, and Fracassini called a meeting in the summer of 1907 in Molveno, that was also attended by Baron von Hügel.[19] A week later, the encyclical *Pascendi* was issued; it forced the group to attempt to coalesce its divergent opinions and concepts, resulting in its dispersal.

[17] M. Guasco, *Fermenti nei seminari del primo '900* (Bologna 1971), 178–79.

[18] Regarding Francesco Lanzoni (1863–1929), rector of the Seminary of Faenza from 1890–1917, author of numerous local hagiographical studies and a fundamental work about *Le diocesi d'Italia dalle origini al principio del sec. VII* (Rome 1927), see the collection of articles *Nel centenario della nascita di mons* (Faenza 1964), and L. Bedeschi, *Lineamenti dell'antimodernismo. Il caso Lanzoni* (Parma 1970).

[19] Regarding this meeting, which has been a secretive affair for a long time and was often incorrectly seen as a sort of council of European modernism, see P. Scoppola, op. cit., 235–44, and L. Bedeschi, *Humanitas* 24 (1969), 658–77; 25 (1970), 482–91.

CHAPTER 33

*Intervention of Ecclesiastical Authority
and the Integralist Reaction*

Roman Intervention

The solemn condemnation of modernism did not take place until 1907. However, there were plenty of indications of the impending papal ban. During the first months of the pontificate, on 13 December 1903, Loisy's main works were put on the Index. Some months later, the encyclicals *Ad diem illum* (2 February 1904) and *Iucunda sane accidit* (12 March 1904) urgently warned against the *novarum rerum molitores,* who, with great scholarly efforts, questioned the history of early Christianity.

In December of the same year, the Pope admonished the bishops to practice uncompromising severity toward seminarians with overly liberal attitudes who lacked the proper respect for the scholarly efforts made "by our great teachers, Church Fathers, and interpreters of revealed doctrine."[1] Similar warnings were contained in a letter, addressed to the rector of the Institut Catholique in Paris at the beginning of the following year,[2] and in a lecture to the students of the French Seminary in Rome[3] containing a rather overt reference to Loisy. In the fall of 1904 two excellent exegetes, Father Genocchi of the Roman Seminary and Father Gismondi of the Gregoriana, were replaced by two professors who fundamentally rejected the application of critical methods to the text of the Holy Scriptures. One of them, Father A. Delattre, had just sharply criticized Father Lagrange and the "new exegetical school." In August 1905 Father Fleming was replaced as secretary of the Biblical Commission by Dom L. Jannsen, a scholastic theologian who did not possess specific competency in the field of exegesis, and overtly conservative consultants were appointed, eliminating the original balance between the various factions. The consequences of these changes were soon noticeable. While the first two reports of the commission regarding actual sayings in the Bible (13 February 1905) and biblical stories that only seemed to be historical (23 June 1905) handled the problem with moderation,[4] the subsequent conclusions regarding the Mosaic authenticity of the Pentateuch (27 June 1906) and the Johannine authenticity of the fourth Gospel were much more reactionary in nature.[5] Both schools, even in Rome, negated each other, because one recommended tolerance and patience in order not to discard the wheat with the chaff, while the other was uncompromising, focusing on the most radical viewpoints. This school more or less enjoyed the trust of the Pope, especially since the imprudence of many of the Italians who disseminated the new ideas had led him to believe that orthodoxy, for which he carried the responsibility, was seriously threatened, even though he had to admit that, in the field of exegesis, circumspective open-mindedness was prudent.[6]

---

[1] Address of 12 December 1904 (ASS 37 [1904–05], 435).
[2] Letter of 22 February 1905 (ASS 37 [1904–05], 555–57).
[3] A. Houtin, La question biblique au 20e siècle, 215–16.
[4] ASS 37 (1904–05), 666; 38 (1905–06), 124–25.
[5] ASS 39 (1906–07), 377–78; 40 (1907), 383–84. The first of these responses inspired a little book written by von Hügel, The Papal Commission and the Pentateuch, about which Bollandist Delehaye wrote: "Let us hope that it will open the eyes of the Father of all faithful, who is truly compromised due to the mediocre tools he is using" (1 December 1906, quoted by M. de la Bédoyère, The Life of Baron von Hügel, 187).
[6] See especially Le Père Lagrange au service de la Bible, 158–59.

After 1904, in Rome, the Swiss K. Decurtins launched a vehement struggle against Blondel, Laberthonnière, and others. By the end of 1905 Loisy and the progressive exegetes had particularly attracted the curiosity of the Holy See. But the wave of the reform movement in Italy vacillated, enlarging the list of urgent concerns and drawing attention to other problems that were discussed more and more frankly. In December 1905 the bishops of the provinces of Turin and Vercelli issued a joint pastoral letter, which, for the first time in an ecclesiastical document, used the word "modernism." The admonishments contained therein were taken to heart by many other bishops.[7] The following year brought additional measures: While the Congregation of the Index, on 14 April, condemned the novel *Il Santo* by Fogazzaro and Laberthonnière's books, by now several years old, Monsignor De Lai and Cardinal Gennari instigated systematic control of the Italian seminaries. Several professors were recalled from their teaching chairs without being granted an opportunity to defend themselves. Thus a gloomy atmosphere of suspiciousness developed in Rome. Everywhere, the approaching storm was felt.[8]

This storm finally broke in the course of 1907. Within a few months more and more solemn *acta* were issued. On 17 April, in the context of a consistorial address,[9] Pius X turned rigorously against the *neoreformismum religiosum,* which was spreading with increasing audacity. At the end of the same month, the prefect of the Index Commission issued a warning to the Milan group of the *rinnovamento.*[10] On 14 June Pius X sent a brief to the Viennese Professor Commer,[11] congratulating him for having hacked to pieces the errors of the main representative of Reform Catholicism, Herman Schell. On 17 July the decree *Lamentabili sane exitu* was published by the Holy Office,[12] over which it had been brooding for several years, containing a revealing list of statements which two Parisian theologians had extracted from Loisy's "little books."[13] The decree condemned sixty-five theses concerning the authority of the ecclesiastical teaching office, the inspiration and historical value of the books of the Holy Scriptures, the terms revelation, dogma,

---

[7] Analysis of these pastoral letters and quotations from them in the brochure *Un allarme dell'episcopato italiano contro ii reformismo religioso* (Genoa 1906).

[8] Regarding the atmosphere in Rome during 1906, see also *Correspondance Blondel-Valensin* I, 262–63, and M. de la Bédoyère, op. cit., 181–82.

[9] *ASS* 40 (1907), 266–69.

[10] Text in *Rinnovamento* 1 (1907), 610. Cf. P. Scoppola, *Crisi modernista,* 212–16.

[11] *ASS* 40 (1907), 392–94.

[12] *ASS* 40 (1907), 470–78. Cf. F. Heiner, *Der neue Syllabus Pius' X.* (Mainz 1907). Regarding the theological value of the document, cf. J. Rivière, op. cit., 341–46.

[13] Cf. P. Dudon, *BLE* 32 (1931), 73–96, and R. Aubert, *EThL* 37 (1961), 557–78.

and faith, certain aspects of Christological dogma, which had been questioned in recent disputes, the origin of the sacraments, the constitution of the Church and the nature of Christian truth in general.[14] And finally, on 8 September, the encyclical *Pascendi* was issued.[15] Since its intent was not to describe exactly the thoughts of the individual instigators of modernism, but rather to present the reflection of their ideas in the consciousness of the community, it started out with a somewhat contrived synthesis of modernism, blaming the various errors on agnosticism, which disputes the value of the rational argumentation in the religious realm, and on the philosophy of immanence, which ignores that the origin of religious truth rests in the needs of life. This philosophy created the dogma unfolding in the course of life on the basis of reason and experience. Likewise, the need "to give religion a *corpus* perceivable through the senses" created the sacraments; the books of the Holy Scriptures contain the experiences collected by the faithful of Israel and by the first disciples of Christ; the Church is a fruit of the collective consciousness, and the only task of authority is to give expression to the emotions of the individual. The encyclical stigmatized the modernistic conception of biblical criticism and the purely subjective methods of apologetics, as well as the demands of reform modernism. It concluded its third, disciplinary part by enumerating a series of practical measures ("remedies") to halt the further spread of evil, above all in the seminaries (renewed obligation to study scholastic philosophy and theology, supervision of reading material, *consilia vigilantiae* in every bishopric).

The encyclical was immediately greeted with exuberant expressions of joy by the conservatives, who had desired it for a long time.[16] Many

---

[14] About fifty theses came from Loisy's works (regarding the exactness with which they reflected his viewpoints, see É. Poulat, *Histoire, dogme et critique,* 109–12); three theses were taken from Houtin, one from Le Roy, and one from the Newman disciple Dimmet, whose work *Le pensée catholique dans l'Angleterre contemporaine* was put on the Index a few days later, as was *Dogme et critique* by Le Roy.

[15] *ASS* 40 (1907), 593–650. See A. Michelitsch, *Der biblisch-dogmatische Syllabus Pius' X. samt der Enzyklika gegen den Modernismus* (Graz, Vienna 1908; in the appendix are several articles from the German and Austrian press that had been devoted to the two papal documents). Frequently, the edition of the encyclical *Pascendi* was ascribed to P. Billot, Msgr. Sardi, and others; however, today we know who the real editors were: P. J. Lemius, O.M.I., was responsible for the dogmatic part (after the Pope had discarded as unsatisfactory several drafts prepared by other theologians), and Cardinal Vives y Tutó for the pragmatic part (cf. *BLE* 47 [1946], 143–61, 242–43). Regarding the theological value of this document, see J. Rivière, op. cit., 364–67.

[16] This was to be anticipated, and Cardinal Maffi, one of the few relatively open-minded Italian prelates, indulged in an illusion when he declared: "Let us hope that the positive impact of the encyclical will not be spoiled by the *zelanti,* who are finding new excuses for their violent excesses and their customary gripes" (F. Crispolti, *Pio IX . . . Ricordi personali* [Milan 1932], 128).

moderates deplored the purely negative tone of the encyclical, yet they were glad that ambiguities, which gradually threatened to become dangerous, had been eliminated. Those who were attracted by the exponents of modernism reacted much less vehemently than had been expected, even though they almost unanimously considered the encyclical "a caricature rather than a picture of modernism" (Sabatier). Tyrrell believed himself able to predict that the encyclical would compel the "right wing of modernism to align itself more closely with the left wing," since the encyclical did not differentiate between reasonable progressivism and the "rendezvous of all heresies" based on agnosticism and immanentism, simply schematically reconstructing both. In reality, the opposite happened: For some, this painful condemnation by the Pope was the criterion revealing to them the fact that they implicitly stood outside of the Church. Consequently, they openly broke with the Church, depending on the individual case, with more or less restraint; and since they had to abandon hope of being able to reform the Church from within, some carried the radicalism of their viewpoints even further, quickly ending up in pure rationalism.

In most of them, however, loyalty to the Church was victorious. Thus most everyone submitted, creating the impression later on that the modernist crisis had simply been a matter of individual, rather isolated personalities. Unquestionably, the masses of believers had not been seized by the wave of modernism. But at least in France and, to a lesser extent, in Italy, the clergy who were informed about the development of scriptural studies, and a number of young Catholic intellectuals had felt strongly attracted to the new movement. These people were dissatisfied with the theological training at that time and conscious of the need for adjusting to the circumstances. Therefore they were enthusiastic over the pioneers who had paved the way. In contrast to some of these very pioneers, they would never have thought of continuing their research outside of the Church. For example, É. Poulat compared the attitude of Loisy with that of his young pupil Abbé L. Vénard, who never considered following Loisy's refusal to submit to the Roman condemnations, and he analyzed correctly their fundamentally different reactions: "While Loisy, with the certainty of a technician, draws the plan (of a necessary development), anticipating its various stages, Vénard wants to cling to the authority of the Church. For the Church, he boldly reconnoiters as a guerrilla who is aware that he is not the whole army and that he is nothing without the army. An expert who grates on the nerves of the ignorant, Loisy follows his blueprint precisely, only paying attention in order to calculate correctly and to leave nothing out. Vénard, in contrast, gives preference to his mind, while adjusting his steps to the awkward pace of the Church, differentiating between justified criticism and the slow process of adjusting to its accomplishments. Loisy conceptualizes and analyzes a historical process of change, Vénard participates in a process of organic adaptation. Both may have the same ideas, but they are not equally in agreement with the Church as an external institution."[17]

The agnostic and immanentist system, superficially reconstructed by the encyclical, was so obviously in contradiction to traditional Christian belief that it was fully normal for many true progressives to depart openly from it and renounce it. Even though submission to the anathema of the encyclical took place within a large framework, it was nevertheless extremely painful for many who observed an increase of hope for an impending adjustment of Catholicism to the changing attitudes, and therefore felt the danger of a more profound schism between the Church and the intellectual world of the West.[18] Many shared the opinion of the "Erasmus of modernism" (J.-M. Mayeur), Monsignor Mignot, who had declared: "There is no Christian conscience that does not reject with the whole force of its faith all errors condemned by the encyclical."[19] However, he also wrote that this encyclical erred in "limiting itself to condemnation without defining what one can say without being a modernist."[20] Or they thought like the philosopher V. Delbos, a marvelous Catholic layman: "The encyclical has one all-too-visible *lacuna*: it consists of the negligence toward or the ignorance of the deeper causes which incited the so-called modernist movement."[21]

---

[17] É. Poulat, *Histoire, dogme et critique,* 313–14. This analysis considers "the amazing psychological flexibility of the religious consciousness, which is not a matter of weakness caused by the lack of logic, but rather a matter of numerous capabilities at its disposal to express itself." This flexibility was clearly illuminated by the most recent progress made in the humanities. Thus, the analysis requires an elaboration of the strict appraisal by T. Gallarati-Scotti, who ascribed the great number of submissions to the *povertà di coscienze e di caratteri* (*Vita di A. Fogazzaro,* 493). Especially in Italy, this element was important, but it is not the only and not even the main explanation.

[18] Vicar General Birot wrote this in metaphorical language to his friend G. Frémont, who considered the exposé of the encyclical "excellent" (A. Siegfried, *L'abbé Frémont* II [Paris 1932], 505): "It condemns the most absurd naturalistic system ever devised, but I submit with sadness because this doctrinary sternness is based on *contrived* ambiguity because it condemns friend and foe alike. The Pope is like the colonel of the artillery shooting from the top of a hill into the troops of both fronts engaged in heavy fighting down in the plains and simultaneously destroying his own best troops" (quoted by É. Poulat, op. cit., 443).

[19] *Semaine religieuse d'Albi* (28 September 1907), 553–55.

[20] Letter to F. von Hügel, 5 October 1907, quoted in É. Poulat, op. cit., 480, n. 89.

[21] Letter to J. Wehrlé, 30 September 1907, quoted in *Correspondance Blondel-Valensin* I, 357–64. He did not feel touched personally, but the tone of the encyclical thoroughly upset him: "How can one persuade that many souls . . . not to doubt the benevolence of the Church?" Regarding the edition of the declaration of submission of the *Annales de philosophie chrétienne* to the encyclical, see ibid., 367–70.

Even though almost everyone submitted to the ecclesiastical authority, there were a few residual pockets of resistance. Loisy published a new little book, *Simples refléxions sur le décret Lamentabili et l'encycle Pascendi,* the tone of which was as ironical as it was aggressive. In order to stress the significance of the booklet, he published simultaneously two thick volumes on *The Synoptic Gospels,* which were far more radical than his previous studies. But it was precisely this development which caused many of his former admirers to fall away; and his excommunication on 7 March 1908 made him a loner. Tyrrell suffered the same fate, after having already been denied the sacraments by his bishop at the end of October 1907, following the publication of several articles in opposition to the encyclical in the *Times* and in the Italian press. At first Minocchi submitted, announcing he would discontinue the publication of his *Studi religiosi.* But after having been charged by his friends with servility, he soon held a public lecture on the earthly paradise and the dogma of original sin. He achieved a great deal of attention because he negated the historical character of the first chapter of Genesis. After the *suspensio a divinis,* Tyrrell rejected submission, and in October 1908 he took off his clerical garb. From then he strove for a more socialistic humanitarianism, seeing in Christianity nothing more than a contingent form of the religion of the absolute. In Germany and Austria, a number of leading personalities of Reform Catholicism also protested against the encyclical: Monsignor Ehrhard, professor at the theological faculty of Strasbourg, turned against the practical measures forming the last part of the encyclical, since they prohibited, in his opinion, any kind of scholarly work; Professors Schnitzer of Munich and Wahrmund of Innsbruck opposed in harsher terms the misdeeds of ultramontanism and Roman absolutism, but these were overt manifestations of academic liberalism and not doctrinary modernism.[22]

Aside from these open protests, there was a series of anonymous criticisms.[23] The most remarkable, though rather superficial throughout, were, in France, the brochure *Lendemains d'encyclique,* in which Monsignor Lacroix, the very liberal bishop of Tarentaise, had collaborated,[24]

[22] Msgr. Ehrhard, who had declared that the doctrinal system ascribed to the modernists by the encyclical was incompatible with dogma, confirmed again, in a memorandum to the press, his Catholic loyalty, and the Holy See was satisfied with removing his prelature. Professor Schnitzer, being much more critical, was initially suspended *a divinis,* later excluded from receiving the sacraments. Regarding the Wahrmund case that resulted in diplomatic tensions between the Vatican and Vienna, see Engel-Janosi II, 87–103. Regarding the rare cases of modernism in Austria, ibid., 143–44.

[23] Regarding the frequently exaggerated significance of the anonyms and pseudonyms in modernist literature, see É. Poulat, op. cit., 621–77, esp. 640–42.

[24] Regarding the brochure *Werk eines Pfarrers der Diözese Autun* signed *Catholici,* see J. Rivière, op. cit., 379–81, and É. Poulat, op. cit., 650. At the instigation of the Kraus

and particularly, in Italy, *Il Programma dei modernisti—Riposta all'enciclica di Pio X,* a document published on 28 October 1907 and quickly translated into French, German, and English. Monsignor Fracassini collaborated on the scriptural section, but the author was Buonaiuti,[25] who, in contrast to other leading modernists, preferred to stay in the Church in order to continue from within the reform work that he had started. It is uncertain where the true Buonaiuti really revealed himself, in the *Programma,* the tone of which was rather moderate, or in the much more radical *Lettere di un prete modernista,* published several months later, likewise behind the veil of anonymity.[26]

These pockets of resistance, which, in spite of the unrest in the first few months, was rather insignificant, inspired the antimodernist reaction that had long remained sporadic and isolated. But since the modernist movement was confined to the circles of intellectuals, only a very few bishops deemed useful the effort of devoting a pastoral letter to it.[27] Nevertheless, with the exception of Germany, they organized the *consilia vigilantiae* required by the encyclical in order to prevent suspect publications by the clergy. There were also isolated attempts to expose the modernist authors hiding behind a pseudonym. The greatest attention was caused by the fact that L. Saltet attributed the articles against the Trinitarian and Marian dogmas, signed by A. Dupin and G. Herzog, to Abbé Turmel.[28] On the other hand, numerous theologians dealt with commentaries on the papal documents, but their refutations usually

---

Society, it was translated into German under the title *Antwort der französischen Katholiken.* Regarding Msgr. Lucien Lacroix (1854–1922), founder of the *Revue du clergé français,* who contributed several anonymous articles, liked to call himself "the bishop of the modernists," and resigned as bishop of Tarentaise after the issuance of the encyclical, see M. Hudry, "Un évêque républicain au moment de la Séparation," *Vieux Conflans,* nos. 65–66 (1965), 3–37, and A. Vidler, *A Variety of Catholic Modernists,* 105–8.

[25] Concerning the *Programma dei modernisti,* see D. Grasso, *Il cristianesimo di E. Buonaiuti* (Brescia 1953), 28–35, and P. Scoppola, op. cit., 269–73. Against Fracassini's will, Buonaiuti revised his pages.

[26] Regarding the *Lettere,* see V. Vinay, *E. Buonaiuti,* 43–53, and P. Scoppola, op. cit., 273–79.

[27] Except in Italy, where modernism was given attention for its reforming and social aspects. The episcopates of Prussia and Bavaria published a joint letter in January 1908. In French-speaking countries, the most popular document was the pastoral letter by Cardinal Mercier, who defended Scholasticism against Kantian philosophy, which he perceived to be the root of modernist errors (*Œuvres pastorales* I [Brussels 1911], 363–82; reprinted in brochure form: *Le Modernisme* [Brussels 1908], German translation [Cologne 1908], including a lecture dealing with the same topic given at the University of Louvain).

[28] Regarding the affair involving Turmel, not resolved until 1929, see, in addition to his biography by F. Sartiaux (Paris 1931), J. Rivière, op. cit., 486–505. About P. Lejay's case, see ibid., 501–2, n. 5.

referred to abstract modernism as presented in the encyclical. Only a few seemed to have recognized the real problems that were maladroitly posed by the modernists; and even if their studies intended to exceed the level of mere general comprehension, their arguments frequently appeared to be rather simplistic.[29] Among the laudable exceptions in France were the articles of the Jesuits Lebreton and de Grandmaison, as well as the *Lettres sur les études ecclésiastiques* by Mignot, in which he tried to prove to what extent the condemnation of modernism justified new scholarly studies; in Germany, the exceptions were an article by F. X. Kiefl published in *Hochland* and a collection of lectures held some time later at the University of Freiburg and published under the title *Jesus Christus.*

The systematic suppression of the modernist movement's last vestiges after the issuance of *Pascendi* was mainly the work of the Holy See itself, living for several years in an atmosphere of panic. With more and more reactionary leanings, the Index Commission[30] as well as the Biblical Commission[31] intensified their activities. Furthermore, new apostolic visitations in the Italian seminaries directly responsible to the Curia were decreed and suspect teachers were recalled, often merely on the basis of unfounded denunciations.[32] Even though, according to Loisy's own words, modernism was in a state of "complete dissolution,"[33] two years after its condemnation in 1907, Pius X was still greatly worried about the continued existence of certain clandestine operations, which were extremely exaggerated. Thus he believed the Church was still "in a state of siege" and he deemed it necessary to take further measures. On 1 September 1910, in his motu proprio *Sacrorum antistitum,*[34] the Pope demanded from all the clergy a special oath, the so-called antimodernist

---

[29] For example, see the appropriate criticism of the *De immutabilitate traditionis contra modernam haeresim evolutionismi* (1907), written by P. Billot, in H. Holstein, *La Tradition dans l'Église* (Paris 1960), 129–34.

[30] Cf. A. Boudinhon, *Revue du clergé français* 75, 215–27. After it was translated into Italian, the *Histoire ancienne de l'Église* by Msgr. Duchesne was condemned on 22 January 1912, in spite of the imprimatur of schoolmaster S. Palatii.

[31] Cf. J. Levie, *La Bible, parole humaine et message de Dieu* (Bruges, Paris 1928), 88.

[32] Aside from the works of L. Bedeschi, see M. Guasco, *Fermenti nei seminari,* 121–54.

[33] In *RH* 102 (1909). Regarding the weakness of Italian modernism, quickly dispersing into small groups with the most varied tendencies, see the letter of S. Jacini to von Hügel written at the very moment the journal *Rinnovamento* ceased publication around the end of 1909 (*RStRis* 56 [1969], 245–47). One of the many other signs of the inevitable decline of modernism after 1907 was the failure of the plans for the creation of an international information agency that had been drawn up by Msgr. Lacroix and Paul Sabatier (a liberal French Protestant who had observed the movement from its inception with passionate interest). Even the founding of the *Revue moderniste internationale* in Geneva in 1910 was but transient ardor.

[34] *AAS* 2 (1910), 655–80.

oath. This involved a statement of faith that had been adjusted to the already condemned versions of modernism, including the statement formulated by Pius IV. The first section formulated in five points the proof for the existence of God, the value of the basis for faith, the founding of the Church through Christ, the immutability of dogma, and the intellectual character of the act of faith. A second part demanded submission to the decree *Lamentabili* and the encyclical *Pascendi* and called for their affirmation. This text did not add anything essential to the *acta* of Pius X, however it was an official summary, the goal and purpose being to request from every priest his expressed solemn affirmation, in order to expose the crypto-modernists. The clergy submitted without much open resistance. In the Church at large, there were not more than approximately forty exceptions.[35] In Germany, however, this measure caused considerable unrest in the name of scholarly freedom; and finally, upon the request of the episcopate, the German theological universities were relieved of the oath.

But not only the Germans feared the disastrous consequences of the anti-modernist suppression upon Catholic scholarship. Today there is agreement that the rejuvenation, commenced under Leo XIII, was seriously hampered throughout a whole generation.[36] Primarily in Italy, where suppression was particularly relentless, almost the entire clergy was prohibited from serious studies, enlarging the critical shortcomings in the area of contemporary culture that have remained one of the great weaknesses of Italian Catholicism to the present day. But elsewhere the fear that Christian scholarship could possibly move in directions considered adventurous by Church authorities caused numerous Catholic theologians to withdraw to strictly historical work, or, even worse, to confine themselves to the reiteration of textbook formulas, speculating only on harmless marginal matters in the framework of a rather narrow-minded Neo-Thomism.[37]

---

[35] One more detail should be noted: Pius X personally empowered Frs. Semeria and Genocchi to take this oath with a proviso. Even more peculiar: he allowed Semeria to publish in certain well-controlled journals, but under a pseudonym. In this manner, he placed Semeria's talents in his service, deflating his influence at the same time.

[36] In order to demonstrate that he was not an opponent of scholarly work, Pius X had announced in his encyclical *Pascendi* the establishment of an international institute for progressive research. Its members were chosen on the basis of rather one-sided criteria, causing the institution to be stillborn (some information in L. von Pastor, *Tagebücher*, 482–511).

[37] The twenty-four theses of the Congregation of Studies of 27 July 1914 concerning the basic doctrine of Saint Thomas are a typical manifestation of this attitude. More open-mindedness was reflected in the founding of the *Rivista di Filosofia neoscolastica* in 1909 by P. Gemelli, O.F.M., and, in Louvain, the efforts of Msgr. Deploige, who tried to integrate sociology into Neo-Thomism (M. Defourny, *Annuaire de l'Université catholique de Louvain* 81 [1927–29], XCVII–XCVIII).

The results on the whole were not as negative as is sometimes maintained. Even in the field of exegesis, where serious studies were largely condemned to sterility in spite of the founding of the Pontifical Biblical Institute in 1909,[38] some remarkable achievements were made: In 1908, *Biblische Zeitfragen* was founded, a popular collection; in 1912 there followed the founding of the *Alttestamentlichen und Neutestamentlichen Abhandlungen,* edited by J. Nikel and M. Meinertz; the publication of *La théologie de S. Paul* by F. Prat, S.J., (1908–12); and the commentary of Father Lagrange regarding the Gospel of Saint Mark (1911). In the area of patrology and dogmatic history, French authors were gradually able to compete with names like Ehrhard, Bardenhewer, and Rauschen: J. Tixeront, a student of Duchesne, published, between 1905 and 1912, a *Histoire des dogmes,* which, for its time, was not without merit. Father J. Lebreton did pioneering work with his *Origines du dogme de la Trinité* (1910). The same applies to J. Lebon in Louvain and his *Monophysisme sévérien* (1909). The growing interest in Near Eastern Christian literature was reflected in the *Corpus scriptorum christianorum orientalium,* continued by the Catholic universities of Louvain and of America after its establishment by J.-B. Chabot in 1902. In 1907 the *Görres-Gesellschaft* under the leadership of Monsignor Kirsch opened a Section for Archaeology, aimed at furthering Christian, classical, and Near Eastern archeological studies and the research of problems posed by religious history. In 1912 F. J. Dölger at the University of Münster established a new teaching chair for General Religious History and Comparative Religious Studies, and he investigated in his lectures the extent to which Christian thought and the original Christian rites felt the influence of the paganism surrounding them.[39] A year earlier, while in France the first Catholic textbook on the history of religions, *Christus,* was published under the direction of P. Huby, P. W. Schmidt, S.V.D., founder of the journal *Anthropos* (1906), had collaborated in Louvain with Father Bouvier, S. J., in the organization of the first Catholic Week for Religious Ethnology;[40] and another German, J. Schmidlin, had founded the *Zeitschrift für Missionswesen* and the first Catholic *Institut für Missionswissenschaft.*[41] Literary history was brilliantly represented by

[38] The Pontifical Biblical Institute was entrusted to the Society of Jesus under the direction of the very conservative P. J. Fonck. It was to be the counterpart of the École Biblique in Jerusalem directed by Father Lagrange, who was under suspicion by Rome. Cf. *S. Pio X promotore degli studi biblici, fondatore del Pont. Istituto biblico* (Rome 1955), 23–42.

[39] Regarding Franz Dölger (1879–1940), the first Catholic theologian who took account of the history of religion school, see T. Klauser, *F. J. Dölger, Leben und Werke* (Münster 1956).

[40] Cf. *RHE* 13 (1912), 747–51.

[41] Cf. *50 Jahre katholische Missionswissenschaft in Münster, 1911–1961,* ed. by J. Glazik (Münster 1961).

the German Baumstark, the Englishmen Bishop and Fortescue, and the French Benedictines Cabrol, Férotin, and Leclercq. The last mentioned published, in 1907, the *Dictionnaire d'archéologie chrétienne et de liturgie,* followed by the *Dictionnaire d'histoire et de géographie ecclésiastiques* in 1912. The appearance of new journals was another sign of the scholarly activities in these difficult years. Worth noting are the historical journals, such as the *Zeitschrift für schweizerische Kirchengeschichte* (1907), the *Revue d'histoire de l'Eglise de France* (1910), the *Archivum franciscanum historicum* (1908), and the *Archivo iberoamericano* (1914), but also strictly theological journals such as *Theologie und Glaube* (1909) of the Philosophical Theological Institute of Paderborn; but above all, the *Revue des sciences philosophiques et théologiques* (1907) of the French Dominicans of Le Saulchoir,[42] and the *Recherches de science religieuse* (1910) of the Jesuits of the province of Paris.[43]

The modernists had posed real problems for discussion, problems that could not be solved by merely condemning modernism. After all, they questioned the relationship between theology and its sources (the Bible, documents of the old tradition, decisions of the ecclesiastical teaching office) and the nature of their homogeneity with divine revelation, down to its technically most sophisticated form.

Of the few theologians trying to find a positive answer to the questions raised by Loisy, Tyrrell, and Le Roy, two merit special mention: Father de Grandmaison, S.J.,[44] who, in this difficult time, helped with his moderate and reasonable (in the opinion of Blondel and Loisy) articles to lead the confused public through the treacherous cliffs of modernism and integralism, however without totally penetrating the problems; and primarily Professor Father Gardeil, O.P.,[45] who, despite his limitations, appears more and more as the forerunner. His influence was initially confined to France, but later, thanks to his students, radiated far beyond French borders. His work reached a peak in the two studies of apologetic and theological methodology long to remain classics: *La crédibilité et l'apologétique* (Paris 1908, second completely revised edition: 1910),

---

[42] Cf. M. Jacquin, *RSPhTh* 40 (1956), 632–35. Concerning the leanings of this school, that was first inspired by Father Gardeil and later by Father Lemonnyer, cf. M. D. Chenu, *Une École de théologie, le Saulchoir* (Kain, Étiolles 1937).

[43] Cf. J. Lecler, *RSR* 48 (1960), 7–39.

[44] Regarding Léonce de Grandmaison (1868–1927), director of the *Études* and founder of the *Recherches de science religieuse,* see J. Lebreton, *Le P. L. de Grandmaison* (Paris 1932). His main articles are compiled in the volume *Le dogme chrétien. Sa nature, ses formes, son développement* (Paris 1928).

[45] Regarding Ambroise Gardeil (1859–1931), see H. Gardeil, *L'œuvre du P. A. Gardeil* (Paris 1956). Also R. Aubert, *Le problème de l'acte de foi* (Louvain ²1950), 393–450; M. D. Chenu, *RSPhTh* 40 (1956), 645–52; Y. Congar, *DThC* XV, 443.

which became the object of vehement controversies, above all on the part of Blondel; and *Le donné révélé et la théologie* (Paris 1910), a study intended to resume the work done by Cano regarding the problems of the beginning of the twentieth century. Germany and Austria, the first to deal with historical theology, did not contribute a lot to these methodological discussions. Highly respected at that time, the work of the Viennese Professor Commer or that of the Jesuit C. Pesch (for example his *Theologische Zeitfragen,* 6 vols., 1910/16) seems very disappointing today. The contribution of the Latin countries was practically nonexistent.

Integralism

Hand in hand with the suppression of modernism by Church authorities went a campaign of denunciations that increased throughout the pontificate and poisoned the atmosphere of its last years. It may seem peculiar that this campaign unfolded from the very moment when modernism, after the condemnations of 1907, seemed to be in the process of decline. One of the most active early proponents of orthodoxy, A. Cavallanti,[46] explained this fact in the following manner: "Arianism, Pelagianism, and Jansenism, having disappeared after their condemnation by the Church, left a trail of errors even more subtle and less obvious than that of modernism, errors that became known as semi-Arianism, semi-Pelagianism, and semi-Jansenism. Likewise, today, modernism, fatally exposed, has left after its departure other kinds of errors, sprouting all over like seeds and threatening to ruin, or ruining, many a good Catholic. . . . I repeat, there is a semimodernism that, although not as ugly as its antecedent, is much more deceptive and insidious, a modernism that proposes to be a synthesis of all heresies."[47]

Where did "semimodernism" begin? And where, moreover, did the "modernistic tendencies" and the "modernistic mental constitution," as the *Corrispondenza romana* called it, begin? The danger of abuse was particularly great because most of these irresponsible censors were not very competent in the area of theology and especially in the field of exegesis. Furthermore, they belonged to those minds who are completely indifferent to foreign ideas. Several months after the publication

[46] Concerning him, see *CivCatt* (1917) III, 370; also É. Poulat, *Intégrisme,* 434–37.

[47] Lecture of 16 November 1908, summarized in *La critique du libéralisme* 1 (1908–09), 421–23. On 5 February 1909, the *Corrispondenza Romana* wrote similarly: "Today, the danger lies in propaganda trying to be modern rather than in the radically modernistic propaganda." In 1913, Msgr. Benigni protested against those people who wanted to reduce modernism to its most radical form, stating: "As if fever is only present when forty degrees centigrade are measured" (quoted by É. Poulat, *Intégrisme,* 340).

of *Pascendi,* Cardinal Ferrari already had to take a strong stance against the excesses, writing in his pastoral letter of Lent: "It is sad that some are obliged, even publicly, to act excessively, detecting modernism almost everywhere and denouncing it, and that they even want to suspect men of modernism who are far from it." There was hardly a single Catholic scholar who was not exposed to their attacks in the course of these years, to accusations that violated, in many instances, justice as well as love of one's fellow man. Even many deserving institutes were victims of such regrettable polemics, such as the École Biblique of Jerusalem, the theology faculty of Fribourg (almost suspended by Pius X), the Institut Catholique of Paris, numerous seminaries that had made efforts to improve the quality of studies, and many others.

These zealots have entered history under the nickname of "integralists." They called themselves "integral Catholics": in contrast to the efforts of liberal Catholics and modernists (whom they often threw in one and the same pot) wanting to water Catholicism down, they intended to confirm "the integrity of their Romanism: the entire Roman Catholicism (doctrine and praxis) and nothing but."[48] Whatever their debatable methods may have been, many of them were more than just theologians envious of competitors who might want to deprive them of the favor of the younger generation. In view of the dangers threatening their faith, they simply considered their crusade a sacred duty, and the repeated encouragements they received from the Pope were bound to strengthen their convictions.

On the one hand, the integralists had no scruples over denunciations, clandestine methods, and even espionage;[49] on the other hand, they fought with their visors open: with books and brochures, like those of the Jesuit J. Fontaine, whom É. Poulat considered "a remarkably well-preserved witness of an intellectual species, whose role is supposed to have been important,"[50] and with a series of journals (with rather limited circulations) controlled more or less by the integralists. In Italy, there was the *Unità cattolica,* financially supported by Pius X, *Verona*

---

[48] Declaration of the *Agence internationale Roma* (*AIR*) of 19 June 1913, quoted in É. Poulat, *Intégrisme,* 132. One of the main press channels of the movement, the *Vigie,* wrote on 5 December 1912: "We are integral Roman Catholics, which means that we prefer over everything and everybody not only the traditional doctrine of the Church in regard to absolute truths, but also the directives of the Pope in the area of pragmatic contingencies. The Pope and the Church are one." Poulat pointed out (op. cit., 522) that "the most ambitious successors of Pius X often showed rather less enthusiasm for Leo XIII."

[49] Often covered up by those in high places, as was shown in the Perciballi affair (cf. É. Poulat, *Intégrisme,* 588–89).

[50] *DHGE* XVII, 819–21.

fedele and the *Riscossa* of the Scotton brothers; in France, *La foi catholique* by B. Gaudeau and *La critique du libéralisme* by É. Barbier, both appearing in 1908, *L'Univers,* looking for revival in integralism, and, after 1912, *La Vigie,* both journals dependent on the Assumptionists, thanks to Father Salvien;[51] in Belgium, the *Correspondance catholique* of the lawyer Jonckx; in the Netherlands, *De Maasbode,* whose chief editor M. A. Thomson was the soul of Dutch integralism; and in Poland the *Mysl Katolicka.*

To what extent were all these activities coordinated and directed by one center and what role did the Holy See really play? In view of the fact that the integralists worked partly in the dark, the answer has remained unclear for a long time, especially since the Roman archives were made accessible to the general public with considerable delay. But the curtain was partly lifted in 1921, though under circumstances which did not completely appease the conscientious historians. New information was provided in 1950 on the occasion of the beatification of Pius X. A tremendous step toward the illumination of the situation was recently made by É. Poulat with exemplary professional conscientiousness. He succeed in analyzing the workings of the "international antimodernist secret operations" that had been organized by Monsignor Benigni,[52] a prelate of the secretariat of state: the *Sodalitium Pianum,* often simply referred to by its initials S. P., or by the camouflaging name *La Sapinière,* which Benigni wanted to fortify with an institutional religious basis in the manner of today's secular institutes. After the discovery of 1921 there was a tendency to consider Benigni as the soul of the entire integralist movement; he was supposed to have acted without the knowledge of Pius X, who is said to have known nothing of his often disputable methods. *La Sapinière* was regarded as a pressure group with remarkable but secret powers in the Church. Today the reality appears much more modest and at the same time more official than had been presumed. Except for the *Correspondance de Rome,* which was to provide the world press with religious news written in "the right spirit," the confidential bulletins promulgated by Benigni were but a "cascade of unfortunate attempts," and the S. P. had never more than about fifty members in all of Europe. However, the group was in contact with a

---

[51] Regarding P. Salvien, A.A., whose proper name was Charles Miglietti (1873–1934), and who served the *Maison de la Bonne Presse* from 1896 until 1923, see É. Poulat, *Intégrisme,* 286–87.

[52] Regarding Msgr. Umberto Benigni (1862–1934), raised in the spirit of the "counter-revolutionary" Catholicism of the *Syllabus* and the *non expedit,* who tried with tireless energy to form, together with a few friends, the *dernier carré des incorruptibles,* see *Disquisitio circa quasdam obiectiones . . . . ,* 197–204) É. Poulat, *Intégrisme,* 61–70.

number of individuals who formally did not belong to it, but shared its convictions, mainly with Abbé Barbier and Father Salvien, who had great influence in the *Bonne Presse*. With other opponents of modernism, however, the relations of this group were a lot more reserved. The documents published in the meantime have thrown a completely new light on the often rather fundamental differences separating the minds summarily labelled with the collective term "integralists." Wanting to avoid any kind of political exposure and to move exclusively on religious grounds, Benigni distanced himself from the *Action française* and its members. He considered men like Cardinal Billot and Abbé Gaudeau too soft. He mistrusted Abbé Thompson, the German Kaufmann, and the Austrian Maus. He was on bad terms with Merry del Val, since the secretary of state adroitly applied the brakes to the headlong initiatives of Benigni, who, in turn, charged him with diplomatic restraint.[53] Benigni's relations to the Society of Jesus grew increasingly cooler as well, even though many of its members defended the most traditional positions with narrow-minded intransigence until the end of the pontificate.

In his investigations, É. Poulat succeeded in dispelling the myth about the infamous integralist conspiracy. He discovered that the situation was much more complicated than had been presumed for a long time; mainly, he was able to "reduce the S.P. to its real dimensions" and to prove that the ideological world of integralism went far beyond the circle of the *Sodalitium Pianum* and its sympathizers.[54] It was also proven that there was no longer a reason to maintain that Pius X had no knowledge of Benigni's activities. It is certain that the Pope supported *La Sapinière* and that he not only knew of the activities of its founders, but also approved and encouraged them. Benigni informed him daily through Monsignor Bressan and was regularly ordered to make delicate inquiries. It also seems to be obvious that the Pope never reprimanded Benigni seriously for the manner in which he conducted the tasks entrusted to him, as he had often done with other militant integralists, for example in the case of Abbé de Töth of the *Unità cattolica;* and that he

[53] After analyzing the new documents, Poulat came to the following conclusion: "We definitely must relinquish the fairy tale: Benigni, the man of Merry del Val; the secretary of state who tries to persuade a good and devout Pope, having given him the reins, to be unyielding" (op. cit., 77).

[54] It is easy to forget that the initiative for these sanctions did not always come from Rome. M. Bécamel recently demonstrated this (*BLE* 72 [1971], 258–88) in regard to the recall of Msgr. Batiffol from his post as rector of the Institut catholique of Toulouse in 1907: mainly responsible for this were the archbishop and his entourage (pressured by the local reactionary circles). See also J. Daoust, *MSR* 9 (1952), 251–62, regarding the role that the archbishop of Rouen, Msgr. Fuzet, played (his campaign against Msgr. Baudrillart was not approved by Pius X).

personally covered up a sort of ecclesiastical secret police, one which does not seem permissible to us today,[55] but which he appears to have deemed justified in view of the dramatic situation that he felt the Church was entangled in.

The integralistic reaction reached its climax during 1912 and 1913. In 1912, Father Lagrange, among others, was forced to leave Jerusalem, and the *Revue biblique* almost had to cease its publication.[56] At the beginning of 1913, the entire fifth series (1905–13) of the *Annales de philosophie chrétienne* was put on the Index, a measure that was intensified a few weeks later when its director, Father Laberthonnière, was prohibited from publishing anything whatsoever, without being given the opportunity to defend himself.[57] The same decree of 5 March 1913 had also put the *Sainte Chantal* of Abbé H. Bremond on the Index, a condemnation which was less serious, but nonetheless significant. Bremond also attempted a renewal in the field of hagiography, that is, he wanted to replace the traditional picture of a saint with a human face, but now, every attempt at renovation was suspect; this attitude applied not only to areas directly involving the faith but also to the manner of representing Church history or the life of the saints, if these manners were inspired by "secular methods." The Bollandists narrowly avoided condemnation[58] (something Monsignor Duchesne failed to accomplish), only because of the powerful protection of Cardinal Mercier.

For the integralists, the danger of innovation and secularization did not exist only in the fields of exegesis, theology, philosophy, or Church

---

[55] We may assume that he did not know everything and, "had he been better informed, would have objected to certain measures." If one were to appraise Pius X's course of action in the suppression of modernism, certain distinctions would have to be made. First, in regard to time: during the first few years of his pontificate he was intent on not annoying those people who deserved, in his opinion, a reprimand (see, e.g., the letter of 1906 quoted in P. Stefanini, *Il card. Maffi* [Pisa 1958], 277). From 1910 on, the anxiety which permeated his life ("the error spreading these days is much more murderous than that of Luther," he wrote in 1911 to Msgr. Bonomelli [*Dal Gal, Il papa S. Pio X,* 183]), compelled him to present himself more and more uncompromisingly and to extol the opinion that "the danger of the evil justified the extraordinary means" (É. Poulat, *Intégrisme,* 218). By the way, Pius X tried to respect the rights of the bishops as much as possible (several times, he charged the integralists with not taking them sufficiently into account). On the other hand, he had a very authoritarian concept of the rights of the hierarchy in regard to the common priests: This explains the often harsh procedures against them when he was of the opinion that he had to defend sound dogma.

[56] See the autobiographical pages entitled *L'année terrible* in *Le P. Lagrange au service de la Bible,* 200–15.

[57] Some details in A. Blanchet, *Histoire d'une mise à l'Index,* 149–55. The dossier that resulted in the condemnation had been handed in by the *Action française.*

[58] An encyclical of the Congregation on Studies announced that the *Légendes hagiographiques* of P. Delehaye were not to be used in Italian seminaries.

history, but also in the area of relations between the Church and society, at that time called "sociology." In the efforts of the Christian Democrats, no matter of what persuasion, they saw the spirit of liberal Catholicism, stigmatized by Pius IX in the *Syllabus,* revived in a new version. Unfortunately, they made no distinctions between men like Murri, the French *Abbés démocrates,* the *Sillon* group or the trade-union headquarters in Mönchen-Gladbach. The program, presented to the collaborators of the *Sodalitium Pianum,* climaxed in the following declaration: "We are opposed to the exploitation of the clergy and the Catholic Action with the intention of luring them from the sacristy and rarely allowing them to return."[59] At first glance, one may be surprised at such a viewpoint when observing that several integralistic leaders, such as Benigni in Italy, Maignen in France, Decurtins in Switzerland, and many others had been ardent admirers of *Rerum novarum.* But it is precisely Leo XIII's first program of social Catholicism to which they remained loyal. In this program, the Pope expressly contrasted, for the benefit of the bourgeois world which had emerged from the revolution of 1789, the Christian social order resting on Christ's Kingdom over human society to "social atheism." These men charged the Christian democrats of the new generation with increasingly using their social concerns and their conviction of the independence of secular life as a pretense to liberate themselves from ecclesiastical tutelage.

These facts, in the context of which the term "pragmatic modernism" was sometimes used, increasingly engrossed the integralists, and, even the Holy See, especially after the condemnations of 1907 had diminished the threat of doctrinaire modernism. It is interesting to find that problems of such a nature were the almost exclusive subject of Benigni's international correspondence, which has recently become available.

Naturally, in the various countries these incidents, labelled "blunders," were more varied than had been the case in regard to the problems of dogma. In Italy, attention was first directed toward the action that Murri and his disciples, who will be discussed in the next chapter, intended to carry on in the political arena. After they had failed and the ecclesiastical authorities had regained control of the Catholic movement, the Catholic press became their main concern. As mentioned in chapter 12, there were two opposing opinions regarding the press: According to one opinion, the Catholic newspapers, under direct control of the clergy, were to be official interpreters of the Holy See's thoughts and to preach to "a peaceful audience of devout citizens" (M. Vaussard) a strict policy of "religious defense," in agreement with the Catholic "thesis" regarding the rights of the Church within society; according to

[59] Quoted in *Disquisitio circa quasdam obiectiones . . . ,* 265–66.

the other opinion, the Catholic press was to try to reach the ear of the upper class, which had largely adopted the liberal concept of society in order to make it familiar with the Catholic viewpoint concerning problems at hand. The controversy was: *stampa di concentrazione* or *stampa di penetrazione*. The Pope preferred the first solution, as represented by newspapers such as *Osservatore Romano* and the *Voce della verità* in Rome, the *Unità cattolica* in central Italy, and the *Difesa* in Venetia. Around 1907, under the direction of a former president of the Catholic movement, Count Grosoli, a society was formed that was generally called *Il Trust*. It published newspapers with other, much less parochial tendencies, such as the *Corriere d'Italia* and the *Avvenire d'Italia*.[60] These newspapers became the target of the integralist groups. Because of one such newspaper, the *Unione* of Milan, a regrettable collision of opinions occurred in 1911 between Pius X and Cardinal Ferrari.[61] On 2 December 1912, the Pope officially condemned the papers published by *Il Trust*.[62]

In France, numerous attacks were launched against "social modernism," supported by the *Action française* and others. Through the assistance they received from Rome, many victims finally succeeded in evading a condemnation, as for example the Jesuits of the *Action populaire*.[63] But there were also rather painful incidents: For example, F. Anizan, the superior general of the Brothers of Saint Vincent de Paul, was denounced in Rome by a priest from his own congregation, and, in 1914, after an apostolic visitation, he and his entire council were suspended from office.[64]

In view of the international interest that the case of *Le Sillon* aroused then and continues to arouse today, *Le Sillon* is still worth a closer look. This movement owes its founding to a few young people who, like many other students, strove for reconciliation between Catholicism and a society indoctrinated by the ideas of 1789. One of these young men was Marc Sangnier,[65] who, having a profound influence on his com-

---

[60] Cf. (A. Giorgi), *G. Grosoli* (Assisi 1960), 83–103; L. Bedeschi, "Significato e fine del Trust grosoliano," *Rassegna di politica e di storia* (1964), 7–24; R. Aubert, "Premessa ad una storia dell' 'Avvenire,'" *Humanitas* 22 (Brescia 1967), 488–512.

[61] Regarding this serious incident that is often quoted as an example of the excesses resulting from the antimodernist suppression, see *Disquisitio circa quasdam obiectiones . . . ,* to be supplemented and refined by the article by M. Torresin, utilizing the diocesan archives of Milan: *Memorie storiche della diocesi di Milano* 10 (1963), 37–304.

[62] *AAS* 4 (1912), 695.

[63] The affair can be recapitulated on the basis of numerous unpublished documents compiled by P. Droulers, op. cit.

[64] Cf. É. Poulat, *Intégrisme*, 419–22.

[65] Regarding Marc Sangnier (1873–1950), see, in addition to the work by J. Caron (cf. biblio., this chap.), M. Barthelemy-Madaule, *M. Sangnier* (Paris 1973).

rades, turned the original study group into an active movement (1899). He took various initiatives which, due to his extraordinary energy and his noble eloquence, were immediately very successful. He founded circles for social studies, in which young intellectuals and young workers got together on a basis of equality. He established institutes which entered into competition with the socialist peoples' universities, and he organized public debates about problems and questions of the day. The movement, thanks to some strong local personalities also invading the provinces, quickly took on the form of a crusade aiming at the re-Christianization of democracy by winning the masses back for the Church and by reconciling the Church with the Republic. At first, the movement kept its distance from the liberal Catholics, being too far removed from the world of the workers, and from the Christian democrats, whom it charged with doing little more than preferring reforms of the institutional order to the more urgent task of morally educating the individual, in whom, assisted by the indispensable intellectual forces, the true spirit of democracy should be developed, without which democratic institutions would be delivered to a disastrous fate. On the one hand, a blustering Messianism was expected to sweep people off their feet through the impact of a charismatic spell, and therefore it was suggested that they be simply assembled in a fraternal community where no rigid organization would be able to suffocate their creative energy. On the other hand, many members patiently and gradually wanted to transfer the Christian ideal to the present social order; the existing organization was to obtain control over the responsibility for leading the state. This difference of opinion caused a serious crisis during 1905. However, the internal disputes did not impair the impact of Le Sillon. A more serious crisis appeared on the horizon after 1906, when the movement began to be active in politics, propagating a program according to which Christians in a pluralistic democratic society were to strive for a particularly strong influence, of course with mutual respect for different opinions. This new orientation changed the denominational group, essentially based on the apostolate, into a movement that invited, often in a rather provocative manner, non-Catholics, Protestants, even freethinkers to participate (Sangnier called this new institution le plus grand Sillon). By necessity, this development had an unsettling effect on the ecclesiastical authorities who tried to keep the Catholic youth under their exclusive control. Young priests and seminarians joining a movement that wanted to constitute itself without any official sanction by the hierarchy posed new problems, especially since many of them utilized Sangnier's declarations about the citizen's freedom of conscience in order to justify their independence from their superiors in other areas as well. Several bishops had already reacted to the new situation in 1907, and from this moment on the Vatican also acted. At first, Pius X had expressed his sympathy for these young Catholics' idealism, oriented toward religious activities; but he grew increasingly uncertain, especially since he was informed rather tendentiously. To be sure, there were incidents that justified concrete charges, such as the relentless criticism with which *Le Sillon* attacked those Catholics who did not share in its enthusiasm for republican democracy, or the intention to declare this democracy an obligation derived from Christian morality rather than the subject of free elections. Carelessness in terminology and Sangnier's increasingly harsh procedures completely compromised the movement. In February of 1909, Cardinal Luçon, the archbishop of Rheims, sent a serious reprimand to Sangnier, which resulted in the intensification of the campaign launched for months against him by the conservative press headed by the integralists. Encouraged by Benigni, Abbé Barbier took great pains to create the suspicion that *Le Sillon* smacked of modernism, since it paid homage to the concept of democratic authority condemned in the encyclical *Pascendi*. On the other hand, Pius X considered the new orientation of *Le Sillon*, with which it wanted to evade the ecclesiastical authority, unacceptable. For the Pope, any plan aiming at a modification of society was a matter of the moral order for which the Church alone was responsible. On 25 August 1910 he sent a letter to the French episcopate,[66] in which he defined three kinds of errors on the basis of authentic Sillonist texts, which had been frequently "distorted or simplified" (J. Caron) because they were taken out of their objective or historical context: 1) statements that are not in agreement with the traditional Catholic doctrine of society, since they are reminiscent of the "theories of the so-called philosophers of the eighteenth century, of the Revolution, and of liberalism, which had been often condemned"; 2) an illegitimate demand for autonomy from the ecclesiastical hierarchy in regard to areas belonging to the realm of morals, a demand worsened by the eclecticism of the alliance with non-Catholics;[67] 3) finally, as a consequence of this work, "promiscuity": modernist infiltrations which would compel the Sillonists to forget Christ's divinity and to "speak only of His sympathy for all human suffering and His urgent appeals to love thy neighbor and to practice brotherhood," and which would result in the Sillonists form-

[66] *AAS* 2 (1910), 607–33. Regarding the sources on which these documents seem to rest, cf. J. Caron, op. cit., 707–11.

[67] As a practical solution, the Pope demanded the division of the movement into strictly denominational diocesan groups subject to the bishop. M. Sagnier and his friends submitted without any reservation. However, the suggested solution resulted in the disappearance of the very element that had made the movement so original. Consequently, it quickly faded away.

ing only "a scarce tributary to the great flow of apostasy which had been organized in all countries for the purpose of establishing a world Church that would have no dogma, no hierarchy, and no rules governing the spirit."

Received with enthusiasm by the entire rightist press, this condemnation was taken by the leftists as a confirmation of the incompatibility of the Church and the modern tendencies within society. This impression was fortified by the fact that numerous influential circles in Rome and Pius X himself were benevolent toward the *Action française,* a royalist group of the extreme right that was led by Charles Maurras and usually supported the integralist opponents of Christian democracy. "It advocates the principle of authority, it defends the order," the Pope told the Catholics of the left who saw the *Action française* as an un-Christian conception of the state, aimed at elevating the reason of the state to the ultimate value. The Pope was grateful to Maurras for his sarcastic assaults on the kind of democracy perpetuated by the anticlerical parliaments of France and Italy and he was grateful that he had created a "teaching chair for the *Syllabus*" in order to preach a counterrevolutionary concept of society based on tradition and the hierarchy. He even went so far as to call this agnostic "a good defender of the Holy See and the Church,"[68] without taking into consideration the fact that Maurras had praised the Catholic Church for having succeeded in moderating the destructive content of the message of the "Hebrew Christ" through wisdom derived from ancient Rome. In 1913, after another offensive against Maurras that was supported by several bishops, "leading personalities" interceded with the Pope, presenting the denunciations as "a trap set by the demo-liberals." Nevertheless, after initial hesitation, the Pope sent Maurras's works to the Congregation of the Index; yet, though the congregation unanimously agreed on a condemnation (26 January 1914), he did not issue it,[69] because he was afraid that a condemnation of the journalist who, in his opinion, was one of the strongest opponents of the modernists and the anticlerical groups, would only serve their cause.

Germany, scarcely affected by the modernist crisis in the true sense of the word, did not have to suffer too much from the antimodernist reaction on a doctrinal level, even though some Catholic scholars were

---

[68] But not a defender "of faith," as C. Bellaigue had written absentmindedly. He postdated by one year the declaration delivered on 6 July 1913 (cf. A. Ansette, *Études* 279 [1953], 391–92).

[69] See the content of the dossier in the *Index librorum prohibitorum*, ed. of 1930, pp. XXVIII–XXXI. Concerning the condemnation, see A. Latreille, *Cahiers d'histoire* 10 (1965), 388–401.

subject to measures which hardly seem justified today.[70] In the last years of Pius X's pontificate, Germany was violently shaken by integralist assaults of a political and social nature. Details about the so-called Center controversy and the opposition crystalizing after 1904 within the trade unions will be discussed later (chap. 35). This opposition was dealing with tensions between the Berlin group that had remained loyal to the old formula of the Catholic worker association and the much stronger Cologne group demanding interdenominational trade unions that would be willing to cooperate with the Socialists to defend professional interests. This double conflict required a fundamental decision as to what extent the laity was able to take on responsibility for its activities in the secular realm without the hierarchy's intervention. The integralists were convinced (and Pius X agreed) that religion was indeed the foundation of social order. Therefore, if one were to solve the political and social problems outside of the control of the ecclesiastical authorities, one would question the traditional concept of the "Christian civilization" and thus run the risk of committing an error in the area of doctrine. Consequently, the Christian trade unions, organized as they were everywhere in western Europe around the turn of the century, were charged with emphasizing their economic and social tasks instead of their ultimate moral and religious purpose. They were especially indignant about the Cologne group going so far as to organize the defense of the workers on a neutral professional basis, enabling cooperation with non-Catholics and even with Socialists.

On the one hand, Pius X wanted to uphold the principles that, in his opinion, should guide every Christian society, and therefore he assailed the efforts to declericalize secular life. On the other hand, he had to take into account the strength of the Cologne group, which was backed by the majority of the German episcopate and enjoyed the clandestine support of the nuncio in Munich.[71] For those reasons, the entire situation was fundamentally different from that of Le Sillon. Therefore, the Pope looked for a compromise and, in September 1912, issued the encyclical Singulari quadam,[72] unconditionally sanctioning the Berlin

---

[70] When F. Maier accepted the invitation to write the commentary for the first three books of the Gospel for the so-called Bonner Bibel prepared by F. Tillmann, his solution to the synoptic problem was considered daring, and after several fascicles he had to be replaced by another man.

[71] Regarding the mitigating action of the nuncio in respect to the various controversies that had been incited under the flag of the antimodernist reaction (his measures were not always appreciated by many a Roman group), see A. Walz, Andreas Kard. Frühwirth (Vienna 1950), 328–47. Regarding the history of the encyclical, see L. Hardieck, WZ 109 (1959), 169ff.

[72] AAS 4 (1912), 657–62.

proposal, but conceding that the other plan could also be "tolerated" to prevent a more serious malady, that is, thesis and hypothesis. However, this papal intervention did not succeed in easing the controversies raging over several years; on the contrary, it agitated the situation even more, since both parties had reason now to cheer. The conflicts also flared up again in France. There, the integralists took advantage of the encyclical, using it to revive their assaults against Christian democracy.[73] Then the *Civiltà cattolica* published two articles by P. G. Monetti,[74] a theologian to whom the Pope liked to listen. These articles were directed against the principle of the trade-union system and culminated in the statement: "It includes many things absolutely opposed to the true spirit of the Gospel, and there is no use in baptizing it Christian; when two terms are so ill-matched, one should not try to combine them." This article was obviously inspired. It was a test, a prologue for a new, much more pointed papal document. This document was intended to warn the Christian trade unions of a development that would drive them gradually away from the social ideology which Pius X considered the only legitimate one, since it agreed with the Catholic concept. However, this was denied by several apologetic historians. Those people, who were convinced that the Pope had been victimized by an obsolete "model" in the sociological sense of the word and was intent on proceeding with the adjustment of the Church to the development of modern society, tried to forestall this new threat. Cardinals Maffi and Mercier, the general of the Jesuits, Fathers Wernz, Toniolo, Harmel, and others discreetly interceded, and Pius X himself finally preferred to postpone the scheduled measures. Thus, the Christian democrats had finally been victorious over their integralist opponents in this "last great battle of the pontificate" (É. Poulat).

At that time, the excesses of the "witch hunt" had gradually caused a resistance that, in contrast to frequent appraisals, did not wait for the pontificate of Benedict XV in order to manifest itself more or less openly.[75] This resistance progressively focused on a few prelates who

---

[73] An official letter by Cardinal Merry del Val to A. de Mun of 7 January 1913 (see R. Talmy, *Les syndicalisme chrétien*, 122–24) was the first success for them; however, during the following months, the tensions eased.

[74] *CivCatt* (1914) I, 385–99, 546–99. Regarding the affair and its consequences, see A. Zussini, *L. Caisotti de Chiusano e il movimento cattolico dal 1896 al 1915* (Turin, 1965), 154–96.

[75] The letters of Msgr. Benigni (published by É. Poulat) clearly show that the integral Catholics grew increasingly anxious about the development of the situation after 1913, and that their encouraging pleas in view of the "liberal" counteroffensive became more and more numerous.

had been concerned for years over the development of the situation and the direction it had taken,[76] and around a number of Jesuits who had anticipated that Pius X's successor was bound to continue this development and that this turn of events also had to be anticipated. Several respected journals of the Society of Jesus such as the *Stimmen der Zeit,* publicly risked protests after 1913,[77] in which Father Lippert brandished the "hunt for heresies" as one of the most regrettable phenomena of the antimodernist reaction. Likewise, the *Civiltà cattolica* published the complaints, issued by Prince zu Löwenstein on the occasion of the Congress of Metz, regarding the assaults of "certain" integralists against the social Catholics.[78] A little later, the French Jesuit journal severely criticized the "denunciations without any kind of discernment."[79] For those who were informed, it was no secret that the Jesuits, reacting in this manner to the excesses of the integralists, were backed by the general of the society and two of his main assistants, Fathers Ledóchowski and Fine.

Pius X, whose bitter complaints about his "isolation" in the struggle on behalf of the integralist orthodoxy can be better understood in this context, did not conceal his dissatisfaction. In October 1913 he had assigned the management of the *Civiltà cattolica* to Father Chiaudano, who wholeheartedly shared his opinion, and of whom the integralist paper *La Vigie* wrote that he would lead the Roman journal back to the "relentless determination" from which it wanted to depart and that he would "revive the beautiful days of Pius IX."[80] The brief addressed to the Society of Jesus on the occasion of the centennial celebration of its restoration did not leave any doubt, by virtue of the indifference with which it was composed, about the Pope's disappointment about the "blunders" with which he felt compelled to charge the Society. It appeared as if he even contemplated relieving Father Wernz of the direction of the Society and replacing him with Father Matiussi, who had

---

[76] Among others, Cardinal Piffl, archbishop of Vienna; Cardinal Amette, archbishop of Paris; most German bishops; Cardinal Mercier, the archbishop of Mechelen; in Italy the Cardinals Maffi, Svampa, Capecelatro, Richelmy, and even the cardinals of the Curia, Casetta, prefect of the Congregation of Studies, and Steinhuber, S.J., prefect of the Index.

[77] 85 (1913), 358–62; cf. 87 (1914), 249–58.

[78] 1913, III, 612. Concerning this intervention of the *Civiltà,* see G. de Rosa, *L'Azione cattolica* II (Bari 1954), 132–38.

[79] "Critiques négatives et tâches nécessaires," *Études* 138 (1914), 5–25. Cf. J. Lebreton, *Le P. L. de Grandmaison* (Paris 1932), 187–93.

[80] Cf. É. Poulat, *Intégrisme,* 335–37. It is remarkable that Pius X, on the occasion of his appointment, expressed the desire that the *Civiltà* should serve as a model to all *sincere et integre catholici* journalists.

close contacts with the integralists.[81] But at this very moment, the almost simultaneous death of the "white Pope" and the "black Pope" brought an end to this particularly painful aspect of the suppression of modernism by the antimodernists.

[81] Cf. G. Cassiani Ingoni, *Vita del P. W. Ledochowski* (Rome 1945), 71–73, and *Disquisitio circa quasdam obiectiones,* 10–11.

The Holy See and the European Governments

CHAPTER 34

The Roman Question and Italian Catholicism
The Non expedit in the Pontificates of Pius X,
Benedict XV, and Pius XI (until 1925)

Giuseppe Sarto, later Pope Pius X, participated as bishop of Mantua and subsequently as patriarch of Venice in the struggle of active integralism regarding the Roman question and the critical, aloof attitude toward the unified Italian state. However, he was quite sensitive toward the basic problems of the political society of Italy being dominated, after the bloody incidents of May 1898 and the King's assassination in 1900, by anxieties, antagonism, and accusations. The Pope was worried that during the elections the Socialists would support the radicals who stubbornly continued their anticlerical campaign, inspired by the Freemasons, and refused to allow the Church to influence social life (education, schools, social welfare, charity) with respect to the essential internal national aspect of the "Roman question." In order to create a counterweight against such alliances between the radicals and the new social forces in the spirit of more open-mindedness for the democratic authorities, but also of a more aggressive laicism, Cardinal Sarto approved agreements for the purpose of defending religious values and institutions, to be concluded with the Liberals on the occasion of the administrative elections. Moreover, in Mantua and Venice, Sarto had an opportunity to observe and appraise personalities, situations, and programs of the militant Catholics, and he did not entirely reject contacts with "transigent" and arbitrating groups.

Also as Pope, Sarto adhered to his guidelines of "conservative reformism" in the face of Catholic activism (Aubert); he was amicable toward the demands of the most ardent activists, but only within clearly defined limits and in a certain framework, thus keeping in check the initiatives and the men who perpetrated them and put them in action. As far as the Catholic movement in Italy is concerned, Pius X forced those men who had supported the policies of Leo XIII to step into the background, and he introduced new methods of government that were oriented toward direct, unbureaucratic relations with the leading figures of the movement and the spokesmen of various factions. These contacts were made via the secretariat of state. Officially, however, the secretariat of state continued to be responsible, even though Pius X knew that its new leader, Cardinal Merry del Val, was not familiar with Italian Catholicism and was primarily anxious to preserve its authority, the discipline, and the direction from above.

In this manner, Pius X mainly preferred the personal leadership of men of his special trust who stood outside of the Secretariat of State and its offices. Among these advisers, some Fathers of the Society of Jesus were given particular responsibility. Moreover, as editors of the *Civiltà cattolica,* they obtained increased influence for this journal by making it the voice of the papacy. These men were Fathers Santi, Passavich, and Brandi. They had direct access to the organization and the successes of the organized Catholics, one of them in regard to Germany, the second one in regard to Belgium and France, and the third in regard to the United States. They were ordered to prepare drafts of papal documents and served as intermediaries between the papacy and the leaders of the Catholic movement, obtaining reports and declarations and passing on suggestions and reprimands.

It was the wish of Pius X as well as his predecessor that the decisions made at the top, according to his concept of papal authority, should emanate from the people; however, the laity and the active circles of the clergy were in disagreement and tried to drive a wedge between the members of the Curia and the Pope himself, causing the official directives to be somewhat contradictory and ambiguous. In 1904 it was decided that the *Opera dei congressi,* celebrating its thirtieth anniversary, be suspended. At the same time, the dependence of the Catholic movement and its organizations on the ecclesiastical authority was increased through instructions for the reorganization of the centralized cadres, based on the encyclical *Il fermo proposito* (11 June 1905).[1] The Pope found himself bitterly disappointed as far as the people and institutions acquiescing in his intentions were concerned.

Also in regard to the formally approved *Non expedit,* Sarto began to introduce innovations; case by case, mitigations and exceptions were permitted aiming at the elimination of radical and socialist candidates. At the general elections, the liberal candidates were supported, provided they had agreed to assent to the demands of the Catholics regarding schools, family (rejection of divorce), and the religious institutions. By backing the liberal deputies constituting the parliamentary majority of Prime Minister Giolitti, Pius X wanted to make a gesture of détente toward the Italian state. In return, he expected some kind of willingness

[1] Text: *Insegnamenti pontifici* no. 4; *Il laicato,* 201–31, nos., 323–74.

to oblige in the Roman question, if only in two respects: in regard to the bilateral regulation of the position of the Holy See in Rome and in regard to a mutual agreement about the definition of the legal status of ecclesiastical institutions in Italy.

However, the expectations were not fulfilled. The prime minister from Piedmont indeed pursued a policy of cooperation, assisted by an obliging parliamentary majority despite opposition throughout the country and in the Chamber of Deputies. He listened to the demands and employed ecclesiastical spokesmen in his service. Yet in regard to relations between Church and state, and consequently the relations to the Holy See, he adhered to the customary attitude. He upheld the theory that state and Church could be compared to parallels determined to run abreast of each other without ever meeting. Therefore, the Vatican also returned to its formal and rigid stance. Concerning the Catholic movement, this resulted in a stronger emphasis of its dependence on the Holy See, but also in an intensification of the public activities of Catholics in the communal administrations and in economic and social organizations (savings and loan banks in the country, worker auxiliaries, emigrant welfare, community halls, the political-religious and popular-polemical press, professional organizations, e.g., of elementary school teachers). All these activities resulted in more and more frequent contacts with the world of politics; in public opinion and in peoples' representations, the programs were synchronized and there were meetings pursuing the goal of exerting pressures on the official authorities in favor of the groups that were represented.

Thus, on the level of administrative elections (which had been strongly supported all along) as well as in the area of "political" elections (handled more indirectly), the problem of elections became the priority of the movement, whereby, aside from the "economic-social union," an "election union" was particularly significant during the preparations for the elections.

One of the last decisions made by Leo XIII was the appointment of a new president of the *Opera dei congressi,* Count Grosoli of Ferrara, a man who was sympathetic toward the ideas of Toniolo and to the demands of youth. As the editor of Catholic daily papers, he was bound to occupy an outstanding position. This meant that Leo XIII had begun to employ more venturesome principles of social democracy, and that he finally regarded as a social movement what had seemed to him to be a religious-clerical movement. At the Catholic Congress of Bologna (November 1903), the new democratic spirit had had an opportunity to assert itself through motions and democratic ballot procedures, persuading everyone that the groups had moved closer and that the progressive ideas and their authors had found followers. This was not the case within the traditional five actions. On the contrary, following Paganuzzi, who had been replaced by Grosoli, the "old ones" had incited an alarmist campaign against the new leadership, and in the following year they succeeded in taking the majority of the central committee of the *Opera dei congressi* away from Grosoli. Nevertheless, the Pope confirmed him; but shortly afterward (19 July 1904), the *Osservatore Romano* disapproved of a letter which Grosoli had sent to the Catholic Committees on 15 July 1904. Referring to the statement that "the matter of absolute, effective freedom and independence from the Holy See was the main goal of Catholic Action," Grosoli had insisted in this letter that the Catholics were subject to the authority of the bishop not only in regard to their religious, but also their economic and social initiatives, and that they were to abstain from political elections. However, significantly evoking their national consciousness and referring to demands regarding changing realities, he said: "Within the inalienable rights of the Holy See, Catholics consider historical epochs and events milestones on a path leading into the future and they are intent to assure that their work, carried on in this life, not be hindered by matters that are dead in the national consciousness."[2]

Grosoli again handed in his resignation, and this time it was accepted. Subsequently, in a letter by Cardinal Secretary of State Merry del Val to the Italian bishops, the *Opera dei congressi* was declared suspended, with the exception of its second section, which was still chaired by Medolago Albani. The Catholic Action was to be dependent on the hierarchy of the Church. It had to relinquish the principle of determining the leadership through elections and to forego regional autonomy, thus returning to rigid Roman centralism and an organization of dioceses. "At general congresses and at smaller meetings, parliamentary procedures had to be abandoned and decisions could no longer be made through plebiscite."[3]

Grosoli did not succeed in persuading Murri to return to the organization and to adopt the guidelines of the *Opera dei congressi*. Through the problems he had raised, he had caused a crisis of conscience among the militant Catholics. This was not only of concern to the organization, its goals and methods, and forced it to decide whether Catholics were to follow the directives of the *Opera dei congressi* or Christian democracy; but it also called into question the validity of the *Non expedit* and the restrictive measures of the Vatican regarding the democratic activity of the Catholics.

At this point in time, in July 1904, the social movement showed a balance that was impressive even after being divided regionally: a total

---

[2] A. Gambasin, *Il movimento sociale . . . ,* op. cit., 552.
[3] Ibid., 552–54.

of 2,432 organizations, 642 of them in Venetia, 677 in Lombardy, 106 in Tuscany, 27 in Umbria, 99 in the Marches, 37 in Latium, 17 in the Abruzzi mountains, 37 in Campania, 17 in Apulia, 5 in the Basilicata, 8 in Calabria, 3 in Sardinia, and 125 in Sicily. These 2,432 organizations consisted of 774 associations established for the purpose of mutual assistance, 21 people's secretariats, 107 productive and consumer-oriented associations, 170 professional unions or workers' associations, 33 farm labor societies, 43 farmers' associations, 29 associations for collective tenants, 69 banks, 855 rural loan associations, 40 workers' banks, 154 cattle insurance federations, and 187 democratic propaganda societies.[4]

The Catholic movement was now facing a dilemma: on the one hand, it had to continue and intensify the multiplicity of social work, and the organizations and their organizers had to take into account the demands raised by the world of workers and farmers. These groups were primarily affected by industrialization, subjected to new living conditions, and repeatedly overrun by crises emanating from the existing world-wide crises. Moreover, the Catholics wanted to establish themselves according to the model of the socialist organizations, trying to show them that Christianity possessed the social strength to liberate the masses from their misery and utilizing all means at their disposal. On the other hand, Catholic activism, by virtue of its loyalty to the Pope, had to follow the papal directives that were spelled out in *Il fermo proposito* of 1905 and in the new "statutes" that had been painstakingly prepared by laymen in 1906. These statutes were the result of intensive consultations with Pius X's advisers and obviously tried to copy many aspects of the Catholic organizations with experience in foreign countries.

The overall structure had been simplified; in place of the five sections of the *Opera dei congressi,* three great national unions were formed. The biggest and most extensive union was the People's Union, comparable to the *Volksverein* of the German Catholics. It consisted of individual members and intended to train them socially and religiously through the traditional values of piety and love. It replaced the first section of the *Opera dei congressi,* unfolding its activities during the Social Weeks, according to the French model. The second section of the *Opera dei congressi* had been essentially retained under the new name Economic Social Union and had the task of educating people as to the principles of an economic order (based on Christian ethics rather than liberalism and socialism) and of creating the appropriate organizations. The activities of the Catholics in the administrative field, gaining more and more significance, were to be furthered and directed by a third organ that was

[4] Ibid., 558.

significantly called the Election Union of the Italian Catholics. In regard to practical procedures, the main emphasis was placed on the disciplinary element, which was to curb the drive toward extensive social action and toward political involvements.

The task of adjusting the movement to these structures and the duty to obey the directives of the hierarchy, without sacrificing its vitality and impetus, were challenges to leaders and groups alike. In the spirit of Murri, the more active and impatient ones among them subsequently broke away from the movement and divorced themselves from the Catholic Action, ultimately joining forces with the radicals and socialists. This precipitated the loss of many members. The most crucial point troubling them was the matter of autonomy. It caused the most tensions, if only because the demand for autonomy included the limitations imposed by the encyclical *Non expedit,* with all its principle and tactical requirements. In 1905, autonomous groups of "Christian democracy" were formed.

In view of the election of deputies in 1904, some people who, like Bishop Bonomelli under Pope Leo XIII, had pleaded for reconciliation with the government, asked the new Pope to cancel the *Non expedit.* They were joined by laymen who were more successful as spokesmen of the well-meaning, yet impatient activists from the provinces. One of them, Bonomi, the future deputy of Bergamo, was also asked to mediate the issue by advisers of Minister President Giolitti and Minister Tittoni, who compared the degree of Catholic voting in the administrative elections to the degree of abstention in political elections and took account of the political strength of the Catholics.[5] In a conference dealing with the *Non expedit,* Bonomi was told by Pope Pius X: "Follow your conscience, the Pope will be silent."[6] Subsequently, the Catholics participated in the parliamentary elections in Bergamo, Cremona, and Milan, gaining several chamber seats for Catholic deputies, thanks to agreements with the Liberals.

On the part of the Holy See, this was a small concession, eventually resulting in the suspension of the *Non expedit.* The Vatican reserved the right to grant dispensations whenever the bishops deemed them necessary and demanded them. This was a consequence not so much of sympathy with the Liberals as of fear of the advancement of socialism,

---

[5] At the supplementary elections in Bergamo in June 1904 under the regime of the *Non expedit,* 2,465 had voted in favor, 3,875 had withheld their vote; the radical candidate, with the help of the Socialists, had received 1,330 votes, and the moderate candidate 924. Cf. D. Secco Suardo, *Da Leone XIII a Pio X* (Rome 1967), 384.

[6] P. Zerbi, *Il movimento cattolico in Italia da Pio IX a Pio X. Linee di sviluppo* (Milan 1961), 85.

which was considered a threat to the religiosity of the people and to the stability of the foundations of the Italian state, a state that was now felt to be stable and in need of protection from the turmoils of revolution.

The Catholic movement continued to take a defensive stance. It protested against any kind of assault on the authority and reputation of the Church, as well as on the religious convictions and customs of the common people. It charged liberal principles with such assaults and showed its strength in unanimous cooperation with the Pope. Not without tensions, this strength consisted of several factors, such as class identity, the progressive ascent of the lower classes, religious devotional enthusiasm, and the pastoral policy of the hierarchy. The leadership was dominated by those who loyally upheld the faith and wanted to lead it to victory. These factors also affected the political action in regard to its spiritual as well as its practical application. In regard to political activity, which was particularly emphasized under Pius X through the mitigation of the *Non expedit,* the offensive attitude crystallized in various forms; so did the intention to exert influence on the social, economic, and religious structures in the spirit of the Church and according to its requirements.

This line was particularly extolled by the moderate clerical group that was part of the Catholic movement and of the Italian politics dominated by Giolitti and his governmental methods. It had a parallel in the so-called "reformist" tendency of socialism, provided that this kind of socialism wanted to take the democratic route toward the realization of its economic and social goals and distanced itself from revolutionary syndicalism and anarchism. The moderate clerical group was a result of the meetings of Catholics and Liberals that took place under the auspices of the journal *La rassegna nazionale* (founded in 1879), an official mouthpiece of the Catholics favoring reconciliation. Under Pius X this journal was brought into ill repute for its sympathies toward Reform Catholicism. Advocates of an election alliance with the Liberals were conservative "intransigents" who were concerned with the economic and social order threatened by the collectivist program and the syndicalist agitation of the Socialists, as well as with the so-called "progressive intransigents," who felt driven to political action in order to be able to influence the official institutions in the spirit of Christian social ethics. The alliance's criteria pertaining to the characteristics expected of the candidates were defined by the Pope himself in 1908 when he said to the future bishop of Bergamo, Radini Tedeschi: "If they are neither sectarian nor socialist candidates, if they offer sufficient prospects for being elected and pledge to uphold the principles of order and public welfare, they should be supported; if Freemasons, anticlerical, socialist, or even worse candidates run for election, Catholic candidates agreeable to amicable factions should be nominated."[7] These directives can be found in the so-called *Patto Gentiloni,* which was signed prior to the elections of 1913 (the first elections in which all men, i.e., 24 percent of a population that had increased to 36 million, had the right to vote). The *Patto* was given the name of Gentiloni, the current president of the Catholic Election Union. It demanded of the liberal candidates the following: the private educational system is not to be burdened with difficulties; the introduction of religious instruction in community schools is to be favored; the institution of divorce is to be rejected; social legislation is to be furthered; and the candidate should be concerned with representing the Catholic professional associations in governmental employment bureaus. Customary defensive concerns took precedence over the social program. This reflected consideration for the liberal allies, as was demanded by the conservative wing, but not condoned by the Catholics, who had a socially more progressive attitude. Gradually the Christian trade-union system, supported by laymen and young priests, made itself felt through unions of farm laborers and of male and female workers, especially in the textile factories of northern Italy, who were accustomed to agitations for wage demands and knew how to use strikes as a weapon. Thanks to the Gentiloni pact, thirty-three Catholic representatives moved into Parliament and, no less significant, about two hundred deputies of the government party were elected due to the votes of Catholics.

Several Catholic groups in the southern part of Italy leaned toward political action as a natural consequence of the social movement, yet were predisposed against an alliance with the Liberals. Their spokesman was a Sicilian priest, Don Luigi Sturzo (born in 1871 in Caltagirone), who justified the opposition of the Catholics against the lay state based on dissatisfaction with the economically disadvantaged south, which was dominated by shrewd businessmen. Sturzo's restraint toward the liberal state rested on the fact that this state was engaged by Giolitti for the purpose of power in a system of business interests and such corruption that the prime minister from Piedmont was named "minister of corruption" by Socialists who also came from the south. Out of opposition against this centralistic, bureaucratic state, Don Sturzo recommended furthering the local autonomy of the communities and counties under the regime of the *Non expedit.* Wishing greater regional autonomy, he actively worked toward this end by founding, for instance, an association of communities.[8] According to his intentions, the incorporation of

---

[7] D. Secco Suardi, op. cit., 558.

[8] Cf. L. Sturzo, *"La croce di Constantino." Primi scritti politici e pagine inedite sull'azione cattolica e le autonomie communali, a cura di G. De Rosa* (Rome 1958), (cf. above all 263–300, *Il programma municipale dei cattolici*).

Catholics into political life was to proceed in an autonomous manner, and one was to work towards the goal of "preparing with restraint." This goal was reached in 1919 with the founding of a nondenominational (formally not subject to the hierarchy) Italian People's Party (*Partito Popolare Italiano*).

Murri proceeded from a different position, totally rejecting the liberal, lay state and sharing in this regard the ideas of the intransigent circles. However, he soon planned to create, in opposition to the *Risorgimento* government, a political organization within the Catholic movement that was to put into action the Catholic social program by seizing power through elections. In a sensational campaign, Murri, the priest from the Marches, rejected the structural, hierarchical rigidity of the Catholic Action precipitated by the "instructions" of Pius X. Murri founded a denominational Catholic party, the *Lega democratica nazionale*, giving it a program that was aimed not only at a reform of the state but also of the Church. Through this, he risked two condemnations: a religious-political condemnation, following the collapse of Catholic unity, and the dogmatic condemnation threatening him as a disciple of modernism. With the support of the radicals, Murri was nominated as a parliamentary candidate. But in 1907 he was suspended *a divinis* and in 1909 excommunicated, even though personalities of the Curia, such as Cardinal Agliardi, continued to give him respect and understanding.

This National Democratic League was soon abandoned by intellectuals, trade-union leaders, and members of community and provincial administrations who could not accept Murri's "political modernism." In 1911, supported by Don Sturzo, they founded the Christian Democratic League; it was one of the elements from which the Italian People's Party subsequently emerged.

There was another significant meeting between the Catholic movement and political organizations: Catholic personalities and representatives of institutions patronizing the missions and the care of Italians in foreign countries met with the proponents of the new nationalist tendencies who considered such institutions instruments of national significance to be utilized in the age of colonialism for purposes of foreign politics. This resulted in the furthering of several Catholic works that were concerned with religion and culture in foreign countries and especially with the care of Italians who had emigrated to North and South America (in 1911 alone, the number of emigrants amounted to over half a million). The consequence of this were closer relations between Catholic leaders and the *Risorgimento* state.

Nevertheless, the active Catholics were still distrustful of and disappointed with the Italian state. The religious-social efforts of the Catholics encountered resistance and the Giolitti government was determined to keep the Catholics, in contrast to the Socialists, from advancing in politics. Therefore, it avoided making concessions to the Vatican that could have compelled Pius X to give the activity of the organized Catholics more leeway. The conciliatory gestures of the bishops and Catholic organizations on the occasion of the fiftieth anniversary of the unified state in 1911 entailed reprimands of the Vatican that sounded almost intransigent.

The Catholic movement had in the meantime invaded the cultural realm. In academia, it was represented by Toniolo and Contardo Ferrini, professor of Roman law, who was sympathetic to the Milan circles, as well as by the philosophers Petrone in Naples, Acri in Florence, and Bonatelli in Padua. Highly respected even in university circles were the conciliatory Cardinal Capecelatro, the astronomer Cardinal Maffi of Pisa, and Monsignor Talamo who was trying to establish contact between the Neo-Thomist renaissance and social studies in the *Rivista internazionale di scienze sociali*. Finally there was the young biologist Agostino Gemelli, who had converted from militant atheism to become a Franciscan friar. After 1909, he emphasized that the Catholic movement must also permeate the universities, thinking of his own plan of a Catholic university which he indeed founded in 1921. The problems of religious consciousness appeared also in literature committed to the cause, such as in novels by Fogazzaro, or works by poets such as Giulio Salvadori, and they found expression in avant-garde journals of the early twentieth century like *La voce* and *L'acerba* of Papini and Prezzolini. The plea for a merging of modern culture and Christianity in the area of historical studies and Scriptural exegesis grew increasingly more intense within the circles of the movement. The most representative groups were those of Buonaiuti, Genocchi, and Fracassini in Rome and the Milan group gathered around the journal *Il rinnovamento* and including T. Gallarati Scotti, A. Casati, and A. Alfieri, who were in contact with the Barnabite Father Semeria and Bishop Bonomelli.[9] However, this cultural orientation of the Catholic movement fell victim to the suppressive measures against antimodernism because it was reminiscent of concepts that were condemned by the encyclical *Pascendi*. The Catholic movement for decades to come was affected by these steps.

As the Catholic movement knew how to interpret the currents in the educated classes as well as in the masses, it succeeded in assuming leadership in the social and political upswing. From then on, its own development coincided more and more with the history of Italy as it emerged from the *Risorgimento*. Its exponents in both chambers, in the

---

[9] N. Raponi, *T. Gallarati Scotti tra politica e cultura* (Milan 1971).

administrative bodies, in the press, in the pastoral management of dioceses and parishes soon faced the world conflict that confronted Italy with a choice between war and peace. At first, the Catholics were inclined toward neutrality, in part because of solidarity with the new Pope, Benedict XV (Della Chiesa), who decisively announced his neutrality. People who played an outstanding role and circles that were politically most committed, especially those who were close to the nationalists, were carried away by the appeals to intervene in the war and to fight on the side of the Allies against the Central Powers, on the grounds that this would bring about the completion of national unification. Remembering the spirit of the *Risorgimento,* the Catholics found intervention in the war to be an opportunity to prove their loyalty to the state. The government soon realized the political weight of the practicing Catholics and took their representative Filippo Meda into the Boselli Cabinet (1916).

In August 1917 the Pope called for a peace that would know neither victors nor vanquished, terming war "a senseless slaughter." This reflected negatively on the Catholics and raised doubts about their loyalty, even though, in agreement with the attitude of the Holy See (declarations of Cardinal Secretary of State Gasparri in 1915), they had rejected attempts of foreign powers to raise the Roman question to an international level.

Willing to deal with the problems of the postwar years pertaining to religious, moral, and socio-political issues, the exponents of the Catholic movement in 1919 founded the Italian People's Party (*Partito popolare italiano*). They approached the problems at hand with a concept of state and society that had matured in the course of their study of the struggles and experiences of the previous four decades.[10] With the approval of the Holy See, the party declared itself "non-denominational," thus removing the last obstacle set up by the *Non expedit.* As a result of Catholic Action under the direction of the bishops, the various Catholic organizations were able to pursue their responsibilities to the different sectors of religious education and culture. Members of the People's Party were all Catholic representatives, the leaders and active members of Catholic societies and "white" trade unions. From this time on, their influence was obvious. It was not coincidental that this very same year, at the Peace Conference of Paris, the first deliberations over negotiations regarding the Roman question took place between Prime Minister Orlando and Monsignor Cerretti.[11] These talks were interrupted by the

[10] St. Jacini, *Storia del Partito Popolare Italiano* (Milan 1951).
[11] Cf. E. Orlando, *Su alcuni miei rapporti di Governo colla S. Sede* (Rome 1930); F. Margiotta Broglio, *Italia e S. Sede dalla granda guerra alla Conciliazione* (Bari 1966), 43–58 (political and juridic aspects).

government crisis and the stubborn resistance of certain anticlerical elements.

The success of the Catholics, due to the proportional representation of 1919 in the elections (the People's Party furnished over one hundred deputies), gave the Catholics a very strong position and the equally responsible task of aligning the parliamentary majority behind the government in the event of a major economic and political crisis. At the same time, in complete independence, the "white" trade-union organization unfolded, but not without slogans of class struggles and a radicalism that negatively affected the People's Party and relations to the hierarchy. The Catholics had to accept sharing the responsibility for the government in an atmosphere that was tense because of the emergence of new political forces and factionalism, which prevented the emergence of any dominant majority. In the elections of 1921, under Prime Minister Giolitti, the People's Party refused to enter into agreements with the liberal government party. Strengthened (with 107 deputies), it returned to the chamber and forced a compromise regarding a temporary government that was rejected by Giolitti. Pressured, on the one hand, by socialists who had in mind the model of the Russian proletarian dictatorship and, on the other hand, by Fascist combat veterans who were soon assisted by the economic and political right wing, a government crisis emerged in which Catholic solidarity broke down. The conservative faction that had allies in the hierarchy and even in the Vatican, refused to align itself with the Socialists in Parliament, instead pressing for the acceptance of the alliance offered by the Fascists and their supporters. The Fascist program had, on the one hand, antidemocratic and nationalistic features, but was, on the other hand, ill disposed toward the Freemasons and benevolent toward the institutions and personalities of the Church.

Under the new Pope, Pius XI (Ratti), who was raised in a middle class and tolerant environment, the Vatican lessened the impact of the coup d'état of October 1922, legalized by King Emmanuel III, and allowed the formation of a wing of "national" Catholics in the People's Party that favored the new political course. Leaders of this wing joined Mussolini's "national" government in 1922.

The revision of the anticlerical traditions of the *Risorgimento* state had been initiated by the Catholics; the Italian People's Party had continued it systematically through legislation and administrative measures. However, now it seemed as if the renovation in important areas was conducted by forces that were unrelated to the Catholic movement or actually stood in opposition to it. Thus it was Mussolini's government that had the Cross installed in schools and courtrooms, reintroduced religious instruction in elementary schools, made denominational schools equal to public schools, officially recognized the Catholic University of Sacro Cuore in Milan, increased the state subsidies for the salaries of the clergy, exempted the higher clergy from military service, increased state subsidies for ecclesiastical buildings, paid greater respect to Church dignitaries, and participated in the great religious celebrations. The new government was also willing to revise the legislation regarding the Church system according to the wishes expressed by the clergy. In view of these concessions offered to Church life in Italy, the Holy See simply consigned the People's Party to the fate of an opposition party, its purpose, in the eyes of the Vatican, having been the political defense of religious ecclesiastical interests. Its leader, Don Sturzo, was asked to resign. In his capacity as priest, he was not to give rise to misunderstandings but clearly demonstrate that the Vatican, despite the opposition of the People's Party, took a benevolent and reserved stance toward Mussolini's government.

The maintenance of religious ecclesiastical interests toward the state was assumed by the hierarchy, and the new government indicated that it preferred to deal with ecclesiastical authorities rather than the representatives of an opposition party. But the attitude of the Holy See was not without reserve. In 1924, for the benefit of Mussolini's government, the Pope reprimanded the anti-Fascist collaboration between the *popolari* and the Socialists that resembled the collaboration between the Center Party and the Social Democrats in the German Empire and specifically in Prussia, but distanced himself from the government by condemning the Fascist violence that was perpetrated on individuals and institutions of the Catholic Action and by voicing his objections to the new totalitarian trade-union legislation, which resulted not only in the termination of the People's Party but also in the end of the Catholic workers' movement. When Minister A. Rocco set up a commission for the reform of the law on ecclesiastical matters, to which, with the tacit agreement of the Holy See, three clergymen were to belong, the Pope personally emphasized (in an address on 18 February 1925) that no decision by this commission could be accepted as long as the Roman question was not solved, whereupon the Minister announced (May 1925) that the problem would be taken up again on "a broader basis."

This implied a confirmation of the *Non expedit,* i.e., of papal control over Italian politics. This resulted in a new climate for a bilateral examination of the Roman question, which was regularized eventually in the Lateran treaties of 1929. In the meantime, directly through the bishops, the Holy See intensified its influence on Catholic attitudes and institutions. Even the structure of the Catholic Action underwent a reform that on the basis of a *Non expedit* emanating from the other side limited the Catholic movement. But the Catholic movement continued to exist, though with somewhat abated energy, especially among the youth and the student associations which were willing to offer resistance to the harassments of the government and Fascist violence. Dissatisfaction with and accusations against the hierarchy even reached the Lateran treaties,[12] which introduced (in a certain sense) yet another phase in the Catholic movement of Italy, the phase of reconciliation (*Conciliazione*), which was interpreted and experienced in different ways.

[12] Cf. G. L. Ferrari, *L'azione cattolica ed il regime, edizione postuma a cura di E. Rossi* (Florence 1956), and shorter: M. Bendiscioli, *La politica della S. Sede 1918–1938* (Florence 1939), 74ff. Its thirtieth anniversary served as an occasion to critically review the *Conciliazione*. Significant is the contribution of the Oratorian from Brescia, Cardinal G. Bevilacqua, "Trent'anni dopo i patti lateranensi," *Humanitas* (February 1959), 182–90.

CHAPTER 35

German Catholicism between Kulturkampf *and World War I*

In 1886/87, peace[1] in the matter of Church policies was restored, and until the end of the Empire it would not be seriously questioned. Bismarck's successors Caprivi (chancellor of the Reich from 1890 until 1894), Hohenlohe (1894–1900)[2] and Bülow (1900–09) successfully wooed the Center Party; Caprivi, who tried to alleviate the internal tensions that had built up under Bismarck, made concessions to Poland. In 1891, a Polish prelate, Florian von Stablewski (1841–1906),[3] who was committed to his nation, was assigned the episcopal see of Gnesen. Some of the severities of the retained sections of the *Kulturkampf* legislation were moderated. In 1890 the Expulsion Law was repealed and the exemption of theologians from active military duty was granted. In 1891 the Prussian dioceses were repaid the funds that had been suspended during the *Kulturkampf*. In 1894 the Redemptorists and the Holy Ghost Fathers, who had also been included in the Jesuit Law, were allowed to return; however, the efforts of the Center Party regarding the suspension of this exception law were only partially successful: In 1904 at least ARTICLE 2, which had permitted the internment and expulsion of individual Jesuits, was stricken.[4] In 1902 a Catholic

[1] Cf. chap. 3, pp. 70–73.
[2] Cf. chap. 1, p. 34.
[3] H. K. Rosenthal, "The Election of Archbishop Stablewski," *Slavic Review* 28 (1969), 265–75.
[4] Regarding the arguments about the Jesuit law continuing into the last phases of the Empire, see B. Duhr, *Das Jesuitengesetz* (Freiburg 1919).

theological faculty was established at the Imperial University of Strasbourg. It soon received papal approval. However, the resistance of the Liberals to the Elementary School Bill drafted by Minister of Cultural Affairs von Zedlitz-Trützschler (1892) in agreement with the Center and the Conservatives showed all too clearly the limits of the compromise; reverting to the most ardent *Kulturkampf* polemics, this opposition involved the struggle "against the obscurantist spirit" and was finally successful.

In spite of this, the process of normalization was probably furthered by Wilhelm II and Pius X alike. During his thirty years in office, the Emperor stressed in his many often ill-conceived statements the Protestant character of his House and the Empire; but he also found understanding words for the Catholics and for Catholic institutions. He sincerely wished the mitigation of the denominational differences.[5] He was particularly interested in the Benedictine order and the Catholic missions, since they were also useful in terms of colonial policy.

The state's right to participate in the appointment of high Church officials, as well as the election of bishops and the nomination of voting cathedral canons during the "royal" months was still exercised,[6] but the bishops' elections that had burdened the relationship between Church and state until the *Kulturkampf* were not interfered with any longer.[7] The government of Wilhelm II successfully effected the elevation of Prussian bishops to cardinals,[8] and the Emperor himself had a vital interest in the improvement of the German influence in Rome, which

[5] See mainly K. Bachem, *Zentrumspartei* VI, 262–77, and R. Morsey, *Katholiken und Nationalstaat*, 40–43. Not very informative: M. Buchner, *Kaiser Wilhelm II., seine Weltanschauung und die deutschen Katholiken* (Leipzig 1929), and S. Merkle, *Die katholische Kirche: Deutschland unter Kaiser Wilhelm II* III (Berlin 1914).

[6] See mainly N. Trippen, *Erzbischofswahlen in Köln,* 294–463; also: A. G. Scharwath, "Eine staatliche 'Nachweisung' geeigneter Bischofs- und Domherrenkandidaten der Diözese Trier aus dem Jahre 1902," *AMrhKG* 20 (1968), 335–46; G. Knopp, "Kirchliche Personalpolitik im Düsseldorfer Reichspräsidium vom Ausgang des Kulturkampfes bis zum Ende der Monarchie," *AHVNrh* 173 (1971), 157–81; F. G. Hohmann, "Bischofswahlen in Paderborn," *WZ* 122 (1972), 265–82.

[7] Such interventions were initiated by the Curia, which, in the wake of the perfected centralism, tried to limit the chapter's suffrage. This prepared the initiative regarding the law of free papal appointments which the Curia had enacted following the overthrow of the Central European monarchies that had a voice in such matters. In Germany, Nuncio Pacelli participated in this offensive (N. Trippen, op. cit., 448f.).

[8] In 1893 and 1903 respectively, Kopp (Breslau) and Krementz (Cologne) were appointed. Krementz's successor Fischer and von Hartmann were appointed in 1914. In spite of efforts in Berlin, only Krementz's direct successor Hubert Simar was not elevated to cardinal during his short time in office (1899–1902); this was partly due to Leo XIII's impression that his election had been too much influenced by the government (Trippen, op. cit., 294–344).

had always been minor. His wish to have a German cardinal appointed to the curia was not fulfilled, because the Emperor's own adviser on Church policy, Cardinal Kopp, skillfully opposed this plan. Kopp had refused since the conclusion of the *Kulturkampf* to share his role of mediator between Rome and Berlin with anyone.

In spite of concentrating on internal Church reforms, Pius X never neglected diplomacy, and thus he endeavored to establish good relations with the antirevolutionary Empires of Austria and Germany.[9] On several occasions he demonstratively assured Wilhelm II and Bülow, the guarantors of the existing order, of his sympathy, which survived the break of the Center Party with the Chancellor (1906). The Vatican repeatedly confused the political with the ecclesiastical sphere. This was the case when Erzberger and other Center Party deputies criticized the imperial colonial administration, causing a break (that was also provoked by Kopp), and when the Vatican reprimanded them for ingratitude toward the Chancellor, who was friendly toward the Church.[10] Supported by Kopp, Bülow entertained good relations with Rome. All in all, the example set by Bismarck in the septennate controversy continued to have an effect in Berlin: The *Reich*'s government often tried to solicit internal political assistance from the Vatican and to preserve or increase the distance between the Curia and the growing democratic tendencies. Bülow's successor Bethmann Hollweg (after 1909) adhered to the ecclesiastical political balance. A temporary cooling off between Rome and Berlin only occurred because of the backlash that was caused in Germany by the struggle of the Curia against modernism.[11] The efforts of Pius X (less intense than those of his predecessor) regarding the establishment of a nunciature in Berlin were not successful. They failed because of the opposition of the Berlin imperial court and many influential Protestant circles; but Cardinal Kopp and the Center Party, still fearing for their independence, did not want a nuncio in Berlin either.

After the nineties, the German Catholics and their political representatives began to integrate the Church into the national state. In spite of earlier scepticism, Windthorst had made the first steps in this direction. His successor Ernst Lieber (1838–1902)[12] led the party completely out

---

[9] Schmidlin, *PG*, 94ff; cf. also Engel-Janosi II, 55, 149–52.

[10] Cf. *Bülows Denkwürdigkeiten* II (Berlin 1930), 272f.

[11] Only recently, statements by Bethmann and his adviser Kurt Riezler have been discovered that are directed against the Vatican's antimodernism, but favor the Center (K. Riezler, *Tagebücher, Aufsätze, Dokumente,* intr. and ed. by K. D. Erdmann [Göttingen 1972], 170–74).

[12] Biographies by M. Spahn (Gotha 1906), H. Cardauns (Wiesbaden 1927), and K. Wolf, *Nassauische Lebensbilder* 4 (1950); E. Deuerlein, *StL*[6] V, 393f.

of the opposition into which it had been forced during the *Kulturkampf,* making it an indispensable support for the policies of Caprivi, Hohenlohe, and Bülow.[13] In pursuit of this aim Lieber disengaged himself from the governmental minority, consisting predominantly of noblemen from Silesia and supported by Cardinal Kopp, and introduced more national, but at the same time more democratic policies. In the spirit of Windthorst, Lieber's course aimed at strengthening the *Reichstag* and at the complete parliamentarization of the Empire, from which his party could expect the most effective increase of its influence. Moreover, there were tensions among the right wing that had already come to the fore in the trade-union controversy and resulted (after 1918, when the majority of the party had begun to favor the republic) in the migration of the Catholics of the right toward the German Nationals. Following the end of the *Kulturkampf,* the number of Catholics voting for the Center Party slowly and steadily decreased.[14] The essential motives for the existence of the party were no longer valid. Frequently, political and economic interests began to take precedence over the appeal for denominational solidarity.

Peter Spahn (1846–1925), Adolf Gröber (1854–1919), and Georg von Hertling, bourgeois notables like Lieber, continued after his death the policy of "national cooperation." The role of opposition, with which the Center, after the break with Bülow, had to content itself, did not bring a change of course. This break was particularly significant because a new type of leadership emerging from the lower middle class and the workers, exemplified in Matthias Erzberger (1875–1921),[15] began to assert itself.

The Center Party did not only support the social policies of Wilhelm II because they were compatible with its old objectives. Only the Center's approval enabled the enactment of all the great "national" legislative bills, ranging from Caprivi's trade treaties, the Civil Code, and the improvement of the navy, to the imperial budget reforms under Bülow. The sanctioning of Wilhelm II's navy policy was an expression of the unconditional will to fulfill a national duty. This was an understandable reaction to the earlier charges of "hostility toward the Empire," a reaction that reflected the mood of the citizens at that time, yet was doubtful in terms of its impact.[16] Nonetheless, the Center Party on the basis

---

[13] Very extensive presentation: K. Bachem, *Zentrumspartei* VI; summary: R. Morsey, *Katholiken und Nationalstaat,* 48–57.

[14] J. Schauff, *Die deutschen Katholiken und die Zentrumspartei* (Cologne 1928).

[15] K. Epstein, *Matthias Erzberger und das Dilemma der deutschen Demokratie* (Berlin, Frankfurt 1962); R. Morsey, *Zentrumspartei 1917–1923,* passim; id., *StL*[6] III, 36ff.

[16] Equally dubious parallels occurred in France and Italy. The Catholics wanted to prove their patriotism, which was questioned by the majorities in those countries where they

of its experiences collected during the *Kulturkampf* continued to promote civil rights, a significant contribution to the constitutional development of Germany.[17] The Catholic association system, especially the *Volksverein,* also supported the democratization of society.

The Center Party managed to enter "the antechamber of power" by way of its national policy, but it did not proceed further.[18] The leadership positions in the Empire and Prussia remained inaccessible to the Catholics; and also in the other areas of state administration, they were unable to achieve participation on an equal footing.[19] Even in Bavaria it was not until 1912, after forty years of liberal regimes, that Hertling, an exponent of political Catholicism, occupied the highest position of government. Weighty remnants of *Kulturkampf* legislation continued to exist. It was not until 1917 that the Jesuit Law was completely suspended. The Center Party's so-called toleration proposal failed to introduce to the imperial code of law the guarantees for ecclesiastical liberty provided by the Prussian constitution that had been suspended during the *Kulturkampf.* Consequently it also failed in suspending the restrictions to which the Catholic Church in some predominantly Protestant federal states (e.g., Saxony, Mecklenburg, Brunswick) was still subject.[20]

The most prominent figure in the Prussian episcopate until World War I was Cardinal Kopp. It was only in the last years of his life that he was increasingly isolated, mainly because of his inflexibility in the trade-union controversy. The differences between him and the bishops of the Rhineland, a remnant of the last phase of the *Kulturkampf,* had been moderated. After all, the bishops had to concede that the mediation of Kopp, criticized by them, was totally compatible with Leo XIII's

---

were in the minority or had been pushed aside by the recent political development. Therefore, they aligned themselves with the aggressive nationalism that led to World War I.—The problem as a whole needs to be researched. Important information, although treating the German development too isolatedly, is to be found in H. Lutz, *Demokratie im Zwielicht,* 21, 24ff., 33ff., 43–52. Cf. also the collective volume prepared by G. Rossini, *Benedetto XV, i Cattolici e la prima guerra mondiale* (Rome 1963), passim.
[17] Thus, the Center resisted the anti-Semitism invading the right wing. Cf. P. G. J. Pulzer, *Die Entstehung des politischen Antisemitismus in Deutschland und Österreich 1867–1914* (Gütersloh 1966), 219–23, etc.; R. Lill, *Kirche und Synagoge,* ed. by K. H. Rengstorf, and S. von Kortzfleisch, II (Stuttgart 1970), 380–85.
[18] R. Morsey, *Katholiken und Nationalstaat,* 53–56.
[19] Cf. A. Klein, *Die Personalpolitik der Hohenzollernmonarchie bei der Kölner Regierung* (Düsseldorf 1967), 75–114, 125–29.
[20] K. Bachem, *Zentrumspartei* VI, 101–25, 225–35, 291–94. Cf. among the extensive literature of brochures: M. Erzberger, *Der Toleranzantrag der Zentrumsfraktion des Reichstages* (Osnabrück 1906).

intentions. Korum, Kopp's opponent in the game of Church policies at that time, was later to become Kopp's frequent ally. The integralism they had in common brought them together. Kopp's relations with Cardinals Krementz and Antonius Fischer of Cologne (1840–1912, in 1902 archbishop, 1903 cardinal)[21] remained cool, even though both sides were in agreement about most ecclesiastical matters. The archbishops of Cologne and the majority of their suffragans were largely influenced by the Center Party of the Rhineland and the *Volksverein* with its democratic tendencies, as far as their political and socio-political stance was concerned. They also supported the Christian trade unions that had emerged in the nineties from the Catholic workers' associations in western Germany and continued to be backed predominantly by Catholics, though they were interdenominational. The militant atheism of the free (social-democratic) trade unions had caused the formation of the new organization. They enabled the Catholic and Protestant workers efficiently to represent their professional interests while respecting their religious convictions. The workers' associations led by priests now dealt only with the spiritual care of their members. The Christian trade unions employed all means necessary for the workers' struggle, even the strike. But since they only strove for evolutionary improvements rather than revolutionary change of the existing system, they were supported by the Prussian government in many instances. Their public relations were handled by the *Volksverein*. This reformism of the West, often merging with the remnants of critical distance toward the Prussian state, went too far according to Kopp's opinion. He insisted on patriarchal authoritarian concepts and wanted to integrate Catholicism unconditionally into the state of Wilhelm II and its rigid backward social structure. He was assisted by those magnates whose influence on the Center Party's politics was fading. Kopp knew how to deal with the power of the Center. However, his relationship to the party leadership, from which he frequently tried to extricate the representation of ecclesiastical interests in the political arena, was always tense and grew increasingly worse after Erzberger's rise.

In Bavaria,[22] Archbishop Franz von Bettinger of Munich (1850–1917, archbishop after 1909)[23] supported the *Volksverein* and the Christian trade unions. That he did not become cardinal until 1914 was due to governmental doubts about his leanings. The government would have preferred the elevation of the younger, more intelligent and at the

---

[21] Biography by J. Schmitz (Cologne 1915); Trippen, 358–423, etc; J. Torsy, *LThK*² IV, 155.

[22] K. Möckl, *Die Prinzregentenzeit* (Munich 1972), 228–344.

[23] Biography by K. von Preysing (Regensburg 1918); M. J. Hufnagel, *LThK*² II, 323.

same time more conservative Bishop Michael von Faulhaber (1869–1952)[24] of Speyer, who owed his office to royal nomination. Among the bishops of southwest Germany, Paul Wilhelm Keppler (1852–1926, since 1898 bishop of Rottenburg),[25] respected by his contemporaries as a religious writer, must be mentioned. He had inaugurated a constructive biblical and homiletical renewal, but occupied a very conservative position in the controversy over Reform Catholicism. Cultural inferiority, the most crucial inheritance of the *Kulturkampf*, was a heavy burden for the Catholics.[26] That it grew worse for a while had two causes: The perpetuators of the predominantly Protestant or liberal national culture denied the Catholics full participation. For example, academic teaching positions were generally difficult to obtain. Moreover, most Catholics remained, often preferred to remain, in the self-sufficient isolation that they had escaped to from the onslaught of the liberal offensive. The authoritative defensive of papal doctrine that had climaxed in Pius X's struggle against modernism aggravated or hindered the new ideas of the modern world. Thus the German Catholics were initially unable to provide adequate answers to the growing self-criticism of liberalism. Instead, they retreated into a superficial adaptation of the sham culture of the Wilhelmian era. The criticism of capitalism voiced by apologists and social reformers, such as Franz Hettinger, Georg Ratzinger, and Albert M. Weiß,[27] remained defensive and espoused obsolete concepts of society. The anti-liberalism of the convert Julius Langbehn, temporarily supported by Bishop Keppler, contained, aside from the irrationalism and voluntarism which initially affected the developing youth movement, ambivalent elements that appeared in different places around the turn of the century and eventually paved the road for totalitarian ideologies.[28]

Likewise, around the turn of the century, an active minority took up a more adequate rational confrontation with the intellectual forces of the time. The initiatives were provided by the representatives of Reform

[24] M. von Faulhaber was elevated to cardinal in 1921.

[25] A. Donders (Freiburg 1935); A. Hagen, *Rottenburg* III, 94–97, 119–29, etc; P. Bormann, *LThK*[2] VI, 118f; cf. above, p. 428.

[26] Two objective accounts: G. von Hertling, "Der deutsche Katholik und die Wissenschaft," *Jahresbericht der Görres-Gesellschaft für das Jahr 1896* (Cologne 1897); speech of Deputy Fehrenbach at the Catholic Convention in Bonn: 47, 1900.

[27] Well-known works: F. Hettinger, *Aus Welt und Kirche*, 2 vols. (Freiburg [5]1902), *Apologie des Christentums*, 5 vols. (Freiburg [10]1914–18); G. Ratzinger, *Die Volkswirtschaft in ihren sittlichen Grundlagen* (Freiburg [2]1895); A. M. Weiß, *Apologie des Christentums*, 5 vols. (Freiburg [4]1904–08), *Die religiöse Gefahr* (Freiburg 1904), *Liberalismus und Christentum* (Trier 1914). Cf. chap. 12.

[28] Langbehn's main work, *Rembrandt als Erzieher* (Leipzig 1890), had several editions. Cf. O. Köhler, *LThK*[2] VI, 783f.

Catholicism,[29] some of whom, out of opposition to papal centralism as well as to political Catholicism, had ventured too far into nationalism. The most significant contributions were provided by Carl Muth and his friends, who initiated in *Hochland,* founded in 1903, the liberation of Catholic belles lettres from an apologetical and backward-looking parochialism. Their opponent in the ensuing literary controversy was Richard von Kralik, representing the traditional concepts in *Gral.*[30]

The controversy over Reform Catholicism and *Hochland* carried on throughout the last decade led to vehement disputes over the political or denominational character of the Center Party and over the permissibility of interdenominational Christian trade unions.[31] These had partially grown out of older, aforementioned differences, but were also caused by the integralism of Pius X and his disciples. The liberal-democratic "Cologne Faction" and the patriarchal-integralistic "Berlin-Breslau Faction" confronted each other in the "Center Party controversy" as well as in the "trade union controversy." Members of the first group were the West German Center Party with its paper *Kölnische Volkszeitung,* the *Volksverein,* the Christian trade unions, and the West German Catholic workers' associations. A minority was integralist, chiefly the association of Catholic workers' societies, located in Berlin, that claimed to represent their members socio-politically, but actually served the interest of the employers through its patriarchalism and by neglecting to utilize the weapons of the trade unions. Its leaders were Roeren, Bitter, and Duke Oppersdorff (deputies of the Center who later left the party) and von Savigny. The integralists were supported by Cardinal Kopp and Bishop Korum. Through Kopp, as well as through the international organization of Prelate Benigni,[32] they had contact with the Vatican, whose full approval they enjoyed.

The papal historian Ludwig von Pastor, an integralist on friendly terms with Pius X and living in Rome at that time, interpreted the interdependence between the various controversies with the following words: "The controversy between Kralik and Muth dealt with the same question that was the object of the controversy between the disciples

---

[29] Cf. chaps. 29 and 15.

[30] Literature controversy: A. W. Hüffer, *Carl Muth als Literaturkritiker* (Münster 1959); F. J. Schöningh, *StL*[6] IV, 112ff. Cf. also the contributions by F. Fuchs, J. Nadler, M. Ettlinger, P. Funk, and F. Herwig, *Wiederbegegnung von Kirche und Kultur in Deutschland, Festgabe für Carl Muth* (Munich 1927), esp. 38–56, 61–75f., 86–110, 375ff.

[31] Center and trade union controversies most extensively described in K. Bachem, *Zentrumspartei* VII, 156–325. See also Schmidlin, *PG* III, 98–104, 158f., 164ff.; E. Deuerlein, *ThQ* 139 (1959), 40–81; id., *StL*[6] III, 943–46; E. Ritter, *Katholisch-soziale Bewegung,* 313–51; R. Morsey, *Zentrumspartei 1917–1923,* 33–41; É. Poulat, *Intégrisme,* 198ff., 234–44, etc.; O. Schröder, *Aufbruch und Mißverständnis,* 353–68.

[32] Cf. chaps. 33, 490.

and opponents of the *Kölnische Volkszeitung*. Some, and I am one of them, look for salvation in a courageous and frank confession of the Catholic point of view; the others, and Muth belongs to them, want to adapt to the opponent by acquiescing to the utmost. . . ."[33] The implication contained therein is typical of the integralists who thoughtlessly doubted the loyalty to the Church of people who disagreed with them. The leaders of the integralists, especially Benigni and his assistants, were known to have spied on their internal ecclesiastical opponents and to have accused them of heresy. Theological modernism, which developed primarily in France, Italy and England, was condemned in 1907. After this date, they turned their full attention to German developments. The procedures of the Cologne faction were considered just as dangerous as the theological innovations that had not gone quite as far. As a matter of fact, the Center majority pursued the declericalization of public life feared by the integralists, and the objective separation of the spiritual and the temporal. Pius X considered this a serious danger. He insisted that all organizations sustained by Catholics should remain in direct dependence on the hierarchy.

When the Center Party was founded, the leadership and the majority insisted that it be a political party, claiming and obtaining independence from the ecclesiastical authority in political matters.[34] But after Lieber's death, an integralist minority again voiced the demand, favored by the new course Pius X had taken, for more consideration of Catholicism in regard to party policy. In order to counteract this, Julius Bachem (1845–1918), after 1869 editor-in-chief of the *Kölnische Volkszeitung,* in 1906 wrote the famous essay "Wir müssen aus dem Turm heraus," published in the *Historisch-Politische Blätter.* This caused a dispute. Bachem warned against unrealistic conceptions of the Christian state and against abuse of the denominational principle. He demanded political and socio-political cooperation between Catholics and Protestants and the expansion of the party toward an interdenominational Christian people's party. His proposal, based on Windthorst and the tradition of the Center Party and projecting the ideas of Stegerwald and Brüning, became the program of the Cologne Faction. Its forerunners, among them many clergymen, were of the opinion that the Church was to interpret the general norms of morality, but that their actual application to politics and socio-politics was a matter to be dealt with by Catholics versed in these areas. The main paper of the "Cologne Faction," the *Kölnische Volkszeitung,* was supported by most publications of the Center Party, by the *Historisch-Politische Blätter* and *Hochland.*

[33] L. von Pastor, *Tagebücher, Briefe, Erinnerungen,* ed. by W. Wühr (Heidelberg 1950), 508.
[34] Cf. chap. 1, p. 30; chap. 3, pp. 59f., 71f., 74.

The integralists accused the Cologne Faction of curbing papal authority, of wanting to deprive public life of ecclesiastical influence, and of threatening the integrity of Catholic Germany. Some, especially in the Benigni circle, went further. They took up Counter-Reformation slogans, maintaining that the Cologne group was propagating a national Catholicism that would lead to Protestantism. Pastor believed that the Cologne Faction was based on "Gallicanism."[35] Cardinal Kopp, encouraging and supporting the integralist offensive with the increasing stubborness of old age, spoke of the "infestation of the West,"[36] claiming "that *Hochland* was de-Catholicizing the educated classes, while the *Volksverein* was accomplishing the same within the lower classes through its support of the trade unions."[37] All in all, the *Volksverein* and the Christian trade unions were rejected most vehemently because they dealt with tasks the Church was claiming without, however, paying attention to the hierarchy. The trade unions were repudiated because they were interdenominational and used strikes, a weapon that was revolutionary in conservative eyes. The outcome of the dispute would have been clear had it been carried on in Germany only. The great majority of the politically active Catholics, especially in the west and south of Germany, rejected integralism. Bishops Kopp and Korum were unable to persuade their colleagues. Cardinal Fischer protected the *Volksverein*. Furthermore, in 1910, he effected the resolution of the Bishops' Conference in Fulda, permitting membership in trade unions, provided they did not violate Christian morality and would not meddle with religious matters.

But the integralists refused to recognize these limitations. It was to the advantage of the Church's opponents, who profited from the controversy. The integralists clung to the dispute and carried it to the Curia, involving it for the last time in an internal German ideological struggle. In Rome, the mood was different from Fulda. Pius X and Merry del Val disapproved of the Cologne Faction. They disapproved of the *Kölnische Volkszeitung* because it had contradicted the Curia in the controversy involving Ehrhard and Schell. In a sensational speech at the Catholic Convention in Essen in 1906, Cardinal Serafino Vannutelli had declared that those who obeyed the Pope had to obey him in all matters. However, numerous protests had compelled the Vatican to correct this statement. A papal brief addressed to Cardinal Fischer confirmed the freedom of the German Catholics in nonreligious matters. However, Pastor, following a papal audience in 1907, remarked: "I noticed clearly

---

[35] Pastor, 549.
[36] Concerning Kopp's role in the trade union controversy, see R. Morsey, *Kopp*, 54ff. Cf. also C. Weber, *ArSKG* 26 (1968), 327–34.
[37] Pastor, 513.

that the Pope did not approve of the German Center Party's request for absolute independence from any kind of ecclesiastical authority. Indeed, such political independence is too easily transferred to the ecclesiastical realm."[38] Five years later, at the peak of the trade-union controversy, Pius X, in a conversation with Pastor, reiterated "that he absolutely refused the efforts of Julius Bachem and his disciples. He said openly that his reprimand was not directed against the many loyal Catholics of Germany but only against those who followed the *Kölnische Volkszeitung*. It was not their opponents who were disturbing the unity of the Catholics, but rather this very paper." Merry del Val went even further, including in his criticism Cardinal Fischer and the majority of the German bishops, as well as Nuncio Frühwirth of Munich, who was said to lean too far toward the Cologne faction.[39] Frühwirth, the general of the Dominican Order until 1904, was quite antimodernistic. However, in Munich after 1907, he had become convinced that the belligerent manner in which the integralists conducted themselves in the controversies concerning literature, the Center Party, and the trade unions was not justified.[40] The Pope and his chief political adviser were not willing or able to examine critically the great amount of information that was forwarded. They believed only what they wanted to believe. Nonetheless, the Pope directly intervened in the Center controversy only once, in 1914, when the Cologne faction had essentially established itself. Derived from a lecture, the essay by the leader of the Center in Baden, Pastor Theodor Wacker (1845–1921),[41] and entitled "Zentrum und kirchliche Autorität," was put on the Index because its emphasis on the independence of the party could be misunderstood. The disproportional severity of this measure suggests that the men around the Pope had indeed waited for an excuse to act. In other respects, the Pope had to exercise restraint; on the one hand, because the political independence of the Center Party had been recognized by his predecessor and confirmed, after all, by himself after Vannutelli's speech; on the other hand, because the party acted with caution in regard to Rome, taking the initiative in ecclesiastical matters only after consulting with the bishops.

Nonetheless, Pius X's course severely burdened the Church policies of the Center Party. For instance, the Vatican's intransigence in regard to the modernist controversy hampered the support of the toleration proposal. In particular, the party had to cushion the various vehement

---

[38] Pastor, 474.
[39] Pastor, 542, 544f.
[40] A. Walz, *Andreas Kardinal Frühwirth* (Vienna 1950), 328–47.
[41] Biography by J. Schofer (Karlsruhe 1921); H. Sacher, *LThK*² X, 906.

parliamentary debates that had been caused by the Borromeo encyclical and the antimodernist oath. The encyclical *Editae saepe* (29 May 1910),[42] issued on the occasion of the three hundredth anniversary of Borromeo's canonization, honored Saint Charles Borromeo as a model of a true reformer, as opposed to the false reformers such as the modernists and the men of the Reformation of the sixteenth century, against whom Borromeo had fought. The latter were charged in the encyclical with revolt against ecclesiastical authority and blind obedience to the sovereign. Quoting the Epistle to the Philippians, they were called "enemies of the cross of Christ . . . , whose mind is looking for things temporal . . . whose God is the stomach." This metaphor, taken from the vocabulary of the religious struggles of the sixteenth century and congealed into a cliché in the Curia, incurred the outrage not only of the German Protestants. The efforts toward interdenominational cooperation suffered a severe setback. Following protests of the governments of Prussia, Bavaria, and Saxony, and upon the recommendation of the German bishops, the Curia finally did not insist on the official publication of the encyclical in Germany. The Pope himself felt obliged to appease Germany: in several pronouncements he assured Germany and the German sovereigns of his respect. Through his secretary of state he explained that the Curia had not intended to insult the German nation. With respect to the antimodernist oath, a compromise was necessary also. This was almost as injurious to the reputation of the Curia as the previously employed sternness, and it could have been avoided had the situation been assessed more realistically. Following similarly vehement discussions, the theological faculties of the state universities were exempt from the oath. Even Kopp had supported this compromise, because otherwise the continuation of the faculties would have been seriously threatened.

For the integralist efforts toward Roman intervention, the trade-union controversy, with its moral-theological implications, was more appropriate than the essentially political Center Party controversy. At that time, the Vatican was not sufficiently familiar with the problems of a modern economy. Following a trip to Rome, Cardinal Fischer believed it possible to announce in a pastoral letter the Vatican's neutrality in the controversy of the two German factions, but a papal pronouncement of May 1912 clearly sided with the Berlin group rather than the Cologne one. With insufficiently deliberated arguments the Pope reasoned that religion must penetrate the whole individual and therefore his economic enterprises as well. Cardinal Kopp and his allies almost obtained a formal papal condemnation of the Christian trade unions then strug-

[42] *AAS* 2 (1910), 357–80. Cf. Bachem VII, 330–75.

gling for a Christian as well as a democratic solution to the labor problem, offering at that time the only effective alternative to the antiecclesiastical workers' associations. At the last minute, Cardinal Fischer and his close ally, the Franciscan Bishop Bernard Döbbing, an adviser to the Pope, were able to reach a limited compromise.

The encyclical *Singulari quadam* (24 September 1912),[43] concluding the controversy, began with a warning against the "undefined inter-denominationalism" (that was not even espoused by the trade unions) and continued with the reiteration of the reminder, uncalled for in this context, of the principle, not even questioned by the German Catholics, that the social problems could not be solved without recourse to religion and moral law. The Pope unconditionally praised the ecclesiastical workers' associations, supporting their monopoly in Catholic countries. However, subsequently he conceded that in other countries Catholics were allowed to cooperate with non-Catholics in order carefully to elevate the working class (*cautione adhibita*) and that, in the exceptional case of Germany, interdenominational trade unions could be tolerated. He made the membership of Catholic workers dependent on their simultaneous membership in the Catholic workers' associations and on the proviso that trade unions would not interfere with the doctrine of the Church. The first of these conditions unnecessarily burdened the workers, the second one ignored the goals of the trade unions. At least, they were now able to continue with their activities. They had no difficulties adhering to the conditions of the *Singulari quadam* and to prevent further conflicts with Rome. In spite of the Vatican's sympathies for the integralists, the trade-union controversy helped the progressive faction in German Catholicism achieve partial success. But the distrustful *tolerari potest* of the Pope encouraged the integralists to continue to discredit the trade unions, thus causing more unrest. Shortly before his death (4 March 1914), Cardinal Kopp himself rejected a conciliatory interpretation of the encyclical. In 1913, the trade unions already had to defend themselves against assaults by the opposition in a sensational trial that was played up by the antiecclesiastical press.

Cardinal Fischer died on 30 July 1912. Thus he was unable to witness the results of the action initiated by him. Due to the Curia's drastic interference with the suffrage rights of the cathedral chapter of Cologne, he was succeeded by Bishop Felix on Hartmann (1851–1919, after 1911 Bishop of Münster),[44] who was close to the integralist, as well as to the national-conservative course of Cardinal Kopp, but who did

---

[43] *AAS* 4 (1912), 657–62. Regarding the history of the encyclical, see L. Hardick, "Bischop Bernhard Döbbing," *WZ* 109 (1959), 143–95, esp. 169ff.
[44] Trippen, op. cit., 448–63.

not possess his leadership qualities. But even in this manner, full success could not be achieved: Hartmann tried hard to contribute to the preservation of the existing political and social structure, thus apparently establishing a good relationship with Wilhelm II. However, he had to pay attention to the realities of his new diocese and to be content with the activity of the Christian trade unions and the *Volksverein*.[45]

[45] Regarding the development on the whole, see W. Spael, *Das katholische Deutschland . . . 1890–1945* (Würzburg 1964).

CHAPTER 36

Separation of Church and State in France

Voting on the Separation Law (1899–1905)

The emotions aroused by the Dreyfus affair had played a significant role in the failure of reconciliation. Likewise, the separation of Church and state in France was the result of a series of circumstances that gradually deteriorated the relations between the two powers. Basically, neither Pierre Waldeck-Rousseau nor Émile Combes, his successor to the ministerial office in 1902, intended a separation. However, they were led on this path by their personal decisions as well as by political measures demanded by the majority and the compelling force of circumstances. Certainly, many had long regarded the annulment of the concordat a natural consequence of the development, especially after the fateful outcome of the *Ralliement*. However, the internal and external reasons for avoiding the schism were just as strong during the time of the Republic as they had been twenty years before, even though the regime had meanwhile found stronger support among the Catholic voters. When Pius X categorically refused to recognize the law of 2 December 1905, a law introducing into France the "most radical separation system imaginable," the republican government was willing to make a few concessions in order to limit the effects of the law and to avoid at any cost the danger of a religious conflict.

An investigation must first deal with a series of legislative measures whose severe amendments resulted in the separation laws. The "logic of the laws" must not conceal the deep emotions with which these measures were enacted and applied. The ministries stood under the supervision of the majority in the parliament that was ready to strike as soon as the question of congregation and Church was raised. The elections of April 1902, which concerned this topic, resulted in a majority of 339 deputies who belonged to the "bloc" (composed of the Democratic

Union, Socialists, Radicals, and Radical Socialists). The strong core of this "bloc" (200 deputies) was comprised of the representatives of the bourgeoisie of those medium-sized and small cities that were radically anticlerical. One of their loyal representatives was Émile Combes. Formerly a seminarian, he had left Catholicism and turned to medicine and propaganda for the Radicals. This brought him a senatorial seat in his department of Charente-Inférieure. The usual fanaticism of both parties, raked by the press with relentless personal assaults and caricatures, was not without influence on the attitude of the politicians. Preceeding the separation, the expulsion of about twenty thousand members of religious orders between 1903 and 1904 nourished radicalism on both sides. The population frequently supported the resistance of the order members. The demonstrations often ended in bloodshed (in Nantes in 1903, two people died, in Lyon on 8 December of the same year, one person was killed).

In November 1899 Waldeck-Rousseau proposed his bill on the religious congregations. He did not intend it as an aggressive interpretation of the policy of the *défense républicaine.* He had long desired to remedy the lack of any kind of regulation regarding the freedom of association in French law. His aim was to eliminate a new coalition, favored by legal uncertainty, between the nonauthorized congregations and an antirepublican social elite. He was intent on precluding the kind of threat to which the republicans had been exposed on 16 May 1877 and during the appeal of the Dreyfus trial. Moreover, as a statist jurist, he wanted to bring the various forms of ecclesiastical life under the control of the state. This was the background for the measures against the Assumptionists, the prohibition of bishops appointing members of orders to teaching posts and seminaries, and, finally, for the investigation of the property of congregations which he had ordered to be registered in the fall of 1900. In Toulouse, on 20 October, he reiterated the theme of Gambetta, that is, the statement on the clandestine social influence of the congregations on education and the upper echelons of government.

The bill proposed by Waldeck-Rousseau on associations required religious congregations to obtain a license from the government, but at the same time it opened up possibilities for numerous agreements. However, supported by a delegation of groups from the left, the commissions of both chambers gave the bill an expressly anticlerical character. From then on, the admission of congregations which, according to ARTICLE 14, were prohibited from playing an educational role required legal authorization. Strict control of their properties and forced liquidation in case of nonadmission were suggested. The law of 1 July 1901 was, in terms of its spirit, far different from the draft of Waldeck-

Rousseau. The religious associations were excluded from the freedom generously granted to others. This was "the beginning of the struggle." After the autumn, several congregations had dissolved themselves voluntarily, but 700 foundations of female congregations and about 150 male congregations had applied for their authorization. After the enactment of the law, the minister proved to be indulgent and obliging, after Théophile Delcassé had left him in no doubt that for reasons of foreign policy the French did not want a break with the Holy See.

The situation was different in the case of Delcassé's successor, Émile Combes (after 1902). Waldeck-Rousseau was quick to make clear that he did not want the religious struggle launched by Combes. On 27 June 1903, before the Senate, he declared his opposition to Combes's absolutely rigid and uncompromising policy of execution.[1] From all officials Combes demanded, in his words, "strict republican discipline." Contrary to the promises of his predecessor, he declared in June/July 1902 that all schools opened within the period of one year by congregations, even though licensed, were in violation of the law. All schools of nonauthorized congregations were, without exception, affected by this verdict. In the following months almost 12,000 schools were closed, resulting in spontaneous protests especially in Brittany. This total laicization was crowned by the law of 7 July 1904, which denied all members of orders the freedom to teach. Again, 2,500 schools, among them the popular ones of the *Frères des Écoles chrétiennes,* had to be closed. In regard to the congregations, the Chamber approved a government proposal which provided for the denial of all licenses, with the exception of five missionary congregations. The dissolution of congregations was planned for Easter 1903. Some congregations preferred to voluntarily dissolve themselves. However, many others exercised passive resistance in order to draw attention to the coercion concealed behind these measures. Often, the religious who decided to emigrate were cheered by demonstrations of sympathy by the local inhabitants, as was the case on 29 April 1903 with the monks of the Grande-Chartreuse near Grenoble. The government had overestimated the value of the monastery's properties and the treasury made little profit from them.

The vehement protests of the episcopate against all these measures compelled the government to attack the hierarchy. In the summer of 1902, after almost all seventy-four bishops had signed a petition for the purpose of defending the congregations and protesting the interpretation of the law regarding cooperatives, the officials resorted to the regulation that prohibited the bishops from joining together and presenting requests as a legal body. They turned all signatures en bloc over to the

---

[1] A. Latreille, R. Rémond, *Histoire du catholicisme en France* III (Paris 1962), 499.

council of state which was applying the old and senseless procedure of the *appel comme d'abus* against the bishops. The income of the three initiators of the petition, the bishops of Seéz, Besançon and Nice, was canceled. Even the conciliatory bishop of Orléans, Monsignor Touchet, was included in this sanction. During the last months of Leo XIII's pontificate, the standing conflict over the the government's right to nominate bishops for elections also flared up again.[2] The rigid attitude of the aging Pope in this matter was symptomatic of his situation. Pius X, on the other hand, clearly meant to prove his desire for peace when he accepted the rule that officially sanctioned the nomination by the government. Nonetheless, in June 1904 Rome did not hesitate to summon the two bishops of Dijon and Laval who were charged by their subjects with excessive indulgence toward the state authorities and experienced difficulties in their relations with the clergy and the administration of their diocese. The government forbade the two prelates to travel to Rome.[3] These "summons" were issued a few weeks after a serious diplomatic incident had occurred on the occasion of Émile Loubet's (president of the Republic) visit to Rome. For the first time in the course of improving relations with Italy, the government had agreed to this official visit to the Quirinal, disregarding the advice Cardinal Rampolla had offered in the last months of the previous pontificate and giving no consideration to the Vatican. The sharp protest of the Vatican was published by Jean-Léon Jaurès. The fact that this document questioned the presence of the nuncio in Paris was considered a challenging threat by the left. With a majority of 427 votes, the Chamber resolved to recall the French ambassador to the Holy See. This was the prologue to the break in diplomatic relations following the citation of the two bishops of Dijon and Laval to Rome on 30 July.

Combes's ministry came to an end on 14 January 1905 when the Socialists refused to endorse the anticlericalism of the Radicals. Combes's bill of 10 November to separate Church and state was replaced by a new, more liberal one under his successor J.-B. Bienvenu-Martin. During the debate extending from March into the summer, Aristide Briand, reporting for the commission, pleaded for the absolute neutrality of the state in religious matters in order that the Church "be completely at liberty to organize itself, live, and develop in accordance with its rules." Things changed at the end of April when a large majority voted in favor of ARTICLE 4 (formulated by Jaurès, the leader of the Socialists). According to the article, religious communities were to follow the general organizational structure of their religion after they had

---

[2] R. P. Lecanuet, *L'Église de France sous la troisième République* III (Paris 1930), 364–87.
[3] M. Denis, *L'Église et la République en Mayenne, 1896–1906* (Paris 1967), 155ff.

announced their intention to adhere to its rules. This article reflected the lesson learned from the failure of the religious policies of the French Revolution. It precluded any attempt to form a state church that would have challenged the established churches. Instead, it amounted to a spiritualistic interpretation of the revolutionary tradition.[4]

The entire legislative package, approved by the Chamber on 3 July (with a vote of 341 to 233) and by the Senate on 6 December, was not applied until a year later. The law perpetuated the spirit of the legislation of the revolution: neutrality and complete continence on the side of the state in religious matters, including salaries and subsidies. The buildings were declared property of the state or the community. Partially, they were given to the communities to practice their religion, but in the case of conflict, the council of the state, whose hostile attitude was well known, had the right to make a decision.

Execution of the Separation Law (1906–24)

The majority of Catholics considered this law a predatory incursion devised by the state. They had reason to assume that this law created the basis for the destruction of religion and its social impact. Nonetheless, at the end of the nineteenth century, certain groups within Catholicism were still willing to establish contact with the democratic society. They were agreeable to cooperation with the liberal efforts of certain advocates of the law, hoping to achieve with their help a tolerant execution of the law.

Jaurès himself, whose role in the preparation of the law was described above, relied on the support of certain groups of the clergy, ". . . without having to go as far as Loisy . . . . with François Lenormant, the great Christian and scholar, or with Monsignor d'Hulst, or even with Abbé Duchesne, or with the Institutes of Toulouse and Paris, which tried, not without risks, to utilize some of the results of modern criticism for the benefit of traditional exegesis. If only some priests, enthusiastic democrats with liberal spirits, were to stand up and be supported by their religious communities. . . ."[5]

Around 1900, Marc Sangnier, a young engineer from the Parisian middle class, founded a study group that courageously appeared in public with discussion groups, congresses, as well as a project designed to educate the people. The group intended through spiritual indoctrination to prepare the faithful to practice personal responsibility

---

[4] Regarding ARTICLE 4 and its comments, especially the comment of Jaurès of 20 April 1905, cf. J.-M. Mayeur, *La séparation de l'Église et de l'État* (Paris 1966), 61–76.
[5] J.-M. Mayeur, op. cit., 70.

in a democracy. In 1905, the *Sillon* movement had five strong regional groups outside of Paris: in the north, the east, in Limousin, Aquitaine, and Brittany. This movement, whose efforts included sound spiritual and intellectual education as well as social activities, gained some support among the lower and middle classes of the cities and in the rural areas of the east and Brittany. Since 1904, in the region of Lyon, the *Chronique du Sud-Est* had supplied the staff of the *Semaine sociale,* a sort of traveling university which conducted annual seminars on topical or fundamental issues. At that time, the *Chronique* included two hundred groups scattered throughout the Rhône Valley. In 1904, the Jesuit Fr. Leroy founded another movement in Rheims, whose purpose was to disseminate information and be active among the workers. Its *Action populaire* as well as the *Semaines sociales* exist to this day. The Catholic Action of the French youth also undertook a program of social and trade-union related activities.[6] This social involvement was enhanced by lively intellectual activities. When preparing the law, Jaurès had especially the centers of Paris and Toulouse in mind; but the *École de Lyon* that evolved around the new journal *Demain* (1905/07) should be included. The vitality of this group turned again to biblical (Lagrange), historical (Duchesne), and philosophical (Blondel and Laberthonnière) studies.[7] After the elections of 1902, the *Action libérale,* founded in 1901 by Albert de Mun and Jaques Piou, held its ground in the field of politics. The *Action libérale populaire* gained many supporters in the north and in Isère.[8]

These movements were forced to take a somewhat reserved stance toward the separation law. This restraint, in view of the conditions to which the Catholics were subjected, was also exercised by the best known representatives of these movements: M. Sangnier and (in the Chamber) Abbé J. Lemire. The Catholic press intensified its aggressiveness and, within the right wing, the *Action française* separated from *Sillon* at that time. The leading ranks had no difficulties convincing the rural population that the Republic was persecuting religion itself. This idea was also propagated by the majority of the clergy. Among the bishops, however, many shied away from a situation which entailed a complete break with the official authorities and, after the elections of 1906, many of them searched for a modus vivendi. The opposite opin-

---

[6] J. Caron, *Le Sillon et la démocratie chrétienne* (Paris 1967); P. Droulers, *Politique sociale et christianisme: Le P. Desbuquois et l'Action populaire* (Paris 1969); C. Molette, *L'association catholique de la jeunesse française* (Paris 1968).

[7] Cf. in vol. IV of R.P. Lecanuet, *L'Église de France sous la troisième République* (Paris 1930), the chapters that were edited by P. Laberthonnière himself.

[8] J.-M. Mayeur, *Un prêtre démocrate, l'abbé Lemire . . .* (Paris 1968), 300; P. Barral, *Le département de l'Isère sous la IIIᵉ République* (Paris 1962), 341.

ion, rejecting any kind of concession to the political situation at hand and having come to terms with the predicted separation, was extolled by those prelates who referred to "liberal" traditions (François Turinaz, bishop of Nancy) as well as those who had taken an intransigent attitude (Anatole de Cabrières, bishop of Montpellier). Their number increased by the new bishops who were exclusively appointed and installed by the Pope, especially those seventeen bishops whom Pius X had appointed at the same time in 1906. In 1906 the antimodernist condemnations increased in Rome. They foreshadowed the encyclical *Pascendi* and the letter of 25 August 1910 in which the Pope asked M. Sangnier to dissolve the *Sillon* movement. The bishops lobbied for this intransigence because they were alarmed by the infiltration of modernist tendencies, which found disciples among the seminarians and the younger clergy. In view of these conditions, the forces of resistance from the leading ranks of the French Catholics down to the common people had a great deal of significance. However, restraint had to be practiced in this regard, because the elections of May 1906 assured the return and even an increase of the majority of the "bloc." These elections focused not on the religious question but rather on the social problem which remained in the forefront until 1914.

The execution of the separation law was dependent on the Roman directives. Its enactment was almost immediately followed by its condemnation through the encyclical *Vehementer nos* of 2 February 1906, but this did not preclude the possibility of searching for a solution which would insure the religious life of the Church. Such attempts, however, could not imply the recognition of a law prepared without the Holy See. Rome was suspicious of everything that could be taken as acceptance of a precedent and thus influence the concordat situation of the Church in other countries. On the other hand, the government, when preparing the execution of the law, had taken a rather inept and insulting measure. It ordered the churches to take an inventory of all their properties, which were to become that of the state. In March 1906, after a smooth start, these inventory practices caused grave incidents in Paris, Marseille, and especially in the rural areas. The incidents were recorded by J. M. Mayeur.[9] They took place, above all, in areas with strong religious practices (in the lowlands of the west and in the south of the Massif Central, in the Jura, and in French Flanders). In the north and in the Haute-Loire two people died as a result of the unrest. This incipient revolt in the Christian rural areas compelled the government to back down and the inventory activities were discontinued. These incidents were related to the second condemnation of the law through the encyc-

[9] J.-M. Mayeur, *La séparation* . . . , 199.

lical *Gravissimo officio* of 10 August 1906. Under these conditions, the negotiations over the wording of a law that was impossible from a legal point of view were extremely difficult. This was the reason for convening three consecutive episcopal conferences in May and September 1906 and in February 1907. None of the conferences could come to an agreement about the kind of diocesan associations that had been attempted in some dioceses, for instance in Bordeaux. After the law had been enacted, both parties rejected the alternative of "usufruct," which considered the Catholics in their churches users without legal title. When they refused to obtain the official permission required for public gatherings, this offense was ridiculed as a "Mass delict."[10]

The total refusal to cooperate forced the legislators to interpret the law moderately, unless they desired to worsen their already questionable position. The communities were required to let the faithful use the cult buildings free of charge. State council and courts referred to ARTICLE 4, assuring the right of the bishops to stop encroachments of schismatic religious communities that had formed in Toulouse, Lyon, and in the west around some pastors who were rebelling against the diocesan authorities. Thus, when executing the law, the administration even functioned as an "executive organ of the episcopal jurisdiction" (Axel von Campenhausen). The Roman intransigence not only forced it to practice a liberal course, but caused a strengthening of the authority of the hierarchy over the lower clergy, of the clergy over the faithful, and, one could add, of Roman authority over the Church of France.[11]

Nonetheless, the overall balance of the first years was very disquieting to the Church. The confiscation of buildings and the lodgement of bishops and parish priests at their own expense in other buildings entailed material losses and great administrative disorder. The cancellation of stipends and salaries especially caused a rapid decrease of clerical appointments, because the seminarians, mostly of humble background, were unable to cover the cost of their education. The seminaries' student body was reduced by half, and even in areas with traditionally numerous clerical candidates (Rodez, Saint-Brieuc) a decline was felt. The spontaneously developing organizations for clerical appointments, seminary associations and associations of priests were indications of the seriousness of a situation that could not really be improved through such measures. Before the outbreak of World War I, the school conflict flared up again and was intensified by the attitude of the nationalists,

---

[10] L.-V. Méjan, *La Séparation des Églises et de l'État* (Paris 1959), 249–415.
[11] A. v. Campenhausen, *Staat und Kirche in Frankreich* (Göttingen 1962). See also J.-M. Larkin, "The Vatican, French Catholics and the Associations Cultuelles," *The Journal of Modern History* 36 (Sept. 1964), 298–317.

who were willing to make the interests of the Church their own business.

In spite of this difficult situation, which was intensified until 1914 by the antimodernist criticism of the renewal efforts, the French Catholics found ways and means to respond to the severe challenges they were facing. The statement that the disestablishment of the Church of the concord, radically changed the Church's behavior within French society is justified.[12] In this respect, it is significant that the initiatives in the nineties to strengthen the social impact of Christianity increased. They were supported by prelates such as Léon Amette (Paris), Pierre Coullié (Lyon), and Pierre Dadolle (Dijon). The societies that considered it their duty to waken the Catholics' interests in social affairs and to educate them accordingly, increased their activities. Especially prominent were the *Action populaire,* headed by P. Desbuquois, the *Semaines sociales,* whose activities attracted a large audience, and the social secretariats existing in Paris and the provinces after 1908. The *Action Catholique de la Jeunesse française* was asked to delegate apostolic responsibility to its lay members (Pius X's letter to J. Lerolle of 22 February 1907).[13] Finally, most scholars, unperturbed by the ecclesiastical censures during the modernist crisis, insisted on bearing witness to the truth of the Catholic Church. This is documented by the *Annales de philosophie chrétienne* (until 1913) and the *Bulletin de la semaine,* replacing the journal *La quinzaine.*[14] Characteristic for these prewar years is the revival of religious interest within the intellectual circles, mainly among the youth and even at the universities, as was documented by Joseph Lotte, a friend of Péguy. Finally, the war slowly brought the various social groups closer together again. Comradeship in the trenches, where believers and nonbelievers, priests and laymen fought side by side, contributed substantially to the alleviation of anticlerical prejudices. In 1919, the population of Alsace-Lorraine was not forced to accept the separation law, in order to spare religious feelings. There, priests and pastors continued to receive their salaries from the state, and religious instruction was offered in public schools. This exception, motivated by political expediency, contributed to normalizing the relations between Church and state. It was also significant that during the enforcement of the separation law French schools in foreign countries, especially in the Near East, continued to enjoy the support of the French state.

---

[12] J.-M. Mayeur, *La séparation . . . ,* 193.

[13] C. Molette, op. cit., 518–20.

[14] Not to be confused with *Les Cahiers de la quinzaine,* which were joined by authors who had returned to the faith under the influence of Charles Péguy.

The contacts between Paris and the Vatican were officially resumed in 1915, especially after the mediation of the superior of Saint Louis des Français. After Clemenceau had resigned from the political scene, Briand restored diplomatic relations. The new nuncio, B. Cerretti, was solemnly received in Paris in May 1912. At the same time, a deputy of the leftist Center, Célestin Jonnart, was appointed ambassador to the Vatican. Jonnart declared that the government intended "to let the moral forces dominating the world compete to restore peace," without infringing upon the republican laws (*Le Radical* of 29 May 1921). The Holy See granted the French government the right to examine the credentials of episcopal nominees. Finally, in November 1922, exhaustive negotiations began, dealing with the plan to replace the religious associations of parishes that had fallen under the influence of laymen with diocesan associations that were to be subject to episcopal jurisdiction. Thanks to the very active preparations of the texts by Louis Canet, adviser for religious affairs at the Quai d'Orsay, and to the subsequent memoranda of the bishops of Nice (Henri Chapon) and Arras (André Julien), the resistance of the majority of the French episcopate and the restraint of the Holy See could be overcome. At the beginning of his pontificate, Pius XI was persuaded to relinquish guarantees in the form of legislation so that the plan would not fail in the wake of reviving anticlericalism. The diocesan associations were finally constituted through administrative channels. They were headed by the bishop and entitled to administer Church property as well as to accept donations and bequests. On 18 January 1924 the Pope gave his approval by issuing the encyclical *Maximam gravissimamque,* which was endorsed through a letter of 6 February 1924 by the French bishops.[15]

This resumption of relations and this modus vivendi did not mean that anticlerical tendencies had died down. This was demonstrated by the election campaign in the spring of 1925 and by the ensuing policies of the *Cartel des Gauches* (É. Herriot). But this was to be the "last crisis of the Third Republic that was receptive to the revival of the spirit of 1904" (André Latreille). The agreement reached during the postwar era reflected the spiritual development within the Church, which concerned itself with social activities that were more and more divorced from political goals, as well as among the Republicans, who

---

[15] G. Lesage, *Aspects des rapports entre l'Église et l'État en France, de 1919 à 1924 à travers l'action de Mgr. Julien, évêque d'Arras* (Lille 1970); B. Neveu, "Louis Canet, et le service du conseiller technique pour les affaires religieuses au ministère des Affaires étrangères," *Revue d'histoire diplomatique* (April–June 1968), 134–80. Regarding all these questions, cf. the thorough study of H.-W. Paul, *The Second Ralliement: the Rapprochement between Church and State in France in the Twentieth Century* (Washington 1967).

subscribed more and more to a laicism of action rather than belligerent anticlericalism. This marked the establishment of a regime which was entrusted with the relations between the two powers in France in the course of the twentieth century.

CHAPTER 37

The Outbreak of World War I

At the level of international relations, Pius X's pontificate coincided with the "time of crisis" (Duroselle). In 1903, King Alexander of Serbia was assassinated by a group of anti-Austrian officers who tried to make their country the center of Yugoslavian nationalism. From 1905 until 1914 there were five increasingly severe crises: the Franco-German crisis following the Tangier demonstrations of Wilhelm II in 1905, the Austro-Russian crisis following the annexation of Bosnia and Herzegovina in 1908, the Agadir crisis in 1911, the Balkan Wars of 1912–1913, which increased Serbia's prestige, and finally the crisis of July 1914 that caused World War I. Even though there was new hope every time that war was successfully circumvented, the approach of a catastrophe could be felt, the approach of a war that would be much more devastating than earlier ones, due to progress in armament and the general introduction of conscription. In the last years of his life, Pius X spoke more and more about the imminent catastrophe.

In view of the increase in nationalism and imperialism and the increasing threat of an expanding conflict, the reaction of Catholic groups appears disappointing in retrospect. In the course of the two years before the war of 1914–1918, ecclesiastical groups as well as the faithful themselves joined more and more openly in the glorification of national feeling. This chauvinism and the general resignation explain the enthusiasm with which the Catholics from both camps (with few exceptions[1]) unanimously supported the fighting, rejecting, all in all, Benedict XI's repeated attempts to end this "useless slaughter."[2]

In Germany, many Catholics followed the leaning of the Protestants and became more and more receptive to everything relating to "national

[1] Above all the Catholic Irish because of their animosity toward England and some of the Italian Catholics, at least during the first year (cf. P. Scoppola, "Cattolici neutralisti e interventisti alla vigilia del conflitto," *Benedetto XV, i cattolici e la prima guerra mondiale* [Rome 1963], 95–151).
[2] See Part III.

greatness." To be sure, the Catholic associations stayed away from Pan-Germanism and occasionally even condemned its excesses, but the Center Party had relinquished its opposition to armament policies after 1897, and, in 1904, Chancellor von Bülow praised the party for its "German national policies." The development of the international situation in the following ten years, coinciding with the incorporation of the Catholics into the bourgeois national state, encouraged this development, and Erzberger was one of its representatives.[3]

In Austria, the Catholic intellectuals shied away from such chauvinism. However, nationalism was very active among the members of the Christian Socialist Party between 1909 and 1914. The leading ecclesiastical circles showed no evidence of pacifist tendencies, rather they placed their moral influence with few exceptions in the service of the dynasty and the preservation of the old Empire, which was being undermined by the demands of the various Slav minorities.

In Italy, the weight of the Roman question often kept the Catholics from manifestations of patriotism. But by the turn of the century, a patriotic development had commenced. It intensified in view of the colonization efforts in Libya, which even the *Civiltà cattolica* presented as a crusade against Islam, though the Holy See had tried to compel the Catholic press to practice restraint. The phenomenon was most noticeable in the south. But from then on, the Catholics wanted to prove almost everywhere that no one could compete with them in terms of patriotism. Even Filippo Meda succumbed to this exaltation for a while. Moreover, the incidents of conflicts between the organized Catholic movements and the extreme nationalists of Corradini increased. In 1910, when trying to solicit the support of the Catholics, Corradini had only found response among the disciples of Murri. In the elections of 1914, he campaigned as a candidate in the region of Vicenza, supported by the episcopate and Catholic Action.[4]

In France, the majority of the clergy and the large Catholic journals emphasized the supposedly close relation between religious experience and patriotic enthusiasm. Following the Dreyfus affair, it was commonplace to consider "the enemies of the army," "the friends of Germany," and "the destroyers of Catholicism" to be one and the same. Demonstrations of this kind multiplied on the occasion of the beatification of Joan of Arc in 1909. In 1911, Secretary Caillaux suggested a policy of détente toward Germany and giving it a small part of the

---

[3] There is no satisfactory study on this subject, therefore see K. Bachem, *Vorgeschichte, Geschichte und Politik der deutschen Zentrumspartei* VI and VII (Cologne 1929–30).
[4] Cf. G. De Rosa, *Storia politica dell'Azione cattolica in Italia* II (Bari 1954), 304–37, 364–81; G. Spadolini, *Giolitti e i cattolici 1901–1914* (Florence ²1960), 232–82.

French colonial Empire. But he found that almost all French Catholics and a great number of Christian democrats and Sillonists turned against him.[5] The *Société Gratry pour le maintien de la paix entre les nations,* when founded in 1907 by Vanderpol, an engineer from Lyon, could only solicit seven hundred members. Two years later, it changed into the *Ligue des catholiques français pour la paix.* In 1913, when Vanderpol, supported by the bishop of Liège, tried to organize an international Church congress in order to pave the way for better Franco-German relations, only four French bishops were willing to send a representative. This was the reason why Vanderpol decided in 1911 to expand his plan and establish a *Ligue internationale des pacifistes catholiques,* which was to work on public opinion to try to prevent a forced solution of the problem and to insist on the use of international arbitration. In view of the situation, the league was located in Brussels and the positions of president and secretary general were entrusted to Belgians.[6]

The aloofness of many Catholics toward pacifist movements cannot merely be justified with the old medieval tradition according to which military bravery is closely related to Christian virtues. It also rests in the fact that the instigators of antimilitary demonstrations around 1900 were almost always socialists, anarchists, or Freemasons. At that particular time this meant: enemies of the Church. It is characteristic that Pius X principally granted approval to the Carnegie Endowment for International Peace,[7] an American foundation of Protestant origin (letter of 11 June 1911), while rejecting a similar request by Vanderpol's *Ligue Internationale.* To be sure, the Pope had repeatedly condemned the use of weapons as a means to settle conflicts between nations and had demanded arbitration. When Cardinal Vannutelli praised the conquest of Libya by the Italians as a crusade, the Pope called him to order.[8] However, one cannot but concede that the Holy See did not try seriously enough until 1914 to curb the general tendency of the European Catholics to be enthralled by the nationalistic movement. The Holy

[5] A thorough study of nationalism among the French Catholics during the period of the Dreyfus affair and World War I does not exist. A few references can be found in M. Vaussard, *Histoire de la Démocratie chrétienne* I (Paris 1956), 67–69, and in *HistCathFr,* 542–43. Also E. Weber, *The Nationalist Revival in France 1905–1914* (Berkley 1959).
[6] Compared to the nineteenth century, antimilitarism declined, but it was still quite popular among the Belgian Catholics for practical rather than ideological reasons. They feared that the young people would lose their faith when drafted into the army and fall victim to immorality. Cf. Lehouck, *Het antimilitarisme in België 1830–1914* (Antwerp 1958), 44–77.
[7] *AAS* 3 (1911), 473–74.
[8] Cf. G. De Rosa, op. cit., 330–31. Also see the offical proclamations that were published in the *Osservatore Romano* between 20 and 30 October 1911, attempting to moderate the enthusiasm for the war.

See's benevolent attitude toward the *Action française* of Maurras and Daudet, pioneers of the *nationalisme intégral,* supports this impression.

The attitude of the Holy See at the moment of the outbreak of World War I is still a topic of discussion. When the Austrian ambassador informed Pius X about the ultimatum that was issued by Vienna and sent to Sarajevo on 23 July, the Pope declared his willingness to arbitrate between the two countries and he emphasized his intention to exercise a moderating influence on both governments. But what did really happen in the course of the following days?

The Pope's doctor, Marchiafava, declared during the beatification process: "I remember him telling me that he himself wrote to the Emperor of Austria, imploring him to do everything in his power to prevent the declaration of war, but it was in vain."[9] A. de Cigala,[10] whose report has been quoted frequently, added: "When the Austrian ambassador informed Pius X of the fait accompli and asked him in the name of the Emperor to bless the Austrian weapons, he answered: "Tell the Emperor that I can neither bless the war nor those who wanted it. The Emperor should consider himself lucky not to have received the curse of Christ's deputy." Some hagiographers went one step further and maintained that the Pope had contemplated the excommunication of Franz Joseph and discussed his intention with Cardinal Ferrata.[11]

However, Cardinal Merry del Val declared: "I do not think that it is absolutely clear that he wrote a letter to the Emperor of Austria."[12] In the Roman and Austrian archives, not a trace of such a letter was found, so that the testimony of Dr. Marchiafava appears to be rather questionable. It seems to be even more doubtful in view of another document, which is equally unverifiable, but sounds entirely different. A few days before Pius X died, one of his secretaries told a friend of the Austrian ambassador confidentially that the Pope had been asked by several parties to intervene in behalf of peace and that his response was the following: "The only monarch in whose behalf I would intervene is the Emperor and King Franz Joseph, because he was always loyal to the Holy See. But I cannot intervene on his behalf precisely because the

---

[9] *Processus Ordinarius, Roma* II, 1702–5.
[10] *Vie intime de S.S. le pape Pie X* (Paris ²1926), 219–21.
[11] The letter of the Pope addressed to Franz Joseph dated 13 August 1914 and published in the French and Italian press is obviously a forgery which the secretary of state did not deem necessary to deny (cf. A. Hudal, op. cit., 283–84). At that time the rumor was circulated that Merry del Val had joined the Austrian camp and influenced the Pope in order to prevent his official protest.
[12] *Processus Ordinarius, Roma* II, 898.

war of Austria-Hungary is quite just."[13] He is supposed to have added that Russia was totally responsible for the expansion of the conflict.

Aside from these rumors, for which "reliable documents are missing that could prove their authenticity" (Hudal), there are two documents at our disposal which are more reliable, but pose problems of interpretation. On the one hand, we have the letter of the Bavarian legate Baron Ritter, who wrote on 26 July: "The Pope approves the decisive steps Austria took toward Serbia."[14] On the other hand, there is the detailed report of the Austrian legate Count Pállfy, (of 29 July)[15] regarding a conversation he had had two days earlier with Cardinal Merry del Val: "The memorandum addressed to Serbia was considered extremely harsh by the cardinal, but he approved of it nevertheless, at the same time indirectly expressing hope that the Monarchy would be able to endure the conflict. The Cardinal thought that it was a shame that Serbia had not been "crushed" earlier because at that time it might have been accomplished without taking unforeseeable risks." The diplomat added: "This statement coincides with the Pope's ideas, because in the last few years His Holiness frequently expressed regret about Austria-Hungary's failure to put her dangerous neighbor in its place." When these texts were published, the Cardinal countered with a summary of the conversation: "It is true that I said to Count Pállfy after the terrible crime of Sarajevo that Austria had to remain firm and that it had a right to authentic reparations and the protection of its existence, but I never expressed the hope or the opinion that Austria would not take up arms."[16]

What can we conclude from these texts? Unquestionably, we have to consider that a diplomat tends to declare a carefully phrased or simply implied opinion to be an official statement in order to prove that he has succeeded in persuading his opponent that his country was perfectly justified. One should also take into account that some people might have been of the opinion that the Holy See's restraint would finally remove the old Emperor's last inhibitions. On the other hand, it is clear that the slogan "Austria has to remain firm," which Merry del Val admitted to have used, was conducive to encouraging Vienna to impose its reign on Belgrade, even though Serbia had already responded to the Austrian ultimatum in conciliatory terms (25 July). Even on 27 July, the secretary of state and other diplomats were justified in assuming that a

---

[13] Quoted in Engel-Janosi II, 150–51.
[14] *Bayerische Dokumente zum Kriegsausbruch,* ed. by P. Dirr, III (Munich 1925), 206.
[15] *Österreich-Ungarns Außenpolitik. Diplomatische Aktenstücke* VIII (Vienna 1930), 893–94.
[16] *L'Osservatore Romano,* 20 August 1914, 22 October 1923; cf. ibid., 22–23 May 1936.

confinement of the conflict would be possible, at least as long as Russia had not taken a clear stand. When she finally did, she caused a chain reaction of hostilities all over Europe.

In any case, one fact can not be disputed: "A number of documents prove that in the decisive months of the summer of 1914 the Vatican was rather favorably inclined toward Austria-Hungary, in fact, one is tempted to say: surprisingly favorably" (Engel-Janosi). It would be exaggerated to speak about the Vatican's dependence on Austria. This can be documented by the fact that, on 24 June 1914, a concordat with Serbia was signed, even though the Austrian diplomats had tried persistently to prevent this because they considered it to be an encouragement for Yugoslavianism.[17] Pius X, however, had great respect for the old Emperor Franz Joseph. After all, just a few years ago, he had appeared as the model of a Catholic sovereign when he walked in the procession of the Most Blessed Sacrament of the Altar on the occasion of the Eucharistic Congress in Vienna wearing his full-dress uniform. The Pope had placed even more hope on the Austrian successor to the throne, Archduke Franz Ferdinand. His assassination deeply disappointed him. Above all, since France's break with Rome, Austria was the only large Catholic state in Europe. Moreover, Austria provided protection against German Protestantism as well as against Orthodox Slavism. There are indications that Pius X and Merry del Val considered Serbia the malignant cell that would eventually infect even the existence of the Habsburg Monarchy. They believed that a weakening of the Austrian influence in the Balkans and on the Danubian plains would favor Russia, the main enemy of Catholicism in the Near East.

Is it possible that the sympathies the Pope and his secretary of state expressed for Austria (which does not necessarily mean that they intended war) also included Germany? In certain French circles, Pius X was charged with having been "the Pope of the Triple Alliance." It is true that the Pope, as a result of his more conciliatory stance toward Italy, did not have the same reasons to bear a grudge against the allies that Leo XIII had. It is also true that the German influence in the Vatican increased during his pontificate. On the one hand, this development was the normal consequence of the break of diplomatic relations by France and of the discontent of the leadership of the religious orders in this country with the measures taken against the congregations. On the other hand, this development resulted from the fact that Rome tended to favor the "safe" principles and dogmas of German Catholicism as opposed to the dangerous French progressivism in the matter of

---

[17] Cf. C. Alix, *Le Saint-Siège et les nationalismes en Europe* (Paris 1962), 111–14, and É. Poulat, *Intégrisme et catholicisme intégral* (Paris-Tournai 1969), 527–28.

exegesis and philosophy.[18] It is quite possible that the Vatican found satisfaction in the idea that the godless and immoral French would learn a lesson. In view of imminent war, the Pope did not raise the voice of a prophet condemning war, but rather confined himself to a somewhat meek appeal to all peoples to pray.[19] He certainly did not restrain himself because he watched the approach of a catastrophe with pleasure, but rather because he reasoned that the Holy See's position was diplomatically weak and did not permit initiatives such as Pius XII would attempt twenty-five years later at the dawn of World War II. He may also simply have been too tired and old, lacking the energy necessary to act in a hopeless situation.

In fact, a month earlier, Pius X had celebrated his eightieth birthday, and for the last year his health had been a cause of concern. He died almost unexpectedly on the night of 19 August and left his successor with the new and difficult problems that the commencing war posed for the Church.

[18] The following assessment by a neutral party seems noteworthy: The American Cardinal O'Connell was asked by Mrs. B. Storer to exercise his influence and "to preserve the friendly feeling which has grown stronger between Germany and the Vatican." He answered her in January 1910: "I wish to assure you that the Holy Father and the cardinal secretary of state are very practical men and that they understand perfectly the value of the staunch sterling character of the Germans and the methods and maneuvers of the French, which are the same the world over" (*CHR* 40 [1954–55], 141–42).
[19] *Dum Europa fere* of 2 August 1914 (*AAS* 6 [1914], 373).

PART THREE

The Expansion of Catholic Missions
from the Time of Leo XIII until World War II

The striking lack of representation of missionary interests at the First Vatican Council reflected the fact that ecclesiastical circles were caught up in European interests. As we demonstrated earlier, the participating missionary bishops were active, but in terms of numbers and influence they were a small group.[1] The fact that the Council adjourned abruptly and the missionary proposals were never presented is not the reason for the fact that no effective initiatives for the propagation of the faith emanated from it. The real impulse came from outside, especially from the growing and prevailing imperialism or colonialism, in whose wake the missions had recently assumed truly worldwide scope.[2] The earlier colonial powers, England and France, were joined by a united Germany. Russia expanded its empire in the east and south and thus exercised an antimissionary influence because, in agreement with Western powers, especially England, it impeded the preaching of the Gospel in such countries as Tibet and Afghanistan. In Africa, the Islamic faith, a political force in the Ottoman Empire, penetrated even the black population.

CHAPTER 38

Missions in the Shadow of Colonialism

Initially, a false understanding of the missionary concept impaired worldwide and open-minded missionary activities. This concept originated during the First Vatican Council among the authorities of the Congregation for the Propagation of the Faith. Missionary work was primarily understood to mean activities among the Christians of the Eastern churches and the Catholic immigrants in North America.[3] In the context of the last few years of Pius IX's pontificate, this attitude is understandable; but it can still be found in the first years of Leo XIII's reign. While the Near Eastern Churches enjoyed papal attention (the

---

[1] Regarding the mood among the missionaries, see, for instance, the letter of 31 December 1869 by P. Le Doré (later the general of the Eudists), who had accompanied a bishop of the Antilles to the council (in R. Aubert, *Vaticanum I* [Mainz 1965], 295).

[2] Delacroix III, uses the words *La grande expansion des missions* to characterize this period.

[3] Even in our century, the priests in America were considered the "classic" missionaries. The decisive significance of the Congregation for the Propagation of the Faith in regard to the development of the American Church is evident in the collection of documents compiled by F. Kenneally (*United States Documents in the Propaganda Fide Archives* I [1673–1844], II [1845–62] [Washington 1966–68]). The editor of this work, A. Tibesar, states in the introduction: "Perhaps in no other country was the Congregation of Propaganda Fide more successful in fulfilling its purpose than in the United States of America after our independence" (I, xiii).

Pope sent several proclamations and directives), the pagan missions, according to Roman archives, were neglected.[4] On 3 December 1880 the Pope issued the encyclical *Sancta Dei Civitas,* but it is incorrect to call it a missionary encyclical.[5] In 1884, he praised the activities of the missionaries and called them *Evangelii praecones.* However, he did so on the occasion of the dedication of the North American College in Rome.[6]

This view of the pagan mission changed after the reform of the Curia by Pius X on 29 June 1908;[7] as a result of it, the activities of the Congregation for the Propagation of the Faith were principally limited to non-Christian areas. The reform deprived the Congregation of its authority over seven archbishoprics and forty-seven bishoprics in Europe (England, Scotland, Ireland, Holland, and Luxemburg) and thirty archdioceses with 147 suffragan bishoprics in Canada and the United States. As far as the Near Eastern Churches were concerned, the system of 1862 remained in force. They continued to be subject to the prefect of the Congregation for the Propagation of the Faith, with its own special secretary. Finally, in 1917, a Congregation for the Eastern Churches was established, thus relieving the Congregation for the Propagation of the Faith of its last responsibility. On the basis of the reform of 1908, missionaries as missionaries were subject to the Congregation for the Propagation of the Faith. However, as members of religious orders they were responsible to the Congregation for Religious.[8] Moreover, a number of areas for which the Congregation for the Propagation of the Faith had been responsible (e.g., matters of faith, of marriage, of rites and liturgy) were now transferred to other administrative branches.

During the pontificates of Leo XIII and Pius X, home missionary activities were increased and strengthened. This was necessary for two reasons: because of the expansion of missionary tasks (especially after the colonization of Africa) and because of the new Italy depriving the Congregation for the Propagation of the Faith of some of its respon-

---

[4] Schmidlin, *PG* II, 500–36, in accordance with the documents, devoted more than half of his study to the northern, the Russian, and the Middle Eastern missions.

[5] *Acta Leonis* I, 171–77. The encyclical contains a warm commendation of the activities of the Society for the Propagation of the Faith in Lyon and the Association of the Holy Childhood in Paris. However, the work of the Christian schools in the Middle East is considered equally valuable.

[6] *Acta Leonis* II, 88–92: *Litterae Apostolicae* of 25 October 1884. Praise of the missionaries: p. 88.

[7] N. Hilling, "Die rechtliche Stellung der Propagandakongregation nach der neuen Kurialreform Pius' X," *ZM* (1911), 147–58.

[8] This gave the leaders of orders the right to voice their opinion about the activities of their members in the missions. Consequently, they became much more interested in missionary work.

sibilities.[9] Therefore, the existing missionary societies were strongly recommended and supported by popes and bishops alike. However, since several of these organizations (e.g., the *Leopoldinen-Stiftung* in Vienna and the *Ludwigs-Missionsverein* in Munich, etc.) served almost exclusively the American and Near Eastern missions, new societies arose, such as the Africa Society of the German Catholics (from 1888–1917),[10] the *Werk vom heiligen Petrus für den einheimischen Klerus,* founded in 1889 by Stéphanie Bigard and her daughter Jeanne, the *Missionsvereinigung katholischer Frauen und Jungfrauen* (1893), the *Petrus-Claver-Sodalität,* suggested by Countess Maria Theresia Ledóchowska in 1894, and many more.[11]

In conjunction with the increase of material support, the number of missionary personnel increased. The first third of the nineteenth century was marked by the founding of French missionary societies, while the second third was marked by the establishment of new Italian associations, which were later joined by the missionaries of Parma (Saveriani, 1895)[12] and the *Consolata* missionaries of Turin (1901).[13] The German missionary groups were (for the most part) formed in the last third of the century. Because of the *Kulturkampf,* the first group settled in nearby Holland, where Arnold Janssen founded the Society of the Divine Word (Steyl, 1875).[14] From here, he tried to move into Germany. In 1889, he began work, with permission of the government, in Mödling near Vienna and in 1892 in Neisse (Silesia). The actions of the missionaries in Steyl signaled the creation of German provinces by French and Italian societies. Thus, the following groups were allowed to settle: the Pallottines in Limburg (1892), the Oblates of Mary Immaculate in Hünfeld near Fulda (1895), the Holy Ghost Fathers in Knechtsteden (1895), the White Fathers in Trier (1896), and the Sacred Heart Missionaries in Hiltrup near Münster (1896).

Conceived differently was the missionary work started in 1882 by the Austrian Trappist Franz Pfanner and his disciples in Mariannhill (South

---

[9] Schmidlin, *PG* II, 502. All protests were in vain, and not until the Lateran Treaties of 1929 did they receive compensation.

[10] In connection with Lavigerie's antislavery societies in other countries. The Africa mission profited from the epiphany collection instituted by Leo XIII through his letter of 20 November 1890 (*Acta Leonis* IV, 112–16).

[11] B. Arens, *Die katholischen Missionsvereine* (Freiburg 1922), gives more information about the various countries.

[12] *I Missionari Saveriani nel primo centenario della nascita del loro fondatore Guido M. Conforti* (Parma 1965).

[13] "Il Cinquantennio delle Missioni della Consolata," *Missioni Consolata* 53 (Turin 1951), 101–94.

[14] F. Bornemann, *Arnold Janssen, der Gründer des Steyler Missionswerkes 1837–1909* (Steyl 1970).

Africa). From this community of Trappists, elevated to abbey in 1885, there grew over the years the nonmonastic missionary society of Mariannhill.[15] In 1883/84, the Swiss Benedictine monk from Beuron, Andreas Amrhein, laid the cornerstone for similar monastic missionary communities, first in Reichenbach and later in Saint Ottilien. His intention was to develop the missionary component prior to the monastic.[16]

Home missionary activities were also closely involved with the ecclesiastical efforts to improve the relations between Church and state that were disrupted after 1870, especially in Germany during the *Kulturkampf* and in France during the Republic. The establishment and development of German missionary societies or religious provinces was related to this problem. They owed their establishment to the legislation terminating the *Kulturkampf* and the improved relations between Bismarck and Leo XIII.[17] Two outstanding diplomatic accomplishments of Leo XIII deserve mentioning: his role as arbitrator in the controversy between Spain and Germany over the ownership of the Caroline Islands, a role which he had been offered by Bismarck and in which he decided in favor of Germany; and his open and courageous support of Lavigerie in his campaign against slavery.[18] The diplomatic successes and the receptive personality of Leo XIII permitted him to turn to such non-Christian sovereigns as the Emperor of Japan[19] and Dowager Empress Tz'u-hsi of China and thank them, in writing, for their goodwill toward the foreign missions.[20] While Leo XIII put his diplomatic skills into the service of propagating the faith, Pius X's chief concern in

---

[15] J. Dahm, *Mariannhill. Seine innere Entwicklung sowie seine Bedeutung für die katholische Missions- und Kulturgeschichte Südafrikas 1882—1909* (Mariannhill 1950).

[16] F. Renner, *Der fünfarmige Leuchter. Beiträge zum Werden und Wirken der Benediktinerkongregation von St. Ottilien*, 2 vols. (Sankt Ottilien 1971).

[17] The papal letter to the bishops of Prussia (6 January 1888) emphasized the humanitarian and missionary significance of the colonial policies of their nation (*Acta Leonis* XIII, 183–91).—In a letter to the archbishop of Cologne (20 April 1890), the Pope expressly asked the German Catholics to participate in the Christianization of Africa (ibid. IV, 44–47). These papal words were the result of Bismarck's efforts to get German missionaries for the German colonies.

[18] Lavigerie was the exponent of Leo XIII's relations to France (cf. mainly Xavier de Montclos, *Le Toast d'Alger. Documents 1890–1891* [Paris 1966]). Bismarck played a similar role in Germany. The history of the founding of Saint Ottilien is a striking example of this (cf. F. Renner, op. cit. I).

[19] *Acta Leonis* II, 121–22: letter of 12 May 1885.

[20] *Acta Leonis* II, 134–35: letter of 1 February 1885.—Unlike previous papal letters, this one was answered, which can be documented by the fact that the Japanese delegate thanked the Pope for it on the occasion of the fiftieth anniversary of his priesthood (ibid. IV, 228).

regard to the missions was of a pastoral nature. He recognized the potential of crossfertilization between home country and missions.[21]

The propagation of the faith abroad was totally dependent on the colonial power which directly or indirectly dominated the country or the area. All colonies conquered by Russia, even those solely populated by non-Christians, were off-limits to Catholic missions, as were the countries of the Ottoman Empire and its successor states. These countries, especially England and France, pursued a rather ambiguous missionary policy. Among the non-Islamic populations they tolerated missionary activities, after the turn of the century openly supporting and furthering them. However, among the Islamic populations they forbade and hindered any kind of missionary work.[22]

Everywhere, the missionaries were incorporated into or subjugated to the imperialist system. Real freedom of propagation of the faith barely existed in any of these countries. These facts, which had not been discovered until recently, do not mean that the missionaries voluntarily supported the political and economic systems. According to contemporary reports, most missionaries were scarcely aware of the political impact of their work. And even those who seemed to later generations to have been particularly active in the political arena simply wanted to demonstrate their patriotism, which was constantly questioned by the colonial administration.[23]

Asia

The amalgamation of political power and apostolic activities produced numerous difficulties. The patronate in Asia offers ample evidence for this. After the unpleasant circumstances around the middle of

---

[21] Schmidlin, *PG*, III, 116, 121f. Cf. B. Arens, *Papst Pius X. und die Weltmissionen* (Aachen 1919).

[22] For example, in the Malayan states, in the many independent areas of India governed by Hindu or Islamic maharajahs, in British or French Sudan, and in large areas of Indonesia, any kind of missionary activity, even pastoral work among the Christians, was forbidden until after World War II.—This historical background is often overlooked when, in recent publications, the missionaries are accused of having neglected the dialogue with the Muslims, because a dialogue requires a partner; however, the missionaries were systematically isolated.

[23] Another fact needs to be considered: Like all other contemporaries, the missionaries received an education oriented towards imperialism, especially the whites working in the colonial administrations or in trade and business abroad.—Cf. Leo XIII's encyclical issued to the faithful in France (16 February 1892, *Acta Leonis* II, 39) in which he praised the French missionaries because they had spread the *"renom de la France et les bienfaits de la religion catholique"* in distant lands.—A Villanyi, "Mittel und Wege kolonialer Kirchenpolitik," *ZMR* 47 (1963), 33–46.

the century and the controversies of the Congregation for the Propagation of the Faith with Portugal, Leo XIII finally succeeded in 1886 in settling the unfortunate conflict through a new concordat, at least in principle.[24] (Two years earlier, in the interest of the Indian Church, he had appointed an apostolic legate and closed seven parishes in Goa.) Of course, this was a compromise, because the King managed to obtain the confirmation of the patronate through the archdiocese of Goa, which had been elevated to patriarchate, and through its suffragan bishoprics (Damao, Cochin, Meliapur). Consequently, the double jurisdiction continued, and Lisbon succeeded in assuring its right to nominate candidates for certain episcopal sees.[25] On the other hand, the government relinquished its right to claim the non-Portuguese areas in India and it recognized the authority of the Apostolic See. Taking advantage of this freedom, the Pope immediately established a proper hierarchy with seven church provinces (Goa, Agra, Bombay, Verapoly, Calcutta, Madras, Pondicherry), and in Ceylon he set up the archbishopric of Colombo.[26] This marked the beginning of visible growth, solidification and strengthening of the Indian Church, which was furthered by the founding of the Papal Seminary of Kandy (Sri Lanka) by the Belgian Jesuits and the instructions of the Congregation for the Propagation of the Faith to the episcopate regarding methods of proselytizing.[27] The Uniate Mar-Thomas Church also grew, obtaining its own apostolic vicariates (Trichur and Kottayam) in 1887 thanks to the efforts of its first delegate, L. M. Zaleski.[28] They were first headed by Latin bishops, after 1896 by native pastors, especially in the Syro-Malabarian apostolic vicariates of Ernakulam, Changanacherry, and Trichur. The bishopric of Quilon developed rapidly, headed by the Swiss Carmelite friar A. M. Benziger (suffragan bishop after 1905, bishop from 1905 until 1931).[29] Extraor-

---

[24] *Acta Leonis* II, 192–96 (letter of 6 January 1886 to the king of Portugal); the Concordat of 23 June 1886, ibid., 205–7. Cf. B. J. Wenzel, *Portugal und der Heilige Stuhl. Das portugiesische Konkordatsrecht* (Lisbon 1958), 189ff.

[25] These sees were Bombay, Mangalore, Quilon, and Trichinopoly. Various communities responsible to the Congregation for the Propagation of the Faith became subject to the jurisdiction of Goa. This displeased the Congregation.

[26] *Acta Leonis* II, 229–39: *Litterae Apostolicae Humanae Salutis Auctor* of 1 September 1886.

[27] The Pope insisted on the training of the native clergy. His reasons included the opinions of Francis Xavier, the clergy's better acquaintance with the country and its people, the small number of European missionaries, and, finally, the possibility that the latter could be expelled from the country (*Acta* V, 165–69: encyclical of 24 June 1893, *Ad extremas Orientis ora*).—The instructions: *Collectanea* II, 286–90 (19 March 1893).

[28] W. Maley, *Patriarch Ladislas Zaleski, Apostolic Delegate of the East Indies* (Bombay 1964).

[29] While he was in office, the number of baptized Christians increased from 87,000 to

dinarily successful was the mission of Chota Nagpur in the north, especially among the natives, the Kols. The conversion movement, accelerating after 1880, was consolidated by the Flemish Jesuit K. Lievens through a multiplicity of activities (training of catechists, writings in the language of the area, and social work).[30] In the seventies, the Jesuits reported a considerable increase of members in the diocese of Madura, where they maintained the most important school in all of southern India: Saint Joseph College, located since 1881 in Trichinopoly. They succeeded in converting many Brahmans, thus penetrating for the first time the world of Hinduism. In addition to the Carmelites and Jesuits, the Capuchin friars (in the north), the Salesians, the Oblates, and the Holy Cross Fathers did missionary work in the country. In 1875, they were joined by the Mill Hill Missionaries. The missionaries of Milan, in India since 1863, started a sizable conversion movement at the end of the century among the Telugus in the vicariate of Hyderabad. After Leo XIII's reorganization of the Indian mission, the development progressed rather slowly under the following pontificate.[31]

Indochina,[32] under British dominion, included Burma, with 3 vicariates established between 1866 and 1870 by missionaries from Paris and Milan. Here, the Karens were converted, while the true Burmese, mainly Buddhists, were less susceptible to Christianity. Moreover, the Malay peninsula fell under the control of the British. It was restored to bishopric in 1888.[33] As in Burma, Christians were not recruited from the ranks of the indigenous population, but from among the Indian and Chinese immigrants, who joined in considerable numbers. This is also true for Siam, which, after a trade agreement with France in 1867, experienced a period of benevolent acceptance of the missions, especially under the long government of King Chulalongkorn, who visited the Pope in 1897 and, upon his return, recommended that the Christian messengers be welcomed as friends. Yet even here conversions took place mainly among the Chinese, while the Thais could not

---

226,000. He proved to be an energetic patron of the native clergy and built dozens of churches. Cf. Fr. Philip, O.C.D., *A Man of God. A Biography of Archbishop Aloysius Maria Benziger* (Trivandrum 1956).

[30] F. Schwager I, 425; in regard to Constantin Lievens (1856–93), see Streit VIII, 453f.; concerning his scholarly works, see ibid., 453f.

[31] In 1910, Pius X added the archdiocese of Simla (English Capuchins) and the bishopric of Ajmer (French Capuchins) to the Indian hierarchy; he separated the vicariate of Kottayam (with a native bishop) from Changanacherry (Syro-Malabar).

[32] Regarding these areas, cf. Le Thanh Khoi et. al., *L'Asie Sud-Est de la fin du XIXe siècle à nos jours,* 2 vols. (Paris 1971).

[33] A suffragan bishopric dependent on the archdiocese of Pondicherry after 1889.

be converted.[34] Even though the French colonial administration frequently put obstacles in the way of the missions, the Church of Laos, after 1899 apostolic vicariate, was able to grow. The Christians of Annam particularly suffered from the consequences of colonial politics. Following the peace treaty between King Tu-Duc and France (1862), there was a decade of relative peace, followed by renewed acts of bloody suppression (which can partly be blamed on some missionaries), one in 1872 and another one in 1886, when the final occupation of the country took place. In the course of these persecutions, 20 missionaries, 30 native priests, and 50,000 Christians lost their lives.[35] In spite of this tragic history in the nineteenth century and the many intrigues by the colonial governments, the number of baptized Christians grew after World War I to about one million and the ecclesiastical hierarchy increased to twelve apostolic vicariates headed by the Parisian Dominicans and to two vicariates headed by the Spanish Dominicans.[36]

Similarly fatal events and, for the future of Christianity, even tragic consequences resulted from the Christianization that followed the colonization of China.[37] The treaties imposed upon the Far East by the Western powers marked the beginning of a new era in missionary history. The various agreements paved the way for the missions throughout the entire country and, aside from acceptance and protection, it provided the Church with financial and social advantages. Yet such missionary policies proved to be harmful as well.[38] The missionaries made insufficient efforts to fashion the communities with the Chinese spirit and sensitivities in mind, and many a conversion was inspired by mate-

---

[34] The first Siamese were ordained in 1880. Cf. F. Schwager, "Aus der Vorgeschichte der hinterindischen Mission," *ZM* 3 (1913), 146–51.

[35] E. Vo Duc Hanh, *La place du catholicisme dans les relations entre la France et le Vietnam de 1851 à 1870,* I (Leiden 1969). J. Nguyen van Phong (*ArchSR* 31 [Jan.–June 1971], 248), takes issue with Vo Duc Hanh's opinion that most Catholics were convinced of the religious and political mission of France in the second half of the nineteenth century (p. 26), and the hate of the white population was one of the main reasons for the persecutions of the Christians (287–92).

[36] Latourette VI, 246–51.

[37] To understand the most recent Chinese Church history, see the competent work of J. Beckmann, "Die China-Mission. Versuch einer kritischen Rechenschaft," *Wort und Wahrheit* 14 (1959), 3–40; id., "Neuerscheinungen zur chinesischen Missionsgeschichte 1945–1955," *Monumenta Serica* 15 (Tokyo 1956), 378–462. This extensive bibliography offers a survey of the development of missions from the middle of the thirteenth into the twentieth century. Cf. B. Wirth, *Imperialistische Übersee- und Missionspolitik dargestellt am Beispiel Chinas* (Münster 1968); see also *NZM* 25 (1969), 317.

[38] A very critical assessment of France's policy of protectionism in Schmidlin, *M,* 466f.; cf. A. Schier, "Alphonse Favier et la protection des missions en Chine (1870–1905)," *NZM* 25 (1969), 1–13, 90–101; id., "La nonciature pour Pékin en 1886," *NZM* 24 (1968), 1–14, 94–110.

rial motives (the so-called rice Christians). In addition, the disciples of a white religion were suspect to the population (e.g., in regard to orphanages) and deeply hated by certain segments, especially the Mandarins and scholars, whose national pride was hurt.[39] The resentments exploded during the Boxer uprising in 1900, an incident which cost the lives of thousands of Catholics and numerous priests. In spite of these setbacks and the revolution of 1911, which put an end to the Manchu dynasty but hardly affected the religious communities, the Catholic Church had 1.4 million members around 1912 (the number had doubled since the turn of the century), and the native clergy included 724 clergymen.[40]

Almost twice as many foreign (especially French, Italian, and German) missionaries devoted themselves at the same time to missionary work all over China. The old established order of the Lazarists,[41] the Jesuits, who produced significant cultural achievements through their educational, scientific, literary, and economic charitable activities in parts of Pohai and Shanghai,[42] the Spanish Dominicans, and the Missionaries of Paris, who administered the large area, all profited following the peace of Tientsin from the establishment of new religious societies. The first to bring in reinforcements were the Scheut Fathers. They had an exceedingly difficult vicariate in Mongolia. By establishing Christian villages, its members succeeded in settling complete communities around the center of the Ordos mission.[43] One of the pioneers of this enterprise was Alfons Bermyn (1878–1915), later vicar apostolic.[44] It

---

[39] J. Schütte, *Die katholische Chinamission im Spiegel der rotchinesischen Presse. Versuch einer missionarischen Deutung* (Münster 1957). In his conclusion, the author describes the weaknesses and shortcomings of the China mission: "In spite of its external involvement with politics, the Catholic China mission on the whole recognized its true religious goal and tried consistently to realize it. The repeated charge that the foreign missionaries were political spies and agents of imperialist powers is unfounded and was rejected" (381).

[40] Regarding the position of the Church in China (and Japan), see J. Schmidlin, *Das gegenwärtige Heidenapostolat im Fernen Osten* (Münster i. W. 1929).

[41] O. Ferreux, "Histoire de la Congrégation de la Mission en Chine 1699–1950," *Annales de la Congrégation de la Mission* 127 (Paris 1963), 3–530.

[42] Especially the University of Aurora, the College of Zikawei, and the studios of Tusewe together with the famous observatory.

[43] L. van Hecken, *Les réductions catholiques du pays des Ordos. Une méthode d'apostolat des missionnaires de Scheut* (Schöneck-Beckenried 1957); cf. id., *Les Missions chez les Mongols aux temps modernes* (Brussels 1949). Around 1900, the mission had about 371 members.

[44] Many new documents regarding this pioneer of the Mongolian mission (after 1900, he headed the vicariate apostolic of Southwest Mongolia) can be found in J. van Hecken, *Mgr. Alfons Bermyn. Dokumenten over het missieleven van een voortrekker in Mongolië (1878–1915)*, 2 vols. (Wijnegen 1947); J. van Oost, *Missionnaire de Scheut Monseigneur Bermyn, Apôtre des Ortos* (Louvain 1932).

was here that Monsignor Hubert Otto began his missionary activities.[45] He later transferred to the Kansu province which had been assigned to the Oblates of Mary Immaculate. He headed the vicariate apostolic of northern Kansu from 1890–1921. Following the Milanese missionaries (1869 in Honan) and the Spanish Augustinian friars (1879 in northern Honan), the Divine Word Missionaries arrived in the southern part of Shantung in 1882. Under the vicars apostolic J. B. Anzer[46] and A. Henninghaus,[47] they made rapid and solid progress, for which their schools were largely responsible. In 1885 assistance was sent to North Shensi by the Seminary of Peter and Paul in Rome, and in 1906 the Institute of Parma sent help to northern Honan. All attempts by the Parisians to Christianize Tibet failed due to the strong resistance of the Lamas. The Spanish Dominicans worked in Formosa (from 1859), however, they encountered obstacles after the Japanese occupied the island in 1895.[48]

In order to further the expansion of the Chinese mission, which claimed Leo XIII's particular attention and love, the Pope divided it into five regions (1879), keeping in mind the future local synods that had been negotiated at the First Vatican Council. He also increased the dioceses by fifteen and, in 1883, issued more detailed instructions to the missionaries in China.[49] It was indeed necessary to awaken the missionary spirit because in many cases the interest was not in gaining new territory, but consolidation within the established area.[50] Therefore, the regional synods, appointed after the eighties, strongly emphasized the conversion of the pagans. The meetings were also important for the closer collaboration of the often colorful missionary personnel and for a more uniform organization of missionary procedures. The synods all attempted to eliminate other shortcomings, such as the missionaries' insufficient training and acclimatization to the land and its people, the neglect of the upper classes and intelligentsia in the press and the schools, and the rather arbitrary and not sufficiently planned way in

---

[45] C. van Melckebeke, *Notre bon Monseigneur Otto. 1850–1938* (Scheut, Brussels 1949). Regarding Msgr. Otto, cf. Streit XII, 581f.

[46] Regarding J. B. Anzer (1851–1903), cf. Streit XII, 592ff.

[47] Regarding Augustin Henninghaus (1862–1939), ibid. XIII, 8ff.

[48] A. Züger, "Die katholische Kirche auf Formosa," *NZM* 14 (1958), 276–96. The Dominicans, who had been on the island since 1859, had not been very successful: in 1919, the number of Catholics was only 4,400.

[49] *Collectanea* II, 187–196.—Regarding the development of the hierarchy under Leo XIII, cf. Schmidlin, *PG* II, 527; under Pius X, ibid. III, 134f.

[50] Ibid., 192: "Sed quum gentilium conversio ad Christum Dominum in cuius cognitione vita aeterna omnium hominum sita est, finis praecipuus missionum existat, ad eam toto animo intendere Vicarii App. conentur."

which the Chinese Church was provided with a clergy and episcopate.[51] The elimination of these inadequacies was demanded by a group of missionaries who were attracted by the positive characteristics of the Chinese and, supporting the so-called Tientsin method, advocated turning away from Europeanism.[52] The establishment of a nunciature was to serve the same purpose, but the plan proposed by the Chinese failed because France opposed it.[53] Neither under Leo XIII nor under Pius X could the project be realized. The often abused protectorate was opposed by Vincent Lebbe (1877–1940), who was extremely active, but also assailed by many. He was a disciple of the spirit of the Gentry group and can be considered the pioneer of a new direction of missionary work in China: thorough indigenization.[54]

At the end of the century, the Western powers and Japan concluded treaties with Korea as well; they proved to be beneficial to the Church. Following the persecutions (1803–13, 1827, 1838–46, 1866–69) and the last edict (1881), Christianity was able to gain ground on the basis of the agreements of the eighties, in spite of some reverses in Taikyu in 1887. Religious freedom was not impeded after 1895 by the establishment of the Japanese protectorate, although the authorities attempted to propagate the official Shinto cult. Monsignor Félix-Clair Ridel, after 1869 vicar apostolic of Korea, did not arrive in the country until 1877. He was arrested the following year and deported to China. Like his successors Blanc and Mutel, he was a member of the Missionaries of Paris who, disregarding the hostile atmosphere on the peninsula, had sent more and more personnel there.[55] Mutel held the office of vicar apostolic of Korea from 1890 until 1911. After the division into two dioceses, Seoul and Taikyu (1911), he administered the former. The growth of the new Church was furthered by the founding of vocational

---

[51] J. Beckmann, *Die katholische Missionsmethode in China in neuester Zeit (1842–1912)* (Immensee 1931).

[52] Ibid., 22, 44, 93, 101f., 106f., 195 in regard to this new orientation.

[53] L. Wei Tsing-sing, "Le Saint-Siège, la France et la Chine sous le pontificat de Léon XIII. Le problème de l'établissement d'une nonciature à Pékin et l'affaire du Pei-t'ang 1880–1886," NZM 21 (1965), 18–36, 81–101, 184–212, 252–71.

[54] The founder of the *Société des Auxiliaires des Missions* (S.A.M.) is an ambiguous figure. Even the study of J. Leclercq, *Vie du Père Lebbe* (Toulouse, Paris 1955, [5]1961) was criticized. Cf. J. Levaux, *Le Père Lebbe, Apôtre de la Chine moderne* (Brussels 1948); also J. Beckmann, *Die China-Mission* (n. 37), 3; id., NZM 4 (1948), 309f., about Lebbe's ideas. These were incorporated into the missionary encyclical of Benedict XV, *Maximum illud*, and into other documents.

[55] Concerning Ridel (1830–84), see Streit X, 426–28. Marie-Jean-Gustave Blanc (1844–90) came to Korea in 1876. He was the vicar apostolic of Korea from 1884 to 1890 (Streit X, 436–38); Gustave-Charles-Marie Mutel, 1854–1933 (Streit X, 433).

and trade schools by the Benedictines of Saint Ottilien, located in Seoul after they established their monastery there in 1909.[56]

Due to the influence and pressures from outside (treaties with the European powers) and the ensuing accessibility of the country to modern Western civilization, the Church in Japan seemed to face a promising future.[57] By 1889 it enjoyed full religious freedom. The persecution decrees had been abolished in 1872/73. The improvement of the situation was aided by the friendly relations between both Leo XIII and Pius X and the royal court.[58] Slowly conversions increased: in 1882, there were 28,000 Catholics, by 1890 the number had grown to 54,000. The Japanese bishops met that same year for their first synod in Nagasaki and, in 1891, Rome proceeded with the establishment of a hierarchy, with Tokyo becoming an archbishopric and Nagasaki, Osaka, and Hakodate suffragan bishoprics.[59] In 1896 the Trappists, the male as well as the female branch, began their prolific activities in Tobetsu near Hakodate. However, most of the work still rested on the shoulders of the Paris Missionaries. They were soon joined by other missionary societies: the Spanish Dominicans of the Philippines in the apostolic prefecture of Shikoku (1904), the Divine Word Missionaries (apostolic prefecture of Niigata, 1912) and the Franciscans in Hokkaido (apostolic prefecture of Sapporo, including Hokkaido, Sakhalin, and the Kuril Islands, 1915), and the (German) Jesuits who founded the Sophia University in the capital (1913). In 1887, the Marianists arrived, earning praise for their work in secondary schools. And finally, there were the female societies (among others, those of Saint Paul and Saint Maurice).

All these groups devoted themselves to the care of the Christians, the training of the Japanese clergy and the catechists, the education of the converts, the press, and social work.[60] Around the turn of the century, however, the disillusioned and disappointed missionaries had to admit that their high hopes could not be fulfilled because the number of baptized had decreased and the number of converts were very few.[61]

---

[56] F. Renner, "Der Ruf an die Benediktiner nach Korea und Manchukuo," F. Renner, op. cit. II, 391–428; A. Kaspar, P. Berger, *60 Jahre Benediktinermission in Korea und der Mandschurei* (Münsterschwarzach 1973). In 1890, Korea had 18,000 Catholics; in 1912: 79,000.

[57] J. Laures, *Die katholische Kirche in Japan* (Kaldenkirchen 1956).

[58] *Acta Leonis* II, 134f.; Schmidlin, *PG* III, 135.

[59] *Acta Leonis* IV, 222–31: *Litterae Apostolicae Non maius Nobis* of 15 June 1891.

[60] J. van Hecken, *Un siècle de vie catholique au Japon 1859–1959* (Tokyo 1960).

[61] In many respects, this situation is reminiscent of the period following World War II. The Protestants were in a much more advantageous position, and their part in modernizing Japan was more significant. The reason may be that their missionaries came mainly from America and England, countries after which the Japanese modeled their adaptation to the western civilization.

The reasons for this are numerous. Money and personnel were lacking. However, the underlying causes are more complex. Among them were the religious scepticism of the Japanese, their passionate desire for purely material, economic progress, their resentment of European teachers, and the fact that they considered Christianity an intrusion. Moreover, there was the identification of the Japanese national character with Shintoism. After the decline of Buddhism, Shintoism became the state religion, the embodiment of the national ideal and the supporting pillar of the new empire. It was an obstacle to the development of the Church, especially since it was extensively propagated throughout the educational system, the military, and all schools. Finally, the missionary process itself had its flaws, which were recognized by a few of the missionaries: The Japanese world had not been penetrated sufficiently, the religions of the country had not been studied, and indirect work, such as literary endeavors, had been neglected. A more thorough study of language and culture, especially of the religious concepts of the Japanese, was needed.[62]

The only Asian country with a Catholic majority, the Philippines, went through the most critical phase of its ecclesiastical history around the turn of the century.[63] If one is interested in the cause of the events which almost brought the Church to the brink of its existence there, one will have to investigate, on the one hand, the characteristics of the political-ecclesiastical constellation within the Spanish colonial empire and, on the other hand, the American intervention, with its many detrimental consequences. Without diminishing the astonishing accomplishments of the Iberian mother country and especially the missionaries,[64] one is compelled to notice that the system, especially on the ecclesiastical level, had considerable shortcomings: it did not aim at independence, but rather tried to preserve dependence on Spain by employing paternalistic methods. Supported by the Freemasons, nationalistic tendencies opposing the foreign dominion grew stronger in the course of the nineteenth century. The native clergy took the same direction because, having been confined to inferior positions, it felt disadvantaged.[65] This placed the clergy into growing opposition to the

---

[62] Schmidlin, M, 479f.; J. Beckmann, *Weltkirche und Weltreligionen* (Freiburg i. B. 1960), 102f., describes the first indications of religious strife in the country.

[63] F. X. Clark, *The Philippine Missions* (New York 1945); "Fourth Centenary of the Evangelization of the Philippines," *Boletín Ecl. de Filipinas* 39 (Manila 1965), 1–352; "IV Centenario de la Evangelización de Filipinas," *Boletín de la Provincia de San Nicolás de Tolentino de Filipinas* 55 (Marcilla, Navarra 1965), 53–303.

[64] In this regard, Streit IX, offers impressive documents; cf. ibid., introduction p. X, J. Dindinger's plea defending the messengers of faith.

[65] In the nineteenth century, their number was relatively large, however, they were

Spanish religious orders whose members clung to their old (economically lucrative) positions and who seemed to guarantee loyalty toward the political power. What was originally devised as a colonial reform, slowly took a course toward separation and, in the struggle with the religious, developed even anticlerical features. Pressured by the rebels, Spain deported the monks and expropriated their estates (1897). However, it was too late. Asked for help by the nationalists, America declared war in 1897. But instead of being given into the hands of the patriots, the country became the property of the United States.[66]

The presence of the new power produced drastic changes for the Church: the separation of Church and state (for which the faithful were not prepared), lay legislation which prohibited religious instruction in schools and thus caused religious deprivation,[67] stress on ideological neutrality of the state university (founded in 1911), which alienated the educated from the Church, the infiltration of Protestantism and numerous sects, and, last but not least, the antagonistic attitude of groups indoctrinated by America who considered Christianity a thorn in their side. Finally, in 1912, in the course of the nationalistic turmoils and under the leadership of Gregorio Aglipay, a secular priest from the Philippines (1860–1940), some of the Catholics separated from Rome and formed the *Iglesia Católica Filipina Independiente*.[68] After initial spectacular successes (50 of the 825 Philippine priests and about 1 million of the 8 million Catholics converted to Aglipayism), the membership slowly declined, especially after 1907 when the Church began to recover from the setback.[69] Aware of the critical situation, Leo XIII had begun in 1902 to reorganize Church life, establishing an apostolic

---

generally kept from heading parishes and episcopal offices (yet there were twelve indigenous bishops during the Spanish era).

[66] The most thorough study of this transition: P. S. de Achútegui, M. A. Bernad, *Religious Revolution in the Philippines,* 2 vols. (Manila 1960–66).

[67] F. T. Reuter, "American Catholics and the Establishment of the Philippine School System," CHR 49 (Washington 1963), 365–81.

[68] Achútegui and Bernad prove clearly that this separation is rooted in nationalism, that it is a reaction to the political as well as religious domination by the Spaniards. Cf. also I. R. Rodríguez, *Gregorio Aglipay y los orígenes de la Iglesia Filipina Independiente 1898–1917,* 2 vols. (Manila 1960); N. P. Cushner, "Gregorio Aglipay and the Philippine Independent Church," NZM 18 (1962), 142–47. Cushner also describes the official doctrine of the schismatic Church.

[69] P. S. Achútegui, M. A. Bernad, *Documents Relative to the Religious Revolution in the Philippines. The Religious Coup d'État 1898–1901. A Documentary History* (Manila 1971). Aglipayism deteriorated for many reasons (in 1960 only 5 percent of the population adhered to it): decline of anti-Hispanic sentiments, revitalization of the Catholic Church, return of all estates to the Catholics, the movement's lack of international reputation, its increasing approach toward Protestantism.

delegature and four new dioceses.[70] On the basis of a treaty with Rome, the missionaries, even the Spanish ones, could return. The old orders, continuing their activities, were aided by more recent missionary societies, following the urgent appeal of the Pope to alleviate the dire need for priests: the Mill Hill Missionaries (1906), the Scheut Fathers (1907), the Missionaries of the Sacred Heart (1908), and the Divine Word Missionaries (1909). At the Thomas University in Manila (licensed in 1916), the Dominicans resumed their work. Pius X himself made efforts to convene a plenary council, which met in 1907 in the capital, headed by the delegate Ambros Agius. The real missionary work was done by the Jesuits (on Mindanao), the Scheut Fathers among the Igorots (northern Luzon), the Negritos, and the immigrant Chinese, while the Divine Word Missionaries, with equal success, took care of the Abras.[71]

Under the rather intolerant colonial power of the Dutch,[72] the Catholic Church was able to develop in Dutch East India after it resettled there in the first half of the century.[73] In the twentieth century, the Jesuits were the only ones, supported by a few secular priests (after 1859), to work in the apostolic vicariate of Batavia, which included the entire huge area of the archipelago.[74] After the formation of the first ecclesiastial districts (1905: the apostolic prefecture of Dutch Borneo, 1911: Sumatra, 1913: the Lesser Sunda islands) and the arrival of new societies (the Missionaries of the Sacred Heart, the Capuchin friars, and the Divine Word Missionaries), the Catholics were able to compete with the Protestants, especially on the Lesser Sunda islands, where exceedingly active communities developed. Progress was also due to the work of the various female congregations. The Ursulines and the female

---

[70] *Acta Leonis* VIII, 141–50: *Litterae Apostolicae Quae, mari sinico* of 17 September 1902: Lipa, Tuguegarao, Capiz, Zamboanga; the apostolic prefecture of Palawan was established in 1910. In his letter, the Pope emphasized the necessity for the development of a native clergy and missionary activities in the pagan regions.

[71] J. Schmitz, *Die Abra-Mission auf Nordluzon/Philippinen von 1598–1955* (Sankt Augustin 1964); Engl. ed.: *The Abra Mission in Northern Luzon, Philippines. 1598–1955* (Cebu City 1971); regarding the beginnings of Church life, see F. Schwager, "Die Mission auf den Philippinen," *ZM* 4 (1914), 198–236.

[72] K. M. Panikkar, *Asien und die Herrschaft des Westens* (Zurich 1955), passes harsh judgment upon the colonial powers (p. 103). See also F. Schwager, "Die ostindische Inselflur," *ZM* 3 (1913), 306–10.

[73] J. A. T. Weltjens, *De Vrijheid der Katholieke Prediking in Nederlands-Indië van 1900 tot 1940* (partial publ. of a dissertation of the Gregoriana—Djakarta 1969).

[74] After 1881, the Mill Hill Missionaries worked among the Chinese and Dajaks on British North Borneo. In Dutch India, there were only sixteen official missions at the beginning of the twentieth century. This situation reflects Catholicism's difficult position in Holland.

Franciscans were joined in 1885 by the Sisters of Charity from Tilburg, who founded their first school in Padang (Sumatra); the Sisters of the Society of Jesus, Mary, and Joseph settled in Minahassa (Celebes).[75] Planting the seeds for the later growth of the Indonesian Church, these pioneers included a respectable number of missionaries who excelled in the area of language, e.g., the Jesuit Cornelius J. F. le Coq d'Armandville (1846–96), who in 1884 discovered the Portuguese Latin songs in Sika (Flores),[76] and Fr. Franciscus van Lith, the founder of the Mission of Central Java. After his arrival in 1896, he closely studied the culture of the country, desiring to enrich it through contacts with Christianity. His method of influencing the social milieu through a carefully educated elite bore rich fruit.[77]

The missions in the Pacific also had to cope with the explosive atmosphere of colonial expansion. The fact that all islands in the Pacific were divided among the Western powers had its impact on the course of Christianization.[78] Due to the presence of the greatest colonial power, Great Britain, Protestantism had a considerable head start, which motivated the Catholics, particularly the French, under the pontificates of Leo XIII and Pius X, to increase their activities. Continuing into most recent times, the denominational competition was occasionally intensified by national rivalries, the Protestant missionaries relying on England and the Catholic ones on France.[79] Because of this, they were accused of political activities, but today scholars assess the situation with more restraint. Though taking advantage of the assistance of the protective and colonial powers, the missionaries were mainly interested in assuring the success of their work: the Christianization of the people in question.[80]

---

[75] A. Mulders, *De Missie in Tropisch Nederland* ('s-Hertogenbosch 1940); regarding the situation around 1913, cf. K. Streit, "Die katholische Mission" (in Dutch India), *ZM* 3 (1913), 310–29; A. Djajasepoetra, "Het 75 jarig bestaan van de St. Claverbond," *Missienieuws Jezuiten* (Nijmegen 1965), Jan. 4–6; a series of other articles about the seventy-five years of missionary work on Java can be found here.

[76] Streit VIII, 486; B. Biermann, "Lieder der Florinesen," *NZM* 10 (1954), 141–45.

[77] Streit VIII, 829; L. van Rijckevorsel, *Pastoor F. van Lith. S. J. De Stichter van de Missie in Midden-Java 1863–1926* (Nijmegen 1952).

[78] *Les missions dans le Pacifique. Journal de la Société des Océanistes (cahier spécial, XXV* [Paris 1970]; R. Jaspers, *Die missionarische Erschließung Ozeaniens. Ein quellengeschichtlicher und missionsgeographischer Versuch zur kirchlichen Gebietsaufteilung in Ozeanien bis 1855* (Münster 1972).

[79] J. Schmidlin, "Missionsmethode und Politik der ersten Südsee-Missionare," *ZMR* 26 (1936), 255–63; A. Perbal, *Les missionaires français et le nationalisme* (Paris 1939), takes issue with Schmidlin's viewpoint.

[80] According to A. A. Koskinen, *Missionary Influence as a Political Factor in the Pacific Islands* (Helsinki 1953).

All in all, we can say that each one of the three societies primarily involved in missionary work settled in a different geographic area. The Picpus Fathers settled in the eastern Pacific. Even though their vicariates on the Hawaiian Islands (where Damian Deveuster died in 1889 in the service of the lepers on Molokai) and on the Gambier, Society, Marquesas, Paumotu, and Tubuaï Islands were all stagnating, they reached out toward the Windward Islands (1888) and later the Cook Islands (1894). In the central Pacific, the Marists (1887) expanded their area of work to the New Hebrides. When establishing the vicariate apostolic (New Hebrides, 1904), they had only twelve hundred faithful. However, at their headquarters on the Wallis and Futuna Islands, the life of the Church flourished. It also developed satisfactorily on the Fiji Islands under Julien Vital (after 1887 vicar apostolic) and on the Tonga Islands. They did not return to the Solomon Islands, which they had to abandon after forty years of difficult trials, until 1897 when the apostolic prefecture of the Southern Solomon Islands was established (in 1912 a vicariate apostolic).[81] During the revolt of 1878 on New Caledonia, they shared the fate of the colonial power and, fleeing under the protection of the French, paid their share with a number of lives.[82] Pierre-Marie Bataillon (1810–77), bishop of the Marists, deserves credit for having dared to improve the education of the native clergy. Failures and setbacks did not discourage him. He made his last and most decisive move when founding the seminary in Lane (Wallis Islands), where his successor was privileged to ordain the first four Polynesian priests in 1886. In the western Pacific, we find mostly the Sacred Heart Missionaries. From 1881 on, they took care of the huge Melanesian-Micronesian dual vicariate.[83] On the Bismarck Archipelago, New Britain,[84] New Ireland and the Admiralty Islands, they witnessed a remarkable increase in their communities around the turn of the century, and they were also successful on the Gilbert Islands under Monsignor Joseph Leray (after 1882 vicar apostolic of those islands). However, the apostolate on the Marshall Islands did not prosper. On Guam (Mariana

---

[81] P. O. 'Reilly, H. Laraey, "Bibliographie des presses de la mission mariste des Îles Salomon," *Journal de la Société des Océanistes* 25 (1969), 257–92.

[82] R. Dousset, *Colonialisme et contradictions. Études sur les causes socio-historiques de l'Insurrection de 1878 en Nouvelle-Calédonie* (Paris 1970); reviewed by G. Höltker, *Anthropos* 66 (1971), 294f.; A. Saussol, "La mission mariste et la colonisation européenne en Nouvelle-Calédonie," *Journal de la Société des Océanistes* 25 (1969), 113–24.

[83] It dates from 1844; cf. Streit XXI, 127; J. Bertolini, "L'Océanie dans les Archives générales des Missionnaires du Sacré-Cœur," *Journal de la Société des Océanistes* 25 (Paris 1969), 359–82.

[84] *Pioniere der Südsee. Werden und Wachsen der Herz-Jesu-Mission von Rabaul 1882–1932* (Commemorative ed. [Hiltrup 1932]).

Islands), German Capuchin friars replaced the Augustinian Recollects who had been driven out by the Americans in 1898.[85] From Austrialia, the Sacred Heart Missionaries traveled to New Guinea, settling first on Thursday Island (1884) and later on Christmas Island (1885). From here, Fr. L.-A. Navarre, later vicar apostolic, and Fr. St. E. Verjus (1860–90), who was well known and later elected chief, Christianized the British area.[86] In the Dutch section, we find the Sacred Heart Missionaries after 1903. In German New Guinea, the Society of the Divine Word laid a solid foundation for Catholic Christianity at the end of the last century. The Marists continued their work among the Maoris in the south of New Zealand (Wellington), the Mill Hill Missionaries in the north (Auckland). There were only three somewhat significant missionary attempts among the aborigines of Australia: the efforts of the Jesuits after the eighties in the north, of the Benedictines of New Norcia,[87] who received the new vicariate of Kimberley in 1887 and founded the daughter mission of Drysdale River, in 1910[88] and, finally, the attempts of the Trappists in Broome, which was given to the German Pallotines in 1900.

An important first step in all these missionary enterprises was the establishment of the apostolic delegature for Australia, New Zealand, and Oceania.[89] At the outbreak of World War I, the number of Catholics in the nineteen mission districts of the South Seas was one hundred ninety thousand, a truely unique accomplishment in the history of missions, demonstrating the endless optimism of the pioneers of the faith in an area that presented more difficulties than anyone could imagine.

Africa

During the same period, the African mission experienced a similarly stormy development. Although it had been in the background in the middle of the nineteenth century, it now became a focal point of interest. On the one hand, it profited from Europe's growing interest in the

[85] C. Lopinot, "Zur Missionsgeschichte der Marianen und Karolinen," *NZM* 15 (1959), 305–08.
[86] Concerning Verjus, cf. Streit XXI, 279ff.; A. Dupeyrat, *Papouasie. Histoire de la Mission 1885–1935* (Issoudun, Paris 1935); B. de Vaulx, *Histoire des missions catholiques françaises* (Paris 1951), 506–31.
[87] R. Salvado, *Memorias históricas sobre la Australia y la Misión Benedictina de Nueva Nursia* (Madrid 1946).
[88] *AAS* 2 (1910), 410f.; in regard to earlier missionary attempts by the Jesuits, cf. R. M. Berndt, "Surviving Influence of Mission Contact on the Daly River, Northern Territory of Australia," *NZM* 8 (1952), 81–95, 188–92.
[89] *Litterae Apostolicae,* 15 April 1914: *Sylloge,* 83f.; expanding over all the Pacific islands: ibid., 108 (20 May 1919).

dark continent. On the other hand, it took advantage of the possibilities which opened up when the colonial powers occupied large areas of land.[90] The criticism that the missionaries were thinly disguised lackeys of the colonial authorities is refuted by the facts. With the exception of a few, the missionaries stayed away from wordly dealings. Not infrequently, conflicts arose with the administration because the missionaries felt obliged to represent the side of the Africans.[91] The Gospel was not always preached with the same enthusiasm and success. In White Africa (north of the Sahara) it gained hardly any ground, but, along the equator, Catholicism encountered the strongest response. Towards the south, the response gradually decreased.[92]

In North Africa Christianity encountered the strongest resistance. From here the Islamic faith was to start its victorious course into the center of the continent. It was an element which the Christian churches had to face in many areas.[93] Out of concern for the Muslim population, the authorities did not permit missionary activities in many areas or they imposed restrictions (e.g., in British Sudan, today's Ghana, and in Cameroon). For a long time, there was no real Islamic mission, until Cardinal Lavigerie became archbishop of Algeria in 1867 and introduced drastic reforms. In his first pastoral letter, he demanded the right to deal with the Arabs and he was, indeed, given greater freedom.[94] In

---

[90] L. H. Gann, P. Duignan, *Colonialism in Africa 1870–1960,* 2 vols. (London 1970); vol. II: 1914–60.—At times, the missionaries were the only whites settling anywhere. In some places, they followed trade or any firmly established foreign power. Partially, the intentions of the missions were identical with those of colonial policies (F. Blanke, "Mission und Kolonialpolitik," *Europa und der Kolonialismus* [Zurich 1962], 91–122; id., *Missionsprobleme des Mittelalters und der Neuzeit* [Zurich 1960]; F. Jäger, "Die Kolonisation Afrikas durch die Europäer—eine Kulturleistung," *Universitas* 17 [1962] 851–57.

[91] E. Dammann takes issue with those who consider any kind of colonial activity an error: "In some individual cases, the ties may have been too close. However, in general, a negative judgment is not justified. The earlier situation should not be measured by today's standards. Where else could and should missions have developed if not here?" (*Das Christentum in Afrika* [Munich, Hamburg 1968], 144; cf. ibid., 23f.).

[92] J. Beckmann, *Die katholische Kirche im neuen Afrika* (Einsiedeln 1947); W. Bühlmann, *Afrika. Die Kirche unter den Völkern* I (Mainz 1963).

[93] J. Beckmann, op. cit., 327–55: "Die Auseinandersetzung mit dem Islam"; G. Simon, *Die Welt des Islams und ihre Berührung mit der Christenheit* (Gütersloh 1930); C. Tiltak, "Die Neuausbreitung des Islam im 20. Jahrhundert," *Saeculum* 5 (1954), 359–75.—By 1950, 85 million of the 150 million Africans had converted to the religion of the prophet; 45 million were natives.

[94] Streit XVII, 743 (*Lettre pastorale,* 1867). Napoleon III granted him this right, Mac-Mahon protested. Regarding the conflict with MacMahon, see M. Emerit, *RH* 223 (1960), 63–84.

1800, he was allowed to educate and baptize orphans whom he had collected in villages (Saint Cyprian, 1873, and Saint Monica, 1875). He also founded the first missions among the purely Muslim Berbers.[95] His disciples, the White Fathers, were supported by the Jesuits, for whom their general, Fr. Roothaan, a genius with vision, had devised a bold program.[96] Subsequently, the White Fathers moved toward the southeast, toward Shanija (three stations). The White Sisters opened a hospital in Biskra. By 1906, the number of Muslim converts had increased to eight hundred and the catechumens to two hundred within thirteen missions. This seems to be a small number, but in view of its principal significance, it represents an important achievement.

Lavigerie formulated his methodical principles regarding missions in his instructions to the missionaries (1878–79). Essentially, they are still valid, and they also inspired other societies in their behavior toward the Muslims.[97] He initially forbade preaching a specifically Christian message, as well as the baptism of individual candidates. He recommended instead the indirect apostolate (charity, schools, orphanages, visits with the natives), hoping to prepare the ground gradually.[98] The same course was taken by the "Apostle of the Sahara," Charles de Foucauld (1858–1916).[99] The primate of Africa demanded of his sons that they know the language, adapt to the life-style of the people who were to be converted, and practice friendship and active charity. Foucauld tried to put these principles into practice in Beni-Abbés and later in Tamanrasset. The White Fathers moved their post into the Sahara desert, where they settled in Gardaia, El Goléa, and Uargla, thus adding to the vicariate of Sahara (1891) the prefecture of Gardaia (1901), which was served by the hermit Foucauld.

In West Africa, the activities of Catholic missionaries began in the black independent state of Liberia. The efforts made on behalf of this country show what kind of obstacles were in the way of missionary

---

[95] J. Tiquot, *Une expérience de petite colonisation indigène en Algérie. Les colons arabes-chrétiens du Cardinal Lavigerie* (Algier 1936).

[96] A. Villanyi, "La fondation de la mission algérienne dans la correspondance du Père Général Roothaan," *NZM* 18 (1962), 196–207, 289–304; 19 (1963), 29–42. In a letter of 20 October 1849, Roothaan wrote: "Allez sans bruit dans les tribus voisines comme hôte et comme ami. C'est une œuvre de patience et d'un long dévouement" (ibid., 32).

[97] *Instructions de son Éminence le Cardinal Lavigerie à ses Missionaires* (Maison-Carrée 1927).

[98] J. Perraudin, *Lavigerie. Ses principes missionaires* (Fribourg 1941); J. Mazé, "Les idées principales du Cardinal Lavigerie sur l'Evangélisation de l'Afrique," *RHM* 2 (1925), 351–96.

[99] Streit XX, 475–91: bibliography; J. F. Six, *Itinéraire spirituel de Charles de Foucauld* (Paris 1958); id., "Le Père de Foucauld et ses recherches de fondations évangéliques," *Rev. d'Asc. et de Mystique* 36 (1960), 64–72.

work: unhealthy conditions, the Islamic faith penetrating from the north, the strong presence of Protestantism.[100] In many places, the colonial administration added to the difficulties. After their missionary attempts in the first half of the century failed, American secular priests and the Holy Ghost Fathers[101] returned in 1884. But the tropical climate decimated their numbers and they were replaced in 1903 by the Montfort Fathers. When they gave up, the prefecture was given to the Society of African Missions, headed by the courageous Étienne Kyne.[102] The two societies mentioned above, the Spiritans and the Lyon group, took care of a number of areas in West Africa around the turn of the century. Some of them seemed promising (southern Nigeria, the Ivory and the Gold Coast, Lower Volta, Dahomey, the Bight of Benin).[103] More missionaries arrived, such as the Pallottines in Cameroon in 1890. It was important for them that they began in 1901 to take care of the Yaundes (living near today's capital).[104] They contributed a great deal to the acquisition of large communities through farming and the development of small businesses, as well as an extensive school system where German was spoken almost exclusively. The female Pallottines took care of the women. In the north, in Adamaua, the priests of the Sacred Heart from Sittard took on responsibility, while the Divine Word Missionaries, mostly of German descent, moved into Togo in 1892, where they taught, developed agriculture, trained craftsmen, and worked a printing press (in Lomé).[105]

[100] E. Dammann (op. cit., 24–58) lists as some of the predominantly Protestant missionary areas in Africa Gambia, Sierra Leone, Liberia, Ghana, Kenya, Tanzania, Malawi, Zambia, Rhodesia, the Republic of South Africa, Lesotho, Swaziland, Botswana, South West Africa; the predominantly Catholic areas are Portuguese Guinea, Guinea, the Ivory Coast, Togo, Dahomey, Equatorial Guinea, Cameroon, São Tomé, Príncipe, Gabun, Congo (Brazzaville), the Central African Republic, Zaïre, Angola, and Portuguese East Africa.

[101] The archbishop of Philadelphia sent his vicar general Barron to Liberia in 1840. He was joined by some Spiritans. Cf. H. J. Koren, *The Spiritans. A History of the Congregation of the Holy Ghost* (Louvain 1958).

[102] During the first sixty-five years, this society lost almost four hundred members in West Africa (283 priests and 110 sisters). Cf. R. Guilcher, *La Société des Missions Africaines. Ses origines, sa nature, sa vie, ses œuvres* (Lyon 1956); P. Falcon, "Bilan historique de l'action des Missions Africaines sur le continent noir," *Revue Française d'Études Politiques Africaines* 56 (Paris 1970), 12–36.

[103] See F. Schwager II, 85–112; R. Wiltgen, *Gold Coast Mission History 1471–1880* (Techny, Ill. 1956): The author deals with practically all of West Africa.—Along the Ivory Coast, the Africa Society (active after 1895) used a steamship to maintain contact between the stations located on the coast.

[104] P. Hermann Nekes studied the language of the Yaundes (cf. Streit XVIII, 778–80).

[105] H. W. Debrunner, *A Church between Colonial Powers. A Study of the Church in Togo* (London 1965): especially about the Protestant missions; K. Müller, *Geschichte der katholischen Kirche in Togo* (Kaldenkirchen 1958); H. W. Gensichen, "Die deutsche

After 1839, when France began to sign treaties with kings and chiefs in the territory around the equator, gradually expanding the French Congo, the first missionaries started to arrive: in 1844, the Holy Ghost Fathers in Gabun and four years later the Sisters of the Immaculate Conception of Chartres. The Spiritans took care of the vicariate of Loango on the coast and the vicariate of Ubangi, which was responsible for the northeastern, the largest part of the colony (1890).[106] This district was first headed energetically by Bishop P.-P. Augouard (1852–1921). In spite of the lowliness of the population, he never doubted their Christianization. Suffering great privation, he took daring trips throughout the huge territory, founding missions in strategic places. Though he was always concerned with the well-being of the missions, he also rendered outstanding political service to his country, but France did not reward him.[107]

The area around the equator and central Africa belonged to those regions of black Africa that had been a focal point for preaching the Gospel since the fifteenth century. Libermann, Monsignor Bessieux, Mère Javouhey, and Monsignor de Marion-Brésillac planned to explore the Sudan, the enormous territory between the Atlantic ocean, the Sahara, Abyssinia, and the Congo.[108] Even though they were unable to penetrate the interior of the continent, their attempts resulted in solid foundations on the coasts of Guinea and Senegal. Others planned to approach the center of Africa from the north along the Nile river, instead of from the west. In 1847, a year after the vicariate apostolic of Central Africa was established, the Congregation for the Propagation of the Faith itself sent out pioneers: Monsignor Annetto Casolani, Maximilian Ryllo, S.J., Emmanuele Pedemonte, S.J., and two trainees of the Congregation, Ignaz Knoblecher and Angelo Vinco. They made it all the way to Khartoum, where they failed in the attempt to found a mission.[109] There was another point from which some attempted to reach the desired goal. After a 999-day trip, Stanley had explored the course of the Congo River and discovered its mouth near Boma (1877).

Mission und der Kolonialismus," *KuD* VII, 1962, 136–49.

[106] Streit XVIII, 152, 268.

[107] Streit XVIII, 252ff.; G. Goyau, *Monseigneur Augouard* (Paris 1926); A. Perbal, "Le nationalisme de Mgr. Augouard," *RHM* 15 (1938), 385–407.

[108] A. Tanghe, "Essais de pénétration missionaires dans l'Afrique centrale," *NZM* 8 (1952), 230–33.

[109] Vicariate apostolic of Central Africa: *Ius Pontificium* V (Rome 1893), 361; in regard to the various individuals, cf. Streit XVII, 552f., 564f., 602f., 605f., 625f.; M. B. Storme, "Origine du Vicariat Apost. de l'Afrique Centrale," *NZM* 8 (1952), 105–18; id., "La renonciation de Mgr. Casolani, Vicaire Apostolique de l'Afrique Centrale," *NZM* 9 (1953), 290–305; R. Gray, *A History of the Southern Sudan 1839–89* (Oxford 1961).

Africa's secret was found. Now, the missionaries were able to penetrate the Congo area from the west.

In this enterprise King Leopold II (1865–1909) played a unique role.[110] In 1876 he invited the Geographic Conference to Brussels. He was primarily interested in maintaining control of the initiative to explore the interior of Africa, pursuing the idea of Belgium's colonial expansion. During the debates about the establishment of international strongholds, most participants held the opinion that missionaries should help the explorers and traders to civilize the country. Leopold made sure that the final decisions were not in the hands of the missions because he had his own plans in this regard. Since the Belgian Catholics were sceptical, he informed the Holy See. Pius IX and his successor welcomed the royal plan.[111] Trying to pursue his policy, the monarch established the *Association Internationale Africaine.* In 1885, on the basis of the Berlin Conference, the independent state of the Congo was created. At first it was the private property of Leopold, after 1908 it became part of the Belgian kingdom. Aside from abolishing the slave trade and elevating the morals of the natives, the King was clearly interested in their Christianization. For that purpose, he pursued the establishment of the vicariate apostolic of the Belgian Congo (1888),[112] which was assigned to the Scheut Fathers because the King gave preference to his countrymen.[113]

The Congregation of the Immaculate Heart of Mary began its work and, subsidized by the government, gathered primarily slaves and children in closed settlements. This system was used in the Kasaï mission (1904, apostolic prefecture), one of the most beautiful settlements of the Scheut Fathers.[114] A similar method (the so-called *Fermes-chapelles,*

---

[110] P. A. Roeykens, *Les débuts de l'œuvre africaine de Léopold II 1875–79* (Brussels 1955).

[111] P. A. Roeykens, *Le dessein africain de Léopold II. Nouvelles recherches sur sa genèse et sa nature 1875–76;* id., *Léopold et la Conférence géographique de Bruxelles 1876;* id., *La période initiale de l'œuvre africaine de Léopold II. Nouvelles recherches et documents inédits 1875–83. Tome X,* fascs. 1–3 (Brussels 1956–57).

[112] Streit XVIII, 198.

[113] E. de Moreau, *Les missionaires belges de 1804 jusqu'a nos jours* (Brussels 1944); L. Anckaer, *De evangelizatiemethode van de missionarissen van Scheut in Kongo 1888–1907* (Brussels 1970).—With the exception of the White Friars (vicariate of Upper Congo), the old missionaries had to leave their stations.

[114] M. B. Storme, *Het Onstaan van de Kasai-Missie* (Brussels 1961): regarding the first negotiations between 1881 and 1891 and the transferal of the Kasai mission (Luluabourg); id., *Pater Cambier on de stichting van de Kasai-Missie* (Brussels 1964). P. E. Cambier (1865–1943) was the founder of the mission. Its history from 1891 until 1894 is described on the basis of documents (id., *Konflikt in de Kasai-Missie* [Brussels 1965]). The civil authorities caused the most problems for the development of missionary activities; in this book, the author deals with the conflict of March 1894–June 1895.

including economic and cultural institutions) was employed by the Jesuits, settled in Kwango after 1893.[115] Thanks to the efforts of the Scheut Missionaries and the King it was possible to attract new missionary personnel: in 1894 the Trappists, in 1897 the Priests of the Sacred Heart of Jesus (Stanley Falls), in 1898 the Premonstratensians (northern Congo), in 1899 the Redemptorists (Matadi at the lower portion of the Congo River).[116] Here they were joined by many more missionaries from other orders and societies than anywhere else in Africa in the twentieth century. In spite of the enormous difficulties (slave trade, "Congo tortures," the population's stubborn belief in paganism, tropical diseases), the number of Christians increased (1910: fifty thousand; 1921: three hundred seventy-six thousand). In several areas, missionary activities began rather late, for instance in Ruanda-Urundi (around 1900), but after the twenties they were marvelously successful.[117] These results give an impression of the efforts made by Catholic Belgium on behalf of its colony.

Another advance into the interior of Africa was made from the east, after Livingstone had explored new possibilities and Leopold II's initiatives had aroused the interest of missionary circles. Three societies offered their services to the Congregation for the Propagation of the Faith, proposing to Christianize these promising regions. In 1877, Fr. Augustin Planque (1826–1907),[118] the first general of the Lyon Missionaries, offered to pursue this task. A year earlier, his priests had settled around the mouth of the Nile with the special assignment of reporting the results of the explorations, which were immediately known in Egypt, to the Roman authorities.[119] In 1878 Lavigerie wrote his extensive *Mémoire secret* for the Congregation for the Propagation of the Faith. In it he suggested ways and means for swift Christianization and the elimination of slavery.[120] The (tendentious) article resulted in the assignment of the missions in central Africa to the White Fathers on

---

[115] L. Dénis, *Les Jésuites belges au Kwango 1893–1943* (Brussels 1943).

[116] M. Kratz, *La mission des Rédemptoristes belges au Bas-Congo. La période des semailles 1899–1920* (Brussels 1970). Initially, they had no real concept for their missionary work. Therefore, they followed at first the *Fermes-chapelles*, later the *Écoles-chapelles* (according to the Protestants). Not until after 1921, along with the development of Kimbanguism, did they attempt definite accomodation.

[117] J. Perraudin, *Naissance d'une Église. Histoire du Burundi chrétien* (Usumbura, Burundi 1963).

[118] Regarding Planque, see Streit XVIII, 148f.

[119] M. B. Storme, *Rapports du Père Planque, de Mgr. Lavigerie et de Mgr. Comboni sur l'Association Internationale Africaine* (Brussels 1957).

[120] His attempt to penetrate Central Africa from the Kabyle mission had failed. In regard to his memoirs, cf. Streit XVII, 865f.; concerning his antislavery campaign, see F. Renault, *Lavigerie, l'esclavage et l'Europe*, 2 vols. (Paris 1971).

24 February 1878, four days after the election of Leo XIII.[121] The third person to promise establishing missions in the area of the great lakes was the vicar apostolic of central Africa in Khartoum, Monsignor Daniel Comboni, who, in contrast to Lavigerie, was in favor of the efforts made in Brussels. These areas belonged to his district.[122]

In 1878, starting from Zanzibar, the first caravan of White Fathers headed toward the interior of Africa. In Tabora, they separated into two groups. One, under the leadership of Fr. Léon Livinhac, traveled toward Lake Tanganyika. The other group, which had lost its leader, turned toward Lake Victoria.[123] Fr. Simeon Lourdel (1853–90) succeeded in negotiating with King Mtesa of Uganda. After a fine beginning, the mission got caught in the net of politics. Upon pressure by the Muslims (around the middle of the nineteenth century, the Arabs had entered the area via Zanzibar) and because of Mtesa's fear of British aggression, the missionaries had to leave the country in 1882, at least until after Mtesa's death (1884). His son, suspicious that the European missionaries were pioneers of the colonial powers, agreed. In October 1885, the Anglican Bishop Hannington was murdered, and in May of the following year, a large number of Christians became victims of the persecutions, among them even servants at the court of Charles Lwanga.[124] In 1894, when Britain took charge of the protectorate, a period of peace returned. However, particularly during the time of turbulence, the number of baptisms increased,[125] in spite of the strict requirements by the White Fathers. Thus the threat of the Muslims in the period before World War I was eliminated and Christianity was on the way to becoming a Church of the people.[126]

[121] With his allegations that the conference in Brussels was Protestant, Freemason, and anticlerical in spirit, the archbishop wanted to frighten Rome and incite the Propaganda to act swiftly. He was successful.

[122] The basic work about the evangelization efforts in Central and Equatorial Africa during the nineteenth century: M. B. Storme, *Evangelisatiepogingen in de binnenlanden van Africa gedurende de XIXe eeuw* (Brussels 1951).

[123] Regarding the *pénétration laïque et religieuse* from the east, cf. R. Heremans, *Les établissements de l'Association Internationale Africaine au lac Tanganika et les Pères Blancs. Mpala et Karéma 1877–85* (Tervuren 1966). Between 1879 and 1885, Lavigerie sent forty-six missionaries to the two missions of Nyanza and Tanganyika in order to outdo the *Association* and the Protestants in every respect and to establish a Christian kingdom.

[124] Among the victims were also Anglican Christians. The beatification of the twenty-two martyrs of Uganda took place on 6 June 1920, their canonization on 18 October 1964 (G. Goyau, "Le Cinquantenaire des Martyrs d'Ouganda," *RHM* 13 [1936], 321–40; Streit XVIII–XX, passim; biblio. also in A. Mulders, op. cit., 406f.).

[125] The situation of the Christians was aggravated by the presence of the Arabs as well as by the tensions between the Catholics and the Protestants.

[126] J. V. Taylor, *Die Kirche in Uganda. Das Werden einer jungen afrikanischen Kirche* (Stuttgart 1966). This is a model for the study of a local church. The author indicates the

The Congregation for the Propagation of the Faith responded to this upswing by dividing the old district Nyanza into three vicariates, North Nyanza (Uganda), South Nyanza, assigned to the disciples of Lavigerie, and the Upper Nile, which was given to the Mill Hill Missionaries who used similar methods successfully.[127] The Consolata Missionaries in near-by Kenya (since 1902) were hampered by the fact that the coast was totally Muslim.[128] Toward the south, in East Africa (today Tanzania), Germany had colonial interests. Its protectorate received its final borders in 1890 through the Helgoland Treaty.[129] The Holy Ghost Fathers, in this area after 1863, moved their positions from Bogamayo to Kilimanjaro. They placed great emphasis on economic enterprises and colonization. The White Fathers had more visible successes around the turn of the century in the interior of Africa, in the four vicariates east of Lake Victoria and Lake Tanganyika where they rigorously applied the catechumenate's discipline (according to the directives of their founder). In spite of bad setbacks (during the uprisings of 1889 and 1905), the German Benedictines of Saint Ottilien (after 1888) developed a new mission in Dar es Salaam (1902: vicariate apostolic), which pursued pastoral, educational, and agricultural activities.[130] The Trappists of Mariannhill were briefly engaged (1887–1907) in German East Africa. A shortsighted measure caused them to be recalled from their promising cultural work in the two missions of Gare and Irente in the Usumbura Mountains contrary to the desires of the German colonial administration.[131] During the first East African Episcopal Conference in Dar es Salaam, in July 1912, it became clear that the area, with its seven flourishing vicariates, was outgrowing its status as a mission and that seeds of a native Church had sprung up, for which a well-structured

---

rivalries between the three religions. At that time, this implied choosing between the Arabian, French, or British power.—In 1884, there were 10,000 Christians and 60,000 catechumens in Uganda; in 1904: 86,000 Christians and 135,000 catechumens.

[127] H. P. Gale, *Uganda and the Mill-Hill Fathers* (London 1959): a critical study of the conflicts between the Muslims, the Protestants, the Catholics, and the pagans.

[128] Establishment of the vicariate apostolic of Kenya: Streit XVIII, 1183.

[129] J. Schmidlin, *Die katholischen Missionen in den deutschen Schutzgebieten* (Münster i. W. 1913); S. Hertlein, *Aufbau der Kirche in Tansania* (Münsterschwarzach 1971).

[130] F. Renner, "Die Benediktinermission in Ostafrika—eine Überschau," F. Renner, *Der fünfarmige Leuchter* II (Sankt Ottilien 1971), 123–52; L. Kilger, "Die Missionsgedanken bei der Benediktinergründung von St. Ottilien und die Übernahme der Afrikamission," *ZMR* 24 (1934), 213–28; J. Eggert, *Missionsschule und sozialer Wandel in Ostafrika* (Bielefeld 1970).

[131] H. Stirnimann, "Mariannhiller Trappisten in Deutsch-OstAfrika 1897–1907," *NZM* 25 (1969), 167–80.

catechumenate and the diligent cultivation of religious and liturgical life were characteristic.[132]

In the middle of the nineteenth century, a simply catastrophic situation had resulted from the practice of the patronate in the territories of Portugal in West and East Africa. As good and as necessary as it may have been at one point, this institution was largely to blame for the decline of the missions, running parallel with the collapse in the motherland. The efforts of the Spiritans to take over the abandoned areas found little response until, in 1865, they received permission to work there. One year later they were able to begin. There were five priests in all of Angola.[133] The leadership of the order gradually arrived at the conviction that only missionaries under Portuguese leadership were able to produce fruitful results. Therefore, the Swiss Father J. G. Eigenmann set out to found a settlement or a school of his order in Portugal. In 1869 he was appointed head of the Congo seminary in Santarem, the birthplace of the Portuguese province of the Holy Ghost Fathers. The first priest from the school of Eigenmann, Father José Maria Antunes, went to the mission in Huila (south of Angola) in 1882 to reorganize it.[134] Fathers H. Carrie, C. A. Duparquet, Monsignor L. A. Keiling, and Antunes were all especially important in the tedious new beginning and the slow ascent of the mission.[135] The revolution in the homeland (1910), followed by the separation of Church and state, destroyed a large part of the work abroad. The situation was even worse in the Portuguese part of East Africa, where, after the expulsion of the Jesuits, only a few secular priests were left, mainly Goans, to assure the religious care of the Christians. The Jesuits turned to the heathen missions again in 1881 in the lower portion of the Zambezi river. Due to the relentless climate, they lost thirty-seven members in twenty years. Nevertheless, they managed the founding of several new centers and smaller communities, until they had to leave in 1911. The Divine Word Missionaries, admitted through political pressure, gave a guest performance, so to speak, because they were expelled in 1918.[136] It is not

[132] *Beschlüsse der ersten Konferenz der afrikanischen Bischöfe im Juli 1912* (Kath. Miss. Druckerei, Dar es Salaam 1912).

[133] A. Brásio, *Spiritana Monumenta Historica. Series Africana I, Angola*, vol. I, *1596–1867* (Pittsburgh, Louvain 1966); cf. review by J. Beckmann, *NZM* 24 (1968), 232f.; C. Ferreira da Costa, *Cem anos dos Missionários do Espírito Santo em Angola 1866–1966* (Nova Lisboa, Angola 1970).

[134] Brásio, *Spiritana Monumenta Historica. Series Africana. I, Angola*, vol. II, *1868–1881* (Pittsburgh, Louvain 1968); cf. review by J. Beckmann, *NZM* 25 (1969), 227.

[135] Concerning Carrie, see Streit XVIII, 530, concerning Keiling, ibid., 483ff.

[136] F. Schwager II, 149f.; P. Schebesta, *Portugals Conquistamission in Südostafrika. Missionsgeschichte Sambesiens und des Monomotapareiches 1560–1920* (Sankt Augustin 1966).

surprising that there were only about five thousand Catholic Africans in this vast country at the beginning of World War I.

Eight of the Jesuits who had been driven out of Mozambique, mostly Austrians and Poles, settled in 1910 in neighboring northern Rhodesia.[137] The Society of Jesus had long endeavored to found a permanent settlement there. Fathers Joseph Moreau and Jules Torrend from the Zambesi mission (in southern Rhodesia) were permitted to settle in Tongaland.[138] Pioneers of the agricultural development of northern Rhodesia, they taught the population modern methods of agriculture and cattle breeding. They were also accomplished in the areas of linguistics and ethnology, especially Torrend, who gained a reputation with his research of the Bantu languages.[139]

In 1879, the Zambezi expedition set out from Cape Town. Headed by the Belgian Jesuit Father Henri Depelchin (1822–1900), an experienced Indian missionary, the group of six priests (among them the German Fathers Anton Terörde [died in 1880] and Karl Fuchs) and five laymen arrived at Victoria Falls in 1880.[140] They established the first station in the land of the Tongas. In spite of the massive reinforcement of fifty-one members which the Society received the following year, they were unable to hold their ground in the northern part of the Zambesi until the beginning of the twentieth century. In the northern region of today's Zambia, the area between Lake Bangwenlu and Lake Nyasa, the White Fathers laid the foundation for their mission among the Bembas (1895). They were headed by Father Joseph Dupont (1850–1930), who was appointed first vicar apostolic of Nyasa in 1897 when this district was separated from the Tanganyika mission.[141] Even though the "wild" tribe of the Bembas had to be trained to settle down, the mission under Bishop Dupont,[142] mainly by way of education and new agricultural methods, reached a remarkable level (1911: six thousand Catholics, fifty-seven catechumens, eighteen thousand pupils).

---

[137] S. Reil, *Kleine Kirchengeschichte Sambias* (Münsterschwarzach 1969), 34–37; R. L. Rotberg, *Christian Missionaries and the Creation of Northern Rhodesia 1880–1924* (Princeton 1965).

[138] S. Reil, op. cit., 32–34.

[139] Regarding Torrend, cf. Streit XVIII, 176f.; concerning Moreau, see ibid., 626f.

[140] J. Spillmann, *Vom Cap zum Sambesi. Die Anfänge der Sambesi-Mission. Aus den Tagebüchern des P. Terörde S. J. und aus den Berichten der anderen Missionare dargestellt* (Freiburg 1882); excerpts from the diaries of Depelchin and Charles Croonenbergh in *Diaries of the Jesuit Missionaries at Bulawayo 1879–1881* (Salisbury 1959).

[141] S. Reil, op. cit., 22ff.—In 1913, the division into the vicariates of Bangweulu and Nyasa occurred (Streit XX, 618).

[142] Dupont had a lot of conflicts with the British colonial authorities. They accused him of pursuing political goals in favor of France.

From the beginning, a number of White Fathers qualified as linguists and their studies rendered invaluable services to their successors.[143]

Aside from the Muslim north, the Catholic missionaries did not encounter anywhere the kind of difficulties they had to cope with in the south of the dark continent.[144] Since they appeared rather late (middle of the nineteenth century), the Roman Church had trouble catching up with the headstart of the Protestants who had worked in these areas intensively. This situation was aggravated by the customary intolerance of the Boers, partly by the British residing in the country since 1806, by the racial differences, and by the numerous sects and African splinter groups which had begun before the turn of the century.[145] In the northern part of German South West Africa, the Oblates of Mary Immaculate arrived and began work in 1896 (at the end of the seventies, the Spiritans had failed) in the prefecture of Lower Zimbabwe, founded in 1892. They also succeeded the missionaries of Lyon north of the Orange Free State (1882) and worked in Transvaal. But progress was slow, even though the Jesuits and Dominicans sisters who had been called from Augsburg to Grahamstown to organize a college could report modest success around 1876 among the Xhosas (east of the Cape of Good Hope area). Statistics may illuminate the situation: in 1911, the number of Catholics in the South African Union (with 4.7 million non-Europeans) was thirty-seven thousand, the Protestants had 1.4 million faithful.[146]

The work was difficult, yet there were two areas in which the Catholics excelled: Basutoland deserves first mention (Lesotho).[147] The Oblates, active in this mountainous and remote region since 1862, managed to establish an influential position, partly owing to their friendly relations with the chiefs. The Sisters of the Holy Family, who arrived in 1865, trained a dozen native sisters by 1912. After 1908, the Men-

[143] Louis Guillermé, Eugène Pueth, Louis Molinier, Georges Schoeffer.

[144] B. Hutchinson, "Some Social Consequences of XIXth Century Missionary Activity among the South African Bantu," *Africa* 27 (London 1957), 160–77.

[145] Cf. E. Dammann, op. cit., 53, 160ff., incl. extensive biblio. regarding the post-Christian movements in Africa.

[146] W. E. Brown, *The Catholic Church in South Africa. From its Origins to the Present Day* (London 1960). The author expresses regret about the Church having missed its chances. He attributes this to the excessively cautious attitude of the vicars apostolic, who tried to avoid any kind of aggravation and scandal and left creative work to others, especially at the beginning of the twentieth century.—Cf. also J. E. Brady, *Trekking for Souls* (Cedara, Natal 1952).

[147] M. Bierbaum, "Die Entwicklung der katholischen Mission in Basutoland," *ZMR* 1 (1938), 133–44.

zingen Sisters assisted with social work.[148] The other flourishing mission was located in Natal, which had been assigned to the Oblates in 1850 as a vicariate. This was the center of Mariannhill founded in 1882 by German Trappists under the leadership of Abbot Franz Pfanner (1825–1909).[149] Their life-style, based on Benedictine rules, facilitated social and economic activities which were mandatory in view of the local circumstances. They acquired a large complex of land, settled Bantus, and organized an impressive educational system (with a school, seminary, small businesses, printing press, and hospital).[150] The women were cared for by the Sisters of the Precious Blood.

Finally, the island of Madagascar should be mentioned (elevated to vicariate apostolic in 1885). Experiencing difficulties due to pressures from the pro-Protestant governments of the sixties and seventies, the Jesuits were nevertheless able to expand their activities. After they were temporarily deported during the occupation of the country by France and during the turmoils at the end of the century, they received assistance in 1896 from the ranks of the Lazarists,[151] two years later from the Spiritans,[152] and in 1899 from the missionaries of La Salette. In 1906, the French *Kulturkampf* affected the East African islands and dealt the Church a severe blow. This did not stop its growth, however, but rather caused a constructive process of internal cleansing.

Reviewing the missionary activities under the pontificates of Leo XIII and Pius X, one must describe this period as epoch-making and highly

---

[148] In 1914 the number of Catholics was around 15,000. Basutoland became an apostolic prefecture in 1894, a vicariate apostolic in 1909 (Streit XVII, 404, 1183).

[149] J. Dahm, *Mariannhill. Seine innere Entwicklung sowie seine Bedeutung für die katholische Missions- und Kulturgeschichte Südafrikas. I. Zeitabschnitt: Von der Gründung Mariann-Hills 1882 bis zur Trennung vom Trappistenorden 1909* (Mariannhill, Natal 1950).—Long before Mariannhill was founded, the German Protestant missionaries had started in other parts of Africa to work particularly with the rural population, and they had taken similar paths.—See A. Roos, *Mariannhill zwischen zwei Idealen* (diss., Innsbruck 1962), 13–99, regarding the tragic life of Pfanner, who had established eleven missions, which caused him to be in conflict with the rules of his order. Consequently, he was recalled in 1893.

[150] G. M. Lautenschlager, *Die sozialen Ordnungen bei den Zulus und die Mariannhiller Mission von 1882 bis 1909* (Reimlingen 1963).—Likewise, the research accomplishments in Mariannhill were quite remarkable, e.g., the studies of Zulu language and history by W. Wanger (1872–1943) and A. T. Bryant (1865–1953). See Streit XVIII, 493–95; XX, 17–19. Mariannhill also made the first courageous attempt to publish a truly African religious textbook: the great Wanger catechism of 1912 in the Zulu language. Cf. L. A. Mettler, *Christliche Terminologie und Katechismus-Gestaltung in der Mariannhiller Mission 1910–1920* (Schöneck-Beckenried 1967).

[151] P. Coste, "Saint Vincent de Paul et la Mission de Madagascar," *RHM* 4 (1927), 26–61, 217–50.

[152] G. le Faucheur, "Madagascar et les Spiritains," *RHM* 5 (1928), 407–37.

important for Africa as well as the Pacific. Almost everywhere, new communities were established. Quantitatively as well as qualitatively remarkable feats were accomplished in such a short time span. But the missions were now outgrowing the first phase and trying to achieve independence and a character of their own. Even though the missionaries were indebted to the spirit of their time, they remained loyal to their true mission, the preaching of the Gospel.[153]

[153] H. Jedin offers the following conclusion: "On the whole we may say that most of the missionaries were able to preserve the independence of evangelization, and the "natives" were quite capable of differentiating between colonialism and mission activity" ("Weltmission and Kolonialismus," *Saeculum* 9 [1958], 393–404, quot. 401).

CHAPTER 39

The Development of New Churches

World War I clearly interrupted the missionary activities. The missionary work that had seemed so very promising before the outbreak suffered severe reverses during the upheaval. After the peace was signed, missionary work experienced a decisive new orientation. Well aware of the multiplicity of relationships and tensions between colonialism and missions, the chief authorities of the Church were intent on de-politicizing missionary work. On the other hand, they focused more and more on the independence of the established communities. The period of the pontificates of Benedict XV and Pius XI entailed a basic rejection of Europeanism and can be called an era of increased adjustment to the peoples who were to be converted. Even though the past still had its effect here and there, the model of the native church was clearly in everyone's mind.[1]

The consequences of the war were first felt in the economic sector and in personal life.[2] The subsidies from the home countries decreased considerably or dried up completely. The countries directly involved in the war were affected, while the neutral countries, at least partially, filled the gaps. In spite of an early hope that the colonies might be

[1] It should not be forgotten that, at that time, the colonial areas covered two-thirds of the globe and that, of the world's population of 2 billion people, 700 million were subjected to foreign rule (cf. G. Balandier, "Die koloniale Situation: ein theoretischer Ansatz," R. v. Albertini, *Moderne Kolonialgeschichte* [Cologne, Berlin 1970], 105–24; R. Delavignette, *Christianisme et colonialisme* [Paris 1960], 19).
[2] X. Bürkler, "Der Weltkrieg 1914–18 und die Mission," *Kath. Missionsjahrbuch der Schweiz* 11 (Fribourg 1944), 22–29; cf. the war-mission reviews in *ZM*, 1915–19.

spared the devastations of the war, hostilities also broke out in the German protectorates. In those areas where no actual fighting took place, the missionary activities suffered noticeably from the recall of numerous missionary personnel. This was particularly true in the case of French citizens, whose departure left many a region abandoned,[3] and in the case of the Italian missions, though to a less devastating degree. The missions of the Germans were particularly burdened by the events of the war. In many places, the missionaries were expelled, imprisoned, or deported, which affected the settlements badly. This happened to the Pallottines in Cameroon, the Divine World Missionaries in Togo, and the Benedictines in East Africa, who all were forced to leave. The German missionaries in British India suffered a similar fate. However, they were able to stay in German South West Africa and, to some extent, in the Far East.[4] The spiritual damages of the war had more impact than the material and personnel losses. The belligerent Western nations, representing Christianity, also infected the missions with the idea of nationalism. In their disunion, they presented an annoying picture to the non-Europeans, causing the halo that had surrounded the white races to fade.

In order to heal the wounds inflicted by the war, many missionaries returned to their communities after the peace treaty, particularly from the victorious countries, such as the French. The Catholic Church found it easier to recruit replacements for those areas that the missionaries had been forced to leave. This allowed the Church (in some areas) to catch up more rapidly than the Protestants. On the basis of ARTICLES 438 and 122 of the Versailles Treaty, the German missionaries found their missionary freedom limited. However, in retrospect the destruction of the unity of mission and colonial power was a salutary move, even though it was one-sided.[5] At least this was the beginning of the dissolution of the close ties between national and missionary interests, of the liberation of the missions from the burden of colonialism, and of once again focusing on the supranationality of the Church and its mission.[6]

---

[3] During the war, 5,000 French missionaries were drafted: in the summer of 1915, for instance, more than 200 Paris Missionaries, as compared to 200 White Friars and the same number of Lazarists.

[4] At the outbreak of the war, approximately 1,100 German priests, 850 clergymen and brothers and 2,000 sisters worked in all missionary regions. By the end of the war: 192 priests, 76 brothers and 249 sisters were expelled; 126 priests, 220 brothers and 76 sisters were imprisoned or interned.

[5] Cf. W. Holstein, "Die Mission in den völkerrechtlichen Verträgen und Verfassungen der Neuzeit," *Basileia, Festschrift für Walter Freytag* (Stuttgart 1959), 106–27, esp. 117f.

[6] F. Kollbrunner, "Abkehr vom Europäismus und universale Haltung im Missionswerk 1919–59," *NZM* 28 (1972), 117–32; id., "Die einheimische Kirche als Konsequenz der Katholizität (1919–1959)," *NZM* 29 (1973), 10–27.

It is to Benedict XV's credit that he dealt with this question courageously. In a situation of extreme national pathos, he offered clarification, rigorously uncovering the weakness of the missionary activity of the Church (the nationalistic attitude of individual representatives and the colonialist missionary methods).[7] Since he partially overcame Europeanism, also introducing a change in missionary theology, he deserves the name "Missionary Pope" as much as his successor, who, following Benedict's ideas, set out to realize the program outlined in *Maximum illud*. There is no doubt that the apostolic letter of 30 November 1919 was the Magna Carta of the modern missions.[8] The initiative is said to have been made by Guido Conforti, the founder of the Missionaries of Parma. The Dutch Redemptorist and long-term prefect of the Congregation for the Propagation of the Faith, Cardinal Willem van Rossum, is considered to have had decisive influence on the writing of the document.[9]

During the time of Leo XIII, who loved openness and space, the universal responsibility of the Church was already clearly visible. Through his concern for the salvation of all mankind, he brought the missions back into the fold of the Church, integrating the doctrine of the mission into that of the Church. At the same time, in contrast to his predecessors, he assessed the situation of the non-Christians more positively.[10] Pius X, on the other hand, almost completely neglected the "others"; therefore hardly perceiving their true nature. He seemed to turn exclusively inward and did not include the missions in his reform

[7] Amidst the climax of nationalism it was not easy to preserve impartiality; both camps expressed their discontent with the Pope. *Cf.* G. Maron, "Die römisch-katholische Kirche von 1870 bis 1970," *Die Kirche in ihrer Geschichte. Ein Handbuch,* ed. by K. D. Schmidt and E. Wolf, vol. 4, no. 2 (Göttingen 1972), 214f.

[8] This is not an encyclical; the text can be found in *Sylloge,* 113–28; Germ.—in Marmy, *Auf der Maur,* 7–25; Lat.-Germ. in Glazik, *Päpstliche Rundschreiben,* 18ff. The Magna Carta is discussed in J. Beckmann, *La Congrégation de la Propagation de la Foi face à la politique internationale* (Schöneck-Beckenried 1963); Delacroix III, 128f.; A. Rétif, *Les Papes contemporains et la mission* (Paris 1966), 40: *le premier grand document missionnaire du siècle.*

[9] In regard to Conforti and *Maximum illud,* cf. J. Paventi, "Tres Encíclicas o una Trilogía misionera," *Misiones Extranjeras* 3 (Burgos 1952), 88–104; J.-M. Drehmanns, "Le Cardinal van Rossum et l'Encyclique Rerum Ecclesiae," *Le Bulletin des Missions* 25 (1951), 227–30: "Il (*sc.* van Rossum) *élabora le projet de 'Maximum illud'* " (228). Regarding Lebbe's influence, cf. J. Glazik, "Die Missions-Enzyklika 'Maximum illud' Benedikts XV. (1919)," W. Sandfuchs, *Das Wort der Päpste* (Würzburg 1965), 65–74 (esp. 66).

[10] The best presentation of the integration of Church and mission: P. Wanko, *Kirche— Mission—Missionen. Eine Untersuchung der ekklesiologischen und missiologischen Aussagen vom I. Vatikanum bis "Maximum illud"* (diss., Münster 1968), 42ff. A continuation of this study in F. Kollbrunner, *Die Katholizität der Kirche und die Mission in der kirchenamtlichen, ekklesiologischen und missionswissenschaftlichen Literatur der Zeit von "Maximum illud" bis "Princeps Pastorum" 1919–59* (diss., Gregoriana, Rome 1970).

plan—a fatal limitation of the idea of restoration, which caused Church and mission to be separated again and appear to be divided and unrelated entities.[11] This was changed by Benedict XV, who resolutely opened the Church to the missions and restored them as a basic function of the Church itself. His reintroduction of the plural *ecclesiae* into the ecclesiastical perception of the Popes (the expression had previously been used in an abstract sense) had far-reaching consequences for his concept of the missions. The recognition that the entire Church is composed of individual churches suggests that one not speak of the propagation of the faith in merely general terms but that one plan in concrete terms the formation of new individual Churches.[12] In the final analysis, this view emanated from the fact that the Church was taking its catholicity seriously.

With his new ecclesiological, missiological concept, Benedict offered a basic answer to the postwar conditions. In *Maximum illud* he focused on a series of urgent individual problems.[13] First, he clearly rejected the nationalistic attitude of certain missionaries, emphasizing the ecclesiastical nature of the missions. Those, he said, who "think more of the wordly than of the heavenly fatherland" and confuse the interests of the nation with those of the Gospel bring Christianity under suspicion of being the concern of the foreign state under whose mandate and as whose agents the missionaries act. He did not hesitate to stigmatize such an attitude as *pestis teterrima.* The truely "Catholic" missionary is intent only on representing Christ, not his own nation.[14] The Pope developed a missionary strategy that was rooted in mercy: The missionary will never meet anyone with disrespect, no matter how lowly he may be. Rather, "through all the kindness of Christian mercy" he will try to win him to the Gospel. When he defined missionary activity, Benedict also emphasized its ecclesiastical character. It is not exclusively the Pope (as was the case with his predecessors) who stands in the face of Christ and obeys his missionary order, but the Church as a whole.[15] He therefore

---

[11] P. Wanko, op. cit., 67ff.

[12] Cf. Motu proprio *Dei providentis* of 1 May 1917, pertaining to the establishment of the Congregation for the Eastern Churches (a step that was also important theologically): *AAS* 9 (1917), 529. Benedict uses the plural (*particulares ecclesiae*) in regard to the people in the Middle East, but he also deals with the missionary churches.

[13] Cf. the reviews of the papal document (which do not discuss the theological questions): G. Goyau, *Missions et missionnaires* (Paris 1931), 169–81; M. Grösser, "Das Missionswesen im Lichte des päpstlichen Sendschreibens 'Maximum illud,'" *ZM* 10 (1920), 73–86; A. Huonder, "Das Missionsrundschreiben Benedikts XV.," *StdZ* 98 (1920), 433–41.

[14] Elsewhere he says: "Memineritis non hominum debere vos imperium propagare, sed Christi, nec patriae quae hic est, sed patriae quae sursum cives adiicere" (*Sylloge,* 120).

[15] The Church as a whole is obligated to obey Jesus Christ; this is expressed in the

impressed on the missionaries (mainly their leaders) not to be satisfied with their achievements, but "to strive for the salvation of all people without exception." In order to accomplish this, the leader will, in the true "Catholic" spirit, involve other missionary institutions, if necessary, regardless of whether they are a member of a foreign order or nation. This was clearly aimed at the narrow-minded esprit de corps of the missionary societies. With his recommendation to discuss and resolve common problems with the neighboring areas, the Pope tried to combat any kind of particularism, replacing it with the spirit of cooperation.

The goal of missionary work, as the Pope envisioned it, is, in addition to the conversion of individuals, the founding of churches.[16] This requires a native clergy that could "one day take charge of its people." Because the future of new churches is dependent upon the existence of thoroughly trained priests, this task, resting on the universality of the Church, demands the special attention of the responsible missionary staff. Benedict considered this the only way to acclimate the Church and the only possibility to do justice to the characteristics of the people or to harvest its treasures for the benefit of the Church. Unfortunately, the life of the Christian communities is neglected by the papal considerations—they are merely the *terminus ad quem* of the missionary efforts and their own significance does not come to the fore. Nevertheless, the Pope attempted not only to turn to the Church at home, but contemplated the problems from the perspective of the missions themselves.[17]

The principles outlined in *Maximum illud* were completed in the instructions to the Congregation for the Propagation of the Faith, entitled *Quo efficacius* (6 January 1920).[18] Referring to the classic passage according to which Christianity should not be alien to any nation, these instructions remind the missionaries to understand their task as a spiritual and religious one. They are asked to practice strict neutrality in political matters and forbidden to propagate their own laws and customs in the foreign country.[19] Benedict tried to instill new energy into apostolic activities. This is demonstrated, on the one hand, by his measures

---

beginning of the letter: "Divini mandati memor, Ecclesia numquam, labentibus saeculis, cessavit adhuc traditae divinitus doctrinae partaeque humano generi per Christum salutis aeternae nuntios et administros in omnes partes mittere" (*Sylloge,* 114).

[16] The individual aspect takes priority in *Maximum illud,* however, the Pope acknowledges both the individual and the social element.

[17] Schmidlin, *PG* III, 252, already recognized this peculiarity of the letter.

[18] *Sylloge,* 131–35.

[19] The prophetic words in the instructions of the Propaganda of 23 November 1845 (*Collectanea* I, 544f.) about the dangers of politics in the missions should not be ignored; ibid., the progressive ideas concerning the elimination of the native episcopate.

to increase the missionary hierarchy (he established twenty-eight apostolic vicariates and eight prefectures as well as a delegation for Japan, Korea, and Formosa [1919][20]) and his order to conduct apostolic inspections (e.g., in China and South Africa); and, on the other hand, by his initiatives regarding the missionary relief system at home. In order to make the papal project more effective for the native clergy, he assigned its supervision to the Congregation for the Propagation of the Faith, thus locating it in Rome. The *Unio Cleri pro Missionibus,* founded in 1915 by the energetic Father Paolo Manna (1872–1952)[21] and Bishop G. M. Conforti of Parma and approved in 1916, was incorporated in 1916 in the Roman headquarters. The Union of Priests and Missionaries quickly expanded into Canada, Germany, and Switzerland. Finally, during this pontificate, several missionary seminaries were established (for the purpose of founding missions manned by secular priests), such as the seminary of Maynooth-Galway (Ireland, 1917), of Almonte (Canada, 1919), of Burgos (Spain, 1919), of Montreal (Canada, 1921), and of Bethlehem Immensee (Switzerland, 1921).[22] Many of these progressive activities under Benedict XV and later under Pius XI came about thanks to the open-mindedness of van Rossum, who is rightfully considered the pioneer of the Catholic "world mission." After all, he did away with Europeanism, pushed for adaptation, and worked toward the training and development of the native clergy under the supervision of native bishops.[23]

The missionary programs that Benedict XV initiated during his relatively brief pontificate were continued by Pius XI and put into action. The prefect of the Congregation for the Propagation of the Faith of both papal administrations made sure that a continuity was preserved.[24] By emphasizing certain aspects initiated by his predecessor, Pius XI shifted the focal point to the theme of universality, to the independence of the new churches and to their growing roots in the native soil, thus to indigenization.[25] The preaching of the Gospel all over the world is the

[20] *Sylloge,* 112f.: *Litterae Apost.* of 26 November 1919.
[21] P. G. B. Tragella, *Un'anima di fuoco P. Paolo Manna* (Naples 1954).
[22] The Society for Foreign Missions of Maryknoll, U.S.A., was founded in 1911 (B. Arens, *Handbuch der katholischen Missionen* [Freiburg ²1927], 65–72). Regarding the Foreign Missionary Society of Bethlehem (Immensee), see R. Rust, *Die Bethlehem Missionare* (1962).
[23] Van Rossum (born 1854) was prefect of the Propaganda from 1918 until his death in 1932; cf. N. Kowalsky, *LThK* IX, 59f.; J. O. Smit, *W. M. Kardinal van Rossum* (Roermond 1955).
[24] Cf. J.-M. Drehmanns, op. cit.
[25] J. Schmidlin, "Pius XI. als Missionspapst," *ZMR* 27 (1923), 233–43 (incl. biblio. concerning the missionary aspect of this pontificate); M. Ledrus, "La doctrine missionnaire de S. S. Pie XI," *NRTh* 56 (1929), 481–94.

most essential task of the papal office, Pius XI declared at the beginning of his pontificate[26] (in 1922, the centennials of three missions were celebrated).[27] In cooperation with the Pope, the entire episcopate has an obligation toward the task of mission because it represents the universal Church.[28] The Pope required the same efforts from the priests, telling them at the first international congress of the *Unio Cleri* in Rome (3 June 1922) that the missionary apostolate is not just to be pursued by a special task force but by the entire Church, so that every church would gradually develop into a cell active in missionary work.[29] According to the Pope, the secret of the universality of the Church rests in charity. Love of God and one's fellow man extends it and allows it to grow roots in areas where the population does not know Christ yet. The Church is not primarily self-serving, but exists to serve all.[30] According to his maxim that missions should have priority among Catholic works,[31] he opened during the Sacred Year the mission exhibition of the Vatican, which lived on in the founding of a missionary ethnological museum in the Lateran (1926). Furthermore, in order to awaken the missionary spirit in the entire Christian community, he declared in 1927 the second to the last Sunday in October to be observed as Mission Sunday. In 1922 he moved the Society for the Propagation of the Faith to Rome, incorporated it into the Congregation for the Propagation of the Faith and elevated it to a papal work (with new statutes). In 1929, he also initiated the coordination of the three most important organs (Childhood of Jesus, Propagation of the Faith, and Work of Saint Peter). He probably did this hoping to solicit more funds and to distribute them

---

[26] Three hundred years after the establishment of the Propaganda and the canonization of Francis Xavier and one hundred years since the beginning of the work of the propagation of the faith.

[27] The beginning of the Motu proprio of 3 May 1922: "Romanorum Pontificum in hoc maxime versari curas planum est oportere, ut sempiternam animarum salutem, Iesu Christi regno per orbem terrarum dilatando, quaerant . . ." (*AAS* 14 [1922], 321–26). Cf. the famous Pentecost homily of 4 June 1922 (*Sylloge*, 196–202): He felt obligated to the *paternità universale*.

[28] *AAS* 18 (1926), 68f.

[29] *AAS* 14 (1922), 198f.; concerning the general statutes of the missionary society of priests of 1926, see *AAS* 18 (1926), 230–36. The entire first part of *Rerum Ecclesiae* is devoted to the mobilization of the Christian world for the missions.

[30] "Because the Church was born for nothing but the propagation of Christ's kingdom all over the world so that all of mankind may partake in eternal salvation" (Marmy, Auf der Maur, 27); cf. ibid., 30f. (*Rerum Ecclesiae*). Pius speaks of quantitative as well as qualitative Catholicity (cf. A. Seumois, "La Charité Apostolique, fondement moral constitutif de l'activité missionnaire," *NZM* 13 [1957], 161–75, 256–70).

[31] In the consistory of 23 May 1923, he spoke about the "maximum sanctissimumque omnium catholicorum operum, quale est opus missionum" (*AAS* 15 [1923] 248).

more fairly, but also in order to dissolve the regional national ties of the large missionary societies.

Another matter to which the Pope devoted his attention was outlined in detail in Pius XI's encyclical *Rerum Ecclesiae* (1926). Its main passages deal with the founding, solidification, and independence of the new churches.[32] Three years earlier, the Congregation for the Propagation of the Faith sent directives to the missionary societies that clearly aimed at the assimilation of the church into the missionary district.[33] The work of the foreigners could be considered concluded as soon as the new foundation had established its own leadership, churches, native clergy, and funds, in short, as soon as it no longer needed the help of others. At that stage its existence would no longer be threatened if the missionaries should be deported or fresh recruits from Europe should be reduced. For the creation of a church, *Rerum Ecclesiae* demanded: an autochthonous clergy that would be compatible with the European clergy; autochthonous orders that would correspond to the expectations and interests of the natives as well as to the regional conditions and circumstances; an autochthonous monastic system because the contemplative monasteries offer irreplaceable contributions to the development of an individual church;[34] autochthonous catechists, and an elite of laymen whose careful training could be of invaluable importance for the future of Church and country.[35] The words of Pius XI's encyclical were carried out in practice. In 1926, at the celebration of the Feast of Christ the King, he himself ordained six Chinese bishops, one year later a Japanese, and in 1933 three more Chinese, a Vietnamese, and an Indian. In spite of all obstacles, this was a decisive breakthrough toward independence. This tendency was also noticeable in the intensive development of the missionary territories: by the end of his pontificate, there were 116 new vicariates and 157 prefectures. The Pope pursued the goal of stabilizing the growing churches by sending out apostolic delegates (e.g., Monsignor Costantini to China in 1922, Delle Piane to the Belgian Congo in 1930) and by convening local synods (1924: the

---

[32] *Sylloge,* 240–58: *De sacris missionibus provehendis Rerum Ecclesiae* (28 February 1926); German: Marmy, Auf der Maur, 26–49.

[33] Decree of the Propaganda of 20 May 1923, *Lo sviluppo* (*Sylloge,* 213–17).

[34] The Popes rarely discuss this (rather important) concern of monachism. Regarding the numerous native orders and congregations developing in India, see P. Rayanna, *The Indigenous Religious Congregations of India and Ceylon* (Tallakulam, Madura 1948); concerning the contemplative orders in Africa, cf. *Grands Lacs* (Namur, Jan. 1956); I. Auf der Maur, "Werden, Stand und Zukunft des afrikanischen Mönchtums," *NZM* 23 (1967), 284–95, 24 (1968), 21–35; P. Gordan, "Aufgaben und Probleme des benediktinischen Mönchtums in Afrika," *NZM* 16 (1960), 186–92.

[35] Pius XI devotes one chapter to the assistance provided by missionary doctors.

council of Shanghai and all of Japan, 1924/27: the synods of South Africa) which tried to apply the directives from Rome to the respective situation.

In a letter to the ecclesiastical leaders in China (16 June 1926)[36] Pius XI expressed another first principle: the idea of accommodation.[37] In order to fend off the persistent charges that missionaries were pursuing political interests, the Pope once more emphasized in this letter the purely religious character of ecclesiastical activities. He continued stressing that no one could dispute the fact that the Church demonstrated the desire to adapt to the character of a people.[38] The justified aspirations of a nation with a rich culture and tradition, he declared two years later in a message to the same country, should not be ignored.[39] Therefore, upon the request of the bishops of Manchuria in 1935, he permitted the Christians in that area to observe certain Confucian ceremonies, provided they exercise pastoral expedience.[40] This ended an exceedingly deplorable chapter in the history of the Far Eastern missions: the unfortunate conflict over rites. Similarly, the Congregation for the Propagation of the Faith allowed the Japanese faithful to attend certain events of a national or family-related nature. The instruction in this matter referred to principles that had been devised in 1659 and were surprisingly broad-minded.[41] Two other initiatives by Rome point in the direction of indigenization. The "exceedingly Catholic initiative" requesting that the religious activities be adapted to Japanese characteristics and tradition is praised because the risky enterprise of a Christian Japanese art was somewhat crucial for the Church on these islands.[42] On the other hand, the missionary leaders encouraged the artistic creativity of the natives on the occasion of the first exhibition of

---

[36] *Ab ipsis: Sylloge,* 259–64. In regard to Pius XI's relations to the China mission (first Council, 1924; ordination of Chinese bishops, etc.), cf. L. Wei Tsing-sing, *Le Saint-Siège et la Chine de Pie XI. à nos jours* (Sotteville-lès-Rouen 1971).

[37] F. Kollbrunner, "Die Akkommodation im Geist der Katholizität 1919–59," *NZM* 28 (1972), 161–84, 264–74; the first monograph was published by J. Thauren, *Die Akkommodation im katholischen Heidenapostolat. Eine missionsmethodische Studie* (Münster 1927). Cf. J. Masson, *Le testament missionarie de Pie XI* (Collection *Xaveriana März,* Louvain 1939).

[38] *Sylloge,* 263: "Nemo ignorat . . . Ecclesiam ad eas, quae cuiusvis nationis aut regni propriae sunt, leges aut constitutiones, sese accommodare."

[39] *Sylloge,* 308f. (1 August 1928).

[40] *Sylloge,* 479–82 (28 May 1935).

[41] *Sylloge,* 537–40 (26 May 1936); the instructions of 1659: *Collectanea* I, 42f.: "Do not try and do not expect these people to change their ceremonies, their customs, and their traditions unless they are in blatant conflict with religion and ethics. . . . Faith is not in the habit of overthrowing or fighting a people's customs and traditions if they are not bad; on the contrary, it wishes to preserve them unharmed."

[42] Letter to Apostolic Delegate P. Marella of 1 June 1935 in *Sylloge,* 483.

religious art in the Congo, justifying it as an expression of the catholicity of the Church, which was willing to absorb the spiritual values of a nation into its tradition.[43] This document demonstrating the spirit of accommodation of the Roman headquarters was written by Celso Costantini, the long-term prefect of the Congregation for the Propagation of the Faith (1935–1953) and the patron of autochthonous Christian art.[44] Finally, in view of the missions in Africa, a letter of 1938 should be mentioned, because it favors the adoption of burial ceremonies (Matanga) in the Belgian Congo and thus advocates the liturgical adaptation which was finally turned into a program by the Second Vatican Council.[45]

To what extent were the ideas propagated by the two Popes and espoused in numerous proclamations applied to everyday missionary life? The ecclesiastical documents show a certain discrepancy between theory and practice. But if we want to be fair, we have to admit that, particularly between the two world wars, the Roman declarations had an effect on history, though maybe to a different degree, depending on the case.[46] First of all, they succeeded in interesting Christians in the world apostolate, for instance the Dutch, who were exceedingly active, and the Catholics in the United States, who developed more and more missionary responsibility, or Spain, which sent many friars to South America. If the Church as a whole had not become more missionary in nature, we would not be able to understand the expansion of the missionary work during this period in which catholicity was realized to a unique extent.[47] For example, during the pontificate of Pius XI, the number of Catholics in India grew from three to 3.5 million, in Indo-China from one to 1.5 million. In spite of many obstacles, their numbers also grew considerably in the Pacific. But especially the African missions, mainly in the areas around the equator, witnessed such an upswing that the missionaries had a hard time accomplishing their work.[48] Even in areas that had no great achievements to report, things were stirring, as in South America, where several missionary dioceses

[43] Sylloge, 543f.: letter to Apostolic Delegate Delle Piane of 14 December 1936.—J. Beckmann, "Die Stellung der katholischen Mission zur bildenden Kunst der Eingeborenen," Acta Tropica 2 (1945), 211–31.

[44] C. Constantini, L'arte cristiana nelle missioni (Vatican City 1940).

[45] Sylloge, 576–78: letter of 14 July 1938 to Apostolic Delegate Delle Piane.

[46] See the critical comments in J. Glazik, "Mission der Kirche im Zeichen des Konzils," ZMR 48 (1964), 149–75 (esp. 170–72); W. Bühlmann, Sorge für alle Welt (Freiburg 1967), 88: "They (sc. Maximum illud and Rerum Ecclesiae) were unable to influence reality."

[47] Schmidlin, PG III, 197–209.

[48] A. Tellkamp, Die Gefahr der Erstickung für die katholische Weltmission (Münster 1950); L. Grond, "Wachstum der Kirche und Priestermangel in Afrika," NZM 16 (1960), 142–46.

and twenty new missionary districts were established among the Indians.[49] The mission of the Indians and blacks in North America (which the Catholics began rather late),[50] where several societies were involved, and the activities among the Eskimos in the north, where Christianization was mainly attempted by the Oblates,[51] progressed to everyone's satisfaction.

However, in another area the positive influence of the two Popes was more visible: in the energetically pursued education of a native clergy and the assignment of the Church leadership to local bishops. This breakthrough at that time can be considered an epoch-making event in the recent history of the missions, even though a lot may have been lacking in regard to the independence of the new Churches.[52] The principles extolled by Benedict XV and Pius XI (regarding the need, possibility, and usefulness of a native clergy and episcopate) were not new, they were embedded in a three-hundred-year-old Roman tradition. However, particularly regarding the demands pertaining to the office of bishop, these principles seemed shocking to many, sometimes even revolutionary.[53] Opposition did not fail to appear: some used the tactic of procrastination, others, for reasons of racial prejudice, warned of hastiness, even though Father Gabet, in a memorandum of 1848, had already refuted their arguments in detail.[54] Disregarding the opposition,

---

[49] Most rewarding in this regard were the successful efforts to establish a native clergy. In 1925, the Bavarian Capuchin Bishop Guido Beck founded for his huge territory in Araucania (Chile) a seminary from which the first full-blooded Indians graduated in 1933. Cf. Noggler, *Vierhundert Jahre Araukanermission* (Schöneck-Beckenried 1973).—In Yarumal (Colombia), the native Bishop Miguel Angel Builes initiated the founding of the Papal Missionary Seminary of Saint Francis Xavier (1927). Today, it is responsible for several missionary regions.

[50] A. Tellkamp, "Zur Geschichte der Missionierung der Neger in den USA," *NZM* 4 (1948), 45–63. Since 1871, this mission was in the hands of the Mill Hill Missionaries, the Spiritans, the missionaries of Lyon and Steyl, the American society of the Josephites (in existence since 1892), and, after World War II, the brothers of Scheutveld. The smaller number of Catholics is due to the historical circumstances of the past. The first American seminary for blacks, founded in 1920 by the Steyl missionaries in Bay St. Louis, trained, by 1960, thirty-seven S.V.D. members (cf. M. Meier, *Die Negermission SVD im Süden der USA* [diss., Gregoriana, Rome, part 4 printed, Steyl 1961]).

[51] Since 1932, there has been a female society of Eskimos; P. Duchaussois, *Femmes héroïques, les Sœur Grises Canadiennes aux Glaces Polaires* (Paris ²1933); id., *Aux Glaces Polaires. Indiens et Esquimaux* (Paris 1935). Cf. A. Freitag, "Die katholischen Missionen Amerikas," *ZMR* 25 (1935), 152–77.

[52] G. B. Tragella, *Una nuova Epoca nelle storia delle Missioni* (Milan 1933).

[53] J. Schmidlin, "Der Sieg der eingeborenen Missionshierarchie," *ZMR* 24 (1934), 1–19; cf. the disputes of the two spokesmen Lebbe from China and Gille for India.

[54] J. Beckmann, *Der einheimische Klerus in den Missionsländern. Eine Übersicht* (Fribourg 1943); id. (ed.), *Der einheimische Klerus in Geschichte und Gegenwart. Festschrift L. Kilger* (Schöneck-Beckenried 1950); included is an essay about P. Gabet by G. B. Tragella, "Le vicende d'un opuscolo sul clero indigeno e del duo autore," 189–202.

Rome helped the cause to succeed. The statistics are striking proof of this.[55] Two examples may serve the point. First: China, which proceeded quickly after 1920. By 1939 it had more than two thousand autochtonous priests, and in approximately twenty districts natives were responsible for the fate of the Church. A historic milestone was the establishment of the hierarchy (1946): twenty-one Chinese were appointed bishop and seven apostolic prefects.[56] Second: After many disappointments and unsuccessful attempts, Africa had, after World War I, 148 native clergymen. By 1939, their number had grown to 358. The first two black bishops (Madagascar and Uganda) were consecrated in 1939 under Pius XII. While the natives were entering the ranks of the clergy and the episcopate, the large orders, such as the Franciscans, Dominicans, and Jesuits opened their doors to the communities in the Far East. Furthermore, the natives were granted independence through the constitution of provinces and monasteries, or they were allowed to develop their own branches within the monastic system (e.g., the Carmelites in India, the Cistercians in China, Japan, and Vietnam). At any rate, there the Church demonstrated that it was overcoming racial prejudice,[57] which certainly did not free it from the responsibility to develop individual ways of training the clergy, depending on the various peoples, in order to break away from an all too Western education.[58]

Finally, if we consider the efforts made toward a qualitative catholicity, which means the Church's willingness to get involved in the cultural, social, and religious traditions of the mission countries, we have to admit that between 1914 and 1939 this was not the dominant concern. Certainly, a native clergy and episcopate were created with indigeniza-

---

[55] A. Freitag, "Die Fortschritte des einheimischen Klerus und der einheimischen Hierarchie in den Missionsländern der letzten dreißig Jahre (1920–50)," *Festschrift L. Kilger* (n. 54), 203–32; I. Ting Pong Lee, "Episcopal Hierarchy in the Missions," *ED* 13 (1960), 181–225.

[56] J. Beckmann, "Die hierarchische Neuordnung in China. Ein geschichtlicher Überblick," *NZM* 3 (1947), 9–24.

[57] J. Beckmann, "Einheimischer Klerus und Rassenfrage," *NZM* 11 (1955), 1–14. "One of the most gratifying aspects of the recent missionary epoch is the fact that, after overcoming the last obstacles, the foreign missionaries of all nations unanimously supported the papal directives and tried in any way possible to apply them" (11).

[58] In the past, isolated attempts were made to adjust the education of the clergy. Nevertheless, it remains a task of the future which can only be accomplished through cooperation of foreign missionaries and native priests. See T. Ohm, "Die philosophisch-religionswissenschaftlich-theologische Ausbildung des indischen Klerus," *Festschrift L. Kilger* (n. 54), 233–50; H. Köster, "Zur theologischen Ausbildung des chinesischen Klerus," *TThZ* 61 (1952), 289–316; A. Morant, *Die philosophisch- theologische Bildung in den Priesterseminaren Schwarz-Afrikas* (Schöneck-Beckenried 1959); C. W. Forman, "Theological Education in the South Pacific Islands: a Quiet Revolution," *Journal de la Société des Océanistes* 25 (1969), 151–68.

tion in mind. But precisely this step had to be made first. Foreigners cannot completely adapt the Church to the characteristics, customs, and traditions of a people. This is essentially the task and the obligation of a matured native elite. The urgent need for acclimatization and decolonization in terms of spirit and religion did not surface to the level of awareness until the era of political colonialism approached its end. Nonetheless, the missionaries laid the foundation for such a change, and in that regard they followed the directives of the Pope, though perhaps not always with the (in retrospect) desirable energy. To vindicate them one could say that the will to adapt to the mentality of the land and the people was in many respects a lot stronger than we can imagine.[59] This is proven by the efforts regarding the languages and the native literature (which cannot be praised enough),[60] the creation of a Christian terminology,[61] the indigenization of the Bible,[62] and research in the area of ethnology and religious studies.[63] At their general chapter meeting in 1926, the White Fathers decided to prepare a study center for the Muslim missionaries, an initiative to which the *Institut des Belles Lettres Arabes* (and its periodical *Ibla*) owes its existence. Among the missionaries in India, the Belgian Jesuits dealt with the relations between Hinduism and Christianity, e.g., the two Sanskrit scholars Father Dandoy and Father Johanns (with his famous work *To Christ through the Vedanta*).[64] The Parisian missionaries had outstanding linguists and reli-

[59] Regarding the Chinese missions, see J. Beckmann, "Die Stellung der katholischen Missionare zur chinesischen Kultur," *Missionsjahrbuch der Schweiz* 9 (Fribourg 1942), 41–67: "Without being too optimistic, it is justified to say that the Church in China is on its way to becoming a true people's Church, that is to say, the Catholic Church is about to enter into close alliance with the Chinese intellectual and cultural life." (67); cf. J. Rossel, *Dynamik und Hoffnung* (Basel 1967), 25.

[60] The *Bibliotheca Missionum* offers a wealth of material illustrating these efforts. See J. Beckmann, "Werden, Wachsen und Bedeutung der Bibliotheca Missionum," *De Archivis et Bibliothecis Missionibus atque scientiae Missionum inservientibus: Festschrift Rommerskirchen* (Rome 1968), 33–57; one of the most distinguished Catholic Africa linguists: P. G. van Bulck, S. J., *Les recherches linguistiques au Congo Belge* (Brussels 1948); concerning one of the most eminent experts of Swahili, cf. W. Bühlmann, "P. Charles Sacleux CSSp Missionar und Wissenschaftler (1856–1943)," *NZM* 4 (1948), 17–32; A. Huppenbauer, "Afrika-Missionare im Dienst der Sprachforschung," *Acta Tropica* 2 (1945), 262–70.

[61] W. Bühlmann, *Die christliche Terminologie als missionsmethodisches Problem* (Schöneck-Beckenried 1950); A. Capell, "La traduction des termes théologiques dans les langues de l'Océanie," *Journal de la Société des Océanistes* 25 1969), 43–70.

[62] J. Beckmann (ed.), *Die Heilige Schrift in den katholischen Missionen* (Schöneck-Beckenried 1966).

[63] Regarding the prerequisites for the Christianization of Africa, see E. Dammann, op. cit., 101ff.: "Sprache, Völkerkunde, Religionen, sprachliche Praxis"; 130ff.: biblio.

[64] Concerning G. Dandoy (1882–1962), cf. Streit XVII, 224f.; he was the founder and editor of the monthly journal *The Light of the East* (1922–46); regarding P. Johanns

gion scholars. Therefore, Vietnam witnessed the most enlightened investigation of its culture and especially the religious tradition of Buddhism in the Orient.[65] In Japan, some missionaries conducted similar studies.[66] There were even steps made toward a native theology, as in India and China,[67] and in many places the liturgy was on its way to finding a form of expression which was more in line with the people's feelings.[68] In regard to Africa we need to remember the invaluable contributions of the native catechists and sisters (by 1939, the number of female congregations was 242 and included 1,529 members) regarding the solidification of the Church. These examples remind us not to pass general judgment on the missionaries and their guilt or insufficient willingness to adapt.

The new theological discipline called missiology participated energetically in the efforts toward the formation of new churches in the period between the wars, primarily through an eloquent defence of the native clergy and episcopate.[69] The creation of missiology was, on the one hand, an expression of the strengthened desire of the Catholics for missions, on the other hand, it had a stimulating and cleansing effect on missionary activities. The Protestants conducted mission studies much

---

(1882–1955), see Streit XVIII, 252–54 (including a summary of *To Christ through the Vedanta*); P. Johanns, *La pensée religieuse de l'Inde* (Paris, Louvain 1952).

[65] One of the greatest scholars of the Far East is L.-M. Cadière (1869–1955), who also pioneered religious ethnology; cf. Streit XI, 435ff.

[66] P. Aimé Villon (1843–1932), to mention only one of the many missionaries from Paris, left us thirteen extensive manuscripts containing studies of Buddhism; in 1938, the Jesuits began publishing the *Monumenta Nipponica;* see *NZM* 1 (1945), 145–50.

[67] Regarding India, cf. J. R. Chandran, *Library of Indian Christian Theology. A Bibliography* (Madras 1969); cf. *NZM* 27 (1971), 302. P. Henri Bernard-Maître, S. J., wrote a *Brevis Introductio in Philosophiam sinicam* (Sienshien 1940). Maurus Heinrichs, O.F.M., used a series of studies about Chinese philosophy and cultural history in the *Collectanea Commissionis Synodalis* (1936ff.) for teaching in the seminaries.

[68] A. Schmid, "Rites camerounais et liturgie catholique," *Festschrift L. Kilger* (n. 54), 275–95; J. L. van Hecken, "Le mouvement liturgique au Japon en faveur de la célébration eucharistique 1865–1962," *NZM* 26 (1970), 18–27, 94–113; I. Auf der Maur characterizes the period from 1920 until 1945 in " 'Rückschlag und Besinnung': Beitrag der Benediktiner-Missionare von St. Ottilien in Tansania zur liturgischen Erneuerung 1887–1970," *NZM* 27 (1971), 126–35, 188–200; A. Plangger says about Rhodesia: "So far, cultural adaptation occurred mainly on the terminological and linguistic level. . . . Broad conceptual adaptations are still modest and rare" ("Shona Gebetbücher. Ein Beitrag zur Geschichte der Shona-Frömmigkeit," *NZM* 26 [1970], 28–39, 127–36).

[69] General introductions to Catholic missiology: P. de Mondreganes, *Manual de Misionología* (Vitoria 1933, Madrid ²1947); A. Mulders, *Inleiding tot de Missiewetenschap* ('s-Bosch 1937, Bussum ²1950); J. E. Champagne, *Manuel d'action missionnaire* (Ottawa 1947); S. Paventi, *La Chiesa Missionaria* (Rome 1949); A. Seumois, *Introduction à la Missiologie* (Schöneck-Beckenried 1952).

earlier. In 1867 Alexander Duff (1806–78), a Scottish missionary who used to work in India, succeeded in establishing a missiological teaching chair in Edinburgh, which only lasted until 1905.[70] The international mission conference in Edinburgh in 1910 made a new start by stressing the importance of this discipline for activating the home base. Above all, the Protestants of the United States followed the appeal and, by 1930, sixty out of sixty-eight schools taught missiology in one form or another.[71] Gustav Warneck (1834–1910) is considered the true founder of the discipline on the Protestant side. He introduced it to its rightful place in theological teaching.[72]

Under Warneck's influence, Joseph Schmidlin, an energetic man from Alsace (1876–1944), seized the Catholic initiative in Münster,[73] after Robert Streit, O.M.I. (1875–1930),[74] Anton Huonder, S. J., of Chur (1858–1926), and Friedrich Schwager S.V.D. (1876–1929)[75] had done the groundwork. After 1910 Schmidlin was lecturer for mission studies and, after 1914, the first Catholic full professor. He attended in a critical and systematic manner to the entire discipline with its various branches (theory of mission, missiology, missionary history, law, etc.). After some resistance, he took charge of the editorial office of the first Catholic missiological periodical, the *Zeitschrift für Missionswissenschaft,* which he published (with the exception of one short period) without interruption until 1937, making it the voice of many a thorough study. The basic works of the new discipline gradually emanated from his work for the journal: *Einführung in die Missionswissenschaft* (1917, 1925), *Katholische Missionslehre im Grundriß* (1919, 1923)—called "an event" in the Catholic world—*Katholische Missionsgeschichte* (1925), and the two-volume *Das gegenwärtige Heidenapostolat im Fernen Osten* (1928).[76]

---

[70] O. G. Myklebust, *The Study of Missions in Theological Education* I (Oslo 1955); cf. review in *NZM* 12 (1956), 146–49.

[71] Id., *The Study of Missions in Theological Education* II, 1910–1950 (Oslo 1957); cf. review in *NZM* 15 (1959), 224f.

[72] The first missionary theory is contained in his five-volume work *Evangelische Missionslehre* (1892–1905).

[73] A biography of him is still lacking; however, a study of his early years in Alsace seems to be planned in honor of his one hundredth birthday. L. Riegert, "Ein Apostel aus dem Sundgau: Joseph Schmidlin 1876–1944," *L'Alsace,* 2 July 1971, 11; different aspects of his life and work in J. Glazik (ed.), *50 Jahre katholische Missionswissenschaft in Münster 1911–1961* (Münster 1961); J. Beckmann, "Universitätsprofessor Dr. Josef Schmidlin," *Schweiz. Kirchenzeitung* 112 (1944), 234–36.

[74] J. Pietsch, *P. Robert Streit OMI. Ein Pionier der katholischen Missionswissenschaft* (Schöneck-Beckenried 1952).

[75] Among other books, he published *Europäismus im Missionsbetrieb* (Aachen 1921).

[76] He was capable of gaining recognition for his discipline, but he made few friends, shocking most people with his brusque behavior.

Assisted by the *Internationales Institut für missionswissenschaftliche Forschungen,* founded by Schmidlin in 1911, the *Bibliotheca Missionum* was published (among other works). This work had been started by Streit in 1916 and continued by Johannes Dindinger, O.M.I. (1881–1958)[77] and Johannes Rommerskirchen, O.M.I.[78] It is an exemplary tool, which now includes about thirty impressive volumes. In regard to recent literature, it should be supplemented by the *Bibliografia Missionaria* (Rome 1935ff.).[79] Because of his opposition to National Socialism, Schmidlin was forced to retire in 1934 and to resign from the *Zeitschrift für Missionswissenschaft* in 1937. He died in 1944 in the Struthof concentration camp near Schirmeck.

The tireless efforts of this innovator bore fruit. His students especially carried missiology across the German borders. Their success was probably aided by recommendations from Rome.[80] Indeed, after Münster, missiological teaching chairs were established in Munich (1919), in Rome (1919 at the Congregation for the Propagation of the Faith), Nijmegen (1930), Ottawa (1932), Vienna (1933), Comillas (Spain), and Fribourg (1940).[81] At other universities, lectures were given, as at the Institut Catholique of Paris after 1923, in Louvain after 1927, and in Lyon. Real missiological departments were established in 1932 at the Gregoriana and the Propaganda College in Rome. Elsewhere, but not until after 1939, academic institutes were added (Fribourg, Nijmegen, Ottowa).[82] By the outbreak of World War II, thanks to these institutions and the efforts of individual scholars, this new academic discipline already had a sizeable number of missiological journals, series, and compilations, especially regarding sources. In the meantime, practitioners and experts debated acute problems at conventions such as the *Semaines de Missiologie* (Louvain, since 1922).

During the first phase of the development of Catholic mission studies, Germany produced men who made the young discipline respectable. Otto Maas, O.F.M. (1884–1945) distinguished himself through his mis-

---

[77] Concerning him, cf. *NZM* 7 (1959), 64–66 (J. Beckmann).

[78] Regarding his 60th birthday, cf. *NZM* 15 (1959), 64–66 (J. Beckmann).

[79] J. Beckmann, "Die Bibliotheca Missionum. Zur Vollendung der ersten Serie," *Priester und Mission* (Aachen 1963), 237–50.

[80] Pius X welcomed the missiological efforts in Germany (Schmidlin, *PG* III, 119); Benedict XV announced a teaching chair for missiology in Rome in *Maximum illud* (*Sylloge,* 121f.); Pius XI demanded that missionary work be studied in a scholarly manner (cf. Schmidlin, *PG* IV, 192, his critical comments regarding Pius XI).

[81] J. Beckmann, "Die Universität Freiburg und das katholische Missionswerk," *Festgabe an die Schweizer Katholiken* (Freiburg 1954), 155–67.

[82] A. Mulders, "Missiewetenschappelijk Leven," *Het Missiewerk* 26 (1947), 1–15; J. Beckmann, "Die Pflege der Missionswissenschaften in den einzelnen Ländern," *NZM* 5 (1949), 19–29.

siological historical studies of the Franciscan missions in China, New Mexico, and Indochina.[83] His Franciscan brother Dorotheus Schilling (1886–1950) devoted his research to Japanese missionary history, primarily to the activities of the Jesuits, later to the missionary work of the Franciscans.[84] Benno Biermann, O.P. (1884–1970) critically investigated the contributions of the Dominicans in regard to the propagation of the faith (especially in the New World), and for decades he studied the fascinating person of Las Casas.[85] Anton Freitag S.V.D. (1882–1968), the first one to get his Ph.D. under Schmidlin, devoted his energy thenceforth to missiology.[86] Johannes Peter Steffes (1883–1955) enriched the discipline by incorporating religious studies. Subsequently, Schmidlin expanded his journal after 1928 to a *Zeitschrift für Missions- und Religionswissenschaft.*[87] Wilhelm Schmidt S.V.D. (1868–1954) offered new ideas through ethnology and philology when founding *Anthropos.*[88] Through Thomas Ohm, O.S.B. (1892–1962), at first professor of missiology in Salzburg, later in Münster, the scholarly investigation of foreign religions became the focal point.[89] Missiology was relatively weak in France. Georges Goyau (1869–1939) taught missionary history at the Institut Catholique in Paris. He also determined the character of the *Revue d'Histoire des Missions* during its regrettably brief period of publication (1924–1939). In Italy, a student of Schmidlin, Giovanni Battista Tragella (1885–1968), mediated German missiology by translating several books and thus instilling new impulses into the missionary system at home.[90] Pioneering studies in the area of sinology and Chinese missionary history (especially about Matteo Ricci) were made by the Jesuit Pasquale d'Elia (1890–1963), professor at the Aurora University of Shanghai and subsequently at the missiological depart-

---

[83] *NZM* 2 (1946), 305f.; this volume deals with earlier representatives of missiology: Paul Andres, Maurus Gahn, and Josef Jung-Diefenbachs.

[84] Ibid. 6 (1950), 223–26.

[85] Ibid. 20 (1964), 50–54; 26 (1970), 219f.; B. Biermann, *Las Casas und seine Sendung. Das Evangelium und die Rechte der Menschen* (Mainz 1968).

[86] *ZMR* 49 (1965), 222–24; *NZM* 24 (1968), 205f.

[87] *NZM* 11 (1955), 142f.

[88] J. Beckmann, "Mission und Ethnologie, Zum Tode von P. Wilhelm Schmidt SVD," *NZM* 10 (1954), 293–96; J. Henninger, "Im Dienste der Mission: 60 Jahre Anthropos 1906–1966," *NZM* 23 (1967), 206–21.

[89] *NZM* 18 (1962), 305–311. T. Ohm, *Machet zu Jüngern alle Völker. Theorie der Mission* (Freiburg 1962).—This list shows how the number of the first German missiologists has diminished—and there are very few replacements.

[90] For instance, he translated Schmidlin's history of the missions into Italian (3 vols., Milan 1927–29). His three-volume history of the seminary of Milan gained quite a reputation (*Le Missioni Estere di Milano nel quadro degli avvenimenti contemporanei* [Milan 1950/1959/1963], cf. *NZM* 24 [1968], 203–5).

ment of the Gregoriana.[91] Essays valuable in regard to missiology and ethnology are contained in the *Annali Lateranensi* (after 1937), which was edited by Michael Schulien S.V.D. (1888–1968) for three decades.[92] In Louvain, missiology could only settle on the fringes of academia. There, Pierre Charles, S.J. (1883–1954), not really a specialist, yet very sensitive to the concrete reality, pointed in new directions and insisted that "implanting the Church" was the main missionary goal.[93] Adelhelm Jann (1876–1945), Swiss Capuchin, focused his missiological-historical work on Bishop Anastasius Hartmann. For the purpose of his investigation he founded the *Monumenta Anastasiana*.[94] Also oriented toward history was Laurenz Kilger, O.S.B. (1890–1964). Immediately after World War II, in cooperation with Johannes Beckmann, S.M.B. (1901–1971), he founded the *Neue Zeitschrift für Missionswissenschaft,* a courageous enterprise.[95] Beckmann's interests (he as well as Kilger were students of Schmidlin) included all aspects of his discipline, but his exceedingly rich work is also dominated by history.[96] In Spain, missiology flourished unexpectedly after the Civil War, especially missionary history, so that the *Archivo Ibero-Americano* (1914–1936, 22 vols.), which was important for the missionary history of the Franciscans, could be continued after 1941.[97] Aside from the Franciscans, the Catholics in the United States paid little attention to this discipline, in spite of the general upswing of missions in this country. It was regrettable that this branch of theology was also lacking in the mission churches themselves. But this is understandable in the case of a discipline that is still struggling for recognition, even though the missions needed it most.[98]

It is obvious from the names mentioned that the strength of missiology during the period of its consolidation lay in the area of mission history, even though it accomplished a great deal in other areas as well, e.g., in mission studies. By investigating the past as objectively as possi-

---

[91] *NZM* 20 (1964), 146f.: information about the Fonti Ricciane.
[92] Ibid. 5 (1949), 143–47; 24 (1968), 304f.
[93] Ibid. 10 (1954), 136f.
[94] Ibid. 2 (1946), 131; W. Bühlmann, "P. Adelhelm Jann, Pionier der schweizerischen Missionswissenschaft und Missionsbewegung," *Geist und Geschichte. Gedenkschrift zum 50jährigen Bestehen des Lyzeums am Kollegium St. Fidelis in Stans* (Stans 1959), 149–69.
[95] *NZM* 20 (1964), 161–67 (obituary of Kilger); J. Beckmann, "Von der alten zur neuen Zeitschrift für Missionswissenschaft," *NZM* 1 (1945), 1–11; J. Baumgartner, *Missionswissenschaft im Dienste der Weltkirche. 25 Jahre NZM* (Schöneck-Beckenried 1970).
[96] J. Baumgartner, "In Favorem Missionum. Zum Ehrendoktorat von Prof. Dr. Joh. Beckmann," *NZM* 26 (1970), 82–93; id., obituary: *NZM* 28 (1972), 1–9.
[97] *NZM* 2 (1946), 143–46. Manuel Giménez (1896–1968) was a respected Las Casas scholar.
[98] This postulate is still waiting to be realized.

ble and thus creating a benevolent understanding for the missionary efforts within the other camp, the intensive historical research in regard to missions resulted in a relaxation of the often tense relationship between Catholics and Protestants. This was quite an accomplishment.[99] Aside from theoretical debates which are still carried on today,[100] two problems played an important role. The first was the question of the missionary goal.[101] Against the background of complicated interrelations, the discussion is dominated by two major trends: the theory of the *Plantatio Ecclesiae* and the salvation of the non-Christians. However, the viewpoints gradually merged and one could say that the missionary goal is the implantation of the Church with the conversion of the people in mind.[102] The other frequently discussed problem deals with accommodation. The urgency of this matter resulted from the changes within the missionary field, the rejection of Europeanism.[103] Several things were realized: adaptation is the requirement for the implantation of Christianity into the people. Adaptation emanates by necessity from the essence of the Church itself. It is the realization of its catholicity and occurs when cultures meet. This complex of problems became more complicated after World War II, when the exceedingly difficult situation of the countries in the Third World began challenging the new discipline to provide new answers.[104]

[99] J. Beckmann, "Der Einfluß der Missionswissenschaft auf die Beziehungen der christlichen Konfessionen," *Kath. Missionsjahrbuch der Schweiz* 25 (Freiburg 1958), 28–35; J. Beckmann, "Missionsgeschichte und Ökumene. Zum Tode von Kenneth Scott Latourette 1884–1968," *NZM* 25 (1969), 210–14; id., "Die Bedeutung der Missionsgeschichte für die praktische Missionsarbeit," *Scientia Missionum ancilla. Festschrift A. Mulders* (Nijmegen, Utrecht 1953), 124–37.
[100] See H. Adamek, "Über die Integration der Missionswissenschaft in die Forschungs- und Lehrpraxis der evangelisch-theologischen Fakultäten," *Ev. Miss. Zeitschrift* 26 (1969), 106–10; F. Kollbrunner, "Der Ort der Mission in der Theologie," J. Baumgartner (ed.), *Vermittlung zwischenkirchlicher Gemeinschaft* (Schöneck-Beckenried 1971), 247–63.
[101] H. Kruska, "Zum katholischen Missionsdenken der Gegenwart," *Ev. Miss. Zeitschrift* 10 (1953), 33–45.
[102] A. Seumois, *Vers une définition de l'activité missionnaire* (Schöneck-Beckenried 1948).
[103] J. Müller, *Missionarische Anpassung als theologisches Prinzip* (Münster 1973).
[104] J. Beckmann, "Forderungen der gegenwärtigen Missionslage an die Missionswissenschaft," *NZM* 8 (1952), 241–50; T. Ohm, "Die katholische Weltmission—gestern und heute," *ZMR* 39 (1955); id., "Die Missionswissenschaft," *ZMR* 45 (1961), 189–96 (tasks for the future: 193ff.).

BIBLIOGRAPHY

GENERAL BIBLIOGRAPHY

The General Bibliography in vol. VIII (p. 337) contains a large part of material also pertaining to this volume. The following bibliography is of a supplementary nature listing particularly more recent works. The bibliography on individual countries (II, 3) should be supplemented with the systematic bibliography in II, 4–9. Biographies, memoirs, and diaries are included in the bibliographies to individual chapters.

I. GENERAL HISTORY

T. Schieder, ed., *Handbuch der europäischen Geschichte* VI (Stuttgart 1968); R. Lill, *Politische Ideologien und nationalstaatliche Ordnung. Festschrift für Th. Schieder* (Munich 1968); L. Capéran, *Histoire contemporaine de la laïcité française*, 3 vols. (vol. 4 not yet publ. by the Institut catholique de Toulouse) (Paris 1958–61); P. Sorlin, *Waldeck-Rousseau* (Paris 1966); id., *La société française* I: *1840–1914* (Paris 1969). R. C. K. Ensor, "England 1870–1914," *Oxford History of England* XIV (London 1936); G. M. Young, *Victorian England. Portrait of an age* (London 1957); F. Fonzi, *Crispi e lo "Stato di Milano"* (Milan 1965); A. W. Salomone, *Italy in the Giolittian Era. Italian Democracy in the Making, 1900–1914* (Philadelphia 1960); R. Konetzke, *Geschichte des spanischen und portugiesischen Volkes* (Leipzig 1939); L. Sánchez Agesta, *La revolución liberal* (Madrid 1955); H. Jeschke, *Die Generation von 1898* (Heidelberg 1934); T. Schieder, *Das deutsche Kaiserreich von 1871 als Nationalstaat* (Cologne and Opladen 1961); E. R. Huber, *Deutsche Verfassungsgeschichte seit 1789* IV (Stuttgart 1969); P. Alter, *Die irische Nationalbewegung zwischen Parlament und Revolution* (Stuttgart 1971); O. Halecki, *Grenzraum des Abendlandes. Eine Geschichte Ostmitteleuropas* (Salzburg 1957); P. Kovalevsky, *Bildatlas der Kultur und Geschichte der slawischen Welt* (Basel and Vienna 1964); R. Portal, *Les Slaves. Peuples et nations* (Paris 1965); F. R. Dulles, *The United States since 1865* (University of Michigan 1959); Postan, M. M. and Habakuk, H. J., eds., *Cambridge Economic History of Europe* 4 (Cambridge, England) 1965; Parker, W. N. and Pounds, N. J. G., *Coal and Steel in Western Europe* (Bloomington, Indiana 1957); Moller, Herbert, ed., *Population Movements in Modern European History* (New York 1964); Dickinson, R. E., *The West European City: A Geographical Interpretation* (London 1951); Briggs, Asa, *The Making of Modern England, 1783–1867: The Age of Improvement* (New York 1959); Bell, H. C., *Lord Palmerston*, 2 vols (Hamden, Conn. 1936); Curtis, L. P., *Coercion and Conciliation in Ireland, 1880–1892* (Princeton 1963); Wright, Gordon, *France in Modern Times: 1760 to the Present* (Chicago 1960); Brogan, D. W., *The French Nation: From Napoleon to Petain, 1814–1940* (London 1961); Holborn, Hajo, *A History of Modern Germany* 3 (New York 1968); Webb, Robert K., *English History, 1815–1914* (Washington, D.C. 1967); Rich, Norman, *Germany, 1815–1914* (Washington, D.C. 1968); Macartney, C. A., *The Habsburg Empire, 1790–1918* (London 1969); Langer, William L., *European Alliances and Alignments, 1871–1890* (New York 1931).

II. CHURCH HISTORY

1. GENERAL CHURCH HISTORY

G. Maron, "Die römisch-katholische Kirche von 1870–1970," K. D. Schmidt and E. Wolf, *Die Kirche und ihre Geschichte* 4 and 2 (Göttingen 1972); K. Algermissen, *Konfessionskunde,* revised by H. Fries et al. (Paderborn 1969).

2. PAPACY

Stanislao da Campagnola, *I papi nella storia* II (Rome 1961); G. Schwaiger, *Geschichte der Päpste im 20. Jh.* (Munich 1964; new ed. in Deutscher Taschenbuchverlag no. 482 [1968]); C. Falconi, *I papi del ventesimo secolo* (Milan 1967); H. Hermelink, *Die katholische Kirche unter den Pius-Päpsten des 20. Jh.* (Zurich 1949); C. Alix, *Le Saint-Siège et les nationalismes en Europe, 1870–1960* (Paris 1962); D. Secco Suardo, "Da Leone XIII a Pio X," *Collana di storia del movimento cattolico* no. 18 (Rome 1967); K. O. v. Aretin, *Papsttum und moderne Welt* (Munich 1970); E. T. Gargan, ed., *Leo XIII and the Modern World* (New York 1961); F. Engel-Janosi, *Österreich und der Vatikan 1846–1918,* 2 vols. (Graz 1958–60) (of general interest); *Il cardinale Gasparri e la Questione Romana (con brani delle Memorie inedite),* ed. by G. Spadolini (Florence 1973); G. Franz, *Kulturkampf. Staat und katholische Kirche in Mitteleuropa von der Säkularisation bis zum Abschluß des preußischen Kulturkampfes* (Munich 1954); id., (G. Franz-Willing), *Kulturkampf gestern und heute. Eine Säkularbetrachtung* (Munich 1971); H. E. Feine, *Kirchliche Rechtsgeschichte. Die katholische Kirche* (Cologne and Graz 1964); N. del Rè, *La Curia Romana* (Rome 1970); L. Bedeschi, *La Curia Romana durante la crisi modernista* (Parma 1968); id., *Riforma religiosa e Curia Romana all'inizio del secolo* (Milan 1968); *La Correspondance de Rome 1907–1912* (later ed. Milan [1972], 3 vols., ed. by É. Poulat); *L'ordinamento dei seminari da S. S. Pio X a Pio XII* (Rome 1958).

3. THE CATHOLIC CHURCH IN INDIVIDUAL COUNTRIES

GERMANY: R. Lill, *Die ersten deutschen Bischofskonferenzen* (Freiburg, Basel, and Vienna 1964); E. Gatz, *Die deutschen Bischofskonferenzen 1872–1881* (in preparation); W. Spael, *Das katholische Deutschland im 20. Jh.* (Würzburg 1964); *Der Katholizismus in Deutschland und der Verlag Herder. 1801–1951* (Freiburg i. Br. 1951); W. Kramer, *Zeitkritik und innere Auseinandersetzung im deutschen Katholizismus im Spiegel der führenden katholischen Zeitschriften, 1895–1914* (diss., Mainz 1955); K. Buchheim, "Der deutsche Verbandskatholizismus. Eine Skizze seiner Geschichte," B. Hanssler, *Die Kirche in der Gesellschaft* (Paderborn 1961), 30–83.

The Social Question: W. Schwer and Franz Müller, "Der deutsche Katholizismus im Zeitalter des Kapitalismus," *Kirche und Gesellschaft* VI (Augsburg 1932); P. Jostock, *Der deutsche Katholizismus und die Überwindung des Kapitalismus. Eine ideengeschichtliche Skizze* (Regensburg 1932); id., *Die katholisch-soziale Bewegung der letzten hundert Jahre in Deutschland* (Cologne 1958); id., *Katholische Arbeiterbewegung in der Geschichte der christlichen Arbeiterbewegung Deutschlands* (Cologne 1963); J. Höffner, *Die deutschen Katholiken und die soziale Frage im 19. Jh.* (Paderborn 1954); E. Ritter, *Die katholisch-soziale Bewegung Deutschlands im 19. Jh. und der Volksverein* (Cologne 1954); K. H. Brüls, *Geschichte der katholisch-sozialen Bewegung in Deutschland* (Münster 1958); E. Filthaut, *Deutsche Katholikentage 1848–1958 und soziale Frage* (Essen 1960); J. J. Stegmann, "Geschichte der sozialen Ideen im deutschen Katholizismus," H. Grebing, ed., *Deutsches Handbuch der Politik* 3 (1969), 325–560.

Church and State: H. Bornkamm, *Die Staatsidee im Kulturkampf* (Munich 1950); R. Morsey, "Bismarck und der Kulturkampf," *AKG* 39 (1957), 232–70; id., *Die deutsche Zentrumspartei 1917–1923* (Düsseldorf 1966; also important for the decade preceeding 1914); id., ed., *Zeitgeschichte in Lebensbildern. Aus dem deutschen Katholizismus des 20. Jh.* (Mainz 1973) (biographies of Cardinal G. Kopp, J. Bachem, G. v. Hertling, F. Hitze, P. Spahn, K. Trimborn); E. Schmidt-Volkmar, *Der Kulturkampf in Deutschland 1871–1890* (Göttingen 1962); K. Buchheim, *Ultramontanismus und Demokratie* (Munich 1963); H. Lutz, *Demokratie im Zwielicht. Der Weg der deutschen Katholiken aus dem Kaiserreich in die Republik* (Munich 1963); C. Weber, *Kirchliche Politik zwischen Rom, Berlin und Trier 1876–1888* (Mainz 1970); id., *Quellen und Studien zur Kurie und der vatikanischen Politik unter Leo XIII.* (forthcoming); R. Lill, *Die Katholiken und Bismarcks Reichsgründung: Reichsgründung 1870/71,* ed. by T. Schieder and E. Deuerlein (Stuttgart 1970), 345–65; id., *Die Wende im Kulturkampf* (Tübingen 1973); A. Gnägi, *Kirche und Demokratie* (diss., Zurich 1970); K. Erlinghagen, *Die Säkularisierung der deutschen Schule* (Hanover 1972).

AUSTRIA-HUNGARY: M. Csáky, *Der Kulturkampf in Ungarn* (Graz, Vienna, and Cologne 1967).

The Social Question: J. Wodka, *Kirche in Österreich* (Vienna 1959); F. Engel-Janosi, *Österreich und der Vatican,* 2 vols. (Graz 1958–60); F. Funder, *Aufbruch zur christlichen Sozialreform* (Vienna and Munich 1953); id., *Vom Gestern ins Heute* (Vienna and Munich 1971); C. Allmayer-Beck, *Vogelsang. Vom Feudalismus zur Volksbewegung* (Vienna 1952; of general interest); G. Silberbauer, *Österreichs Katholiken und die Arbeiterfrage* (Graz 1966); I. A. Hellwing, *Der konfessionelle Antisemitismus im 19. Jh. in Österreich* (Vienna, Freiburg, and Basel 1972).

SWITZERLAND: K. Fry, *Kaspar Decurtins,* 2 vols. (Zurich 1949–52; of general interest); J. Meier, *Der Schweizer Katholische Verein* (Lucerne 1954); U. Altermatt, *Der Weg der Schweizer Katholiken aus dem Ghetto* (forthcoming).

FRANCE: E. Lecanuet, *L'Église de France sous la IIIᵉ République,* new ed., II–IV (Paris 1930–31); A. Latreille and R. Rémond, *Histoire du catholicisme en France* III (Paris 1962); R. Rémond, *Les deux congrès ecclésiastiques de Reims et de Bourges, 1896–1900* (Paris 1964); A. Baudrillart, *Vie de Mgr d'Hulst,* 2 vols. (Paris 1921–25); J.-M. Mayeur, *Un prêtre démocrate, l'abbé Lemire* (Paris and Tournai 1968).

Church and State: J. Gadille, *La pensée et l'action politiques des évêques français au début de la IIIᵉ république,* 2 vols. (Paris 1967); J.-B. Woodall, *The Ralliement in France. Origins and History, 1876–1894* (New York 1961); A. Sedgwick, *The Ralliement in French Politics, 1890–1898* (Cambridge, Mass. 1965); L. V. Méjan, *La séparation de l'Église et de l'État en France. L'œuvre de Louis Méjan* (Paris 1959); A. v. Campenhausen, *Staat und Kirche in Frankreich* (Göttingen 1962); J.-M. Mayeur, *La séparation de l'Église et de l'État* (Paris 1966); M. Vaussard, *Histoire de la démocratie chrétienne* (Paris 1956); J. Caron, *Le Sillon et la démocratie chrétienne* (Paris 1967); P. Castel, *Le Picard et le P. Bailly dans les luttes de presse* (Rome 1962); P. Sorlin, *"La Croix" et les Juifs* (Paris 1967); P. Pierrard, *Juifs et catholiques français. De Drumont à Jules Isaac* (Paris 1970).

The Social Question: E. Barbier, *L'histoire du catholicisme libéral et du catholicisme sociale en France, 1870–1914,* 5 vols. (Bordeaux 1923–28) (integralist perspective; a great deal of documentation); H. Rollet, *L'action sociale des catholiques en France, 1871 à 1914,* 2 vols. (Paris 1948–58); G. Le Bras, *Histoire de la pratique religieuse en France,* 2 vols. (Paris 1942–44); C. Molette, *L'Association catholique de la jeunesse française, 1886–1907* (Paris 1968); H. I. Terhünte, *Die religiöse Lage der Katholiken Frankreichs in der 3. Republik* (1919); H. Platz, *Geistige Kämpfe im modernen Frankreich* (Kempten 1922).

ITALY: G. Spadolini, *L'opposizione cattolica da Porta Pia al '98* (Florence 1961); id., *Giolitti e i cattolici, 1901–1914* (Florence 1960); D. Secco Suardo, *I cattolici intransigenti* (Brescia 1962); P. Scoppola, *Coscienza religiosa e democrazia nell'Italia contemporanea* (Bologna 1966); id., *Spiritualità e azione del laicato cattolico italiano*, 2 vols. (Padua 1969); F. Magri, *L'azione cattolica in Italia (1775–1939)* (Milan 1953); L. Civardi, *Compendio di storia dell'Azione cattolica italiana* (Rome 1956); L. Ambrosoli, *Il primo movimento D. C. in Italia (1897–1904)* (Rome 1958); G. De Rosa, *Storia politica dell'A. C. in Italia 1905–1919* (Bari 1954), new ed. in 2 vols. (1966); A. Gambasin, "Il movimento sociale nell'Opera dei congressi (1874–1904)," *AnGr* no. 91 (Rome 1958); M. C. Casella, *Religious Liberalism in Modern Italy*, 2 vols. (London 1966); G. Candeloro, *Il movimento cattolico in Italia* (Rome 1953) (Marxist interpretation); R. F. Esposito, *La Massoneria e l'Italia* (Rome 1969); C. Bello, *Geremia Bonomelli* (Brescia 1961); A. Albertazzi, *Il cardinale Svampa e i cattolici bolognesi* (Brescia 1971).

BELGIUM—THE NETHERLANDS—LUXEMBURG: A. de Moreau, *L'Église en Belgique* (Brussels 1945), 239–63; P. van Zuylen, "La Belgique et le Vatican en 1879," *Revue générale Belge* (1954), 1707–34, 1901–15, 2065–81; (1955), 67–86; A. Simon, *La liberté de l'enseignement* (Brussels 1952); id., *Le cardinal Mercier* (Brussels 1960); R. Reszohazy, *Origines et formation du catholicisme social en Belgique. 1842–1909* (Brussels 1958); P. Gérin, *Les origines de la démocratie chrétienne à Liège*, 2 vols. (Brussels 1958–59); L. J. Rogier, *Katholieke Herleving, Geschiedenis van Katholiek Nederland sinds 1853* (The Hague 1957), 276–348; E. Donckel, *Die Kirche in Luxemburg von den Anfängen bis zur Gegenwart* (Luxemburg 1950).

SPAIN: J. M. Cuenza, *Estudios sobre la Iglesia española del xix* (Madrid 1973).

BRITISH EMPIRE: Maisy Ward, *The Wilfrid Wards and the Transition*, 2 vols. (London 1934–38); J. G. Snead-Cox, *Life of Herbert Vaughan*, 2 vols. (London 1910); E. Oldmeadow, *Francis cardinal Bourne*, 2 vols. (London 1940–44); L. I. McCaffrey, *The Irish Question, 1800–1922* (Lexington 1968); Alexis de Barbezieux, *L'Église catholique en Canada* (Montreal 1934); E. Gautier, *Le catholicisme au Canada* (Ottawa 1934); D. de Saint-Denis, *L'Église catholique au Canada* (Montreal 1956); V. Harvey et al., *L'Église et le Québec* (Montreal 1961); J. Hulliger, *L'enseignement social des évêques canadiens, 1891–1950*; F. Engel-Janosi, 2 vols. *Österreich und der Vatican* (Graz 1958–60); E. Winter, Laval University 1961); P. Savard, *Jules-Paul Tardivel* (Quebec 1967) (of general interest); J. E. Murtagh, *Australia. The Catholic Chapter* (New York 1947); P. Ford, *Cardinal Moran and Australian Labour Party* (London 1966); R. Fogarty, *Catholic Education in Australia, 1806–1950*, 2 vols. (Melbourne 1959).

THE SLAVIC WORLD: A. M. Ammann, *Abriß der ostslawischen Kirchengeschichte* (Vienna 1950); F. Engel-Janosi, 2 vols. *Österreich und der Vatican* (Graz 1958–60); E. Winter, *Byzanz und Rom im Kampf um die Ukraine 955–1939* (Leipzig 1942); id., *Rußland und die slawischen Völker in der Diplomatie des Vatikans 1878–1903* (Berlin 1950); id., *Rußland und das Papsttum* II: *Von der Aufklärung bis zur großen sozialistischen Oktoberrevolution* (Berlin 1961); id., *Rom und Moskau. Ein halbes Jahrtausend Weltgeschichte in ökumenischer Sicht* (Vienna 1972), 145–232.

LATIN-AMERICA: E. Ryan, *The Church in the South American Republics* (London 1934); J. L. Mecham, *Church and State in Latin America* (North Carolina Press 1934); W. v. Schoen, *Geschichte Mittel- und Südamerikas* (Munich 1953), 343–665.

THE UNITED STATES: Nolan, ed., *Pastoral Letters of the American Hierarchy, 1792–1970* (Huntington 1971); T. T. McAvoy, *A History of the Catholic Church in the United States*

(Notre Dame 1969); id., *The Great Crisis in American Catholic History 1895–1900* (Chicago 1957); T. Roemer, *The Catholic Church in the United States* (London 1950); C. J. Barry, *The Catholic Church and German Americans* (Milwaukee 1953) (critical of the Ireland-Keane group); H. A. Buetow, *The Story of Catholic Education in the United States* (New York 1970); F. J. Zwierlein, *Theodore Roosevelt and Catholics, 1882–1919* (Rochester 1956); R. D. Cross, *The Emergence of Liberal Catholicism in America* (Cambridge, Mass. 1958); J. T. Ellis, *The Life of James card. Gibbons,* 2 vols. (Milwaukee 1952); J. H. Moynihan, *The Life of John Ireland* (New York 1953).

The Social Question: H. Browne, *The Catholic Church and the Knights of Labor* (Washington 1949); M. Karson, *The Catholic Church and Unionism* (New York 1951); A. I. Abell, *American Catholicism and Social Action, 1865–1950* (Notre Dame 1963).

4. HOPES FOR UNIFICATION

CONTACT WITH THE ANGLICAN CHURCH: J. J. Hughes, *Absolutely Null and Utterly Void* (London 1968); id., *Stewards of the Lord. A Reappraisal of Anglican Orders* (London 1970); id., "Zur Frage der anglikanischen Weihen. Ein Modellfall festgefahrener Kontroverstheologie," *Quaestiones disputatae* 59 (Freiburg i. Br. 1973; original in German).

THE INDEPENDENT AND UNIATE CHURCHES—PAPAL HOPES FOR UNIFICATION: D. Attwater, *The Christian Churches of the East,* 2 vols. (Milwaukee 1961–62); A. Brunello, *Le Chiese Orientali e l'Unione. Prospetto storico statistico* (Massimo and Milan 1966); J. Casper, "Die orientalische Christenheit," *Christus und die Religionen der Erde. Handbuch der Religionsgeschichte* III, ed. by F. König (Freiburg 1951), 643–729; R. F. Esposito, *Leone XIII e l'Oriente cristiano. Studio storico-sistematico* (Rome 1961); E. v. Ivánka et al., *Handbuch der Ostkirchenkunde* (Düsseldorf 1971); F. Heiler, *Die Ostkirchen.* Revision of *Urkirche und Ostkirche.* In cooperation with H. Hartog, ed. by A. M. Heiler (Munich and Basel 1971); A. S. Hernández, *Iglesias de Oriente. Puntos específicos de su teología* (Santander 1959); R. Janin, *Les Églises orientales et les rites orientaux* (Paris 1955); id., "Les Églises orientales," C. Poulet, *Histoire du christianisme. Époque contemporaine* (Paris 1957), 489–545; M. Lehmann, *Österreich und der christliche Osten* (Vienna 1970); H. Musset, *Histoire du christianisme, spécialement en Orient* 3 (Harissa and Jerusalem 1948–49); J. Hajjar, *Le christianisme en Orient. Études d'histoire contemporaine 1684–1968* (Beirut 1971); B. Spuler, *Gegenwartslage der Ostkirchen in ihrer nationalen und staatlichen Umwelt* (Frankfurt a. M. 1968); B. Stasiewski, "Geschichtliche Überlegungen zur kirchlichen Trennung zwischen Orient und Okzident," *Das Christentum des Ostens und die christliche Einheit* (Würzburg 1965), 13–40, W. de Vries, *Der christliche Osten in Geschichte und Gegenwart* (Würzburg 1951); G. Zananiri, *Catholicisme oriental* (Paris 1966); N. Zernow, "Die Ostkirchen und die ökumenische Bewegung im 20. Jh.," R. Rouse and St. C. Neill, *Geschichte der Ökumenischen Bewegung 1517–1948* II (Göttingen 1958), 317–58.

5. HISTORY OF THE MISSIONS

R. Streit, *Bibliotheca Missionum* III, XXIV, XXV (America); VIII, XXVII (India); IX (Philippines); X (Japan, Korea); XI (Indochina); XII–XIV (China); XVII–XX (Africa); XXI (Australia, Oceania (Freiburg i. Br. 1951ff.); J. Glazik, *Päpstliche Rundschreiben über die Mission von Leo XIII. bis Johannes XXIII.* (Münsterschwarzach 1961; Lat. and Germ.); Kenneth Scott Latourette, *A History of the Expansion of Christianity* V–VII (New York and London 1943–45); A. Mulders, *Missionsgeschichte. Die Ausbrietung des katholischen Glaubens* (Regensburg 1960); T. Ohm, *Wichtige Daten der Missionsgeschichte* (Münster 1961); J. Jennes, *A History of the Catholic Church in Japan* (Tokyo 1959).

6. ORDERS AND CONGREGATIONS

P. Schmitz, *Histoire de l'ordre de saint Benoît* (Maredsous 1948–56); A. Wulf, *Compendium of the History of the Cistercian Order* (Milwaukee 1944); C. Grolleau and G. Chastel, *L'ordre de Cîteaux. La Trappe* (Paris 1954); A. Walz, *Wahrheitskünder. Die Dominikaner in Geschichte und Gegenwart* (Essen 1960, gen. Germ. version of the *Compendium* . . .); C. Hollis, *The Jesuits: A History* (New York 1969); J. Monval, *Les Assomptionnistes* (Paris 1939); E. B. Lüthen, *Die Gesellschaft des Göttlichen Heilandes* (1911); R. Pfeiffer, *Joh.-B. Jordan* (Rome 1920); E. Federici, *G. B. Jordan* (Rome 1948); H. Fischer, *Arnold Janssen* (Steyl 1919); S. Sinningen, *Katholische Frauengenossenschaften Deutschlands* (Düsseldorf 1944; biblio.); R. Hostie, *Vie et mort des ordres religieux* (Paris 1927), 223–80.

7. PIETY—ITS EXPRESSION IN THE ARTS AND LITERATURE

A. Rohrbasser, *Heilslehre der Kirche. Dokumente von Pius IX. bis Pius XII.* (Fribourg 1953); R. Graber, *Die marianischen Weltrundschreiben der Päpste in den letzten hundert Jahren* (Regensburg 1951); A. Mayer-Pfannholz, "Das Kirchenbild des 19. Jh. und seine Ablösung," *Die Besinnung* 3 (Nuremberg 1948), 124–44.

LITURGICAL MOVEMENT: W. Trapp, *Vorgeschichte und Ursprung der liturgischen Bewegung* (Regensburg 1940); O. Rousseau, *Histoire du mouvement liturgique* (Paris 1945), 201–30; J. Hacker, "Die Messe in den deutschen Diözesan-, Gesang- und Gebetbüchern von der Aufklärung bis zur Gegenwart," *MthSt(H)* 1 (1950), 68–132; Anton L. Mayer, "Die Stellung der Liturgie von der Zeit der Romantik bis zur Jahrhundertwende," *ALW* 3 (1955), 1–77; H. A. Heiser, *Die Durchführung der Kommuniondekrete in der ganzen Welt* (Wiesbaden 1932); P. Hellbernd, *Die Erstkommunion der Kinder in Geschichte und Gegenwart* (Vechta 1954).

EUCHARISTIC CONGRESSES: E. Lesne, *Cinquantenaire des congrès eucharistiques internationaux* (Lille 1931). R. Aubert, "Die Eucharistischen Kongresse von Leo XIII. bis Johannes XXIII.," *Concilium* 1 (1965), 61–66.

REFORM OF THE BREVIARY: T. Narbutas, *La reforma del breviario romano por Pío X* (Santiago de Chile 1949).

THE SIGNIFICANCE OF THE BIBLE: B. Dreher, *Die biblische Unterweisung im evangelischen und katholischen Religionsunterricht* (Freiburg i. Br. 1963), 11–81.

CHURCH MUSIC: K. G. Fellerer, *Geschichte der Katholischen Kirchenmusik* (Düsseldorf 1949), 143–62; F. Romita, "La preformazione del Motu proprio di S. Pio X sulla musica sacra," *Monitor ecclesiasticus* 86 (1961), 395–497; P. Combe, *Histoire de la restauration de chant grégorien d'après des documents inédits* (Solesmes 1969).

CHURCH ART: I. Herwegen, O.S.B., *Das Kunstprinzip der Liturgie* (Paderborn 1920); id., *Kunst und Mysterium* (Münster i. W. 1929); K. Clark, *The Gothic Revival* (London 1950); K. Andrews, *The Nazarenes. A Brotherhood of German Painters in Rome* (Oxford 1964); R. Ironside and J. Gere, *Pre-Raphaelite Painters* (London 1948); A. Kamphausen, *Gotik ohne Gott. Ein Beitrag zur Deutung der Neugotik und des 19. Jh.* (Tübingen 1952); A. Mann, *Die Neuromantik* (Cologne 1966); J. Kreitmaier, S.J., *Beuroner Kunst. Eine Ausdrucksform der christlichen Mystik* (Freiburg i. Br. 1923); St. Waetzoldt, "Bemerkungen zur christlich-religiösen Malerei in der zweiten Hälfte des 19. Jh.," *Triviale Zonen in der religiösen Kunst des 19. Jh.* (*Studien zur Philosophie und Literatur des 19. Jh.* 15 [Frankfurt a. M. 1971]).

SPIRITUAL LIFE: H. Weinert, *Dichtung aus dem Glauben* (Heidelberg 1948); C. Moeller, *Littérature du XXᵉ siècle et christianisme* (Paris 1953ff.). A. Simon, *La Littérature du péché et de la grâce, 1880–1950* (Paris 1957); M. Bougier, *Essai sur la renaissance de la Poésie catholique de Baudelaire à Claudel* (Montpellier 1942); W. Spael, *Das Buch im Geisteskampf. 100 Jahre Borromäusverein* (Bonn 1950); O. Köhler, *Bücher als Wegmarken im deutschen Katholizismus: "Der katholische Buchhandel Deutschlands"*, ed. by the Vereinigung des katholischen Buchhandels (Frankfurt a. M. 1967); G. Rossini, ed., *Aspetti della cultura cattolica nell'età di Leone XIII* (Rome 1961).

8. POLITICAL AND SOCIAL DOCTRINE—SOCIAL AND POLITICAL CATHOLICISM

PAPAL SOCIAL AND POLITICAL DOCTRINES: R. Kothen, *L'enseignement social de l'Église* (Louvain 1949) (texts of doctrines issued by the Popes from Leo XIII to Pius XI); E. Muhler, *Die Soziallehren der Päpste* (Munich 1958); J. Schasching, *Die soziale Botschaft der Kirche von Leo XIII. bis Johannes XXIII.* (Vienna 1963); G. Jarlot, *Doctrine pontificale et histoire, L'enseignement social de Léon XIII., Pie X et Benoît XV vu dans son ambiance historique* (Rome 1964).

LEO XIII: P. Mourret, *Les directives politiques, intellectuelles et sociales de Léon XIII.* (Paris 1920); W. Schwer, *Leo XIII.: Klassiker der katholischen Sozialphilosophie* (Freiburg 1923); O. Schilling, *Die Staats- und Soziallehre des Papstes Leo XIII.* (Cologne 1925); id., *Christliche Gesellschaftslehre* (Freiburg i. Br. 1926); P. Tischleder, *Die Staatslehre Leos XIII.* (Mönchen-Gladbach 1925–27); id., *Staatsgewalt und katholisches Gewissen* (Mönchen-Gladbach 1926); L. P. Wallace, *Leo XIII and the Rise of Socialism* (New York 1966).

RERUM NOVARUM: G. Gundlach: *Veröffentlichung der Görres-Gesellschaft, Sektion Sozial-und Wirtschaftsgeschichte* no. 3 (Paderborn 1931) (also *Quadragesimo anno*); O. v. Nell-Breuning, *Die soziale Enzyklika: Erläuterungen zum Weltrundschreiben Pius' XI. über die gesellschaftliche Ordnung* (Cologne 1932; 2d ed., 1950; including important comments regarding *Rerum novarum*); M. Allendorf, *Zur Geschichte der Sozialenzykliken des Vatikans* (diss., Humboldt Univ., Berlin 1963).

DOCTRINE OF PROPERTY: O. v. Nell-Breuning, "Die Eigentumslehre," J. Strieder et al. (ed. of the *Görres-Gesellschaft*), *Die soziale Frage und der Katholizismus* (Paderborn 1931); K. H. Grenner, *Wirtschaftsliberalismus und katholisches Denken* (Cologne 1967); F. Beutter, *Die Eigentumsbegründung in der Moraltheologie des 19. Jh.* (Paderborn 1971).

SOCIAL AND POLITICAL CATHOLICISM: A. M. Knoll, *Der soziale Gedanke im modernen Katholizismus. Von der Romantik bis Rerum novarum* (Vienna and Leipzig 1932); L. Leutner, *Das Erwachen der modernen katholischen Sozialidee. Die Entwicklung im 19. Jh. bis Rerum novarum* (Vienna 1951); J. N. Moody, ed., *Church and Society: Catholic Social and Political Thought and Movements, 1789–1950* (New York 1953); M. P. Fogarty, *Christian Democracy in Western Europe, 1820–1953* (London 1957); G. Brakelmann, *Die soziale Frage des 19. Jh. II: Die evangelisch-soziale und die katholisch-soziale Bewegung* (Witten 1962); C. Bauer, "Bild der Kirche—Abbild der Gesellschaft," *Hochland* 48 (1956); new ed.: *Deutscher Katholizismus* (Frankfurt 1964), 9–27; Hans Maier, *Revolution und Kirche. Studien zur Frühgeschichte der christlichen Demokratie, 1789–1901* (Freiburg 1965); id., *Kirche und Gesellschaft* (Munich 1972); M. Bendiscioli, "Chiesa e società nei secc. XIX e XX," *Nuove questioni di storia contemporanea* I (Milan 1967), 325–447; Verluis, *Beknopte Geschiedenis van de Katholicke Arbeidersbeweging* (1949); Götz Briefs et al., ed. by the Catholic Social Institute of the Archdiocese of Cologne, *Das Bild des Arbeiters in der katholischen Sozialbewegung von den Anfängen bis zur Gegenwart*

(Cologne 1960); S. H. Scholl, ed., *150 ans de mouvement ouvrier chrétien en Europe de l'Ouest* (Paris 1966); L. R. Sanseverino, *Il movimento sindacale cristiano dal 1850 al 1939* (Rome 1950); K. H. Schürmann, *Zur Vorgeschichte der christlichen Gewerkschaften* (Freiburg i. Br. 1958); K. Buchheim, "Christliche Parteien," *StL* II 467–75 (international survey, biblio.).

9. HISTORY OF THEOLOGY

NEO-SCHOLASTICISM: P. Dezza, *Alle origini del Neotomismo* (Milan 1940); id., *I neotomisti italiani del secolo XIX,* 2 vols. (Milan 1942–44); R. Aubert, "Aspects divers du néo-thomisme sous le pontificat de Léon XIII.," *Aspetti della cultura cattolica nell'età di Leone XIII.* (Rome 1961), 133–227; A. Walz, "Sguardo sul movimento tomista nel secolo XIX fino all'enciclica Aeterni Patris," *Aquinas* 8 (1965), 351–79; H. Vorgrimler and R. Vander Gucht, *Bilanz der Theologie,* 3 vols. (Freiburg i. Br. 1969), esp.: F. van Steenberghen, *Die neuscholastische Philosophie* (vol. 1), R. Aubert, *Die Theologie während der 1. Hälfte des 20. Jh.* (vol. 2); K. Eschweiler, *Die zwei Wege der neueren Theologie. G. Hermes-M. J. Scheeben* (Augsburg 1926); M. J. Scheeben, *Handbuch der katholischen Dogmatik,* 7 vols., ed. by J. Höfer et al. (Freiburg 1941–57; incl. biblio.); F. S. Pancheri, *Il pensiero teologico di M. Scheeben e S. Tommaso* (Padua 1956).

M. BLONDEL AND HIS SCHOOL: R. Scherer, Introduction to: *M. Blondel, Das Denken* (Freiburg i. Br. 1953), VIII–XXXII; R. Aubert, *Le problème de l'acte de foi, données traditionnelles et résultats des controverses récents* (Louvain 1950), 227–511; J.-P. Golinas, *La restauration du Thomisme sous Léon XIII et les philosophes nouvelles. Ètude de la pensée de M. Blondel et du Père Laberthonnière* (Washington 1959); A. Hayen, *Bibliographie blondélienne* (Messina 1953); *Laberthonnière. L'homme et l'œuvre,* ed. by P. Beillevert (Paris 1972); E. Lecanuet, *La vie de l'Église sous Léon XIII* (Paris 1930), 384–543.

THE BIBLICAL QUESTION (cf. "MODERNISM"): A. Loisy, *Mémoires,* 3 vols. (Paris 1930–31); A. Houtin, *La question biblique chez les catholiques de France au XIXᵉ siècle* (Paris 1902); id., *La question biblique au XXᵉ siècle* (ibid. 1906); J. Chaine et al., *L'œuvre exégétique et historique du R. P. Lagrange* (Paris 1935); L.-H. Vincent, "Le Père Lagrange," *RB* 47 (1938), 321–54; F. M. Braun, *L'œuvre du Père Lagrange* (Fribourg 1943); *Le Père Lagrange ou service de la Bible, Souvenirs personnels* (Paris 1967).

THE "MODERNIST" CRISIS: O. Schröder, *Aufbruch und Mißverständnis. Zur Geschichte der Reformkatholischen Bewegung* (Graz 1969); A. Gisler, *Der Modernismus* (Einsiedeln 1912); J. Rivière, *Le modernisme dans l'Église* (Paris 1929); *The Modernist Movement in the Roman Church* (Cambridge 1934); id., *A Variety of Catholic Modernists* (Cambridge 1970); É. Poulat, *Histoire, dogme et critique dans la crise moderniste* (Paris and Tournai 1962); id., *Intégrisme et catholicisme intégral* (Paris and Tournai 1969); J. Ratté, *Three Modernists, A. Loisy, G. Tyrrell, W. L. Sullivan* (New York 1967); F. Rodé, *Le miracle dans la crise moderniste* (Paris 1965); C. Porro, *La controversia cristologica nel periodo modernisto* (Milan 1971); M. Ranchetti, *Cultura e riforma religiosa nella storia del modernismo* (Turin 1963); P. Scoppola, *Crisi modernista e rinnovamento cattolico* (Bologna 1969); L. Bedeschi, *I cattolici disubbidienti* (Naples and Rome 1959); id., *Il Modernismo e Romolo Murri in Emilia e Romagna* (Parma 1967); M. Guasco, *R. Murri e il modernismo* (Rome 1968); M. de la Bédoyère, *The Life of Baron von Hügel* (London 1951); L. F. Barmann, *Baron F. von Hügel and the Modernist Crisis in England* (Cambridge 1972); F. Parente, *E. Buonaiuti* (Rome 1970); L. Bedeschi, *Lineamenti dell'antimodernismo. Il caso Lanzoni* (Parma 1970); E. Weinzierl, ed., *Der Modernismus. Beiträge zu seiner Erforschung* (Graz, Vienna and Cologne, 1973), which includes: R. Lill, "Der Kampf der römischen Kurie gegen den 'praktischen' Modernismus: Die Päpstliche Autorität im katholischen Selbstverständnis des 19. und 20. Jh.," 109–23.

BIBLIOGRAPHY TO INDIVIDUAL CHAPTERS

Part One

The Problem of Adapting to the Modern World

Introduction: *The World Plan of Leo XIII: Goals and Methods*

SOURCES

ASS 11–35 (Rome 1878–1903); *Leonis XIII Pont. Max. Acta,* 23 vols. with index (Rome 1881–1905; reprint Graz 1971); *Epistolae encyclicae,* 6 parts (Freiburg i. Br. 1878–1904; Lat. and Germ.); *Leonis XIII Allocutiones, Epistolae et Constitutiones,* 8 vols. (Bruges 1887–1911); *Scelta di atti episcopali del card. G. Pecci ora Leone XIII* (Rome 1879); *Leonis XIII Carmina, Inscriptiones, Numismata,* ed. by J. Bach (Cologne 1903); *Discorsi,* ed. P. de Franciscis (Rome 1882); A. Mercati, *Raccolta di Concordati* I (Rome 1952); *Œuvres pastorales de S. E. le Cardinal Pecci,* 2 vols. (Bruges and Lille 1888–92); *Lettres de Pecci, 1843–1846,* ed. by A. Simon (Brussels and Rome 1959).

On the conclave: Mullé de la Cerda, *Reseña histórica del último conclave y biografía de León XIII* (Madrid 1878); Journal of Cardinal H.-M.-G. Bonnechose: L. Besson, *Vie de S. E. le cardinal Bonnechose* II (Paris 1887); R. de Cesare, *Il Conclave di Leone XIII* (Città di Castello 1888).

Memoirs and letters: A. Perraud, *Mes relations personnelles avec les derniers papes Pie IX et Léon XIII 1856–1903* (Paris 1917); D. Ferrata, *Mémoires,* 3 vols. (Rome 1920); K. v. Schlözer, *Letzte römische Briefe* (1882–94 [Berlin 1924]; P. M. Baumgarten, *Römische und andere Erinnerungen* (Düsseldorf 1927); C. Benoist, *Souvenirs I 1883–93* (Paris 1932); G. Someria, *I miei quattro Papi* I (Milan 1930); F. Crispolti, *Pio IX–Pio XI, Ricordi personali* (Milan 1939); *Lettere di Giuseppe Toniolo,* ed. by G. Anichini, 3 vols. (Rome 1952–53); F. X. Kraus, *Tagebücher* (cf. chap. 29), 383–758; L. v. Pastor, *Tagebücher—Briefe—Erinnerungen* (cf. chap. 29) 111–416; H. des Houx, *Souvenirs d'un journaliste français à Rome* (Paris 1886).

Nunciatures: G. de Marchi, *Le nunziature apostoliche dal 1800 al 1956* (Rome 1957; chronologically arranged list of nuncios with appointment and sanction according to countries).

The press: *Osservatore Romano* (1878ff.; since 1870 semiofficial paper of the Vatican); *La Civiltà Cattolica* (1878ff.); in Schmidlin, *PG*, 377, and in the other biographies the positive press comments, even from the liberal and Socialist camp, are quoted; the wording and selection need to be examined; F. Jürgensmeier, *Die katholische Kirche im Spiegel der Karikatur der deutschen satirischen Tendenzzeitschriften von 1848–1900* (1969) 216–29, 230–47, passim.

LITERATURE

In addition to the general church histories listed in the General Bibliography, see the older documents of that time (cf. chap. 22), especially F. Mourret, *Histoire générale de l'Église,* 9 vols. (1909–21), pertinent vols. 8 and 9; P. M. Baumgarten, *Die katholische Kirche unserer Zeit,* 2 vols. (Munich 1899–1902); E. Jarry, *L'Église contemporaine,* 2 vols. (Paris 1936).

New assessments of the pontificate: E. T. Gargan, ed., *Leo XIII and the Modern World* (New York 1961); Stanislao da Campagnola, *I papi nella storia II* (Rome 1961); G. Schwaiger, *Geschichte der Päpste im 20. Jahrhundert,* (Munich 1964; new in Deutscher Taschenbuchverlag no. 482 [1968] 28–49); D. Secco Suardo (cited in chap. 5); K. O. v. Aretin, *Papsttum und moderne Welt* (Munich 1970); G. Maron, *Die römisch-katholische Kirche von 1870 bis 1970;* K. D. Schmidt and E. Wolf, *Die Kirche und ihre Geschichte* 4, 2 (Göttingen 1972), 203–8, passim; I. E. Ward, "Leo XIII, 'the Diplomat pope,'" *Review of Politics* 28 (1966), 47–61; C. Weber (biblio. to chap. 3).

Biblio. on the various countries and the individual topics, cf. the respective chapters.

BIOGRAPHIES

Schmidlin, *PG* II (Munich 1934), 331–589, is still considered "one of the most thorough . . . presentations" (R. Lill).—The purely popular biographies, of which the German ones are particularly numerous (see Schmidlin, *PG,* pp. XIX–XXII), are noteworthy as documents of the papal consciousness.—C. Tesi-Passerini and G. Cinquemani, *Leone ed il suo tempo,* 3 vols. (Turin 1890–92); C. de T'Serclaes, *Le Pape Léon XIII,* 3 vols. (Paris and Bruges 1894–1906), annalistic; according to the foreword of Vol. III, Pope Leo read the proof sheets, advice-note by Rampolla; H. des Houx, *Histoire de Léon XIII* (Paris 1900); L. K. Goetz, *Leo XIII., seine Weltanschauung und seine Wirksamkeit* (Gotha 1899; Protestant); B. O'Reilly, *Vie de Léon XIII* (Paris 1887); N. Schneider, *Leo XIII., sein Leben und Wirken* (Kempten 1903; "with Duke Pecci's support"); M. Spahn, *Leo XIII.* (Munich 1905); J. Fèvres. *Vie de Léon XIII,* 2 vols. (Paris 1908); Walter Goetz in *Meister der Politik* III, ed. by E. Marcks and K. A. v. Müller (Stuttgart 1924) 381–403 (best assessment from the Protestant side; cf. below); E. Vercesi, *Tre Papi: Leone XIII, Pio X, Benedetto, XV* (Milan 1929); A. Buttè, *Il papa Leone XIII* (Milan 1931); E. Soderini, *Il pontificato di Leone XIII,* 3 vols. (Milan 1932–33; "using the materials made available to him by the Pope himself"); R. Fülöp-Miller, *Leo XIII.* (Zurich 1935); F. Hayward, *Léon XIII* (Paris 1937; foreword by Cardinal A. Baudrillart); G. Monetti, *Leone XIII,* 3 vols. (Rome 1942); R. Aubert, *Léon XIII: I cattolici italiani dall'800 ad oggi* (Brescia 1964), 191–220.—Misc.: A.-J. Boyer d'Agen, *La jeunesse de Léon XIII* (and cf. below) (1897); J. Kraikin, *L'infanzia e la giovinezza di un papa* (Grottaferrata 1914); W. Lorenz, *Die Jugend des J. Pecci: StdZ* 165 (1959/60) 415–23; A.-J. Boyer d'Agen, *La prélature de Léon XIII* (Paris 1907); id., *Msgr. J. Pecci 1838–46* (Paris 1910); P. van Zuylen, "La nonciature Pecci," *Rev. gén belge* 126 (Brussels 1931) 258–76; N. Hilling, "Die kirchliche Gesetzgebung Leos XIII," *AkathKR* 93 (1913); 94 (1914); *Un témoin* (=Cardinal F. D. Mathieu), *Les derniers jours de Léon XIII et le conclave* (Paris 1904).—Pertaining to the various papal actions, cf. the respective chapters.

VATICAN AND CARDINALS: L. Teste, *Léon XIII et le Vatican* (Paris 1880); id., *Préface au Conclave* (Paris 1873); J.-J. Thierry, *La vie quotidienne au Vatican du temps de Léon XIII* (Paris 1963).—Cardinals (according to the dates of their appointment): J.-B. *Pitra* (1863); see vol. VIII; Gustav F. v. *Hohenlohe* (1866): vol. VIII; P. *Cullen* (1866): M. J.

Curran (Dublin 1955); L. *Oreglia* (1873): Schmidlin, *PG* II, index; *Franchi* (1873): Schmidlin, *PG* II, index; J. H. *Guibert* (1873): J. Paguelle de Follenay, 2 vols. (Paris 1896); M.-H. Graf v. *Ledóchowski* (1875): this vol., Chaps. 1 and 3; H. E. *Manning* (1875): J. Fitzsimons (London 1951); V.-A. *Dechamps* (1875): M. Becqué, 2 vols. (Louvain 1956); *Bartolini* (1875): Schmidlin, *PG* II, index; *McCloskey* (1875): J. Farley (London 1918); J. B. *Franzelin* (1876): Hocedez III, 133–40, index; L. *Parocchi* (1877): Schmidlin, *PG* II, index; Pastor, *Tagebücher,* index; L. *Nina* (1877): Schmidlin, *PG* II, index; J. H. *Newman* (1879): vol. VIII, chap. 9; T. M. *Zigliara* (1879): Hocedez II and III, index; J. *Hergenröther* (1879): S. Merkle in *Lebensläufe aus Franken,* ed. by A. Chroust (Munich 1919), 188–97; B. Lang: *ThPQ* 93 (1940) 302–9; L. *Jacobini* (1879): Schmidlin, *PG* II, 458–62; L. *Pie* (1879): vol. VIII; C.-M. A. *Lavigerie* (1882): this vol. chap. 6; W. *Czacki* (1882): this vol., chap. 3, n. 4; G. Aloisi *Masella* (1883): this vol., chap. 3, n. 8; C. *González Díaz Tuñón* (1884): A. Walz, *Compendium* . . . (Rome 1948), 621f.; P. F. *Moran* (1885): Schmidlin *PG* II, 500; this vol., chap. 9; P. *Melchers* (1885): H. M. Ludwigs (Cologne 1909); C. *Mazzella* (1886): *ECatt* VIII, 526f.; Hocedez III, 263f., index; J. *Gibbons* (1886): J. T. Ellis, 2 vols. (Milwaukee 1952); E. A. *Taschereau* (1886): D. de Saint-Denis, *L'Église cath. au Canada* (Montreal 1956); this vol., chap. 9; M. *Rampolla* (1887): T. Cramer-Klett in *Hochland* 11, 2 (1914), 1–9; B. *Ceretti* (Rome 1928); E. Vercesi, *Tre Segretari di Stato: Consalvi, Rampolla, Gasparri* (Venice 1932); Engel-Janosi, index; Serafino *Vannutelli* (1887): Schmidlin, *PG* II, index; F. X. *Kraus,* index; P. L. *Goossens* (1889): J. Muyldermans (Mechelen 1922); F.-M. B. *Richard de la Vergne* (1889): this vol., chap. 30; G. *Mermillod* (1890): C. Comte (Paris 1924); H. J. *Gruscha* (1891): O. Posch (diss., Vienna 1947); H. *Vaughan* (1892): J. G. Snead-Cox, 2 vols. (London 1910); P. Thureau-Dangin (Paris 1911); this vol., chap. 9; G. *Sarto* (1893): cf. Part II of this vol.; G. v. *Kopp* (1893): F. X. Seppelt in *Zs. f. Gesch. Schlesiens* 50 (Wroclaw 1916) 295–308; id., *Gesch. des Bistums Breslau* (Berlin 1929), 121–26; P. *Krementz* (1893): P. Höveler (Düsseldorf 1899); L. *Galimberti* (1893): this vol., chap. 3; Engel-Janosi, index; Angelo di *Pietro* (1893): De Marchi (see under Sources); A. G. *Ferrari* (1894): G. B. Penco, *Un grande cardinale* (Milan 1959); A. *Gotti* (1895): *Il Carmelo* 5 (1906), 15 (1916), 33 (1934); A.-L.-A. *Perraud* (1895): G. d'Orgeval-Dubouchet (Paris 1907); A. Houtin, *Évêques et diocèses* I (Paris 1908), 5–42; F. *Satolli* (1895): L. Hertling, *Gesch. der kath. Kirche in den Vereinigten Staaten* (Berlin 1954), 225f., 232ff.; A. *Agliardi* (1896): Pastor, *Tagebücher,* 229, 251f.; Engel-Janosi, index; D. *Ferrata* (1896): U. Stutz, *Die päpstl. Diplomatie unter Leo XIII nach den Denkwürdigkeiten* [cf. above, Sources] D. *Ferratas* (Berlin 1926); F.-D. *Mathieu* (1899): E. Renard (Paris 1925); J. C. *Vives y Tutò* (1899): A. M. de Barcelona (Barcelona 1951); *Respighi* (1901): Schmidlin, *PG* II, index.

The Situation in the Various Countries until 1914

1. *The* Kulturkampf *in Prussia and in the German Empire until 1878*

Sources

N. Siegfried (i.e., V. Cathrein), *Aktenstücke betreffend den preußischen Culturkampf* (Freiburg 1882); *Aktenstücke betreffend die Fuldaer Bischofskonferenzen 1867–1888* (Cologne 1889); L. Bergsträsser, *Dokumente des politischen Katholizismus* II (Munich 1923); O. v. Bismarck, *Die gesammelten Werke* VIc: *Politische ɔchriften 1871–1890,* ed. W. Frauendienst (Berlin 1935); XI: *Reden 1869–1878,* ed. W. Schüßler (Berlin 1929); *Die Vorgeschichte des Kulturkampfes. Quellenveröffentlichung aus dem Deutschen Zentralarchiv,* ed. A. Constabel, introd. by F. Hartung (Berlin 1956).

Literature

J. Bachem, *Preußen und die kath. Kirche* (Cologne 1887), 80–110; H. Brück, *Gesch. der kath. Kirche in Deutschland im 19. Jahrhundert* IV, 1, ed. J. B. Kißling (Münster 1907); J. B. Kißling, *Geschichte des Kulturkampfes im Deutschen Reich* II, III (Freiburg 1913, 1916); F. Vigener, *Ketteler* (Munich and Berlin 1924), 612–722; K. Bachem, *Vorgeschichte, Geschichte und Politik der deutschen Zentrumspartei* III (Cologne 1927; reprint, Aalen 1967); Schmidlin, *PG* II, 179–89; H. Bornkamm, *Die Staatsidee im Kulturkampf* (Munich 1950); Aubert, *Pie IX,* 384–92; G. Franz, *Kulturkampf. Staat und kath. Kirche in Mitteleuropa von der Säkularisation bis zum Abschluß des preußischen Kulturkampfes* (Munich 1954), 185–246; id., (under the name of G. Franz-Willing), *Kulturkampf gestern und heute, Eine Säkularbetrachtung* (Munich 1971), 27–72; R. Morsey, "Bismarck und der Kulturkampf," *AKG* 39 (1957), 232–70; id., "Probleme der Kulturkampf-Forschung," *HJ* 83 (1964), 217–45; K. Buchheim, *Ultramontanismus und Demokratie* (Munich 1963), 215–308; Bihlmeyer-Tüchle III, 406–10; E. Schmidt-Volkmar, *Der Kulturkampf in Deutschland 1871–1890* (Göttingen 1962); W. P. Fuchs, "Ultramontanismus und Staatsräson. Der Kulturkampf," *Staat und Kirche im Wandel der Jahrhunderte,* ed. by W. P. Fuchs (Stuttgart 1966), 184–200; E. R. Huber, *Deutsche Verfassungsgeschichte seit 1789* IV (Stuttgart 1969), 49–54, 60f., 651–767; R. Lill, "Die Katholiken und Bismarcks Reichsgründung," *Reichsgründung 1870/71,* ed. by T. Schieder and E. Deuerlein (Stuttgart 1970), 345–65; C. Weber, *Kirchliche Politik Zwischen Rom, Berlin und Trier 1876–1888* (Mainz 1970); G. Maron, "Die römisch-kath. Kirche von 1870 bis 1970," *Die Kirche in ihrer Geschichte. Ein Handbuch,* ed. by K. D. Schmidt and E. Wolf, vol. 4, no. 2 (Göttingen 1972), 201ff., 256–59; E. Gatz, *Die deutschen Bischofskonferenzen 1872–1881* (in preparation).

Individual Dioceses and Provinces: M. Höhler, *Gesch. des Bistums Limburg* (Limburg 1908), 322–65; A. Bertram, *Gesch. des Bistums Hildesheim* III (Hildesheim and Leipzig 1925), 313–26; E. Gatz, "Bischöfliche Einheitsfront im Kulturkampf? Neue Funde zum Kirchenkonflikt im Bistum Hildesheim," *HJ* 92 (1972), 391–403; L. Ficker and O. Hellinghaus, *Der Kulturkampf in Münster* (Münster 1928); G. Dettmer, *Die ost-*

und westpreußischen Verwaltungsbehörden im Kulturkampf (Heidelberg 1958); W. Jestaedt, *Der Kulturkampf im Fuldaer Lande* (Fulda 1960); H. Lepper, "Die kirchenpolitische Gesetzgebung der Jahre 1872–1875 und ihre Ausführung im Regierungsbezirk Aachen," *AHVNrh* 171 (1969), 200–258; Weber, *Kirchliche Politik* (see above, Trier, Rhine province); N. Trippen, *Das Domkapitel und die Erzbischofswahlen in Köln 1821–1929* (Cologne and Vienna 1972), 249–76; F. G. Hohmann, "Domkapitel und Bischofswahlen in Paderborn 1857–1892," *WZ* 122 (1972), 192–282.

INDIVIDUAL PERSONALITIES (the extensive Bismarck bibliography is not listed; there are no critical biographies of most Catholic leaders): Empress Augusta: M. v. Bunsen (1940); W. Goetz in *NDB* 1, 451f.—Eberhard: A. Ditscheid (Trier 1911).—Falk: E. Förster (Gotha 1927); R. Ruhenstroth-Bauer, *Bismarck und Falk im Kulturkampf* (Heidelberg 1944); S. Skalweit in *NDB* 5, 6f. —For the following, see vol. VIII in this series: Ketteler (chap. 6), Ledóchowski (chap. 8, no. 6), Mallinckrodt (chap. 8), Melchers (chap. 8, n. 5), Moufang (chap. 8; in add. G. May in *AMrhKG* 22 [1970], 227–36), the brothers Reichensperger (chap. 6). For Förster and Krementz, see above, this chapter, nn. 15 and 16.—Mühler: W. Reichle (Berlin 1938).—Windthorst: E. Hüsgen (Cologne 1907); E. Deuerlein in *StZ* 169 (1961/62), 277–97; W. Spael (Osnabrück 1962); R. Lillin *Politische Ideologien und nationalstaatliche Ordnung. Festschr. f. Th. Schieder* (Munich 1968), 317–35; R. Morsey in *StL* VIII, 712ff.

2. Tensions in the Austro-Hungarian Monarchy (1878–1914)

LITERATURE

Vol. VIII, chaps. 8 and 19. In addition: L. v. Pastor, *Tagebücher, Briefe, Erinnerungen,* ed. W. Wühr (Heidelberg 1950); A. Hudal, *Die österreichische Vatikanbotschaft 1806–1918* (Munich 1952); J. Wodka, *Kirche in Österreich* (Vienna 1959); F. Engel-Janosi, *Österreich und der Vatikan* II, 2–173; M. Csáky, *Der Kulturkampf in Ungarn* (Graz, Vienna and Cologne 1967); F. Funder, *Vom Gestern ins Heute* (Vienna and Munich 1971); G. Adriányi, "Friedrich Graf Revertera, Erinnerungen (1888–1901)," *AHPont* 10 (Rome 1972), 241ff.; I. A. Hellwing, *Der konfessionelle Antisemitismus im 19. Jh. in Österreich* (Vienna, Freiburg and Basel 1972).

3. The Conclusion of the Kulturkampf in Prussia and in the German Empire

SOURCES

As in chap. 1 (except the edition of Constabel). In addition: O. Pfülf, "Aus Windthorsts Korrespondenz," *Stimmen aus Maria Laach* 82, 83 (1912); K. v. Schlözer, *Letzte römische Briefe 1882–04,* ed. L. v. Schlözer (Berlin and Leipzig 1924); O. v. Bismarck, *Die gesammelten Werke* XII, XIII: *Reden 1878–1897,* ed. W. Schüßler (Berlin 1929–30); *Vatikanische Akten zur Geschichte des deutschen Kulturkampfes,* ed. R. Lill, Part 1:1878–80 (Tübingen 1970), Part 2: 1880–87 (in preparation).

LITERATURE

As in chap. 1, especially the works by Kißling (vol. 3), K. Bachem (vols. III, IV), Franz-Willing, Morsey, Schmidt-Volkmar, E. R. Huber and C. Weber. In addition: E.

Lefebvre de Béhaine, *Léon XIII et le Prince de Bismarck . . .* , *Introduction par G. Goyau* (Paris 1898); C. Crispolti and G. Aureli, *La politica di Leone XIII da Luigi Galimberti a Mariano Rampolla* (Rome 1912); J. Heckel, "Die Beilegung des Kulturkampfes in Preußen," *ZSavRGkan* 19 (1930), 215–353, reprinted in: J. Heckel, *Das blinde, undeutliche Wort Kirche,* ed. S. Grundmann (Cologne and Graz 1964), 454–571; E. Soderini, *Il Pontificato di Leone XIII* III (Milan 1933); H. Mann, *Der Beginn der Abkehr Bismarcks vom Kulturkampf 1878–1880 unter bes. Berücksichtigung der Politik des Zentrums und der Römischen Kurie* (diss., Frankfurt a. M. 1953); R. Lill, "Die Wende im Kulturkampf," *QFIAB* 50 (1970), 227–83, 52 (1972), 657–730; in book form (Tübingen 1973); C. Weber, *Quellen u. Studien zur Kurie u. vatikan. Politik unter Leo XIII.* (in preparation).

4. The Development of Catholicism in Switzerland

LITERATURE

Vol. VII, chaps. 7 and 20; vol. VIII, chap. 8; Schmidlin, *PG* II, 482–85; U. Stutz, 29–46; G. Franz, *Der Kulturkampf* (1954), 154ff.; K. Fry, *Kaspar Decurtins,* 2 vols. (Zurich 1949–52), on the basis of archival material, offers above and beyond the biography of this politician a lot of information about the internal problems of Swiss Catholicism; G. Beuret, *Die kath.-soziale Bewegung in der Schweiz. 1848–1919* (diss., Zurich, Winterthur 1959, with biblio.); L. Schihin, *Sozialpolitische Ideen im schweizerischen Katholizismus. 1798–1848* (diss., Zurich 1937), offers, in regard to the case of the poor, information about the early paternal mentality and fear of socialism; B. Prongué, *Le mouvement chrétien-social dans le Jura bernois, 1891–1961* (Fribourg 1968); R. Ruffieux, *Le mouvement chrétien-social en Suisse romande, 1891–1949* (Fribourg 1969); U. Altermatt, *Der Weg der Schweizer Katholiken aus dem Ghetto* (Cologne, in preparation).

5. Italian Catholics between the Vatican and the Quirinal

LITERATURE

Vol. VIII, chaps. 17, 18, and 20.

1. COLLECTIONS OF SOURCES: H. Bastgen, *Die Römische Frage. Dokumente und Stimmen,* 3 vols. (Freiburg i. Br. 1917–19); A. C. Jemolo, *La questione romana* (Milan 1938); *Insegnamenti pontifici n. 4, 1748–1956. Il Laicato,* ed. the monks of Solesmes, ed. Ital. (Rome 1958); P. Scoppola, *Dal neoguelfismo alla democrazia cristiana* (Rome 1957).

2. HISTORICAL SURVEYS OF PIONEERS: V. Veggian, *Il movimento sociale cristiano nella seconda metà del sec. XIX* (Vicenza 1902); R. della Casa, *Il movimento cattolico italiano,* 2 vols. (Milan 1905); R. Murri, *Dalla Democrazia Cristiana al Partito Popolare Italiano* (Florence 1920); F. Olgiati, *Storia dell'azione cattolica in Italia* (Milan 1920); E. Vercesi, *Il movimento cattolico italiano (1870–1922)* (Florence 1922); M. Vaussard, *L'Intelligence catholique dans l'Italie du XXe siècle* (Paris 1921); G. B. Valente, *Aspetti e momenti dell' azione sociale dei cattolici in Italia (1892–1926),* ed. F. Malgeri (Rome 1968); G. della Torre, *I cattolici e la vita pubblica italiana,* ed. G. De Rosa, 2 vols. (Rome 1962); M. Zanatta (pseudonym of A. De Gasperi), *I tempi e gli uomini che prepararono la "Rerum novarum"* (Milan 1928 and 1945); F. Magri, *L'azione cattolica in Italia (1775–1939)* (Milan 1953).

3. MORE RECENT HISTORICAL WORKS: G. Candeloro, *L'azione cattolica in Italia* (Rome 1949); id., *Il movimento cattolico in Italia* (Rome 1953) (Marxist interpretation); L. Riva, *Sanseverino. Il movimento sindacale cristiano* (Rome 1950); G. De Rosa, *L'azione cattolica. Storia politica 1874–1904* (Bari 1953); id., *Storia politica dell'A. C. in Italia 1905–1919* (Bari 1954) (cf. review by F. Fonzi in *Humanitas* VIII [1963], 694–98; IX [1954], 1120–30). New ed. in 2 vols. (1966); F. Fonzi, *I cattolici e la società italiana dopo l'Unità* (Rome 1953); G. Spadolini, *L'opposizione cattolica da Porta Pia al 1898* (Florence 1954); A. Martini, *Studi sulla questione romana e la conciliazione* (Rome 1963); D. Secco Suardo, *Da Leone XIII a Pio X* (=*Collana di storia del movimento cattolico* no. 18 [Rome 1967]); several authors, *Spiritualità ed azione del laicato cattolico italiano,* 2 vols. (Padua 1969) (cf. review by S. Tramontin in *RSTI* 26 [1972], 154–74); A. Gambasin, *Il movimento sociale nell'opera dei congressi (1874–1904)* (=*AnGr* no. 91 [Rome 1958]); id., "Il movimento sindacale italiano" in S. H. Scholl, ed., *150 anni di movimento operaio cattolico nell'Europa centro-occidentale* (Padua 1962); G. Rossini, Ed., *Aspetti della cultura cattolica nell'età di Leone XIII* (Rome 1961); L. Ambrosoli, *Il primo movimento D. C. in Italia (1897–1904)* (Rome 1958); C. Brezzi, *Cristiano sociali e intransigenti (L'opera di Medolago Albani fino alla "R. N.")* (Rome 1971); Complete bibliography: *Archivio per la storia del movimento cattolico in Italia* (Milan 1967); M. Bendiscioli, "Chiesa e società nei secc. XIX e XX," *Nuove questioni di storia contemporanea* I (Milan 1967), 325–447; C. Maronciu-Buonaiuti, *Non expedit* (Rome 1971).

4. SPECIFIC TOPICS: (a) The development in different parts of the country: Lombardy: Aside from the monographs about D. Albertario, F. Meda, Rezzara (Bergamo), Tovini (Brescia), Bonomelli (Cremona), cf. A. Zaninelli, *Le leghe "bianche" nel cremonese (1900–21)* (Rome 1961); L. Ambrosoli, *Profile del movimento cattolico milanese nell'Ottocento* (Milan 1960); B. Malinverni, *La scuola sociale cattolica di Bergamo (1910–32)* (Rome 1960).—Veneto: The biographies of Paganuzzi, Rezzara, the Scottons in: A. Gambasin, *Il movimento sociale nell'opera dei congressi;* biblio. in ibid., 585–96; E. Reato, *Le origini del movimento cattolico a Vicenza (1860–91)* (Vicenza 1961).—Piedmont: A. Zussini, *L. Caisotti di Chiusano e il movimento cattolico dal 1896 al 1915* (Turin 1970); M. L. Salvadori, *Il movimento cattolico a Torino 1911–15* (Turin 1969).—Tuscany: G. P. Cappelli, *La prima sinistra cattolica in Toscana* (Rome 1962); M. Stanghellini and U. Tintori, *Storia del movimento cattolico lucchese* (Rome 1958); P. L. Ballini, *Il movimento cattolico a Firenze 1900–19* (Rome 1969).—Naples: P. Lopez, *E. Cenni e i cattolici napoletani dopo l'unità* (Rome 1962); A. Cestaro, *La stampa cattolica a Napoli 1860–1904* (Rome 1965).—Calabria: P. Borzomati, *Aspetti religiosi e storia del movimento cattolico in Calabria (1860–1919)* (Rome 1970).

(b) The movement and organizations: B. M. Brogi, *La lega democratica nazionale* (Rome 1959); C. Giovannini, *Politica e religione nel pensiero della lega dem. naz. 1905–1915* (Rome 1968); G. Licata, *La "rassegna nazionale". Conservatori e cattolici liberali attraverso la loro rivista* (Rome 1968); O. Confessore, *Conservatorismo politico e riformismo religioso. La "rassegna nazionale" 1898–1908* (Bologna 1971); G. Marcucci Fanello, *Storia della Federazione Universitaria Cattolica Italiana* (Rome 1971). Regarding the *Rinnovamento,* cf. N. Raponi, *Tommaso Gallarti Scotti tra politica e cultura* (Milan 1971).

(c) The journals as an expression of the Catholic movement: several authors, *Aspetti della cultura cattolica nell'età di Leone XIII* (Rome 1961); G. De Rosa, ed., *Antologia della "Civilta cattolica"* (Rome 1971).

(d) The relationship to Italy's history: F. Chabod, *Storia della politica estera italiana dal 1870 al 1896.* I. Premesse (Bari 1951); L. Valiani, "L'Italia dal 1876 al 1915," N. Valeri, ed., *Storia d'Italia* IV (Turin 1965); C. A. Jemolo, *Chiesa e stato in Italia negli ultimi cento anni* (Turin 1955).

(e) Individual personalities: G. Toniolo, *Opera omnia* (Vatican City 1947), especially *Lettere*, 3 vols. (1952–55); E. da Persico, *G. Toniolo* (Verona 1928) (rather belletristic); F. Vistalli, *G. Toniolo* (Rome 1954); A. Vian, *G. B. Paganuzzi* (Rome 1950); G. Roncalli, *Radini Tedeschi, vescovo di Bergamo* (Bergamo 1916); 2d ed. by G. De Luca (Rome 1963); C. Bellò, *Geremia Bonomelli con documenti inediti* (Brescia 1961); F. Gregori, *La vita e le opere di mgr. G. B. Scalabrini* (Turin 1932); E. Vercesi, *Don Davide Albertazio* (Milan 1922); A. Novelli, *F. Meda* (Milan 1921); E. Micheli, *F. Meda . . .* (Parma 1948); M. Vaussard, *L'intelligence catholique en Italie*, op. cit., 85–132; F. Meda, *Scritti scelti*, ed. G. P. Dore (Rome 1959); A. Cistellini, *G. Tovini*, foreword by G. B. Montini (Brescia 1954); C. Brezzi, *Cristiano sociali e intransigenti. L'opera di Medolago Albani* (Rome 1971); G. Sacchetti, *La reazione cattolica. Scritti e discorsi con introduzione di G. De Rosa* (Rome 1967).

6. *The Failure to Reconcile Catholics and the Republic in France*

SOURCES

Cardinal D. Ferrata, *Mémoires. Ma nonciature en France* (Rome 1921); A. Siegfried, *L'abbé Frémont (1852–1912)*, 2 vols. (Paris 1932); C. Benoist, *Souvenirs* (Paris 1932–34); X. de Montclos, *Le toast d'Alger. Documents, 1890–1891* (Paris 1966).

LITERATURE

E. Lecanuet, *L'Église de France sous la IIIe République* II–IV (Paris 1930–31, reprint); A. Latreille and R. Rémond, *Histoire du catholicisme en France* III (Paris 1962); L. Capéran, *Histoire contemporaine de la laïcité française*, 3 vols. (vol. 4 not yet issued by the Institut catholique de Toulouse) (Paris 1958–61); id., *L'anticléricalisme et l'affaire Dreyfus, 1897–1899* (Paris 1948); H. Rollet, *Albert de Mun et le parti catholique* (Paris 1947); id., *L'action sociale des catholiques en France*, 2 vols. (Paris 1948–58); J. Gadille, *La pensée et l'action politiques des évêques français au début de la IIIe république*, 2 vols. (Paris 1967); J. Tournier, *Le cardinal Lavigerie et son action politique* (Paris 1913); J.-B. Woodall, *The Ralliement in France. Origins and History, 1876–1894.* (New York 1961); A. Sedgwick, *The Ralliement in French Politics, 1890–1898* (Cambridge, Mass. 1965); M. Montuclard, *Conscience religieuse et démocratie* (Paris 1965); J.-M. Mayeur, *Un prêtre démocrate, l'abbé Lemire 1853–1928* (Paris 1968); "Les congrès nationaux de la démocratie chrétienne à Lyon, 1896–1898," *RHMC,* July/Sept. 1962; "Droites et Ralliés à la Chambre des députés au début de 1894," *RHMC,* April/July 1966; R. Rémond, *Les congrès ecclésiastiques de Reims et de Bourges* (Paris 1964); P. Sorlin, *"La Croix" et les Juifs* (Paris 1967); P. Pierrard, *Juifs et Catholiques français* (Paris 1970).

7. *On the Road to Conservatism: Belgium, the Netherlands, and Luxemburg*

SOURCES

Pastoral letters of the bishops (index): *Lettres pastorales des évêques de Belgique, 1800–1950* IV: 1868–1883, V: 1883–1906, VI: 1906–1926 (Brussels, n.d.); *Akten der Kongresse der Katholiken in Lüttich* 1887, 1889, 1890, and in Mechelen 1891 and 1909; C.

Woeste, *Mémoires* I–II (Brussels 1927–33); id., *Échos des luttes contemporaines,* 2 vols. (Brussels 1906); A. Verhagen, *25 années d'action sociale* (Brussels, n.d.); A. Vermeersch, *Manuel social. La législation et les œuvres en Belgique* (Louvain 1900).

LITERATURE

BELGIUM: Vol. VIII, chap. 18; C. Doset, Ed., *Un siècle de l'Église en Belgique,* 2 vols. (Cortrai 1934); A. de Moreau, *L'Église en Belgique* (Brussels 1945), 239–63; P. van Zuylen, "La Belgique et le Vatican en 1879," *Revue générale Belge* (1954), 1707–34, 1901–15, 2065–81, (1955), 67–86; A. Simon, *La liberté de l'enseignement* (Brussels 1952); M. Becqué, *Le Cardinal Dechamps,* 2 vols: (Louvain 1956); J. Muyldermans, *Cardinal Goossens* (Mechelen 1922); A. Simon, *Cardinal D. Mercier* (Brussels 1960); L. De Raeymaeker, *Le Cardinal Mercier et l'Institut Supérieur de Philosophie de Louvain* (Louvain 1952); R. Reszohazy, *Origines et formation du catholicisme social en Belgique. 1842–1909* (Brussels 1958); P. Gérin, *Les origines de la démocratie chrétienne à Liège,* 2 vols. (Brussels 1958–59); L. de Saint-Moulin, "Contribution à l'histoire de la déchristianisation. La pratique religieuse à Seraing depuis 1830," *Annuaire d'histoire liégeoise* 10 (1967), 33–126; W. Rombauts, *Het Paasverzuim in het bisdom Brugge* (Louvain and Paris 1971); F. Petri, "Belgien, die Niederlande und Luxemburg (1867–1918)," in T. Schieder, ed., *Hdb. der europ. Geschichte* VI (Stuttgart 1968), 465–93.

THE NETHERLANDS: L. J. Rogier, *Katholieke Herleving, Geschiedenis van Katholiek Nederland sinds 1853* (The Hague 1957), 276–348; G. Brom, *Herleving van de wetenschap in Katholiek Nederland* (The Hague 1930); I. Wietlox, *H. Schaepman,* 3 vols. (1960); G. Brom, *Fr. Ariëns,* 2 vols. (1941); J. Colsen, *P. Poels* (1955).

LUXEMBURG: E. Donckel, *Die Kirche in Luxemburg von den Anfängen bis zur Gegenwart* (Luxemburg 1950).

8. *The Church of the Iberian World between Revolution and Reaction*

LITERATURE

Vol. VIII, chaps. 10 and 18.

SPAIN: Schmidlin, *PG* II, 441–47; J. Becker, *Relaciones diplomáticas entre Espāna y la S. Sede durante el Siglo XIX* (Madrid 1908); R. Konetzke, *Geschichte des spanischen und portugiesischen Volkes* (Leipzig 1939), 368–80, 393–99, id. in: T. Schieder, ed., *Hdb. der europ. Geschichte* VI (Stuttgart 1968), 503–33 (considering church history); J. N. Schumacher, "Integrism. A Study in XIXth Century Spanish Politico-Religious Thought." *CHR* 48 (1962/63), 343–64; M. Llorens, "El P. Antonio Vincent. Notas sobre el desarollo de la acción católica en España," *Estudios de Historia moderna* 4 (Barcelona 1954), 393–440; J. F. Pastór, *Weltanschauung und geistiges Leben in Spanien* (Wroclaw 1931); L. Sánchez Agesta, *La revolución liberal* (Madrid 1955); H. Jeschke, *Die Generation von 1898* (Heidelberg 1934).

PORTUGAL: Z. Giacometti, *Quellen zur Geschichte der Trennung von Staat und Kirche* (1926); Schmidlin, *PG* II, 447f.; G. S. da Silva Dias, *Correntes do sentimento religioso* (Coimbra 1960); R. Konetzke, op. cit. (1939), 386–90 id., op. cit. (1968) 533–38.

LATIN AMERICA: *Acta et decreta concilii plenarii Americae latinae anno 1899 celebrati,* 2 vols. (Rome 1900); cf. A. Bellesheim in *AkathKR* (1901), 38–63 (with introductory description of the situation); Schmidlin, *PG* II, 448–54; E. Ryan, *The Church in the*

South American Republics (London 1934); J. L. Mecham, *Church and State in Latin America* (North Carolina Press 1934); E. Samhaber, *Die Neue Welt. Wandlungen in Südamerika* (Freiburg i. Br. 1949; essayistic, but more from the perspective of church history than in: *Südamerika* [Hamburg 1939]); L. Zea, *Dos etapas del pensamiento en Hispanoamérica. Del romanticismo al positivismo* (Mexico City 1949); W. v. Schoen, *Geschichte Mittel- und Südamerikas* (Munich 1953), 343–665. Biblio. regarding general Latin American history in A. P. Witaker in *HM* X (Berne 1961), 788f.

9. Catholic Self-Awareness in the British Empire

LITERATURE

THE UNITED KINGDOM OF GREAT BRITAIN AND IRELAND: Vol. VII, chap. 21; vol. VIII, chap. 9; also E. Taylor, *The Cardinal Democrat* (London 1908); G. Goyau, *Autour du catholicisme social* II, 220–45; III, 194–231; IV, 71–85; K. Waninger, *Der soziale Katholizismus in England* (Mönchen-Gladbach 1914); I. Bolten, *Katholisches aus England* (Mönchen-Gladbach 1928; popular, but informative); C. Hollis in I. N. Moody, ed., *Church and Society* (New York 1953), 809–42; W. G. Gorman, *Converts to Rome in the United Kingdom during the last 60 years* (London 1910); J. G. Snead-Cox, *Cardinal Herbert Vaughan. 1892–1903,* 2 vols. (London 1910); E. Oldmeadow, *Cardinal Francis Bourne, 1903–1935,* 2 vols. (London 1940, 1944); Maisy Ward, *The Wilfrid Wards and the Transition,* 2 vols. (London 1934–38).

General history: P. Kluke in T. Schieder, ed., *Handbuch der europ. Geschichte* 6 (1968), 269–72, biblio.

IRELAND: A. Bellesheim, *Geschichte der kath. Kirche in Irland* III (Mainz 1891); J. Pokorny, *Irland* (1916); P. K. Egan, *The Influence of the Irish on the Catholic Church in America in the 19th Century* (Dublin 1968; a twenty-two-page summary, with biblio.); E. Larkin, "Economic Growth, Capital Investment and the Roman-Cath. Church in 19th Century Ireland," *AHR* 72 (1966), 885–905; L. I. McCaffrey, *The Irish Question, 1800–1922* (Lexington 1968); cf.: M. R. O'Connell in *CHR* 58 (1972) 415f.; P. Alter, *Die irische Nationalbewegung zwischen Parlament und Revolution* (Stuttgart 1971).

CANADA: Vol. VII, chap. 9; vol. VIII, chap. 9; Alexis de Barbezieux, *L'Église catholique en Canada* (Montreal 1934); E. Gautier, *Le catholicisme au Canada* (Ottawa 1934); D. de Saint-Denis, *L'Église catholique au Canada* (Montreal 1956); V. Harvey et al., *L'Église et la Québec* (Montreal 1961); P. Savard, *Jules-Paul Tardivel* (Quebec 1967).

AUSTRALIA: Vol. VIII, chap. 9; J. E. Murtagh, *Australia. The Catholic Chapter* (New York 1947); G. Walter, *Australien. Land und Leute, Mission* (Limburg 1928), *Bericht eines Missionars;* P. Ford, *Cardinal Moran and the Australian Labour Party* (London 1966).

10. The American Way

LITERATURE

Vol. VII, chap. 9; vol. VIII, chap. 9; H. J. Nolan, ed., *Pastoral Letters of the American Hierarchy, 1792–1790* (Huntington 1971), cf. J. T. Ellis in *CHR* (1972), 388–93; J. T.

Ellis, *A Select Bibliography of the History of the Catholic Church in the US* (New York 1947); T. Maynard, *The Story of American Catholicism* (New York 1941, 1949); T. Roemer, *The Catholic Church in the United States* (London 1950); J. T. Ellis, *American Catholicism* (New York 1956; review, critical of J. G. Shea and T. Maynard); id.: *New Cath. Encyclopedia* 14 (1967), 425–48 (esp. considering the question of immigration); best complete presentation: T. T. McAvoy, *A History of the Catholic Church in the United States* (Notre Dame 1969); P. Guilday, *A History of the Councils of Baltimore, 1711–1884* (New York 1932); Schmidlin, *PG* II, 494–500; III, 114ff.; J. T. Ellis, *The Life of Cardinal Gibbons* (Milwaukee 1952); J. H. Moynihan, *The Life of Archbishop J. Ireland* (New York 1953); *M. Corrigan-Memorial*, compiled and published by J. M. Farley (New York 1902); regarding the controversy over the emigrants' loss of faith: L. Hertling, 162–66; C. J. Barry, *The Catholic Church and German Americans* (Milwaukee 1953; is negative about the Ireland-Keane group); about the Irish influence: P. K. Egan (biblio. for chap. 9); F. Downing in J. N. Moody, ed., *Church and Society* (New York 1953), 843–904; H. Browne, *The Catholic Church and the Knights of Labor* (Washington 1949); S. Bell, *Rebel, Priest and Prophet. A Biography of Dr. Edw. McGlynn* (New York 1937); T. T. McAvoy, *The Great Crisis in American Catholic History. 1895–1900* (Chicago 1957); P. E. Hogan, *The Cath. University of America. 1896–1903* (Washington 1949); J. T. Ellis, *The Formative Years of the Catholic University of America* (Washington 1946); W. E. Garrison, *Catholicism and the American Mind* (Chicago 1928); J. Mannix, *The American Convert Movement* (New York 1923); L. C. Feiertag, *American Public Opinion in the Diplomatic Relations between the United States and the Papal State* (Washington 1933); R. D. Cross, *The Emergence of Liberal Catholicism in America* (Cambridge, Mass. 1958).

11. *Catholicism in the Slavic World until 1914*

LITERATURE

THE RUSSIAN EMPIRE: W. Gribowski, *Das Staatsrecht des Russischen Reiches* (Tübingen 1912); F. Haase, *Die katholische Kirche Polens unter russischer Herrschaft* (Breslau 1917); A. Boudou, *Le Saint-Siège et la Russie. Leurs relations diplomatiques au XIXe siècle* II: *1848–83* (Paris 1925); A. Petrani, *Kolegium Duchnowne w Petersburgu* (Lublin 1950); "Kościoły katolickie ob. łać. na obszarach Rosji (1772–1914)," *SPM* II (Rome 1955), 467–97; E. Winter, *Rußland und das Papstum* II (Berlin 1961), 340–567; B. Stasiewski, "Die kirchliche Organisation der deutschen katholischen Siedler in Rußland," *Festschrift für Margarete Woltner zum 70. Geburtstag* (Heidelberg 1967), 270–83; G. Simon, *Konstantin Petrovič Pobedonoscev und die Kirchenpolitik des Heiligen Sinod 1880–1905* (Göttingen 1969).

THE THREE PARTITIONS OF POLAND: J. S. Pelczar, *Pius IX i Polska* (Miejsce Piastowe 1914); K. Völker, *Kirchengeschichte Polens* (Berlin and Leipzig 1930); G. Manteuffel-Szoege, *Geschichte des polnischen Volkes während seiner Unfreiheit 1772–1914* (Berlin 1950); J. Umiński, *Historia Kościoła* II, ed. by W. Urban (Oppeln 1960); F. Manthey, *Polnische Kirchengeschichte* (Hildesheim 1965); G. Rhode, *Kleine Geschichte Polens* (Darmstadt 1965); W. Urban, *Ostatni etap dziejów kościoła w Polsce przed nowym tysiącleciem 1815–1965* (Rome 1966, biblio.); Z. Olszamowska-Skowrońska, "Tentatives d'introduire la langue russe dans les églises latines da la Pologne orientale 1865–1903," *Antemurale* 11 (1967), 47–169; B. Stasiewski, "Tausend Jahre polnischer Kirchengeschichte," *Kirche im Osten* 10 (1967), 56–60; *Księga tysiąclecia katolicyzmu w Polsce*, 3 vols. (Lublin 1969); *Le millénaire du catholicisme en Pologne* (Lublin 1969); B. Kumor, *Granice metropolii i diecezji polskich* 966–1939 (Lublin 1969–71); E. Jabłońska-Deptuła, "Duchowieństwo zakonne a sprawa narodowa w połowie XIX wieku," *Znak* 24 (1972), 481–504.

THE HABSBURG MONARCHY: A. Hudal, *Die österreichische Vatikanbotschaft 1806–1918* (Munich 1952); R. A. Kann, *Das Nationalitätenproblem der Habsburgmonarchie. Geschichte und Ideengehalt der nationalen Bestrebungen vom Vormärz bis zur Auflösung des Reiches im Jahre 1918*, 2 vols. (Graz and Cologne 1964); R. W. Seton-Watson, *A History of the Czechs and Slovaks* (Hamden 1965); F. Prinz, "Die böhmischen Länder von 1848 bis 1914," *Hdb. der Gesch. der böhmischen Länder* III, ed. by K. Bosl (Stuttgart 1968), 103–23; A. Wandruszka, "Österreich-Ungarn vom ungarischen Ausgleich bis zum Ende der Monarchie (1867–1918)," *Hdb. der europ. Gesch.* VI, ed. by T. Schieder (Stuttgart 1968), 354–99.—See this vol., chap. 2.

SOUTHEASTERN EUROPE: H. Wendel, *Der Kampf der Südslawen um Freiheit und Einheit* (Frankfurt 1925); M. Spinka, *A History of Christianity in the Balkans* (Chicago 1933); J. H. Ledit, *The Church in the Balkans* (New York 1949); J. Radonić, *Rimska kurija i južnoslovenske zemľe od XVI do XIX veka* (Belgrade 1950); G. Stadtmüller, *Geschichte Südosteuropas* (Munich 1950); G. Wolfrum, "Die Völker und Nationalitäten," *Osteuropa-Handbuch Jugoslawien*, ed. by W. Markert (Cologne and Graz 1954) 14–36; R. Kißling, *Die Kroaten. Der Schicksalsweg eines Südslawenvolkes* (Graz and Cologne 1956); G. Jäschke, "Das osmanische Reich vom Berliner Kongreß bis zu seinem Ende (1878–1920/22)," *Hdb. der europ. Gesch.* VI, ed. by T. Schieder (Stuttgart 1968), 539–46; G. Rhode, "Die Staaten Südosteuropas vom Berliner Kongreß bis zum Ausgang des I. Weltkrieges (1878–1918)," ibid., 547–609; E. Schramm-von Thadden, "Griechenland vom Beginn der Dynastie Glücksburg bis zum Frieden mit der Türkei (1863–1923)," ibid., 610–17; A. Tarnovaliski, *Msgr. Andreas Canova. Bulgariens erster Kapuzinermissionar und Bischof 1841–1866* (Bressanone 1968); H. D. Schanderl, *Die Albanienpolitik Österreich-Ungarns und Italiens 1877–1908* (Wiesbaden 1971).

The Development of Catholicism in Modern Society

12. Catholicism in Society as a Whole

Sources

Encyclicals of Leo XIII: *Quod apostolici* (1878); *Arcanum illud* (1880, marriage); *Humanum genus* (1884, Freemasons); *Libertas* (1888); *Sapientiae christianae* (1890); *Rerum novarum* (1891); *Longinqua Oceani spatia* (1895); *Militantis ecclesiae* (1897, education).

Contemporary theoreticians (especially regarding the question of property): C. Périn, *De la richesse dans les sociétés chrétiennes*, 2 vols. (Paris 1861); F. Le Play, *La réforme sociale en France*, 2 vols. (Paris 1864); M. Liberatore, *Principii di economia politica* (Rome 1889); G. Toniolo (cf. above chap. 5); C. v. Vogelsang, *Ges. Aufsätze über socialpolitische und verwandte Themata* (Augsburg 1885–87); F. Hitze, *Capital und Arbeit und die Reorganisation der Gesellschaft* (Paderborn 1880); *Die Quintessenz der socialen Frage* (Paderborn 1880); H. Pesch, *Liberalismus, Sozialismus und christliche Gesellschaftsordnung* (Freiburg 1898); id., *Lehrbuch der Nationalökonomie*, 5 vols. (Freiburg i. Br. 1905–23); V. Cathrein, *Der Sozialismus* (Freiburg i. Br. 1890, 1923); A. Lehmkuhl, *Theologia moralis*, 2 vols. (Freiburg i. Br. 1883, 1890); A. M. Weiß, *Apologie des Christentums* 4, 5 (=*Soziale Frage und soziale Ordnung*) (Freiburg i. Br. 1892, 1904); T. Meyer, *Die christlich-ethischen Sozialprinzipien und die Arbeiterfrage* (Freiburg i. Br. 1904); G. J. Waffelaert, *De iustitia*, 2 vols. (Bruges 1885–86); A. Vermeesch, *Quaestiones de iustitia* (Bruges 1901); A. Stöckl, *Das Christentum und die großen Fragen der Gegenwart auf dem Gebiet des geistigen, sittlichen und sozialen Lebens*, 3 vols. (Mainz 1879–80); F. Schaub, *Die Eigentumslehre nach Tomas v. Aquin und dem modernen Sozialismus* (Freiburg i. Br. 1898).

Literature

Translations of and Commentaries on Rerum Novarum: G. Gundlach: *Veröff. der Görres-Gesellschaft, Sektion Sozial-und Wirtschaftsgeschichte*, no. 3 (Paderborn 1931) [with *Quadragesimo anno*]; R. Kothen, *L'enseignement social de l'Église* (Louvain 1949; texts of doctrinal statements by the Popes from Leo XIII to Pius XII); P. Jostock. *Die sozialen Rundschreiben:* Leo XIII: "Über die Arbeiterfrage"—Pius XI: "Über die gesellschaftliche Ordnung" [texts and commentary] (Freiburg i. Br. 1960); J. Schasching, *Die soziale Botschaft der Kirche von Leo XIII. bis Johannes XXIII.* (Vienna 1963; aside from the texts of *Rerum novarum, Quadragesimo anno,* and subsequent social encyclicals, an introduction, 11–68); P. Mourret, *Les directives politiques, intellectuelles et sociales de Léon XIII* (Paris 1920); W. Schwer, *Leo XIII.: Klassiker der katholischen Sozialphilosophie* (Freiburg 1923); O. v. Nell-Breuning, *Die soziale Enzyklika: Erläuterungen zum Weltrundschreiben Pius' XI. über die gesellschaftliche Ordnung* (Cologne 1932, 1950; including important remarks about *Rerum novarum*); J. Haessle, *Das Arbeitsethos der Kirche nach Thomas von Aquin und Leo XIII.* (Freiburg i. Br. 1923); E. Muhler, *Die Soziallehren der Päpste* (Munich 1958); G. Boni, *Il pensiero sociale di Leone XIII e Pio XI . . .* (Bergamo

1932); M. Allendorf, *Zur Geschichte der Sozialenzykliken des Vatikans* (diss., Humboldt Univ., Berlin 1963); G. Jarlot, *Doctrine pontificale et histoire. L'enseignement social de Léon XIII, Pie X et Benoît XV vu dans son ambiance historique* (Rome 1964); R. L. Camp, *The Papal Ideology of Social Reform, 1878–1967* (Leiden 1969).—Regarding the history of the development of *Rerum novarum:* G. Antonazzi, *L'enciclica R. N.* (Rome 1957).

THE PROBLEM OF "CATHOLICISM": C. Bauer, "Bild der Kirche—Abbild der Gesellschaft," *Hochland* 48 (1956), new: "Deutscher Katholizismus" (Frankfurt 1964), 9–27; id., "Wandlungen der sozialpolitischen Ideenwelt im deutschen Katholizismus des 19. Jh.," J. Strieder et al., eds., *Die soziale Frage und der Katholizismus* (Paderborn 1931), 11–46.

GENERAL PRESENTATIONS: G. Goyau, *Autour du catholicisme social,* 5 "series" (Paris 1901–12); O. Schilling, *Die Staats-und Soziallehre des Papstes Leo XIII.* (Cologne 1925); id., *Christliche Gesellschaftslehre* (Freiburg i. Br. 1926); E. K. Winter, *Die Sozialmetaphysik der Scholastik* (Vienna 1929); O. v. Nell-Breuning, "Die Eigentumslehre," J. Strieder, et al. (cf. above); A. M. Knoll, *Der soziale Gedanke im modernen Katholizismus. Von der Romantik bis Rerum novarum* (Vienna and Leipzig 1932); W. Schwer, "Krisen der kath.-sozialen Bewegung und ihre Lehren," *Soziale Revue. Kath. internationale Quartalschrift* 31, 1 (Munich 1930), 1–9 (regarding W. Schwer, see N. Monzel in *Hochland* 42 [1949/50] 309f.); J. N. Moody, ed., *Church and Society: Catholic Social and Political Thought and Movements. 1789–1950* (New York 1953); W. Bredendiek, *Christliche Sozialreformer des 19. Jh.* (Leipzig 1953); L. Leutner, *Das Erwachen der modernen kath. Sozialidee. Die Entwicklung im 19. Jh. bis Rerum novarum* (Vienna 1951); S. Hedler, *Die katholischen Sozialisten. Darstellung und Kritik ihres Wirkens* (diss., Hamburg 1952); L. P. Wallace. *Leo XIII and the Rise of Socialism* (New York 1966) (the Catholic Church as a dam against socialism); F. Beutter, *Die Eigentumsbegründung in der Moraltheologie des 19. Jh.* (Paderborn 1971); H. Maier, *Kirche und Gesellschaft* (Munich 1972; recent history, but also including problems of the nineteenth century).

INDIVIDUAL COUNTRIES: Cf. the biblios. of chaps. 1–10 and chap. 13; also in regard to France: C. Calippe, *L'attitude sociale des catholiques français au XIXe siècle* (Paris 1911); E. Barbier, *L'histoire du catholicisme libéral et du catholicisme sociale en France, 1870–1914,* 5 vols. (Bordeaux 1923–28; integralistic perspective, rich documentation); W. Gurian, *Politische und soziale Ideen des französischen Katholizismus. 1789–1914* (1929), here: 239–312; G. Hoog, *Histoire du catholicisme social en France, 1871–1931* (Paris 1946); J. B. Duroselle, *Les débuts du catholicisme social en France* (Paris 1951; goes up to 1870, but important description of previous history); Dansette [cited in Chap. 16] II, 180–215, 397–436 (after 1898).

Germany and Austria: S. Merkle, "Die katholische Kirche," S. Körte, ed., *Deutschland unter Kaiser Wilhelm II.* (1914); M. Meinertz-H. Sacher, *Deutschland und der Katholizismus,* 2 vols. (Freiburg 1918); W. Schwer-Franz Müller, "Der deutsche Katholizismus im Zeitalter des Kapitalismus," *Kirche und Gesellschaft,* VI (Augsburg 1932); P. Jostock, *Der deutsche Katholizismus und die Überwindung des Kapitalismus. Eine ideengeschichtliche Skizze* (Regensburg 1932); id., *Die katholisch-soziale Bewegung der letzten hundert Jahre in Deutschland* (Cologne 1958); J. Höffner, *Die deutschen Katholiken u. die soziale Frage im 19. Jh.* (Paderborn 1954); K. H. Grenner, *Wirtschaftsliberalismus und katholisches Denken* (Cologne 1967); K. Buchheim, *Ultramontanismus und Demokratie. Der Weg der deutschen Katholiken im 19. Jh.* (Munich 1963); F. J. Stegmann, "Geschichte der sozialen Ideen im dt. Katholizismus," H. Grebing, ed., *Dt. Hb. der Politik* 3 (1969), 325–560; J. B. Kißling, *Geschichte der deutschen Katholikentage* II (Mainz 1923);

P. Siebertz, *Karl Fürst zu Löwenstein. 1834–1921* (Munich 1924); F. Funder (cited in chap. 2).

THE POLITICAL SITUATION: Cf. chaps. 1–11 and chap. 14.

THE QUESTION OF SCHOOLS: Aside from biblio. in the chaps. on individual countries: J. A. Burns-B. J. Kohlbrenner, *A History of Catholic Education in the US* (New York 1937); H. K. Beale, *History of Freedom of Teaching in American Schools* (New York 1941); F. Larroyo-A. L. Lacombe (Latin America): *New Cath. Encyclopedia* 5 (1967), 157–62; P. Verhaegen, *La lutte scolaire en Belgique* (Ghent 1905); M. Spahn, *Der Kampf um die Schule in Frankreich u. Deutschland* (Munich 1907); K. Erlinghagen, *Die Säkularisierung der deutschen Schule* (Hanover 1972), 43, 48, 58f., 73ff.

CATHOLIC ORGANIZATIONS: Cf. biblio. in the chaps. on individual countries; Wetzer-Welte, ed., "Vereinswesen," *Kirchenlexikon* 12 (1901), 707–60; A. Retzbach, *Das moderne kath. Vereinswesen* (1925) (countercritique of societies); K. Buchheim, "Der deutsche Verbandskatholizismus. Eine Skizze seiner Geschichte," B. Hanssler, *Die Kirche in der Gesellschaft* (Paderborn 1961), 30–83; A. Pieper, *Sinn und Aufgaben des Volksvereins* (Mönchen-Gladbach 1926), 25–41, about the history of its founding, containing organization and statutes; E. Ritter, *Die kath.-soziale Bewegung Deutschlands im 19. Jh. und der Volksverein* (Cologne 1954; literary estate of August Pieper and Chancellor Wilhelm Marx included; up to p. 130 good summary [with biblio.] about the development of social theory, also in the Center Party).

THE CATHOLIC PRESS: H. Keiter, *Hdb. der kath. Presse* (1895, 1909); *New Catholic Encyclopedia, Catholic Press, World Survey* 3 (New York 1967), 283–327, according to countries, partially with historical retrospective; J. Morienval, *Sur l'histoire de la presse catholique en France* (Paris and Colmar 1936). Regarding *La Croix:* E. R. Lacoste, *P. Bailly* (Paris 1913); id., *F. Picard* (Paris 1932); De Moine, *"La Croix"—cinquantenaire* (Paris 1933); R. Kokel, *P. Bailly* (Paris 1942); R. d'Harcourt in *StL* V, 207f.; P. Castel, *Le P. Picard et le P. Bailly dans les luttes de presse* (Rome 1962); R. J. Marion, *La "Croix" et le Ralliement* (diss., Worcester, Mass. 1957).

The press in Italy: E. Lucatello, "Giornalismo Cattolico," *ECatt* VI (1951), 458–62; cf. chaps. 5, 33, 34. Regarding *Osservatore Romano:* G. B. Casoni, *Cinquant'anni di giornalismo* (Bologna 1907); C. Crispolti, *Rimpianti* (Milan 1922).

In Germany: K. Löffler, *Gesch. der kath. Presse Deutschlands* (Mönchen-Gladbach 1924); K. Bachem, *Josef Bachem. Versuch einer Gesch. der kath. Presse*, 2 vols. (1912–13): II: until 1860 (as a history of the preceding period important for the subsequent development); W. Kisky, *Der Augustinusverein zur Pflege der kath. Presse von 1878–1928* (Düsseldorf 1928).—On the *Vienna Reichspost:* F. Funder, *Vom Gestern ins Heute* (Vienna 1952).

13. *The Social Movements*

LITERATURE

ON THE THEORIES: Cf. chap. 12.—International presentations and collections: J. N. Moody (cited in chap. 12); M. P. Fogarty, *Christian Democracy in Western Europe. 1820–1953* (London 1957); G. Briefs et al., eds. of the Catholic Social Institute of the Archdiocese of Cologne, *Das Bild des Arbeiters in der kath. Sozialbewegung von den*

Anfängen bis zur Gegenwart (Cologne 1960); G. Brakelmann, *Die soziale Frage des 19. Jh.* II: *Die evangelisch-soziale und die katholisch-soziale Bewegung* (Witten 1962); H. S. Scholl, ed., *150 ans de mouvement ouvrier chrétien en Europe de l'Ouest* (Louvain 1966).

ON INDIVIDUAL COUNTRIES: France: M. Vaussard, *Histoire de la Démocratie chrétienne* (Paris 1956); H. Rollet, *L'Action sociale des catholiques en France. 1871 à 1914,* 2 vols. (Paris 1947, 1958).—Belgium: R. Reszohazy (cited in chap. 7).—Italy: F. Magri, A. Gambasin (cited in chap. 5).—Switzerland: G. Beuret (cited in chap. 4).—Germany: K. H. Brüls, *Geschichte der kath.-sozialen Bewegung in Deutschland* (Münster 1958); E. Filthaut, *Deutsche Katholikentage 1848–1958 und soziale Frage* (Essen 1960); J. Joos, *Kath. Arbeiterbewegung in der Gesch. der christl. Arbeiterbewegung Deutschlands* (Cologne 1963); E. Naujoks, "Die kath. Arbeiterbewegung und der Sozialismus in den ersten Jahren des Bismarckschen Reiches," *Neue Deutsche Forschungen,* ed. by H. R. G. Günther and E. Rothacker, Vol. 228 (Berlin 1939), Abt. Neuere Geschichte, Vol. 6, ed. by R. Stadelmann [in favor of Bismarck, but material on Chaplain Gronenberg, etc.]; M. Berger, *Arbeiterbewegung und Demokratisierung. Die . . . Gleichberechtigung des Arbeiters im Verständnis der kath. Arbeiterbewegung . . . zwischen 1890 und 1914* (diss., Freiburg i. Br. 1971).—Austria: F. Funder (cited in chap. 2); G. Silberbauer, *Österreichs Katholiken und die Arbeiterfrage* (Graz 1966); F. Bischof, *Kard. Gruscha und die soziale Frage* (diss., Vienna 1959).—United States: Henry D. Browne, *The Catholic Church and The Knights of Labor* (Washington 1949); A. I. Abell, *American Catholicism and Social Action, 1865–1950* (Notre Dame 1963).

CHRISTIAN TRADE UNIONS: Information about the international situation in: Fogarty; K. H. Schürmann, *Zur Vorgeschichte der christl. Gewerkschaften* (Freiburg 1958); L. R. Sanseverino, *Il movimento sindacale cristiano dal 1850 al 1939* (Rome 1950); M. Karson, *The Catholic Church and Unionism* (New York 1951); J. Zirnheld, *Cinquante Années de Syndicalisme Chrétien* (Paris 1937) (13–76 the development toward the *Confédération Française des Travailleurs chrétiens* [CFTC]); L. Deuerlein, "Gewerkschaftsstreit," *StL* III, 943–46.—R. Morsey, ed., *Zeitgeschichte in Lebensbildern. Aus dem deutschen Katholizismus des 20. Jahrhunderts* (Mainz 1973), portraits of Cardinal G. Kopp, J. Bachem, G. v. Hertling, F. Hitze, P. Spahn, K. Trimborn et al.—In general, cf. chaps. on individual countries.

14. *The Relationship to the State and the Parties*

Encyclicals of Leo XIII: *Diuturnum illud* (1881); *Immortale Dei* (1885); *Libertas* (1885); *Au milieu des sollicitudes* (1892); *Graves de communi* (1901).

LITERATURE

C. Crispolti and G. Aureli, *La politica di Leone XIII da L. Galimberti a M. Rampolla* (Rome 1912); F. Mourret, *Les directives politiques, intellectuelles et sociales de Léon XIII* (Paris 1920).—Aside from biblio. for chap. 12 (especially the works of O. Schilling and F. Mourret): P. Tischleder, *Die Staatslehre Leos XIII.* (Mönchen-Gladbach 1925–27); id., *Staatsgewalt und katholisches Gewissen* (Mönchen-Gladbach 1926).—History of the assessment of democracy by Catholicism: A. Pieper in *StL* I, and H. Peters in *StL* II, 589–92; Hans Maier, *Revolution und Kirche. Studien zur Frühgeschichte der christlichen Demokratie, 1789–1901* (Freiburg 1965); K. Buchheim, "Christliche Parteien," *StL* II,

467–75; A. Gnägi, *Kirche und Demokratie* (diss., Zurich 1970), 149–60.—Cf. biblio. for the chaps. on individual countries.

15. *The Position of Catholicism in the Culture at the Turn of the Century*

SOURCES

Encyclicals of Leo XIII: Praise of technological progress, passim, such as in *Sapientiae christianae* (1890), *Rerum novarum* (1891); Criticism of civilization: *Inscrutabili* (1878); *Exeunte iam anno* (1888); *Annum ingressi* (1902).

Scholarship: universities: *Annuaire de l'université catholique de Louvain; Univ.-cath. de Louvain—Bibliogr. 1834–1954* (Louvain 1900–1954).—*Die Universität Fribourg* (Basel 1939).—Regarding Washington: chap. 10.—C. Roy, *L'université de Laval et les fêtes du cinquantenaire* (Quebec 1903). *Instituts catholiques* (France): G. Delépine in *Catholicisme* V (1963), 1756–63.

Congresses: L. Pisani, "Les congrès scientifiques internationaux des catholiques," *Revue du clergé français* (1898); *Compte rendu du 3ᵉ Congrès scientifique international des catholiques* (Brussels 1895); *Compte rendu du 4ᵉ Congrès scientifique* (Fribourg 1897–98).

Societies: *Jahresberichte der Görres-Gesellschaft* (1880f.); On the Leo Society: *Die Kultur* (Vienna 1899–1919).

New journals: historical journals: this series, vol. I, 35–56; theological and philosophical journals: aside from *ZKTh* (Innsbruck 1877ff.), cf. chap. 20.

On the problems: G. v. Hertling, *Das Prinzip des Katholizismus und die Wissenschaft* (Freiburg i. Br. 1899); G.-P. Fonsegrive-Lespinasse, *Le catholicisme et la vie de l'esprit* (Paris 1898); id., *L'évolution des idées dans la France contemporaine de Taine à Péguy* (Paris 1917); F. Brunetière, *Essais sur la Littérature contemporaine* (Paris 1892); id., *Questions actuelles* (Paris 1907); id., *Discours de combat,* 3 vols. (Paris 1895ff.); R. Murri, *Battaglie d'oggi,* 5 vols. (Rome 1903–8); C. Sonnenschein, *Aus dem letzten Jahrzehnt des italienischen Katholizismus* (Elberfeld 1906) =*Broschüren des Windhorst-Bundes* no. 1; C. Schulte, *Die Kirche und die Gebildeten* (Freiburg i. Br. 1919).

Literature and the Arts: cf. chaps. on individual countries and chaps. 18, 19.

LITERATURE

Cf. chaps. 18–22, 29–32, 35. W. Schwer, "Die kirchliche Entfremdung des neuzeitlichen Bürgertums," *BZThS* (1930), 307–20; F. Schneider, *Bildungskräfte im Katholizismus der Welt* (Freiburg i. Br. 1936); R. Agraiu, *Les Universités catholiques* (Paris 1935); In this regard, see the studies about the individual universities in the chapters on individual countries.—H. Rost, *Die wirtschaftliche und kulturelle Lage der deutschen Katholiken* (Cologne 1911); W. Kramer, *Zeitkritik und innere Auseinandersetzung im dt. Katholizismus im Spiegel der führenden kath. Zeitschriften. 1895–1914* (diss., Mainz 1955); W. Spael, *Das Buch im Geisteskampf. 100 Jahre Borromäusverein* (1950); O. Köhler, "Bücher als Wegmarken im dt. Katholizismus," *Der. kath. Buchhandel Deutschlands,* ed. by the Association of the Catholic Bookstores (Frankfurt a. M. 1967) (review from the beginning of the nineteenth century until the present); *Der Katholizismus in Deutschland und der Verlag Herder. 1801–1951* (Freiburg 1951).—H. Platz, *Geistige Kämpfe im modernen Frankreich* (Kempten 1922); M. Bougier, *Essai sur la Renaissance de la Poésie catholique de Baudelaire à Claudel* (Montpellier 1942); A. Simon, *La littérature du péché et de la grâce. 1880 jusqu'à 1950* (Paris 1957); C. Moeller, *Littérature du XXᵉ siècle et christianisme* (Paris 1953ff.); H. Weinert, *Dichtung aus dem Glauben* (Heidelberg 1948).

SECTION THREE

Forms of Piety

16. *Externalization and Internalization of Nineteenth-Century Spirituality—Beginnings of the Eucharistic Congress Movement— Veneration of Saint Thérèse of Lisieux*

LITERATURE

Vol. VIII, chap. 15. Also: A. Mayer-Pfannholz, "Das Kirchenbild des 19. Jh. und seine Ablösung," *Die Besinnung* 3 (Nuremberg 1948), 124–44; S. Beissel, "Zur Geschichte der Gebetbücher," *StdZ* 77 (1909); H. Brück and J. B. Kißling, *Geschichte der katholischen Kirche in Deutschland* IV/2 (Mainz 1908); H. J. Terhünte, *Die religiöse Lage der Katholiken Frankreichs in der 3. Republik* (1919); G. Le Bras, *Histoire de la pratique religieuse en France*, 2 vols. (Paris 1942–44); A. Dansette, *Histoire religieuse de la France contemporaine* II, 1–286 (also non-Catholic publications).

EUCHARISTIC PIETY: E. Dumoutet, *Le désir de voir l'hostie* (Paris 1926); R. Aubert, "Die Eucharistischen Kongresse von Leo XIII. bis Johannes XXIII.," *Concilium* 1 (1965), 61–66.

DEVOTION TO THE SACRED HEART: J. Stierli et al., *Cor Salvatoris* (Freiburg i. Br. 1956), esp. 163ff.

DEVOTION TO MARY: E. Campana, *Maria nel culto cattolico*, 2 vols. (Turin 1945); E. Villaret, *Les Congrégations Mariales* (Paris 1947); A. Walz, *Saggi di storia rosariana* (Florence 1962); J. Stierli, *Die Marianischen Kongregationen*, 2 vols. (Leipzig 1947); R. Graber, *Die marianischen Weltrundschreiben der Päpste in den letzten hundert Jahren* (Regensburg 1951).

THE LITURGICAL MOVEMENT: In addition to A. Trapp, 282–367; Anton L. Mayer, "Die Stellung der Liturgie von der Zeit der Romantik bis zur Jahrhundertwende," *ALW* 3 (1955), 1–77; J. A. Jungmann, *Missarum sollemnia* I (Freiburg i. Br. 1952), 208–11; T. Klauser, *Kleine abendländische Liturgiegeschichte* (Bonn 1965), 121–23; J. Hacker, "Die Messe in den deutschen Diözesan-, Gesang- und Gebetbüchern von der Aufklärung bis zur Gegenwart," *MthSt(H)* 1 (1950), 68–132.

CHARITY: In addition to A. Foucault (see vol. VIII, chap. 2, n. 28): W. Liese, *Geschichte der Caritas* II (Freiburg i. Br. 1922); L. Werthmann, *Die Ziele des Caritasverbandes für das kath. Deutschland* (Freiburg 1899); K. Borgmann, *L. Werthmann. Aus seinen Reden und Schriften* (Freiburg 1958); W. Röhrich: *JCW* 2 (Freiburg i. Br. 1928), 25–36; A. Eckert, "Aus meinen Erinnerungen an L. Werthmann," *Caritas* 59 (1958), 285–310.

On Charles de Foucauld and Thérèse Martin (Thérèse of Lisieux), cf. below.

17. The Organization in the Old and New Orders—Inner Reform and the Power of Attraction

LITERATURE

General: J. Zürcher, ed., *Päpstliche Dokumente zur Ordensreform* (1954); R. Hostie, *Vie et mort des ordres religieux* (Paris 1972) 223–51 (sociological).—Benedictines: P. Schmitz, *Histoire des l'ordre de saint Benoît* (Maredsous 1948/56).—Dominicans: A. Walz, *Kardinal Frühwirth* (Vienna 1950); id., *Wahrheitskünder. Die Dominikaner in Geschichte und Gegenwart* (Essen 1960).—Franciscans: best summary yet: H. Holzapfel, *Geschichte der Franziskaner* (Munich 1909).—Jesuits: R. García-Villoslada, *Manual de Historia de la Compañía de Jesús* (Madrid 1954); H. Becher, *Die Jesuiten* (Munich 1951); J. Stierli, *Die Jesuiten* (Fribourg 1955; short history of the spirituality of the order, with biblio.); C. Hollis, *The Jesuits. A History* (New York 1969), cf.: E. McDenmott in *Cath. Hist. Rev.* 58 (1972) 76f.—Redemptorists: M. De Meulemeester, *Histoire Sommaire de la Congrég. du T. S. Rédempteur* (Louvain 1958).—Salesians: *Don Bosco nel mondo* (Turin 1959; statistics, atlas).—Assumptionists: J. Monval, *Les Assomptionnistes* (Paris 1939).—Missionaries of Steyl: H. Fischer, *Arnold Janssen* (Steyl 1919) (cf. biblio. for chap. 38).—Salvatorians: E. B. Lüthen, *Die Gesellschaft des Göttlichen Heilandes* (1911); R. Pfeiffer, *Joh.-B. Jordan* (Rome 1920); E. Federici (Rome 1948).

18. The Dispute over Church Music

LITERATURE

K. Weinmann, *Geschichte der Kirchenmusik, mit besonderer Berücksichtigung der kirchenmusikalischen Restauration im 19. Jh.* (Munich 1906, 1913; Weinmann was president of the General Cecilia Association from 1873 to 1929); O. Ursprung, *Die katholische Kirchenmusik* (Potsdam 1931) 250–85: E. Bücken, ed., *Hdb. der Musikwissenschaft;* K. G. Fellerer, *Der gregorianische Choral* (Regensburg 1936); id., *Geschichte der kath. Kirchenmusik* (Düsseldorf 1949) 143–62; F. Haberl, "Cäcilianische Kirchenmusik," *Zs. f. Kirchenmusik* 74 (Cologne 1954), 121–32; F. Krieg, *Katholische Kirchenmusik* (Teufen and St. Gallen 1954) (the historical parts by E. Tittel; 53, 134–42, with biblio.); P. Combe, *Histoire de la restauration de chant grégorien d'après des documents inédits* (Solesmes 1969); H. Hucke, "Die Anfänge des Cäcilienvereins," *Musik und Altar 22* (Freiburg i. Br. 1970) 159–78; K. G. Fellerer, "Grundlagen und Anfänge der kirchenmusikalischen Organisationen F. X. Witts," *KmJb* 55 (1971), 33–60; J. M. Bauduccio, "Relazioni del P. A. De Santi SJ con la congr. dei Riti circa la musica sacra dal 1887 al 1902," *AHSJ* 42 (1973), 128–60.

19. Church Art in the Nineteenth and Twentieth Centuries

(This biblio. offers only a selection. Treatises, catalogues, reports of meetings, congressional files, and articles are only listed in exceptional cases.)

LITERATURE

RELIGION AND ART: C. Meyer, *Über das Verhältnis von der Kunst zum Kultus. Ein Wort an alle gebildeten Verehrer der Religion und der Kunst* (Zurich 1837); F. Spitta, *Gotteshaus und Kunst* (Strasbourg 1895); A. Ehrhard, *Katholisches Christentum und moderne Kultur* (Mainz and Munich 1906); G. F. Hartlaub, *Kunst und Religion. Ein Versuch über die Möglichkeit neuer religiöser Kunst* (Munich 1919); I. Herwegen, O.S.B., *Das Kunstprinzip der Liturgie* (Paderborn 1920); id., *Kunst und Mysterium* (Münster i. W. 1929); R. Guardini, *Vom Geist der Liturgie* (Freiburg i. Br. 1921); id., *Von heiligen Zeichen* (Rothenfels a. M. 1922); J. van Acken, *Christozentrische Kirchenkunst. Ein Entwurf zum liturgischen Gesamtkunstwerk* (Gladbach 1923); G. Mensching, *Die liturgische Bewegung in der evangelischen Kirche. Ihre Formen und Ihre Probleme* (Tübingen 1925); C. Gröber, *Kirche und Künstler* (Freiburg i. Br. 1932); W. Stählin, *Berneuchen* (Kassel 1939); P. Larsch and R. Kramreiter, *Neue Kirchenkunst im Geist der Liturgie* (Vienna and Klosterneuburg 1939); K. B. Ritter, *Die Liturgie als Lebensform der Kirche* (Kassel 1946); T. Klauser, *Richtlinien für die Gestaltung des Gotteshauses aus dem Geist der römischen Liturgie* (Münster i. W. 1955); F. Kolbe, *Die liturgische Bewegung* (Aschaffenburg 1964); U. Rapp, O.S.B., *Konzil, Kunst und Künstler. Zum VII. Kapitel der Liturgiekonstitution* (Frankfurt a. M. 1965); T. Filthaut, *Kirchenbau und Liturgiereform* (Mainz 1965); D. F. Debuyst, O.S.B., *Architecture moderne et célébration chrétienne* (Brussels 1966); W. Birnbaum, *Die deutsche evangelische liturgische Bewegung* (Tübingen 1970).

CHURCH ART IN THE NINETEENTH CENTURY: A. Reichensperger, *Vermischte Schriften über christliche Kunst* (Leipzig 1856); K. Clark, *The Gothic Revival* (London 1950); A. Addison, *Romanticism and the Gothic Revival* (Philadelphia 1938); A. Kamphausen, *Gotik ohne Gott. Ein Beitrag zur Deutung der Neugotik und des 19. Jh.* (Tübingen 1952); C. Gurlitt, *Die deutsche Kunst des 19. Jh.* (Berlin 1899); R. Zeitler, *Die Kunst des 19. Jh.* (*Propyläen-Kunstgeschichte* 11 [Berlin 1964]); D. Lenz, O.S.B., *Zur Ästhetik der Beuroner Schule* (Vienna 1912); J. Kreitmaier, S. J., *Beuroner Kunst. Eine Ausdrucksform der christlichen Mystik* (Freiburg i. Br. 1923); A. Cingria, *La Décadence de l'Art Sacré* (Lausanne 1917); *Triviale Zonen in der religiösen Kunst des 19. Jh.* (*Studien zur Philosophie und Lit. des 19. Jh.* 15, Frankfurt a. M. 1971); G. Germann, *Gothic-Revival in Europe and Britain* (London 1972); A. Meyer, *Neugotik und Neuromanik in der Schweiz. Die Kirchenarchitektur des 19. Jh.* (Zurich 1973); H. Sedlmayr, *Verlust der Mitte* (Salzburg 1948); N. Pevsner, *Wegbereiter moderner Formgebung* (Hamburg 1957).

CHURCH ART IN THE TWENTIETH CENTURY: T. Wieschebrink, *Die kirchliche Kunstbewegung in der Zeit des Expressionismus 1917–1927* (diss., Münster i. W. 1932); P. R. Boving, O.F.M., *Kirche und moderne Kunst* (Bonn 1922); P. P. Regamey, *Kirche und Kunst im 20. Jh.* (Graz, Cologne and Wien 1954); P. Metz, *Abstrakte Kunst und Kirche. Studie über die Kunst in der Heilsgeschichte* (Nuremberg 1954); H. Schnell, *Zur Situation der christlichen Kunst* (Munich 1962); J. Plazaola, S. J., *El arte sacro actual* (Madrid 1965).

CHURCH ARCHITECTURE IN THE NINETEENTH AND TWENTIETH CENTURIES: E. Kaufmann, *Architecture in the Age of Reason. Baroque and Post-Baroque in England, Italy and France* (Cambridge, Mass. 1955); P. Hautecœur, *Histoire de l'architecture classique en France* VII (Paris 1963); A. Reichensperger, *Die christlich-germanische Baukunst und ihr Verhältnis zur Gegenwart* (Trier 1852); H. Lützeler, *Der Kölner Dom in der deutschen Geistesgeschichte* (Bonn 1948); A. W. N. Pugin, *True Principles of Pointed or Christian Architecture* (London 1841); id., *An Apology for the Revival of Christian Architecture in England* (London 1843); W. Weyres and A. Mann, *Hdb. der rheinischen Baukunst des 19. Jh., 1800–1880* (Cologne 1968); G. Palm, *Von welchen Prinzipien soll die Wahl des Baustyls insbesondere des Kirchenbaustyls geleitet werden?* (Hamburg 1845); A. Mann, *Die Neuromanik* (Cologne 1966); F. Schumacher, *Strömungen zur deutschen Baukunst seit 1800* (Leipzig 1935); J. Gerhardy, *Praktische Ratschläge über kirchliche Gebäude, Kirchengeräte und Paramente* (Paderborn 1895); R. B. Witte, *Das katholische Gotteshaus*

(Mainz 1951); W. Weyres and O. Bartning, *Kirchen. Handbuch für den Kirchenbau* (Munich 1959); H. Muthesius, *Die neuere kirchliche Baukunst in England* (Berlin 1901); H. Lützeler, *Der deutsche Kirchenbau der Gegenwart* (Düsseldorf 1934); R. Schwarz, *Vom Bau der Kirchen* (Würzburg 1938, Heidelberg 1947); F. Pfammater, *Betonkirchen* (Zurich 1948); H. Baur and F. Metzger, *Kirchenbauten* (Zurich and Würzburg 1956); R. Schwarz, *Kirchenbau. Welt vor der Schwelle* (Heidelberg 1960); J. Pichard, *Les églises nouvelles à travers le monde* (Paris 1960); H. Muck, S. J., *Sakralbau heute* (Aschaffenburg 1961); H.-E. Bahr, *Kirchen in nachsakraler Zeit* (Hamburg 1968); C. M. Werner, *Das Ende des "Kirchen"-Baus. Rückblick auf moderne Kirchenbaudiskussionen* (Zurich 1971); H. Schnell, *Der Kirchenbau des 20. Jh. in Deutschland* (Munich and Zurich 1973).

PROTESTANT CHURCH ARCHITECTURE: G. Langmaack, *Evangelischer Kirchenbau im 19. und 20. Jh.* (Kassel 1971); P. Brathe, *Theorie des evangelischen Kirchengebäudes. Ein ergänzendes Kapitel zur evangelischen Liturgik* (Stuttgart 1906); M. Meurer, *Der Kirchenbau vom Standpunkt und nach dem Brauche der lutherischen Kirche. Geistlichen, Kirchenpatronen und Kirchenvorständen zur Orientierung dargeboten* (Leipzig 1877); O. Mothes, *Handbuch des evangelisch-christlichen Kirchenbaues* (Leipzig 1898); W. Distel, *Protestantischer Kirchenbau seit 1900 in Deutschland* (Zurich 1933); O. Bartning, *Vom neuen Kirchenbau* (Berlin 1919); O. Bartning, *Vom christlichen Kirchenbau* (Cologne 1928).

PAINTING AND INTERIOR DESIGN: F. Novotny, *Painting and Sculpture in Europe 1780–1880* (Harmondsworth 1960); J. W. v. Goethe (J. H. Meyer), *Neudeutsche religiös-patriotische Kunst* (*Über Kunst und Altertum* I, 1817); K. Andrews, *The Nazarenes. A Brotherhood of German Painters in Rome* (Oxford 1964); H. Schrade, "Die romantische Idee von der Landschaft als höchstem Gegenstande der christlichen Kunst," *Neue Heidelberger Jahrbücher* (1931); R. Ironside and J. Gere, *Pre-Raphaelite Painters* (London 1948); G. Brundu, "Preraffaelismo e Purismo," *Enciclopedia universale dell'Arte* X, 943–48; S. Waetzoldt, "Bemerkungen zur christlich-religiösen Malerei in der zweiten Hälfte des 19. Jh.," *Triviale Zonen in der religiösen Kunst des 19. Jh.* (*Studien zur Philosophie und Literatur des 19. Jh.* 15, [Frankfurt a. M. 1971]); J. Kreitmaier, S.J., *Von Kunst und Künstlern. Gedanken zu alten und neuen künstlerischen Fragen* (Freiburg 1926); G. Hexges, O.F.M., *Ausstattungskunst im Gotteshaus* (Berlin 1934); R. Koch, *Das Kirchengerät im evangelischen Gottesdienst* (Hamburg 1935); A. Henze, *Kirchliche Kunst der Gegenwart* (Recklinghausen 1954).

SECTION FOUR

Teaching and Theology

20. *The Encyclical* Aeterni Patris

COMMENTARIES

F. Ehrle (1880), newly ed. by F. Pelster (Rome 1954); G. Cornoldi, *La riforma della filosofia promossa dall'enciclica "Aeterni Patris" di S. S. Leone XIII* (Bologna 1880); other contemporary commentaries: Schmidlin, *PG* II, 394 (footnote).

LITERATURE

A. Walz, "Sguardo sul movimento tomista nel secolo XIX fino all'enciclica Aeterni Patris," *Aquinas* 8 (1965), 351–79; R. Aubert, "Aspects divers du néo-thomisme sous le pontificat de Léon XIII," *Aspetti della cultura cattolica nell'età di Leone XIII* (Rome 1961), 133–227.—Regarding the history of Neo-Scholasticism after 1879: chap. 21.

21. *Neo-Thomism, Neo-Scholasticism, and the "New Philosophers"*

LITERATURE

Cf. chap. 20.—M. Grabmann, *Die Geschichte der katholischen Theologie* (Freiburg i. Br. 1933, photoprint, Darmstadt 1961), 218–81; Hocedez III, 45–52, 110–20, 235–322, 351–83; G. Söhngen, "Neuscholastik," *LThK* VII, 923–26; O. H. Pesch, "Thomismus," *LThK* X, 160f.; R. Aubert, *Aspects* (cited in chap. 20); id., "Die Theologie während der 1. Hälfte des 20. Jh.," H. Vorgrimler and R. Vander Gucht, *Bilanz der Theologie* II (Freiburg i. Br. 1969), 7–14; F. van Steenberghen, "Die neuscholastische Philosophie," ibid. I, 352–63; in regard to ethical theology: J. G. Ziegler in ibid. III, 316–28; in regard to apologetics: J. Schitz in ibid. II, 201–20 (also about M. Blondel).—On individual philosophers and theologians, cf. chapter footnotes, also chap. 15.

22. *The Theory of Church History*

LITERATURE

On ecclesiastical historiography: this series, vol. I, pp. 35–56; Hocedez III, 64–91, 142–72; L. Scheffzyk, *F. L. von. Stolbergs "Geschichte der Religion Jesu Christi". Die Abwendung der kath. Kirchengeschichtsschreibung von der Aufklärung und ihre Neuorientierung im Zeitalter der Romantik* (Munich 1952).

On the history of various problems: this series, vol. I, pp. 1–11; A. Franzen, "Theologie der Geschichte und theologischen Kirchengeschichte," *Oberrhein. Pastoralblatt* 67 (1966), 395–400; J. Ratzinger, "Das Problem der Dogmengeschichte,"

Arbeitsgemeinschaft f. Forsch. Nordrhein-Westfalen, Geisteswiss., no. 139 (Cologne 1966); H. Dickerhof, "Kirchenbegriff, Wissenschaftsentwicklung, Bildungssoziologie und die Formen der kirchlichen Historiographie," *HJ* 89 (1969), 176–202; R. Kottje, ed., *Kirchengeschichte heute—Geschichtswissenschaft oder Theologie?* (Trier 1970); P. Stockmeier, "Kirchengeschichte und Geschichtlichkeit der Kirche," *ZKG* 81 (1970), 145–62; *Concilium, Internat. Zs. f. Theol.* 6 (1970), no. 8/9, with articles by G. Alberigo, R. Aubert, Y. Congar et al.; O. Köhler, "Die Kirche als Geschichte," *Mysterium salutis* IV/2 (in preparation).

23. The Question of the Bible

LITERATURE

A general history of Catholic Bible studies in the nineteenth century does not exist.—On Catholic exegesis after the sixteenth century: V. Baroni, *La Contre-Réforme devant la Bible* (Lausanne 1943); id., *La Bible dans la vie catholique depuis la Réforme* (Lausanne 1955).—A short summary of the "Question Biblique" during Leo XIII's pontificate in: Hocedez III, 124–41; A. Wikenhauser and Josef Schmid, *Einleitung in das NT* (Freiburg i. Br. 1973), 8ff.; briefly describes the situation until *Divino afflante Spiritu* (1943), introducing "a new epoch for Catholic Bible Studies."—The best analysis of the problems is provided by the studies about Albert (Marie-Joseph) Lagrange: J. Chaine et al., *L'œuvre exégétique et historique du R. P. Lagrange* (Paris 1935); L.-H. Vincent, "Le Père Lagrange," *RB* 47 (1938), 321–54; F. M. Braun, *L'œuvre du Père Lagrange* (Fribourg 1943); *Le Père Lagrange au service de la Bible, Souvenirs personnels* (Paris 1967). Negative, but with information: A. Houtin, *La question biblique chez les catholiques de France au XIXᵉ siècle* (Paris 1902).—J. Coppens, *Le chanoine A. van Hoonacker* (Paris 1935).—The Jesuit Franz von Hummelauer, suspended from exegetical research, has not yet been appraised, except by L. Koch (*Jesuitenlexikon,* 833).—The traditional position: cf. A. Delattre, S.J., *Autour de la question biblique* (Paris 1904); L. Fonck, *Der Kampf um die Wahrheit der Heiligen Schrift seit 25 Jahren* (Innsbruck 1905).

24. The Condemnation of Americanism

Cf. chap. 10, especially T. T. McAvoy, *Crisis* (1957); id., *New Catholic Enc.* 1 (1967), 443f.; Hocedez III, (1947), 190–94; L. Hertling, 230–44; E. Lecanuet, *L'Église de France sous Léon XIII* (Paris 1931), 544–602.

25. Papal Hopes for Unification—The Independent Eastern Churches and the Uniates

LITERATURE

Cf. Gen. Biblio.; also "Päpstliche Unionshoffnungen": L. K. Goetz, *Leo XIII. Seine Weltanschauung und seine Wirksamkeit, quellenmäßig dargestellt* (Gotha 1899); B. Arens, *Papst Pius X. und die Weltmission* (Aachen 1919); F. Portal, "Le rôle de l'amitié dans l'Union des Églises," *La Revue catholique des idées et des faits* 11 December 1925, 5–8; A. Gratieux, *L'Amitié au service de l'Union, Lord Halifax et l'abbé Portal* (Paris 1951); A.

Hudal, *Die österreichische Vatikanbotschaft 1806–1918* (Munich 1952); R. Aubert, "Un document de la fin du XIXe siècle relatif aux facteurs non théologiques de Désunion entre chrétiens," *1054–1954. L'Église et les églises, neuf siècles de douloureuse séparation entre l'Orient et l'Occident* II, ed. by L. Beauduin (Chevetogne 1955), 429–35; G. Florowski, "Die orthodoxen Kirchen und die ökumenische Bewegung bis zum Jahre 1910," R. Rouse and S. C. Neill, *Gesch. der Ökumenischen Bewegung 1517–1948* I (Göttingen 1957), 231–96; O. S. Tomkins, "Die Römisch-Katholische Kirche und die ökumenische Bewegung 1910–1948," ibid. II (Göttingen 1958), 359–484; J. Alameda, *Las Iglesias de Oriente y su Unión con Roma* (Vitoria 1960); O. Rousseau, "Les attitudes de pensée concernant l'unité chrétienne au XIXe siècle," *L'Ecclésiologie au XIXe siècle* (Paris 1960), 351–73; W. de Vries, *Orthodoxie und Katholizismus. Gegensatz oder Ergänzung?* (Freiburg, Basel and Vienna 1965); C. Soetens, "Les catholiques belges et le rapprochement avec les Églises d'Orient dans la seconde moitié du XIXe siècle," *RHE* 66 (1971), 83–115; J. Hajjar, *Zwischen Rom und Byzanz. Die unierten Christen des Nahen Ostens* (Mainz 1972).

THE INDEPENDENT EASTERN CHURCHES. RUSSIA: J. Wilbois, *L'Avenir de l'Église russe. Essai sur la crise sociale et religieuse en Russie* (Paris 1907); W. Gribowski, *Das Staatsrecht des Russischen Reiches* (Tübingen 1912); A. Herman, *De fontibus iuris ecclesiastici Russorum. Commentarius historico-canonicus* (Rome 1936); J. S. Curtiss, *Church and State in Russia. The last years of the Empire 1900–1917* (New York 1940); A. M. Ammann, *Abriß der ostslawischen Kirchengeschichte* (Vienna 1950); J. Chrysostomus, *Die religiösen Kräfte in der russischen Gesch.* (Munich 1961); I. Smolitsch, *Gesch. der russischen Kirche 1700–1917* I (Leiden 1964); K. Onasch, "Grundzüge der russischen Kirchengeschichte," *Die Kirche in ihrer Gesch. Ein Handbuch* III, ed. by K. D. Schmidt and E. Wolf (Göttingen 1967), 1–133; G. Simon, "Kirche, Staat und Gesellschaft," *Rußlands Aufbruch ins 20. Jh. Politik—Gesellschaft—Kultur 1894–1917,* ed. by G. Katkov, E. Oberländer, N. Poppe, G. v. Rauch (Olten and Freiburg i. Br. 1970), 199–233.

AUSTRIA-HUNGARY AND SOUTHEASTERN EUROPE: A. Hudal, *Die serbisch-orthodoxe Nationalkirche* (Graz and Leipzig 1922); J. Mousset, *La Serbie et son église 1830–1904* (Paris 1938); G. G. Arnakis, *The Near East in Modern Times* I (Austin and New York 1969); J. Kondrinewitsch and E. v. Ivánka, "Die Orthodoxie in der Donaumonarchie und im Balkan von 1690 bis heute," *Hdb. der Ostkirchenkunde,* op. cit., 187–97.

THE FOUR OLD ORTHODOX PATRIARCHATE CHURCHES: C. Korolevsky, *Histoire des Patriarcats Melkites,* 3 vols. (Rome 1910–11); "Ekklesia X: Die Orthodoxe Kirche auf dem Balkan und in Vorderasien," ed. 45, *Gesch., Lehre und Verfassung der Orthodoxen Kirche* (Leipzig 1939); ed. 46: "Die orthodoxen Patriarchate von Konstantinopel, Alexandrien, Antiochien, Jerusalem und das Erzbistum von Cypern" (Leipzig, 1941); G. Vismara, *Bisanzio e l'islam. Per la storia dei trattati tra la Cristianità Orientale e le potenze Musulmane* (Milan 1950); J. Totzke, "Die alten Patriarchate Alexandrien, Antiochien und Jerusalem," *Una Sancta* 14 (1959), 300–307; 15 (1960), 203–12; C. Dahm, *Die Kirche im Osten. Macht und Pracht der Patriarchen* I (Offenburg 1964); F. W. Fernau, *Patriarchen am Goldenen Horn. Gegenwart und Tradition des orthodoxen Orients* (Opladen 1967); M. Lacko and P. Chrysostomus, "Gesch. und jetziger Stand der orthodoxen Kirchen," K. Algermissen, op. cit., 171–202; R. Potz, *Patriarch und Synode in Konstantinopel. Das Verfassungsrecht des ökumenischen Patriarchates* (Vienna 1971).

THE NATIONAL CHURCHES IN THE MIDDLE EAST: C. Fink, "Die getrennten Kirchen des Morgenlandes," *Morgenländisches Christentum. Wege zu einer ökumenischen Theologie,* ed. by P. Krüger and J. Tyciak (Paderborn 1940), 23–48; P. Kawerau, *Amerika und die orientalischen Kirchen. Ursprung und Anfang der amerikanischen Mission unter den National-alkirchen Westasiens* (Berlin 1958); *Hdb. der Orientalistik,* Pt. 1, Vol. 8, Sec. 2, ed. by B. Spuler (Leiden and Cologne 1961); A. S. Atiya, *A History of Eastern Christianity* (London 1968); W. de Vries, "Die getrennten Kirchen des Ostens," K. Algermissen op. cit., 79–170; id., "Die 'nationalen Kirchen' des Nahen Ostens und das 'Uniatenproblem,'" *Hdb. der Ostkirchenkunde,* op. cit., 198–217.

THE UNIATE CHURCHES: A. Fortescue, *The Uniate Eastern Churches. The Byzantine rite in Italy, Sicily, Syria and Egypt* (New York 1923); B. J. Kidd, *The Churches of Eastern Christendom from A.D. 451 to the Present Time* (London 1927); P. Werhun, "Gesch. der Union in Byzanz und Südosteuropa," *Der christliche Osten,* op. cit., 294–310; id., "Gesch. der Union im ostslawischen Raum," ibid., 311–35; P. Krüger, "Die Unionen im Orient und Ägypten," ibid., 336–49; H. Engberding, "Die mit Rom vereinten Kirchen," *Morgenländisches Christentum,* op. cit., 49–61; C. de Clercq, *Histoire des Conciles d'après les documents originaux* XI, 2 (Paris 1952); I. Totzke, "Die 'Unierten.' Zum Problem der mit Rom in kirchlicher Gemeinschaft stehenden Orientalen," *Una Sancta* 14 (1959), 9–22; J. Alameda, *Las Iglesias de Oriente y su Unión con Roma* (Vitoria 1960); F. X. Siess, *Die Patriarchalverfassung der Unierten Kirche* (Erlangen 1960); F. Heyer, "Die katholische Kirche vom Westfälischen Frieden bis zum Ersten Vatikanischen Konzil," *Die Kirche in ihrer Gesch.* IV, ed. N, op. cit. (1963), 1–195; J. Madey, *Kirche zwischen Ost und West. Beiträge zur Geschichte der Ukrainischen und Weißruthenischen Kirche* (Munich 1969); M. Lacko, "Unionsbewegungen im slawischen Raum und in Rumänien," *Hdb. der Ostkirchenkunde,* op. cit., 218–35; J. Hajjar, *Zwischen Rom und Byzanz. Die unierten Christen des Nahen Ostens* (Mainz 1972).

Part Two
Defensive Concentration of Forces

Introduction: *Pius X, a Conservative Reform Pope*

SOURCES

ASS, 36–41 (1903–8); *AAS* 1–6 (1909–14); *Lettere,* ed. by N. Vian (Rome 1954); L. v. Pastor, *Tagebücher,* ed. by W. Wühr (Heidelberg 1950), 414–611; R. Merry del Val, *Pio X, impressioni e ricordi* (Padua 1949); C. Bellaigue, *Pie X et Rome* (Paris 1916); F. Crispolti, *Ricordi personali* (Milan 1932), 85–139; *Beatificationis et Canonizationis Servi Dei Pii Papae X Positio super introductione causae* (Rome 1942); *Positio super virtutibus* (Vatican City 1949); *Disquisitio circa quasdam objectiones modum agendi Servi Dei respicientes in modernismi debellatione* (Vatican City 1950, important documents); in addition, the records of the processes (Rome, prof. 1923–31, and apost. 1943–46; Venice, prof. 1924–30 and apost. 1944–46; Mantua, prof. 1924–27 and apost. 1945–46; Treviso, prof. 1923–26 and apost. 1944–46).

LITERATURE

GENERAL PRESENTATIONS: Schmidlin, *PG* III, 1–177; *DThC* XII, 1716–40; *A Symposium on the Life and Work of Pius X* (Washington 1946); H. Hermelink, *Die Kath. Kirche unter den Piuspäpsten des 20. Jh.* (Zurich 1949), 3–23, passim; Stanislao da Campagnola in *I papi nella storia* II (Rome 1961), 1078–1101; C. Falconi, *I papi del ventesimo secolo* (Milan 1967), 17–103, 387–89; G. Schwaiger, *Gesch. der Päpste im 20. Jh.* (Munich 1968), 49–71, 206–7; Y. de la Brière, *Les luttes présentes de l'Église,* 2 vols. (Paris 1913–14); M. Pernot, *La politique de Pie X* (Paris 1910); id., *Le Saint-Siège, l'Église catholique et la politique mondiale* (Paris 1924; liberal viewpoint); Aventino (=C. Bélin), *Le gouvernement de Pie X. Concentration et défense catholique* (Paris 1912; conservative viewpoint); *Ce qu'on a fait de l'Église* (Paris 1912; polemical, but informative); É. Poulat, *Histoire, dogme et critique dans la crise moderniste* (Paris and Tournai 1962), 662–64; J. M. Javierre, "La diplomacia pontificia en los estados europeos, 1903–14. Fuentes y bibliografía," *Salmanticensis* 11 (1964), 343–73.

BIOGRAPHIES: Since a satisfactory biography does not yet exist (list in *Salmanticensis* 11 [1964], 353–54), we recommend primarily: R. Bazin, *Pie X* (Paris 1928); E. Vercesi, *Il pontificato di Pio X* (Milan 1935); F. De Carli, *Pio X e il suo tempo* (Florence 1941); C. Ledré, *Pie X* (Paris 1952; the most detailed biography; see also id., *RHEF* 40 [1954], 249–67); G. Dal Gal, *Il papa santo Pio X* (Padua 1954; very one-sided, but offers many details); P. Fernessole, *Pie X. Sa vie et son œuvre,* 2 vols. (Paris 1952); N. Vian, *S. Pius Pp. X* (Padua 1958); P. V. Facchinetti, *L'anima di Pio X* (Milan 1935); F. Antonelli, "La santità di Pio X," *Rivista di vita spirituale* 6 (1952), 121–32.

GIUSEPPE SARTO BEFORE HIS PONTIFICATE: A. Marchesan, *Pio X* (Einsiedeln 1905); D. Ireno, "La formazione di S. Pio X nel Seminario di Padova," *Studia patavina* 1

(1954), 286–317; E. Bacchion, *G. Sarto arciprete di Salzano* (Padua 1925); N. Vian, *San Pio X a Venezia* (Rome 1958); id., *Sulla soglia di Venezia* (Florence 1964).

THE CONCLAVE: G. Berthelet, *Storia e rivelazione sul conclave del 1903* (Turin 1904). The essential issues can quickly be obtained from the article by F. D. Mathieu, "Les derniers jours de Léon XIII et le conclave," *Revue des deux mondes* 362 (1904), 241–85 (a few additional details from his diary in E. Renard, *Le cardinal Mathieu* [Paris 1925], 390–415); Prince B. v. Bülow published in his memoirs (I [Berlin 1930], 619–23) an extensive letter by Cardinal Kopp of 4 August 1903; other details given by M. Landrieux, "Le conclave de 1903. Journal d'un conclaviste," *Études* 299 (1958), 157–83; the French diplomatic correspondence was appraised by H. Néant in *Revue d'histoire diplomatique* 77 (1963), 97–111, the Austrian diplomatic correspondence by Engel-Janosi II, 1–47. On the veto, see also Z. Obertyński, "Kard. Puzyna und sein Veto," *Festschr. F. Loidl* III (Vienna 1971), 177–95.

THE CURIA UNDER PIUS X: L. Bedeschi, *La Curia Romana durante la crisi modernista* (Parma 1968); cf. M. Guasco in *Humanitas* (1968), 814–17, and G. Martina in *RSTI* 23 (1969), 230–34.

The Reform Work of Pius X

26. Reorganization of the Roman Curia and Codification of Canon Law

LITERATURE

ON THE ENTIRE COMPLEX OF REFORMS: N. Hilling, *Die Reformen des Papstes Pius X. auf dem Gebiete der kirchenrechtlichen Gesetzgebung,* 3 vols. (Bonn 1909–15; chronological) and id. in *AkathKR* 95 (1915), 78–112, 283–99, 457–86, 639–58; 96 (1916), 60–73, 244–70, 408–30, 550–68; 97 (1917), 67–81, 245–59, 397–408, 563–75 (systematic); H. E. Feine, *Kirchliche Rechtsgeschichte. Die kath. Kirche* (Cologne and Graz 1964), 699–719 (biblio.).

ON THE REFORM OF THE CURIA: *DDC* IV, 997–1004; V. Martin, *Les cardinaux et la Curie und Les congrégations romaines* (Paris 1930); N. del Rè, *La Curia Romana* (Rome 1970), see above all: *Romana Curia a beato Pio X Sapienti consilio reformata* (Vatican City 1951; cited as *Rom. Curia*), especially the second chap. by G. Feretto about the stages of preparation (as yet unpublished documents). Regarding the old biblio., see Schmidlin, *PG* III, 34, n. 14. See also L. Bedeschi, *La Curia Romana durante la crisi modernista* (Parma 1968).

ON THE REFORM OF CANON LAW: P. Gasparri, "Storia della codificazione del diritto canonico," *Acta Congressus iuridici internationalis* IV (Rome 1937), 1–10; N. Hilling, op. cit.; I. Noval, *Codificationis juris canonici recensio historico-apologetica* (Rome 1918); A. Knecht, *Das neue Kirchliche Gesetzbuch. Seine Geschichte und Eigenart* (Strasbourg 1918); U. Stutz, *Der Geist des Codex iuris canonici* (Stuttgart 1918); M. Falco, *Introduzione allo studio del "Codex iuris canonici"* (Turin 1925); F. Cimetier, *Les sources du droit ecclésiastique* (Paris 1930), 150–97; *DDC* III, 909–40; Agatángel de Langasco in *Revista española de derecho canónico* 10 (1955), 457–75 (about the role of Cardinal Vives).

27. Eucharistic Decrees and Liturgical Renewal

SOURCES

A. Bugnini, *Documenta pontificia ad instaurationem liturgicam spectantia 1903–1935* (Rome 1953).

LITERATURE

EUCHARISTIC DECREES: C. Zerba, *Nel cinquantenario del Decreto "Quam singulari"* (Vatican City 1961); J.-M. Derély, *NRTh* 73 (1951), 897–911, 1033–48; id., ibid. 77 (1955), 506–12; *DThC* III, 539–52; *DSAM* II, 1282–89; J. A. Hardon, *ThSt* 16 (1955), 493–532; H. A. Heiser, *Die Durchführung der Kommuniondekrete in der ganzen Welt* (Wiesbaden 1932; *ZAM* 8 [1933], 162–66; P. Hellbernd, *Die Erstkommunion der Kinder in Geschichte und Gegenwart* (Vechta 1954).

LITURGICAL REFORMS OF PIUS X: N. Hilling, *AkathKR* 96 (1916), 550–68 (old biblio., see 557, n. 6); 97 (1917), 245–59; O. Rousseau, *Histoire du mouvement liturgique* (Paris 1945), 201–30; T. Narbutas, *La reforma del breviario romano por Pío X* (Santiago de Chile 1949); J. M. Lecea Yabar, *Pastoral litúrgica en los documentos pontificios de Pío X a Pío XII* (Barcelona 1959); H. Vinck, "Les réformes liturgiques de 1911–1914" (unpubl. diss. of the Institut supérieur de Liturgie, Paris 1971); Schmidlin, *PG* III, 46–53.

CHORAL REFORM: K. G. Fellerer, *Der gregorianische Choral im Wandel der Jahrhunderte* (Rome 1936); E. Moneta-Caglio, "L'attività musicale di S. Pio X," *Bolletino ceciliano Nov. 1964;* id., *Musica sacra,* 84–86 (Milan 1961–63); F. Romita, "La preformazione del Motu proprio di S. Pio X sulla musica sacra," *Monitor ecclesiasticus* 86 (1961), 395–497; P. Combe, *Histoire de la restauration du chant grégorien* (Solesmes 1969); F. M. Bauducco in *CivCatt,* 1961, III, 583–94; 1963, I, 240–53; 1968, III, 243–52 (about the role of A. de Santis); id., *Bolletino ceciliano* (1964), 75–92; G. Zaggia, *L. Bottazzo e la restaurazione della musica sacra* (Padua 1967); E. Valentini, *Un campione del movimento ceciliano, G. Grosso* (Turin 1962); H. Vinck in *ELit* 86, (1972), 290–98; E. Moeller, "C. Bellaigue et Pie X," *QLP* 21 (1936), 40–65; "Il Pont. Istituto di musica sacra 50° di fondazione," *Bolletino degli Amici del Pont. Ist. di Mus. sacra* 13 (1961).

BEGINNING OF THE LITURGICAL MOVEMENT: A. Haquin, *Dom Lambert Beauduin et le renouveau liturgique* (Gembloux 1970); B. Fischer, "Das 'Mechelner Ereignis' vom 23. 9. 1909," *LJ* 9 (1959), 203–19; A. Bernareggi in *SC* 78 (1950), 81–102.

28. *Concern for Pastoral Improvements: Seminaries, Catechetical Instruction, Catholic Action*

LITERATURE

PIUS X AND THE CLERGY: Schmidlin, *PG* III, 40–43; N. Hilling in *AkathKR* 95 (1905), 283–99; A. M. Lanz, "Pio X e la Spiritualità del clero diocesano," *CivCatt,* 1952, I, 141–50; G. Lenhart, *Der Priester und sein Tagwerk im Licht des Papstprogramms* (Freiburg i. Br. 1913).

THE REFORM OF SEMINARIES: M. Bargilliat, *Romanorum Pontificum Pii IX, Leonis XIII et Pii X monita et decreta de institutione clericorum in seminariis* (Paris 1908; see also *Enchiridion clericorum* [Rome 1938]); *L'ordinamento dei seminari da S. S. Pio X a Pio XII* (Rome 1958); M. Guasco, *Fermenti nei seminari del primo '900* (Bologna 1971); id.: *Storia contemporanea* 2 (1971), 863–74; N. Hilling in *AkathKR* 95 (1915), 95–112.

CATECHETICAL INSTRUCTION: G. Dal Gal, *Beato Pio X papa* (Padua 1951), 401–9; P. Stella, "Alle fonti del Catechismo di S. Pio X," *Salesianum* 23 (1961), 43–66; A. Balocco, "Un memorabile trentennio nella storia della catechesi, 1905–1935," *Rivista lassalliana* 36 (1962), 3–27; B. Dreher, *Die biblische Unterweisung im evangelischen und katholischen Religionsunterricht* (Freiburg i. Br. 1963), 11–81.

CATHOLIC ACTION: L. Civardi, *Compendio di storia dell'Azione cattolica italiana* (Rome 1956); Mgr. de Bazelaire, *Les laïcs aussi sont l'Église* (Paris 1958).

The Modernist Crisis

LITERATURE

The studies written immediately after the crisis are tendentious, but they are valuable by virtue of their testimony. See especially: A. L. Lilley, *Modernism, a Record, and a Review* (London 1908); K. Holl, *Der Modernismus* (Tübingen 1908); P. Sabatier, *Les modernistes* (Paris 1909); A. Gambaro, *Il modernismo* (Florence 1912); J. Schnitzer, "Der katholische Modernismus," *Zeitschrift für Politik* 5 (1912), 1–218 (also the volume of documents in the collection *Klassiker der Religion* 3 [Berlin 1912]); A. Houtin, *Histoire du modernisme catholique* (Paris 1913); M.-D. Petre, *Modernism. Its failure and its fruit* (London 1918); E. Buonaiuti, *Le modernisme catholique* (Paris 1927).

So far, there are three comprehensive histories: J. Rivière, *Le modernisme dans l'Église* (Paris 1929, with old lit., cf. *RevSR* 4 [1930], 676–92, and É. Poulat, *Histoire, dogme et critique dans la crise moderniste* [Paris and Tournai 1962], 41, 289–92, 295), and A. Vidler, *The Modernist Movement in the Roman Church* (Cambridge 1934). Also: É. Poulat, "'Modernisme' et 'Integrisme'. Du concept polémique à l'irénisme critique," *ArchSR* 27 (1969), 3–28; id. in *RSR* 58 (1970), 335–550; 59 (1971), 161–78; A. Vidler, *A Variety of Catholic Modernists* (Cambridge 1970); M. Ranchetti, *Cultura e riforma religiosa nella storia del modernismo* (Turin 1963); O. Schröder, *Aufbruch und Mißverständnis. Zur Geschichte der reformkatholischen Bewegung* (Graz 1969); L. da Veiga Coutinho, *Tradition et histoire dans la controverse moderniste* (Rome 1954); P. de Haes, *La résurrection de Jésus dans l'apologétique des 50 dernières années* (Rome 1953); C. Porro, *La controversia cristologica nel periodo modernista* (Milan 1971); P. Scoppola, "Recenti studi sulla crisi modernista," *Rivista di storia e letteratura religiosa* I (1965), 274–310.

29. Reform Catholicism in Germany

LITERATURE

A thorough study of this theme is lacking. See the summaries in *LThK* VIII, 705–7, *LThK* VIII, 1085, and in *RGG* V, 896–903; also an extensive study in J. Rivière, op. cit., 75–81, 288–93, 416–27, in A. Gisler, *Der Modernismus* (Einsiedeln 1912), 133–54, 642–50, and esp. in O. Schröder, op. cit., 369–431.

Regarding the most important leaders, see in this chapter: for Schnell n. 9; for Ehrhard n. 11; for Kraus n. 5; for P. Funk n. 19; for Schnitzer n. 18.

See also A. Hagen, *Der Reformkatholizismus in der Diözese Rottenburg* (Stuttgart 1962); A. ten Hompel, *Indexbewegung und Kulturgesellschaft* (Bonn 1908); W. Spael, *Das katholische Deutschland im 20. Jh.* (Würzburg 1964).

30. The Beginning of the Crisis in France

SOURCES

A. Loisy, *Mémoires*, 3 vols. (Paris 1930–31; cf. M.-J. Lagrange, *M. Loisy et le modernisme* [Paris 1932] and É. Poulat, *Une œuvre clandestine d'H. Bremond* [Rome 1972]); A.

Houtin and F. Sartiaux, *A. Loisy. Sa vie, son œuvre,* ed. with footnotes by É. Poulat (Paris 1960; cf. A. Vidler, *A Variety of Catholic Modernists,* 29–33); A. Houtin, *Une vie de prêtre. Mon expérience* (Paris 1926); P. Alfaric, *De la foi à la raison. Scènes vécues* (Paris 1965); J. Turmel, *Comment j'ai donné congé aux dogmes* (Paris 1935); id., *Comment l'Église romaine m'a donné congé* (Paris 1937); J. Guitton, *Dialogues avec M. Pouget* (Paris 1954); J. Chevalier, *P. Pouget. Logia* (Paris 1955); *Au cœur de la crise moderniste. Le dossier inédit d'une controverse,* ed. by R. Marlé (Paris 1960; cf. É. Poulat, *Histoire, dogme et critique,* 40–41, 513–15, 587, and *Revue belge de philologie et d'histoire* 41 [1963], 1164–66); M. Bécamel, "Lettres de Loisy à Mgr. Mignot," *BLE* 67 (1966), 3–44, 81–114, 170–94, 257–86; 69 (1968), 241–68; M. Blondel and A. Valensin, *Correspondance 1899–1912,* 2 vols. (Paris 1957); M. Blondel and J. Wehrlé, *Correspondance,* ed. by H. de Lubac, 2 vols. (Paris 1966); M. Blondel and L. Laberthonnière, *Correspondance philosophique,* ed. by C. Tresmontant (Paris 1961); H. Bremond and M. Blondel, *Correspondance,* ed. by A. Blanchet, I–II (Paris 1970–71); H. Bernard-Maître, "'Histoire et dogme' de M. Blondel d'après les papiers inédits d'A. Loisy," *RSR* 57 (1969), 49–74; id., "Lettres d'H. Bremond à Loisy," *BLE* 69 (1968), 3–24, 161–84, 269–89; B. Neven, "Lettres de Mgr. Duchesne à A. Loisy et à Fr. v. Hügel," *Mélanges de l'École française de Rome* 84 (1972), 283–307, 559–99; R. Aubert, "Aux origines de la réaction antimoderniste. Deux documents inédits," *EThL* 37 (1961), 557–78.

The literary estates of Loisy and Houtin are kept in the Bibliothèque nationale in Paris; those of Blondel in the Institut supérieur de philosophie in Louvain; those of Laberthonnière are kept by the Oratorians of Paris; those of Mgr. Mignot in the archbishopric of Albi and in the bishopric of Rodez.

LITERATURE

Aside from the general works by Rivière, Vidler, Houtin, etc. (p. 616), see primarily: É. Poulat, *Histoire, dogme et critique dans la crise moderniste* (Tournai and Paris 1962; cf. *RH* 230 [1963], 262–67), with useful appendix: "Pseudonymes et anonymes modernistes" (621–76). Also: A. Houtin, *La question biblique au XXᵉ siècle* (Paris 1906); R. Aubert, *Le problème de l'acte de foi* (Louvain 1950), 265–92; F. Rodé, *Le miracle dans la crise moderniste* (Paris 1965).

On A. Loisy, aside from his biography by Houtin-Sartiaux (above, with a complete list of his works, 303–24), see also: F. Heiler, *Der Vater des katholischen Modernismus, A. Loisy* (Munich 1947); M. Dell'Isola, *A. Loisy* (Modena 1957); R. Boyer de Sainte-Suzanne, *A. Loisy entre la foi et l'incroyance* (Paris 1968); R. Aubert, *Die Wahrheit der Ketzer,* ed. by H. J. Schultz (Stuttgart 1968), 172–83, 349–57; D. Baader, "Der Weg Loisys . . . ," *FreibThSt,* 1974.

On M.-J. Lagrange and M. Blondel, see biblio. to chap. 23 and chap. 21, ns. 19 and 20.

On P. Batiffol, see J. Rivière, *Mgr Batiffol* (Paris 1929) and A. Houtin, *Ma vie laïque* (Paris 1928), 150–55. On J. Turmel, see F. Sartiaux, *J. Turmel prêtre, historien des dogmes* (Paris 1931) and A. Vidler, *A Variety . . . ,* 56–62.—On Mignot, Houtin, Bremond, Laberthonnière, and Le Roy, see below, ns. 12, 13, 15, 17, and 19.

31. *The Crisis in England*

SOURCES

For Tyrrell: T. M. Loome, "A Bibliography of the Published Writings of G. Tyrrell," *Heythrop Journal* 10 (1969), 280–314; supplement, ibid. 11 (1970), 161–69; *G. Tyrrell's*

Letters 1898–1909, ed. by M. Petre (London 1920); *Lettres de G. Tyrrell à H. Bremond,* ed. with footnotes by A. Louis-David (Paris 1971); other letters in M. Petre, *Autobiography and Life of G. Tyrrell* (below), in A. Loisy, *Mémoires* (Paris 1930–31), and ed. by J. H. Graham in *The Month* 226 (1968), 178–85; 231 (1971) 111–19, and by T. M. Loome in ibid. 229 (1970) 95–101, 138–49; many, as yet unpublished letters in the British Museum, Manuscripts Section. Also F. v. Hügel, "Father Tyrrell. Some memorials of the last 12 years of his life," *Hibbert Journal* 8 (1909/10), 233–52.

For von Hügel: *Selected Letters 1896–1924,* ed. by B. Holland (London 1927; the selection intended to cleanse him from the suspicion of modernism); *Letters to a Niece,* ed. by G. Greene (London 1928); *Spiritual Counsels and Letters,* ed. by D. Steere (London 1964); other important letters in A. Loisy, *Mémoires;* regarding the unpublished letters and diaries, see T. M. Loome, op. cit. (below), 295. Also: M. Petre, *My Way of Faith* (London 1937).

Literature

J. Rivière, op. cit., esp. 82–85, 102–6, 192–222, 265–74, 300–307, 389–401; A. Vidler, *The Modernist Movement,* esp. 143–81, 204–12; id., *A Variety,* 109–90; M. Ranchetti, op. cit., 58–74; M. Ward, *The Wilfrid Wards and the Transition* II (London 1937), 134–420; M. Petre, *Von Hügel and Tyrrell* (London 1937); id.: *Congrès d'histoire du christianisme,* ed. by P. Couchoud, III (Paris 1928), 226–47.

On Tyrrell: M. D. Petre, *Autobiography and Life of G. Tyrrell,* 2 vols. (London 1912); R. Gout: *L'affaire Tyrrell* (Paris 1910); J. Stam, *G. Tyrrell* (Utrecht 1938); D. Grasso, "La conversione e l'apostasia di G. Tyrrell," *Gregorianum* 38 (1957), 446–80, 593–629; R. Boudens, "G. Tyrrell and Card. Mercier," *Église et théologie* 1 (Montreal 1970), 313–51; P. Scoppola: *Humanitas* 22 (Brescia 1967), 705–38; G. Daly, "Some Reflections on the Character of G. Tyrrell," *Heythrop Journal* 10 (1969), 256–74; J. A. Laubacher, *Dogma and the Development of Dogma in the Writings of G. Tyrrell* (Louvain and Baltimore 1939); J. F. O'Grady, *The Doctrine of Nature and Grace in the Writings of G. Tyrrell* (Rome 1968).

On von Hügel: M. de la Bédoyère, *The Life of Baron v. H.* (London 1951); M. Nédoncelle, *La pensée religieuse de F. v. H.* (Paris 1935); L. Barmann, *Baron v. H. and the Modernist Crisis in England* (Cambridge 1972); J. Steinmann, *F. v. H.* (Paris 1962; cf. *Revue belge de philologie et d'histoire* 41 [1963], 1162–63); J. Heaney, *The Modernist Crisis, v. H.* (London 1969; cf. *Heythrop Journal* 10 [1969], 315–19); T. Loome in *DR* 91 (1973), nos. 302–4.

On Modernism in the United States: T. McAvoy: *RPol* 21 (1959), 71–74; J. Ratté, *Three Modernists, A. Loisy, G. Tyrrell, W. L. Sullivan* (New York 1967); J. Leinhard, "The 'New York Review' and Modernism in America," *RACHS* 82 (1971), 67–82.

32. *The Crisis in Italy*

Sources

E. Buonaiuti, *Pellegrino di Roma* (Rome 1945); S. Minocchi, "Memorie di un modernista" (manuscript in the Biblioteca Nazionale of Florence; edition prepared by A. Agnoletto; excerpts in *RicRel* 19 [1948], 148–67, and *Itinerari* nos. 47–48 [1961], 29–52); G. Semeria, *I miei tempi* (Milan 1929); F. Lanzoni, *Le Memorie,* ed. by G. Cattani (Faenza 1958); *Centro Studi per la storia del modernismo. Fonti e documenti* I (Urbino 1972;

letters prepared by Buonaiuti); A. Fogazzaro, *Lettere scelte,* ed. by T. Gallarati Scotti (Milan 1940); O. Morra, *Fogazzaro nel suo piccolo mondo, dai carteggi familiari* (Bologna 1960); A. Fogazzaro and G. Bonomelli, *Corrispondenza,* ed. by C. Marcora (Milan 1968); R. Comandini, "Echi della crisi modernista in un carteggio inedito di G. Meloni con A. Fogazzaro," *Studia Patavina* 16 (1969), 60–96; P. Scoppola, "Gli anni del modernismo nelle carte inedite di F. Salimei," *Humanitas* 22 (1967), 705–38. In regard to the reaction against Modernism, see *CivCatt* after 1901.

LITERATURE

Aside from the general works by Rivière, Vidler, Ranchetti, etc., see: P. Scoppola, *Crisi modernista e rinnovamento cattolico* (Bologna 1969; basic, cf. *RStRis* 49 [1962], 491–98; and *Revue belge de philologie et d'histoire* 41 [1963], 1159–62); L. Bedeschi, *I cattolici disubbidienti* (Naples and Rome 1959); id., *Il Modernismo e Romolo Murri in Emilia e Romagna* (Parma 1967; unpublished letters, 277–354); id., *Linneamenti dell'antimodernismo, il caso Lanzoni* (Parma 1970); M. Guasco, *R. Murri e il modernismo* (Rome 1968; biblio.); C. Giovannini, *Politica e religione nel pensiero della Lega Democratica Nazionale* (Rome 1959); F. Manzotti, "'Plebei' cattolici fra integralismo e modernismo sociale (1904/08)," *Convivium* 26 (1958), 423–45. See also M. C. Casella, *Religious Liberalism in Modern Italy,* 2 vols. (London 1966), and the other works by L. Bedeschi (below, biblio. to chap. 33).

On the group of the *Rinnovamento:* P. Scoppola, op. cit. chap. 4; M. Ranchetti, op. cit., 117–29, 191–226; F. Fonzi, "St. Jacini jr e il 'Rinnovamento,'" *RStRis* 56 (1969), 183–254; O. Confessore, "Sulle origini del 'Rinnovamento,'" *Rivisto di storia e letteratura religiosa* 4 (1968), 328–37; N. Raponi, *T. Gallarati Scotti tra politica e cultura* (Milan 1971).

On Genocchi, Fracassini, Minocchi, Buonaiuti, Semeria, and Fogazzaro, see this chap., nn. 1–4, 6, and 14.

33. *Intervention of Ecclesiastical Authority and the Integralist Reaction*

SOURCES

The main documents regarding Rome's measures against Modernism were compiled by A. Vermeersch, *De modernismo* (Bruges 1910).

On the integralist reaction: see mainly (F. Antonelli and G. Löw) *Disquisitio circa quasdam obiectiones modum agendi servi Dei Pii X respicientes in modernismi debellatione* (Vatican City 1950) and É. Poulat, *Intégrisme et catholicisme intégral* (Tournai-Paris 1969; with an introduction and informative footnotes; renders obsolete: N. Fontaine [=L. Canet], *Saint-Siège, Action française et catholiques intégraux,* Paris 1928). Also: *La Correspondance de Rome 1907–1912* (reprint Milan [1972], 3 vols.), the weekly journal by Msgr. Benigni, containing numerous essays; the memoirs and correspondences mentioned in chaps. 30–32; *Le P. Lagrange au service de la Bible. Souvenirs personnels* (Paris 1967); [P. Naudet], *Ce qu'on a fait de l'Église* (Paris 1912; about the author, see É. Poulat, *Histoire dogme et critique dans la crise moderniste* 662–64); L. Bedeschi, *Lettere ai cardinali di don Brizio* (Bologna 1970); id. in *Nuova rivista storica* 54 (1970), 125–76; 55 (1971), 90–132; 56 (1972), 389–412; id. in *Rivista di storia e letteratura religiosa* 6 (1970), 350–67; 7 (1971), 278–98; C. Marcora in *Studi storici in memoria di Mons. A. Mercati* (Milan 1956), 201–43.

LITERATURE

J. Rivière, *Le modernisme dans l'Église* (Paris 1929), 329–549; P. Scoppola, *Crisi modernista* . . . (Bologna 1969), 327–64; D. Grasso, "I modernisti e la 'Pascendi,'" *Divinitas* 2 (1958), 150–76.

On the integralist reaction, aside from the aforementioned basic works of É. Poulat, see: *DThC,* tables 2294–2303; R. Lill, "Der Kampf der römischen Kurie gegen den 'praktischen' Modernismus," *Die päpstliche Autorität im kath. Selbstverständnis des 19. und 20. Jh.,* ed. by E. Weinzierl (Salzburg 1970), 109–23; P. Droulers, *Politique sociale et christianisme. Le P. Desbuquois et l'Action populaire. Syndicalisme et intégristes 1903–18* (Paris 1969); L. Bedeschi, *Lineamenti dell'antimodernismo. Il caso Lanzoni* (Parma 1970); A. Blanchet, *Histoire d'une mise à l'Index, la 'Sainte Chantal' de l'abbé Bremond* (Paris 1967); M. Becamel in *BLE* 71 (1970), 262–73.

On *Le Sillon:* J. Caron, *Le Sillon et la démocratie chrétienne 1894–1910* (Paris 1967).

On *L'Action française:* E. Weber, *The Action française* (Stanford 1962) and the research report by V. Nguyen in *Revue d'histoire moderne et contemporaine* 18 (1971), 503–38.

The Holy See and the European Governments

34. *The Roman Question and Italian Catholicism*

BIBLIOGRAPHY

1. COLLECTIONS OF SOURCES (cf. the biblio. in chap. 5): *Acta Pii X*, 3 vols. (Rome 1905–7); R. Aubert, "Documents relatifs au mouvement catholique sous le pontificat de Pie X," *RSTI* 12 (1958), 202–43, 334–70; A. Toniolo, *Saggi politici*, ed. S. Majerotto (Rome 1957); F. Meda, *Scritti scelti*, ed. G. P. Dore (Rome 1959); G. Della Torre, *I cattolici e la vita pubblica italiana*, ed. G. De Rosa, 2 vols. (Rome 1962); R. Murri, *Battaglie d'oggi*, 4 vols. (Rome 1904); L. Sturzo, *Opera omnia* (appearing in Bologna 1950ff.); id., *Dall'idea al fatto*, ed. G. De Rossi (Rome 1920); id., *Chiesa e Stato* (Bologna 1958); *La Civiltà cattolica 1850–1945, anthology*, ed. G. De Rosa (Rome 1967); *L'Azione, antologia di scritti 1902–22*, ed. C. Bellò (Rome 1967; journal-newspaper of Cremona); A. Gemelli and F. Olgiati, *Vita e pensiero 1914–64*, (Milan 1966); *Civitas, 1919–25*, ed. B. Malinverni (Rome 1963).

2. THE HISTORICAL CONTEXT: Several authors, *30 anni di storia politica italiana* (Turin 1968); L. Salvatorelli, *Storia del Novecento* (Milan 1957); G. Giolitti, *Memorie della mia vita* (Milan 1945).

3. SPECIAL TOPICS (cf. biblio. in chap. 5): L. Salvatorelli, *Giolitti* (Milan 1928); G. Spadolini, *Giolitti ed i cattolici, 1901–14* (Florence 1960); M. Guasco, *R. Murri ed il modernismo* (Rome 1968); G. Corradi, *Liberali e cattolici nelle Marche, 1900–13* (Urbino 1970); A. Canaletti Gaudenzi, *L. Sturzo. Il pensiero e le opere* (Rome 1945); G. Petrocchi, *Don Luigi Sturzo* (Rome 1945); F. Rizzo, *L. Sturzo e la questione meridionale* (Rome 1937); F. Magri, *Un pioniere dell'azione sociale cristiana, Angelo Mauri 1873–1936* (Milan 1956); P. Bondioli, *P. Agostino Gemelli. Un profilo* (Milan 1926); M. C. Rossi, *Fr. L. Ferrari, Dalle Leghe bianche al P. P. I.* (Rome 1965); Several authors, *Benedetto XV, i cattolici e la prima guerra mondiale* (Rome 1963); *La parola e l'opera di Benedetto XV durante il conflitto mondiale* (Florence 1916); F. Meda, *I cattolici nella guerra mondiale* (Milan 1928); G. Quadrotta, *Il Papa, l'Italia e la guerra, con prefazione di F. Scaduto* (Milan 1915); E. Vercesi, *Il Vaticano, l'Italia e la guerra* (Milan 1925).

35. *German Catholicism between* Kulturkampf *and World War I*

LITERATURE

H. Brück, *Gesch. der kath. Kirche in Deutschland im 19. Jh.* IV, 2, ed. J. B. Kißling (Münster 1908); K. Bachem, *Vorgeschichte, Geschichte und Politik der deutschen Zentrumspartei* V–VII (Cologne 1919–30; reprint, Aalen 1967–68); Schmidlin, *PG* III, 94–104, 156–59, 164ff.; Bihlmeyer-Tüchle III, 411ff.; G. Maron, *Die römisch-kath. Kirche von 1870 bis 1970* (see in chap. 1), 260ff.

E. Ritter, *Die kath.-soziale Bewegung Deutschlands und der Volksverein* (Cologne 1954),

129–351; H. Philippi, "Kronkardinalat oder Nationalkardinalat. Preußische und bayerische Bemühungen an der Kurie 1900–1914," *HJ* 80 (1961), 185–217; id., "Beiträge zur Gesch. der diplomatischen Beziehungen zwischen dem Deutschen Reich und dem Hl. Stuhl 1872–1909," ibid. 82 (1963), 239–62; Buchheim, *Ultramontanismus und Demokratie*, 309–536; H. Lutz, *Demokratie im Zwielicht. Der Weg der deutschen Katholiken aus dem Kaiserreich in die Republik* (Munich 1963); R. Morsey, *Die deutsche Zentrumspartei 1917–1923* (Düsseldorf 1966; also important for the decade before 1914); id., "Die deutschen Katholiken und der Nationalstaat zwischen Kulturkampf und erstem Weltkrieg," *HJ* 90 (1970), 31–64; id., "Georg Kard. Kopp, Fürstbischof von Breslau (1887–1914), Kirchenfürst oder 'Staatsbischof'?," *Wichmann-Jahrbuch für Kirchengeschichte im Bistum Berlin* XXI–XXIII (1967–69), 42–65.—Cf. the sections on Germany in chaps. 12–15.

36. Separation of Church and State in France

SOURCES

Livre blanc du S. Siège. La séparation de l'Église et de l'État en France. Exposé et documents (Paris 1906); *Une campagne du Siècle. La séparation des Églises et de l'État*, H. Brisson . . . (Paris 1905); *Les fiches pontificales de Monsignor Montagnini* . . . (Paris 1908); J. de Narfon, *La séparation de l'Église et de l'État. Origines, étapes, bilan* (Paris 1922); E. Combes, *Mon ministère. Mémoires (1902–1905)* (Paris 1957); Z. Giacometti, *Quellen zur Geschichte der Trennung von Staat und Kirche* (Tübingen 1926); L. V. Méjan, *La séparation des Églises et de l'État* (foreword by G. Le Bras; biblio.) (Paris 1959).

LITERATURE

Aside from the mentioned works by Lecanuet, Latreille, and Mayeur, see F. Mourret-Carreyre, *Précis d'histoire de l'Église* III (Paris 1929); J. Brugerette, *Le prêtre français dans la société contemporaine* II–III (Paris 1935–38); L. Capéran, *L'invasion laïque. De l'avènement de Combes au vote de la Séparation* (Paris 1935); P. Sorlin, *Waldeck-Rousseau* (Paris 1966); J.-M. Mayeur, *La séparation de l'Église et de l'État* (Paris 1966); J. Caron, *Le Sillon et la démocratie chrétienne* (Paris 1967); C. Molette, *L'association catholique de la jeunesse française, 1886–1907* (Paris 1968); A. v. Campenhausen, *Staat und Kirche in Frankreich* (Göttingen 1962); E. Appolis, "En marge de la Séparation. Les associations cultuelles schismatiques," *RHEF*, 1963; G. Le Bras, *Le Conseil d'État, régulateur de la vie paroissiale. Trente ans de Séparation* (Paris 1950); Fontaine (L. Canet), *Saint-Siège, Action française et catholiques intégraux* (Paris 1928); B. Neveu, "Louis Canet et le service du Conseiller technique pour les Affaires religieuses au Ministère des Affaires étrangères," *Rev. d'Hist. diplom.* (April/June 1968); M. J. M. Larkin, "Loubet's Visit to Rome and the Question of Papal Prestige," *The Historical Journal* IV (1961), 97–113; id., "The Vatican, French Catholics and the Associations Cultuelles," *The Journal of Modern History* XXXVI (1964), 298–317; id., "The Church and the French Concordat, 1891 to 1902," *EHR* LXXXI (1966), 717–39; id., *Church and State after the Dreyfus Affair: the Separation issue in France* (London, in preparation); J. McManners, *Church and State in France 1870–1914* (London, SPCK, 1972); G. Laperrière, *La Séparation des Églises et de l'État à Lyon, étude d'opinion publique* (Lyon, Centre d'histoire du catholicisme, 1973).

37. *The Outbreak of World War I*

LITERATURE

Engel-Janosi II, 148–52; J. Nobécourt, *"Le Vicaire" et l'histoire* (Paris 1964), 120–23, 130–31; A. Hudal, *Die österreichische Vatikanbotschaft 1805–1918* (Munich 1952), 281–84; P. Fernesole, *Pie X* (Paris 1954), II, 440–50; E. Adamov, *Die Diplomatie des Vatikans zur Zeit des Imperialismus* (Berlin 1932), 72–73; P. Renouvin and J. B. Duroselle, *Introduction à l'histoire des relations internationales* (Paris 1964), 235–36, 254–56.

Part Three

The Expansion of Catholic Missions from the Time of Leo XIII until World War II

38. Missions in the Shadow of Colonialism

39. The Development of New Churches

SOURCES AND LITERATURE

R. Streit, *Bibliotheca Missionum* III, XIV, XXV (America); VIII, XXVII (India); IX (Philippines); X (Japan, Korea); XI (Indochina); XII–XIV (China); XVII–XX (Africa); XXI (Australia, Oceania); J. Rommerskirchen, *Bibliografia Missionaria* (Rome 1936ff.); *Acta Leonis XIII,* 8 vols. (Bruges and Paris 1887–1910); *Acta Sanctae Sedis* (*ASS,* Rome 1865–1908); *Acta Apostolicae Sedis* (*AAS* Rome 1909ff.); *Collectanea S. Congregationis de Propaganda Fide,* 2 vols. (Rome 1907); *Sylloge praecipuorum documentorum recentium Summorum Pontificum et S. Congregationis de Propaganda Fide* (Rome 1939); J. Glazik, *Päpstliche Rundschreiben über die Mission von Leo XIII. bis Johannes XXIII.* (Münsterschwarzach 1961; Lat. and Germ.); E. Marmy and I. Auf der Maur, *Geht hin in alle Welt. Missionsenzykliken der Päpste Benedikt XV., Pius XI., Pius XII. und Johannes XXIII.* (Fribourg 1961).—J. Schmidlin, *Papstgeschichte der neuen Zeit* II (Pius IX, Leo XIII); III (Pius X, Benedikt XV); IV (Pius XI) (Munich 1934–39); id., *Katholische Missionsgeschichte* (Steyl 1925); S. Delacroix, *Histoire universelle des missions catholiques* III (*Les missions contemporaines 1800–1957*) (Paris 1958); F. Schwager, *Die katholische Heidenmission der Gegenwart* II (Africa) (Steyl 1908); IV (*Vorderindien und Britisch-Hinterindien*) (Steyl 1909); K. B. Westmann and H. von Sicard, *Geschichte der christlichen Mission* (Munich 1962); Kenneth Scott Latourette, *A History of the Expansion of Christianity* V–VII (New York and London 1943–45); id., *Geschichte der Ausbreitung des Christentums,* condensed ed. (Göttingen 1956); A. Mulders, *Missionsgeschichte. Die Ausbreitung des katholischen Glaubens* (Regensburg 1960); T. Ohm, *Wichtige Daten der Missionsgeschichte* (Münster 1961); B. Arens, *Handbuch der katholischen Missionen* (Freiburg 1925); H. Bernard-Maître, "China," *DHGE* XII, 693–741; J. Jennes, *A History of the Catholic Church in Japan* (Tokyo 1959).

INDEX